Two Wars
We Must Not Lose

What Christians Need to Know About Radical Islamists,
Radical Secularists, and Why We Can't Leave the Battle
Up to Our Divided Government

By Bill Hecht

CONCORDIA
THEOLOGICAL
SEMINARY
PRESS

Cover Image:
Architect of the Capitol. Use of photo above, which was graphically altered for the cover,
does not imply endorsement by the Architect of the Capitol or the United States Congress
of the views expressed in this book.

Back Cover Image:
EA Photography

Cover Design:
Colleen. M. Bartzsch

The views expressed in this book are those of the author and do not necessarily reflect the views
and policies of the Concordia Theological Seminary Press or Concordia Theological Seminary,
Fort Wayne, Indiana.

Published by
Concordia Theological Seminary Press
6600 North Clinton Street
Fort Wayne, Indiana 46825

Printed on acid-free paper in the United States of America.
Set in Garamond Premier Pro.
Manufactured by Mignone Communications, Inc,. Huntington, Indiana.

Table of Contents

Acknowledgments

I am indebted to so many people for their encouragement and assistance in my research and writing of this book. But this book would never have been possible without the dedicated efforts of the Rev. David Mahsman and my very talented wife, Susan, who is an extraordinary writer.

David has performed a herculean task of carefully editing a book that covers many different topics, some of which required technical explanations and many footnotes. To add to his challenge, some material in the book was written considerably earlier and required constant revisions as events and circumstances changed. He deserves as much credit for this book as its author.

Susan has revised and rewritten enough different sections of this book that she qualifies as a co-author. This was especially true in the chapters dealing with our American heritage, the Culture Wars, political activities, and the requirements of Lutheran citizenship. In some of these areas she had as much knowledge and experience as I did. She was always invaluable when it came to grammar and spelling. (I am more of an expert in matters relating to grammatical correctness of biblical Hebrew and New Testament Greek than the King's English. This was not especially helpful in writing this book. But in South Georgia, I grew up on good ole Southern English.)

I would be remiss if I failed to note that this book would never have been written but for the persistence of Dr. Dean Wenthe. As president of Concordia Theological Seminary, Fort Wayne, Dr. Wenthe invited me to address an assembly of the faculty and student body on these subjects. After the address, I was flattered when he suggested that I must write a book. I would ultimately agree to undertake such a time-consuming project after repeated phone calls and a generous offer that the Fort Wayne seminary would like to publish the book.

Dr. Larry Rast, who succeeded Dr. Wenthe as president of the seminary, followed up on Dean's offer to have the seminary publish this book. Larry also spent some of his valuable vacation time reading several chapters of the book. This resulted in some helpful suggestions and encouragement that I devote the time to get the book ready for publication prior to the 2012 elections, while there is particular interest in political issues.

During his term as LCMS president, my longtime friend Dr. Jerry Kieschnick read some of the early material now included in the book and insisted that such a book would be valuable to our church body. About a year after Dr. Matt Harrison became president of the LCMS, the book was in a more developed form. Matt asked to read some of the chapters in their unedited form and became convinced that we must get the book published. He has been extremely generous in finding time in his busy schedule to read the developing material and offer valuable editorial suggestions. I no longer had any choice but to spend all the time necessary to complete my book.

Dr. David Scaer, a classmate of mine at Concordia Seminary, St. Louis, and a longtime family friend, found time in his schedule as a professor at the Fort Wayne seminary to help facilitate the publication of the book. His suggestions and editing were invaluable as well. Also, I can never adequately express my appreciation for the relentless efforts of Jayne Sheafer, Colleen Bartzsch, and other members of the seminary staff, including a number of graduate students who spent hours proofreading the text of this book. They set aside other endeavors to make possible the publication of this book in a timely fashion.

I met Dr. Tom Coburn in 1994 when he made his first trip to D.C. after having decided to run as a Republican in Oklahoma's ancestrally Democrat Second District in northeast Oklahoma. My longtime dear friend, now senior Oklahoma Senator Jim Inhofe, brought the doctor to my table in the Capitol Hill Club. We bonded immediately. Coburn was a devout Southern Baptist. While we would not agree on all doctrinal issues, we were in total agreement on moral and social issues. Who better than an obstetrician who has delivered some 4,000 babies to become a champion in defense of unborn babies? The congressional district he would represent included the area in which the "Five Civilized Tribes" from Alabama and Georgia located after President Jackson's "Trail of Tears," a forced march on which 4,000 Cherokees died. Many babies in this district with pockets of poverty were brought into this world by Dr. Coburn at little or no charge. (This reminded me of growing up in South Georgia during the depression.)

Dr. Coburn has strong convictions about the unsustainable direction in which this country is travelling—fiscally and otherwise. He hopes to make a difference. As one with similar strongly held convictions, I can tell the difference between being stubborn and being committed. (We agree on most issues. On the few occasions when we disagree, we are so strong willed that we usually agree to disagree.) Senator Coburn has become a valuable member of the U.S. Senate. As one of the most conservative senators, unlike the few hard-core libertarians, Dr. Coburn understands that the U.S. Congress has the responsibility to govern. He is capable of reaching across party lines to reach a bipartisan compromise without sacrificing his principles. Senator Coburn enjoys a personal relationship with the likes of President Obama and Majority Leader Harry Reid. He has also become an essential ally of Senate Republican Leader Mitch McConnell. Coburn is not shy about making his voice heard and is making a difference. I am humbled that he found time during the hectic final days before the adjournment of this Congress to read a draft of my book. Knowing him so well, I knew he would never agree to write a recommendation without reading the manuscript. I certainly appreciate his trust and generous comments in his Foreword.

I owe a special debt of gratitude to the brilliant Michael Schwartz. As chief of staff to Senator Coburn, Michael is one of the busiest men on Capitol Hill and has exerted major influence on the conservative movement in the Nation's Capital. He generously gave of his time to read even some of the unedited chapters of this book. Michael, I will always remember your expert counsel, your informed suggestions, and your persuasive advice. I am very fortunate to be able to call you my friend.

Obviously, space does not allow me to give credit to all of those who have helped make this book possible. I must point out that this is not intended to be a biographical account of my life, including my 40-plus years on the Washington scene. (Numerous congressman and senators have encouraged me to write such an account, since few people have been in the Nation's Capital longer and seen more than I have. I will leave such memoirs to succeeding family generations, and much will be left out even in such an account.) The biographical material in this book is included only to help the reader understand my background and to establish the validity of the case that is being made in various sections of this book.

Foreword

By the Rev. Dr. Matthew C. Harrison
President, The Lutheran Church—Missouri Synod

Step into Bill Hecht's D.C. office and you immediately observe a menagerie of political memorabilia, a 40-year collection of photographs and handwritten notes from presidents, senators, chiefs of staff, and cabinet members. In the unpretentious space the waft of cigar smoke directs the nose to Bill's corner, a modest room, totally unpretentious, a desk piled with reports and papers. He offers a cigar and finds deep joy in the shared billows, opens with the warmest welcome, invites you to sit down on the low couch, styled a decade or three in the past.

The conversation is lighthearted but ribbed with profound and enduring issues: government, politics, national interests, international policy, the U.S. Constitution, congressional hearings, Middle East affairs, Islam, and more. Every issue is punctuated with stories of political personages and events. In addition to presidents, Bill knows and has known personally virtually every player in the House and Senate, and those around them, for 40 years. The repartee flows effortlessly between politics, religion, and philosophy. He's lived it all.

Trained in the Missouri Synod's demanding system of theological education, Bill served as a campus pastor in Oklahoma before delving full-time into politics in the 1960s and then becoming a lobbyist on the Hill. Like the contradictions inherent in so much of American life, Bill carries out his much-maligned vocation with honor and deep devotion to his Lutheran Christian convictions. His list of charitable endeavors is long, working countless gratis hours for his church and others. He's one of those rare men whom I always leave thinking I did not have enough time to spend with him.

At his octogenarian threshold, Bill has performed a herculean task. In his office is a large frame window facing Capitol Hill—a window on America as it were. Bill has been more than an observer; he's lived events, which have taken place in the purview from that window for decades.

Now he has a story to tell. This great nation is at a turning point, a moment of crisis upon which our republic is so tenuously placed that we face not only the decline, but the very demise of America as a republic of free people unless the tide is turned. The assault, which threatens the republic, as Hecht so thoroughly and eloquently demonstrates, is being waged on two fronts, that is, by militant Islamists and by radical secularism. Failing to grasp what Islam is, we can have no idea of the wisdom or folly of international and domestic policy with respect to the Muslim world. Bill untangles and lays before us the force of Mohammed's modern disciples. He also carefully unfolds the string of horrendous Supreme Court decisions, which have landed this nation in a moral and ethical impasse, precisely the opposite of that which of our Founders envisioned.

As valuable as anything in the book is the chapter on the religion of the Founders, which with careful and calm precision points out that Ben Franklin and Thomas Paine were probably the only deists among them. Jefferson, Washington, Adams, and even the deist Franklin were all deeply committed to the premise that America could only survive if its people were a religious people. That meant that the U.S. Constitution and particularly the First Amendment were constructed precisely to protect the states and their religious citizens *from* the encroachment of federal power. Now we live, since 1947, with precisely the opposite reality. And the results are all around us: cultural and ethical demise on virtually every measurable front.

With calm Lutheran precision, clearly understanding the two distinct realms that are not to be mixed (state and church), Hecht calls religious citizens to action for the sake of the future of this great nation. I for one am convinced. The time to sit quietly while religious rights are eroded at pace with consequent socio-cultural demise is over.

Foreword

By the Honorable Tom A. Coburn, M.D.
United States Senator, Oklahoma

Bill Hecht is both a pastor and a patriot, and both aspects of his experience are evident in this important and timely book. America is in mortal danger due to a combination of two very different enemies: Islamic jihadists and politically correct secularist elitists.

Bill Hecht offers considerable detail on the history and nature of Islam, with special emphasis on the emergence of extremist sects that have given rise in the past century to the Muslim Brotherhood and such violence as the attack on the World Trade Center of Sept. 11, 2001, as well as suicide bombers and similar acts of mayhem that have become commonplace in recent years. While he emphasizes that this violent extremism is not typical of Muslims, it nevertheless has a long pedigree in the Islamic world, going all the way back to the time of Mohammed. The people who carry out these attacks are well funded, intelligent, and absolutely dedicated to conquering the world for Allah.

Americans will never learn this from the mainstream media because the media are dominated by a political correctness that requires the truth to be suppressed in order to accommodate a secularist ideology. That very political correctness renders us incapable of defending ourselves against the jihadists.

It was not always so. From the beginning and well into the 20th century, Americans understood that our society was rooted in a Christian worldview. But certain elites found a secularist worldview more attractive, and they were handed a great victory with a 1947 Supreme Court decision in which Justice Hugo L. Black, a one-time hero of the Ku Klux Klan, picked up Thomas Jefferson's metaphor of a "wall of separation" between church and state and turned it into the charter for establishment of secularism as the national religion. Ironically, Jefferson had used that phrase to reassure the Danbury Baptists that the government would never interfere in their religious affairs. Since then, the courts have expanded this secularist theme in an attempt to scrub any trace of Christian heritage out of American public life.

The secularists and the jihadists have practically nothing in common except their shared disdain for America's Christian heritage.

Americans need to understand these twin threats. We need to know the historical and ideological roots out of which Islamic terrorism grows. We need to recognize that secularist elitism is not our authentic constitutional tradition. And we need to throw off the shackles of political correctness and face the truth.

Even though Bill Hecht's book is addressed to his fellow Christians, and especially to his brothers and sisters of the Lutheran communion, it is important for all Americans, even those with no particular faith commitment.

Preface

The purpose of this book is to challenge Christians, especially Lutheran pastors and lay people, to accept their citizenship responsibilities at this crucial time in our nation's history. My hope is that the book will serve as a research tool to help the reader better understand the nature and seriousness of the threats we face.

The subjects addressed are controversial and produce strongly held opinions. The discussion of how difficult it is for a radically divided government and country effectively to confront these serious threats is based in part on personal experience. I have labored to be as objective as possible without sacrificing any of my own strongly held convictions.

Not one ounce of energy has been wasted on being "politically correct." On the other hand, I believe the Lord I strive to serve expects me always to "speak the truth in love." So, I have agonized over choosing words that accurately record the facts at my disposal without giving offense to any who disagree with my conclusions. This is not an easy task!

The two threats I address are 1) the war declared on America by radical Islamist terrorists, and 2) the "cultural war" being waged by radical secularists on the traditional moral and spiritual foundations of our country. The first war I discuss is of relatively recent appearance on American soil, but the Muslim-Christian struggle stretches over almost 14 centuries. The second threat, the secularists' war, began with a few skirmishes shortly after our nation's founding, reached the serious planning stages in the early part of the 20th century, and began in earnest in the 1940s.

The success of either of these two wars would destroy our way of life passed on to us by our forefathers.

When the liberal or politically correct elites refuse to use the word "Muslim," "Islamic," or even "Islamist" in describing the terrorists who continue to attack America and her allies, they not only are being intellectually dishonest but are placing our country at even greater risk. When we fail to identify the deeply religious motivation of these terrorists by their own clear admission, we are not furthering Muslim-Christian relations. We are simply ignoring the facts at our own peril, and most likely theirs as well. Peace-loving moderate or secular Muslims don't want such radicals committing terrorist acts in the name of Islam and giving their religion a bad name. We must all seek to understand the source and nature of their fundamentalist beliefs in order to promote better relations between Muslims and Christians, as well as among majority-Muslim nations and majority-Christian nations. It is very important to learn to disagree without being unnecessarily divisive, but it is more than that.

It is impossible to understand al-Qaeda, the late Osama bin Laden, or zealous Islamist terrorists without understanding at least some of the most basic characteristics of the world's two largest religions and their historic struggles. We cannot change history, but we can and *must* learn valuable lessons from an unbiased study of history. For one thing, it was absolutely inevitable that Islam would be on a collision course with Christianity from Islam's founding in the 7th century. There were too many similarities between the basic tenets of these two religions as well as too many dramatic theological differences to make reconciliation possible. This should not mean that mutual respect and peaceful coexistence cannot be achieved in today's world.

Both Christianity and Islam are exclusive religions whose adherents believe they have received God's *final* revelation. Their most basic doctrines are absolutes that by definition are incapable of compromise. (With the exception of some small sects that are statistically insignificant in a global context, this is not the case with other major world religions.) Christians and Muslims similarly accept a divinely inspired holy book, the Bible and the Koran respectively, which they believe contains the totality of God's final revelation. Christians and Muslims also believe that God expects them to share His final message with others throughout the world. Both religions believe they have a command from God to proselytize until the entire world has heard His message.

Historically, orthodox Christians have believed that Jesus Christ is the promised Messiah, the Savior promised by God to Adam and Eve after their fall in the Garden of Eden. According to Christian beliefs, this promise was repeated consistently to Abraham, Moses, David, and all the children of Israel by the prophets throughout the Old Testament. Essential doctrines taught in the New Testament and established as absolute tenets of the Christian faith by all the early church councils include the virgin birth of Christ; that Jesus Christ is the Son of God and has both a divine and human nature; that His sinless life fulfilled God's law; Jesus' crucifixion and resurrection; salvation by grace through faith; the doctrine of the Holy Trinity; the bodily resurrection of all the dead on the last day when Christ returns to judge the world; and the sacraments of Baptism and Holy Communion. The Athanasian Creed, one of the three ecumenical Christian creeds, bluntly states that those who reject the basic Christian doctrines cannot be saved.

It is a fact that heretical sects throughout the history of Christianity have challenged one or more of these Christian doctrines. It is also true that before, during, and after the Reformation, differences developed over certain teachings of the Christian church, but most do not involve doctrines considered to be absolutely essential to salvation. In the 20th century, "modernist" or liberal theologians and philosophers, while still claiming the "Christian" label, nonetheless challenged virtually all of the historic beliefs of Christianity. (Such challenges do not happen among Islamic theologians or philosophers.)

Just as Christianity teaches of God and Scripture, so Islam teaches that Allah gave Mohammad his *final* revelations, which had been only partially revealed to other prophets, most prominent of whom were Adam, Abraham, David, and Jesus. Judaism and Christianity became totally obsolete when Allah chose to give his final and total revelation to his prophet Mohammad.

While Muslims do share with Christians some beliefs (e.g., belief in angels, the devil, Judgment Day, and the existence of heaven and hell), the suggestion recently advocated by liberal or politically correct theologians and philosophers that dialogues should take place between the two religious communities on commonality of doctrinal beliefs is a mirage. Those who contend that Judaism, Christianity, and Islam are three great Abrahamic religions with basic common beliefs obviously have never read the Koran. The Koran clearly states that "Ibrahim [Abraham] was not a Jew nor a Christian but he was (an) upright (man), a Muslim, and he was not one of the polytheists" (Koran 3:67). Jesus is referred to as the "Messiah" in the Koran, but this means only that He was one of the early prophets pointing to the final prophet, Mohammad. The Koran says, "Christians say: The Messiah is the son of Allah; these are the words of their mouth; they imitate the saying of those who disbelieved before; may Allah destroy them; how they are turned away!" (9:30). The Koran quotes Jesus as saying, "Surely I am a servant of Allah: He hath given me the Book and made me a prophet" (19:30).

There clearly is no common ground for a dialogue on the basic doctrines of Christianity and Islam (or historic Judaism) unless Christians and Jews are willing to submit to the monolithic unity of, and absolute authority of, Allah and the finality of the prophet Mohammad. Unlike liberal Christian theologians and some church leaders and their Jewish counterparts, Muslim theologians or leaders do not question the basic doctrines of Islam. There is no such precedent of any recognized Islamic authority in antiquity or modern times ever even raising any question about basic Muslim doctrines.

A Muslim's right to accept without question the fundamental principles of his or her faith is not the issue. We would all respect such a basic human right. In return we would expect them to respect our right to hold the Christian faith with the same level of conviction. Any potential dialogue in which the starting point would be recognition of the Muslim doctrine of God and the prophethood of Mohammad is a contradiction in terms.

This is not to say that we should not promote civil dialogues about how we can live peacefully in the same world without sacrificing the basic beliefs of our mutually exclusive religions. Questions relating to freedom of religion whereby

Muslims could live in majority-Christian countries without fear of retaliation and Christians could also live in majority-Muslim countries without fear of discrimination and persecution should and must be addressed. We should honestly respect mutual rights to proclaim our religions freely without concern that any converts would experience retaliation. This is a basic human right that all religions should promote and respect.

Whereas Muslims (unlike Christians) have never even debated fundamental doctrines of their religion, they have extensively studied and disagreed on practical applications of *jihad* and Islamic law. Over the centuries, four major schools of jurisprudence in Sunni Islam and basically one in Shi'a Islam have spent as much time and written almost as many volumes on these subjects as Christian scholars have on Christian doctrines. The term "fundamentalism" applies to *jihad* and Islamic law in the Muslim tradition in a similar way the same word applies to doctrine or interpretation of Holy Scripture in Christianity. (The fact that Islam has never had a "Reformation" is noted by many non-Muslim scholars.)

Radical Islamist terrorists have no disagreements with devout Muslims of all stripes over Islamic doctrine. Because their disagreements arise over "holy war" and Islamic law, it seems logical that mainline Muslims would be anxious to join Christians and others in efforts to marginalize and defeat these terrorists who commit horrible acts in the name of their religion. It not only is dangerous but counterproductive to deny that such terrorists are not religiously motivated. The late Osama bin Laden, other al-Qaeda leaders, and the leaders of the other Islamist terrorist organizations repeatedly quote the Koran, the teachings of Mohammad, and Muslim authorities through the ages to justify their attacks. Muslim leaders say such terrorists are perverting the true teachings of Islam and Mohammad. These moderate Muslim spokesmen may well be correct to some degree. But the fact is that these Muslim terrorists believe with a religious zeal arguably unmatched in history that they are carrying out the commands and teachings of Allah and Mohammad. Without such a religious fanaticism they could never motivate their followers to eagerly seek martyrdom in such acts as suicide bombings and indiscriminate destruction of civilians, including fellow Muslims. We must all seek to find the roots of such devotion on the part of these terrorists.

One of the most dramatic dissimilarities between Christianity and Islam involves their respective commands to spread their messages of salvation. Mohammad led his armies in conquering and converting Arabia by persuasion or force. He commanded his successors, the caliphs, to conquer the surrounding lands, which were mostly Christian, in the name of Islam. People of the Book, initially Christians and Jews, were not forced to convert to Islam but were allowed to live in these conquered countries under strict rules of subservience if they paid a special tax. They were allowed even to practice their religions under controlled conditions that would not offend believing Muslims. They were to recognize that they were by definition inferior to those who had accepted the religion of Allah, and they had no legal rights in an Islamic society. For example, Muslims do not question what they believe to be Allah's literal command: "Fight those who do not believe in Allah, nor in the latter day, nor do they prohibit what Allah and His Apostle have prohibited, nor follow the religion of truth, out of those who have been given the Book, until they pay the tax in acknowledgment of superiority and they are in a state of subjection" (Koran 9:29).

During the so-called "golden age of Islam," as well as today, a few "secular" Muslim rulers relaxed some of the rules and allowed more freedom for non-Muslims. ("Secular" has a different meaning in the Muslim world than in Christendom. The strict teachings of the Koran require a theocracy. Referring to a Muslim ruler as "secular" does not mean he is not devout in his Islamic faith but that he recognizes some type of separation between religion and the state.) The eminent scholar on Islam, Dr. Bernard Lewis, contends that Islamic conquest did not necessarily require forced conversion but established the conditions that encouraged conversion.

In absolute contrast, the Christian religion was spread by a persecuted and often despised minority, beginning with the apostles and their followers. Frequently, early Christians who refused to denounce their faith in Christ literally were fed to the lions. They had no armies and conquered no lands by force in the name of Christianity for centuries after Christ established His Church.

After the Roman Emperor Constantine converted to Christianity, things did change. While there are few historical examples of forced conversions to Christianity brought about by conquest, there are numerous examples of discrimination against Jews and persecution of those considered to be Christian heretics. When we cast stones of criticism at Muslim atrocities during their conquest of Christian lands in history, we must in humility admit that Christian history has its share of deeds that greatly offended the Lord of the Church as well.

However, the "politically correct" myth that Jewish residents and heretical Christians welcomed with open arms the conquering Muslim armies in Christian-controlled lands in the 7th and 8th centuries is totally refuted by the history of these conquests and the rule they established. There were some examples of mistreatment of Jews and Christian heretics by Christian rulers at this time in history, but in the vast majority of the cases the abuse was much less severe—and certainly no worse—than that suffered under the conquering Muslims.

Christian leaders—popes, patriarchs, and rulers—deserve their share of criticism for the Crusades, but these events must be evaluated in the context of the historical circumstances. The split between the eastern and western branches of Christianity left the Christian lands in the East vulnerable to attack from Muslim armies. Had Christendom been united and willing to provide mutual defense, the invading Muslim forces might have been hesitant to invade Palestine, Syria, and other Christian-controlled countries in the early years. It took more than 400 years of Muslim aggression, with the Christian Byzantine Empire on the verge of total collapse and virtually confined to Greece, before Pope Urban II called the First Crusade. This Crusade resulted in certain well-known and inexcusable atrocities, but had it never taken place it is almost a certainty that Islam eventually would have conquered all of Europe. Had Greece fallen to the invading Islamic armies, Rome would have become the most coveted target for future Islamic conquest.[1] Once again, we cannot rewrite history, but we must learn from its mistakes.

In my extensive research, I have sought to examine the teachings of Islam and its history by using Muslim sources when possible. More extensively, I have relied on non-Muslim scholars who relate Islamic teachings and history from the most ancient and authoritative Muslim documents. I have made a sincere effort to present facts that are available to mainline or moderate Muslims as well as to Islamic terrorists.

It is clear to me that until Christians and Muslims of good will realize that the fundamentalist teachings of Wahhabism, fueled by Saudi oil revenues, are the main driving force behind Islamic terrorism, no solution can be found.

I repeat in all sincerity that I have made an honest effort to avoid offending sincere Muslims by examining Islamic history. I fully understand that many of these teachings and historical events can be interpreted in more than one way.[2] But serious dialogue that might lead to some solutions cannot take place until such history is understood.

By the same token, I have not intended to offend honest and dedicated liberals who have a different view of the cultural struggles raging in our society today. Liberal voters have the same right to vote for liberal candidates as do conservatives to vote for conservative candidates. Liberal and conservative elected officials have the right and the responsibility to fight for the ideals of those who elected them.

The Founders were careful to establish a Republic, or representative democracy. They were very aware of the potential for abuses and inequities in a pure democracy. Those who are elected are to represent the people to the best of their abilities. It is basically the extreme hard right and hard left who have caused most of the problems. An attempt is made to examine the dangers of such extremes in chapters 2, 3, and 6.

The greatest threat today may be from activist judges, whom I will evaluate in Chapter 6. The irony of all ironies is that the prominent Founder who was most concerned about unelected, activist judges usurping powers not delegated to them by the people was Thomas Jefferson. One of President Jefferson's first actions after his election was to have the newly elected Republican Congress suspend the Supreme Court for 14 months. Jefferson took such drastic action because he was so concerned about the Federalist[3] judges sitting on the high court claiming jurisdiction over matters clearly preserved by the people for the states. What subsequent judges have wrought in Jefferson's name is indefensible.

As difficult as it may be because of the arrogance of many of these liberal elitists, I have made every effort to keep this dialogue civil. My goal in this book has been to motivate Christians to make their infinitely more-numerous voices heard in such important matters.

Finally, I certainly have not intended to offend anyone in my plea for Christians to take their citizenship responsibilities more seriously. Lutherans have been especially remiss in the area of elective office, as I will illustrate by comparative statistics in Chapter 8.

As we are all aware, the Bible is silent on any particular form of government. Jesus simply told us to "render unto Caesar the things that are Caesar's and unto God the things that are God's." Jesus never called for the violent overthrow of the pagan Roman Empire. He did not even condemn the institution of slavery. He simply taught His followers a system of morality that would make such human bondage impossible for Christians. St. Paul spelled out the practical application for Christians in his letter to Philemon when he told his convert to accept his slave, Onesimus, back into his home not as a slave but as a brother in Christ.

Martin Luther's theology of the two kingdoms—the kingdoms of the right hand (the church) and left hand (the state)—seems totally compatible with the role of Church and State in our founding documents. John Calvin, on the other hand, envisioned a Christian theocracy. The Roman Catholic Church and the Orthodox churches have experienced both systems—the State dominating the Church and the Church dominating the State. It is my opinion that our Founding Fathers got it as close to right as far as sinful human beings are capable.

Those of us who are so blessed to live in the United States of America owe special thanks to God for the blessings He has bestowed upon us along with our unique citizenship responsibilities. When the Declaration of Independence stated that we were "endowed by our Creator with certain inalienable rights," this marked a new experiment in human government. (Unfortunately, it took almost 100 years for the country to finalize this right for all our citizens.)

At the time of our founding, this country was overwhelmingly Christian. Even today polls tell us that some 80 percent to 85 percent or our population continues to describe themselves as "Christians." The strength of our country was, and is, the fact that our Founders built this country on the foundation of Judeo-Christian principles.

These Founders also wisely insisted that freedom of religion is a basic human right essential for a country to remain free. (While the Founders were basically concerned with keeping one group of Christians from denying freedom of religion to other groups of Christians, they also opposed religious coercion.) Subsequent American history has taught us that to deny such freedom of religion to others ultimately would threaten the rights of Christians to worship the God of the Bible according to the dictates of their own consciences.

For such religious freedom to endure, it must also recognize the rights of the relatively few atheists and agnostics—their percentage of the population apparently has remained static at less than four percent since our founding—to refuse to recognize or worship any god.[4] This certainly does not mean, however, that our country must become totally secular or amoral and devoid of all moral and religious values. These "secular humanists," or whatever they call themselves, have had inordinate successes (vastly out of proportion to their numbers) in challenging America's heritage of absolute values because too many Christians have shirked their responsibilities as Christian citizens.

As caring Christians we never want to trample on the rights of minorities, no matter how small their numbers, but we also must not sacrifice the moral heritage of the overwhelming majority of our God-fearing people. In Karl Marx's prophetic words: "A country without a heritage is easy prey."

Unfortunately, some Christians have joined forces with the liberal secularists in opposing some of our traditional moral values. We also want to deal with them in love, but we must not sacrifice moral principles clearly taught in Holy Scripture. We can out-vote them in a loving manner when necessary, but we cannot forsake our citizenship responsibilities in God's left-hand kingdom. God does also govern in the "affairs of men," just as our Founders insisted.

Notes

[1] The myths and complicated facts surrounding the Crusades will be discussed in some detail in Chapter 5.

[2] In the Koran, the earliest biographical account of Mohammad's life (Ibn Ishaq), and the Hadith (the traditions and sayings of the Prophet Mohammad as agreed upon by the community of Islamic scholars some 200 years after Mohammad's death), he is portrayed sometimes as a man of peace and tolerance and at other times as a man of war and intolerance (always at Allah's direction, according to these sources). There is no disagreement among devout Muslims regarding basic doctrines of their faith. The differences relate primarily to *jihad* and Islamic law, as will be explained later when we deal with the life and teachings of Mohammad.

[3] At the time, the word "Federalist" meant "nationalist," or those who believed in a strong central or federal government. The Federalists were typified by Alexander Hamilton and to a lesser degree by George Washington and John Adams.

[4] In February 2008, the prestigious "Pew Forum on Religion and Public Life" released the results of the most in-depth survey on America's "religious landscape" ever conducted. This information will be carefully examined in Chapter 3. This survey found that 2.4 percent of Americans claimed to be "agnostics" and 1.5 percent said they were "atheists."

Introduction

Seventy-year-old men should know better than to attempt writing their first book, when most of their contemporaries are playing golf in Florida or watching their grandsons play high school football. But surprising even to my most energetic self, I found myself, in spite of still working at my full-time job, doing just that. I am in fact doing this in addition to attending most of my grandsons' football, baseball, and basketball games and my granddaughters' dance and piano recitals. My golf game may have suffered a little more. But it had already seen its better days anyway.

Regrettably though, several months into many long days and some longer nights, I was growing weary of researching and reading all the sources needed to do my subject justice. I quite frankly asked myself, "Why am I doing this?"

It was at that point that I turned a page in the book I was reading and stared at a quote that gave me a rather dramatic answer to my self-serving question. It was not as dramatic or life-changing as the lightning bolt that barely missed Martin Luther and caused him to promise he would become a monk, but it answered my question. I happened to reread (from a new source) a Bernard Lewis quote that reminded me why I had an obligation to write this book.

Dr. Lewis, a man who is universally recognized as the western world's leading authority on Islamic history, was quoted in a *Wall Street Journal* article as he explained the problems that America and the rest of what once was known as the "Christian world" confront today because we do not understand the nature of the war we face. Referring to his work for British intelligence during the dark days of World War II, Lewis said, "We knew who we were, we knew who the enemy was, we knew the dangers and the issues. It is different today. *We don't know who we are. We don't know the issues, and we still do not understand the nature of the enemy*"[1] (emphasis added).

It is sadly true that the vast majority of Americans, including most of our political leaders, academics, church leaders, and the news media, do not truly know "who we are" and "still do not understand the nature of the enemy."

This book is not intended to be a technical, scholarly work, but rather an easily readable account of the issues that confront us today, as well as a reference to books and other works that can provide more detail on given topics. While Dr.

Lewis referred in his quote only to one threat—that of radical Islamists—I intend also to make the case that we must know who we are and who the enemy is if we are to respond adequately to another threat as well. This is the threat posed by radical secularists who would destroy the moral and religious foundations of our great nation in the "culture wars."

Both wars are totally religious in nature. The first war is a religious war because these fundamentalist radical Muslim terrorists believe they have a divine obligation to destroy the Great Satan (America) in order to achieve their goal of establishing a world ruled by Islamic law. The second war is religious because these hard-core secularists believe they must completely drive religion from the public square in order to destroy the moral and religious (Judeo-Christian) foundation upon which this nation was built. Their goal is to establish a totally secular society free from the moral restraints inherent in a society founded on religious principles.

These two enemies of the God-given liberties enjoyed in this country for more than 200 years know the stakes and the religious nature of these wars. Unfortunately, the majority of God-fearing, hard-working, and family-oriented Americans don't have the same understanding of the nature of these wars.

While these two wars are totally separate, I do not believe we can lose one war without losing both.[2]

If we lose the culture war and with it our moral and spiritual heritage, we will lose the will and determination to fight the long and drawn out war the fanatical Islamist jihadists are prepared to wage. On the other hand, if we were to lose the war being waged by al-Qaeda and its Islamic terrorist allies, we would lose not only our religious freedoms but most of our other freedoms as well.

Radical Islamists

It is my intention to give a brief summary of Islamic history and the threat from radical Islamic fundamentalists in chapters 4 and 5. The Rev. Dr. Franklin Graham was criticized a few years ago—even President Bush offered mild criticism—for saying that Islam has been a violent religion from its founding. Certainly, Graham made a "politically incorrect" statement, but was the statement in fact correct? I intend to shed light on this question.

The prophet Mohammad himself led the first military mission against a Christian settlement in 631 A.D., apparently to set an example for his followers. The last of the Arabian tribes had submitted to Islam and now he instructed his followers to conquer Christian countries. Mohammad led an attack on Tabuk, a northwestern Arabian city, which was part of the Christian Byzantine Empire. The Byzantine troops deserted the city and little fighting took place. The Christian ruler of Tabuk, along with several other leaders, submitted to Mohammed and agreed to pay the *jizya* (tax) and accept the "protection of the Muslims." *Thus, the first page was written in Islam's wars of conquest of Christian lands.* This war would expand over many centuries.

At one peak of its power, Islam had conquered lands comprising roughly two-thirds of what had been the Christian world. Of special interest to those of us who are trying to comprehend the Islamic terrorists' threats today, as well as to understand their origins, is the fact that in 638, less than three years after Mohammad's death, invading Muslim armies conquered Jerusalem and took control of the Christian and Jewish population in that city. When the Muslims expanded into Syria, Egypt, North Africa, and parts of Europe, including Spain, Portugal, southern Italy, and, briefly, even southern France, they were conquering Christian populations.

Who are these Islamist terrorists and what motivates them? What do they believe? Why do they hate us with such a passion? What caused the disputes and sectarian divides that lead them to hate one another? How can a rational human being believe in a cause with such fervor that he will destroy himself and even his (or her) children in suicide bombings? The answers appear to lie deeply imbedded in their religious beliefs. We must find the time to understand their beliefs and history if we are to know this enemy.

The Muslim confession of faith is not complicated: "*There is no God but Allah, and Mohammad is His Prophet.*" They are taught that Allah in the Koran and Yahweh of the Bible are the same God (Koran 29:46). They believe God sent other prophets, such as Abraham, Moses, and Jesus, but Mohammad was the last. He brought the final revelation and there will be no more.

If anyone says that you or anyone else is quoting the Koran out of context, the proper response is, "What context?" There is very little context in the Koran itself since it is not presented in a linear record but is divided up based on the length of the verses (surahs). The commentaries on the Koran, traditions, and biographies of Mohammad that attempt to establish a context were not even agreed upon until the 9th century at the earliest. It is extremely difficult for the best of scholars to place many, if not most, of the surahs in their historical context.

This is important because Mohammad received his revelations in two distinct periods: the Meccan period from 610 to 622 and the Medinan period from 622 until his death in 632. The Meccan period is a time of peace, tolerance, and persuasion as Mohammad tries to convince the members of his own tribe and others in Mecca that he is God's promised prophet. The Medinan era is a period when Mohammad has political authority, commands his troops in battle, and is himself a fierce warrior. Gentle persuasion was superseded by stronger tactics.

What's more, the Koran teaches a "doctrine of abrogation (*naskh*)" (Koran 2:106), which holds that, while man may not change anything Allah says, Allah can change or supersede any revelation with something better if he chooses. So, verses written in the Medinan period supersede the earlier surahs. Logic says the verses stressing peace and tolerance fit more readily in the early period in Mecca. That puts the verses speaking of holy war (*jihad*) in the period of final revelation in Medina.

We will try to learn as much as possible about what Mohammad believed Allah commanded him to do.

It is most likely self-evident to the reader that, if we are to understand the threat of radical Islamic terrorism today, we must try to learn as much as possible about Islam's prophet, his life, his actions, and the teachings of the religion he founded. Devout Muslims believe that Mohammad led the ideal life and set the perfect example for them to follow. Hundreds of millions of Muslims today still believe that the highest degree of devotion to Allah is to emulate the life of Mohammad.

Mohammed certainly was a highly creative and complex teacher. He inspired and motivated his followers to the point that he commanded absolute loyalty from the vast majority of them. He was a shrewd military commander and a fierce warrior. At times, he showed leniency to the vanquished and, at other times, only the sword.

Is it even possible for Christians, Jews, or others to enjoy real freedom of religion in a Muslim-ruled country? I believe that such an idea is a contradiction in terms of the teachings of Mohammad and the religion he founded. Since Islam teaches that Muslims have accepted God's final revelation, they are by definition superior to those who have refused to accept it.

As Christian clergymen and laymen, we must feel great compassion for Christians who are experiencing persecution and discrimination in Muslim-ruled countries. Equally heartrending is the multitude of cases of Muslims, living in Christian lands, who convert to Christianity and then receive threats—frequently death threats—and who are totally ostracized by family, friends, and their native countries. I will reference books with horror stories written by some of these Muslim converts, as well as by some former Muslims who have simply denounced what they believe to be the oppressive beliefs of Islam without actually having converted to any other religion.

Christianity and Islam alike have seen sectarian divisions. The major divide in Western Christianity, the Reformation, took more than 15 centuries to materialize. For Islam, the split came just a few years after Mohammad's death in 632. The Sunni-Shiite division was caused by an emotional and bloody internal conflict over who was to be Mohammad's successor. It is difficult to understand the complex history of Islam and its very divisive theological disputes. But obtaining at least a basic knowledge of these subjects is essential to understanding today's terrorist threats from certain segments of radical Islam.

The frequently violent Sunni-Shiite struggle, which has now spanned some 1,400 years, was a major factor in the prosecution of the war in Iraq. This major divide in Islam continues to result in bloodshed and a divided government after all American troops have been withdrawn. In addition, there are thousands of sects and sub-sects, clans and sub-clans, tribes and sub-tribes, cults and sub-cults, which often arise from the followers of some Islamic cleric, scholar, or revolutionary leader. These groups frequently provide fertile recruiting grounds for the extremist and terrorist organizations that wage *jihad* or Islamic holy war.

I hope to shed some light on the theological and operational differences between the Sunni and Shiite sects from their beginnings, which should explain their respective roles in the struggles with Islamic terrorists in today's world. We will consider what the "Twelver Shiites" believe and the dominant role they play in Iran and Iraq today. And we will examine the history and goals of al-Qaeda, a Sunni terrorist organization run by Osama bin Laden for almost 30 years until his death. Bin Laden's intention to establish an organization for global terrorist attacks dated back at least as far as 1982.[3] Bin Laden was the emir or commander of al-Qaeda until he was killed by a team of Navy SEALs on May 1, 2011. (After some internal dispute, Ayman al-Zawahiri, al-Qaeda's number-two man under bin Laden, assumed control of the world's most violent terrorist organization on June 16, 2011.)

It is incumbent upon us to analyze the origins and power that the *Wahhabi*-dominated Sunni version of Islam exerts in Saudi Arabia and throughout Islam today. As we examine this matter, it will become clear that the extremist teachings of the fundamentalist Twelver Shiites or the Sunni Wahhabis certainly do not reflect the beliefs of the popular masses in Islam. Rather, the threat to world peace and stability comes from the fanatics and radicals who believe they have a divine command to conquer the infidels.

To make sense of today's terrorist threats, one must also know how various Islamic cults interpret *jihad* (spiritual striving or "holy war" to establish the world wide reign of Islam). And, *sharia* (Islamic law), which is almost always universally oppressive to women and certain minorities, varies not only in the Sunni and Shiite traditions but frequently from country to country. In a number of Muslim countries today, *sharia* law mandates the death penalty for Muslims who convert to Christianity. How can we not keep ourselves informed on such matters when even the Archbishop of Canterbury says that due to the growing Muslim population in England, the U.K. should take steps to accommodate itself to *sharia* law?

The role of the war American troops fought in Iraq will be examined in the context of the "holy war" being waged by Islamic extremists. It will become perfectly clear that al-Qaeda did not declared war on America because we invaded Iraq. This was merely one of the many fronts of al-Qaeda's global terrorist war against America and her allies. We will look briefly at the propaganda effort by some Islamic scholars and apologists. Even more importantly, we will examine a few examples of disinformation being disseminated by Western "scholars" and even by some church "leaders." We will conclude with a discussion of what role Lutherans, especially Lutheran clergymen, can and must play in the life and death struggle with the Islamist terrorists.

During the last 40 years of my professional career in the nation's capital, I have not seen it all, but I have seen much more than most. I have been an eyewitness to some of the most significant—and some of the most troubling—events in our nation's history. The Watergate scandal, the resignation of a president, and the *Roe v. Wade* Supreme Court decision that has resulted in the death of some 50 million babies all occurred during the early years of the 1970s. The 1974 congressional election immediately after Watergate resulted in such a Democrat landslide that the Democrats were within a few seats of having a two-to-one majority in the U.S. House of Representatives. These events were followed by the election of a former governor of Georgia, Jimmy Carter, as president of the United States in 1976.

During the Carter administration, some good things happened. But in my opinion, history will judge this administration harshly for a major foreign policy mistake. This mistake was so serious that it would end up empowering a radical group of Islamic Shiite terrorists. Through some inexplicable neglect or extremely poor judgment on the part of some high-level officials in the Carter administration, the Shah of Iran was allowed to fall from power.

Mohammad Reza Shah Pahlavi was arguably the most enlightened ruler in modern times in this part of the world. The Shah was without question the strongest and most loyal ally the United States had in the Muslim world. After the Shah was forced to flee the country, Ayatollah Ruhollah Khomeini returned from exile in France as a conquering hero and almost immediately consolidated absolute power. Khomeini was a fundamentalist Twelver Shiite and may well have believed himself to be the *Mahdi* (Messiah).

As the revolution was reaching its final days, a group of fanatical armed students occupied the American embassy in Tehran and held 52 U.S. diplomats hostage for 444 days. The Iranian hostage crisis became an embarrassment to America and an inspiration to radical Islamists (especially Shiites). It may well have awakened latent *jihad* (holy war) tendencies among fundamentalist Muslims worldwide. The hostage crisis must have had an unintended consequence for these radicals as well. This foreign policy debacle played a major, possibly decisive, role in the 1980 presidential election and Jimmy Carter's defeat by Ronald Reagan.

The fall of the Shah, America's most powerful and loyal ally in the entire Middle East, helped set the stage for the Islamist terrorists' war being waged against America and her allies today. How this major foreign policy mistake happened and its tragic consequences will be discussed further in Chapter 5.

A major initiative that began under the Carter administration and was continued during Reagan's watch as president would have a significant effect on the ultimate outcome of the Cold War and is recorded in the book *Charlie Wilson's War*. The book and movie by the same title offer an amazingly accurate account of how a little-known Texas congressman, Charlie Wilson, almost single handedly managed to get massive American support for a group of Muslim rebels who were resisting the Soviet invasion of Afghanistan. This ragtag, poorly armed (until Wilson got involved) group of hard-core Islamic resisters, called *mujahedeen*, succeeded in defeating the mighty Russian army after a long and exceptionally bloody war that drained Soviet resources and resolve.

Those who read the book or view the movie get a rare, inside look at the strengths and weaknesses of certain types of American foreign-policy operations. Like the making of sausage, it often is not very pretty.[4]

The most serious flaw in our foreign policy under most administrations and congresses is the lack of an endgame. The same Congress that had given Wilson almost a billion dollars to fight the war refused to appropriate a million dollars to build a school for the poor children after the war ended. The overwhelming majority of the people in Afghanistan never knew that the United States had the slightest role in helping to rid them of the oppressive and brutal Soviet invaders. Those who might have known of our help could not find us when the battles ceased and they wanted now to live normal lives. When the Soviets withdrew from Afghanistan in 1988, we slipped out of the country, taking all possible traces of our involvement with us. I guess we convinced ourselves that our number-one enemy in the Cold War would never find out about our involvement. The average citizen in Afghanistan may have never known of America's massive involvement, but the Soviets knew it from day one.

The unintended and tragic consequences of deserting the Afghan people after helping to drive the Russians out confront us today with a war waged by radical Islamic terrorists who want to destroy us. After we left, and after a period of struggle between tribal warlords, the radical Islamic Taliban consolidated total power in 1996. (It should be pointed out that the *mujahedeen* and their leaders made no secret of the fact that they desired to establish in Afghanistan a fundamentalist Islamic regime patterned after some of their early-medieval theocracies under strict Islamic [*sharia*] law.)

The Afghan people were burdened with heartless masters who would make the Russians look like benevolent rulers. A recent CNN documentary examined life in Afghanistan under the Taliban, especially in the more remote areas, which they still control today. Included were scenes of horror as younger women committed suicide, frequently leaving young children behind, in a desperate attempt to protest the horrible treatment of women under the rule of the Taliban.

Osama bin Laden started terrorist training camps in Afghanistan in 1986 and founded al-Qaeda in 1988. He established al-Qaeda as a "humanitarian" organization to keep records and notify the families of the *mujahedeen* killed in Afghanistan. Al-Qaeda would evolve into the vehicle for his global terrorist network. (Could the U.S. have helped broker a stable, moderate Islamic regime in Afghanistan with a proactive foreign policy after the Soviets withdrawal? Unfortunately, we will never know!)

The Taliban is a radical fundamentalist Islamic movement with a total commitment to *jihad*. This movement, which eventually bin Laden virtually controlled, would become the ideal venue for him after his return to Afghanistan in 1996. After the war in Afghanistan ended, bin Laden returned to his homeland, Saudi Arabia, for a few years, where he ended up under house arrest for much of the time. He then fled Saudi Arabia for Sudan. During some five years in Sudan, bin Laden and his top assistants developed the al-Qaeda terrorist organization and directed a number of terrorist attacks. When his Sudanese hosts could no longer provide protection for him, he and his most loyal followers returned to the safe haven of Afghanistan to plan and execute their terrorist activities—culminating in the 9/11 attacks on American soil. (A more detailed account of these activities will be presented in Chapter 5.)

Failed American foreign policy decisions in Iran ended up creating a radical Shiite theocracy that nurtured a culture of *jihad* for Twelver Shiites and their glorification of martyrdom. Haphazard and uncoordinated foreign policy activities in Afghanistan, with no thought of an endgame, created a Sunni Islamic government there with a fanatical commitment to Sunni *jihad* activities throughout the world. The Soviets would never have dreamed of invading Afghanistan in 1979 had the Shah still been in power with the world's fourth largest and modernly equipped army standing in their way. Saddam Hussein would never have allowed himself even to entertain the thought of invading Kuwait a decade later if the Shah's powerful army would still have been in place.

We did not realize the tragic consequences of such foreign policy failures until Sept. 11, 2001. Even then, very few understood the history behind one of the two most devastating attacks on American soil in our history. Only Pearl Harbor rivals the horror of 9/11.

When the 9/11 tragedy hit, the country came together for a period of patriotic unity. President Bush's strong and forceful response to these radical Islamic terrorist attacks was widely supported by the country and its elected officials in the beginning. Almost all of my Democratic friends in D.C., including a few members of Congress, privately told me, "Thank God George Bush is President!" The invasion of Afghanistan was almost universally supported. Initially, the Iraq invasion and the overthrow of Saddam Hussein also were widely supported, if not overwhelmingly so.

On the substantive side, I am not in this case necessarily criticizing the foreign policy of the Carter or Reagan administrations or those officially charged with the responsibility to conduct foreign policy. The Afghanistan-*mujahedeen* operation was so congressionally driven and cloaked in such secrecy (with all the CIA involvement) that I doubt those charged with making and conducting foreign policy knew much about what was going on. They were supposed to be above the fray. The Cold War was of such paramount importance at the time that I doubt many of the best and brightest in these administrations ever gave much thought to a future Islamic *jihad's* threat. (Obviously, President Carter and President Reagan had to authorize such a major CIA operation. I now know from very reliable sources that Reagan enthusiastically supported the undertaking as long as no American combat troops were involved.)

I am fearful that few of those in positions of authority in our country have taken the time to undertake an in-depth study of Islamic history and realize how it has bred a radical terrorist element over the last 1,400 years. I fear that too many of our leaders, as well as our scholars, get caught up in the politically correct concerns of not wanting to offend the vast majority of Muslims in the world who want to live in peace and harmony.

The Muslims I know personally are among the nicest, friendliest, and most accomplished people one could ever hope to meet. We certainly do not want to give offense to such people. Yet we must be fair and realistic about the threats we face. This is one reason I have consented to write this book. I hope to reach and motivate those who are most capable of informing and motivating people with the truth.

Radical Secularists

Meanwhile, there is yet another war that demands our attention and about which too many people are woefully ignorant. This war involves the cultural struggles that have plagued us to a certain extent since our nation's founding, but which have been raging in our society since the 1940s.

As I noted in the Preface to this book, our elected representatives generally seek to serve the people as best they can. Most of the problems have been caused by those on the extreme left and extreme right.

I added that the greater threat comes from activist judges. And, arguably the most egregious example of judicial activism in American history is found in the majority opinion written by Justice Hugo Black in *Everson v. Board of Education* in 1947. It was in that opinion that Black wrote, "The First Amendment has erected a wall between church and state. That wall must be kept high and impregnable. We could not approve the slightest breach."

In *Everson*, Black uses the "wall of separation" metaphor that appears in a letter written Jan. 1, 1802, by Thomas Jefferson to a Baptist association in Danbury, Conn. Black does this to justify his revisionist interpretation of the religious clause in the First Amendment. This Supreme Court decision[5] in effect reversed some 150 years of judicial history concerning the proper relationship between church and state as intended by those who drafted, debated, amended, and passed the First Amendment in the First United States Congress.

Neither Black nor any of the other justices voting in the majority seemed to have had any interest in what the states that ratified the First Amendment understood it to mean.[6] What's more, Justice Joseph Story, appointed to the Supreme Court by President James Madison, and several other prominent early justices made significant and defining comments on the "religious clause" in the First Amendment, but none are even considered in this radical and revisionist decision. It is obvious that Justice Black was determined to ban religion from the public square—and he was not going to let the facts stand in his way.

The almost total lack of knowledge[7] of Hugo Black's early background as a defense attorney in Birmingham, Ala., and his actions that led to his election to the U.S. Senate will be examined in some detail in Chapter 6. The stage was set by Black's successful, but racist and anti-Catholic, defense of a barber-turned-Methodist-minister of all charges for the cold-blooded murder of a Catholic priest.

With his newly acquired celebrity status, Black joined the Ku Klux Klan and was elected Alabama's junior senator in 1926. When FDR appointed him to the Supreme Court in 1937, Black's strict (perhaps fanatical) separationist views were already concrete because of his obsessive fears of an increase of Catholic power in America. In the next 10 years, the American Civil Liberties Union (ACLU) and their secularist allies such as "Protestants and Other Americans United for Separation of Church and State"[8] would fan the fires of rabid fear over perceived growing Catholic influence. They ranted about the wealth of the Catholic Church and the ever-expanding number of Catholic parochial schools, that they contended might threaten public education and democratic values.[9]

The brilliant, complex—and sometime verbose—Thomas Jefferson will receive special attention when I deal with the Founding Fathers. Jefferson's attitude toward the role of religion in government, as well as his personal religious convictions, which are complicated, shifting and sometimes seemingly inconsistent, will receive special attention.[10]

Suffice it to say at this point that Jefferson's personal religious persuasion went from Anglican to Deist to Unitarian to "Christian" Unitarian,[11] as will be discussed and documented. His public actions as governor of Virginia and as president of the United States are perhaps even more complex and complicated. Two examples that I hope will whet the appetite for further detail and that are sure to drive the secularists to near despair relate to Jefferson's actions as president.

One: If President Jefferson did in fact intend to erect a "wall of separation" between church and state,[12] it must have been a very low wall that he could easily step over. Two days after Jefferson penned the letter to the Danbury Baptists that is so authoritatively quoted by Black, Jefferson comfortably stepped the "wall" to attend a Christian worship service in the U.S. House of Representatives. He would continue such a practice of church attendance on most Sundays during the remaining seven years of his presidency.

Two: Dr. Daniel Dreisbach emphasizes how President Jefferson condoned federal government assistance to religion as necessary and desirable under certain circumstances. Dreisbach notes, "During his presidency, for example, Jefferson negotiated a treaty with the Kaskaskia Indians that appropriated federal dollars for 'the support of a [Catholic] priest' and 'the erection of a church.'"[13]

Dreisbach, as well as many other recognized scholars, freely admits that Thomas Jefferson was more of a "separationist than virtually all his contemporaries." Unlike the other first seven or so American presidents (and nearly all the members of the earliest congresses), Jefferson was opposed to the President issuing religious proclamations, such as for days of prayer and fasting. This was a state matter. However, by words and deeds, Jefferson unequivocally demonstrated that he had no intention of banning religion from the public square.

Like virtually all of the founding fathers, Jefferson harbored a strong fear of the Catholic Church. He also expressed grave concerns that an attempt might be made to establish a "Protestant Popedom." But almost always a practical man, Jefferson needed to fix a problem. The Kaskaskia Indians needed to educate their children. Jefferson needed their peace and friendship. It certainly would not hurt for these Indian children to get a dose of the Christian religion on the American government's dime. Jefferson obviously reasoned at the time that there were too few Catholics in America to pose a problem.

For the sake of discussion, a theoretical case could be made that things might have been different had the ACLU, AUSCS, and their secularist allies been around at the time. Such secular humanists, who have always challenged the moral and religious foundation on which this nation was founded, could have filed lawsuits as fast as the ink would dry.

They could have argued that the courts should immediately ban the Congress from allowing their facilities to be used for religious purposes. The President should have been ordered by the judges not to step foot on federal property to attend a Christian worship service. The congressmen and senators who might be attending such worship services would have been charged with violating the Constitution and Bill of Rights that many of them had drafted, passed, and sent to the states for ratification.

The Congress could have been charged with flagrantly violating the "establishment clause" of the "religion clause" in the First Amendment that they had so carefully debated, amended numerous times, and finally passed just a dozen years earlier. The elite secularist scholars at the ACLU and the other such organizations almost certainly would have chosen to go to court to explain to these men what they really meant. Such farmers, 18th-century-trained lawyers, and clergymen were not really equipped to understand the niceties of the law, even if they wrote it.

If such founding secularist "watchdogs" would have existed at the time, they might have had trouble finding the right court in which to file their lawsuits. The Supreme Court still was not meeting when President Jefferson started joining the members of Congress, cabinet members, and others attending these early worship services due to Jefferson's suspension of this court.

Such a theoretical ACLU-led coalition might have found it difficult to find standing in any early American court, since the overwhelming majority of the men serving as judges at the time were devout, practicing Christians.

Jefferson's treaty with the Kaskaskia Indians would certainly have been viewed by these hypothetical secular elites as an even more serious breach of the Constitution and the Bill of Rights. The president and the U.S. Congress financing a Catholic school and spending federal dollars to build a Catholic church would almost certainly have been viewed by such an imaginary transposition of a modern-day secularist coalition as totally destroying the "wall" of separation of church and state.

They could not have resisted cries for "impeachment" of the President—and the Congress—for "high crimes and misdemeanors" and any other even more serious charges they could come up with. How dare these country bumpkins in Congress fail to understand the real meaning of the "establishment clause" they had placed in the First Amendment? President Jefferson had just explained to them, and the rest of the country, a couple of years earlier that they had established a wall between church and state that could never be breached.

I probably should not appear to be making light of such serious problems faced by our country today. My only defense would be that this is an attempt to offer an overly simplified, highly metaphorical analysis to characterize how most of the secularist elites treat the majority of ordinary, Christians Americans. When these "politically correct" secular elites adopt—almost universally—the demeaning "of course" strategy[14] based on the implication of "how stupid can you be" to describe traditionalist Americans, we must understand their intentions.

"Of course," we are a secular country! "Of course," our Founders intended strict separation of church and state and built a legal "wall" to keep the two from ever mingling or influencing each other! "Of course," religion—especially the Christian religion—has no place in "the public square," because religion is a purely private matter for home and church and must be left behind when Christians venture into the political or civic arena! When one questions their source of authority for their "of course" conclusions, you usually feel that the short answer offered is, "Because we said so" and "We know better."

Obviously, as dedicated and concerned Christian Americans, we should always take the "high road" in our efforts to defend the moral and spiritual values bequeathed to us by our forefathers. I have become convinced, however, that if we don't understand the "low road" strategy of our opponents, we will be unable to mount a "high road" game plan to successfully compete in this high stakes contest.

The other Founder who will receive special attention in the section of the book dealing with the Founding Fathers is, unsurprisingly, James Madison. Madison is perhaps even more complex and sometimes more contradictory in his writing and actions than Jefferson, the man frequently referred to as Madison's mentor. Madison is often called the "father" of the Constitution and the "author" of the Bill of Rights. The latter title is certainly more accurate than the former.

James Madison's personal religious convictions are sketchy, to say the least. We know that he was raised an Anglican and became an avid Calvinist under the influence of the Rev. John Witherspoon during his days as a student at Princeton. Having completed Princeton's four-year undergraduate curriculum in two years, Madison was Princeton's first graduate student. He spent much of his year as a graduate student trying to decide if he wanted to study for the Holy Ministry. We know that he held the Evangelicals in high esteem later in life, and there is not a shred of evidence that he ever became a Deist or a Unitarian.

It is not surprising that the secularists quote some of Madison's writings in the later years of his life to promote their secular goals. It is a little surprising that virtually none of these secular elites, at least in the name of academic honesty, seem to have read his drafts and amendments as well as his debate surrounding Congress' adoption of the "religion clause" in the First Amendment. As we shall see in this book, Madison's clearly stated goal was to prevent Congress from establishing a "national" religion or from interfering with anyone's right to freely practice their religion.

Today's secular elites, including the ACLU, appear to give Madison a total pass on his actions as a congressman and president. As a congressman, Madison sat on the House committee that established federal salaries for chaplains and supported the Northwest Ordinance,[15] for example. As president, he allowed military chaplains to be paid from the federal treasury, designated days of prayer and fasting, and attended Christian worship services in the U.S. Capitol.[16]

When this country was founded as a representative democracy "conceived in liberty," it was an experiment in many ways. There was no historical blueprint to rely upon. But there were perhaps some primitive examples in certain Greek "city-states" such as Sparta and in the republicanism of early Rome. And, in the *Second Treatise of Civil Government* and other writings of John Locke, there were many sound ideas.

The liberal establishment taunts Locke's contention that man is endowed with "natural rights" and has the right to rebel against an oppressive government as forming the foundation of our government. Locke is frequently also credited with advocating a government by the "consent of the governed," which is the bedrock of our founding principles. Some 70 years earlier, in November 1620, the Pilgrims who landed at Plymouth Rock adopted the Mayflower Compact. All 41 men who had arrived on the Mayflower signed this written agreement to establish a government whose laws were based on the consent of the governed. Some 150 years later, John Adams would refer to the Mayflower Compact as the foundation of the U.S. Constitution.[17]

We owe a debt of gratitude also to Charles de Secondat, baron de Montesquieu, for our concept of the separation of the executive, legislative, and judicial branches of government. In his *The Spirit of the Laws,* published in 1748, he eloquently espouses the doctrine of the separation of powers.

We owe nothing but scorn to Jean-Jacques Rousseau, who denied original sin and insisted that man should be free to follow his natural proclivities, and is correctly identified by Edmund Burke as the reason for the excesses of the French revolution.

What made the American Revolution unique in history and so successful was that America's Founders turned to a more ancient and much more reliable source for the founding of this country: THE HOLY BIBLE. Locke's thesis that man was endowed with certain "natural rights" is only true to the extent that one understands that these rights come from God.

Thomas Jefferson stated this truth much more accurately when he wrote in the Declaration of Independence that we are "endowed by our Creator with certain inalienable rights." The fact that the success of the young country depended on the blessings of the God of the Bible is stated by virtually every Founding Father. If there was near unanimity on anything among the Founders, it would have been the fallen nature of man. They were like Will Rogers, who when asked if he believed in original sin, responded, "Sir, not only do I believe in it, I have seen it."

It should be noted that discussing the role of religion in the founding of America is made difficult—almost impossible—to articulate in a dispassionate dialogue since a number of the most prominent Founders rejected the miraculous elements in the New Testament. Jefferson, Adams, Franklin, and some of the less significant founders, such as Thomas Paine and Ethan Allen, did not accept the divinity and the atonement of Jesus Christ. (Some scholars, all the liberals, and some of the conservatives insist that Washington and Madison also fall into that category. Since neither left us much information on their religious beliefs, we will not know for sure until the Day of Judgment.)

The secularists have used such facts to discredit the belief that our country was founded on a Judeo-Christian moral foundation. They boldly proclaim that this proves that these Founders wanted the Christian religion to play no role in the Public Square. This is academically, and in some cases personally, dishonest considering the undeniable facts clearly stated in documents written by these Founders. But it is contrary to the politically correct culture that dominates today's Public Square to even imply that a person must have faith in Jesus Christ as his or her personal Savior in order to inherit the paradise He has prepared for His followers. The politically correct have created a culture of "universalism" (i.e., that many roads lead to heaven if you just strive to be a good person and do good works), which may be their most important achievement in furthering their goal of creating a secular society.

A recent conversation I had with a group of Republican congressmen who are good friends illustrates just how pervasive this culture of universalism has become. This group was not made up of my regular running buddies, but I am close enough to most of them that we had discussed religion on previous occasions. They all were conservative, pro-life, pro-traditional marriage, and none of them had ever shown any interest in being politically correct in their political careers. A couple of them had a special interest and some expertise in the beliefs of the Founders.

We were discussing this very topic, the role of religion in our founding. I had just offered the Franklin quotes (which I will record below to make my point) where he says that Jesus' teachings are by far the superior moral standards of all history. I then made a sincere off the cuff remark that I was sorry that Ben Franklin didn't believe in the divinity of Christ because I would love to meet him in heaven. I was immediately pelted with sharp questions.

How could I possibly know that Franklin would not be in heaven?

"Simple," I replied. "The Bible tells me so!"

As I explained in detail what Jesus taught, I realized just how widely politically correct universalism had spread.

The documented fact of the matter is that the Age of Reason and the Enlightenment had taken its toll on a few of the more intellectual and best known Founders. They were suspicious of the miraculous, which they believed could not be justified by scientific methods. However, they quote without expressing reservations Moses' receiving the Ten Commandments, the exodus from Egypt, and the promise given to Abraham and his leading the Israelites into new lands at God's direction, for example.

They appear to have a similar problem that St. Paul encountered with his audience of Greek religious scholars on Mars' Hill. Many of these men had spent much of their lives studying the gods and religions and had erected an altar "TO THE UNKNOWN GOD." They listened intently to Paul as he spoke of the almighty God who had created all things. They might have accepted the Day of Judgment and that God had sent the message of salvation to men on earth, but when Paul proclaimed that God had given assurance that Christ was the one with that message by raising Him from the dead, this was too much for the ears of highly educated religious scholars to accept.

Jefferson, Adams, and Franklin had no doubts that Jesus was the greatest teacher of morality in all history. They wanted to make sure this young country was founded on such solid principles to ensure its survival. Consider their own words.

I know of no example where any of the "Big Six" (as I will call Franklin, Washington, Adams, Jefferson, Madison, and Hamilton) had anything but ridicule for Thomas Paine's famous tract "The Age of Reason," which strongly attacks biblical Christianity and advocates a form of deism totally foreign to the Christian religion. Paine sent a copy of his manuscript to Benjamin Franklin, who many consider to be the least religious of the Founders, for his comments before publication. Franklin tersely wrote back that he had carefully read the manuscript and advised him not to publish the tract since the "consequence of printing this piece will be a great deal of odium drawn upon yourself, mischief to you, and no benefit to others."

John Adams, who some contend was no more personally religious than Franklin, wrote in his diary[18] of the strongly anti-Christian tract, "The Christian religion is, above all the religions that ever prevailed or existed in ancient or modern times, the religion of wisdom, virtue, equity and humanity, let the Blackguard [scoundrel, rogue] Paine say what he will ...."

Adams, who by his own admission had become a Unitarian, also wrote in his diary:

> "Suppose a nation in some distant region should take the Bible for their only law book, and every member should regulate his conduct by the precepts there exhibited! Every member would be obliged in conscience, to temperance, frugality, and industry; to justice, kindness, and charity towards his fellow men; and to piety, love, and reverence toward Almighty God.... What a Utopia, what a Paradise would this region be."[19]

Adams missed the most important message of the Bible, the message of salvation in Jesus Christ, but he certainly seems to recognize the value of its teachings for the moral foundation of a nation.

In a letter to Charles Thomson, the long-time secretary to Congress, on Jan. 9, 1816, Thomas Jefferson made his personal beliefs very clear. He refers to his "Bible," which he had revised by cutting and pasting—at the same time eliminating all the passages in the Gospels involving any miracles. He wrote that his version "is a document in proof that I am a real Christian, that is to say, a disciple of the doctrines of Jesus, very different from the Platonists, who call me infidel and themselves Christians and preachers of the gospel, while they draw all their characteristic dogmas from what its author never said nor saw."

Sadly, like Franklin and Adams, the "enlightened" Jefferson's reason would not allow him to accept the virgin birth and resurrection of Jesus Christ. But none of these Founders had the least doubt that Jesus was God's messenger who taught God's transcendent moral values so essential for their experiment of a government ruled by a free people. Obviously, the vast majority of the other Founders who were Bible-believing Christians were thrilled to accept their advice.

The Founders all knew that for this fragile republic to succeed, its citizens must be subject to God's law, which they basically incorporated in the nation's laws. They all believed that moral Christian behavior was essential for the well-being of this country. (Even Thomas Paine, the obvious darling of the secularists, said as much on several occasions.)

Americans certainly should be grateful for the part, sometimes major, played by many political philosophers. The guidance contained in earlier documents that were concerned with the establishment of a just and free society was similarly valuable. America, for example, owes a major debt to John Locke (however, not nearly as great a debt as the liberal elitists would have us believe). In some ways our debt to Montesquieu is even greater. The English Bill of Rights, the Magna Carta, and the Toleration Act of 1689 are but a small sampling of political documents that influenced our Constitution. But in *How to Ruin the United States of America*, Ben Stein and Phil DeMuth describe what our Founders really relied upon:

"As Jacques Maritain said in *Man and the State*, 'Far beyond the influences received either from Locke or the XVIII Century Enlightenment, the Constitution of this country is deeply rooted in the age-old heritage of Christian thought and civilization.' Maritain goes on to assert: 'This Constitution can be described as an outstanding lay Christian document tinged with the philosophy of the day.'"[20]

Even Thomas Jefferson, the man vilified by the Federalists in the 1800 presidential election as an "atheist" and so extensively praised by modern-day secularists as erecting a "wall of separation" between church and state, had this to say in his Second Inaugural Address in 1805:

"I shall need, too, the favor of that Being in whose hands we are, who led our forefathers, as Israel of old, from their native land and planted them in this country."

On another occasion, Jefferson got even more explicit when he wrote: "I have little doubt that the whole country will soon be rallied to the unity of our Creator, and, I hope to the pure doctrines of Jesus also."[21]

The only self-described deist of the well-known Founders, Benjamin Franklin, always known for memorable statements, offered this gem: "Whoever shall introduce into public affairs the principles of primitive Christianity will change the face of the earth." President John Adams, the Congregationalist turned Unitarian, made this well-known observation: "Our Constitution was made only for a moral and religious people. It is wholly inadequate to the government of any others."[22]

Professor Stephen Carter of Yale Law School sheds considerable light on how modern-day Americans—living in a country of religious pluralism (still small in terms of percentage of population, but significant in terms of numbers)—should understand the religious climate at the time of our founding. Carter strongly defends religious freedom and tolerance of all religions in today's America because history has taught us the value of such an approach. On the other hand, Carter warns against putting "words in the mouths" of our Founders that they never spoke or wrote. They were concerned about keeping one Christian sect, or some combination of two or three such sects, from gaining a predominate position and denying the other Christian sects in the United States from freely practicing their religion. (Carter's *The Culture of Disbelief* and *God's Name in Vain* are must-reads on this subject.)

Six of the original colonies had an established church. Eleven (12, if you count parts of New York) had a religious test for holding elective office. Pennsylvania was the first state to allow that privilege of holding office to Catholics in 1790 and subsequently to Jewish Americans. It is difficult to argue that America was not founded as a "Christian nation." It certainly was a nation of Christians.

When Alexis De Tocqueville returned to France in 1831 after a nine-month visit to the States, he wrote, "There is no country in the whole world in which the Christian religion retains greater influence over the souls of men than in America."

In fairness to all sides, an attempt will be made in this book, especially in chapters 3 and 6, to distinguish between the American Left and traditional liberals, who have come to be known in modern times as "New Deal" liberals. The American Left, which has been around in one form or another since our founding days, is certainly not a monolithic entity itself.[23] The American Left, which at times included some religious sects, always had in common a "scorn for what is and hopes for what could be," as Daniel Flynn notes in his revealing book, *A Conservative History of the American Left* (Crown Forum, 2008). They were always seeking some type of "utopia" on earth. Capitalism—more specifically, "private property" in most cases—was inherently inequitable and therefore unjust in their minds. There must be a redistribution or equal sharing of the wealth.

Many of those with a casual interest in early American history, as well as historical scholars, are aware of the first communist experiment in American history. The pilgrims who landed at Plymouth Rock were greeted with an edict from their British investors banning the ownership of private property. From 1620 to 1623, the Plymouth colony suffered hunger and other hardships brought about by the requirement to share equally all their resources in communal living.

Even among a totally Christian colony, when one of their stated goals for immigrating to the New World was to spread the Gospel, communism failed miserably. It simply runs counter to man's sinful nature. They would thank God for William Bradford—a man they elected as their governor 30 times—for saving the Plymouth colony. He gave each family enough land to grow their crops, feed their families, and have some left over to pay those who invested in the colony.

A few history buffs may know of some prominent members of the American Left at certain times in history—for example, Roger Baldwin who founded the ACLU in 1920; perhaps also some of Baldwin's contemporaries and friends, such as Margaret Sanger, the eugenicist so admired by Adolf Hitler and the founder of Planned Parenthood; and maybe even the anarchist "Red Erma" Goldman, who was deported to Russia in 1919.

Few Americans other than the historians know two of the most important intellectual leaders of the American Left: Roger Owen and Henry George.[24] Both men challenged the economic system and the very principles of the American government with some limited success during the 19th century and the early years of the 20th century. The bigger concern is what lasting influence they may have had on the modern-day radical left and how far to the left the hard left has moved today's more extreme liberals.

Robert Owen was born in Wales, where he became part owner of a cotton mill. Later, in Scotland, he acquired another mill after marrying the daughter of the mill owner. He launched into reforms to remove small children from working in the factories; shortened the work hours for older children; and established stores, clinics, and other amenities in connection with his factories. He gained fame, amassed considerable wealth, and set out to reform Great Britain according to his model. When he felt rejected by only a marginal response from the British government, he immigrated to the United States to establish local communes, which he contended would become utopian communities.

Believing himself to be the most popular man in the world, Owen charged into the States in 1824, confident he could transform American society into a Utopia by convincing the government to adopt his comprehensive philosophy. Such a philosophy, initially called communism[25] and then socialism,[26] grew out of Owen's list of needed and popular reforms to abuses he believed were inherent in a capitalist system.[27] Owen's comprehensive philosophy probably evolved as he ran his cotton mills and observed other industries around him. He would also unfold such a philosophy in an evolving manner in his public addresses. Meanwhile, Owen started his communes (such as the one he expected to be his showcase, in New Harmony, Ind.) in an effort to illustrate how communal socialism would enhance the lives of the people.

Amazingly, shortly after arriving on American soil, Robert Owen secured meetings with outgoing President James Monroe and incoming President John Quincy Adams. (Within his first year or so in America, Owen would meet with seven of the first eight American presidents.) Even more surprisingly, Owen was afforded the opportunity to advocate his political philosophy before a joint session of the U.S. Congress. Owen's pleas for a socialist Utopia apparently received polite skepticism.

However, on July 4, 1826, before almost 1,000 followers at his principle commune in New Harmony, Owen issued his "Declaration of Mental Independence." In this speech, he gives considerable details about his dream of his brand of socialism in America. The speech contained too much that ran counter to the work ethics and moral values of the overwhelming majority of Americans at the time. Owen identified private property, traditional religion, traditional marriage, and the traditional family as the primary sources of evil, inequity, and greed in human societies. Marriage based on individual property promotes the individual family over the human family and individual interest over group interest. Society must raise children, or they will learn the bad habits of their parents.

Owen's dream of an earthly paradise in America ended in structural failure before the close of the 1820s, but not without leaving behind the seeds of economic socialism and the destruction of American values. Daniel Flynn makes this astute observation about Robert Owen:

> "Robert Owen would feel more at home in a world with gay marriage and easy divorce, which excludes nativity scenes and the Ten Commandments from the public square, and where courts grant government the 'right' to redistribute property from rightful owners

to covetous developers. This is because that is the world Robert Owen helped make" (emphasis added).[28]

Henry George, the son of a Philadelphia printer of religious books, travelled extensively West and East trying to earn a comfortable living, but succeeded only in piling up debts. He ended up type-setting his own book, *Progress and Poverty*. This book, published in 1879 and virtually unknown to modern Americans, sold 3 million copies. *Progress and Poverty* was the most widely read non-fiction book in the English language, save only the Holy Bible, prior to the 20th century. Flynn points out that Henry George—not his contemporary Karl Marx—was the "American Left's intellectual leader during the 1880s."[29]

George lived during what Mark Twain described as the "Gilded Age,"[30] or the Second Industrial Revolution following the end of the War Between the States and "Reconstruction." This period was dominated by the super-industrialists who built the factories, railroads, the coal mines, and steel mills. Among the biggest names were Cornelius Vanderbilt, John D. Rockefeller, Andrew Mellon, Andrew Carnegie, and J.P. Morgan. They were also the great American philanthropists who built colleges, hospitals, museums, and public libraries, and promoted the arts, for example.

As a young man, George saw wealth everywhere but personally found only poverty. After detailing in his book all the workplace problems and social inequities brought about by the polarization of wealth as he saw it, he came up with his "simple" solution. The problem was not "capital" as Marx would insist, because workers created capital. For George, the problem was not all private property, but private "land ownership." George's solution: a "single tax" on land "equivalent to its annual worth." This would lead to public ownership and "in effect, force property holders to rent land from the state." Flynn quotes George:

> "To extirpate poverty, to make wages what justice commands they should be, the full earnings of the laborer, we must therefore substitute for the individual ownership of land a common ownership."[31]

The American Left has consistently sought to find ways to redistribute the nation's wealth. They never have seemed to understand the dynamics of a marketplace inhabited by free citizens. Some government regulations are necessary, but they should be limited.

Henry George was eventually so overshadowed by Marx that he is almost totally unknown to history. But many of George's socialist ideas have continued to influence the modern American Left, even if they barely know his name.

A brief look at the American Left in the 20th century (and into the 21st century) is justified in this book for two reasons: first, because of their efforts to undermine the moral and religious foundations of this country in the cultural wars;

and second, because of their well-financed efforts to move traditional political liberals farther to the left and their not-too-veiled attempts to dominate, if not to take over, the Democrat Party.

The old Marxists of the 1930s, '40s, and '50s are no longer relevant as far as their political and economic theories are concerned. The damage they did to our national security and the lasting influence they exerted on our opinion-molding institutions are still evident. Many of the radical leftists of the 60s, such as Tom Hayden and Bill Ayers, are still around promoting in various ways their extremist left-wing agendas.

But much more dangerous are the radical left-wing billionaires, typified by George Soros, who are pouring hundreds of millions of dollars into left-wing think tanks and political organizations and activities. Bit players like Michael Moore have gone so far left that they are not attracting many converts but are energizing the hard-core left. There is no question that under our constitutional system of government, the hard left has the right to advocate their political philosophy, as long as they do not advocate the violent overthrow of our government.

As noted in the Preface, radical secularists and elitists in the various disciplines have the right to be heard, but they do not have the right to insist that they speak the definitive word just because they say so. To put new words with entirely different meanings into the Founders' mouths is not merely arrogant, but it is a total distortion of the words of the Founders and the documents they produced. The founding documents, specifically the Constitution and Bill of Rights, were to be the unequivocal authority for how America was to be governed. Changes in how "we the people" are governed could be made *only* through the carefully prescribed process of amending the Constitution.

The role and extent of authority granted to federal judges, including the Supreme Court, were also carefully limited and prescribed. This was done specifically to prevent over-reaching judges from assuming that they knew better what was best for the American people than these simple founders. After all, such judges might conclude, these Founders were farmers, merchants, clergymen, and lawyers who did not have the benefit of the prestigious liberal educations they had received. Such judges might further conclude that the world had changed so much that such simple Founders could not possibly understand today's world. One thing our wise Founders did realize was that arrogance of power is a result of original sin and raises its ugly head in every generation. Therefore, they took the proper steps to control such power-seeking and activist judges whom they knew were sure to follow.

Clearly, a careful study of early American history reveals that the intellects of such men as Thomas Jefferson, James Madison, Benjamin Franklin, George Washington, John Adams, John Marshall, John Jay, Patrick Henry, Joseph Story, and a few hundred lesser-known founders would cause the cumulative intellects of the ACLU secularists and their legions of followers throughout history to dwarf in comparison.

Labels and Political Shorthand

What does it mean when a person is described as being "politically correct" or a "politically correct elitist?" Probably a lot more than you realize unless you are steeped in present-day political parlance.

Such terms as these are most often used in a descriptive context rather than with derogatory connotations. (Of course, these phrases can resonate with both meanings. But most of those described as being "politically correct" are proud of such a description.) Politics is noted for employing "political shorthand" in its discussions. For example, when a person is described as a "movement conservative," this is a reference to the "Goldwater movement," the "Reagan revolution," and a multitude of conservative political organizations.

I submit that a person cannot truly understand the magnitude of the threat we face from the Islamist terrorists and radical secularists if we fail to comprehend how deeply political correctness and elitism has become ingrained in our society.

Just a few examples:

It is not politically correct to refer to certain terrorists as "Islamic" or even "Islamist," even though that is how they describe themselves. It is politically correct to believe that the Crusades are the cause of the Muslim-Christian struggle, and it is insensitive and politically incorrect even to raise the issue of the 400 years of Muslim conquest of Christian lands prior to the Crusades.

It is a total violation of political correctness in our society even to suggest that there are transcendent values that forbid a woman's right to an abortion on demand, a person's *right* to marry someone of his or her own sex, or to forbid pornography—perhaps even involving children. And it is terribly politically incorrect and bigoted even to suggest that salvation is available only through Jesus Christ.

The list goes on and ultimately includes disallowing any legal limitations on an individual's behavior as long as one does not physically harm another person. If you have any doubts about how totally secular the Founders intended for this country to be, the "PC" elitists will give you their definitive word on the subject!

The birth and growth of what has become known as political correctness and elitism was a deliberate and well-planned movement in 20th-century America. Likewise, in the second half of the 20th century, the Goldwater movement and the ultimate election of Ronald Reagan bred what is sometimes described as the counter culture of political incorrectness and as anti-elitism. Conservatives, or traditionalists, finally decided that they must fight back or everything our Founding Fathers had bequeathed to us would be radically altered, if not totally destroyed.

My knowledge of these movements was not acquired in a mere academic exercise. Starting in the Goldwater movement and now having spent more than 40 years in Washington, I have been in the middle of many of these struggles. My career path has enabled me to be involved on numerous occasions with government officials at the highest level, including presidents. Perhaps more importantly, I have participated in literally thousands of conversations with senators, congressmen, key staff members, political consultants and analysts, lobbyists, and think-tank intellectuals who represented all shades of the political spectrum on these subjects. I not only know about political correctness and incorrectness, elitism and anti-elitism, I have witnessed these attitudes in all their manifestations on almost a daily basis for some 40 years.

Political correctness was started as a movement that intended to undermine the Judeo-Christian foundation of our system of government, which had led to American exceptionalism and ultimately to the United States becoming the greatest power on earth—and finally the most humanitarian and generous nation the world has ever known. (Yes, we made our mistakes. Slavery is an example. It was the rule, not the exception, in the world at this time in history. Unfortunately, in America, as in most of the rest of the world, the abolition of slavery was followed by a long period of segregation.)

Capitalism and the free market economy were always subject to abuse and could not be left totally unbridled. However, it turned out to be the most productive economic system in world history.

The prime reason capitalism was so successful is that it is rooted in a realistic understanding of man's fallen nature. Man by his nature is unwilling to work hard just to use only what he needs from the fruits of his labor and to share the rest with others who choose not to work. He needs incentives and rewards because he is a sinful creature. (Shortly after Pentecost, the first attempt to establish "Christian" communism, socialism, or communal living, where everyone shared what they had, is recorded in Acts 4:32-5:11. This experiment failed, even among the earliest Christians, because they were still clothed in sinful flesh and needed constant forgiveness.)

If there was one thing that virtually all the founders agreed upon it was that man is basically sinful.[32] An even more unanimously held principle was the belief in rewards and punishments in the hereafter, which would encourage moral behavior so essential to the survival of this fragile Republic. Dr. James Hutson, longtime chief of the Manuscript Division at the Library of Congress, devotes 42 pages to this subject in Chapter 1 ("A Future State of Rewards and Punishments: The Founders' Formula for the Social and Political Utility of Religion") of his book *Forgotten Features of the Founding*. Hutson is frequently described as the man who has read more of the original documents of the Founders concerning religion than any other man alive.

Our Founding Fathers knew all too well the history of experiments in a republican form of government—the Greek city-states, for example—and why they failed to long endure. They had fallen by the way because of greed, corruption, and rampant immorality. Once again, one of the least personally orthodox "Christians" among the famous Founders, John Adams, said it best when he explained that "our Constitution is only suitable for a moral and religious people."

Adams, who knew the intricacies of the Magna Carta perhaps better than most Founders, also contended that the Mayflower Compact served as the foundation for the U.S. Constitution.

One reason I feel compelled to offer a brief history of these movements and the effects they have had is that these terms afford a writer a relatively accurate version of "political shorthand" in characterizing the views of those identified as authorities—as well as those who are self-appointed authorities. For example, not every liberal takes a politically correct attitude on all subjects. Likewise, not all conservatives adopt a politically incorrect posture on many issues. The bottom line is that such descriptions can be neutral or descriptive rather than always negative. (The use of these terms to characterize a person's views is more precise than the broader category of liberal and conservative.)

The movement that would become known as "political correctness" probably had its beginning at the turn of the 20th century when biblical higher criticism, so rampant in Europe, gained its foothold in America. As modernism began to take control of the liberal Christian denominations, the authority of Holy Scripture began to unravel. This was the breakthrough so coveted by the communists, socialists, and other secularists. Writer Agustin Blazquez contends that the adoption of the term "political correctness" to describe this movement was adopted in Germany in the early 1920s. He explains that the term grew out of the Institute for Social Research, founded in 1923 in Frankfurt, Germany. A group of thinkers from this "Frankfurt School" had banded together to study the dilemma facing Russian communism: why was it not spreading as Marx and Lenin had predicted?[33]

They concluded that Western Civilization was hung up on the individual and not the good of society as a whole. As long as the individual was free to think and express his own opinions, he would never learn that valid ideas come only from the "social group of the masses." Vocabulary must be changed so that one will understand that "vocalizing your belief is disrespectful to others and must be avoided to make up for past inequities and injustices."

The members of the Frankfurt School chose "political correctness" as a positive-sounding and progressive description of their undertaking. Blazquez, who says he was subjected to Castro's brain washing and sophisticated censorship in the name of political correctness before fleeing Cuba, notes that a few years later, in the 1930s, Mao spelled out his "sensitive training" [sic]—another way of saying "political correctness." The author then points out:

> "In 1935, after Hitler came to power, the Frankfurt School moved to New York City, where they continued their work by translating Marxism from economic to cultural terms using Sigmund Freud's psychological conditioning mechanisms to get Americans to buy into Political Correctness. In 1941, they moved to California to spread their wings."[34]

Roger Baldwin was the primary founder in 1920 of the American Civil Liberties Union with the intent of destroying America's Judeo-Christian foundation and replacing it with a country that was totally secular. The ACLU[35] put together a coalition of American communists, socialists, liberal church leaders, and other secularists that would firmly establish the culture of political correctness in 20th-century America. The term "political correctness" to describe the movement developed gradually, but it had taken root by the 1960s when I initially became involved in politics.

Some scholars contend that political correctness took on a life of its own as the movement's favorite expression at the University of Wisconsin, which was a hotbed of liberalism at this time. It drove every issue, including feminism, the anti-war movement, universalism in religion, and the "benefits" of a totally secular society.

Political correctness would spawn an elitist class in America. This development would occur logically, since the movement had flooded academia with politically correct scholars. This was especially true of the Ivy League and many of the other most prestigious colleges, such as the University of California at Berkley and the University of Wisconsin. Such elitists, typified by the likes of Arthur Schlesinger Jr., Robert McNamara, and Henry Kissinger, drove the debate during the Cold War until the coming of Ronald Reagan. (As I consistently point out, these men were not bad people or unpatriotic. They simply had been led to believe that they were smartest men alive—this was probably true in many cases—and that they must save the world from a nuclear holocaust.)

I have been convinced—and pleased to see some Christian scholars begin to pick up on the theme—that the weakness of the worldview of the liberal elitists is their failure to understand original sin. This certainly was not the case with most of the Founding Fathers.[36] A quote from the most famous Founder of them all, General George Washington, typifies their attitude.

Washington, like most of the other Founders, was deeply concerned with how ineffective the Articles of Confederation had proven to be. Morality was on the decline and a Constitution was needed to control the behavior of sinful and greedy men. It should be remembered that the Declaration of Independence explained *why* our country was founded. Men had been "endowed by their Creator" with the right to be free and form their own government. The Constitution was to explain *how* they should be governed and controlled. With all this in mind, George Washington told John Jay in words that reveal his understanding of man's sinful nature:

> "We have probably had too good of an opinion of human nature
> in forming our confederation. Experience has taught us, that men will
> not adopt and carry into execution, measures the best calculated for
> their own good without the intervention of a coercive power . . . . We

must take human nature as we find it. Perfection falls not to the share of mortals."[37]

These "elitists," or "Ivy League elitists" as they are frequently called, could not believe that the Marxists really meant what they said. They had to be posturing to get the best deal possible. In such an enlightened age, these theoreticians and communist leaders had to be basically reasonable and good people. They would eventually respond to détente and negotiated treaties.

There were many talented individuals who finally joined what would later become known as the counter-culture, or the anti-elitist and political incorrectness uprising that had its origins in the Goldwater movement. But Bill Buckley, supported by an extraordinary group of intellectuals, many of whom had escaped Soviet oppression in the Captive Nations, emerged as the leader of this urgent undertaking. (Buckley and the intellectuals he surrounded himself with were every bit as brilliant as the "Ivy League elitists," but there was one major difference that separated the two groups in their worldviews. Buckley's group not only believed in original sin but, like Will Rogers, they had "seen it.")

Chapter 7 is dedicated to the "Culture Wars" and the role that political correctness and creation of a class of secular elites played in this struggle. I lean heavily on two outstanding sources as I make my case. One is Richard John Neuhaus' *The Naked Public Square: Religion and Democracy in America*. The other is Yale Law School Professor Stephen L. Carter.

Neuhaus was my classmate at Concordia Seminary in St. Louis. During our first year at the seminary, we lived only two doors apart in our dorm. Needless to say, we had many discussions—and some arguments—on theology and politics. I am still convinced that I was almost always right on theology. But he did me a service in this area. He was so incredibly smart that I read many of Luther's works and books on theology that I would not have read otherwise. I never liked to lose an argument. In the political realm, I am now convinced he was right most of the time and actually taught me some things that would be useful later on. (I was still a died-in-the-wool Southern Democrat at the time.)

My second primary source, Professor Stephen L. Carter, is perhaps an even more distinguished academician. His two books, *The Culture of Disbelief: How American Law and Politics Trivialize Religious Devotion* and *God's Name in Vain: The Wrongs and Rights of Religion in Politics,* are also essential documents in understanding the Culture Wars. Who could possibly be a better source on elitism in American universities than a black scholar who has also written a book titled *Reflections of an Affirmative Action Baby*? Carter, like Neuhaus, is a careful scholar who offers a wealth of documentation from both sides. Unlike Neuhaus, Carter comes down on the liberal side on some political issues, such as abortion. But he cuts no slack in denouncing the intolerance and arrogance of the politically correct elitists who assume the right to be the final authority on moral issues in the political arena.

I will also include some people and organizations who have decided to fight back in defense of our American heritage. Specifically, the Alliance Defense Fund has taken the lead in battles to defend our religious liberties so carefully bequeathed to us by our Founding Fathers. The tide is turning among the American people, but activist judges continue to represent the biggest obstacle in upholding traditional values.

Overcoming Ignorance

We are facing two enemies—the radical Islamists and the radical secularists. It is the intention of this book to overcome the ignorance about which Dr. Bernard Lewis warns.

In the final chapter, we will attempt to lay out a Lutheran plan of action in which we can perhaps play a unique role in the context of an essential Christian response to these challenges. If we Americans allow our heritage to fall and our moral foundations to crumble, and if we fail to appreciate our responsibilities in this great land of liberty so richly blessed by God, then we will fall easy prey to the adversaries who seek to destroy us. Christians must respond to what I believe to be God's call to arms or we will suffer the same fate as Israel of old!

Therefore, let us now explore who we are, the issues with which we must grapple, and the nature of the enemy with whom we are engaged.

Notes

[1] Quoted in *Faith, Reason, and The War against Jihadism* by George Weigel, 9. I will refer extensively to Dr. Lewis' numerous works throughout this book when discussing Islam and the threats posed by the radical Islamic terrorists

[2] The deep partisan divide over out-of-control government spending and the attendant unsustainable explosion of government debt has further diverted our attention from these two "wars." All of these matters threaten the very survival of the type of country we all hope to bequeath to our children and our children's children. The financial crisis will be addressed in the context of the 2012 elections in Chapter 3.

[3] Abdel Bari Atwan's *The Secret History of al-Qaeda* offers some interesting insights into Osama bin Laden and the terrorist organization he founded. The author spent three days with bin Laden in his Tora Bora hideout in 1996. He is the only western-based journalist to ever have had such an extensive conversation with al-Qaeda's founder. The author has valuable insights, but he is a Muslim with some Muslim bias.

[4] I must offer a disclaimer before anyone runs out and buys the Charlie Wilson book or watches the movie. Some of the language and some of the scenes are vulgar and pornographic. The movie will be offensive to the religiously devout. Those who fall into this category probably are better off just taking my word for the content. The movie also distorts the perceived social habits of the vast majority of members of Congress. Charlie Wilson was a flamboyant, unmarried congressman who was referred to by his friends as "good-time Charlie." I knew him fairly well on a casual basis, and I always regarded him as a nice, happy guy with a lot more depth of conviction than he let show most of the time. He certainly was not the typical member of Congress, though.

[5] Justice Black not only wrote the majority opinion but was clearly the driving force behind the debate and the resulting decision.

[6] The states were absolutely opposed to the U.S. Congress establishing a national church. All matters relating to religion were to be reserved to the states. As we shall see, 11 or 12 of the original 13 states had an established church at some point and/or a religious test for voting.

[7] It is not surprising that almost all non-lawyers, including members of the U.S. Congress, with whom I have raised the subject, knew nothing of Black's background. It was a little surprising that in discussions with prominent lawyers, including some members of the House and the Senate, they knew very little or nothing about his background. Most, however, knew about some of his most notable decisions on the Supreme Court.

[8] They would later change their name to Americans United for the Separation of Church and State (AUSCS) and are heavily influenced by very liberal Protestant clergy in their ranks.

[9] In Chapter 6, the highly respected Dr. Daniel Dreisbach, professor of Justice, Law and Society at American University, will be quoted extensively on these subjects. Dreisbach's *Thomas Jefferson and the Wall of Separation of Church and State* (NYU Press, 2003) is considered in many scholarly circles to be the definitive work on this subject.

[10] Unlike most of the prominent Founders, Jefferson wrote extensively on the subject of his religious faith.

[11] This interesting description is advanced and documented by some scholars to clearly differentiate the vast difference between what Unitarians believed in the founding period as compared with modern times. This term makes the religious classification of Jefferson, Adams, and a few others much more precise, as we will point out when the subject is fully discussed in the book.

[12] This is the only time Thomas Jefferson ever used this metaphor in a religious context. On one other occasion, in January 1798, Jefferson used the "wall of separation" as a metaphor in a letter to Angelica Church, Alexander Hamilton's sister-in-law, to describe the bitter divides between the Federalists and Republicans. This letter is quoted in Daniel Dreisbach's *Thomas Jefferson and the Wall of Separation between Church and State*, 184.

[13] Dreisbach, 183, note 88. He lists sources for other such examples.

[14] Richard John Neuhaus in *The Naked Public Square: Religion and Democracy in America* (Wm. B. Eerdmans Publishing Company, 1996) references the tendency of many modern scholars to contend that "*of course America is a secular society*", 80. He explains that "this way of thinking is of relatively recent vintage." Among other references, he cites the very liberal Supreme Court Justice Douglas as late as 1952 writing in an opinion, "*We are a religious people whose institutions presuppose a Supreme Being.*" These references will be more closely examined in Chapter 6.

[15] The Northwest Ordinance was a very enlightened document initially passed by the Continental Congress (and reauthorized by the First U.S. Congress) to regulate how these territories could become states. This document, which will be further discussed in Chapter 6, advocated the teaching of religion and morality and funded joint efforts between the churches and the federal government to provide education for the children in these territories.

[16] As early as 1850, a subsequent U.S. Congress questioned how these early congresses had justified some of these acts, such as paying chaplains with federal dollars. As we shall see in the body of the book, they overwhelmingly concluded that such actions were totally consistent with our founding documents.

[17] The Compact describes one of the purposes for taking this voyage and establishing this colony as the "Advancement of the Christian Faith."

[18] July 26, 1796.

[19] Feb. 22, 1756.

[20] Ben Stein and Philip DeMuth, *How to Ruin the United States of America*, (New Beginnings Press, 2008), 10. This short and readable book is a very easy and informative read.

[21] For Jefferson, the "pure doctrines of Jesus" meant the standards of moral behavior, the treatment of others, and civic responsibility, since he denied the miraculous aspects of his teaching. While serving as president, Jefferson "cut and pasted" his own New Testament, deleting most of the miracles because he thought they diluted Jesus' pure teachings. This will be further discussed and documented in Chapter 6.

[22] This may sound strange in today's America with a few million Americans who are Jews, Muslims, Hindus, and other non-Christian religions. It certainly did not sound strange at the time, when virtually the entire country was Christian, at least in the generic sense. The 1790 census revealed that there were just under 4 million people in the United States at the time—including more than 600,000 slaves and slightly fewer than 60,000 free blacks. The vast majority would have considered themselves orthodox Christians and most of the rest as Christian in the general sense of the term. There were only slightly more than 2,000 Jews living in the States, most of whom were descendents of the Jews who had landed in New York (New Amsterdam at the

time) in 1654, fleeing persecution in Brazil. A statistically significant number of those of Jewish descent had distinguished themselves during the War of Independence. Those of other non-Christian religions were too statistically insignificant to receive any historical note, with a handful of exceptions.

23 The source that will be used most extensively in this discussion is Daniel J. Flynn's *A Conservative History of the American Left* (Crown Forum, 2008). This 455-page book includes 69 pages of notes that identify primary sources unknown to virtually all Americans except for the most dedicated scholars. Some of this material is very helpful in understanding the influences and differences between modern-day liberals and the hard or radical left. A similar distinction between the conservative movement and the radical right is included in Chapter 3.

24 For an in-depth look at Owen, see Flynn, 19 ff., and at George, 99 ff.

25 Communism meant primarily communal living and equal sharing of all resources. Communism in this context has nothing to do with Marxism, which didn't appear until almost 50 years later.

26 The term "socialism" was actually coined by followers of Owen and meant for them "the transferal of responsibility from the individual to the social." Today, it generally refers only to economics. See Flynn, 24.

27 Capitalism for Owen entailed private property (for him, "the root of all evil") and the profit motive, which creates corporate greed and worker exploitation.

28 Flynn, 19.

29 Flynn, 101.

30 Twain believed this to be a time of glitz, corruption, greed, and guile. He apparently was unimpressed with the fact that during the late 19th century, per capita income and industrial production in the U.S. exceeded any country in the world except the U.K. Of course, all of these countries were having similar problems with working conditions and poverty.

31 Flynn, 100.

32 The vast majority of the 250 most important Founding Fathers were orthodox Protestant Christians. Most of them who spoke on the subject of original sin accepted the Lutheran-Calvinist doctrine of the total depravity of man's fallen nature. However, a few of the most prominent Founders, including Adams, Franklin, and probably Washington, held a softer view that might be characterized by saying that man was "deprived," not "depraved." Adams and Franklin left behind writings on the subject. We can only surmise Washington's attitude from quotes such as the one given below.

33 Agustin Blazquez, "Political Correctness: The Scourge of Our Times," *Newsmax.com*, April, 8, 2002. Accessed Aug. 23, 2012, at http://archive.newsmax.com/archives/articles/2002/4/4/121115.shtml.

34 Blazquez.

35 The name "American Civil Liberties Union" was specifically chosen because it sounded so patriotic and so American. Language was always a major consideration.

36 Some of the founders, most notably Franklin, Adams, and, obviously, Paine, contended that man could not be held accountable by God for the sins of their fathers, including Adam. However, they had no trouble recognizing that man was a sinful creature and must be controlled by laws.

37 As quoted in Thomas S. Kidd's *God of Liberty: A Religious History of the American Revolution* (Basic Books, 2010), 209. Dr. Kidd teaches history at Baylor University. He is also a senior fellow for Baylor's Institute for Studies of Religion. He is a prolific writer who contributes to many prestigious publications and is the author of several books. The *God of Liberty* and *The Founding Fathers and the Debate over Religion in Revolutionary America: A History in Documents* are excellent sources on this subject.

1

From South Georgia
to the Nation's Capital

The task of selecting a few highlights from my life and varied careers to establish my bona fides for writing this book led me to repeatedly confess to myself in sincere humility, "Only in America!" And then to add, "Only by the grace of God!"

It certainly is no exaggeration to say that not a single person in Tifton, Georgia, including my family and certainly my teachers, would have ever guessed that this very average high school student would grow up to become a Lutheran minister. It would have been a laughable fantasy that little Billy Hecht would end up with a 40-year-plus (Lord willing) career in the Nation's Capital where I would become personally acquainted with seven American presidents. (I have been fortunate enough to know five of them pretty well. Similarly, I have personally known the last seven LCMS presidents. I have been so blessed to become close personal friends with five of these outstanding men.)

In the closing days of the 2012 Georgia legislative session, the Georgia house and senate honored three "outstanding Georgians" with a resolution honoring their career accomplishments. I was honored to be one of them. Each recipient was given the opportunity to address the legislature from the speaker's podium in the Georgia House of Representatives. This caused me to spend many hours assessing the challenges I had faced in the 78 years God had so graciously given me on this earth. I chose to emphasize the deeply Christian and Georgia values that had been instilled in me during my formative years. I believe that I bonded with this audience when I told them: "When times got really difficult, I, like Lee Greenwood sings in his famous song that 'my heart goes drifting down that dusty Dixie road,' hear in my mind my momma, daddy or some other familiar voice say: 'Billy, you never give up!' Then I would remember being taught that if your cause is right, God will always find a way to get you through your difficulties."

Perhaps the experience in my Washington years that was the most dramatic and frightening happened on my way to work on that *fateful day of 9/11* in 2001. Less than nine months after George W. Bush placed his left hand on the Holy Bible and raised his right hand to take the oath that would make him the 43rd president of the United States, a cowardly act took place that not only would define his presidency but also would change our nation forever.

On that September morning, I was scheduled to attend a fundraiser at the Republican Senatorial Committee in the Ronald Reagan building on Capitol Hill. I had asked my driver, Vincent, to pick me up around 9 a.m. so we could avoid the rush-hour traffic and have an easy 25- or 30-minute drive to the Hill. As we started out from my home and headed for the highway, I turned on the radio as was my normal habit. Shortly thereafter, the announcer alerted us to the fact that a plane had flown into one of the twin towers of the World Trade Center. How horrible! Maybe it was a freak accident?

Just as we had turned onto Route 110, which runs in front of the Pentagon, this same now-frantic announcer said that the second tower has been hit by another plane. Obviously, this was a planned attack! It seemed like just a minute or two, when we were about a half mile from the Pentagon, that I saw the red flames of a third plane crashing into the far side of the Pentagon. I screamed, "It's the Pentagon!"

Vincent said maybe it's Reagan National Airport (which is only a few miles beyond the Pentagon). I said, "No! It's the Pentagon!" We could not turn around because of the large median strip that divides the highway on the way to the Pentagon. So he hit the gas, and we happened to be the first car to cross under the overpass that connects the Pentagon grounds to a large parking lot on the other side of Route 110. There appeared to be hundreds of civilian and military employees running across the bridge. My first irrational impulse was that we should pull onto one of the ramps and see if we could help.

Visibly shaken but now thinking more rationally than I, Vincent insisted that there was nothing we could do, as everybody was trying to get out. He sped up and almost flew around the ramp leading to Capitol Hill. Amazingly, there were still only a few scattered cars on the highway heading for the Hill. We passed every car on the road until we got into eyesight of the U.S. Capitol and the House office buildings. People were streaming out of all doors. IT NOW APPEARED TO ME THAT THE NATION'S CAPITAL WAS UNDER HOSTILE ATTACK!

I quickly concluded that we would have an easier time getting to my meeting location on the Senate side of the Capitol than down to my office, which was only a couple of blocks away. Surprisingly, we made it to the Ronald Reagan Senate building in about 10 minutes while paying little attention to stop signs and red lights. Wouldn't you know it? There was a large vegetable truck parked right in front of the Reagan building.

I jumped out of the car and frantically summoned a couple of Capitol policemen who were within shouting distance. I urged them to get that truck out of there. As they came running, I rushed into the meeting room. Once again, I was amazed that so many people were still in the room. They actually had heard only part of what was happening. I quickly told them that the Pentagon had been attacked and exhorted them, "I don't know where to tell you to go, but you better get out of here." I jumped into my car. It took us more than half an hour to drive the few blocks from one side of the Capitol to the other.

My secretary, Nelle, was almost beside herself as we reached my office. Her mentally challenged brother was at work at the Commerce Department, and she knew he would be terribly confused and have no idea what to do. I told her to take Vincent and the car and try to go get her brother. I would ride home with my middle son, who works with me. Amidst all the confusion, my son navigated us to the Capital Beltway the back way, through parts of the city he felt no one would ever think of bombing. It still took us more than four hours to make the trip home. As a rule, that commute never took over an hour in rush-hour traffic. My wife was exceptionally frightened because she could not reach our other two sons, as the cell phones were by now constantly busy. Our youngest son had ended up walking five or six miles out of the city until he was able to squeeze into a crowded subway car that would stop near our home.

Personal memories of 9/11 are still very much a part of our lives as we try to do our part in response to this blatant, unprovoked, and dastardly attack by these heartless Islamist jihadists.

From Georgia to the Seminary

The road that led me from a small country town in the deep South into the Lutheran ministry, and ultimately to a career of more than 40 years in the Nation's Capital, was long, with many unexpected twists, turns, and challenges all along the way.

I was born in Tifton, Georgia, in 1933, during some of the darkest days of the Great Depression, in perhaps the most segregated part of the country (with the possible exception of Boston). My daddy, a devout Missouri Synod Lutheran, was born and raised in St. Louis. Upon graduation from Lutheran high school in River Forest, Ill., just as the depression hit in 1928, he was in desperate need of work. Strangely enough, he found a much-needed job in Tifton.

When he arrived in Tifton, Daddy was the only Lutheran in this heavily Baptist and Methodist town. He would not see his dream of having a Missouri Synod Lutheran church finally realized in Tifton until I was in the seminary. (When Peace Lutheran church was founded in Tifton, Daddy was carrying on a Hecht family tradition. His granddaddy, John Hecht, had emigrated from Hanover, Germany, just after the War Between the States had ended. John Hecht would become a large farmer in St. Louis County and play a key role in starting Our Redeemer Lutheran Church in Overland, Mo. Will Hecht, my father's daddy, moved to Miami while Daddy was in high school at River Forest and started a real estate business. Will Hecht almost immediately began a successful effort to establish the first LCMS church in Miami, St. Matthew's Lutheran Church. My efforts to establish two LCMS churches in Oklahoma, which will be described in the following pages, enabled me to carry on this family tradition.

My primary "church" growing up was "The Lutheran Hour" on radio, listening to the powerful sermons of Dr. Walter A. Maier. My mother, a share-cropper's daughter, was a life-long resident of Tift County and had grown up a Baptist. She joined the Lutheran Church after marrying my dad, becoming the second Lutheran in Tifton. I would become the third Lutheran in this small town after being baptized at St. Matthew's in Miami a few months after my birth. (None of such details would make me a logical candidate for the Lutheran ministry.)

My first major turn in the road along the path to my career was when I decided not to return to Auburn University for a second year. Instead, I had decided to attend Concordia Junior College in Fort Wayne, Indiana, to begin my studies for the holy ministry. It was a sudden decision, but I felt strongly that God was calling me to follow this course of action.

Arriving at the train station in Fort Wayne in the middle of the night, already a week late for classes, I may have experienced some temporary second thoughts. Here I was in a northern city that I had heard of for the first time only a few weeks earlier. I didn't know one person in the entire state of Indiana, but I was pretty sure they were all Yankees.

I was "greeted" on the platform at the train station by a Concordia student who did not appear to be especially happy to be out at such a late hour. Detecting my apprehensions, he did assure me that everything would be fine once I was settled in after a few days. Thus my study for the Lutheran ministry was about to begin.

My two years of study in Fort Wayne were both productive and enjoyable. The make-up of the student body was about one half students from public high schools and one half those who had attended high school at Concordia. This turned out to be a major advantage for me because I was almost immediately adopted by the "old timers," the students who had studied Greek, German, and Latin in high school in addition to lots of Bible courses. They were probably fascinated by this kid who spoke with a "funny accent."

The only Greek I knew was the alphabet—from having pledged a fraternity at Auburn. I knew less German and Latin. The professors would know that my name was Billy, but most of the students just called me "Georgia" for the entire two years.

It is impossible for me to overstate the value these buddies were in helping me catch up on the background I lacked for the courses I took in my two years at Concordia. They also taught me a few other things my mother would just as soon I had not learned. When I was growing up down South, Methodists and Baptists really didn't drink strong beverages. Certainly not in front of one another!

Preparing for the ministry at Concordia Seminary in St. Louis was truly a major turning point in my life. Some of my daddy's relatives still lived in St. Louis, and my course of studies leading to my B.A. and B.D. were especially enlightening and enjoyable.

The professors I came to know very well at the seminary molded and refined the theological beliefs my daddy had taught me on an elementary, but soundly biblical, foundation when I was growing up. These professors also would have a lasting influence on my life. I finally learned the value of scholarship if I was going to accomplish the goals I was beginning to set for my life.

I have no doubt that God's hand was involved every step along the way. I certainly made my share of mistakes, but He was always patient with me.

Biblical Hebrew came easy for me, and I briefly considered studying to become an Old Testament scholar. A quarter's course in Arabic with a few real seminary scholars cured me of that radical idea.

Dr. Robert Preus was most responsible for instilling in me a special interest in systematic theology. This interest led me to enroll in a master's degree program in philosophy at Washington University while I was finishing my last two years at Concordia Seminary. This would serve me well, as it turned out, when I served as campus pastor at the University of Oklahoma a few years later.

I always had more than a passing interest in politics, as well as a fascination with Luther's two-kingdom theology. I understood Luther to teach that every citizen had a responsibility in both kingdoms, whether they became a pastor or a lawyer or any other vocation. Like most everyone else who read the newspapers during my time at the seminary, I was concerned about the communist threats to world peace. In some of my philosophy courses at Washington University, I studied Karl Marx and other communists. (As it would turn out, the many courses I took in comparative religions would prepare me to better grasp the severity of the threat posed by the radical Islamist terrorists after 9/11. As will be emphasized in this book, it is impossible to understand the Islamist terrorist's mentality without a basic knowledge of Islam and its history.)

During my final year at the seminary, in 1960, my interest in politics reached the front burner. A Roman Catholic named John F. Kennedy was the Democrat nominee for president. It sounds silly today to be concerned about a Catholic becoming president, doesn't it? I can assure you there was more concern and discussion about a Catholic being president in 1960 than there was about a Mormon, Mitt Romney, running for that office in 2008. The so-called "Mormon issue" continued to be of concern to some voters in the 2012 Republican presidential primary. This was especially evident among some "evangelicals" and other conservative Christian voting blocs. It is unclear at this point if, or how, Democrats will try to use the issue in the 2012 presidential election. Hopefully, in view of the numerous serious threats facing our country today, this concern will not become a defining issue.

After finishing the course work for my M.A. in the summer of 1960, I was ordained and installed as pastor of Faith Lutheran Church in Mt. Vernon, Illinois. As my personality had always dictated for each task I undertook, I threw myself into trying to become the best parish pastor I could possibly be. At the same time,

I believed that God expected me to take my citizenship responsibilities seriously, and so I also became actively involved in Republican politics. Shortly thereafter, I became involved in some of the local anti-communist organizations whose major purpose was to inform people about the threats the communists posed to our country.

During our time in Mt. Vernon, my wife and I experienced joy like we had never known before when God gave us our first son, who was born on my daddy's birthday. As we doted on the most precious baby we had ever seen, we could not stop thanking God for His blessings.

My wife and I also experienced the greatest tragedy of our lives one year and three days after our first-born son came into the world. We lost our second son a day after his birth and a day after I baptized him in the hospital in Mt. Vernon. Dr. Robert Preus preached his funeral service and gave us much-needed comfort when he reminded us that God knows our pain since He gave up His only Son into death on the cross for our sins. Then God raised Him from the dead to assure us of the forgiveness of our sins, including those inherited by our own newborn baby.

The tragic loss of our baby would have a lasting effect on the careers in politics my wife and I eventually would follow. As Bible-believing Christians, we both were always pro-life. But losing a baby really motivates parents to become lifetime crusaders in efforts to preserve human life. When God gives life it is always sacred.

God continued to bless us! As the years passed, our third son and his wife gave us a grandson on Martin Luther's birthday! Dr. Preus came to Washington to baptize two grandsons—my fourth son and his wife had a son just four days later.

I recall that Dr. Preus delivered a powerful baptismal sermon that moved the entire congregation. This wonderful day would always hold special memories for me as it would also be the last time I saw the man who molded my theology and meant so much to our entire family.

Off to Oklahoma

After three happy and successful years in Mt. Vernon, the road in my life took another unexpected turn when I was called to be the campus pastor at the University of Oklahoma (OU).

The time spent in Oklahoma was challenging, exciting, extremely busy, and productive. What's more, it ultimately and quite unexpectedly offered a road that led to my career in politics.

We started a congregation in Norman made up mostly of professors and students, and we closely watched the construction of University Lutheran Chapel just a few blocks from OU's famous football stadium.

My inclination toward organizational skills, political activities, and persuasive abilities may have shown at the building's dedication. Dr. Oliver Harms, then president of The Lutheran Church—Missouri Synod, was the speaker at the Festival Dedicatory Service. He also installed me as pastor during the morning service. (I had chosen to postpone my installation until the building of the Chapel was completed.) Dr. Alfred Fuerbringer, president of Concordia Seminary in St. Louis, was the speaker for the Entrance Dedicatory Worship Service. The Honorable Henry Bellmon, governor of Oklahoma, was the featured speaker at the Festival Banquet. Dr. George Cross, president of the University of Oklahoma, brought greetings at the Festival Banquet. The Rev. A.E. Behrend, president of our church body's Oklahoma District, brought greetings from the district and officially welcomed the chapel into the fold. The Rev. Clarence Knippa, mission secretary for the district (and my boss, I might add), gave a history of Lutheran campus work in Oklahoma. The Honorable William Morgan, mayor of Norman, and the Rev. James Shields, president of the campus ministry association at OU, brought their respective greetings.

We had been blessed with unexpectedly large attendances at the services conducted in our temporary worship facilities (an old fraternity house we had rented). As a result, we stopped construction on the chapel three times to make it larger. The University of Oklahoma was a great campus, and the Oklahoma District was a far-sighted district.

The opportunities and challenges in Norman never seemed to abate. The pastor of the town church, Trinity Lutheran, took a call just as I arrived, and I was asked to serve as vacancy pastor. A few months later, an opportunity to very quickly start a mission church in Moore, a rapidly growing community about 15 miles up the road, roughly half way between Norman and Oklahoma City, presented a challenge we could not ignore.

A number of Moore residents, mostly graduate students at OU, were attending Sunday worship at Trinity Lutheran in Norman. They discovered that another Lutheran synod was canvassing in Moore with the obvious intention of starting a mission. Our Moore Lutherans knew for a fact, they insisted, that most Lutherans living in Moore were Missouri Synod Lutherans. They had no trouble convincing me. There was no time for any red-tape and long considerations with our district. If we let this other synod get the jump on us and start holding services before we did, it would look bad. And, we knew we would never get district's approval to move in once they had started a mission.

We rapidly recruited 25 or 30 Missouri Synod students at OU to help us go door to door in Moore, searching for Lutherans. In less than two weeks, we had rented a dance hall with a piano; dug out some old Lutheran hymnals, a standing cross, and other items for a make-shift altar from Trinity's basement; and held our first worship service in Moore. To our surprise and delight, we had more than 35 attendees for the first worship service in Moore.

We decided that we had better not tell district officials until we were confident that this was going to work in the long run. In the meantime, a group of dedicated Lutheran Christians rushed over to the dance hall early each Sunday morning to clean up the beer cans, prepare the altar, set up the chairs, and ready this large room for a more spiritual purpose. I would race from the 8 a.m. service at Trinity for a 9:30 service in Moore, then back to Trinity for the 11 a.m. worship service.

Thankfully, I never got a speeding ticket. I did slide off an icy road once on my way back to Trinity. Fortunately, I flagged down a sympathetic and very friendly old farmer in a pickup truck. He looked slightly confused as I climbed into his truck with robes, liturgical books, and Bible in hand. I explained to him that I needed to get to Trinity Lutheran by 11 or the service was going to start without a pastor. He assured me he would do his best, but if he slid off the road too, neither one of us would get there anytime soon.

I was only five or 10 minutes late when I stuck my head out of the pastor's study and told the congregation I would be ready shortly. I caught a quick glimpse of my anxious looking wife with our little boy on her lap and saw her breathe a sigh of relief.

Actually I had accidentally and embarrassingly already taught the congregation that sometimes they must be patient with their pastor. I believe that every seminarian has a nagging fear of sleeping through a church service he was to conduct. I can assure you that those of us who are basically night owls live with such a fear. Well, it happened just a month or so after I had begun conducting the 8:00 a.m. and 11:00 a.m. services at Trinity. A long week translated into sermon preparation continuing late into Saturday night. The phone rang early Sunday morning.

"Pastor! Are you coming to church this morning?" asked our organist, Beryl Nash.

"What day is it?" I asked drowsily.

"Sunday," she answered.

Suddenly wide awake, I asked, "What time is it?"

"Five minutes after eight," was the startling answer.

"Tell the congregation I'm on my way and play some of your beautiful organ music," I said as I grabbed for my pants.

Not much more than 15 minutes later, a shabbily dressed, unshaven, and embarrassed pastor pulled into the church parking lot without hitting a thing or running but one red light. Thank goodness I wore only a plain zip-up black robe at the time. I walked out to the altar acting as though I didn't notice the smiling faces in the church. My long-time fear had reached it culmination.

A little over a month after sliding off the road and hitch-hiking to church, I informed a shocked and surprised district mission director, my boss, that he had a new mission congregation in Moore. I very quickly explained that the dedicated laymen there were covering all expenses and that we already had an average attendance of 45. I knew this number was at least comparable with a few of the other mission congregations around the state.

After what seemed like a very long pause (maybe he was getting up off the floor), he asked me calmly but firmly if I would *please* inform him in advance if I decided to start any more mission churches.

After eight or nine months of this "no-cost-to-the-district" arrangement, the Moore mission was growing rapidly and the Oklahoma District decided to call a full-time pastor. Today St. John's Lutheran Church in Moore is one of the larger churches in the Oklahoma District. Maybe this little diversion helped prepare the district officials for the larger-than-anticipated cost of the chapel on the OU campus.

Having arrived in Norman just days before the beginning of the fall semester in 1963, I managed to get accepted into the doctoral program to earn my Ph.D. in philosophy at OU. Prior to the beginning of the second semester, I was offered a part-time job as a teaching assistant in the philosophy department. This turned out to be a major blessing because it greatly increased my visibility as a Lutheran campus pastor.

I received a number of invitations to speak to sororities and fraternities over the dinner hour. Occasionally, members of these sororities and fraternities would return the favor by attending Sunday services *en masse* to hear me preach. This was a wonderful opportunity to share the Gospel with them, and occasionally, a few would become regulars—some even took confirmation instruction and joined University Lutheran.

It did cause me a little theological heartburn when 40 or 50 of these sorority or fraternity members would show up on communion Sundays and I could recognize only one or two of them that I knew were Lutheran. I did not in any way want to trivialize how seriously we Lutherans feel about the sacrament of Holy Communion. On the other hand, I did not want to offend or place any unnecessary obstacles in the way of the faith of these young students. I felt that so many of them were reaching out for an anchor to grasp in the turbulent waters of the troubled 60s. I did not want to do anything that might inhibit them from grasping by God's grace, the only anchor that would never move, because He is the same yesterday, today, and forever.

I hope and pray that I handled these situations in a biblical manner. I would give a fairly detailed statement on the Lutheran teaching about Holy Communion and how seriously we took the act of receiving the true body and blood of Christ. After explaining the need to examine oneself, I would request that they not come to the altar unless they felt they were in total agreement with our teaching about the Lord's Supper. Only God knows for sure if this was the right course of action.

Serving as Lutheran campus pastor and teaching in the philosophy department put me right in the middle of the action at a major university during the radical 60s. Most will recall, either from personal observation or recorded history, that a cultural upheaval made the 1960s the age of situation morality, the sexual revolution, the numerous left-wing hate-America organizations, the women's liberation movement, and drugs, sex, and rock and roll, not to mention "black helicopters" and various sightings of spacecrafts.

These were indeed wild and crazy times. OU was not as bad as some of the even crazier universities. As Merle Haggard would sing, "leather boots were still in style for manly footwear" and at least most of the kids "still respected the college dean." The football players—many of whom took my philosophy courses or attended my chapel services or both—did a good job of protecting the girls' dorms from "panty raids" and other incursions. The "hippies" didn't enjoy challenging the OU defensive line anymore than Texas' or Nebraska's offense did. These hippies also didn't show much appetite for challenging me personally during or after any of the campus debate forums. This may well have resulted from the fact that some of the more patriotic football players who were friends of mine always showed up at these extracurricular events.

The Road to Washington

To better explain the polarization in Washington and our country as I understand it, I probably need to share with you briefly a few details of how I got from the University of Oklahoma to the Nation's Capital. This explanation also will reveal my understanding of a Christian's dual citizenship in the "two kingdoms."

I was the Lutheran campus pastor at the University of Oklahoma, where I also was a teaching assistant in the philosophy department, from 1963 to 1967. These were eventful years, as I have mentioned, to be on any college campus because it was such a period of social unrest. The Vietnam War debate and the civil rights movement were raging in full force.

These were also productive years, since we built a chapel, confirmed more than 150 adults, and had an average year-round chapel attendance of 190. I also was instrumental in influencing five OU students to enroll in various Lutheran seminaries. Probably the best known is Bill Weinrich, who has taught for many years at Concordia Theological Seminary in Fort Wayne. My superiors considered these accomplishments very successful since OU had the smallest Lutheran enrollment of any major university campus at the time.

We also went through the 1964 and 1966 elections during these years. Feeling a strong responsibility as a Christian citizen to fulfill my duties in the "Kingdom of the Left," I also became quite active in the political process.

With a strong concern over the worldwide communist threat and an equally strong fear that our country was severely threatened by moral decay, I struggled over how best to meet my responsibilities as a member of both kingdoms, Church and State.

I met a former state representative from Missouri who was enrolled as a graduate student at OU after he lost reelection in 1964. I confirmed him and his wife and baptized their children. We became close friends and had many theological and political discussions. In 1967, he asked me if he could submit my name as a potential executive director for the Missouri Republican Party. I said "yes," thinking it would probably never happen.

After my interview in Jefferson City, Missouri, the Republican state chairman offered me the job on the spot. I accepted and signed a contract. Later that evening, I was called to be the head campus pastor at the University of Wisconsin, which I believe had the largest Lutheran student enrollment at the time. How much that timing affected my life is still an occasional question in my mind. Unlike at OU, "leather boots" certainly were not "in style for manly footwear" at the University of Wisconsin, and few there seemed to "respect the college dean" at that time. This position probably would not have been a good fit for me at that time in history. Most likely, I would have bonded with many of the football and basketball players at Wisconsin, since athletes most always tend to be more practical and conservative in their beliefs. Such an alliance might have been necessary for my survival at such a liberal university.

Within a few months, I moved to Jefferson City to assume the day-to-day responsibility of running the Republican Party of Missouri under the direction of the Republican State Committee. We carried the state for Richard Nixon in the 1968 presidential election. Until he died, U.S. Attorney General John Mitchell, who was Nixon's campaign manager in 1968, believed that Missouri made the difference.

In 1968, Missouri had two Democrat U.S. senators and a Democrat governor. The Democrats controlled both houses of the state legislature with large majorities. But that year, Jack Danforth was elected attorney general of Missouri. Many believed this was the start of turning this reliable Democrat state into a Republican-leaning state today.

Missouri's senior senator, Christopher "Kit" Bond, a Republican, retired in 2010 and was succeeded by Republican Congressman Roy Blunt in the 2010 election. (Missouri's junior Republican senator at the time, Jim Talent, lost a close election to Democrat Claire McCaskill in 2006. McCaskill is running for reelection in 2012, and this contest is shaping up to be one of the most highly contested races in the country.) The Republican governor did not run for reelection in 2008 and was replaced by a Democrat, Jay Nixon. Nixon is also up for reelection in 2012. A few years ago, the GOP took control of the state legislature for the first time in the state's history. In 1970, Kit Bond was elected state auditor, then governor in 1972. I had run his campaign for Congress in 1968; we lost in a very close race.

Most Missouri politicians I talk to today believe our organizational and recruitment efforts during the 1968 election have paid rich dividends over the years.

After the 1968 election, I ran a couple of campaigns for Congress and took a position with the American Security Council (ASC), an organization concerned about the communist threat at home and abroad. In the latter part of 1970, Dr. Jack Preus, then president of The Lutheran Church—Missouri Synod, asked if I would take a temporary assignment as a public-relations assistant to him to organize an "around-the-world" trip of American church leaders on behalf of the POWs and MIAs in Vietnam. My employer, the ASC, highly approved of this humanitarian effort on behalf of our service men missing or receiving inhumane treatment in communist prison camps in Vietnam.

Within a few months, we had such an overwhelming response from U.S. church leaders that we could tell the North Vietnamese diplomats with whom we met throughout the world that we spoke for 98 percent of the Christians in the United States.

The delegation, headed by Dr. Preus, included Archbishop Joseph Ryan of Alaska, who was a close friend of Pope Paul VI, and Dr. Nathan Bailey, president of the Christian and Missionary Alliance (CMA), which did the major Protestant missionary work in Vietnam and Laos at the time. These two were very important for our mission.

Archbishop Ryan was able to get us a lengthy meeting with the pope at the Vatican. The pope not only agreed with the purpose of our trip, but also authorized Ryan to speak for him as we met with the North Vietnamese.

Dr. Bailey's CMA church had several missionaries who were either missing or had been taken prisoner by the North Vietnamese.

Another member of the delegation was Dr. George E. Sweazey, immediate past moderator of the United Presbyterian Church in the U.S.A. and at the time a professor at Princeton Theological Seminary. He also was a member of an anti-war church group. As the North Vietnamese evaluated the composition of our delegation, his presence made it difficult for them to assume that our mission was political rather than humanitarian.

The fact that Dr. Preus was president of a Lutheran church body undoubtedly explains why Prime Minister Olof Palme of Sweden was willing to assure Preus privately, after our meeting in Stockholm, that for the first time he would use the diplomatic channels of his neutral government to urge the North Vietnam diplomats at the various embassies to meet with our delegation. We ended up spending 29 hours in discussions with North Vietnamese ambassadors and other embassy officials in various capitals around the world.

As I clandestinely kept our American embassy diplomats in the various countries informed of our progress, they were surprised, shocked, and delighted.

The way we were able to make it to Vientiane, Laos, in time for a long-sought appointment with the North Vietnamese ambassador was so extraordinary I was convinced it involved divine intervention. After a long, tiring day that started at daylight and in which we had inspected all American POW facilities in South Vietnam, including the so-called "tiger cages," I received an urgent message after I reached our hotel. The North Vietnamese ambassador in Vientiane had found a slot in his extremely busy schedule to meet with our delegation the following afternoon. This was the news we had been desperately hoping to hear. The problem was that all flights were totally booked for the following morning. Dr. Preus was way too tired to deal with it. In what had become routine procedure, he just said: "Billy, I know you will be able to figure it out."

I frantically called everybody I could think of in Saigon and surrounding areas. No one at the American embassy had any ideas. U.S. Ambassador Ellsworth Bunker had said that using any U.S. military aircraft was out of the question. He was already ticked at me for using political pressure from a U.S. senator, who was in Saigon at the time, to cause him to get *all* U.S. POW camps ready for our visit. I decided to have a drink.

I visited with a few American soldiers on the streets of Saigon on my way to the door of a well-known international bar. I sat down at the bar and asked for a Beefeater martini. At that point, a distinguished-looking gentleman slid into the seat next to me and said: "Hi Yank! I see you also like Beefeater martinis." (He possibly knew who I was, since this wasn't my first trip to this highly recommended establishment.) "What brings you to Saigon, ole chap?" he continued. I mentioned a little bit about our delegation of church leaders and quickly asked: "Why are you here?" My ears perked up when he told me that he had recently been appointed to head up the UN inspection team that travelled mostly between Saigon and Hanoi. (I knew a great deal about their role.)

As a light turned on in my head, I rapidly told him about the humanitarian mission of these church leaders and how we had just returned from inspecting all POW camps in the South. Detecting an interest on his part, especially when he asked me about the conditions in two or three of these camps, I launched into our dilemma in getting to Vientiane the next day. I suddenly hoped he might have some suggestion. But I literally almost fell off the bar stool when he mentioned that the UN plane was flying to Vientiane in the morning. Never shy or bashful, I bluntly asked: "Is there any way my delegation could go with you?"

Without answering my question, he excused himself to go to the bathroom. He was gone for so long I began to fear he had decided to leave and get out of this situation. (My guess later was that he had called some members of his group and possibly someone he knew in our embassy to check out my story.)

When he finally returned (I had convinced myself that a full-blooded Englishman would never leave an undrunk Beefeaters martini), he got right to the point. We might be able to accommodate your group, but the necessary logistics might be too difficult. He explained that he would have to see all of our passports along with some biographical material on each person. "No problem," I responded, I have the passports and biographies in my briefcase right here. When I laid the passports in front of him, he was convinced. He obviously knew that if we had more than one passport that our State Department had to be strongly supportive of our mission.

He gave me explicit details about how to get my delegation through security and be escorted to the UN plane. Early the next morning, I had a haggard group of preachers at the proper gate at the airport. We made our meeting right on time with the North Vietnamese ambassador in Vientiane. This meeting would play a major role in the success of our mission.

Surprised State Department officials later explained to me that we were the only Americans ever to fly on the UN plane except for a handful of high ranking American government officials with a specific charge. God's hand was unmistakably the driving force in this crucial development.

We ended up spending four extra days in Vientiane, Laos, at the end of our month-long trip waiting for a Russian plane to come through on its way to Hanoi. Based on the discussions I was having with the first secretary of the Vietnamese embassy in Laos, I am convinced they spent several days in Hanoi trying to decide whether to allow some members of this high-powered delegation to actually visit the POWs in Hanoi. At 6 a.m. Friday, the first secretary called to inform me that they had decided it was just too dangerous for any of us to visit because of the American bombings.

Upon my return to the United States, I wrote a featured news letter for the ASC publication titled "Not Quite Ready for Inspection." However, the people at the State Department and the White House responsible for the POW-MIA efforts were all convinced that our mission was responsible for improved treatment of the American POWs in North Vietnam. Dr. Preus privately briefed President Nixon on our trip and preached at the White House Sunday-morning service a few weeks later. Incidentally, in addition to the president, the vice president, most of the cabinet, Billy Graham, and several other prominent religious leaders were in attendance, but Dr. Preus had the entire service.

After tying up all the loose ends of the trip, which included extensive contacts with POW and MIA wives and other family members with whom I had developed a close relationship, and doing a few other projects for Dr. Preus, I went back full time to the ASC. In this capacity, I got to know Dick Ichord, a conservative Democrat congressman from Missouri, quite well.

Ichord, chairman of the House Committee on Internal Security, offered me a job as "special assistant to the chairman." He assured me that I could spend a reasonable amount of time dealing with the families of the missing and the prisoners in Vietnam. This had become almost an obsession with me because the families were so desperate for any news of their loved ones or any information about how the war was progressing. I was able to become an unofficial intermediary for them with the White House and the Congress.

So, I was off to Washington in the summer of 1971.

This long story explains how I was able to come to Congress with a Democrat after having been so involved with the Republican Party and Republican campaigns. This was a wonderful experience for me, but I do not believe there is any way this could happen today. Could an active and committed Republican serve as the top staffer for a Democrat committee chairman in the House of Representatives? No way in today's climate! The ideological climate was so different in the Capitol in those days.

Parenthetically, the work I did for the American Security Council and the Democrat chairman of the House Committee on Internal Security unknowingly prepared me for the most important role I would ever play in the political process. A former FBI special agent and Sears executive, John Fisher, was asked by Gen. Robert Woods, retired chairman of Sears Roebuck, to establish an inclusive anti-Communist educational organization. That organization, which would become known as the American Security Council (ASC), acquired the largest private library of works on communism (Marxism) in America. Founded as a bi-partisan entity and made up of business executives, educators, educational institutions, church groups, and labor leaders, the ASC became the most respected, responsible, and effective anti-communist organization in America. Its founding board of directors would include a who's who of corporate executives, and its membership would eventually include some of the nation's most prestigious educational institutions. Its stated purpose was to educate the American people as to the teachings and threats of communism to America and the free world.

Fisher would put together a star-studded group of retired generals, intelligence officials, and educators in a "Coalition for Peace Through Strength (CPTS)" to lay out a "National Strategy for Peace Through Strength." An unbelievable 2,530 retired admirals and generals would join this "coalition," as would 169 national organizations and 182 local and state organizations. Some 514 universities, colleges, and think tanks would participate in fleshing out the most essential elements in such a strategy. The basic strategy developed in this study would be implemented by Presidents Reagan and George H.W. Bush as a major part of their successful effort to win the Cold War.

In 1967, the Democrat chairman of the House Armed Services Committee, Mendel Rivers, had asked John Fisher to undertake a study of the *comparative strategic military strength of the United States and the Soviet Union*" using only public, unclassified sources. Fisher responded immediately and rapidly assembled a blue ribbon commission chaired by former Air Force Gen. Bernard Schriever. General Schriever was the ideal selection because he had just retired from heading up the U.S. ballistic missile program. Another very prominent commission member was Gen. Thomas Powers, who also had recently retired as commander of the Strategic Air Command of the U.S. Air Force.

A few months later, the commission delivered its completed 103-page study to Chairman Rivers. The detailed study, "The Changing Strategic Military Balance, U.S.A. vs. U.S.S.R.," made banner headlines when it was released to the press. The study documented that the U.S. had recently *changed its goal of a war-winning strategic superiority for a strategy of mutual deterrence*" while the Soviet Union "*is striving hard toward a goal of overwhelming superiority in the decisive field of nuclear weaponry.*" The study further warned that the U.S. would lose its strategic nuclear superiority to the Soviet Union if the recently adopted policy were not quickly changed.

The Johnson administration not only refused to heed the warnings but, in addition, the Secretary of Defense Robert S. McNamara tried to play down the developing mega-tonnage gap by contending that we still had more smaller nuclear warheads. He also pushed back on the recommendations of this panel of experts that we develop our own ABM system to protect against possible incoming Soviet missiles to counter the anti-ballistic missile network being established by the Soviets. He argued that this might be provocative and that we should rely on a policy of détente or peaceful coexistence, and Strategic Arms Limitation Treaty (SALT) negotiations. It should be noted that JFK, LBJ, and Richard Nixon were hardcore anti-communists but their policies were heavily influenced by brilliant but "politically correct" Ivy League elitists. LBJ inherited McNamara from JFK and Nixon became infatuated with the even more brilliant Henry Kissinger. All such men were well-meaning patriots, but their liberal intellectual worldviews would not allow them to believe that these Soviet communist leaders really meant what they said. Surely, they could be convinced to abide by reasonable solutions to prevent a possible nuclear holocaust and just live in peace with one another, they concluded.

(Sixty long years of studying theology, comparative religions, philosophy, and political philosophy, including 50 years of being deeply immersed in politics and the political process, has led me to this strong conviction. Liberal elitists, since at least the Age of the Enlightenment, have based their political philosophies on religious convictions that deny the reality of original sin. In different stages of history, they have refused to recognize how evil the fallen natures of Napoleon, Hitler, Mussolini, Marx, Lenin, Stalin, and all the subsequent Soviet leaders really were. In spite of how strongly and explicitly such leaders expressed their evil intentions, the liberal elitists cling to the "enlightened" belief that such men can be reasoned with if we just treat them as reasonable human beings. The Islamist apologists are falling into this same trap today. The current liberal elitists are totally ignoring the modern "Islamist"[1] movement going back to the founding of the Muslim Brotherhood in 1928. For example, they try to deny that Osama bin Laden and his legions of fanatical followers were motivated by religious beliefs when they caused massive human carnage in suicide attacks. Osama's successors and other Islamist terrorist leaders continue to recruit and inspire their followers to carry out terrorist attacks in religious terms.

(It will be carefully documented in this book that our Founding Fathers were so successful in establishing this Republic because they had no question about the sinfulness of man. Even famous Founders like Adams, Jefferson, and Franklin, who questioned or even denied some miraculous teachings of the Bible, emphasized that the behavior of man must be held in check by moral laws of the state and federal governments. The chief of the Manuscript Division at the Library of Congress, Dr. James Hutson, frequently considered to be the foremost scholar on religion in our founding period, contends that virtually every Founder believed in "a future state of rewards and punishments."[2] Franklin, Jefferson, and Adams believed that a person is rewarded or punished in the afterlife based on their works in this life, not by faith in Christ. But without such a fear of punishment or promise of a reward, man's behavior could not be controlled in our system of government. Dictators and monarchs had ways to control the behavior of their subjects that our Founders abhorred. This subject will be discussed in detail in the section on the faith of our Founders in this book.)

But when the study by the ASC's blue ribbon commission was released, there was a no-nonsense governor in California by the name of Ronald Reagan who totally grasped the severity of this threat. He was an expert on Marxist communism and Russian history after the Bolshevik revolution. Reagan had studied the Soviet leaders, watched their occupation and treatment of the "Captive Nations," and closely followed their so-called "wars of national liberation." He knew that the Marxist philosophy, to which they were totally committed, necessitated world domination in order to create their "utopia" on earth. With a Christian understanding of man's fallen nature, we must *win* the Cold War. "Peace Through Strength" was not merely a slogan; it was a necessity if our Republic was to "long endure."

About the time I became an employee of the ASC after the 1968 campaign, John Fisher launched the effort to establish a "congressional division" of the Coalition for Peace Through Strength. On many of my early trips from St. Louis to Washington, beginning in 1970, I began to learn my way around Capitol Hill. The following year, when I came to work for Chairman Ichord, a conservative Democrat and big supporter of the ASC, I helped ASC President Fisher get this project off to a fast start. As a congressional staffer, with the boss' encouragement, I played an important role in establishing this congressional coalition on the solid bi-partisan foundation Fisher had envisioned. As a top aide for a highly respected Democrat committee chairman, I had easy access to conservative and national-security-oriented Democrats in the House and the Senate.

Reagan would adopt "Peace Through Strength" in his 1980 presidential campaign as a slogan to emphasize his plan and determination to win the Cold War. The fact that a majority of the sitting congressmen and senators were members of the "Congressional Coalition for Peace Through Strength," was of immense value to President Reagan when he unveiled his ambitious plan to rebuild our aging military might. During the time this "Congressional Coalition" was being developed, a total of 277 congressmen and senators would become members. Very importantly, the members of the congressional coalition were almost evenly split between Democrats and Republicans, as Fisher had directed.

During all but two years of Reagan's presidency, the Republicans held a majority in the U.S. Senate. But the U.S. House of Representatives was in Democrat hands during the entire eight years Ronald Reagan was president of the United States. President Reagan and Democrat House Speaker Tip O'Neill developed a close working relationship almost from the beginning. It definitely made it easier for Speaker O'Neill, who was also a national security conservative, to push for the significant increase in defense spending requested by President Reagan, since a majority of the members of the U.S. House of Representatives were also members of the "Congressional Coalition of Peace Through Strength." The Soviets initially tried to match our military buildup, but they were spending almost half of their GDP on defense while we never broke double digits of our GDP. Mikhail Gorbachev, who would become the de facto ruler of the Soviet Union upon being selected as general secretary of the Communist Party of the Soviet Union (CPSU) in 1985, would perhaps inadvertently sum up President Reagan's crowning achievement. In a now-famous lighthearted remark later in life, Gorbachev said that President Reagan "almost spent *us* into bankruptcy."

The Soviet communists would never have despaired of their long-held dream of world domination until it was beyond doubt that America, under President Reagan's leadership, intended to gain and maintain strategic and tactical military superiority. Under Gorbachev's watch, the Berlin Wall would fall, the Cold War would end, and the Soviet Union would dissolve. (There is no debate over the fact that Gorbachev was a much more enlightened Soviet leader than any of the long line of hard core, uncompromising communist leaders who preceded him. I would conjecture that he was the only one of such Soviet leaders who never totally deceived himself about man's fallen nature.

(Gorbachev was baptized and raised as a child in the Russian Orthodox Church. Just a few years ago, in some of his statements, he said that certain events happened according to "God's will." He answered a question about his future with the qualifier "as long as God lets me live." This generated some speculation in the Russian press about whether or not he was a Christian. On a trip to Italy, he visited some Christian shrines in Rome. On March 9, 2008, he paid a surprise visit to the tomb of St. Francis of Assisi. When the Italian press questioned him about this visit, Gorbachev explained that *"His story fascinates me and has played a fundamental role in my life."* He further explained that *"It was through St. Francis that I arrived at the Church"* and it was important that he visit his tomb. Later Gorbachev would dismiss speculations that he was a Christian by saying, *"of course, I am an atheist."* This would lead to a response by a spokesman for the Russian Orthodox patriarch that in Italy he spoke in "emotional terms" and "not terms of faith." The spokesman further expressed the patriarch's belief that Gorbachev was *"still on his way to Christianity. If he arrives we will welcome him."*)

President Reagan, and his successor, President George H.W. Bush, understood that the Communist threat could be defeated only through a policy of "Peace Through Strength." (The return of Vladimir Putin as Russian president should remind us, as our Founding Fathers believed, that "the price of liberty is eternal vigilance.")

Another major benefit of my work with the ASC and Chairman Ichord was that it afforded me a unique opportunity to make a contribution to the efforts of the Reagan campaign to reach out to labor union voters. In my work with the "Missouri Council on National Security" I became good friends with a prominent and powerful labor leader named Ollie Langhorst. Ollie, who was president of the Carpenters Union in Missouri and was on the national board of the Carpenters International Union, had two sons who were career Army officers. Ollie was passionately anti-communist and assured me from the beginning that labor union members as a whole were also passionate about the issue. He demonstrated the truth of that statement when we organized a "Pro America" rally in St Louis to counter the proliferation of so-called "Anti-War" demonstrations. More labor union members than I had ever seen turned out for our march. Some groups of anti-war hippies were scattered on a few occasions along the parade route. (Not surprisingly, virtually all the policemen and other law enforcement officers were supportive of our "Pro-America" march and made sure that this was one of the most successful events in St. Louis history.)

On my first or second day on the job in Washington for Chairman Ichord, I met a member of Congress who was arguably the member of Congress most respected by labor union officials and members.[3] Obviously he was very liberal on labor issues as well as most areas of domestic policy. But he was conservative on social issues and very conservative on national security issues. (This makeup was not unusual at this time in history.) He would soon become one of my best friends as we spent many hours after work socializing together with Ichord and others.

I mention these two men because they played a key (actually indispensible) role in the contribution I made in the political earthquake that created the group of voters now known as the "Reagan Democrats." These Democrats, essential to Republican election victories, are those who are likely to vote for Republican candidates who espouse Reagan principles of government.

In 1979, two of my best buddies, Congressman Tom Evans of Delaware and Congressman Carroll Campbell of South Carolina, took me to dinner to offer me an opportunity I could not refuse. They were putting together a group of congressmen who supported Governor Reagan to become the nominee in the 1980 Republican presidential primary. These Reagan supporters would be made up of 13 congressmen known as the "Core Group."

An often forgotten fact of the world-changing event of Ronald Reagan's election as president are the difficult challenges he had to overcome to win the Republican primary nomination in 1980. Reagan faced a star-studded cast of Republican opponents headed up by former Governor John Connally of Texas, Senate Republican Leader Howard Baker, and George H.W. Bush, who would become Reagan's vice presidential nominee.[4] The fact that at least 18 men, most of whom were well known and qualified, seriously considered becoming candidates is a revealing statistic. When 10 such men actually mounted campaigns, it should have been obvious that prevailing political wisdom was that the nomination was wide open.

Even conservative Republicans worried that Reagan might be too old to finish out a term if elected. If the repeated fact that Reagan would turn 69 just weeks after he would be sworn in, if elected, was a whisper campaign, it was a very loud whisper. Everyone knew that he would be the first person in American history to be sworn in for the first time at such an advanced age. The moderate Rockefeller Republicans had resurrected the slogan used so effectively in the 1976 campaign that "governors can't start wars, presidents can." They were trying to convince voters that Reagan was too extreme in his anti-communist views to be trusted with his fingers on the nuclear button.

The Core Group proved to be essential if not decisive in the Republican primary. (We worked very closely with Senator Paul Laxalt's Thursday Night Group, which included two other Republican senators. This made communications concerning suggested strategies smooth and timely since Senator Laxalt was Governor Reagan's closest friend.) Tom Evans was ideal to head up the group since he was perceived as an Eastern moderate and, equally as important, he had served as co-chairman and chief executive officer of the Republican National Committee. Carroll Campbell, who would become a two-term governor of South Carolina and end up twice in later campaigns on the short list of vice-president candidates, was a master political strategist. Other outstanding congressional Gore Group members included Jack Kemp, who would run for president in future elections and serve as Secretary of Housing and Urban Development; Trent Lott, who would become Republican Senate minority and majority leader; and nine other equally dedicated and prominent members.[5]

Core Group members serving as surrogates gave the campaign credibility in the early and most difficult stages, produced position papers, recruited volunteers, raised money, and all the rest. But few know of their two most important and crucial contributions. One, working closely with Senator Laxalt, a delegation of Core Group members obtained a private meeting with Reagan and convinced him to replace campaign manager John Sears with Bill Casey.[6] Sears had been under heavy criticism by those who blamed his strategy for Reagan's loss to Bush in the Iowa caucus. Sears retaliated by trying to isolate candidate Reagan from all of his other top advisors, including his closest friends. On the very day Reagan won the crucial New Hampshire primary, he notified John Sears that he was being replaced.

The Core Group delegation had met with Reagan when he was in New Hampshire for the famous debate that took place just four days before the primary. They returned to Washington in good spirits but with the alarming news that the campaign was virtually out of money and credit. Eleven of the 13 Core Group congressmen spent the weekend in D.C. desperately making calls to raise immediate money for the Reagan campaign. Amazingly, our group was able to get more than $300,000 wired to the campaign virtually overnight. This was not a large sum of money in the overall scheme of fundraising, but it was crucial at the time since it enabled the campaign to get the Reagan bus up and running to South Carolina for the showdown with Governor Connally. Building on the momentum from the primary win in New Hampshire, the Reagan campaign was able to end the Connally presidential bid in South Carolina where he had been riding high on the support of the South Carolina icon, Senator Strom Thurmond.[7]

Since I spent months with Core Group members as their almost full-time "staffer," which frequently involved eating breakfast, dinner, and supper on weekdays, I would get to know Bill Casey fairly well.[8]

Once the primary was over, Ollie Langhorst and my labor unions' favorite congressman buddy began to lean on me. They were both very unhappy with President Carter. They believed Carter's policies had severely damaged our intelligence agencies, downsized our military, and allowed the Shah of Iran to fall. Their major concerns with Carter revolved around what they believed to be his national security failures. They felt that Reagan could cut heavily into the always reliable labor Democrat vote, and they offered to help. But they both needed the same union concession as the carrot. They needed assurances that if Reagan were elected president, he would not suspend (or try to repeal) the Davis-Bacon Act. This act mandated that prevailing wages must be paid to workers on public-works projects funded by the federal government.[9] I was very familiar with this law because this was one of the few concessions Ichord as a conservative Democrat made to keep the unions off his back.

Ollie told me he would travel around the country in an effort to rally union leaders and workers to the Reagan cause, which would include get-out-the-vote efforts and all the rest, if I could get a promise in the Reagan campaign plank to protect Davis-Bacon. My Democrat congressman friend told me that he would publicly endorse Reagan for president if such a public assurance were made. This would be the first time he had ever endorsed a Republican. I immediately realized that having the endorsement of "Mr. Labor" in congress would be a deal closer if Reagan, who had been a labor union member earlier in his life, had no strong ideological reservations.

I quickly called Paul Russo, a senior aide to Bill Casey, who served as Casey's liaison with the Core Group, among many other duties, to tell him about these offers. I asked Paul if he could help me get a meeting with Casey as soon as possible. I explained that I could not bring this before the Core Group since I was almost positive that all but one of them were opposed to Davis-Bacon. The meeting was arranged in just a few days, when Casey was scheduled to be in Washington. Mr. Casey listened carefully to the two offers of potential help with the union vote. He told me that my visit was timely because they had been discussing the issue and receiving strong opinions on both sides—mostly on the "don't do it" side. He said he would get back to me in a timely manner.

Mr. Casey called me back a week or so later to tell me that they had decided to include in their campaign plank a commitment to protect Davis-Bacon. Furthermore, Governor Reagan was going to make that promise in a campaign speech in the near future. I hung up the phone and called Ollie. He was thrilled and told me he already had his bags packed. I reached "Mr. Labor" congressman later that day and relayed the news. We then agreed that I would fly in to his local airport and discuss the details of how his endorsement could be most effectively carried out. The following week he met me at the gate where my flight arrived and suggested we go sit down in a restaurant that wasn't crowded. As we sat down at a table, he laid a legal-sized yellow pad down that contained many pages of names and phone numbers.

Then he said that for one of a very few times in his life, he was going to have to break a promise but would replace it with an offer as good as the original promise, if not better. "Bill," as I still remember his words almost verbatim, "shortly after I got out of the navy after WW II ended, I was elected to a local office as a Democrat. I have now served as a Democrat in the state house, state senate, and the U.S. House of Representatives for over 50 years. I just can't take the chance of embarrassing my family or longtime supporters by endorsing a Republican, as much as I would like to do so." He then explained that he had almost 600 names and phone numbers on that yellow pad, and "I promise to call every one of them and tell them why they should support Ronald Reagan for president."

"As a matter of fact," he continued, "if you notice the check marks on these pages, they identify the ones I have already called." He then further noted that labor leaders throughout the country will know who he was supporting. Having no choice otherwise, but also having great respect for this man, I thanked him for his help and asked if he would keep me informed of how those he called were responding. He called fairly often and met with me at the Dem Club in Washington on a few occasions to share some optimistic information. I know he made the promised calls because Ollie told me he was surprised by how many labor leaders mentioned that they had been called by this man they so admired.

Politics is certainly never an exact science, and it is always difficult to know for sure who had how much, if any, influence on any major political decisions. Of course I would like to think I played some part in Ronald Reagan's very successful efforts to reach and motivate this key voting bloc of social and national security oriented, mostly Catholic, labor Democrats.[10] These so-called "Reagan Democrats" are essential to Republican election successes.

There has always been a liberal-conservative split in the people's House, a body I considered to be the last hope for freedom and democracy in the world when I first came to Washington. The big difference from today was that there were liberals and conservatives in *both parties.*

In fact, I am sure that at the time I moved to Washington, there were more conservative Democrats in Congress than conservative Republicans. In 1971, there were 255 Democrats in the House and only 180 Republicans, a 75-vote majority. Of the 255 Democrats, a major portion of them were conservatives from the 13 states of the old Confederacy. (The Republicans started the process of defeating some southern Democrats in the Reagan elections. They pretty much wiped them out in the Republican landslide of 1994.)

I realize that it is imprecise to use liberal and conservative in such a broad way during this period of time. Many were probably better classified as moderates, moderate-conservatives, conservatives with a populist slant, etc. I would jokingly say that I knew what a liberal was and what a conservative was, but a moderate was someone who couldn't make up his mind. In truth, many members of Congress at the time were liberal on some issues and conservative on other issues. Many of the southern Democrats had a populist, "old New Deal" bent, even though they would be considered mostly conservative.

How I Became a Lobbyist

It didn't make much difference anyway during my first few years in Washington, because the committee chairmen ran the show in the House almost with an iron fist. In later years, after I became a lobbyist, I would tell my clients that when I first came to Washington, the Congress was Democrat controlled— just as it should have been. Why? Because, I would say, "When I came to work in the Congress, only one full-committee chairman, of all the committees, spoke with a funny accent. That would be Manny Celler of New York, who was chairman of the House Judiciary Committee, because all the rest of them spoke good ole southern English."

After about four years working on the Hill, I took a job in 1975 as vice president of the Tobacco Institute. I held this position for some six years and then proceeded to start my own lobbying firm, which fortunately has enjoyed a great deal of success over the past 31 years. Here's how it came about.

Ronald Reagan's election as president of the United States afforded me the opportunity to dramatically change my career path in the Nation's Capital. Having been very active in the Reagan campaign, as noted above, I was offered a position at the Inaugural Committee for President-elect Reagan's 1981 inauguration as virtually a full-time volunteer—as assistant to Ambassador Bill Mittendorf, the committee's finance chairman. (Since the finance committee raised and distributed the money for all the events, it virtually drove the train at the Inaugural committee.) In this position I had access to all kinds of limos and other donated vehicles, as well as to numerous off-duty policemen and other law enforcement officials who were volunteering their free time to the Inaugural Committee.

Despite the fact that the new Senate had been sworn in for more than two weeks prior to the inaugural ceremonies, the Democrats, who had controlled the Senate for decades, still had not turned over the cars and the security detail to the newly elected Senate majority leader, Sen. Howard Baker of Tennessee.[11] However,

I was able to provide Senator Baker with cars, vans, and a security detail for his use during the inaugural activities.

Since Sen. Baker's top aide was my neighbor, buddy, and fellow youth-football coach, I was able to put together a once-in-a-lifetime deal for an aspiring young lobbyist. My wife and I ended up having the majority leader in our box at the Presidential Gala, which happened to be adjacent to President and Nancy Reagan's box. In addition, I was given a seat in the senator's section on the platform for the swearing in of Ronald Reagan as the 40th president of the United States. To have been seated only some 15 feet from the man I believe to be the greatest U.S. president of the 20th century when he took the oath of office is an honor and privilege I will cherish my entire life.

Ronald Reagan's election, coupled with the Republicans gaining control of the Senate for the first time in more than 20 years, motivated me to leave my position with the Tobacco Institute to start my own lobbying firm with a partner named Stu Spencer,[12] one of Nancy and President Reagan's closest personal friends and the campaign manager of Reagan's two successful campaigns for governor of California.

Stu Spencer and I made strategic decisions in the very beginning about the type of clients we would represent and the type we would not be able to represent. Obviously, we were not going to lobby for issues that would violate our own beliefs and principles. But for us there were even bigger considerations. We both desperately wanted Reagan to succeed in his major policy initiatives. In addition, Stu was known to virtually all the press as one of Reagan's closest friends. Therefore, we had to be careful not to get on the wrong side of any of the new president's early legislative goals. This would be especially sensitive in high-profile issues relating to foreign policy or defense matters.[13] We also both wanted to be of any possible assistance in his number-one goal of making the world safer from the communist threat and ultimately winning the Cold War.

One of our first decisions—not made without a little agony—was not to work for any defense contractors. Everyone knew that President Reagan was going to dramatically increase defense spending, and we did end up turning down a significant number of suitors willing to pay us well. Stu justifiably did not want to give any appearance of abusing his friendship with President Reagan. And in my case, with a strong anti-communist, ASC and intelligence background and commitment, I wanted to be free to lobby congressmen and senators for every weapons system the administration proposed. I certainly did not want to be accused of doing so for personal gain. Members of Congress are usually more willing to listen to a person with strong commitments on an issue.

I mention the policy Stu and I adopted with some pride since it led to one of the most satisfying achievements of my long lobbying career. I was privileged to be at the 25th and last of Senator Laxalt's fabled "Lamb Fries"[14] and be seated next to another of Ronald Reagan's oldest friends and confidants named Bob Gray. I almost fell out of my chair when he told me that on one of the last occasions in which he had a lengthy conversation with Ron (as he called him), before his Alzheimer's had set in, that Reagan mentioned my name. In shock I asked, "What on earth did he say about me?" Bob, who is a number of years older than me, thought for a minute and finally said, "Ron said that you were crucial, played a decisive role or something like that, in passing a key piece of his legislation." As I regained my composure I responded: "What legislation?" Bob said: "I can't remember." Racking my brain I said the only thing I can think of is the bill authorizing the sale of AWACS (Airborne Warning and Control System) to Saudi Arabia. "That's it, that's exactly it," he replied.

This discussion was special and somewhat emotional to me (I teared up a little as my buddy John Boehner is noted for doing) since I thought the only memory President Reagan had of me was that I was one of a long list of his dedicated supporters. This was particularly meaningful since this was President Reagan's first and most difficult foreign policy initiative.[15] (Had Reagan failed to get the final senator—it ended up being a tie vote in the Senate, and the vice president broke the tie—it would have spelled trouble for Reagan's planned extensive military buildup!)

A massive lobbying effort developed because the Congress had to approve this sale, which at the time would be largest arms sale to a foreign buyer in American history. Powerful U.S. senators, typified by Ted Kennedy on the Democrat side and Bob Packwood on the Republican side, condemned the proposal as a threat to the security of Israel.[16] Equally prominent administration officials, eventually including the president himself, joined in the debate, arguing that in fact this would help insure the peace of all countries in the region, including Israel. Israel was taken to task for interfering in American foreign policy. President Reagan would be quoted in the August 12, 1981, edition of the Boston Globe as saying: "*It is not the business of other nations to make American foreign policy.*"

The White House lobbying and political shops mounted an effective and ultimately successful lobbying campaign. They were joined by the Boeing (the primary manufacturer) and other defense lobbyists and a few other lobbyists like me who were simply dedicated to supporting Reagan's foreign policy and defense policies. Of course, the Israeli lobbyists also found and motivated their allies. Many people can justifiably take some credit for the ultimate success of this Reagan initiative. Rounding up the 49 yes votes was a difficult task. Some would say it almost involved "hand-to-hand combat." Multiple meetings, offers of help in the future, and all the other things that are included in lobbying were obviously employed.

Ultimately it came down to the vote of one senator from Iowa named Roger Jepsen. The other 99 senators, 50 "noes" and 40 "yeses," were "in concrete," in language used on the "Hill." Jepsen, who had consistently resisted, was the last hope. I knew Senator Jepsen but was not a close friend. I also knew that he had a religious concern relating to Israel. I contacted my closest friends from Iowa to find out more. I found out that the senator had been raised in the American Lutheran Church but had joined some millenarian denomination later in life. Of course, these groups come up with many of out-of-the-mainstream interpretations of Rev. 20:1-7. Most of them believe in the universal conversion of the Jews on the day of the return of Christ.

Having been told that Senator Jepsen was particularly concerned about Rom. 11:26 ff., which begins, *"And so all Israel shall be saved,"* I came up with a plan. The junior senator from Iowa, who had been elected to the Senate in the 1980 election with Reagan, was a very good friend. I had gotten to know Chuck Grassley during the six years he served in the House and was active in raising funds for his Senate campaign. Chuck was a conservative Baptist[17] and as sincere and dedicated as they come. I called and asked for an appointment to discuss how we might get Jepsen's vote, and I would need some time. Actually, our meeting was almost two hours long as we read through most of the book of Romans. As Chuck took pages of notes I suggested that he start by quoting Rom. 9:6, which states: *"For they are not all Israel, which are of Israel."* Then urge Jepsen to carefully read the first 11 chapters of Romans in order to understand 11:26 in its context. Chuck asked me if I wanted to accompany him to see Roger, and I responded that this was such a delicate subject that it would be better to do it "Senator to Senator." He agreed and left through his side door.

As I exited through the regular door into Senator Grassley's waiting room, I was overwhelmed by how many impatient White House lobbyists were waiting. They began to give me grief about monopolizing the senator's time when they desperately need to talk to him about getting Senator Jepsen's vote. I didn't tell them that we had been engaged in Bible study. (That was a private matter.) I tried to assure them that we had covered that subject from every angle.

"Chuck has just left out the side door to talk to Roger, and our fate is in his capable hands," I tried to reassure them. They were not happy with me at that time. That would change the next day when Majority Leader Baker called the bill up for a vote and it passed when Jepsen voted "aye." A few sort of apologized to me the next time I saw them. Two of my better friends in the group actually called and thanked me for my help.

Chuck Grassley and I never referred to our biblical strategy again until I mentioned it to him just in passing some two years later. I believe only someone with a theological background could have successfully devised such a strategy. Only a few people knew the full story. I was thrilled that somebody told Reagan what had happened. It would be more than 25 years later that I was convinced myself that encouraging Senator Jepsen to read all of Romans made the difference. This happened when I found a book I had purchased and never read about the powerful Jewish lobby. Paul Findley, a former long-time congressman from Illinois, had written a book titled *They Dared To Speak: People and Institutions Confront Israel's Lobby.*

Findley listed in his book the names of a number of congressmen and senators this lobby claimed to have defeated because of a vote or votes they had cast that they deemed not to be in the best interest of Israel. In a chapter titled "Church and State," Findley wrote this about Jepsen:

> "Senator Roger W. Jepsen, a first-term legislator from Iowa, told the 1981 annual policy conference that one of the reasons for his 'spirited and unfailing support' for Israel was his Christian faith. He declared that Christians, particularly Evangelical Christians, have been among Israel's best friends since its rebirth in 1948.'" Then turning to Jepsen's crucial vote on AWACS, Findley stated; "Jepsen cited his fundamentalist views in explaining his early opposition to the sale of AWACS to Saudi Arabia but then credited divine intervention as the reason he switched his position the day before the Senate voted on the proposal. On election day, November 6, 1984, Iowans—spurred by the Israeli lobby—did their own switching, rejecting Jepsen's bid for a second term."[18]

This led me to believe that after the biblical discussion Senator Jepsen had with Senator Grassley, he prayed over the issue. This conclusion was based on his words that God revealed to him how he should vote. This is a heavy story and it should be easy to understand why I told very few people about it at the time.[19]

I probably should tell you a little bit about the role of a lobbyist from my vantage point. Why do we have lobbyists? Are they necessary? Do they perform a useful or necessary role in our government?

And, why do we have so many of them? There are more than 30,000 registered lobbyists in Washington—66 for every member of Congress! Also, more than 10,000 associations, organizations, corporations, labor unions, and even churches have offices in the Nation's Capital. All of these groups are there to monitor the proceedings in Congress and the policies adopted by the White House. The overwhelming majority are here to lobby Congress and the Administration. Have we become a nation of lobbyists, as a few wags have suggested?

In a Harris poll, more than 80 percent of the American people think lobbyists have too much power. Are not most lobbyists a bunch of scumbags who intend to thwart the will of the people with their sleazy tactics, mostly for personal gain?

These are all legitimate questions, especially in view of recent lobbying scandals involving millions of dollars and prison time for some lobbyists and members of Congress. They deserve serious answers, since many Americans have had their faith in the American system of government shaken by these revelations of corruption.

Let's start with the basic question: What right do the American people have to send lobbyists to Washington to represent them before their government?

On Sept. 29, 1789, Congress transmitted to the state legislative bodies 12 amendments to the Constitution of the United States for ratification. These 12 amendments, authorized by Congress, were signed by the speaker of the House and the president of the Senate. This first speaker was Frederick Augustus Muhlenberg, a Lutheran minister and member of Congress from Pennsylvania. The president of the Senate was John Adams, the first vice president of the United States.

The state legislators rejected two of the amendments (having to do with Congressional representation and pay). The other 10 amendments, better known as the Bill of Rights, were ratified by the states effective Dec. 15, 1791.

The First Amendment reads: "Congress shall make no law respecting an establishment of religion, or prohibiting the free exercise thereof; or abridging the freedom of speech, or of the press, or the right of the people peaceably to assemble, *or to petition the Government for a redress of grievances.*"

The same First Amendment that forbids the federal government from establishing a national church, protects our religious liberty, and guarantees Americans the right of free speech, including religious speech, also allows American citizens the right to petition their government. Whether or not Americans have a right to lobby the government is answered clearly in the First Amendment.

Most Americans have neither the means nor the ability to lobby the government, so they band together to hire someone to represent them in Washington, in their state capitals, and sometimes even before their local governments. Is it fair that a few of the privileged enjoy the services of these high powered lobbyists and the masses are left out in the cold? The fact is that most Americans, with the possible exception of Missouri Synod clergymen, have a lobbyist in Washington whether they realize it or not.[20] I say "possible exception" because some LCMS clergymen may have wives who are nurses, school teachers, or who work for some corporation, all of whom would have lobbyists. Some Lutheran pastors may even serve as chaplains for fire, rescue, or police departments or belong to some group such as a right-to-life organization, all of which would have some lobbyist serving them.

Farmers, lawyers, doctors, small-business men and women, teachers, older people (the AARP represents more than 40 million people, since 43 million Americans are now on Medicare), the Girl Scouts, the Boy Scouts of America (that's me), most clergymen, union members, builders, and nearly all who have a profession have lobbyists in Washington. (You guessed it! There are no lobbyists for housewives and stay-at-home mothers that I am aware of. There probably should be, but I would guess that many of them still belong to some organizations that have some lobbying representation.)

But aren't most lobbyists sleazy and unscrupulous? No, not by a long shot! Some certainly are—more than I would like. The vast majority, though, are decent, hard-working, and patriotic people who are dedicated to doing their jobs in an honest and effective way. Just like any other profession or trade, a few lobbyists give this honorable and necessary job a bad name.

No profession can change the sinful nature of man. You have corrupt and immoral doctors, lawyers, farmers, teachers, businessmen, factory workers, plumbers, trash collectors, elected officials, and even clergymen. You don't ostracize or abolish the Catholic Church because a tiny fraction of immoral and despicable priests have grossly abused the trust given to them by God. You don't trash the medical profession and stop going to your doctor because an extremely small number of them, through incompetence or neglect, allow an unnecessary death or sexually abuse a vulnerable patient. I'll skip the lawyers and used car salesmen for now.

In a like manner, it would be irresponsible to defame or try to abolish a profession so necessary to the proper functioning of our form of government because of the inexcusable actions of a handful of lobbyists motivated by greed or desire for power. If you break the law as a lobbyist, congressman, or banker, you should go to jail. It's that simple from my point of view.

How can I say that lobbying is so necessary to the proper functioning of our government? For one thing, literally thousands of bills are introduced in Congress every year. Many of them make it to the committee process. During the committee process, a bill is debated and usually amended. Normally, several amendments are agreed to and many more are either withdrawn, not considered, or voted down. Sometime these bills can be hundreds—even thousands—of pages long. Frequently, they are so technical that the wording of a phrase—on rare occasions, even where a comma is placed—can dramatically affect the final interpretation of the bill if it becomes law.

The size of congressional and committee staffs has been significantly increased since my days on the Hill, but they still are limited. When a committee is considering a controversial provision of a bill or amendment, the arguments for and against can be very complex. Lobbyists for and against these provisions become experts on the details, or they bring in experts from the home office, and explain them to the member of Congress and his or her staff. This is a major contribution to the member as he or she makes decisions. I have always made it a practice to give the member the other side of the argument after I have made the case for our point of view. In addition, many matters of great concern to the people are never brought to the attention of congressmen and senators without input from lobbyists.

I view my obligations as a lobbyist from a vantage point similar (though not identical) to my dual responsibilities as a clergyman in the two kingdoms. When I was a pastor, I realized that my primary responsibility was to be a shepherd of the flock over which God had given me charge. My secondary, but still important, responsibility was to be a good citizen and set an example for the people I served. I view it my responsibility as a lobbyist to represent my clients to the best of my ability, but my role as a citizen of this great nation requires me to use my talents and efforts to try to influence our government in a moral and just direction.

I didn't end up in Washington because I was looking for a career change. I was happy and felt that I was making a contribution as a campus pastor. I got into politics and ended up in the Nation's Capital because I wanted to try to make a difference. In my dealings with members of the House and Senate, I try to do my part to make sure our policy makers have all the information necessary to make a decision. I view these as equal responsibilities, which I believe I have successfully balanced over the years.

One other thing that ministers and lobbyists have in common is the importance of their reputations. If a minister loses his good reputation, he may continue to preach and carry out the other duties of the pastoral office, but his effectiveness will be greatly diminished. If a lobbyist loses his good reputation, he may continue to receive his salary or fees, file his reports with his office or clients, and manage to schedule some appointments with members and staffers, but his ability to influence legislation is not simply diminished—it is *gone*. I have witnessed many an occasion when some lobbyist approaches a member of Congress at the Capitol Hill Club (the Republican club) or some restaurant and brings up some legislation of importance to his client. Then, the minute he leaves, the member will say something like, "I wouldn't trust that guy with my dog, much less my wife."

Hard work and sincerity is always highly respected, be you a pastor or a lobbyist. I have made it a point throughout my career never to lie to, or even mislead, a congressman or senator. I always try to show the proper respect to which their office entitles them, even to those who are among my very best friends.

I never ask a member of Congress to violate any of his or her basic philosophical principles. I may have friendly discussions about why I believe a particular vote in a gray area is in the best interest of the country, the party, or one of my clients, and explain that they can cast such a vote without violating their basic principles.

What's more, I am not shy about giving unsought advice about the appearance of some behavior that may in reality be totally innocent. I am sometimes called a "mother hen" in a friendly way, since they know that I have their best interests at heart. After so many years on the job, I have sort of achieved a "senior statesmen" status and am frequently asked for advice. Unfortunately, a few of those you may have read about in the papers came to me for advice after the fact.

Finally, I try not to abuse the friendships I have established over many years. If you don't ask for much when you ask for something about which a congressman has no problem with, you usually get prompt action. One relatively minor example: Just a few days before the August congressional recess in 2006, my wife and I had a fundraising event for our Virginia senator, George Allen, at our home. The event was on a Monday evening, and I happened to run into George at a noon event in D.C. I told him that I expected to have seven or eight of his Senate colleagues and more than 20 members of the House at the event that evening. He cautioned me not to be disappointed if none of the senators showed since there were no votes in the Senate until Tuesday evening. He also mentioned that he had heard that the House would not finished voting until about 7:00 p.m., and with my house 35 or 40 minutes from the Capital, he doubted many would show.

You should have seen the surprise on his face when nine of his Senate colleagues and 26 congressmen showed up. When my very good friend, Senator Saxby Chambliss of Georgia, got up to introduce his colleagues to the crowd, he said, "George, I don't want to hurt your feelings, but we are here because Bill Hecht said we had to come—and he does not ask for much."

Over the years, I have been involved in six presidential campaigns—heavily involved in the two Reagan campaigns and the first George H.W. Bush campaign— and have helped in hundreds of congressional and senatorial campaigns, often in a relatively small way, but a significant number of times in a major way.

I cannot imagine how I could have had a job that would allow me a better opportunity to fulfill my goal of trying to make a contribution to my country through the political process while trying never to forget my responsibilities as a Christian. I believe that God sometimes has many "callings" for us in our lives, and if we listen to Him in humility, He empowers us to carry them out!

It will be clearly documented in this book that our Founding Fathers intended for us as American citizens to always take our Christian faith with us when we enter the "public square." While acknowledging my personal failures due to the frailties of my sinful flesh, I have always tried to do as our Founders intended. If this nation ever forgets the words of one of the most famous and least orthodox Christian Founders, John Adams, we are in grave danger. In 1798, President Adams[21] warned in these frequently quoted words that "Our Constitution was made only for a moral and religious people. It is wholly inadequate to the government of any other."

Notes

[1] The term "Islamist" is used to describe the radical, fundamentalist Muslim terrorists who believe that they have a divine command from Allah to wage *jihad* against the infidels, personified by the U.S., which is considered to be "the Great Satan." This will become evident when we examine radical Islamist terrorism. The term "Islamic," like the word "Muslim," is a neutral description that can be used to identify the majority of moderate followers of Islam as well as the radicals.

[2] James Hutson, *Forgotten Features of the Founding: The Recovery of Religious Themes in the Early American Republic*, (Lexington Books, 2003), 1.

[3] Out of respect I have chosen not to bandy about the name of this now deceased dedicated member of Congress for reasons that will become clear in the following pages. The readers who study the history of the U.S. Congress will have no difficulty in discovering his identity and, I hope, will read about some of his many accomplishments.

[4] Former conservative Democrat Governor Connally, who was seriously wounded in the car with JFK when he was assassinated, was appointed as a Democrat to be secretary of the Treasury under President Nixon and became a Republican in 1973, which made him a celebrity among Republicans. Former Congressman George H.W. Bush had served as ambassador to the UN, director of the CIA, and, importantly in a Republican presidential primary, chairman of the Republican National Committee. Popular and talented Republican

Senate Majority Leader Howard Baker also had great credentials as a candidate. In addition, there were eight well-known individuals who explored and/or were strongly urged by supporters to enter the Republican presidential primary and declined to run. This list included such heavyweights as former President Ford, former Senator and NRC Chairman Bill Brock, and Pennsylvania Senator John Heinz. Two other U.S. senators launched exploratory campaigns and withdrew before the primaries began. Seven other former or presently serving elected officials mounted serious campaigns and withdrew during the primaries.

[5] Some may wonder why we had only 13 original Reagan supporters in the Core Group. For one thing, there were probably no more than another half dozen members of Congress willing to publicly endorse Reagan at this stage of the campaign. Beloved House Republican Minority Whip Bob Michel (who would become House Republican minority leader after the 1980 election) was an early Reagan supporter but did not become a member of the Core Group because of his leadership position. However, he was very helpful and we met daily in his whip office just off of the House floor.

[6] John Sears, Governor Reagan's very brilliant but arrogant 1976 campaign manager, insisted that Reagan's very narrow loss to President Ford in the previous primary would make him the presumptive nominee in 1980. Some early Republican presidential primary polling data tended to support this contention since Governor Reagan's name recognition was almost 100 percent among Republicans. Sears' decision to keep Reagan above the fray and not become involved in the initial visits and debates of the so-called "retail politics" in Iowa, where the first caucus would be held, for example, created a rift with the congressmen in the Core Group. They knew from their visits back to their home districts that these attacks on Reagan were taking a significant toll.

[7] Lee Atwater would see his budding career as a master campaign strategist get a big boost due to his efforts on behalf of Reagan in the South Carolina primary. Carroll Campbell had discovered Lee at a young age in his earlier campaigns. When Lee's fabled election accomplishments were cut short by cancer, I spent several hours at the governor's mansion in Columbia, S.C., with just Governor Campbell and his family. We reminisced and mourned over the loss of our dear friend at such a young age. Then Governor Campbell asked me if I would go represent him at Lee's favorite jazz establishment where they were having a special concert to celebrate his life. I told a packed hall of Lee's friends that the governor had planned to come with me but could not face such a wonderful crowd in his emotional state.

[8] This position turned out to be a great opportunity for me to make a contribution to the Reagan effort and helped me a lot on my career path. I always told people I got to make the calls the members didn't want to make. Often I got to explain why none of the members would be able to attend some local campaign event. I got to attend meetings members couldn't make or didn't want to make. I scheduled meetings and met with congressmen who were potential Reagan supporters, etc.

[9] The act was named after a Republican senator, named James J. Davis, and a Republican congressman, named Robert L. Bacon, who were the original sponsors. President Herbert Hoover signed it into law in 1931. In simple terms, it prevented contractors from bringing in workers who were willing to work for less than union wages in given areas. FDR, Nixon in 1971, and both George H.W. and George W. Bush would suspend Davis-Bacon in times of domestic emergencies (e.g., a depression, floods, or other natural disasters) to stem inflation.

[10] I would get to know Bill Casey even better after he became director of the CIA in the Reagan administration. Stu Spencer and I would represent two foreign governments of interest to Casey. Since we traveled to these countries on some occasions and talked to their top leaders, Casey would suggest that we drop in from time to time and "share" information. We were able on a few occasions to confirm or refute some information he had received from intelligence sources. We knew he was not going to give us much info unless there was something he wanted us to know. But as long as he expressed no reservations about our work, we felt we were doing our job properly. On at least two occasions, Director Casey, who was never known for "small talk," mentioned to me that I had played a "key" or "important" role in the success of the Reagan effort to win over large numbers of labor union voters. I treasure those remarks from a man who had so much to do with Reagan's victory and served our country so well.

[11] Why the delay in turning over power is still a mystery to me. The Democrats in the Senate were obviously in a state of shock. The Republicans had gained 12 long-held Democrat Senate seats in the largest swing since 1958. These include Herman Tallmadge (D-Georgia), Frank Church (D-Idaho), George McGovern (D-SD), Warren Magnuson (D-WA), and Birch Bayh (D-Indiana). This was arguably the most dramatic ideological shift in the history of the U.S. Senate.

[12] Hecht, Spencer and Associates celebrated its 31st anniversary in 2012.

[13] Obviously, over the years on a few occasions we found ourselves on opposite sides from the administration on some domestic spending issues.

[14] Senator Laxalt was the son of a "Basque sheepherder" who spent much of his childhood tending the sheep and their young lambs in the mountains of Nevada near Lake Tahoe. His storied rise as an attorney, governor of Nevada, and U.S. senator is inspiring and vital to American history. During Reagan's presidency, he honored a Basque tradition by holding an annual dinner at the Georgetown Club known as the "Laxalt Lamb Fry." President Reagan himself attended on several occasions and the attendees always included a "who's who" of longtime Reagan supporters and key White House and administration officials. I was so fortunate to be able to attend all of these Lamb Fries, except one that resulted in a heart-to-heart discussion with my scheduler. I was always included primarily because of my role with the Core Group and Laxalt's Thursday night gathering during the 1980 primary and general election campaigns. I had actually hosted a dinner at the Georgetown Club honoring the "1st Anniversary of Reagan's Nomination" in 1981, which President Reagan attended. I consulted frequently with Senator Laxalt about who should be invited and who should speak besides him and me, since I was the master of ceremonies.

[15] Reagan and his top advisors had made the decision that it was necessary to sell five AWACS (Airborne Warning and Control System) planes to help secure the peace in the Middle East. The AWACS plane had a mounted antenna on its top capable of detecting and tracking enemy airplanes within a 175,000 square-mile radius. With the fall of the Shah of Iran and his military might under the previous administration, there was no one capable of maintaining peace in the region. When the Shah, America's best ally in that part of the world, was in power, he could provide stability in the Persian Gulf region. Communism, not radical Islamist terrorism, was the major threat at that time. A massive uproar over selling such sophisticated technology to Saudi Arabia was led by Israel and the Israeli lobby in the U.S. To understand how fierce the headwinds were, it should be noted that at least one poll released in May 1981 revealed that only 19 percent of Americans supported selling AWACS planes to Saudi Arabia.

[16] The argument was not about any fear that Saudi Arabia would attack Israel. Many insisted that Israel must maintain the ability to launch an undetected first-strike attack in order to deter any of the more extreme Muslim countries in or around the Middle East from attacking Israel. It was argued that while Saudi Arabia didn't have the military capacity to attack any country, they would feel obligated to alert other Muslim countries of the movement or location of Israeli military aircraft. President Reagan was confident that no rogue Muslim countries would attack Israel knowing that he was committed to protecting Israel. Reagan believed that if he provided the Saudis with the ability for early detection of a hostile movement against them, he could gain their trust, and he needed their cooperation. It worked in several ways. First of all, they dramatically increased their oil production to enable America to roll back the soaring gas prices. Secondly, they used their considerable influence in the Muslim world to discourage those who wanted to destroy Israel. Thirdly, and of great importance to Reagan, they discouraged any form of support or assistance to the communists, who were trying to increase their influence in this part of the world. As the rulers of the Muslim holy land and the wealthiest nation in the Muslim world, the Saudis maintained considerable influence.

[17] Senator Grassley is a member of a Baptist church that is affiliated with the Baptist General Conference (BGC). The BGC is an evangelical Baptist body that grew out of the "great revival" in the 19th century. Their theology is basically Calvinistic, and they are not into millenarianism.

[18] Paul Findley, *They Dare to Speak Out: People and Institutions Confront Israel's Lobby*, (Chicago Review Press, 2003), 239-240. I strongly disagree with former Congressman Findley's conclusion that the Israeli lobby engineered Jepsen's defeat in 1984. For one thing, the Jewish population in Iowa is very small. For another, this was one of the 1984 races the NRSC was following closely well over a year before the election. They knew that Jepsen was in trouble, but not because of the AWACS vote in 1981. Jepsen is a good man but he had some personal problems that would have amounted to little in most states. Iowa is a state that doesn't much tolerate what it perceives to be arrogance or even minor dishonesty.

[19] I should make a few disclaimers so that no one misunderstands my position. I have always been a strong supporter of Israel as a crucial friend of America in a dangerous part of the world. Israel is an increasingly important ally due to the rise of the radical Islamists. Secondly, Stu and I stood firm on our principles. Not long after the sale of AWACS to Saudi Arabia was approved, we received a very large contract offer from an Arab country. We respectfully returned the written offer with our regrets. We certainly did not want our motives for our efforts in this fight to be questioned. In addition, I was convinced even back then that we could never in good conscience represent a Muslim-ruled country—even a friendly one at the time.

[20] The LCMS has never had an official lobbyist in Washington, D.C., with the exception of yours truly on an occasional ad hoc, voluntary basis when the president of the Synod or some other church official has asked me to help with a problem that needed attention in Washington. I will mention a few such occasions in Chapter 8 when I discuss Lutheran civic responsibilities.

[21] Adams was raised as a Congregationalist but later became a Unitarian. In a like manner, Thomas Jefferson grew up as an Anglican, became a deist during his college days at William and Mary, and later adopted the Unitarian religion. Some scholars describe both men as "Christian Unitarians" since their beliefs had little in common with the radically liberal modern-day Unitarians. It will be documented in the text that both men questioned many of the miraculous teachings in the Bible, but not its moral teachings and authority. However, it will also be noted that the vast majority of the 200 or more most-significant Founders were orthodox Christians.

2

Polarization in Washington: 41 Years on the Front Lines

On Tuesday, Aug. 15, 1995, in an address to the men's luncheon of the International Lutheran Laymen's League convention in Grand Rapids, Mich., I told the audience that we were experiencing the most partisan times in the Nation's Capital in my 24 years of service there. There had been a sea change since my arrival in the summer of 1971.

Eleven years and a few weeks later, I explained to the Fall Tri-District (Atlantic, New England, and New Jersey) Pastoral Conference of The Lutheran Church—Missouri Synod that the situation had worsened to the point that I believed I could make the case that the partisan atmosphere in Washington was the most highly charged and divisive it had been since the years surrounding Lincoln's presidency.

As we face what potentially is the most severe threat to our still-young nation's liberty since we won the Revolutionary War, this strong partisan divide is troubling to say the least. To confront the radical Islamic terrorists successfully, we need a common resolve, not partisan bickering.

What has happened to poison the well in such a dramatic way? The simple answer (but not the full answer) is that in 1994 the Republicans captured control of the U.S. House of Representatives from the Democrats for the first time in more than 40 years.

Forty-two uninterrupted years of a Democrat majority in the House is a long time. So long that many Democrats may have thought control of the House was their natural birthright. It's worse than that when you realize that the Republicans were in the majority for only two years (1953 and 1954). You have to go back another 20 years, prior to the Great Depression, to see previous GOP control. This means the Democrats had controlled the House for 62 of the previous 64 years.

The situation in the Senate was only slightly different. The GOP took control of the Senate in the 1952 election and relinquished it in 1954. In 1980, 28 years later, the Republicans gained control of the Senate for six years, losing it again in 1986 before regaining it in 1994.

It is a painful experience for a political party to relinquish control of either chamber of Congress after having control for so long that it appears to be the natural order of things.

Parenthetically, the Republicans taking control of the Senate in 1980 was a major break in my professional career. As noted in Chapter 1, the takeover factored into the decision Stu and I made to start our lobbying firm. A special memory not previously mentioned was that my wife and I ended up having the new Senate majority leader, Howard Baker, in our box at the Presidential Gala, which happened to be adjacent to President and Nancy Reagan's box. (The fact that the legendary country singer Charlie Pride was the celebrity guest in our box further highlighted our prominent location.)

Each dramatic change in the makeup of Congress—Democrat landslides in 1964 and 1974; the Republican landslide in 1980; and the Republican "tsunami" in 1994—affected the camaraderie and partisan attitudes in both chambers. The changes resulting from the 1994 elections and the events leading up to this election created a polarization, especially in the House of Representatives, that has changed Washington's way of doing business.

But there is more to the story of hostility and partisanship in Washington than just the 1994 change from majority to minority status for the Democrats. For one thing, the circumstances leading up to the 1994 Republican takeover were a major factor. For another, the liberal-conservative split in Congress had probably reached its widest point to date. Finally, the country as a whole was very evenly divided between the two parties and had very strong differences on significant issues facing the nation.[1]

Let's have a closer look at all this.

The Vietnam-era anti-war protests and other activities in the late 1960s and early 1970s led to partisan fights over foreign policy matters while American troops were fighting on foreign soil. This was the first time in American history that Congressmen and Senators had disagreed publicly over a war while our troops were fighting and dying on foreign fields.

Then, in the 1974 mid-term election following the Watergate scandal, the Democrats won 48 Republican-held seats. By bringing their majority to 147 seats— 291 Democrats to 144 Republicans—the Democrats were within one seat of a two-thirds majority. Most of these 48 new Democrats in Congress were hard-core liberals. We jokingly called them "the class of Nixon's revenge," because this mostly young, very liberal freshman class challenged the strong committee and seniority system that had dominated Congress for most of the previous 200 years. These young liberals had the audacity to insist that the votes of *all* committee members should be counted and that members not simply yield to the "institutional wisdom" of the chairman.

Not too long after this, the tide changed again. The Republicans gained 15 House in 1978 seats and another 34 in the Reagan landslide of 1980. These were almost all very conservative Republicans. A few of the 49 new Republican members elected in 1978 and 1980 replaced liberal Democrats from the 1974 election, but most of them took out *conservative* Democrats, mainly in the South.

These elections led eventually to the 1994 Republican congressional landslide, when the Republicans won 53 Democrat seats, including those of the speaker and several long-serving committee chairmen. Almost all these 53 new Republicans were staunchly conservative. The Republicans in 1994 also won eight Democrat Senate seats[2] and took control of the U.S. Senate as well. (The Senate had returned to Democrat control in the 1986 midterm election and remained so until 1994.)

The 1994 election reshaped the Congress. It was not just that the Republicans took control of both chambers, but they decimated the conservative Democrats in the House of Representatives. The make-up of the House now showed 230 Republicans, the overwhelming majority of whom were conservatives, and 205 Democrats, almost all of whom were liberals. The classic liberal-conservative divide that had existed in Congress since its founding, with liberals and conservative in *both* parties, now became more partisan. Why? Because conservatives dominated one party, while liberals dominated the other.

This trend continued in the five elections through 2004. Of the 232 Republican members in the 109th Congress (2005-2006), before a couple of resignations, one would have been hard-pressed to call more than five of them "liberals." Another 15 to 20 might have been described as "moderates," depending on the issue.[3]

The events leading up to the Republican takeover in 1994 involved Republican exposure of mostly Democrat scandals. This caused bad blood that lingered for the 12 years of Republican control after that.

Shortly after he was elected to Congress in 1990, John Boehner of Ohio, one of my best friends and now the speaker of the House, started an insurgent group called "The Gang of Seven." The other six "gang" members recruited by Boehner (a talented and dedicated group of members of Congress, or MCs) were Frank Riggs of California, who lost his seat in 1996, two years after the takeover; former Sen. Rick Santorum of Pennsylvania, who lost his U.S. Senate seat in 2006 after two terms and ran a competitive campaign for the Republican presidential nomination in 2012; former Congressman Jim Nussle, who was White House budget director after losing the Iowa governor's race in 2006; Congressman Charley Taylor, who in 2006 lost his North Carolina House seat; Congressman John Doolittle of California, who won a tough reelection bid in 2006 but retired in 2008; and Congressman Scott Kluge, who would later lose a Wisconsin Senate bid.

The Gang of Seven believed that four decades of Democrat rule had bred corruption in the House—and they set out to expose it. The Democrats have undoubtedly relished the feat of removing six of the Gang of Seven from elective office. Congressman Boehner, however, will most likely remain in Congress as long as he chooses to run and retain the speaker's gavel if the Republicans maintain the majority, as most political prognosticators predict.

Boehner is widely praised for providing Republican leadership in Congress since he was first elected as majority leader in 2006.[4] In 2009, he led the attacks on what he considered the excessively liberal programs being advanced by the Democrat leadership in the House and the Obama Administration. He took the lead on advancing Republican alternatives. Boehner was heavily involved, with the Republican campaign team, in recruitment of high-quality Republican candidates for the 2010 House races. The project was very successful, allowing the Republicans to regain the majority in the House after the 2010 election. Boehner was subsequently elected the speaker of the U.S. House by the Republican caucus with only minor opposition.

The internal partisan wars in the Nation's Capital that led to widespread partisan polarization had their origins in the successful Democrat-led efforts to impeach President Richard Nixon and to force the resignation of Attorney General Edwin Meese later in the Reagan administration. In the aftermath of the Watergate debacle, the affable President Reagan was able to forge bipartisan cooperation primarily with another Irishman, Democrat Speaker Tip O'Neill. The Democrat attacks in Congress that resulted in Ed Meese's resignation shook the foundations of years of bipartisanship that had resulted in sustained economic recovery for the country and a virtual collapse of the Soviet empire, as explained in some detail in Chapter 1.

However, the most significant event that shattered Democrat–Republican collegiality in the Senate (and by extension to the House) happened in 1989. When the 55-45 majority Democrat Senate took the unprecedented action of denying Senate confirmation to one of their own long-serving Members to a cabinet position, all of the long-established precedents of civility in "The Most Exclusive Club"[5] in the world came to an abrupt end. Former Senator John Tower of Texas, President George H.W. Bush's choice for Secretary of Defense, had served almost 24 years in the Senate before his retirement just five years earlier in 1984. This 53-47 vote to deny Tower the opportunity to serve the new president as Secretary of Defense was dramatic, unexpected and even draconian; in modern times he was only the second nominee for a cabinet post and the only former Senator to be denied appointment.[6]

Regardless of the validity of the charges leveled against John Tower by the Democrats in the Senate, especially by those in leadership positions, they had violated the traditional bipartisan statesmanship of the U.S. Senate that had prevailed throughout its history (previously interrupted only by the War Between the States). At least that is the way that the Republicans saw it.

Republican revenge came rapidly when the Democrat speaker of the U.S. House of Representatives, Jim Wright (also of Texas), was forced to resign over purported ethics violations later in 1989. The perceived high profile bipartisan breach by the Democrats in the Senate did not motivate Congressman Newt Gingrich of Georgia to take on Speaker Wright. He had already filed charges with the House Ethics Committee in 1988. But such highly partisan action by the Senate Democrats certainly emboldened the man from Georgia who would become speaker in 1995.

The Gang of Seven sprang into existence in an extremely partisan climate that was coming to a boil. Just a year before Boehner was elected, in 1989, Democrat Speaker Jim Wright of Texas was forced to resign his seat in Congress, mainly over a book deal. He had written a book, *Reflections of a Public Man,* and a large number of lobbyists had bought more copies than they could possibly give away—they may have had to rent space to store them! (Fortunately, I didn't buy a single copy, but I had known Jim Wright for many years. I thought him to be basically a decent man and a good legislator, but I think he got caught up in a system that had been around so long that it took too many things for granted. He was never convicted of any wrong doing.)

The initial charges against Wright had been filed in 1988 with the House Ethics Committee by a brilliant firebrand of a congressman from Georgia by the name of Newt Gingrich. Newt was propelled to election as minority whip by his Republican colleagues by this brazen (at the time) attack on the Democrat speaker of the House. He would become the visionary and leader of the so-called "Republican Revolution" in 1994, and subsequently speaker in 1995.

Now enters the Gang of Seven. While the seven probably were able to uncover a few other minor scandals, their big disclosures had to do with the House Bank and the House Post Office.

For many years members of the House had their own bank, operated by the sergeant at arms, which, among other things, gave cash advances that amounted to interest-free loans. The practice probably started with advances only a few days before paychecks were issued.[7] But over the years and for some members, the period of time before the "loans" were repaid had stretched into weeks and even months, and some of the amounts had become very significant. Some Republican members also used the bank in similar ways, but not nearly to the extent or in such large amounts. In any event, the Democrats were in charge and responsible for running the institutions of the House.

The House Post Office scandal was even worse. All congressmen were allotted a large number of stamps for use with official correspondence. Congressional offices send out enormous volumes of mail, and the stamp allowances were quite significant. Apparently, some members had started turning in their unused stamps from a given period of time for a cash reimbursement to be used for office supplies and other official office needs. It was alleged—and apparently proven in some cases—that a number of these congressmen were having very large numbers of stamps left over and that the reimbursements weren't being used for office needs. Since the Democrats were the party in power and staffed the House Post Office, Republicans weren't granted equal treatment. That turned out to be a major plus for the party out of power.

As the Gang of Seven uncovered and exposed these practices at the House bank and post office, a major scandal erupted. As it turned out, some of the most senior and powerful congressmen were the major abusers of the system. The best example of how intense this scandal became was Illinois Congressman Dan Rostenkowski's stunning loss in the 1994 election. Rostenkowski, who was one of the most senior members of Congress and chairman of the Ways and Means Committee (arguably the most prestigious and powerful committee of the House of Representatives), was both feared and respected by his colleagues. What made the loss so earth shaking was that Danny's district in Chicago was one of the most heavily Democrat districts in America. It was in this climate of Republicans exposing Democrat scandals that the 1994 election, frequently referred to as the "Republican Revolution," took place.

Exposing these abuses undoubtedly was the right thing to do, and it turned out to be very effective. But it also was very polarizing.

The election of 1994 may well have ended the spirit of partisan cooperation forever. Even though more than a few Democrats, especially some in positions of power, were grossly abusing the system, Democrat resentment lingered toward Republicans for uncovering these practices. I'm sure that revenge, as well as a burning desire to return to power, motivated the Democrats to return the favor to the Republicans in 2006.

Republican abuses of power may not have been as widespread and pervasive as those of the Democrats, but the GOP is held to a higher standard, justifiably I believe. I say "justifiably" because my party has positioned itself as the party of honesty, integrity, and traditional American values. We found out how the Republican scandals played out in the election of 2006. I intend to briefly discuss a few of the congressional scandals I have witnessed during my years in Washington later in this chapter.

To further understand this partisan "divide"—*chasm* is probably a better word—consideration of the constant fights between the Republican-controlled Congress and President Bill Clinton and his Democrat administration would be useful.

A battle over the budget and the threatened shutdown of the government in 1995 was the initial event that foreshadowed things to come. Clinton, always an incredibly smart politician, adopted a strategy of pushing some legislative initiatives popular with the Republicans. The best examples are "welfare reform" legislation and a balanced budget, which both the Republican Congress and President Clinton still claim as two of their proudest accomplishments. Clinton, with major cooperation from the Republican members, also pushed free-trade initiatives, such as NAFTA,[8] over the objections of organized labor. This relatively brief period of bipartisan coordination gave way to more intense partisan "wars" as Clinton's indiscretions became public. These fights culminated in the House bringing articles of impeachment against the president and the Senate voting not to convict.

The bitterly fought 2000 presidential election between Gov. George W. Bush and Vice President Al Gore served to further divide an already fractured electorate. The continuous recount in Florida that followed the election added more fuel to the already brightly burning partisan fires.

When the 9/11 tragedy hit, the country came together for a period of patriotic unity. President Bush's strong and forceful response to these radical Islamic terrorist attacks was widely supported by the country and its elected officials in the beginning. Almost all of my Democratic friends in D.C., including a few members of Congress, privately told me, "Thank God George Bush is president!" The invasion of Afghanistan was almost universally supported. Initially, the Iraq invasion and the overthrow of Saddam Hussein also were widely supported, if not overwhelmingly so.

The war in Iraq, which had lasted longer than most had expected, was one of the dominating issues in the 2008 presidential and congressional campaigns and had become a major point of division for the American people. Much of this division has been caused by, or at least intensified by, the heated disagreements over the war in Washington. Following the precedent set during the Vietnam War, major and very public debates have raged in the Congress over the conduct of the war in Iraq and even whether it is justified, at the same time as our troops are fighting on foreign soil. You don't have to be a foreign policy expert to realize that these debates not only have divided our nation but emboldened our enemy. This is especially true when the enemy is composed of religious fanatics who respect neither human rights nor human life. Their jihadist goals are to destroy the "infidels," with no rules or moral restrictions.

This is not the place for a full-blown debate on the war in Iraq, or on the larger war being waged by the Islamic terrorists. I believe I can make persuasive cases both for why we should and should not have invaded Iraq. My conclusion most likely would be that we should not have invaded Iraq, but also that we didn't really have a choice. There was no good alternative.[9]

The reason for this seemingly contradictory conclusion is that the American people, as well as our elected officials, have such minimal knowledge of Islam, its history, and the history of the countries surrounding the Persian Gulf. This is where the clergy is missing an opportunity to play a significant role in confronting a vicious and powerful enemy that poses a real threat to Western civilization and its Judeo-Christian heritage. Who is better equipped than they to study and understand the varied teachings and history of this religion, with its fanatical, radical minority of adherents who are intent upon destroying Israel, the United States, and its allies? It is my belief that it is very difficult, if not impossible, to defeat an enemy you don't understand.

When one examines the major issues dividing our country in light of the partisan struggles cited above, it is easy to understand why we have such a highly polarized nation. Add the nasty fights over the war in Afghanistan[10] and one wonders if there is any reasonable solution. I see none in the near future. Economic issues involving taxes and spending, the abortion fight, the homosexual agenda, stem cell research, gun control, illegal immigration, measures that are necessary to fight the war on terrorism, and even religious liberty issues guaranteed under the First Amendment to the Constitution surface from time to time.[11] Obviously, not all issues break along strictly partisan lines, but there is a strong partisan division on most of them.

Elected officials from both parties try to find issues that expand their support and produce votes. Voters who are active in campaigns try to find candidates who are "right" on issues that are important to them. You can always debate the chicken and egg question, but once a candidate or an elected member finds an issue that appears to be very important to the voters, he is going to fan the flames until it becomes a wedge issue.

To examine the climate in which today's partisan disputes are fought, it is instructive to take a quick look at how the country has changed over the past 45 or so years. Bill Bishop, writing in *The Big Sort: Why the Clustering of Like Minded America Is Tearing Us Apart,* insists that the "ideological" divide that so separates Americans today in politics, religion, life-style, and geographic location had its beginning rather suddenly in 1965. For one example, he notes that in 1964, 75 percent of Americans "trusted the government to do the right thing most of the time." That percentage dropped "to 25 percent just a few years later."[12]

Bishop notes that most "mainline religious denominations had grown uninterruptedly from colonial times, a two-hundred-year record of orderly expansion." But, he contends, such mainline church growth seemed to end abruptly in 1965. Bishop quotes Dr. Martin Marty, then professor of Christian history at the University of Chicago, who describes "the year as the epicenter of a 'seismic shift' in religious life."

> "'From the birth of the republic until around 1965, as is well known, the churches now called mainline Protestants tended to grow with every census or survey,' Marty wrote. After, 1965, the mainline denominations stopped growing or began to shrink as people turned to independent or Evangelical congregations. The six largest Protestant denominations together lost 5.6 million members between 1965 and 1990. 'At least ten of the largest (and theologically more liberal) denominations have had membership losses in every year after 1966,' religious historians David Rooze and Jackson Carroll wrote in 1979."[13]

Bishop's theses is that the "political polarization" that so radically divides the American people and the U.S. Congress is evidenced in and influenced by their religious convictions and where they choose to live. Therefore, typically "Red" (Republican) states and congressional districts tend to get "redder" and "Blue" (Democrat) states and congressional districts tend to get "bluer." True "moderates" have dramatically decreased among the voters[14] and almost disappeared in both houses of Congress from the 1960s until the present time. This causes bipartisan legislative solutions to become rarer, if not impossible, with each new election. The Republicans become more conservative and the Democrats become more liberal.

Bishop further contends that as the nation becomes more "politically segregated," with more and more Americans choosing to live in like-minded neighborhoods, the divide grows deeper. He illustrates that the percentage of moderates in Congress has steadily declined, with a few minor ups and downs, from almost 55 percent of the senators and 45 percent of the U.S. House being described as "moderates" in 1945 to only about 8 percent in the Senate and 11 percent in the House in 2005.[15] (These numbers seem to continue to decline in varying degrees with each new election.)

The number of moderates in the House fell significantly for Republicans in the 2006 election, since they lost 10 of the 18 Republican-held seats carried by Kerry in 2004. Most of the members who lost were Republican moderates. The Democrats gained about an equal number of carefully picked moderate Democrats in this election, so the percentages probably didn't change much as a result of the 2006 election. In the 2008 election, the Republicans lost at least three of their remaining moderates. The Democrats gained 20 additional seats held by Republicans in 2008, and only three or four could be reasonably classified as moderates. So those who could be classified as true moderates in both parties fell below 10 percent for the first time in modern history.

To say that the 2010 election was historic is an understatement of major proportions. When the Republicans won 66 Democrat-held U.S. House seats, while losing only three Republican-held seats for a net gain of 63 congressional districts, it was the largest gain by either party in a mid-term election since 1938. The Republicans had a net gain of six seats in the U.S. Senate and gained five governors' mansions. Had the Republicans not ended up nominating some candidates too "hard right" for their states, they would have gained three, possibly four, more seats in the U.S. Senate.

A more detailed analysis of these elections, and how the various demographic groups voted, will be included at the end of this chapter. But it may be interesting and instructive to note how the elections in the state legislative races that were up for election in 2010 turned out. The Republicans had a net gain of 693 state house and senate seats and now have the most members of state legislative chambers since Herbert Hoover was first elected. Actually and surprisingly, the Democrats now hold only 39 percent of the state legislative seats.

As we explore the growing partisan divide in the country and the Congress, perhaps the much more important question is how far left and how far right these respective groups have become! The available data examined in this book will clearly illustrate that the Democrat electorate as a whole is much more traditionally liberal or moderately liberal than their elected officials.

On the other hand, as the Republicans replenished their previously depleted numbers of elected officials, it will be of value to try to understand how many of their newly elected officials subscribed to a hard-right litmus test on various issues. I suggest that we will find that in most cases, the Republican members of Congress overwhelmingly represent the conservative values of their states and districts. (But it is also a fact that while still a distinct minority, there are more "hard right" or libertarian members—hard right on some issues and hard left on others—in the Republican caucuses than at any time in modern history.)[16]

The challenges facing each party in the future will be further discussed in the next chapter. Once again, I am convinced that if we Christians are to be able to carry out our God-given responsibilities, we must have some understanding of the political process.

The partisan divide growing among the voters and MCs today had not taken a very heavy toll on bipartisanship and camaraderie in Congress when I arrived on the scene in 1971.[17]

Earlier, I mentioned that I came to Washington as a Republican to work for a Democrat committee chairman, and that this was not that unusual at the time. Starting literally on my first day on the job and continuing for almost 20 years, I socialized with Democrats and Republicans together virtually every night when I stayed down on Capitol Hill for receptions, dinners, or just visits to the two clubs. It was the rule rather than the exception for several congressmen from each party to relax together for refreshments at the end of the day and talk things over.

In 2008, I had only five Democrat House members and one Democrat senator at my regulars table at the Capitol Hill Club (the Republican club). During my first 20 years in town, I would have invited that many or more Democrat congressman over to the club on any given night that Congress was in session. More often than not, we would meet up with a number of Republican members, and the entire group would eventually take a short stroll over to the Democratic Club for a nightcap. What partisanship there was during those years ceased when the day's session ended. Then after tying things up in the office, it was time for a little relaxation and fellowship, usually of a bipartisan nature. I guess one reason for such a cordial atmosphere in those days, particularly in the House of Representatives, was that the Republicans weren't really a threat to take control. Unfortunately, when the GOP began to flex its political muscles, the two sides didn't like each other as much as they did when it was one sided.

The formerly friendly atmosphere made my job much easier and helped my career as a lobbyist. At one time, I felt that I knew and was good friends with more

Democrat congressmen and senators than any Republican lobbyist in town. Today, I can say that I know virtually every Republican member of the House and the Senate, most of them pretty well. But I would be exaggerating if I said I had more than 25 or 30 Democrat congressmen, and perhaps four or five Democrat senators, that I could count as fairly good friends. To be honest, I'm sure I don't even personally know half the Democrats in the two chambers today. It hasn't been that long ago when I knew most all of them. Times have surely changed.

Let me say just a little more about my table at the Capitol Hill Club, which I have now had for more than 25 years.

It's a round table just off the bar and comfortably seats nine or 10 people. Many nights, chairs are pulled all over the place, with other tables added. It is usually referred to as either the "Hecht table" or "the table around which the revolution was hatched." That brings us back to the 1994 Republican takeover of the Congress.

The exposure of the House bank and post office scandals by the Gang of Seven in 1993 created a climate of excitement that the Republicans might be able to make major gains in the 1994 elections. Then, the national healthcare plan pushed so heavily by First Lady Hillary Clinton in the early months of her husband's administration began to backfire big time. The famous "Harry and Louise" ads suggesting that it would take away a person's right to choose his or her own doctors caused a national outcry.[18] Republicans nicknamed it "Hillarycare," but she refused to back down for a considerable period of time.

Newt Gingrich, the Republican whip in the House, pounced on the early Clinton administration mistakes, coupled together with the developing bank and post-office scandals—and called for a Republican revolution. By early 1994, we Republicans were convinced that we could take control of the Congress in the upcoming election. By late March or early April of that year, I had put together a spreadsheet with 163 congressional districts that we began to monitor closely. These included a number of Republican-held districts that we had to watch carefully so we did not lose any of them, and a large number of Democrat seats we felt we had a chance of winning.

Every night, Congressman John Boehner; Congressman John Linder of Georgia, a close friend of Newt's; and seven to 10 other House members would gather at "my table" to evaluate the information we had on the targeted districts. We had another 20 or so "regional whips," as we called them, charged with gathering information on the chosen districts in their areas of the country. These "whips" would stop by the table and share any information they had gathered.

Newt had his own table in another part of the room where he strategized with some of his staff members. He would come over to review our information a time or two a night.[19] By the summer of 1994, I had a list of Republican county chairmen from all over the country in our targeted districts who I would call occasionally to see what intelligence I could acquire from them. Six weeks before the election, we flatly concluded that we were definitely going to take the House and had a good shot at the Senate.

(This prediction brought on considerable disbelief and occasional laughter from many who were casually observing our efforts. I had about a dozen clients at the time. When I informed them in a memo that the Republicans were going to take the House, and possibly the Senate, every one of them called to ask if I had taken leave of my senses. I picked the exact number of seats, 53, that we were going to gain, though not all of the exact seats.)

My heavy involvement with Congressman Boehner and many other incumbent congressmen and senators in the 1994 "Republican revolution" was more than just a major milestone in my lobbying career. It certainly was that, though, since I would have close personal relationships with all the new Republican leaders and the new House committee chairmen. I also had gotten to know almost all of the 53 new Republican freshmen, many of them quite well. But much more importantly, especially as the years pass by, through my involvement in the 1994 election I developed a lasting friendship with perhaps a half dozen of the closest friends I have had in my entire life.

For example, John Boehner had already become a pal and constant companion. Our friendship grew stronger as our almost-daily meetings—and always-daily phone conversations—grew in intensity and frequency over the six or so months before the election.[20] Boehner would be elected Republican Conference chairman, the highest position of congressional leadership that anyone had achieved in our history after such a short time in the House (only two terms), since shortly after our founding years. Sixteen years later he would be elected the 61st speaker of the U. S. House of Representatives, a position considered by most as the second most powerful job in the Nation's Capital.

The most lasting impact on my life concerning friendship was getting to know a Republican candidate for Iowa, a fellow Lutheran named Tom Latham. Virtually from his first day in Washington, I began including Latham in my nightly visits with Boehner, usually for drinks and dinner. Latham had forged an especially close friendship with two members of his freshman class: Saxby Chambliss of Georgia and Richard Burr of North Carolina. He suggested that I begin to include them in our dinners—a suggestion I eagerly accepted. This group, which I have referred to as the "fearless foursome,"[21] has stayed together as the closest of friends, while our initial group expanded over the years into a much larger gathering from time to time. It was with great pride, thankfulness to God, and lots of tears that I watched Boehner receive the speaker's gavel as now-senators Chambliss and Burr and Congressman Latham stood just below the speaker's podium—also occasionally wiping their eyes.

Richard Burr and Saxby Chambliss started their distinguished congressional careers in the House after the 1994 election and have further expanded their unselfish service to our country in the Senate. Congressman Tom Latham, who passed on a potential opportunity to serve in the U.S. Senate, has now become the chairman of a powerful Appropriations subcommittee (such appropriation subcommittee chairmen are called "cardinals") and is a highly respected MC—on both sides of the political aisle. Speaker Boehner has no closer friends and advisors than these three men; they have always been a solid source of strength and sound advice to him. This is especially needed now that he has assumed the most awesome responsibility in the U.S. Congress. Boehner unapologetically calls Latham his "best friend."

In my case, I feel extremely privileged to count these four men among my very best friends. Like Boehner, I, too, consider Latham to be my best friend. One thing they have in common—so important to all successful men, especially those in political office—they all have wonderful wives whom I dearly love. It was a joy for me to have Tom's daughter, Jill, Saxby's son, Bo, and Richard's son, Tyler, as interns in my firm during three summers. All three are wonderful—and very successful—young people. My wife and I gratefully consider all of these families as members of our extended family.

These four men have many similar personal characteristics that were very appealing to me from the first time I met each of them. Within five minutes of meeting John Boehner for the very first time, I asked him a question that I have made a point asking thousands of MCs over the years (but very rarely the first time I meet them): "What motivated you to run for Congress?" Instantly he responded: "This country has been good to me and I wanted to give something back!" I got very similar—if not identical—answers from the other three men. I think I may have asked Latham this question when I first met him as a candidate.[22]

Another similarity that impressed me was that they all four came from deeply religious families. As I recall, Boehner told me about being required to attend Catholic Mass very early every morning before sweeping out his father's bar when he was growing up. Saxby and Richard grew up in parsonages. (They were pastors' kids like my sons.) Tom Latham's family were pillars of an American Lutheran Church rural congregation just a few miles from their home.[23] In addition, while they never wore it on their sleeves, their deep patriotism was as evident as their sincerity and support of traditional Christian values. Not by accident, Boehner, Chambliss, Latham, and Burr hold positions in Congress charged with protecting the security of this country. As speaker of the House, Boehner has access to intelligence briefings almost as highly classified as those the president receives. Saxby is the ranking Republican on the Senate Select Committee on Intelligence. Richard is also a member of this committee, and Latham serves on the Homeland Security subcommittee of the House Appropriations Committee.

Two of my other cherished and highly respected friends were also products of the 1994 elections in slightly different ways. They are the two present senators from Oklahoma. Sen. Tom Coburn was elected to the House in 1994; Sen. Jim Inhofe was serving in the House when he was elected to the Senate in 1994. These two steadfast patriots are devout Christians with families much admired by all who know them. America is blessed by the dedication and service of these remarkable men and by the support they and the American people receive from the wonderful families that support them. I would also be remiss if I failed to mention another bright member of the '94 congressional class, who is now also a senator. Sen. Lindsey Graham (R-S.C.), who has become a recognized and outspoken authority on defense and national security policies, is another enduring and admired friend.[24]

On most evenings yet today, at that very same table, some or all of eight or nine senators and some of the 25 to 30 House members who are my very closest friends will stop by for a drink and a visit. Many others also join us on some occasions. We discuss politics and major issues facing the country and frequently religion, which often involves their personal faith. On many occasions, we have lengthy discussions of how we can best defeat the threats posed by radical Islamic terrorists. At other times, we discuss ways to meet the serious challenges of those who would destroy the traditional values upon which this country was founded.

These are men and women in a position to truly affect the future of our country. I feel privileged to have the opportunity to have my say.

The Parties Realign

Most recognized political scholars identify two major ideological shifts and party realignments in modern times: The first had its origins in the election of FDR in 1932 and the unfolding of the "New Deal." The second had its birth in the 1960s with the Goldwater movement and reached maturity in the election of Ronald Wilson Reagan in 1980.

(Obviously, as is the case of all generalities, there are inconsistencies, twists and turns, and temporary shifts of the voters caused by wars, hard times, and a host of other burning issues of short duration. Such aberrations have led other political historians to divide modern political history into numerous periods based on what others believe to be only minor changes in voter behavior. Based on my almost 50 years studying politics and my active involvement in the political process, I believe the two-shift theory is the most viable and inclusive.)

I will forgo a diversion into 19th century politics, a special interest of mine, which establishes the background that forged the political climate that existed at the turn of the 20th century. Instead, I will turn to the early years of that century and simply make a few generalities about the state of the country Franklin Delano Roosevelt inherited when he was sworn in as president in 1933.

The stock market crash in 1929 led to bank failures that sparked a run on deposits and brought America's financial system to its knees. By the time FDR was inaugurated, the unemployment rate was approaching 25 percent. Nature had also been unkind as a horrific drought had created the "dust bowl" in the farm states, which devastated the country's food supply. Poverty, hunger, and despair were rampant throughout the country.

The new president would inherit the Great Depression from President Herbert Hoover. Hoover's political philosophy was so ambiguous that he earlier had been heavily recruited to run for president on the Democrat ticket.

Hoover was elected president on the Republican ticket in 1928 after President Calvin Coolidge chose not to seek reelection. Abandoning Coolidge's policies of low taxes and limited government, Hoover adopted protectionism, isolationism, higher tariffs, including the Smoot-Hawley Tariff Act of 1930, and other disastrous economic policies that fanned the flames of the depression and spread it throughout the world.

Franklin Roosevelt ran for president as a conservative.[25] After his election, Roosevelt quickly surrounded himself with academics and other intellectual elites. Government was soon viewed as the engine to run the nation's economy.

Liberals at the time argued that government-run programs, which took over some functions of private enterprise, were necessary to stimulate the economy. The so-called "Modernist Movement" in Christianity in the early years of the 20th century, with its emphasis on the "Social Gospel" to improve people's lives, enthusiastically supported FDR's social welfare programs.[26] *The age of big government had its birth in Roosevelt's "New Deal" policies*! If the federal government was going to run certain sectors of the economy, it must provide for the people through massive federal programs. These new and ever-expanding social welfare programs would entail ever-increasing government regulations, higher and higher taxes, and a rapidly expanding national debt.[27]

Liberal historians would argue that Roosevelt's government programs were necessary to stimulate the economy and would lead to an economic recovery that eventually ended the depression. Conservative historians insist that Roosevelt's policies severely weakened the private sector; created a "nanny state" and prolonged the Depression. They further contend that only government spending in WW II brought the great depression to an end. Heated debate over the damage FDR's programs did to the long-term viability of the free enterprise system that made this country so unique and so great is certainly legitimate. But the fact that Roosevelt offered hope to our country in its darkest days of despair is rarely debated.

Controversy still rages over whether Social Security, as the prime example, is a government "social welfare" program or a government-run mandatory "social insurance" program. All income earners are required to pay a Social Security tax. But those who pay the least into the program regularly receive by far the greatest return on their investment. (Some insist this is social welfare, especially since the disabled also receive benefits, frequently for many years.) In spite of disagreements over ways Social Security could be more efficiently structured and placed on a more sound economic foundation, few would dispute the necessity of the program as a safety net for the nation's elderly and infirm.

Noted author and popular radio and TV guest Daniel J. Flynn includes in *A Conservative History of the American Left* an interesting and instructive chapter,

"The Paternalist Dynasty III: New Dealers."[28] There is no question that the federal government assumed a "paternalistic" attitude toward the American people that began with FDR's "New Deal" and lasted to varying degrees until the "Reagan Revolution."

Gone were the days when a free people "endowed by their Creator with certain inalienable rights" granted limited and enumerated powers to *their* federal government. The concept of a national government deciding what was best for "we the people" and "granting" the people certain privileges and rights, as long as they adhered to certain federal guidelines, is so foreign to the beliefs of the Founding Fathers that it would be laughable were it not so serious.

Some measure of individual freedom and responsibility was restored to the American people by the "Goldwater movement," which resulted in the election of Ronald Reagan as president of the United States. Such gains in limiting the power of the federal government and restoring the Founders' dreams of a people's republic were not won easily. These accomplishments were always under attack and they are facing new threats today.

FDR's extensive federal programs were further expanded under President Harry Truman's "Fair Deal." However, the role of an activist ever-expanding federal government intruding in virtually every area of the American people's lives reached its apex in Lyndon Johnson's "Great Society." (The seeds of the end of the Roosevelt era were sown in the excesses of the Johnson administration.)

Franklin Roosevelt put together a powerful and long-lasting coalition of Democrat voting groups that, for all practical purposes, lasted through the election of Jimmy Carter as president. Roosevelt had been able to add blacks to the existing Democrat base of white southerners. He solidified the Democrat hold on farmers, labor union members, ethnic groups so powerful in the large northern cities, and the other traditional liberal voting blocs. Certain of these groups began to fracture during the Nixon elections.[29]

Nothing really changed much in how the government was run for almost 50 years until President Ronald Reagan said, "The government is the problem, not the solution." The new voting coalitions that would elect Ronald Reagan had been in the making since the beginning of the Goldwater movement.

Having grown up in the Deep South, I always considered myself a "Southern Democrat." My interest in politics grew substantially during the 1960 presidential campaign. After one reading of Barry Goldwater's *Conscience of a Conservative*, my political views—and as a result my political life—were changed forever. I was a believer. Soon after JFK's victory in 1960, I became actively involved in the anti-communist movement and the "Draft Goldwater Campaign."

After seven years as a volunteer, I became professionally involved in politics in 1967. As an early and enthusiastic participant in the Goldwater movement, I came to know most of the organizational leaders and a few of the intellectual giants of that movement. Those of us involved knew from the beginning that we had two goals that we must deal with simultaneously:

One, we must wrest control of the Republican Party from the liberal "Rockefeller wing." We viewed them as just a liberal Republican version of the Roosevelt Democrats. Despite the conservative setback in the 1964 election, we were still convinced that this would be our easier task.

Two, the more difficult and important challenge was how to control the hard Right and make sure they did not assume prominent roles in the Goldwater movement. Fortunately, most of our leaders recognized this threat from the very beginning. The excesses of some members of the John Birch Society and other anti-communist organizations posed a potential problem. Some Birch Society members, not including founder Robert Welch, were even racist, anti-Semitic, and anti-Catholic. (The libertarian infiltration occurred without most of us understanding the threat it posed to true conservatism. Even Bill Buckley still believed at this time that the two ideologies were compatible. [More discussion of this subject will come later in this book.] I would realize later that while not all libertarians were Birchers, virtually all Birchers were libertarians.) Other Birch Society members wanted segments of the government dismantled and books burned that were being used in some schools. Most advocated a rigid ideological litmus test on all issues.

The movement needed the enthusiastic efforts and financial support of the more reasonable ideologues. But the more radical and unreasonable right-wingers had to go—or at least to exercise no major influence. They could not become the face of the party. This problem virtually solved itself when it became clear that this movement intended to stand on solid conservative principles while avoiding extremes.

Bill Buckley emerged as the intellectual giant of the movement. Buckley did share certain libertarian tendencies and non-interventionist foreign policy goals with some of the more radical intellectuals, such as Robert Welch and Dean Manion. But Buckley's views would evolve as he made extensive intellectual efforts to reason with such people, and ultimately he would famously insist that "conservatism implies a certain submission to reality."

In time, some of the far-right zealots became members of the Libertarian Party. Others, viewing partisan politics as hopeless, abandoned the Goldwater movement and devoted their time and resources to more radical right-wing groups and concentrated on anti-communist efforts. Many hung around and had to be outvoted at committee meetings, political conventions, and in other such forums when possible. Sometimes, they prevailed and passed a plank or elected a leader too uncompromising. This would make it more difficult to elect candidates to political office. As happens all too frequently, many of our people have failed to learn from history, and we are in danger of making some of the same mistakes today.

Barry Goldwater's overwhelming loss to LBJ in the 1964 presidential election (he carried only five Southern states and his home state of Arizona) was a learning experience and a blessing in disguise for the conservative movement. Obviously, we got a major lesson in how not to run campaigns! Yet emboldened by such a landslide victory, LBJ the following year pushed such a radical liberal agenda in Congress that he energized conservatives and brought them out of the woodwork.

Most importantly, conservatives found the *star* the movement desperately needed in this campaign. Our new champion turned out to be an actor and the host of the weekly General Electric Theater named Ronald Reagan. Due to his speech on a paid network TV address in the final months of the Goldwater campaign titled "A Time for Choosing,"[30] Reagan gained his initial prominence as the man to carry the conservative message. Two years later, he was elected governor of California and new life was breathed into the conservative movement.

It is always intriguing to examine how seemingly minor and unrelated events have such a major impact on history. In 1960, Richard Nixon, in an apparent effort to make peace with Nelson Rockefeller, entered into the infamous so-called "Treaty of Fifth Avenue." Under the agreement, Rockefeller was promised control of the platform at the Republican National Convention in return for his support.

After word of this agreement leaked out, it so inflamed conservatives that Dean Manion organized an effort to draft the rising conservative star, Senator Barry Goldwater, to challenge Nixon in the Republican primary. The effort ended up being unsuccessful. Goldwater was a party loyalist and had already pledged his support to Nixon. Goldwater, however, was upset enough by the "*Treaty*" that he ended up giving Manion permission to have the *Conscience of a Conservative* printed. This book, which altered history, was ghost written—or at least co-written—by Brent Bozell, Buckley's one-time roommate at Yale and now his brother-in-law. If this book would not have been written, there never would have been a Goldwater candidacy and, therefore, no Reagan speech that vaulted the future president to national prominence.

Similarly, had Nelson Rockefeller won the Republican presidential primary in California over Barry Goldwater, the results also would have prevented Reagan from accomplishing such a feat.[31] Once again, there would have been no Reagan "A Time for Choosing" speech and most likely no Governor Reagan, and subsequently no President Reagan.

Had Ronald Reagan never been sworn in as the 40th president of the United States, the Berlin Wall might still be standing and the "captive nations" of Eastern Europe might still be suffering under the Soviet yoke. One could only imagine how many other countries' citizens might be consigned to a bleak and dehumanizing life under Marxist rule. We in America could still be concerned about trying to construct hardened underground bomb shelters in the event of a nuclear attack.[32]

It should not be difficult for Christians to see that our God, who gave us the opportunity to live in this great country founded on principles in His Holy Word, still governs in "the affairs of men." When things do go wrong it is because we fail to carry out our God-given civic responsibilities as Christian citizens. Our Founding Fathers were always concerned about what might befall this fragile experiment in establishing a government "of," "by" and "for" the people if the people ever lost their moral compass.

In the 1964 election, the Republicans also lost 36 seats in the U.S. House and two in the Senate, giving the Democrats a two-thirds majority in both houses of Congress. The liberal media gleefully issued the death notice for the conservative movement. This notice might have been in order had it not been for a number of totally dedicated and highly talented intellectual and political leaders who did not have the word "surrender" in their vocabulary. They knew—as did hundreds of thousands of equally dedicated volunteers, such as Bill Hecht and his wife—that the stakes were too high to even consider giving up on our cause since we all believed that the very future of our country was at stake.

Due primarily to the excesses of LBJ's "Great Society" programs, which involved the massive growth of big government, the Republican gains in 1966 were spectacular. (Of course, we were starting from such a low point that we still had little pure Republican influence in Congress. We were now strong enough, however, that coalitions with conservative Democrats became more productive.)

By far the most important thing that came out of the 1966 election cycle was the election of two governors who were destined to become the political leaders of our "conservative" Republican movement. They were Ronald Reagan of California and Paul Laxalt of Nevada.

The old Goldwater movement, by now more accurately identified as the conservative-Republican movement, suffered what *appeared* to be a second major and possibly fatal defeat in 1976 when President Jerry Ford eked out the Republican nomination for president over Reagan. I say "appeared" deliberately. On the one hand, Reagan's nomination in 1976 might have resulted in a defeat and ended the efforts of this 25 or so year-old conservative movement. The country needed the disastrous four years of the Carter administration to be ready for the courageous policies of Ronald Reagan. As it turned out, after three years of political mourning and a nagging concern that our hero might now be too old, the diehard old Goldwater crowd, energized by scores of enthusiastic new leaders, suited up for political battle.

Finally, those of us who had spent a major part of our political lives trying to restore our government to as many of our country's founding principles as possible breathed a long yearned-for sigh of relief when Ronald Wilson Reagan placed his hand on the Holy Bible and took the presidential oath of office. When President Bill Clinton many years later would say that "the era of big government is over," he must have been thinking of Reagan's inauguration. (The struggle never ends as there is a major push today for big government to increasingly run more and more aspects of the lives of our citizens.)

When Ronald Reagan became the 40th president of the United States, he inherited from his predecessor an economy in shambles and a country facing serious national security threats from abroad. The country was experiencing an economic crisis more severe that at any time since the Great Depression. The country was suffering from double-digit unemployment, double-digit interest rates, runaway inflation, gas lines, and confiscatory tax rates. With bipartisan cooperation from a newly Republican-controlled Senate and a long-time Democrat majority in the U.S. House of Representatives, he solved these economic problems.

Reagan persuaded Congress to slash taxes, spurring economic activity that rapidly reduced unemployment and brought down interest rates to a reasonable level. Reagan negotiated with—or pressured—our Middle Eastern allies to restore our petroleum supplies at an affordable price.[33] Reagan's bold initiatives, which relied on the free market rather than the federal government to correct the nation's economic ills, resulted in seven years of sustained economic growth and prosperity.

Iran had made the wise decision to release the American hostages held in Tehran immediately after Reagan was sworn in as America's president. The radical Shiite Islamic leader Ayatollah Khomeini apparently decided that while Reagan might "walk softly," he had no imminent desire to find out how "big of a stick" this fearless new American leader was carrying.

Reagan not only became America's greatest modern-day president, but he also was able to forge a coalition of voters that resulted in an ideological shift and a party realignment that is still basically in place. The charismatic "Great Communicator" was able to develop the "values voters," or social conservatives (made up largely of white Evangelicals and socially conservative Catholics); the "security voters" (composed largely of white men, including many union members, and white women with children) who are concerned about protection from foreign enemies and crime in this country; and the "economic voters," those who want smaller government, lower taxes, and better job opportunities. These groups included young professionals and members of the working class. Reagan's coalition turned the majority of the Italian vote from Democrat to Republican and made major inroads into the Irish vote. This had never happened before.

Reagan was also able to solidify Republican strongholds that included farmers and suburbanites. Many of these voting blocs obviously overlap. Most of them also can desert their new party allegiance temporarily for a variety of reasons. They can vote for change when they tire of their party's extended rule or face a crisis such the financial meltdown.

The Democrats are confronted with the ideological extremists in their party similar to Republican challenges just enumerated. The hard Left and the hard Right have a number of similar characteristics. In both cases they tend to employ a "rule or ruin" philosophy that is adverse to any reasonable compromise. Many political analysts contend that ideological causes move in a circular manner. If one moves far enough to the left and another moves far enough to the right, they will meet eventually at the bottom of the circle.[34]

Perhaps the classic textbook example of the far left and far right coming together at the bottom of the ideological circle occurred on the floor of the U.S. House of Representatives on March 11, 2010.[35] Congressman Dennis Kucinich, an Ohio Democrat who is almost universally recognized as the most far-left or "progressive" Democrat in Congress, introduced a resolution calling for a pullout of all American troops in Afghanistan in 30 days, or an absolute deadline by the end of the year if President Obama believed the 30-day timeline was unsafe.

Texas Congressman Ron Paul, a libertarian[36] who has always run for Congress as a Republican, whole-heartedly joined in support of this resolution, which in no uncertain terms calls for a unilateral surrender to the Taliban and al-Qaeda in Afghanistan. In passionate debate on the floor of the House, Dr. Paul calls the war in Afghanistan an "immoral war" and questions why the U.S. invaded Afghanistan in retaliation for the 9/11 attacks. Unbelievably, Paul insists that he had seen no evidence that Osama bin Laden or al-Qaeda was responsible for the attacks.[37]

(The evidence is so overwhelming in refutation of such claims by Congressman Paul that it is difficult to give a concise answer. Just to touch the tip of the iceberg of evidence: In 1996, Osama bin Laden moved his al-Qaeda from Sudan to Afghanistan when the Sudanese government said it could no longer guarantee him protection due to extensive pressure from the Saudis. The Taliban welcomed him and his entourage with open arms and guaranteed all the protection he and his Islamic terrorists would need. The Taliban protected and helped run the al-Qaeda terrorist training camps in Afghanistan where many of the 9/11 terrorists were trained.

(In 1996, from his safe haven in Afghanistan, Osama ordered his al-Qaeda in Saudi Arabia to bomb the Khobar Towers to kill American soldiers. Later in the year from Afghanistan, bin Laden issued a *"fatwa"* [religious decree] declaring war on America. In February 1998, from their headquarters in Afghanistan, bin Laden and Dr. al-Zawahiri [al-Qaeda's number two] created an umbrella group to coordinate the activities of al-Qaeda and a number of other Islamist terror groups to wage *jihad* against America.

(It was in the time frame of early 1998 that al-Zawahiri convinced Osama bin Laden that they must launch a major attack on America's homeland. Zawahiri successfully contended to Osama that a high-profile attack on the soil of "The Great Satan" would firmly establish their credentials as the undisputed Muslim leaders of global *jihad*. The high ranking al-Qaeda operative, Khalid Sheik Mohammed [KSM], was recruited to help locate the proper targets and plan the attacks. The captured terrorist KSM openly confessed to being the "mastermind" of the 9/11 attacks as far back as 2005.[38])

The point of the Kucinich-Paul coalition is to illustrate the dangers posed by the political extremes in both parties, in this case where radical extremist policies merge. Such an extremist isolationist, non-interventionism foreign policy in modern times goes back at least to the days of Woodrow Wilson. It was a bipartisan effort.

It is important to remember that libertarianism in a philosophical context grew out of a religious controversy. The term was first used by late-Enlightenment free-thinkers who believed in free will as opposed to determinism. As this philosophy was translated into political terms, it contended that man should be absolutely free to make his own decisions unencumbered by any government regulations. (Anarchism and libertarianism are never far apart, as Bill Buckley would point out later in his career.)

The fact that libertarians refused to recognize original sin (or even that man is basically a sinful creature, since they recognized no transcendent moral values) puts them at odds with almost all of the 250 or so men most deserving of being called "Founding Fathers." Nearly all of them were orthodox Christians, and like Will Rogers, they not only believed in original sin but "had seen it." Even the few Unitarians like Jefferson and Adams and the best-known Deist,[39] Benjamin Franklin, who rejected the Calvinist doctrine[40] of the total depravity of human nature, had no illusions as to how evil man could be if left totally unrestrained by laws. Adams rejected the doctrine of predestination because he believed it offered man an excuse for his evil deeds. Adams and Franklin questioned original sin because they felt it unreasonable for a person to be punished for another person's sins. They were concerned with each man's own sins, which must be held in check by government laws. In Adams words, "I am answerable for my own sins because I know they were my own fault; and that is enough for me to know." With the possible exception of Thomas Paine and Ethan Allen, it is not an exaggeration to say that they all agreed with President John Adams (a Congregationalist turned Unitarian) that our representative democracy is suited to govern only "a moral and religious people." They emphatically believed that man had a fallen nature and must be morally constrained by the laws of the nation, taken in large part from the Bible.

Traditional libertarians in America believed in a limited federal government with carefully enumerated powers; absolute individual freedom as long as one did not physically harm another individual;[41] and a strict isolationist foreign policy. When the Democrats were the fiscally conservative, limited-government party (typified by Grover Cleveland, Al Smith, and even FDR, who ran on a conservative platform in 1932), most libertarians supported them.

When FDR greatly expanded government and later asked Congress to declare war on Nazi Germany and Imperial Japan, the vast majority of libertarians defected to the Republican Party. (The Goldwater movement had to deal with some of the most extreme elements of libertarians[42] in the 1960s and 1970s. They were always a threat, as they sought to drive the party in a direction too extreme for the electorate.)

Few on the far left today identify themselves as libertarians, although a small number may say they are "social-issue libertarians" or "foreign-policy libertarians." Most on the extreme left prefer to be called "progressives," or maybe just call themselves liberals in an attempt to play down their extreme positions. Probably as many as 10 to 15 percent of those on the far right in the Republican Party will identify themselves as libertarians (with a small "l") on some issues or say they have libertarian tendencies.

Social Policies and Foreign Policy

Regardless of the labels they use, the dangers posed by those who move too far to the left or too far to the right are the same, or at least very similar. They both believe people should be allowed to live their lives as they choose. They can have as many abortions as they choose, choose any lifestyle they desire, use drugs of their choice, and do whatever they choose to do so long as they do not cause physical harm to another. (Historically, moral damage to society or other individuals has not been of concern to either group.[43] Since they do not believe in original sin or recognize any moral absolutes, they believe a person will make the right decision for his or her own life. That is all that matters to them.)

The only difference between the far left and the far right on social issues is the role of government. The far right or libertarians insist that the federal government should have no role in telling citizens how they should live their lives. The far left or progressives believe that government should pass laws guaranteeing citizens the freedom to make such decisions.

One very consistent libertarian doctrine (shared with equal fanaticism by the far left) is an isolationist or non-interventionist foreign policy. They try to justify such a philosophy by appealing to President George Washington's warning about getting involved in "entangling foreign alliances." Washington, of course, was worried about the U.S. being dragged into the frequent wars between England, France, Spain, and other European powers. America wasn't even a strong enough military power at the time to make much of a difference beyond her own soil and contiguous areas anyway. (Washington may—or may not—have dreamed that one day America would become the world's foremost power. But at the time, America was still struggling just to nurture its fragile but promising young Republic.)

Disagreements about some of FDR's actions and libertarian isolationists' protests aside, America never had an ultimate choice in confronting Hitler's stated goal of world domination.

In spite of U.S. mistakes at the end of World War II that ended up empowering the Soviet Union and her communist allies, the greatest power in the free world could not retreat to its own shores as avid libertarians insisted we should do. A Bill Buckley, who initially shared some libertarian foreign-policy tendencies, realized we must do whatever was necessary to win the Cold War. However, most hardcore libertarians never understood that even if we left the rest of the world alone to fend for themselves against brutal communist takeovers, Soviet-led attacks would eventually reach American soil.

A present-day libertarian isolationist policy in a world so interconnected by trade, travel, modern means of communications, and all the rest is not only impractical but unrealistic. The world is a much smaller place than it used to be. (This obviously doesn't mean that we should enter into all types of "entangling alliances" that are not directly related to our own national security and the protection of the American people. Few, if any, seriously contend that we should volunteer to become the "world's policeman.") With the advent of global Islamic terrorism, a threat at least as real and in many ways more severe than the one posed by the Cold War, such naïve libertarian isolationism ceases to become merely impractical, but potentially lethal.

Jeffery Kuhner's op-ed in *The Washington Times* (Feb. 25, 2010) titled "Conservatives' isolationist dalliance, Ron Paul's foreign policy is bad for the right and America" offers valuable analysis on the subject. After praising Congressman Paul for some of his fiscal policies, Kuhner, who is president of the Edmund Burke Institute, writes concerning Paul's policies: "On foreign policy, however, he is wrong—dangerously wrong. His opposition to the 'welfare-warfare state' is misguided. *A strong national defense is crucial to America's survival, especially in an age of global Islamic terrorism*" (emphasis added).

Thankfully, after Kucinich, Paul, and others (on both sides) concluded the debate on what I call the "surrender to the Taliban resolution," it was overwhelmingly defeated. Congressman Ike Skelton,[44] a Democrat from Missouri and chairman of the House Armed Services Committee, summed up the majority opinion in Congress as he repeatedly cried out: "Have we forgotten the terrorists' attacks on 9/11?" In the end, a coalition of mostly responsible liberal Democrats and conservative Republicans voted against the surrender resolution by a vote of 356-65. Yet the fact that 59 Democrat members of Congress joined Kucinich in supporting this radical left-wing resolution could actually spell trouble for Democrats in the U.S. House.

The above discussion of how the conservative movement (which ultimately led to the election of Ronald Reagan) began and the internal struggles it faced is very timely since some liberals believe that there is the potential for a third major ideological shift in the political landscape in modern times. (Some appear to arrogantly believe they can force such a shift if they take the time to explain repeatedly to the American people what is good for them. I seem to remember that the British tried that approach in the founding days of this country!) The long struggle for the heart and soul of the Republican Party was not only long but difficult, with successes and failures along the way.[45]

Who Supports Whom?

Since the FDR years, the Democrats have been able to count on 1) minorities, 2) labor unions, and 3) liberal activists, all of which they still can count on today. They used to be able to include farmers, ethnic groups (especially the Irish and the Italians), and a strong majority of Catholics, as well as an almost solid Southern vote, but this is no longer the case. To their stable of reliable supporters, they have added the trial lawyers and the feminist groups, such as NARAL and Emily's List. So, at present, the heart of Democrat support appears to be 1) minorities, 2) labor unions, 3) trial lawyers and 4) the feminist groups. Their heaviest voter concentration is in the larger cities.

On the other hand, the Republican vote seems to be heavily concentrated in suburban and rural areas (Nixon is usually regarded as the first Republican candidate to recognize this voter shift) and clustered around three ideological groups that Ronald Reagan so successfully put together during his campaigns: 1) economic conservatives made up of those seeking lower taxes and less government spending; 2) the national-security group concerned initially with the communist threat and now the terrorist threat; and 3) the moral-values vote made up primarily of those concerned with preserving traditional American values. This group is mainly composed of white evangelicals and conservative Catholics.

It seems reasonable to conclude that the almost evenly divided country in partisan terms is based on strong ideological concerns and to a lesser extent geography.

Our country just recently has experienced two historical landmarks. In late 2006, the American population reached the 300 million mark. Almost simultaneously, a report was released showing that for the first time in American history, we have the dubious distinction of having more non-married people than married couples living in homes across this county.

The Sept. 29, 2006, *USA Today* had a front-page story attempting to show that the "marriage gap" and the "fertility gap" had a bearing on the success of the two parties in various congressional districts. Some will disagree with the conclusions, but it is an interesting study. The writer points out that Democrats control all of the top 50 districts with the most residents who have never married. The Republicans hold 49 of the 50 districts with the most married couples. The story makes this observation about the Democrat districts: "The 'never married' group covers a variety of groups who form the Democratic base: young people, those who marry late in life, single parents, gays, and heterosexuals who live together."

The writer continues, "The marriage divide drew attention in the 2004 presidential race. President Bush beat John Kerry by 15 percentage points among married people and lost by 18 percentage points among unmarried people, according to the exit poll conducted by national news media organizations."

The *USA Today* analysis of 2005 data recently released by the Census Bureau turns to the "fertility gap," which reveals that GOP members of Congress represent 7 million more children under 18 than the Democrats, an average of 7,000 more per district.

"Marriage and parenthood define what's different about Democratic and Republican districts even more clearly than race, income, education or geography, *USA Today*'s analysis of Census data found," says the story. "For example, Republicans represent seven of the 50 districts that have the highest concentration of blacks. Both parties are well represented among affluent and well-educated districts."

The newspaper also points out that the Democrats control only one of the top 50 districts with the highest marriage rates. Just for the interest of it, the article also mentions that Nancy Pelosi, who would become the first woman speaker of the House of Representatives, represents the district with the fewest children in the United States. "House Democratic leader Nancy Pelosi, a Catholic mother of five from San Francisco, has fewer children in her district than any other member of Congress: 87,727."

You can't always get the whole picture from statistics, but there is one thing I can tell you for sure: if you position yourself as the party of traditional moral values, you will pay a much higher price than your opposition if you get caught in unacceptable behavior. And that brings us back to the matter of scandals in Washington.

Let me conclude this chapter with a brief discussion of the scandals I have witnessed during my years in the national capital and then my brief assessment of the 2006 election. The two are linked, since the most recent scandals were directly tied to the election. As we will see in the next chapter, this election set the stage for the historic elections of 2008 and 2010. After that we will make some educated guesses about the upcoming and crucial 2012 election.

Scandals

How widespread are scandals in Congress? Aren't all members of Congress, Republican and Democrat, corrupt, just as 78 percent of the American people believe, according to a poll taken just prior to the 2006 election?

The answer is that scandals occur infrequently, are few in number and have involved only a handful of men. I say "men" because, thankfully, we have yet to have a female member of Congress involved in a major scandal.

It is my strong belief, after observing members of the House and Senate up close for more than 41 years, that they pretty well fit the profile the Founders of this Republic had in mind. I have known most of the members of Congress during my Washington tenure, and this would be my description of them as a group: They are a slight cut above the population as a whole. By that I mean that on average, they were a little more successful in their previous endeavors, a little better educated, slightly more patriotic and dedicated, and—maybe surprisingly to the reader—a little more religious. There may be too many lawyers. There are not enough clergymen who don't have a radical "social gospel" agenda. But, as a whole, they reflect the people they represent very well.[46]

The actual number of scandals is tiny among such a large group, but they do make the headlines. Based on media attention, one might think they are as commonplace as getting up to go to work in the morning. In truth, the minuscule minority who abuse the trust of the people give a bad name to the overwhelming majority who are dedicated public servants.

That said, these members do face a vast array of temptations. With so much power, money, and influence concentrated in one place, it is actually surprising that we don't have even more problems. The scandals that do occur are usually, though not always, initiated by those trying to influence members for their own personal gain or political and career advancement. Bear in mind, as I mentioned previously, when you are a member of the party selling itself as the party of moral and traditional values, you are going to pay a much higher price for misbehavior. This is compounded by the "media bias," which is very real and pervasive.

The long-time political writer for *The Washington Post*, Tom Edsall, who recently retired to write more books, made a surprisingly honest and frank statement in an article after his retirement. He said something to the effect that "I am a life-long Democrat and have never voted for a Republican and probably never will." He went on to confess that over his many years, he had observed that his fellow political writers and reporters were always 15 to one as a minimum, but usually 25 to one, Democrat over Republican. He said it is a simple fact that there is going to be a bias no matter how hard you may try to be fair. To illustrate the point, an independent media study found that the political coverage on the three major networks during the 2006 election cycle was 80 percent positive for the Democrats and only 12 percent positive for Republicans.

This is why Republicans must always raise much more money than Democrats to be competitive. They must buy the time and space to get their message out because they are not going to get anywhere near equal treatment in the so-call "earned media," the coverage given by political reporters.

Many people over the years from all walks of political life have said, perhaps not totally in jest, that had LBJ been a Republican, there still would be investigations going on. Nixon's media treatment was much worse than Clinton's. Nixon was forced to resign in disgrace; Clinton's punishment was simply to have his ability to govern impeded for the last three years of his presidency. But neither Clinton nor the Democrats were ever punished at the polls. As a matter of fact, in the mid-term election during Clinton's second term as president, the Democrats made political history by picking up a few congressional seats. That had never happened before.

The party in power at the White House always loses a significant number of seats in the House and the Senate during the mid-term elections during a president's second term. The Clinton exception remained an exception. History once again repeated itself in 2006, adding to the list of Republican woes in that election.

As we enumerate a few old and new scandals, let's start with an event that I personally witnessed from the House gallery in 1983.

A Republican member of Congress from Illinois, Dan Crane, had been caught having sex with a 17-year-old female House page. Ironically, at the same time, a Democrat member from Massachusetts, Gerry Studds, had been caught having homosexual sex with a 17-year-old male House page. The House of Representatives was struggling with how to deal with these two egregious acts by two of its members. There were calls for them both to be expelled from Congress. Perhaps this would have been the proper punishment. A case can be made that both of them should have gone to jail. But that was not going to happen because the age of consent in the District of Columbia was 16 or 17 years old at the time. Partly because of the age of consent problem, the House leadership decided not to expel but to censure the two members.

After the charges were read on the floor of the House against Congressman Dan Crane, he accepted his censure and asked to address the House. In an emotional and tearful statement, he asked for God's forgiveness, his wife's and children's forgiveness, his colleague's forgiveness, and the forgiveness of the voters, whose trust he had betrayed. I'm sure he received God's forgiveness, his family's forgiveness, and his colleagues' forgiveness, but the voters were not as forgiving—he lost his bid for reelection in 1984. The voters had that right and probably should have done what they did, especially in view of the age factor.

In startling contrast, Congressman Gerry Studds defiantly turned his back on his colleagues as the charges against him were read, and he refused to address his colleagues before or after censure was imposed. Instead, he stormed out of the House chamber and held a press conference with his teenaged male lover and denounced the entire process. He was reelected in 1984 and every subsequent election until he retired in 1994. Obviously, Democrat voters hold their elected officials to a different standard. Some would argue that it is the Massachusetts thing, but to my knowledge, only one Democrat has lost an election over a sex scandal in the last 30 to 40 years.

Wayne Hays of Ohio lost his election because of the Elizabeth Ray scandal— she was the secretary who couldn't type—but none of the other Democrats accused of being involved with her suffered any election problems. Senator Ted Kennedy's girlfriend, Mary Jo Kopechne, died in a drowning tragedy in the Chappaquiddick event, but he never had reelection problems in his Senate races, though it may have cost him the opportunity to be president. Wilbur Mills, one-time chairman of the powerful House Ways and Means Committee, an Arkansas Democrat, lost his committee chairmanship because of an affair involving stripper Fanny Fox, but he was reelected to Congress by the voters.

Republicans have always sealed their fate with sexual misconduct. Senator Bob Packwood of Oregon ended up resigning his Senate seat over a number of alleged affairs. Congressmen Tom Evans of Delaware lost reelection because of the Paula Parkinson affair.

Just prior to the 2006 election, Mark Foley, a Republican from Florida, resigned his seat in Congress over e-mail misconduct with former House pages, and the Democrats picked up the seat. Those tied to the Jack Abramoff scandals, most notably Tom DeLay of Texas and Bob Ney of Ohio, both of whom resigned from Congress, had a major effect on the 2006 election as the Republicans lost both seats. Don Sherwood of Pennsylvania asked forgiveness for sexual misbehavior, but the voters refused to reelect him, as they did Curt Weldon, also of Pennsylvania, who was accused of influence peddling.

The 2006 Election

Aside from developing scandals and other problems, the Republicans were bucking the historic "six-year itch" at the beginning of the 2006 election cycle.

Political prognosticators were contending that beginning in 1902, when the House of Representatives was expanded to 435 seats, the average loss was 29 or 30 seats in the House and six in the Senate during the mid-term election in the second term of the party in control of the White House. As noted above, the only exception had been the 1998 mid-term elections.

It is unfortunate that the Republicans hit this number right on the head. Actually, when one factors in all the issues they were facing, it is remarkable that the Republicans did not lose many more seats in the House of Representatives. The only way the Republicans could have possibly fared worse in the Senate was if Senator John Kyle of Arizona would not have pulled out a razor thin re-election victory.

The 2006 election did not signify any major ideological or party realignment among the voters as had happened in 1964, 1974, 1980, and 1994. But it was a warning to the Republicans that they had better get their act together or such a major realignment could result from the 2008 election. There also was more polarization in Congress after the 2006 election, as more Democrats were elected and the liberal-conservative split grew. However, these Democrat gains were caused by Republican scandals and the unpopularity of President Bush. There was no evidence of a major ideological shift among the electorate. (The Democrat trend continued in the 2008 election for reasons that will be explained in the next chapter. But Republicans came roaring back in 2010 with historic gains in the U.S. House and the state legislatures. The outcome of the 2012 election could well set the political tone in America for at least a decade.)

The voters certainly were not saying in the 2006 election that they rejected conservative, traditional American moral values. For example, seven of eight state constitutional amendments upholding traditional marriage passed easily in most cases. The one ballot initiative that failed (in Arizona) also was doing well until a late flurry of TV ads claimed it would threaten cohabitating unmarried heterosexuals, including elderly couples. In virtually all cases, the ballot initiatives defining traditional marriage received more votes than the Republican candidates running in these states. The Democrats wisely went out of their way not to antagonize social-conservative voters in this election. (In the 2006 exit polls, only 20 percent of the voters claimed to be "liberals.")

The political climate could have not been much worse for Republicans as they prepared for the 2006 elections:

- Republican President George W. Bush's approval ratings were hovering in the 30s, primarily due to a very unpopular war in Iraq. Exit polling by AP and the TV news networks revealed that 55 percent of those who voted in 2006 were opposed to the war in Iraq.[47] These polls also indicated that six of 10 voters in general, and seven of 10 among those who described themselves as independents, did not believe the war in Iraq made us safer at home.

- The approval ratings of the U.S. Congress were at an all-time low. Poll after poll revealed that almost two-thirds of the American people were unhappy with the Congress in general, and with the Republicans in particular because they were the party in control.

- Republicans faced hurricane winds in three crucial states that were holding gubernatorial races and where the Democrat nominee won with a 20- to 40-point margin. In a fourth crucial state, the Republican governor had disapproval ratings that made President Bush look good. *The American electorate was angered and disillusioned.*

- On top of it all, there were the well-publicized *scandals*.

As we analyze these factors in some detail, the reader will justifiably ask why the Republicans did not lose 50 or 60 seats in the House and one more in the Senate.

When an R/T Strategies poll was conducted for the *Cook Political Report* in January 2006, only 38 percent of those polled said the country was headed in the right direction. (Right track/wrong track was still 41 percent to 55 percent in the exit polling.) The Republican base—the economic conservatives, the social conservatives, and to some degree the military conservatives—were upset with how the Republicans had governed. Former President Bill Clinton probably inadvertently summed it up best when he made a comment at a large Democrat rally near a microphone he thought was turned off. He told some Democrat heavyweights something to the effect: We (Democrats) are going to defeat the Republicans soundly, not because of what we have done, but "because the

Republicans have forsaken their principles." Larger, rather than smaller, government, wasteful spending, soaring deficits, and, of course, the *scandals*, were dominating the thinking of the Republican base. This is how they saw it and they were not happy!

We should look not only at what happened but why it happened. A number of Republican leaders have made similar statements to this one: "We became so fat and happy after 12 years of Republican control of the Congress that we started acting like Democrats." These sentiments may offend some Democrats, but they resonate throughout the Capital among most Republican Congressmen and Senators. We will explain the toll these concerns took on some voting groups, especially in the light of the scandals.

First, consider these factors in the four key states that were beyond the control of the Republican Congress:

In New York, now-disgraced Governor Eliot Spitzer won by 40 points, and Sen. Hillary Clinton was reelected by 35 percent as the New York Republican Party was in shambles. With the addition of the alleged scandals in New York, it is a testimony to the leadership of Tom Reynolds, who was chairman of the National Republican Congressional Committee, that the GOP lost only three seats, even as he himself barely held on to his seat.

In neighboring Pennsylvania, which was home to other Republican scandals, Democrat Governor Rendell was reelected with 60 percent of the votes; the Republicans lost three seats and barely saved a fourth.

In Ohio, the approval ratings of retiring Republican Governor Bob Taft were in the teens due to purported scandals in state government. The Democrat candidate for governor won with 60 percent of the vote against a good Republican candidate. The only Ohio seat in the U.S. House of Representative lost by the Republicans was the one held by Bob Ney, who was caught up in a high profile Jack Abramoff scandal. It was a fortunate for Republicans that their leader, John Boehner, was an Ohio resident. Had he failed to exert such strong leadership, two or three more seats could have been lost in Ohio.

In neighboring Indiana with no scandals, the Republicans lost three seats, two of which were directly related to the Republican Governor's disapproval ratings. Governor Mitch Daniels, an able and honest politician, had taken several actions that he believed to be in the best interest of the state, but which were highly unpopular. He had raised taxes rather than cut state services; privatized the toll road to a foreign company; and, most unpopular of all—especially with farmers—established daylight saving time for the state.[48]

There were a dozen or so purported scandals involving a few Democrats, but more involved Republicans during the 2006 cycle. Many of these scandals were real and a few were high profile and egregious, but others were rumor driven and media hyped. In any event "the culture of corruption" label stuck.

It all started with the extremely high profile and truly egregious Congressman Randy "Duke" Cunningham graft episode, which involved millions of dollars from a defense contractor. It is always difficult to understand how men of such stature can get involved in corruption and immoral behavior. There are so many examples of how powerful men have been brought to their knees over such acts. These men obviously are all human and therefore sinful like the rest of us. The devil is always cunning in every situation. But exposure of the House bank and post office scandals that helped to bring the Republicans to power was only a dozen years old. How could anyone forget so quickly?

The case of my dear friend Duke Cunningham—a truly religious man, a genuine war hero, and a proud and patriotic family man—is especially hard for me to grasp. Those who saw the movie "Top Gun" will understand my dilemma; Duke was the *original* "top gun." The only explanation that makes sense to me (but in no way excuses his actions) is that Duke had stared death in the face so many times during the Vietnam War that maybe he fooled himself into thinking he was invincible. I am sure he has asked God and his family for forgiveness many times and will continue to do so in his long years in prison.

The terrible political climate for Republicans and the toll the scandals were taking with the voters had created near panic. During the August 2006 recess, the Republican leaders were storming the country and apologizing for their failures and frailties. They were making progress in touting the fact that the Republicans had kept taxes low, helped make the country safer, and would address the deficit in all seriousness as soon as the Iraq war ended. They pleaded with the voters to give them another chance to fulfill their promises, and they warned that the Democrats would raise taxes, increase government spending, and not keep our military as strong as needed.

The message was resonating especially with those concerned about the Islamic terrorist threat and such social issues as abortion and traditional values. When Congress returned from the recess in September, most polls showed the Republican candidates making a dramatic comeback among the voters. It now seemed not only possible but even likely that the Republicans would lose only about a dozen seats in the House and three in the Senate. They were poised to keep the majority in both houses of Congress. You could feel a renewed mood of optimism as you talked to Republican Congressmen and Senators.

Then the "Foley Bomb Shell" seemed to appear from nowhere, shattering Republican optimism.

It did not in fact come out of nowhere because certain reporters had been holding the evidence for some time. They had kept sexually explicit e-mails from Foley to certain House pages under wraps, assuming that Foley would make a run as the Republican candidate for the U.S. Senate from Florida. The specific e-mails encouraging homosexual activities may have been received by former House pages who were now of age, but this didn't matter—Foley had been acquainted with these boys when they were young pages. This was indeed a "dirty trick" by unscrupulous members of the press, but that did not matter.

When it came out that the speaker's office and others in Republican leadership had known about these e-mails for some time, the scandal took on a life of its own. Why had those in leadership not taken some forceful and definitive action when they first learned the facts? The release of these despicable e-mails along with evidence of the lack of timely action by congressional leadership[49] created a wildfire that spread rapidly throughout the country.

The 2006 election numbers for key groups of essential voters for Republicans tells the complete story.

Since the 1980 election, thanks to Ronald Reagan's campaign, around 40 percent of the total Republican votes come from white evangelical Protestants and socially conservative Catholics.[50] In 2006, the Republicans carried the slightly depressed evangelical vote with 68 percent, but this was down from a whopping 78 percent in a very heavy turnout of white evangelicals in 2004.

The GOP also lost a net of 18 percent of the Catholic vote from 2004 to 2006. (The Republicans lost 9 percent, and the Democrats gained 9 percent of this vote.) This is extremely significant since Catholics make up slightly less than one-fourth of the electorate in any given election. In 1960, seven of 10 Catholics identified themselves as Democrats. By 2004, only 44 percent of Catholics did so. Of this 44 percent, some probably would be among the "Reagan Democrats" or "values voters." In the 2006 election, Republicans dropped below 50 percent of the Catholic vote for only the third time since the 1980 presidential election. (President Clinton did win a plurality of the Catholic vote in both the 1992 and 1996 elections.)

The rapidly growing Hispanic vote—which certainly has "values" implications—fell from the 44 percent for Bush in 2004 (an all-time high for Republicans) to somewhere between 26 and 29 percent, depending on which poll you read. This drop could have some minor relationship to the scandals, but it mostly was driven by the extremes to which some Republicans took the illegal-immigration debate.

The biggest hit for the Republicans came from the 26 percent of the voters who identified themselves as Independents, among whom the Republicans dropped by slightly more than a net of 18 percent from the 2004 election.

In this mix we must not lose sight of the fact that exit polls found that 74 percent of voters said that "corruption" was "very" or "extremely" important in determining how they cast their votes.

With all these statistics in mind, the question of how the Republicans lost so *few* seats reappears. The sum total of the national congressional vote in 2006 was 53 percent Democrat and 47 percent Republican. The Democrats won 25 Republican-held seats and held eight of their most endangered seats by 55 percent or less of the vote. On the other hand, the Republicans protected 47 of their seats by only 55 percent or less of the vote—17 of them by 51 percent or less and another eight by 52 percent of less. Had the Republicans lost most of the 25 seats they held by 52 percent or less of the vote, they could easily have been looking at the possibility of being in the minority in the U.S. House of Representatives for another 40-plus years.

The eight or so real or purported Republican scandals, dramatically reinforced by the late-breaking Foley super scandal,[51] drowned out the three or four cases of alleged Democrat misbehavior. Many voters probably included them in the frequently mentioned Republican "culture of corruption." The Republicans were in charge at the time and therefore charged with the responsibility of making the trains run on time. To be redundant: if you are going to claim to be the party defending traditional moral values, you had better "walk the walk" and not just "talk the talk."

The 2006 election changed the political landscape[52] in the Nation's Capital again very dramatically as the Democrats picked up 30 seats in the U.S. House of Representatives and six in the U.S. Senate. The Democrats would continue to control both houses of Congress after the 2008 election and lose the U.S. House in the 2010 election.

The polarization of the two parties in Washington, which is the major theme of this chapter, deteriorated further. The Democrat-controlled Congress was constantly at odds with the Republican White House. Finger pointing and brinkmanship seem to be the order of the day. Bipartisanship became a rare commodity used only on special occasions when it is absolutely essential for the federal government to continue to function. In many respects, it appeared that 2007 and 2008 were much more about the 2008 presidential and congressional elections than about legislation.

It is truly difficult for a radically divided government to function above the level of a bare minimum.

The political and ideological divide between the two parties after the 2006 election marginally increased in both bodies of the U.S. Congress in slightly different ways. The Democrats had become numerically more liberal, and the Republicans had become more conservative as a whole.

Of the 30 Republican House seats lost in 2006, about one-third of them were held by "moderates," primarily from the Northeast. Since there were fewer than 30 members of the "moderate" group to start with, there were probably fewer than 20 such members in the Republican caucus.

The Republican Study Committee, a group made up of the most conservative Republican congressmen (some would call them "right wingers"), claimed a membership of over half of the Republican House members. It is likely that there was the highest percentage of conservative versus moderate Republicans in the history of the House. (This record would stand for only two years, however.)

It is always imprecise to use labels such as "conservative," "liberal," or "moderate." In this case "conservative" means a member is overwhelmingly pro life, pro traditional marriage, pro second-amendment gun rights, in favor of a strong military, in favor of keeping taxes as low as possible, against most new government spending programs, and believes in striving for a balanced budget. The Republican Party can accurately be identified as the conservative party.

Nearly half of the newly elected Democrat members in 2006 ran campaigns proclaiming they were conservative or at least moderate on some of the social issues. The Democrats employed a successful strategy of recruiting candidates who would have more appeal in some of the more conservative Republican districts. Nearly half of the 2006 Democrat class joined the so-called Blue Dog caucus, a relatively conservative Democrat group, increasing its numbers to around 50.[53]

Still, more than half of the new Democrats were very liberal, and most of the incumbent liberal Democrats were returned to the House. As a result, there undoubtedly were more liberal Democrats (and, consequently, fewer conservative Democrats) in Congress than at any time in recent history, with the exception of 1965 and 1966—the two years when Lyndon Johnson was able to get most of his "Great Society" legislation passed.

The term "liberal" is no more precise or totally consistent than the "conservative" label. It is simply a shorthand method of trying to point out the differences between the two parties without extensive elaboration. (I have tried to use the terms without making value judgments while still not concealing my personal convictions.)

(There was a struggle going on for the soul of the Democrat Party, typified by such extreme left-wingers as Howard Dean, Michael Moore, and George Soros on one side and those who many perceived to be responsible liberals, perhaps typified by the Democratic Leadership Council, on the other. We will analyze how this struggle played out in the 2008 and 2010 elections. Further reference to the Moore- and Soros-type radicals and their attempts to consolidate control of the Democrat party will be further discussed in Chapter 6. I will discuss briefly in the next chapter a similar struggle that took place in the Republican Party after the 1964 election.)

The Republican losses and Democrat gains in the U.S. Senate and how they affected the polarization of that body is a very important element as we consider the challenges faced by our country today.

Of the six Republican Senators who lost their reelection bids in 2006, two were among the half dozen or so moderate-to-liberal Republicans. One of those, former Sen. Lincoln Chafee of Rhode Island, was almost universally considered to be the most liberal Republican in the Senate.[54] Another liberal loss was Mike DeWine of Ohio. The other four Republican losses, Sen. Rick Santorum of Pennsylvania, Sen. Conrad Burns of Montana, Sen. George Allen of Virginia, and Sen. Jim Talent of Missouri were all conservative Republicans.

There were fewer conservative Republicans in the U.S. Senate as a result of the 2006 election. However, a larger percentage of the Senate Republicans still were conservatives, since the number of moderate or liberal Republicans was much smaller than the number of conservatives prior to the 2006 elections. In general terms, this means that Republicans in the Senate were predominately conservative on social issues (moral issues such as abortion and traditional marriage, for example) and national-security concerns. They would also be basically conservative on fiscal matters and opposed to tax increases. There would be some disagreement among Senate Republicans, as also was the case with their House counterparts, on earmarks and spending priorities.

Early in the 2006 election cycle, it became evident to most political prognosticators that the Republicans had little chance of holding their Senate seats in Rhode Island, Pennsylvania, and Ohio. As the scandals—even though not Senate related—rocked two of these states and the general political climate for Republicans deteriorated rapidly in 2006, it became increasing obvious that it would be virtually impossible to hold any of these three states.

History illustrates that the two political parties rarely abandon their incumbents absent some egregious scandal. There was none in either of these cases. Yet it appeared as though the worse the situation became, the more millions of dollars the National Republican Senate Committee (NRSC) poured into these states. Many Republicans strongly disagreed with this strategy. There is always a limited amount of money for a party committee to spend. This is not intended as a criticism as much as a statement of fact. Those in party leadership positions sometimes have to make hard decisions. Some are the right decisions, and some are the wrong decisions. Political decisions are never an exact science.

On the other hand, there is little disagreement that the Republicans should never have lost the Senate seats in Virginia, Montana, and even Missouri. They were lost due to a combination of self-inflicted wounds and bad strategic political decisions.[55]

The only *hint* of a political scandal in these three states was in Montana. Rumors of some connection between Sen. Conrad Burns, the only Missouri Synod Lutheran in the U.S. Senate at the time, and disgraced lobbyist Jack Abramoff led to an investigation. Not surprisingly, all purported charges of misbehavior by Senator Burns were dropped as unfounded a few months after he lost his bid for reelection. In spite of the terrible anti-Republican mood in the country and some campaign mistakes, Burns lost by less than 1 percent of the vote. A Libertarian candidate received 3 percent of the vote—any 1 percent of that vote would have resulted in Burns being re-elected. Burns told me that his internal polling had shown the Libertarian candidate receiving only an insignificant 1 percent of the vote.[56] Of the millions and millions of dollars spent by the Republican committees on Senate campaigns, the infusion of a million or less in the final days of this Burns campaign would undoubtedly have resulted in a win. Campaign committees run out of money at some point. Of course, hind sight is always 20-20.

The reelection of Sen. George Allen was never considered to be in serious doubt until he made an unfortunate, innocent, but serious, gaffe.

A young Democrat activist with a funny-looking haircut, reportedly resembling a "Mohawk" hair style, showed up at a series of Allen events. At one of these political events, the senator saw this young man once again prominently positioned in the audience and pointed him out in words that went something like this: "I see that 'Macaca' is with us once again." Allen said publicly, as well as privately to me and many others, that this was a word he made up and that the expression popped into his head because the man appeared to have a "Mohawk" hair cut. It turned out there was a French word with a similar pronunciation that had racial overtones.

The Washington Post jumped all over this slip of the tongue. Allen apologized—unfortunately again and again—and the *Post* continued to run the story *ad nauseum*. The way this controversy was handled was most likely motivated by a larger concern than the Senate reelection campaign. While Allen never directly expressed such intentions, it was widely believed that he was a likely and serious possibility to become the Republican nominee for president. Had Allen won reelection as anticipated, he would have immediately been considered as one of the leading candidates in the Republican presidential primary.

In any event, there is a prevailing opinion that had this gaffe been handled as a normal reelection issue, it would not have greatly affected Allen's reelection to the Senate. If the Allen campaign, according to this political logic, would simply have issued *one* apology stating that this was an unfortunate, light-hearted expression, certainly not intended to offend, the issue might have rapidly faded. Then, if the reporter persisted, take the Ronald Reagan approach: each time the question was re-asked simply say, "I have answered that question; do you want to ask another question?" If the reporter had nonetheless persisted, tell him about America being the shining city on the hill or some similar heartfelt anecdote. It worked for Reagan. Most believe it could have worked for Allen.

One widely held belief is that the Allen campaign staff and consultants believed that this controversy could leave the false impression that George Allen was a racist if not definitively refuted. This would be unacceptable as they launched the presidential campaign.[57] Everyone who knows George Allen knows that he does not have a racist bone in his body. However, the more they tried to explain this relatively innocent event, the worse it got. *The Washington Post*, with its relentless misleading stories, successfully turned this deliberately distorted event into the defining issue of the campaign. Still, if the NRSC would have had held back a million dollars for the last week of this campaign, Allen almost certainly would have won anyway. Again, hindsight is 20-20. In spite of the persistent dirty tricks by the *Post* reporters, Allen lost by only three-tenths of a percent. The election was so close that a recount was under consideration for some period of time after the election. (George Allen is running again for his old Senate seat in 2012 in what now is considered to be a close race. Since Sen. Webb, who defeated Allen in 2006, has chosen not to seek reelection, Allen's opponent is Tim Kaine. Former Governor Kaine was serving as chairman of the Democratic National Committee [DNC] until he announced his Senate campaign. In this capacity, Kaine was President Obama's main defender on "Obamacare" among other very unpopular programs of this president. I expect this race to break in Allen's favor as they get closer to the election.)

In a friendly—or even neutral—election environment for Republicans, Sen. Jim Talent would have had little trouble getting reelected. He had the reputation of being a hard-working and effective senator for his Missouri constituents.

It was evident in the 2006 climate that Talent would need to run a good campaign. Nothing could be taken for granted. This he was well prepared to do. Then, for whatever reason, the decision was made (by a Republican governor) to put the "embryonic stem cell" constitutional-amendment initiative on the November ballot. This initiative was supported by as much as $20 million in advertisements. As a man of strong moral principles, Senator Talent expressed his opposition to this constitutional amendment, which would allow the creation and destruction of human life for use in unproven research.

The fiasco over Rush Limbaugh's question about whether the actor Michael J. Fox had deliberately not taken his medicine for his Parkinson's disease before he cut a TV advertisement for the initiative created much hype. Due to noble efforts by Dr. Jerry Kieschnick,[58] president of The Lutheran Church—Missouri Synod, and other similarly motivated church leaders in Missouri, the ballot initiative passed only narrowly. The initiative had led in double digits prior to their efforts. With few exceptions, Talent's vote count pretty much tracked the vote on the initiative throughout the state. Since Talent lost by such a narrow margin, it is reasonable to assume that he would have won had this initiative not been on the ballot. It certainly became a dominant issue of the campaign.

Of the six newly elected Democrat senators who replaced Republicans, four had presented themselves as "moderate" Democrats in their campaigns. With the addition of the other two, who ran campaigns as committed liberals, most political analysts contend that there were more liberals in the Democrat Senate Caucus than at any time since the two years following the 1964 elections.

As mentioned earlier, the 2006 Senate elections changed the partisan balance significantly, since the Democrats took control with a 51-49 majority. Even if the overall "ideological" divide was only narrowly altered, the switch of party control only magnifies the divide. The party in power always has the ability to stifle even minor dissent much more effectively than when it is in the minority.[59]

A minimum amount of bipartisanship in the Senate was essential during 2007 and 2008, since both parties had an adequate number of votes to sustain a filibuster.[60] This balance of power would change after the 2008 elections. After Senator Arlen Specter switched parties and the Minnesota Senate race was decided by a court decision, the Republicans no longer had the necessary numbers to sustain a filibuster without help from at least one Democrat senator.[61]

(When Sen. Ted Kennedy died Aug. 25, 2009, the Democrats were one vote shy of the 60 votes necessary to break a filibuster and pass Obamacare. The Democrats in Massachusetts were able to appoint a placeholder, Sen. Paul G. Kirk, which would allow them to pass Obamacare in the U.S. Senate on Dec. 24, 2009, with 60 Democrat votes. Scott Brown's election would change that ratio. In the 2010 election, the Republicans gained six more Democrat-held seats, making it more difficult for the Democrats to find seven Republicans to vote with them to break a filibuster.)

Notes

[1] Subsequent elections, especially the elections of 2000, 2006, 2008, and 2010, will be examined in terms of the deepening ideological divide and attending further polarization. This will be helpful in understanding the factors at play in the crucial 2012 election.

[2] The Republicans won six open Democrat-held seats and defeated two incumbent Democrat senators.

[3] The vast majority of these conservative Republicans were classic conservatives, or perhaps better described in what I refer to as "Goldwater-Reagan conservatives." A few libertarians, who had been pretty much ostracized under Reagan's leadership, had begun to infiltrate the Republican ranks at the time. There are more of them today, perhaps as many as two dozen. Libertarians are hard right on fiscal matters and hard left on social issues and national security policies. This subject will be further discussed later in the book.

[4] Republican Majority Leader Tom DeLay resigned as majority leader in September 2005 and was replaced by Congressman Roy Blunt on Sept. 25, 2005, on an interim basis. On Feb. 2, 2006, Boehner defeated Blunt in a close special election for Republican majority leader. When Republicans lost control of the U.S. House in the 2006 elections, Boehner became Republican minority leader, a position he held until being elected speaker of the U.S. House in 2011 after Republicans regained control following the 2010 elections. It all worked out well for both men since Roy Blunt was elected to the U.S. Senate in 2010 and is rising in leadership in that body of Congress.

[5] Lewis L. Gould's *The Most Exclusive Club* (Basic Books, 2006) is a most interesting 100-year history of the U.S. Senate from 1905 to 2005. For those interested in the subject, this is a fascinating read.

[6] The U.S. Senate by a similar margin had turned down President Eisenhower's nomination of Lewis Strauss to be secretary of commerce in 1959. Every president has virtually been granted carte blanche to select his own cabinet. It was unthinkable for a former senator to be denied such a post. Various arguments were offered to deny Tower Senate confirmation. It was said that he was a womanizer, drank too much on some occasions, and was very arrogant. (It would be an interesting exercise to analyze how many of the 53 Senators who voted "no" on confirmation shared some or all of the same alleged problems.) Others contended that he had become too close to many defense contractors in his many years on the Senate Armed Services Committee, especially as chairman of the committee when Republicans were in the majority and in some lobbying activities after his retirement. Still others insist it was payback time by the Democrats to George Bush for what they considered "negative" tactics used in his campaign against Michael Dukakis.

[7] It should be remembered that congressmen were not highly paid in those days. There obviously were extra expenses in carrying out the responsibilities of the office. Members who had little wealth when they were elected lived literally from paycheck to paycheck. The system probably could have been justified when it was instituted, but over time it had gotten out of hand and was being abused.

[8] This free trade agreement appears to be the single best hope for Mexico to stabilize its fragile economy in 2012.

[9] The very successful Bush surge in Iraq would result in at least a temporary defeat of the Islamist insurgents in Iraq. This enabled President Obama to pull out all American troops at the end of 2011. There is significant debate over whether or not this precipitous withdrawal of all American forces will result in a disaster for the weak and divided Iraqi government. Their still-weak and unprepared military would have no hope of defending against a possible invasion by neighboring Iran. I believe that the only up side of the crisis over Iran's determination to develop nuclear weapons is that it has deterred them from dominating the government in Iraq by infiltration if not invasion. This subject will be discussed in more detail in Chapter 3.

[10] As the war declared on America and her allies by the radical Islamic terrorists continues to rage during the Obama administration, polarization dramatically has intensified. Strong disagreements have further divided Republicans and Democrats. But hard-left or "progressive" Democrats have become increasingly in disagreement with the more moderate or "national-security"-oriented Democrats. This subject will be further discussed in the following chapter.

[11] Ironically, most of these issues would never have surfaced for debate in the first 150 years after the adoption of our Constitution. Our Founding Fathers, who had so carefully laid the foundation of this Republic on Judeo-Christian principles, would have thought many of these topics unworthy of moral conversation among ladies and gentlemen.

[12] Bill Bishop, *The Big Sort: Why the Clustering of Like-Minded America is Tearing Us Apart* (Mariner Books, 2009), 90. Bishop co-wrote the book with Robert G. Cushing. They not only appear to have examined virtually all the polling data in existence but also conducted numerous personal interviews throughout the country.

[13] Bishop, 88-89.

[14] A Gallup poll released in summer 2009 revealed that 40 percent of Americans identified themselves as conservative and 22 percent as liberal. This can be deceiving, especially in the case of liberals. The word "liberal" was so successfully demonized by Republicans in recent years that many who lean liberal refused to call themselves "liberals." Some use the word "moderate" to describe their political leanings, since they do not want to be identified with the far left or the far right. Most of the "moderates" lean fairly strongly in the "conservative" or "liberal" direction when polling questions are asked about specific issues.

[15] Bishop, 247.

[16] Perhaps there were significantly more that fill this description when the so-called "Radical Republicans" controlled the Congress after the War Between the States. There might have been more on a percentage basis when we early "Goldwaterites" insisted on a strict litmus test. Of course, we only had enough MCs to fill a few phone booths. Thankfully, Bill Buckley and then Ronald Reagan taught us some political sense. Concerns of the "Tea Party" movement that Republicans had failed to enforce fiscal restraint on government spending when they were last in control of Congress opened the door to libertarian infiltration of this movement. A more detailed account of how this happened will be included in the next chapter.

[17] The Vietnam War had opened up some partisan fissures, but the Democrats were also divided over the war. Watergate created more division but not enough to have much effect on social habits.

[18] The Clinton administration and the Democrat-controlled House of Representatives pushed a crime bill that ended up making them look soft on crime. They also supported the Federal Assault Weapons Ban, stirring up the National Rifle Association, which represented hunters and other conservative voters. Jack Brooks of Texas, who had represented his district for 40 years and was chairman of the House Judiciary Committee, probably lost his election because he voted for this bill. The Democrats gave the Republicans many issues for their campaigns.

[19] Congressman Bill Paxon of New York, chairman of the National Republican Congressional Committee (NRCC), had offices next door to the Capital Hill Club in the Republican National Committee building. Bill would visit the club regularly to review the information we had and to give us some suggestions on districts in which we could be especially helpful. Paxon was in charge of the professional operation. He supervised and directed candidate recruitment, national fundraising for the NRCC, the hiring of consultants, direct mail, and political advertising used by the NRCC. We were an important outside resource for the campaign since resources are always limited. It was a joint effort, but Paxon and Gingrich deserve the major share of credit.

[20] Boehner, not only an inspiring leader but a good campaign strategist, always had plenty of suggestions and instructions for me. He would tell me which candidates to concentrate on in my fundraising efforts, which one to call on his behalf, and many other assignments. It was actually at Boehner's suggestion that I prepared the spreadsheet and developed the list of Republican county chairmen. Knowing about my previous campaign experience, he always took time to listen to my suggestions, accepted some and on occasion passed them on to Newt.

[21] They all love golf and at least two of them are low-handicap golfers. I have enjoyed many rounds with all of them, and they are very competitive on the golf course, as they are in legislative battles. All are good athletes—three were good high school football players and Burr played football at Wake Forest University. "Lose" is not a popular word in any of their vocabularies.

[22] I would have had reason to ask him this question because this was the first time he, or any member of his family, had ever considered running for elective office.

[23] Latham has developed some deep LCMS ties since we became friends. He is now good friends with Dr. Dale Meyer from Dale's Lutheran Hour days and has visited on a number of occasions with the last three LCMS presidents. On many occasions he has responded to my request without hesitation when I need a speaker for an LCMS event or just a dignitary on some occasion. The offer is always outstanding for him to become a card carrying member of the LCMS.

[24] I am also extremely blessed to enjoy a continuing friendships, going back 30 or 40 years, with men such as Sen. Chuck Grassley (R-IA) and Sen. Thad Cochran (R-MS), who are such dedicated and effective public servants. I could fill several pages identifying other MCs who are close friends and have done so much for our country. I will forego that temptation and conclude by mentioning the other senator from my home state of Georgia. Sen. Johnny Isakson, a rising star among the newer members of the Senate, another loyal friend who has no agenda other than what is best for his country and state, shares many qualities with Saxby (the state's senior senator), mentioned above—including an outstanding wife.

[25] This made sense inasmuch as FDR's original mentor was New York Governor Al Smith. Al Smith, a strong advocate of sound fiscal policies, the free market, and states' rights, had lost to Hoover in 1928. Smith had lost this election not because of his conservative policies but because he was a Roman Catholic. (Many political historians believe that Smith's unsuccessful run for president perhaps benefited JFK 32 years later.) In any event, Smith had picked FDR to succeed him as New York's governor. He did not support Roosevelt for the Democrat nomination for president since he was concerned that he might have become too liberal.

[26] Many mainline churches at the time saw government as the instrument to improve the lot of the masses through the "social gospel."

[27] The size of the national debt must be evaluated in terms of its percentage of gross domestic product (GDP) to be totally meaningful. This will be explained more fully as we examine the present financial situation.

[28] Flynn's book will be referenced frequently.

[29] It should be remembered that Nixon won the first time in 1968 in a three-man race that included a southern Democrat governor, George Wallace, who was popular not only in the South but in certain pockets in the North. In his reelection campaign, the radical anti-war movement and the controversy surrounding the Democrat nomination of the radical liberal Senator George McGovern turned off potential Democrat voters.

[30] Parenthetically, as a poor preacher, I made a modest contribution to the cost of the TV time used by Reagan. I belonged to the same social fraternity as did Barry Goldwater. Since Goldwater was the first Sigma Chi to run for president, some prominent Sigma Chi alumni decided the fraternity should raise money nationally for the Goldwater campaign. The money that was raised all over the country from alumni members of our fraternity ended up paying for Ronald Reagan's nationally televised speech.

[31] U.S. history was dramatically changed by Goldwater's narrow 51 percent to 49 percent win over Rockefeller in the California Republican presidential primary in 1964. A late-breaking story about Gov. Rockefeller's marriage to his second wife and the timing of the birth of their baby undoubtedly played a decisive role in Goldwater's victory. It is strange how seemingly minor personal events can radically alter history.

[32] It might even have been worse since some scholars, who have carefully examined information from Soviet defectors, make a credible case that certain Soviet leaders actually considered a "first strike" once they had adequate strategic and tactical military superiority. They hypothesized that under such a scenario, an American president might choose to negotiate some type of surrender, fearful that if he retaliated, it could result in a second Soviet strike that could virtually wipe out major American cities.

[33] I personally played one of the most decisive roles in my lobbying career in rounding up the final vote to pass a bill in the U.S. Senate to sell the AWACS airplane to Saudi Arabia. The president strongly insisted the sale of this highly sophisticated military aircraft to the Saudis was essential to the security of the Middle East.

[34] This undoubtedly explains why certain libertarians and other right-wing extremists occasionally join forces with the ACLU. The ACLU has been the vanguard of the American Left since its founding by Roger Baldwin in 1920.

[35] I personally know congressmen Kucinich and Paul only casually, having met each of them on a few occasions. From conversations with their colleagues, I know them to be honorable and decent men. This certainly is not a

personal attack on either of them. I defend their right to advocate their policies as well as my right to condemn such policies as bad for America.

[36] In 1988, Ron Paul was the Libertarian candidate for president and received 0.5 percent of the total vote.

[37] Fortunately, this would be the last major congressional extravaganza by the hard-left and the hard-right Kucinich and Paul, since neither will return to the U.S. Congress after their present terms end in 2012. Kucinich lost a Democrat primary in Ohio and Paul, after running an unsuccessful campaign in the Republican presidential primary, is retiring from Congress at the end of this term. As strongly as I disagree with their isolationist policies, I never questioned their sincerity. I am sure some likeminded individuals will eventually take up their causes in future congresses.

[38] This subject will be further explained and extensively documented in the sections on "al-Qaeda" and "Osama bin Laden" in Chapter 5 of this book.

[39] My studies of Washington's religious beliefs, which will be elaborated on in Chapter 6, lead me to believe that he never denied the Anglican faith in which he was raised.

[40] Lutheranism is rarely mentioned by the Founders since Calvinism was dominant at the time.

[41] Debate continues over the Libertarian Party's "Statement of Principles," which declares: "We hold that all individuals have the right to exercise sole dominion over their own lives in whatever manner they choose, so long as they do not forcibly interfere with the equal rights of others to live in whatever manner they choose" (emphasis included in Statement).

[42] Some would argue that there are as many types of libertarians as varieties of Campbell's soup. This is obviously true because they are all strong individualists. But many of them brought a hard-right unbending agenda that the liberal press could ridicule relentlessly. Their small numbers in recent times have been increasing at what I consider to be a still-small but alarming rate in the Republican ranks. They were at least partly responsible in the 2010 election cycle for influencing Republican-primary voters to nominate candidates too far to the right for their districts or states. Since many of them have a "rule or ruin" philosophy, the danger always exists for them to support a third-party candidate who will take votes from the Republican, resulting in the election of a liberal Democrat. This threat probably has been minimized for the 2012 election by the fact that the likable Ron Paul was treated with respect in the Republican presidential primary debates. Such respectful treatment speaks well of Paul's standing as a person since the overwhelming majority of conservative Republicans regard his positions on social issues and defense policy to be very extreme. The fact that newly elected Sen. Rand Paul, Ron Paul's son, has endorsed Mitt Romney for president might help to minimize libertarian defections in the 2012 presidential election.

[43] Since the abortion issue became such a major issue in the 1980s, some libertarians argued that on some occasions, individual liberty must be limited based on moral concerns in society. A group called "Libertarians for Life" was formed. Dr. Ron Paul, when he was the Libertarian Party candidate for president in 1988, stated that all abortions from the time of conception should be prohibited by the states.

[44] Ike, a long time friend and fraternity brother, was defeated for reelection in 2010. His loss was a blow to the dwindling number of moderate Democrats who could reach across the partisan aisle. Fortunately, his Republican replacement appears to be a good MC who will represent the district well.

[45] Interestingly enough, after having written a draft, mostly from memory, of how conservatives took over the Republican Party, I picked up a relatively new book that is a definitive treatise on the subject. Professor Donald T. Critchlow's The Conservative Ascendancy: How the GOP Right Made Political History (Harvard University Press, 2007) documents how this movement succeeded against great odds and the successes and failures that followed. Critchlow points out how the intellectual component of the movement was fueled by the writings of intellectuals who had fled Nazi and Communist regimes as well as by such intellectuals as William F. Buckley, Jr. The intellectual Right defended individual rights, the free market, personal liberty, and the evils of an ever-expanding government moving in the direction of failed European socialism. On the other hand, the foot soldiers who manned the grassroots efforts came out of the anti-communist movement. Neither could have succeeded without the other.

[46] As previously noted, generalities are never precise. My generalized description of the membership of the U.S. Congress as a whole is undoubtedly more reliable for the first 25 or 30 years of my tenure in Washington than for the last 10 or 15 years. As I emphasized in Chapter 1, during my earlier years I knew most of the Democrats almost as well as I knew the Republican MCs. That, of course, is no longer the case.

[47] History will be much kinder to President George W. Bush than are his contemporaries. Many very knowledgeable political leaders believe that he will be exonerated by history as a man who took his oath of office to defend his country "against all enemies, both foreign and domestic" with absolute seriousness. George W. Bush made hard and unpopular decisions to defend against the radical Islamist terrorists without concern

for political and personal consequences. I know from personal experience that this president believed with all his heart that he made the difficult decisions and took the necessary action to protect his country.

[48] Governor Daniels' stewardship of Indiana's affairs was so farsighted that he was overwhelmingly reelected in the anti-Republican climate in 2008. His state registered one of the lowest unemployment rates and was in the best financial condition of almost any other state during the harsh economic times of 2009. His record is so outstanding that many Republican heavyweights urged him to enter the 2012 Republican presidential primaries.

[49] There are questions and disagreements about who knew what and when they knew it. There are theories about how the matter was being handled so as to protect the identity of the young men. Some members of the Democrat leadership had to know something about the emails. But none of this would matter to the voters. The Republicans were in charge in the House at the time and they had failed to take immediate and decisive action. That was *the* concern of the voters.

[50] This means that if they received 51 percent of the total vote, 40 percent of that 51 percent came from this bloc of voters.

[51] Republican congressmen from all over the country told me how their personal reelection numbers dropped sharply after the details of Foley soliciting homosexual sex from these former pages became public. Two MCs from marginal districts in Pennsylvania later told me that their own internal-polling numbers dropped by almost 20 percent the first week after the Foley matter became public. They both said that if they would not have had more than a month to recover before the election, they would not have been reelected.

[52] There was no evidence in the polling data that the voters were excited about the Democrats or had experienced a major ideological liberal shift. There was major evidence that such voters were very unhappy and disillusioned about what they perceived as Republicans abandoning their conservative and moral principles.

[53] This group of moderate to conservative Democrats would lose a few members in 2008 and be almost wiped out in 2010.

[54] Chafee dropped his Republican identity and was elected governor of Rhode Island as an Independent in 2010.

[55] The Democrats who won these Senate seats in 2006 are all up for reelection in 2012. Their Senate races are expected to be among the most competitive in the country.

[56] Burns also told me that had his polling data been anywhere close to accurate, they would have paid more attention to the Libertarian candidate, which surely would have resulted in his reelection.

[57] There are many of us who live in the political world who continue to believe that George Allen would be a great candidate for president and even a better president. A significant number of us continue to believe that as young as he is, this remains a future possibility.

[58] Dr. Kieschnick revived the tradition of LCMS leaders taking a public stand on clear moral issues, for which Lutheran Hour Speaker Dr. Walter A. Maier became so well known during the Great Depression. During his tenure as LCMS president, Dr. Kieschnick travelled to three states during the 2008 election defending ballot initiatives defining marriage as between one man and one woman (all of which were passed by the voters). Dr. Matt Harrison, Kieschnick's successor as LCMS president, has picked up on this bold and badly needed precedent and perhaps taken it to a new level. Dr. Harrison has also spoken out boldly in defense of our religious liberties under attack by the present administration. He has become affiliated with an organized group that has launched a campaign to defend such liberties held so dearly by our Founding Fathers. This subject will be explained in considerable detail in Chapter 8, which deals with the civic responsibilities of Lutherans and other Christians to become involved in the Cultural Wars to protect the moral and religious foundation on which our country was built. Luther's theology of the "Two Kingdoms" will serve as a reference point in this chapter.

[59] The "Lieberman threat" afforded the Bush administration the opportunity to more effectively pursue the war being waged by the radical Islamic terrorists. Senator Joe Lieberman had won reelection in 2006 by switching from Democrat to Independent. If he decided to join the Republican caucus, that would create a 50-50 tie. Since the vice president is empowered by the Constitution to break all tie votes in the Senate, the Republicans would reclaim the majority. Senator Lieberman, a liberal on social issues, has a well-deserved reputation as having a better understanding of the nature and severity of the terrorist threat posed by radical Islamists than virtually any other senator in either party.

[60] A filibuster is a time-honored Senate parliamentary procedure allowing unlimited debate that can indefinitely block consideration of a bill until cloture (which requires 60 votes) is invoked. The filibuster was established to protect the rights of the minority. It prevents the majority from sometimes hastily and almost always in a partisan manner pushing through legislation by a simple majority vote. The procedure has been

extensively used by whichever party is in the minority at the time. It has sometimes been used to block needed legislation. In the era of segregation, the filibuster got a bad name, as southern Democrat senators made use of the procedure to block needed civil-rights legislation. Much more often, the filibuster has resulted in bi-partisan cooperation and compromise that has led to more reasonable and sound legislation.

[61] For one full year—almost to the day—after Barack Obama was sworn in as president, the Democrats held a filibuster-proof majority of 60 votes in the Senate. Then, out of the blue, the totally unexpected happened. Scott Brown, a Republican, was elected to the U.S. Senate from Massachusetts in a special election to replace the late Sen. Ted Kennedy. The Republicans now had the 41st vote necessary to sustain a filibuster.

3

Living with the Most Secular President in U.S. History

"There is no attack on American culture more destructive and more historically dishonest than the secular Left's relentless effort to drive God out of America's Public Square."

Newt Gingrich[1]
Rediscovering God in America

ormer Speaker of the House Newt Gingrich and numerous conservative scholars have repeatedly described President Barack Obama as the most "radical" and secular president in America's history. Although these supercharged terms may carry different meanings for different people, at their core they reflect an undeniable and disturbing departure from the simple time-honored belief that "We the People" live, work, worship, and yes, govern as "One Nation under God."

From day one of his administration, President Obama signaled a new interpretation of America. Given his personal background and comfort with and frequent references to "religion" in all its various forms and belief systems, it is not surprising that he has wandered far afield from the religious beliefs and perspectives held by the Founders and the 43 men who preceded him to America's highest political office.

Consider the tone and content the remarks President Obama delivered in his Inaugural Address just a few minutes after being sworn in as President of the United States:

"For we know that our patchwork heritage is a strength, not a weakness. We are a nation of Christians and Muslims, Jews and Hindus—and non-believers. We are shaped by every language and culture, drawn from every end of this Earth."[2]

By saying "we are shaped," President Obama subtlely contends that our laws and foundation of government are not only fluid but reflect a universal notion of righteous governance derived from all viewpoints (including "non-believers").[3]

A Secularism Born Out of Universalism

Research into Obama's background and religious statements has led me to conclude that he is clearly America's most *totally* committed "universalist" president. Although the few Unitarians who have served in our nation's highest office may have believed that all religious roads lead to heaven, Obama may be unique in his apparent conviction that all good *secularists* will go to heaven—if in fact such a place really exists, and whether they desire to go there or not.

Although President Obama's universalist beliefs sadly reflect to varying degrees the attitude of most 21st-century Americans, a strong majority of Americans still do not share Obama's belief that America is a secular country. In February 2008, the Pew Forum on Religion & Public Life released a comprehensive report on America's attitudes toward religion, the "U.S. Religious Landscape Survey."[4] The findings indicate that "most Americans have a non-dogmatic approach to faith" and "do not believe their religion is the only way to salvation." The authors quickly add that this does not mean that the majority of Americans do not take their religion seriously. As a matter of fact, they reported that more than half of Americans say that religion is very important in their lives and "attend religious services regularly and pray daily."

Significantly, 92 percent of Americans believe in the existence of God, and "roughly seven-in-ten Americans say they are absolutely certain of God's existence."

Further, the survey found that 66 percent of American Protestants, 77 percent of American Catholics, and 72 percent of members of Orthodox churches believe that "Many religions can lead to eternal life." Jewish Americans agreed with this statement by an 82 percent majority, as did 56 percent of all Muslims living in America. By almost identical percentages, these religious groups agreed with this statement: "There is more than one true way to interpret the teachings of my religion."

President Obama appears to typify such wide-reaching and selectively accommodating religious views; views that are quick to denounce Christian doctrine as fundamentalist dogma and non-Christian beliefs as pure and noble. (For instance, President Obama gives the impression that he believes that the teachings of Islam, its history, and the obligations of its adherents regarding *jihad* and *sharia* law are monolithic throughout the world. Does our current President actually believe that beyond the most basic Islamic beliefs, the same brand of Islam is taught in the madrassas and mosques in the moderate and tolerant Muslim countries of Indonesia and Turkey as it is taught in Saudi Arabia and Yemen?[5])

The Roots of Obama's Wide-ranging Ideology

A brief look at President Obama's background provides important insight into why many have accused him of taking an anti-Christian bent on matters of church and state. He does appear to have adopted, without critical evaluation, the politically correct myth regarding Jefferson's erecting a "wall of separation" between church and state.[6] A plethora of manuscripts, including several books by Obama himself, have discussed the president's pre-White House days. Similar to most aspects of his presidency, these commentaries tend to the political extremes. Although generally critical of President Obama, *The Obama Nation* by Dr. Jerome R. Corsi,[7] offers concise and commonly accepted biographical information and thus has been largely sourced in the following pages.

Barack Hussein Obama was born Aug. 4, 1961, in Hawaii of a white mother, Ann Dunham, who came from a Kansas family and was a student at the University of Hawaii at the time. His father, most often referred to as Obama Senior, was a native of Kenya. Barack Senior was an intellectually bright young man from a prominent Muslim family of the predominantly Christian Luo tribe in Kenya.

In 1963, Obama Senior was offered a scholarship to Harvard University to study for his Ph.D. He left his wife and child in Hawaii, as there was not enough money to take them along. Shortly thereafter, Ann divorced Barack Senior, reportedly because he had not divorced a first wife he had left in Kenya. Another account holds that Obama Senior divorced Ann based on the provisions of *sharia* law. In any event, Barack Obama sadly never saw his natural father again until he was 12 years old in Hawaii, where he was living with his grandparents. This was the one and only occasion on which he talked to his father in person.

Obama's mother married Lolo Soetoro in 1965, shortly before Obama's fourth birthday. She also had met Lolo at the University of Hawaii, where she was studying for an advanced degree in anthropology. In 1967, Ann moved to Jakarta, Indonesia, with son Barack. Lolo, an Indonesian Muslim, had been summoned back to his home country after a military coup had overthrown the government. In 1970, when Barack was nine years old, his half-sister, Maya Soetoro, was born.

In Obama's 2006 book, *The Audacity of Hope,* he describes the religious beliefs of his parents and religion in his home as a child. He says frankly that "he was not raised in a religious household."[8] Obama describes the religion of his anthropologist mother this way: "For my mother, organized religion too often dressed up closed-mindedness in the garb of piety, cruelty and oppression in the cloak of righteousness."[9] Obama says that in his home, "the Bible, the Koran, and the Bhagavad Gita sat on the shelf alongside books of Greek and Norse and African mythology." He then describes his father's beliefs in terms he could possibly have heard from his mother: "... although my father had been raised a Muslim, by the time he met my mother he was a confirmed atheist, thinking religion to be so much superstition, like the mumbo-jumbo of witch doctors that he had witnessed in the Kenyan villages of his youth."[10]

When Obama was 10 or 11 years old, his mother sent him back to Hawaii to live with his grandparents and attend school, as Ann's marriage to Lolo was deteriorating. Obama's high-school days were difficult times. He struggled to determine who he was, since he had chosen to be a black man living in what may have seemed a white man's world. He quietly turned to reading black authors, including radicals such as Frantz Fanon, who wrote *Black Skin, White Masks* (1952) and *The Wretched of the Earth* (1961).[11] Obama informs his readers in *Dreams from My Father* that he "gathered up books from the library—Baldwin,[12] Ellison,[13] Hughes,[14] Wright, DuBois," which he read in his room at night when his grandparents thought he was doing homework.[15]

The list of authors Obama chose to read in his formative years, when he says in effect that he was trying to find himself, has to be of concern to those familiar with their works. To say that most of them are far left radicals is an understatement. Many of these authors were the types that inspire and motivate Huey Newton, Bobby Seale and others of Black Panther Party notoriety or those like Malcolm X and Louis Farrakhan, heads of the Nation of Islam. All such are racists who advocate black supremacy.

It is probably instructive that Obama chose to read the works of W.E.B. Du Bois as a teenager. Some authorities have speculated that Frank Marshall Davis, who will be discussed in the following pages, recommended that the young Obama read some of his works. Du Bois would have struck a chord with him since he was the first black to ever receive a doctors degree from Harvard University and had founded the short-lived and more radical Niagara Movement, which is considered to be the precursor of the NAACP. Du Bois was one of the co-founders of the NAACP and was suspected of being a communist by J. Edgar Hoover. Whether or not that was the case, Du Bois clearly insisted that capitalism was the cause of racism in America and expressed his preference for socialism. But what might have had the most appeal—or maybe influence—for Obama, was Du Bois' attitude toward religion, which is strikingly similar to that of Obama's mother. In the October 1933 issue of the NAACP's magazine, *The Crisis,* Du Bois as editor published an essay he had written titled "The Church and Religion." (see pp. 236-237). In this essay he claims that theologians have developed doctrines of which "it would be difficult to adduce scientific proof that these hopes and faiths are justified." He criticizes black preachers: "Among Negroes especially today it is most natural for preachers to sneer at the man who is 'merely' good and emphasize the transcendental value of the person who is too dumb to question any fairy-tale forced upon his belief." The only thing that might distinguish Du Bois' attitude toward supernatural myths in the Christian religion from Obama's mother, Ann, is that he seems to find some value in the moral teachings of Christianity.

Such radicals do not appear to be the voices that influenced Dr. Martin Luther King, Jr. As a devout Christian, Dr. King believed in this country, which was founded on Judeo-Christian principles and quickly became the greatest nation in history. He simply wanted for all people of all colors to be able to enjoy the benefits of our society and live peacefully and equally side by side with each other. He did not want to change our free enterprise system; he simply wanted for all to be able to take advantage of it. Unlike the radical so-called black leaders mentioned above, who harbored communist and socialist sympathies, King in effect used their support in the civil rights movement while never supporting their economic ideology.

Radical Mentors

As a high-school student, Obama developed a relationship with Frank Marshall Davis. Davis, a black journalist and poet, was born in Kansas, spent a major part of his adult life in Chicago, then moved to Honolulu in the late 1940s partly because of his communist (Marxist) sentiments.

Like many black intellectuals in the 1930s and '40s, Davis became a communist or joined communists in the struggle against segregation. And like Roger Baldwin who founded the ACLU, he became disillusioned with Soviet communism after Stalin signed the non-aggression treaty with Hitler. The propaganda about income redistribution and a classless society advocated by communists and socialists was appealing to many blacks concerned about race being at the root of their poverty and inferior status.[16]

Davis and Stanley Dunham, Obama's grandfather, had developed a close personal relationship in Hawaii. The time a volatile high-school-aged Obama spent listening to this now-elderly black journalist and poet with socialist and communist views[17] inevitably influenced the developing economic and social attitudes of the young man who would grow up to become president of the United States.

Soon after his college graduation in 1984, Obama's life and career path would change forever when he started working as a community organizer on the Harlem campus of the City College of New York. It was here that Jerry Kellman,[18] who ran a community organizing organization in Chicago, found and brought Obama to Chicago's South Side to head up a community organizing effort. Obama began his work as a community organizer in 1985. In 1989, after his first year in Harvard Law School, he returned to Chicago as a summer intern at the law firm where his future wife, Michelle, worked. His permanent return to Chicago after graduation from Harvard Law in 1991 set the stage for his political career.

During this time in Chicago, Obama met Tony Rezko, Bill Ayers, Bernadine Dohrn, and the infamous Rev. Jeremiah Wright.

The Syrian born Antoin "Tony" Rezko came to Chicago to attend Illinois Institute of Technology after he graduated from high school in Syria. Tony Rezko prospered in Chicago and became involved in Chicago ward politics and eventually part of the Daley machine. In 2008, Rezko was convicted by a federal jury "on 16 out of 24 counts of political influence peddling."[19] Corsi documents Obama's relationship to Rezko:

"As Chicago reporter Evelyn Pringle tells us, Rezko was Obama's 'political Godfather.' Rezko gave Obama his first political contribution, two thousand dollars, on July 31, 1995, when he learned Obama was going to run for Alice Palmer's seat in the Illinois state legislature. Pringle has claimed Rezko's financial assistance was critical to Obama launching his political career: 'Without the fundraising of his political godfather, Rezko, Obama's rise to power would not have occurred.'"[20]

One might be forgiven for failing to spot a corrupt political operative in a city famous for political corruption. But friendships and activities with well-known radical terrorists (Dohrn and Ayers) who hate America and a preacher (Wright) who overtly preaches hatred of America and espouses racism is another question.

William Ayers and Bernadine Dohrn, now Ayers' wife, were not just loyal Americans who disagreed with their country's policies in Vietnam. They were communist anarchists who hated America and everything it stood for. They were willing to bomb public buildings such as police stations, the Pentagon, and the U.S. Capitol. The Vietnam War appeared to be a convenient excuse to attack the institutions of a government they despised. They couldn't have cared less about the 2 to 3 million natives who were slaughtered in the "killing fields" of Cambodia and in Laos and Vietnam after the American withdrawal. Their ultimate goal was a violent overthrow of the American government and its replacement with a communist government.[21]

As a responsibility of my first job in Washington—special assistant to the chairman of the House Committee on Internal Security—I sat through literally hundreds of hours of congressional hearings on the activities of the anti-Vietnam War organizations. Most of these organizations advocated peaceful protest and political activities aimed at changing American policy in Vietnam. A small but significant number advocated violent terrorist acts that impacted the security of the country. The House committee was trying to determine which types of action were being advocated and conducted by the various so-called "anti-War" organizations.

As we investigated the more radical of these organizations—such as the Students for a Democratic Society (SDS) and its successor organizations, the Weathermen and the Weather Underground—the names Bill Ayers and Bernadine Dohrn were most prominent. They were as closely associated with these organizations as Huey Newton was with the Black Panthers. The unrepentant Ayers reveals his true colors in *Fugitive Days: A Memoir* published in 2001 and quoted by Corsi as Ayers describes his efforts to bomb the Pentagon: "Everything was absolutely ideal on the day I bombed the Pentagon. The sky was blue. The birds were singing. And the bastards were finally going to get what was coming to them."[22]

In 2001, Ayers posed for a photo to accompany an interview for *Chicago Magazine* to promote his book. He was standing on the American flag in a defiant pose.[23] And, Corsi points out the irony of a *New York Times* interview with Ayers published Sept. 11, 2001, in which Ayers says in the first lines of the interview, "I don't regret setting bombs. I feel we didn't do enough."[24]

How could one miss Ayers desecrating the American flag in *Chicago Magazine* and an article with Ayers saying he should have set more bombs that appeared in the *New York Times* on the very day that Islamic terrorists destroyed the Twin Towers? That Ayers hosted one of Obama's first fundraisers for his state-senate race, lived in the same neighborhood, and served with Obama on the board of Woods Fund Chicago makes it harder to understand.

Obama's defense that he was only eight years old when Ayers was setting bombs and that he thought Ayers had been rehabilitated seem disingenuous. Almost everyone who follows national security matters would most likely know about Bill Ayers and his unrepentant arrogance.

The American voters were so concerned about the financial problems facing the country, however, that they either did not listen to these revelations or did not care. What's more, the mainstream media virtually ignored Obama's relationship with this radical terrorist. Can you imagine the press' reaction if some Republican candidate would have had such a friendly and uncritical relationship with some unrepentant former Klansman, White Supremacist, or abortion-clinic bomber?

The Reverend Wright Factor

But perhaps the most serious of Obama's long-term relationships was with the Rev. Jeremiah Wright, pastor of Trinity United Church of Christ in Chicago. When Obama was hired in 1985 to be a community organizer, one of his responsibilities was to get the black churches involved in his organizing efforts. Obama needed to belong to one of these black churches. Why he chose Trinity and Wright has been a matter of debate. Regardless of any alleged motives, Obama was baptized by Wright and joined Trinity. He was also married by Wright, who would baptize his two children when they were born.

For some 20 years, Obama frequently sat in the pews at Trinity and heard Wright relentlessly attack America for all her faults and spew forth an ideology that could only be classified as racist. The reason this relationship became a campaign issue was that many of Wright's sermons were reproduced in print and/or audio and video for distribution.

To understand the basis of the teachings and fiery sermons of Jeremiah Wright, it is helpful to have some comprehension of the radical and racist nature of "black liberation theology." Its basic tenets grew directly out of the "liberation theology" of Latin America, which had strong Marxist roots.

The intellectual architect of black liberation theology was the Rev. Dr. James Hal Cone, a professor at Union Theological Seminary in New York. His book, *A*

Black Theology of Liberation, might justifiably be considered the "bible" of black liberation theology. Critics accuse Cone and other prominent black liberation "theologians" of attempting to blend Christianity and Marxism.[25]

Cone describes God's identification with "blackness" in a passage from his book:

> "The black theologian must reject any conception of God which stifles black self-determination by picturing God as a God of all peoples. Either God is identified with the oppressed to the point that their experiences becomes God's experience, or God is a God of racism. ... The blackness of God means that God has made the oppressed condition God's own condition. This is the essence of the Biblical revelation. By electing Israelite slaves as the people of God and by becoming the Oppressed One in Jesus Christ, the human race is made to understand that God is known where human beings experience humiliation and suffering. ... Liberation is not an afterthought, but the very essence of divine activity."[26]

It might be a stretch to expect that Obama, who by his own admission didn't have much interest in religion at the time, would have undertaken an independent study of black liberation theology.[27] However, with a self-confessed burning interest in racism and the colonization of black countries, it would be difficult to conclude that Obama did not read some of the works of James Hal Cone. During this period in Obama's life, Cone was one of the most prominent writers on this subject, along with the likes of Frantz Fanon (whose books Obama had read in high school), Stokely Carmichael, and Malcolm X.

Irrespective of what knowledge of black liberation theology Barack Obama may have had before joining Trinity, he would have received the full blast sitting in the pew and listening to Jeremiah Wright. Wright became involved in the 2008 presidential campaign as a major player after he delivered a sermon in early 2008 defending Obama and criticizing Hilary Clinton. Excerpts from the video version of the sermon include this:

> "Jesus was a poor, black man who lived in a country and who lived in a culture that was controlled by rich white people. The Romans were rich, the Romans were Italian—which means they were European, which means they were white—and the Romans ran everything in Jesus' country. It just came to me with—with—with—within the past few weeks, y'all, why so many folks are hatin' on Barack Obama. He doesn't fit the mold. He ain't white, He ain't rich. And he ain't privileged. Hillary fits the mold. Europeans fit the mold. Giuliani fits the mold. Rich white men fit the mold.... I am sick of Negroes who just do not get it! Hillary was not a black boy raised in a single-parent

home. Barack was! Barack knows what it means to be a black man livin' in a country and a culture that is controlled by rich white people. ... Hillary ain't never been called a nigger! Hillary has never had her people defined as non-persons! Hillary ain't had to work twice as hard just to get accepted by the rich white folks ... or to get a passing grade when you know you are smarter than that C student sittin' in the White House!"

Word of the contents of this sermon leaked out, and in March 2008, ABC News examined the content of dozens of Wright's sermons. Among excerpts released was this from a sermon preached Sept. 16, 2001, just five days after the 9/11 attacks, titled "The Day of Jerusalem's Fall":

"We took this country by terror away from the Sioux, the Apache, the Arawak, the Comanche, the Arapahoe, the Navajo. Terrorism! We took Africans from their country to build our way of ease and kept them enslaved and living in fear. Terrorism! We bombed Hiroshima, we bombed Nagasaki, and we nuked far more than the thousands in New York and the Pentagon and we never batted an eye. ... We have supported state terrorism against the Palestinians and black South Africans and now we are indignant because the stuff we have done overseas is now brought right back to our front yards. *America's Chickens are coming home to roost*" (emphasis added).

Wright said in an April 13, 2003, sermon:

"The government gives them [African Americans] the drugs, builds bigger prisons, passes a three-strike law and then wants us to sing 'God Bless America.' No, no, no, God damn America, that's in the Bible for killing innocent people. God damn America for treating our citizens as less than human. God damn America for as long as she acts like she is God and she is supreme."

All of a sudden Barack Obama's long ties with Rev. Wright, his pastor for 20 years, dominated the campaign news. As the attacks on Obama's relationship with his pastor intensified, Senator Obama gave a speech titled "A More Perfect Union" in Philadelphia March 19, 2008. In it, he condemned certain of Wright's remarks, which he insisted were not made on occasions when he was in attendance at Trinity.

Obama compared Wright to an old uncle who might make comments with which he disagreed and insisted that he could no more disown Wright than he could disown the white grandmother who had raised him. His grandmother had expressed some fear of black men after being panhandled by one at a bus stop. As a young high school student he had apparently felt his grandmother's fears were racially motivated.

Rev. Wright, obviously basking in the national spotlight, on Friday, April 25, 2008, gave an interview on PBS with Bill Moyers; on the following day he delivered a speech to the NAACP; and on Monday, April 28, he gave an address and made himself available for questions at the National Press Club. On each occasion, Wright made more outlandish and racially charged remarks. Among other incendiary comments, Wright defended Louis Farrakhan as one of the most important voices of the 20th and 21st centuries.

Wright refused to back away from remarks made in previous sermons, such as his suspicion that the U.S. might have created the AIDS virus to kill blacks and that America's past acts of terrorism were partly responsible for the 9/11 Islamic terrorist attacks. Wright contended that Obama had to distance himself from him because he was a politician.

Obama had hoped to at least partly defuse the issue with his Sunday, April 27, appearance on Fox News Sunday. But the day after Wright's Press Club remarks, Obama hastily had to hold a short "news conference" on the tarmac of the airport in Wilmington, N.C. Obama emphasized that Rev. Wright does not speak for him and said of his former pastor,[28] "the person I saw yesterday was not the man I met 20 years ago."

In the April 27, 2008, appearance with Chris Wallace on Fox News Sunday, Obama was clearly trying to minimize the importance of his association with Wright. He did, however, make this admission about Wright and the ensuing controversy: "I think that people were legitimately offended by some of the comments he made in the past. *The fact he's my former pastor I think makes it a legitimate political issue. So I understand that*" (emphasis added).

During this controversy, the highly respected pollster Scott Rasmussen conducted a survey indicating that 72 percent of the voters, including 58 percent of black voters, regarded Wright's remarks to be racially divisive. Wright's persistent fanning the flames of this high-profile controversy ultimately forced Obama to resign his membership at Trinity United Church of Christ on May 31, 2008.

The 2008 Election

Less than six months later, the presidential election resulted in a comfortable win for the Democrats, but it was not a major landslide as in the presidential elections of 1964 or 1980. The Democrats became more liberal in the House and the Senate, but there was no compelling evidence of a major and potentially lasting ideological shift among the electorate. (The Republican sweeps of the governorships in New Jersey and Virginia in 2009 refuted such liberal contentions. The Republican victory in the January 2010 special election for Ted Kennedy's former senate seat totally dispelled this myth.)

What do the figures from Obama's election actually tell us? All the hype about a record turnout among the under-30 voters, first-time and newly registered voters, and voters who identify themselves as liberals did not happen. But the overall turnout rate as a percentage of eligible voters[29] was the highest since the 1968 presidential election among Richard Nixon, Hubert Humphrey, and George Wallace.

Those responsible for planning, organizing and executing the Obama campaign may have experienced some luck along the way and enjoyed a highly favorable environment in which to operate, but they took nothing for granted. Master political strategist and former Speaker of the House Newt Gingrich had this to say about the Obama campaign:

> "I have to say, as somebody who cares how you organize campaigns, because I think they're integral to the process of self government, I will be spending a lot of time over the next year studying the [Barack] Obama campaign because I think it's a watershed campaign. I think it sets the standards for the future. It was intriguing. As a practitioner, I want to gather up all of the different analyses made in public by various Obama leaders and just study them to understand it. Because I think it's a marvelous case study in 21st-century use of technology and the oldest traits of strategy and discipline combined together in a very powerful forum."[30]

These words of former Speaker Gingrich, recorded in the "Inaugural Issue of the *Washington Post Magazine*" (published for President Obama's Inauguration), eloquently express the sentiments of those of us who carefully followed and studied this campaign.

For openers, the Obama campaign inherited a very friendly political environment in which to reach out to the various blocs of their targeted voters. They either knew or rapidly figured out how to take advantage of this environment. Change was certainly what the majority of Americans were looking for. The electorate as a whole was suffering from "Republican fatigue," "Bush fatigue," "Iraq fatigue," and "congressional fatigue" (the potential voters did not seem to have figured out that the Democrats had been in control of Congress for the previous two years).

The near collapse of Wall Street and the attendant effects on certain industries (which created major unemployment), coupled with the massive loss of value in retirement accounts, became the *dominant* issue in the campaign. The Bush administration and congressional Republicans received the bulk of the blame since the financial meltdown happened on Bush's watch.

The Bush administration and the Republican congresses were not blameless, but there is plenty of blame to go around. Many experts who can truly fathom the complexities of our financial system believe that the seeds of this problem were planted in 1977. In that year, newly elected President Jimmy Carter, with an overwhelmingly Democrat majority in Congress, pushed through legislation referred to as "The Community Reinvestment Act." Like many other legislative initiatives that have inflicted lasting harm on the country, this legislation had a noble and highly desirable goal, but it encouraged banks to make questionable loans as it sought to provide more people the opportunity to experience the "American dream" by owning their own home.

As noted, the economy would emerge as *the* issue in the campaign as the stock market dive caused 401(k)s to lose value (some wags began to refer to them as "201[k]s") and credit to dry up. The domino effect hit many other industries, and everybody turned to Washington for help. The Democrats immediately saw this as a "wedge" issue and sprung into full campaign mode to blame the "Republican" Bush administration. The vast majority of voters had no idea about the origins of the crisis. Most did not even realize that the Democrats had been in control of both Houses of Congress for the previous two years. That's politics!

Peter Hart was asked in a *Rolling Stone* interview what was the biggest key to Obama's election. He gives a thumbnail sketch,

> "The core he stimulated within the electorate—African-Americans, Latinos, young voters, first-time voters. He ran better than two-thirds in all of those groups, and 95 percent with African-Americans. He took what had been a confined electorate and changed it. In doing so, he put into play states that Democrats never thought they could win—Colorado, New Mexico, Nevada, Indiana and North Carolina, as well as Ohio and Florida".[31]

David Gergen quickly agrees that Hart has properly identified "the millennial generation, the African-Americans as the driving force behind this new coalition." Gergen adds, "It also includes women, suburban voters and others who have been traditional parts of the Democratic voting bloc."

Despite the loud cries of the hard left that Obama had a clear mandate and the election signaled a major shift to the left by the electorate, recognized authorities do not agree. Many features of how the voters cast their votes on ballot measures and state legislative races clearly prove there was no major ideological realignment of the electorate. *Rolling Stone* asked Hart and Gergen, neither of whom has ever been accused of conservative tendencies, "What would it take for Democrats to turn this victory into a lasting majority?" Hart responds very astutely, "There's a big difference between winning an election where the wind was at your back and putting together a permanent coalition that withstands when the wind's at your face. For the Democrats it really depends on the success of an Obama presidency."

Gergen's usually informed opinion is expressed in this way, "The election was more of a repudiation of the Republicans than it was an embrace of liberal ideology." Gergen seems to elaborate on this point when the next question is what Obama should do in the first 100 days of his presidency: "Second, he's got to ask the question 'Do I intend to govern from the center, or from the left?' Americans are moderate. If he attempts to govern from the left, if he overreaches, he'll pay a price for that." Then he comments on what he thinks Obama really believes, which should be taken as a warning to Republicans: "Obama thinks he can move a center-right country to become a center-left country."[32]

Karl Rove in an obvious reference to Obama's magnetic personality, oratorical skills, compelling presence, and possibly his racial appeal, says there are signs that "Mr. Obama's victory may have been more personal than partisan or philosophical." Rove's analysis of the election results in state elections is not only interesting but instructive:

> "Democrats picked up just 10 state senate seats (out of 1,971) and 94 state house seats (out of 5,411). By comparison, when Ronald Reagan beat Jimmy Carter in 1980, Republicans picked up 112 state senate (out of 1,681) and 190 state house seats (out of 5,501). ... In the states this year, five chambers shifted from Republican to Democrats, while four shifted from either tied or Democratic control to Republican control. In the South, Mr. Obama had 'reverse coattails.' Republicans gained legislative seats across the region. In Tennessee both the house and senate now have GOP majorities for the first time since the Civil War."[33]

Obama's comfortable electoral victory and the attendant Republican losses were not caused by a massive liberal shift in ideology among the voters but on the voters' attraction to Obama's personality, Bush and Republican fatigue, and a severe economic downturn. In analyzing the ingredients that made Obama's election possible, the ideological labels of self-described voters were virtually unchanged from 2004. One percent more described themselves as liberals and one percent less as moderates. The 34 percent who labeled themselves conservatives remained unchanged.

As David Gergen reminded his audience, just because 60 percent of the moderates and 20 percent of the conservatives got on the Obama bus for this election ride doesn't mean that many of them will not get off the bus at some point. In fact, after a year's debate in 2009 over so-called "cap and trade" energy policies and health-care reform, nearly all the conservatives who voted for Obama and 30 or 35 percent of the independent Obama voters had already left the bus. More than half of the electorate had concluded that Obama's positions are too liberal and extreme. (This widespread dissatisfaction of the voters was on clear display in the 2010 election as Republicans made gains of historic proportions. They had a net gain of 63 seats in the U.S. House of Representatives and a total of 693 house and senate seats in the state legislatures, as noted in Chapter 1. The voters will have the final say on how they feel about Obama's policies in 2012.)

This does not yet mean they are totally happy with the Republicans, but they are weary of the Democrat agenda.

Polarization Spins Out of Control

Sincere, honest liberals have as much right to pursue their chosen agenda under our system of government as do equally sincere, honest conservatives. In many if not most cases, such partisan splits have served our country well, as they guard against extremes in either direction. The problem is that when the two parties have become so polarized and the divide as wide as it is today, it is very difficult to deal effectively in a civil, bipartisan way with threats as serious as those we now face in our country.

The polarization and the partisan divide in the nation's capital following the 2008 election is perhaps unsurpassed in America's history. The only possible earlier periods of such polarization and partisan politics would be immediately after Thomas Jefferson's election in 1800 or after Abraham Lincoln's elections in 1860 and 1864—a harsh partisan divide would last throughout most of the remainder of the 19th century.

Despite all the campaign rhetoric by candidate Obama and other Democrats about bringing the country together, finding a different way of doing business in Washington, and governing in a bipartisan manner, the exact opposite has occurred. The country is more divided and the electorate is demonstrating more anger than at any time in modern history.

The majority of the electorate had cast their votes in November 2008 based on their desire for change and the longing they felt for hope in a brighter future. Hopes ran high that Barack Obama might actually be able to rise above partisan concerns and truly bring the country together in such a crucial time in our history. But less than a year and a half into Obama's presidency, hope already had turned into anger and anxiety, and there was a peaceful rebellion brewing against much of the change that had been proposed. The majority of Americans had not bargained for change in our form of government or for a redistribution of wealth that looked like some type of democratic socialism. This disappointment was expressed by the voters in the 2010 election results.

Rampant partisan disputes have disillusioned masses of the people. Polling data from conservative, liberal, and non-partisan pollsters alike reveal that the people believe their elected officials in Washington have become "tone deaf" to the voices of the American people. The prevalent attitude is that a culture of arrogance has so engulfed the Capital that no one seems to be listening to the people. (The people spoke loudly at the polls in 2010 and they are trying to determine if that shout has improved anybody's hearing. They will tell us in the 2012 election if they believe anyone received their message.)

The partisan atmosphere in Washington has become so toxic and the chasm between the two parties is so wide that civil discourse has become a rare commodity. Why and how did Washington become so much more radically and apparently irreconcilably divided, and so quickly?

I offer three theories:

1. From the beginning, Obama, many of his advisors, a number of Democrat congressional leaders, and especially the far-left groups that provided the bulk of the financial support and manpower for the election grossly over-read what they believed was an *"election mandate."* (After Bill Clinton was elected president in 1992, he seemed to harbor similar illusions. He made a major push for "Hillarycare" and other measures the voters considered too radical. President Clinton got the message the voters sent in the 1994 landslide election, in which the Republicans took control of both houses of Congress. President Clinton, always a pragmatist, not an ideologue, was quick to realize that Americans wanted a center-right government, not a left-leaning government. He changed course quickly and was easily reelected in 1996 despite his impeachment scandal. There is no evidence that President Obama got the message from the voters in the mid-term elections. If he did, he remained convinced that he had his own destiny.[34])

2. Therefore, a strong case can now be made that Obama is much more of a left-wing ideologue and not just the traditional liberal he portrayed himself to be during the campaign.

3. This leads to the conclusion that the far left may be exercising considerably more influence over this White House and Democrats in Congress than most people realize.

His persistent actions as president clearly demonstrate that Obama has yet to show any inclination to embrace pragmatism in an effort to make government work as did one of his more successful Democrat predecessors, Bill Clinton. It may well be that Obama believes he is destined—and therefore obligated—to accomplish as much of his left-wing agenda as possible. In an interview before the November 2010 election with ABC's Diane Sawyer, aired Jan. 25, 2010, President Obama said he will not back off his agenda despite the political hazards that might lie ahead.

In a story for *CNS.com*, Aug. 21, 2009, writer Fred Lucas noted that Dick Morris, who had been a consultant to President Clinton, had predicted that "Obama is willing to be a one-term president 'to complete a socialist takeover of the United States' before his popularity runs out...."

Dick Morris' claim may sound harsh and extreme to those who do not closely follow the political wars in Washington. A political consultant and advisor to elected officials at the highest levels in both parties, Morris sometimes is given to hyperbole, but he "calls them as he sees them" without any desire to be politically correct. He is highly regarded for his brilliance and political astuteness.

When the 2012 presidential election kicks into high gear, voters will hear a great deal about an "open mike" discussion between President Obama and Russian

President Dmitry Medvedev at the time. In this discussion, that neither leader realized was being heard by others, President Obama tells President Medvedev that "after" his reelection, he will have more "flexibility" in dealing with the controversy over the placement of America's missile defense systems. Medvedev assures Obama that he will discuss this highly sensitive issue with "Vladimir."[35] This remark led national-security conservatives to fear that Obama was signaling potential noncooperation with our European allies who were seeking a nuclear shield on their border. Republican leaders immediately warned that this indicated that Obama's intent, if reelected, is to use such "flexibility" in implementing his radical left-wing agenda at all cost. In plain language, the fear is that while Obama used his initial popularity (and 60-vote Democrat majority in the U.S Senate) to push through massive bailout programs and "Obamacare," such an aggressive policy agenda may be just the tip of the iceberg. In a second term, with no concern for a future election, Obama might well attempt to muscle through socialist-leaning programs that would make the New Deal pale in comparison.

Former Speaker of the House Newt Gingrich told the Southern Republican Leadership Conference in New Orleans April 6, 2010, that Barack Obama is "the most radical president in American history" and oversees a "secular, socialist machine." Associated Press writer Ron Fournier writes that Gingrich told his audience, "Obama's policies—particularly health care and economic stimulus legislation—have put the United States on the road to socialism."

While it may be a stretch to call Obama a "socialist" in the classic or European sense of the term, it is undeniable that many of the major economic policies he has pushed entail socialist trends. The now-famous encounter between "Joe the Plumber" and then-candidate Obama may have inadvertently exposed the economic philosophy and principles most deeply held by Obama. Joe had challenged the Democrat candidate about his intentions to raise taxes on small businessmen making $200,000 or $250,000 a year. Obama asked Joe if he was not willing to "spread the wealth around." Joe responded that such increased taxes would make it impossible for him to own his own business.

The far left may be exercising considerably more influence over this White House and Democrats in Congress than most people realize. The radical left under the leadership of billionaire George Soros designed an extensive plan to take over the Democrat Party in the early 2000s. The movement had an embryonic beginning in 1998 when California software developer Wes Boyd launched a website, *MoveOn.org*, to offer a petition to censure President Clinton in his impeachment trial and "move on." This organization would raise millions of dollars for Democrat candidates and become the driving force behind the "almost" successful candidacy of Howard Dean, the most far-left candidate to come close to becoming the Democrat presidential candidate in 2004.

Soros, who funds many dozens of far-left intellectual "think tanks" and political organizations, spelled out plans to take over the Democrat Party in 2003.

New York Times best-selling authors David Horowitz and Richard Poe extensively documented Soros' intentions in their book *The Shadow Party: How George Soros, Hillary Clinton, and Sixties Radicals Seized Control of the Democratic Party.*

George Soros is a financial genius with a ruthless, checkered past. In a low-key, almost stealth manner, Soros has put together a radical left-wing coalition of organizations, staffed by some of the brightest liberal or left-wing minds and most-accomplished political operatives.[36] With almost unlimited resources, reaching into the hundreds of millions of dollars for each of the election cycles, there has never been anything close to comparable in past political movements.

Horowitz and Poe note that Soros chose an interview with a *Washington Post* reporter to make public the formation of "The Shadow Party" in November 2003 and announced he had pledged record breaking contributions. His hope was this would stimulate giving by others and ultimately result in the defeat of President Bush.

> "He [Soros] chose The Washington Post to carry his message. Soros sat down with reporter Laura Blumenfeld and issued his now-famous call for regime change in the United States. 'America under Bush is a danger to the world,' Soros declared. 'Toppling Bush,' he said, 'is the central focus of my life ... a matter of life and death. And I'm willing to put my money where my mouth is.' Would Soros spend his entire $7-billion fortune to defeat Bush?, Blumenfeld asked. 'If someone guaranteed it,' Soros replied."[37]

After President George W. Bush won reelection and the Republicans gained seats in Congress in 2004, the Soros team redoubled their efforts. With the wind of Republican scandals and Bush fatigue at their backs, the Democrats took control of both bodies of Congress. Without allowing much time to celebrate, the driven Soros directed his team to begin intense efforts to add to the Democrat numbers in Congress and win the White House in 2008. They would in fact add to their numbers of left-leaning members of Congress in the 2008 elections and, most importantly, capture the big prize on Pennsylvania Avenue. The left-wing operatives undoubtedly exceeded Soros' and his radical co-conspirators' wildest dreams.

David Horowitz, a onetime insider in the American communist movement who became an early advocate and intellectual in the development of the New Left, certainly has the background and knowledge to expose today's premier left-wing conspirators.[38] His most recent book, *The New Leviathan: How the Left-Wing Money Machine Shapes American Politics and Threatens America's Future,* co-written with Jacob Laksin, just came off the press in the summer of 2012. In the first chapter, simply titled "The New Leviathan," the authors expose the myth that Republicans are the party of the rich and the super-rich since conservative philanthropists are providing billions to tax-exempt foundations and think tanks to produce a "rightward shift in American politics."

By the mid 1970s, Horowitz would come to a full understanding of the fallacies and evils of Marxism, other forms of communism and socialism, and the far-left's determination to radically alter America's form of government. The American Left not only intended to destroy the capitalist economic system that has made America the most prosperous and generous nation in human history. But they also were determined to tear down the moral and religious foundation of a country, governed by a free people, that together with an economic system which rewarded dedication and hard work were responsible for American ingenuity and exceptionalism. Adding urgency to the far-left's threat were their efforts to weaken our military and force the government to adopt an isolationist foreign policy that could lead to a Soviet Communist takeover of our country.

For a 10-year period, Horowitz made no public mention of his "conversion" (my description) and his determination to do all he could to prevent a left-wing takeover of America. Then Horowitz wrote an article in 1985, published in *The Washington Post*, titled "Goodbye to All That" in which he explained his change of mind and his decision to support Ronald Reagan for president. This public declaration was followed two years later by Horowitz co-hosting a "Second Thoughts Conference" in Washington, D.C. which Sidney Blumenthal described in *The Washington Post* as Horowitz's "coming out" party as a social conservative. Since that time, Horowitz has relentlessly published articles and books, founded publications, regularly edits *FrontPage Magazine*, and is the current president of the David Horowitz Freedom Center.[39] The leaders of the radical left in America have launched numerous campaigns to vilify David Horowitz—a testimony to his effectiveness, in my opinion. They can call him names but they cannot, with a straight face, question his credentials to know who they are and their intentions to move America to the far left. After all, Horowitz was one of their brightest and most celebrated stars for more than 15 years. Horowitz not only came to understand the dangers of the communist threat, but he has also become a recognized scholar on radical Islamist terrorism. In 2004, he published a book titled *Unholy Alliance: Radical Islam and the American Left*.

Horowitz and Laksin refer to what they describe as "the now-famous PowerPoint presentation that former White House official Rob Stein screened for George Soros" and an assembled group of Democrat operatives and fundraisers prior to the 2004 election. His dishonest purpose was to warn them of "the unfairly oversized conservative war chest."[40] They then cite a 1999 report by a "progressive advocacy group" also making such outrageous claims that they attempt to set the record straight—as frightening as it might be. They write:

> "The twin premises of all these narratives, including Stein's PowerPoint, was that conservatives could draw on far superior and unrivaled tax-exempt resources to change the nation's political discourse and move it to the right. Both premises were demonstrably false. As of 2009, the financial assets of 115 major tax-exempt

foundations of the Left identified by our research added up to $104.56 billion. Not only is this total not less than the financial assets of the 75 foundations of the Right, it was more than ten time greater."[41]

In case conservatives missed the warning, Horowitz and Laksin offered an additional striking example: "In 2009, the leading progressive philanthropy, the Bill and Melinda Gates Foundation, had an endowment of more than $33 billion—over three times the total of all seventy-five conservation foundations combined."[42]

In Chapter 3, "The Progressive Money Machine," the authors describe the left-wing takeovers of large tax-exempt trusts established by free enterprise and limited government entrepreneurs, some of whom were also social conservatives. Reading the names of The Woods Fund, The Pew Charitable Trusts, the Rockefeller Brothers Fund, the Carnegie Foundation, the Heinz Endowments, and especially the Ford Foundation, which have fallen under the control of far-left relatives and trustees, is not only depressing but alarming. (It reminds one of reading the aptly named "litany of the dead" of "the captive nations" of Eastern Europe under Soviet control following World War II.) Horowitz and Laksin give extensive detail of the radical left-wing causes supported by these foundations that have been hijacked by the Left. They then explain how the left-wing activists, including communists and communist-sympathizers, have so successfully and extensively infiltrated academia, the press, and other institutions of influence in this country. (This is a subject that will be discussed in more detail in Chapter 6.)

Far-left Democrat members of the House and the Senate are overtaking the traditional liberal members and are already exerting influence beyond their numbers. The biggest threat faced by the Democrats is the struggle for party control between the traditional liberals and the far left.[43]

The political climate seems to indicate not only a new level of political activism but perhaps a new degree of public understanding of certain issues. More than two-thirds of Americans—in numerous polls—believe that government spending is excessive and that government debt is out of control. What the public is having difficulty understanding is why the Obama administration and the Democrats and Republicans in Congress cannot sit down and start with their agreements about the most pressing problems and find reasonable, bipartisan solutions to these needs?

For example, the debate over a ballooning national debt commands considerable attention even as the partisan divide over taxes and government spending continues to increase with the debt. There has been little disagreement that some steps had to be taken to immediately slow the growth of the debt and to produce a plan that will reduce it in succeeding years. But there has long been a genuine ideological dispute that breaks increasingly in a partisan manner between Republicans and Democrats on how to do what needs to be done. The devil has always been in the details, which inevitably are guided by partisan election considerations.

The Financial Crisis

The 2012 election is overwhelmingly about our current financial crisis. The exploding national debt and the enormous unfunded mandates, primarily involving government obligations to Social Security and Medicare, threaten the very survival of this great nation if not addressed immediately. If we fail to solve this crisis or falter in maintaining our military power, there will be no possibility of us surviving as a moral and religious nation. The outcome of this election will almost certainly determine the fate of America and the type of country we pass on to succeeding generations.

The debt problem can be stated simply by pointing out that the U.S government collects slightly less than $1 trillion dollars per year in individual federal income taxes. In addition, roughly another $2.2 trillion comes into the federal coffers from corporate and other federally taxed sources. Yet in spite of such massive revenues, the federal government is now forced to borrow 44 or 45 cents of every dollar it spends. (This number continues to rise as payments to the multitude of federal programs continue to increase.)

The picture becomes very complex when you consider the astronomical nature of the numbers involved. When George W. Bush took office, the national debt that had been accumulated by all previous American presidents stood at $5.7 trillion. When he left office, it had risen to $10.6 trillion, mostly due to the cost of the two wars against the Islamist terrorists and the meltdown of the financial markets. Obama inherited a $10. 6 trillion national debt when he assumed the reins of government. As President Obama approaches the four-year mark, the national debt has hit $15.7 trillion and is growing by $5 billion a day.

Financial experts have always evaluated the severity of the growth of the national debt by comparing it to the growth of the Gross Domestic Product (GDP), i.e., the total economic output of the nation. As long as the economy grows twice as fast as the debt, or close to that mark, the economic situation is considered to be healthy. Former President Bush, President Obama, the Congressional Budget Office (CBO), and many other government agencies—in addition to a multitude of congressmen and senators—agreed that we were on an "unsustainable fiscal path" when the CBO forecast in early 2009 that the national debt would grow to 100 percent of GDP by 2015. Unfortunately, that forecast was inaccurate—we soared to slightly over 100 percent of debt compared to GDP by the third quarter of FY 2011. We are now threatened with the disastrous financial nightmare that has beset Greece, Spain, and Italy.

To make the picture even bleaker, few realize that many very significant inter-governmental debt obligations, such as government guarantees of mutual funds, banks, home loans, and other such items, are not included in the national debt. But by far the most frightening aspect of our economic troubles are the massive unfunded mandates in current law. Our government is required by law to provide some $60 to $100 trillion over the next 75 years to fund Social Security, Medicare, and Medicaid. Government agencies, such as the GAO, project that government payouts for these programs will greatly exceed tax revenues during this period of time. An article in Wikipedia titled *"United States public debt"* explains:

> "The present value of these deficits or unfunded obligations is an estimated $45.8 trillion. This is the amount that would have to be set aside during 2009 so that the principal and interest would pay for the unfunded obligations through 2084. Approximately 7.7 trillion relates to Social Security, while $38.2 trillion relates to Medicare and Medicaid. In other words, health care programs will require nearly five times the level of funding that Social Security does. Adding this to the national debt and other federal obligations would bring total obligations to nearly $62 trillion.[44] However, these unfunded obligations are not counted in the national debt.
>
> "The Congressional Budget Office (CBO) has indicated that: 'Future growth in spending per beneficiary for Medicare and Medicaid—the federal government's major health care programs—will be the most important determinant of long-term trends in federal spending. Changing those programs in ways that reduce the growth of costs—which will be difficult, in part because of the complexity of health policy choices—is ultimately the nation's central long-term challenge in setting federal fiscal policy."[45]

If the Congress and the president are not willing to take on this financial crisis, they have no concern for future generations and the worst nightmare of our dedicated Founders could become a reality. Time is running out!

Obama's Foreign Policy

The initial hints of the type of foreign policy Obama intended to follow were offered early on when he selected the cabinet members responsible for national security and foreign-policy initiatives. As we look at this, I would advance what I believe to be a plausible and perhaps dangerous theory. One the one hand, Obama made the decision, which ran contrary to his nature, that he could not afford the loss of the war in Iraq or Afghanistan. This should please conservatives. On the other hand, the hard left who brought him to the dance and radical "civil libertarians" would be pacified if he issued tolerant and "humanitarian" guidelines concerning intelligence gathering, prosecution of terrorist suspects, and politically correct descriptions of our enemies.

When President Obama asked Secretary of Defense Robert Gates to stay on for at least a couple of years, there was a collective sigh of relief in many quarters. This was interpreted as a signal that he intended to keep our military strong in the face of so many foreign threats.

The appointment of Leon Panetta as director of the CIA turned out to be perhaps President Obama's best selection in dealing with the war on America being waged by the Islamist terrorists.[46]

Since Panetta had Obama's trust and confidence he was the ideal person for such a sensitive position in the administration. Director Panetta was able to strengthen and protect his agency from some dangerous proposals by more liberal administration officials. Many experts in defense and intelligence matters are convinced that Panetta played the decisive role in convincing President Obama to approve the decision to send the Navy SEAL teams into the compound in Pakistan to kill Osama bin Laden. (This was certainly the right decision, but it was risky. Most remembered the disastrous affect the failed rescue attempt of the American hostages in Iran had on President Carter's reelection bid.) Most conservatives have applauded the switch that saw Leon Panetta named Secretary of Defense on July 1, 2011, after Robert Gates announced his retirement. The CIA remains in good hands, since General David Petraeus was sworn in to replace Panetta Sept. 6, 2011.

Obama asking Gates to stay on at the end of the Bush administration was interpreted to mean that the president had decided to stay the course in Iraq and build on the successes of President Bush's "surge." This had been an up and down strategy, but it seemed to work. However, the insistence on pulling out all U.S. forces by a certain date seemed to encourage Islamic extremists, who apparently had hoped to keep the Iraqi government as weak as possible until they could engage Iraqi troops without American support. President Obama's decision to pull all American combat troops out of Iraq by the end of 2011 may turn out to be our worst nightmare![47] The already weak Maliki government became involved in bloody sectarian clashes as soon as the last of the American planes were out of sight. Iraq has virtually no air force and an inexperienced and a small, still poorly trained military. Many experts are now advancing a theory of why Iran has not already invaded, or at least heavily infiltrated, Iraq. The outcry of the free world over Iran's stubborn determination to create nuclear weapons has inhibited their desire to take over Iraq. The thought of having another radical Shiite theocracy in Iraq like the one in Iran creates fears in many Muslim countries as well as in the entire free world.

The situation in Afghanistan and Pakistan was clearly the most imminent and dangerous threat the new president faced. The resurgence of the brutal and radical Taliban (and concurrently al-Qaeda), along with concessions to the Taliban by the Pakistani government, became a just cause of concern. To his credit, Obama decided to send an additional 30,000 troops to Afghanistan. He made the decision (wisely I believe) to follow the precedent of Bush's "surge" in Iraq with one of his own in Afghanistan. (Obama ultimately would approve only 20,000 of the 30,000 troops requested by General Stanley McChrystal.) Even with a smaller force than desired, this strategy proved to be effective in killing many Taliban leaders and their terrorist followers. After McChrystal resigned the position, General David

Petraeus assumed command of U.S and NATO forces in Afghanistan on June 23, 2010, and continued to command a successful operation. (Petraeus, of course, was widely praised as the mastermind behind the "surge" in Iran during the Bush administration.)

We must remember that our mission in Afghanistan has always been to prevent the Taliban from establishing a safe haven for planning and executing global Islamic terrorist attacks in cooperation with al-Qaeda or other terrorist organizations. It was always counterproductive for Obama to insist on an early withdrawal of U.S. and NATO troops. Dangerously, many experts contend, Secretary Panetta promised President Karzai to remove all American troops by the middle of 2013 but to continue to provide "aid and assistance." On his secret surprise visit to Afghanistan on May 1, 2012, the eve of the anniversary of killing Osama bin Laden, President Obama assured Karzai that America would continue foreign aid for economic development for 10 years.

Undoubtedly, the biggest successes[48] in the various fronts of the war against the Islamist terrorists (whom he steadfastly refuses to refer to by their own stated beliefs and mission) came as a result of Obama's willingness to use unmanned drones to target Islamist insurgents. He has greatly expanded this highly effective weapon, first used during the Bush administration, against al-Qaeda and Taliban operatives. Most of such attacks have been launched in and around the lawless border area of Pakistan which feeds into Afghanistan.

Parenthetically, the always brilliant and usually clever Charles Krauthammer wrote an op-ed piece for the June 1, 2012, edition of *The Washington Post* titled "Barack Obama: Drone Warrior." Krauthammer wrote this article in response to the front-page story in *The New York Times*[49] that describes "how, every Tuesday, Barack Obama shuffles 'baseball cards' with the pictures and bios of suspected terrorists from around the world and chooses who shall die by drone strikes. He even reserves for himself the decision of whether to proceed when the probability of killing family or bystanders is significant."

Krauthammer notes in the beginning that he is convinced that this story was not based on a leak or written based on off-the-record conversations. He further stresses that this newspaper article was written with "On-the-record quotes from the highest officials.... This was a White House Press release." Krauthammer speculates that Obama's handlers are trying to make him look like a "tough guy" since he has appeared to be weak in the recent foreign policy arena. For example, Krauthammer continues, the president has looked helpless as the Syrian dictator slaughters his people, ineffective in the nuclear negotiations with Iran, and "treated with contempt" by Russian President Putin when he failed to show for a promised meeting at the G-8 and NATO summits. He adds to this list the backlash of the American people when an attempt was made to use the anniversary of bin Laden's assassination for political purposes.

Krauthammer then contrasts the new macho man to the bleeding heart humanitarian who was horrified by the harsh interrogations of Islamist terrorists under Bush's watch. In his early days as president, Obama wanted to close Guantanamo and the CIA prisons in the war zones. Later he wanted to try the confessed mastermind of 9/11, KSM, in a civilian court in New York City, only a few blocks from the site of the World Trade Center and read the poor would-be Christmas Day bomber his Miranda rights. (Early initiatives by Obama to correct what he claimed to be the inhumane treatment of terrorist prisoners during Bush's presidency will be discussed in detail in following sections of this chapter.)

Now Krauthammer writes that the man who so vilified George W. Bush for allowing harsh interrogations (which never physically harmed anyone, I might add) which enabled the U.S. interrogators to obtain vital information that probably saved thousands, perhaps millions, of American lives, has changed his tune—in Krauthammer's words, "just in time for the 2012 campaign." Krauthammer says of President Obama, "and now you're ostentatiously telling the world that you personally play judge, jury and executioner to unseen combatants of your choosing and whatever innocents happen to be in their company." Charles Krauthammer makes it clear that he is not opposed to using unmanned drones when circumstances dictate. He is simply making the point that dead terrorists don't talk, and therefore provide no timely intelligence that might save many American lives. Krauthammer concludes his article with this message to President Obama:

> "You festoon your prisoners with rights—but you take no prisoners. The morality is perverse. Which is why the results are so mixed. We do kill terror operatives, an important part of the war on terror, but we gratuitously forfeit potentially life-saving intelligence.
>
> "But that will cost us later. For now, we are to bask in the moral seriousness and cool purpose of our drone warrior president."

The Karzai government in Afghanistan is even weaker than the government under al-Maliki in Iraq. (In some fairness, many areas of this vast mountainous country about the size of Texas and ruled by tribal and sub-tribal hierarchies are virtually incapable of being governed.) In any event, the government in Kabul has been characterized as the second most corrupt in the world, and the country has long been the largest producer of poppies that provide much of the world's opium.

In 2011, discussions between Karzai and the American government, he raised the possibility of a negotiated settlement with the Taliban to end the bloody conflict in Afghanistan. The very thought of "peace talks" with the Taliban raised all kinds of red flags, not only among seasoned national security experts but also among human rights activists. Long-time national security and foreign policy scholars conjured up visions of how well that had worked with Hitler and Stalin. Hitler's gas chambers and Stalin's enslavement of the "Captive Nations" in Eastern Europe had left an indelible memory in their minds. Those who have devoted their lives to protecting human rights cried out that the earlier five-year reign of the Taliban had been a human rights nightmare—especially for women and minorities.

In 1996, when Taliban forces captured Kabul, this effectively ended the civil war in Afghanistan and began the Taliban reign of terror. Under the title of the Islamic Emirate of Afghanistan, this militant Islamist political group ruled most of Afghanistan (including 90 percent of the country at the peak of their power) until October 2001, when President Bush ordered the invasion of Afghanistan following the 9/11 attack. (The origin, teachings, and actions of the Taliban will be covered in much more detail in chapters 4 and 5 of this book.)

At this crucial point in the war against the Islamist terrorists in Afghanistan, it is essential to note a few key features about the Taliban that must of necessity factor into any long-term solution. One, most members of the Taliban, and especially their leaders, come from the large, powerful, and influential Pastun tribes. Significantly, Hamid Karzai and his ancestors are also descendents of the Pastun tribes. Secondly, it is widely believed by Pakistani-Afghanistan experts that Pakistan's Inter-Services Intelligence (ISI) was involved in the founding of the Taliban, and was heavily involved, along with Pakistan's military, in the successful Taliban victory in 1996. On the one hand, the ISI and Pakistan military obviously wanted a government in Afghanistan that was friendly to Pakistan. On the other hand, they shared with the Taliban a belief in the radical fundamentalist Wahhabi brand of Islam that dominates Saudi Arabia. The Taliban theocracy in Afghanistan was granted diplomatic relations only by Pakistan, Saudi Arabia, and the UAE.[50]

This history partly explains the sometimes rocky relations the U.S. has experienced since the 9/11 Islamist attacks. The government of Pakistan claims that it ceased to support the Taliban after 9/11, but it still appears to grant them safe passage and a sanctuary in their lawless border regions. Pakistan complained that it was not notified in advance of the SEAL raid that killed Osama bin Laden. Obviously this was a deliberate decision, since most believed that at least elements of the ISI and the military had to know that bin Laden was living in the luxury compound in Abbottabad, Pakistan, for a number of years. Since this compound was located less than a mile from the Pakistan Military Academy, sometimes compared to West Point, most concluded that members of the intelligence service and the military with extremist Islamist sentiments were complicit in bin Laden's lengthy stay in this secure location.

Administration officials rebuffed demands for the CIA to cease the unmanned drone strikes targeting al-Qaeda and Taliban operatives in their hideouts near the Pakistan border. The calls grew louder when a number of Pakistan troops were inadvertently killed in this area. We apologized but made it clear that strikes must continue as long as Islamist terrorists continue to find refuge in such regions.

Another controversy that might involve leaks of highly classified information with major national security implications came to light when the Pakistani doctor who provided confirmation of bin Laden's location was arrested just three weeks after the daring Navy SEAL raid on his compound. Dr. Shakee Afridi, known for providing medical services for the poor in various parts of Pakistan, arrived in Abbottabad on March 16, 2011, to launch a free hepatitis B vaccination campaign. In the early stages of this campaign, he attempted to collected DNA samples from the children living in a plush complex surrounded by high walls, along with many other children in and around Abbottabad. This location was not selected randomly. Our CIA had been observing this compound for some time. On various occasions they spotted an always completely covered mystery man. Initially, some reports were circulated that the DNA testing of the children's swab samples living in the compound confirmed the suspicion that these were the children of the world's most wanted Islamist terrorist. These reports proved to be erroneous.

A *Newsweek* article dated June 18, 2012, probably offers the most accurate details since it was based on interviews with some of those who claimed to have personally witnessed the attempts by the doctor and his staff to get inside the compound. The article reported that it was the unusual security surrounding the compound that confirmed the CIA's suspicions. The article quotes a "senior U.S. official" as explaining that Dr. Afridi's program was real and would have resulted in the vaccination of many children if he would not have been arrested. They contend that although the doctor "couldn't get the DNA samples, he made a valuable contribution to the hunt for bin Laden." *Newsweek* quotes the official as saying, "Dr. Afridi was inadvertently able to confirm what was already suspected—that bin Laden's couriers practiced extraordinary operational security. Was that a key to the raid? No. Was it important? Absolutely."[51]

A month and a half after Dr. Afridi began his immunization program, the Navy SEALs launched their raid. Three weeks later, the doctor was arrested and charged with treason, which could have led to a death sentence. A year later, a Pakistani judge sentenced Dr. Afridi to 33 years in prison on a lesser charge that he allegedly cooperated with the CIA. The Congress responded by symbolically cutting $33 million in foreign aid, a million for each year of Afridi's sentence, to Pakistan. The hot-button question is, how did Pakistani intelligence operatives find out about the role Afridi played in this operation? It appears unlikely such details were leaked by CIA agents in Pakistan who had so carefully guarded the minutest details of this highly successful undertaking![52] The question of whether an intelligence breach may have occurred in this case will be revisited when we examine the most dangerous leaks, involving highly classified national security information, that have occurred under this administration.

It is difficult to deal with the government of Pakistan because they have so many al-Qaeda and Taliban sympathizers in various branches of their government. This comes as a result of the fact that the Wahhabis have built and run the Islamic schools and many of the mosques in this poor country. Saudi oil money continues to spread the radical Wahhabi teachings of Islam that breeds terrorism when taken to the extreme by fundamentalists. Truly moderate Muslims (who fortunately are the strong majority), moderate Muslim countries, and especially moderate Muslim leaders suffer as much—if not more—than non-Muslims when radical fundamentalists become terrorists or sympathizers to the cause of the terrorists.

Almost all of the key government leaders and virtually all of the military commanders in Pakistan are moderate Muslims, but they always have to look over their shoulders for the radical insurgents in their ranks. We must maintain our relationship with Pakistan, not only because of their strategic importance in fighting the terrorists in Afghanistan,[53] but also because Pakistan, like India, has nuclear weapons.

Senator Hilary Clinton's selection as secretary of state was widely praised by moderates and even by many conservatives. Secretary Clinton continues to receive high praise from most Americans, including many of her previous conservative Republican Senate colleagues. With Iran in radical Shiite Islamic hands and on the verge of manufacturing nuclear weapons, the constantly belligerent rogue nation of North Korea with nuclear capability,[54] and the Middle East in general turmoil, she has her hands full. Conservatives, moderates, and many liberals believe that Clinton's hands are the most capable that could have been hoped for in this administration.

A major surprise—and the biggest disappointment—for conservatives was the appointment of Eric Holder as attorney general. Many conservatives—including some conservative Republican senators who voted for his confirmation—believe that Holder has become the major spokesman for the radical left-wing ACLU at the expense of security concerns of a nation facing unprecedented threats from Islamic terrorism. Not surprisingly, he is the new darling of the hard left and self-appointed "civil libertarians." Holder jumped into all the causes important to the hard left from the beginning and remains in the center of most of the major controversies troubling this administration three and a half years later.

Just months after Holder became attorney general, the justice dropped a civil suit brought by the Bush administration against the New Black Panther Party and its chairman for voter intimidation. Two members of this party, also charged, had stood outside a polling station in Philadelphia dressed in paramilitary uniforms, one of whom was armed with a billy club. During a congressional hearing two years later, Holder was asked why such serious charges of voter intimidation were dismissed. He defiantly responded, "When you compare what people endured in the South in the '60s to try to get the right to vote for African Americans, to compare what people subjected to that with what happened in Philadelphia . . . I think does a great disservice to people who put their lives on the line for my people."[55]

Was this obviously heartfelt explanation based on ingrained racism? The fact that he refers to "African Americans" as "*my people*" raises suspicions that race considerations may influence some of his decisions. The American voters had just elected the first black president in the country's history. Even most of those totally opposed to Obama's policies are not unhappy that the color barrier was breached. The overwhelming majority of Americans, with the exception of a handful of white supremacists and a small number of old diehard segregationists, are certainly not proud of the fact that many blacks were denied the right to vote in the old Jim Crow days in the South. (In a few cases in those days, more black voters might have changed the outcome in the Democrat primary—that was all that mattered at the time, since the Democrat nominee was virtually always elected in the general election.)

Apparently Eric Holder decided that it now was time for blacks to punish whites for their past political sins by making efforts to keep them from voting. President Obama had already publically called out the recently sworn-in attorney general for remarks he made at the Justice Department Feb. 18, 2009. During an observance of Black History Month, Holder told Justice Department employees, in what would become known as his "Nation of Cowards" remarks, "Though race-related issues continue to occupy a significant portion of our political discussion and though there remain many unresolved racial issues in this nation, we average Americans simply do not talk enough with each other about race."[56]

In Helene Cooper's March 7, 2009, *New York Times* article, "Attorney General Chided for Language on Race," she quotes President Obama as saying, "I think it's fair to say that if I had been advising my attorney general, we would have used different language."

Such statements have led various political authorities to question Holder's motives in opposing state Voter ID laws. After the hotly disputed 2000 presidential vote in Florida, the results of which determined whether George W. Bush or Al Gore would become the 43rd president of the United States, most states considered steps to prevent voter fraud. With the memory of "hanging chads" and extensive challenges by both parties to the validity of thousands of ballots fresh in their minds, 31 states have now passed laws requiring some type of voter ID. In addition, the Congress in 2002 passed and President Bush signed into law the "Help America Vote Act." This law mandated that those who register to vote by mail or who had not voted in a previous federal election show a photo ID or a copy of some valid document such as a bank statement, utility bill, a paycheck or some other valid government document showing the voter's name and home address. As recently as May 30, 2012, Holder told black church leaders who gathered at the Conference of National Black Churches that a requirement to show a photo ID, for example, at a polling place was "an unfair burden on non-white voters." *The Huffington Post* also notes that in this speech,

> "Attorney General Eric Holder told members of the Congressional Black Caucus and the Conference of National Black Churches on Wednesday that the right to vote was threatened across the country.

"'The reality is that in jurisdictions across the country, both overt and subtle forms of discrimination remain all too common and have not yet been to the pages of history,' Holder told the audience, made up of black church and political leaders, during a faith leaders summit in Washington." [57]

Eric Holder dogmatically continues to insist that all efforts by 30 state legislatures and the U.S. Congress to protect the right of each American citizen to cast *one* vote is motivated by racism.[58] Who gives him the right to accuse in mass those dedicated lawmakers trying to prevent vote fraud of having racist intentions? Poor people of any color would benefit immensely by having a valid ID that would afford them access to privileges that most people take for granted. (Several states have offered free photo IDs to those who cannot afford to purchase them.)

With the 2012 election approaching, many politicians—in and out of D.C.—including a significant number of Democrats, now believe that Eric Holder's unabashed arrogance is creating unwanted and untimely problems for President Obama and could well end his checkered political career. Holder has come under increasing fire over the last year for the way he handled the code-named "Fast and Furious" gunwalking scandal, which reached its boiling point in June 2012.[59] While he is under a contempt of Congress citation for refusing to provide congressionally subpoenaed documents deemed essential for ongoing House and Senate investigations of this failed operation he could be facing even bigger problems. This scandal, which has resulted in the death of many Mexican citizens and at least one Border Patrol agent, Brian Terry, has now been joined by the unveiling of national security leaks[60] that could put untold numbers of Americans in imminent danger. Sen. John McCain, who is almost universally recognized as an authority on national security matters by his colleagues, says that these intelligence breaches are the most serious he has ever seen.

In a story posted on the *Politico* Web site shortly after a Senate oversight hearing on June 12, 2012, writer Josh Gerstein puts Holder's predicament into perspective:

"Republicans unleashed a two-front attack on the attorney general. They assailed him during a regularly scheduled oversight hearing, where he faced new calls for his resignation, and on the Senate floor, where Sen. John McCain (R-Ariz.) introduced a resolution, urging a special counsel for the leak probe.

"Several GOP senators tried to weave the Fast and Furious and leak-related stories into a common narrative. Sen. John Cornyn (R-Texas) linked the two as he called for the first time for Holder to step down.

'There has been zero accountability at the Department of Justice.... The leaking of classified information represents a major threat to national security, and your office will not appoint a special counsel,' Cornyn told the attorney general. 'Meanwhile, you still resist coming clean about what you knew and when you knew it with regard to Operation Fast and Furious. You won't cooperate with the legitimate congressional investigation, and you won't hold anyone—including yourself—accountable.

"'It is more with sorrow than regret and anger that I would say that you leave me no alternative than to join those who call upon you to resign your office,' Cornyn said."[61]

The leaks of highly classified information involving cyber-warfare against Iran and the "kill list" of Islamist terrorists greatly alarmed prominent Democrats charged with intelligence responsibilities, as well as their Republican counterparts. Senator Dianne Feinstein, the highly respected liberal Democrat from California who chairs the Senate Select Committee on Intelligence, appeared at a press conference specifically to condemn such dangerous leaks. Flanked by Sen. Saxby Chambliss of Georgia, the ranking Republican on the committee; Congressman Mike Rogers (R-Mich.), chairman of the House Permanent Select Committee on Intelligence, and Congressman Dutch Ruppersberger of Maryland, the ranking Democrat on the committee, said that such leaks "jeopardize American lives." She added that they complicate our joint efforts with foreign governments[62] as well as our ability to recruit spies to infiltrate terrorist organizations. She emphatically stated, "This has to stop!"

Congressman Ruppersberger approached the microphone to assure the listeners that "The facts will go where they lead." He assured them, "This is bipartisan, Democrats and Republicans working together as Americans." Neither Feinstein nor Ruppersberger have criticized Holder or called for a special prosecutor (at least not publicly). These Democrats would obviously not be in a position to suggest that these leaks were politically motivated in an effort to make the president look strong on national security.

Republicans, like Senators McCain, Chambliss and Lindsey Graham (R-S.C.), as well as House Speaker John Boehner, point out that the information leaked was so sensitive and highly classified that it had to come from "the highest level of government." They don't have much trouble making the case. *The New York Times* article of May 29, 2012, described how every Tuesday Obama selects the terrorists for the week's targets to be killed by drone attacks quotes such sources. These sources give dates and exact quotes from the president and vice president from meetings in the Situation Room with the head of the CIA. (I was told by an impeccable source that, immediately after General Petraeus, who is now the director of the CIA, was informed of the *Times* article, he made a quick trip to the White House to confront the participants in these meetings with the words "shut up!," that they are endangering the security of America. He may have explained to them that if they want to portray the president as a strong leader in national security matters to pick examples that do not in fact compromise our national security.) The Republicans contend, with justification I am convinced, that with Holder selecting U.S. attorneys, even with good reputations, they are put in an awkward position, to say the least. They will be required to investigate high-ranking members of the administration under which they also serve.

Sen. Joe Lieberman (Ind –Conn.),[63] chairman of the Senate Committee on Homeland Security and Governmental Affairs, has joined Republicans in calling for the appointment of a "special counsel" to investigate the security leaks in order to "avoid any appearance of a conflict of interest." Many have noted that as a freshman U.S. senator, Barack Obama was one of the loudest voices calling for a special prosecutor in the Valerie Plame case under the Bush administration. The Bush administration did appoint a special prosecutor, and Scooter Libby, a top aide to Vice President Chaney, ended up spending time in prison. The charges brought against Libby and the outcome of his trial were—and still are—hotly disputed. No one was killed, no lives were placed in eminent danger, and only the cover of one questionable "covert" CIA agent was "blown."[64] The leaking of classified national security material was so minimal in this case involving *one* agent that it is hardly worth mentioning. When you compare this exposure to today's intelligence "leaks," which could have devastating consequences in the war with radical Islamists, the differences are exponential. But President Bush apparently felt so strongly that even the most minor breach of highly classified national security information could not be tolerated that he steadfastly refused to intervene. This was in spite of the fact that almost every conservative in America was crying out against Libby's unjust treatment.

The continuing exposure of sensitive and highly classified national-security information suggests that such leaks are becoming a pattern in this administration. I am beginning to suspect that the leaking of sensitive classified information could replace the old political scandals involving sex and money in previous elections. It is certainly not beyond the realm of possibility that the 2012 presidential election could become known as the "Intelligence-gate" election. The only possible motive for these clearly deliberate leaks, at least in some cases, is that they are motivated by political concerns. (No recognized and respected political authority has even suggested that such actions were driven by a desire to assist our enemies.) I believe that all such leaks have been driven by the desire to enhance President Obama's image as a bold and decisive wartime commander-in-chief!

Let us consider the scandals involving leaks of very sensitive national-security information;

1.   *The New York Times* article, referenced above, using direct quotes from people in the room, describes Obama's dominating role in the Situation Room as he selects the targets on the "kill list" for the pending drone attacks. This may appear effective in a PR campaign,

but look how it affects our enemies. They not only become more fanatically determined to seek revenge on any American target, but they get valuable information on how to detect and avoid such strikes.

2.   The leaking of intelligence concerning the U.S.-Israel cyber-warfare campaign to disrupt Iran's development of nuclear weapons has destroyed its effectiveness. It may have made the president look smart, but it also undoubtedly emboldens the Iranians and causes the Israelis to distrust our reliability as a partner in such an undertaking.

3.   The joint U.S.-Saudi operation to recruit a double agent to infiltrate al-Qaeda in Yemen (known as al-Qaeda in the Arabian Peninsula or AQAP) is now public knowledge. The operative convinced them that he was a willing suicide bomber and persuaded them to give him a new-type non-metallic bomb to smuggle aboard an airplane. U.S. intelligence operatives waited for him outside Yemen, and the bomb is now being analyzed at the FBI's bomb lab in Quantico, Va. They are trying to determine if such a bomb could have been smuggled through airport security. Obama may now look more creative in some voters' minds but the world now know another of our classified secrets. Saudi Arabia might be worried about just how loud our mouth really is. Meanwhile, we can be sure that AQAP is trying to design another bomb that might better evade our airport security.

4.   Undoubtedly the most serious national security breach—certainly in modern times—involves the details released and/or leaked information regarding the Navy SEAL mission that killed Osama bin Laden. The news accounts and TV reports of this daring mission had most Americans glued to their newspapers and TV sets. The follow-up documentaries shortly after the raid and on its first anniversary were spellbinding! They certainly made America's president look strong. But the backlash they created in Pakistan and Afghanistan is, and will continue to be, very costly in terms of American lives and treasure. The propaganda value to al-Qaeda, the Taliban, and other such Islamist organizations for recruiting untold numbers of new terrorist recruits is bad enough. But the number of lives of Navy SEALS, America's bravest and best men, that may be put at risk by this publicity is beyond heartrending! It is totally irresponsible!

5.   All of these reprehensible violations of America's most closely held secrets have made some experts question if loose, or braggadocios, lips were responsible for the fate of the patriotic Pakistani doctor, Dr. Shakil Afridi, who was known by his colleagues as a devout Muslim who said his prayers daily. While also known as a man with a sense of humor who liked to have fun on occasion, he was loved by the poor in

certain Pakistani tribal areas not controlled by radical Islamists as a caring man who provided medical care to those who had no other source for it. Will we sit idly by as he suffers in a Pakistani jail?

As the attorney general, Eric Holder is the top law enforcement officer in America and has the responsibility to seek to punish those responsible for these extremely serious breaches of national security. In this position, he always has had ultimate responsibility for the operations of the ATF, the Border Patrol, and the U.S attorneys stationed around the country. (No senator, congressman, or any other official in a position of authority ever accused Attorney General Holder—and certainly not President Obama—of approving or even knowing about the "gun-walking" program, code named "Fast and Furious," in its early stages.)

In plain language, this program was designed to allow certain high-powered weapons to be smuggled into Mexico so ATF and Border Patrol agents could track them to the Mexican drug cartel leaders who were paying for the guns and using them. This undertaking became high profile and gained tragic notoriety when Border Patrol Agent Brian Terry was murdered Dec. 14, 2010. At the scene of the crime were found two AK-pattern rifles, which were subsequently positively identified as among the weapons that had been "gun walked" into Mexico.

The ever-vigilant and always sincere Republican Senator Chuck Grassley was contacted by the family of the slain Border Patrol agent. He immediately launched an unofficial investigation by writing a letter to the acting director of ATF on Jan. 27, 2011, asking about the "gun-walking" program and whether one such "walked" gun was involved in Terry's murder. Unbelievably, Assistant Attorney General Robert Welch just days later, on Feb. 4, 2011, responded to Grassley's letter and denied that any such program was sanctioned by ATF. Grassley then contacted Congressman Darrell Issa, chairman of the House Committee on Oversight and Government Reform, and asked him to undertake a committee investigation of this operation that appeared to have gotten out of control.

The cautious and always-fair Chairman Issa asked his investigative staff to look into the matter immediately. They would ultimately discover that more than 2,000 such weapons had been "walked" into Mexico and the program had lost track of more than a thousand of these weapons. (There had been 20 arrests of suspected drug cartel leaders and a 53-count indictment had been brought against them. But evidence had also been uncovered of the deaths of many ordinary Mexican citizens as a result of the use of these guns.)

Had Holder and other administration officials cooperated with congressional investigators and turned over the documents requested by Issa's committee, the matter would not have gotten out of hand. But their stonewalling led to congressional subpoenas for documents the staff knew existed. The matter really got out of hand when Holder testified before the House Judiciary Committee (which also had taken an interest in the matter) in May 2011 and claimed that he did not know who authorized Fast and Furious and that he had just found out about the operation "over the last few weeks." Holder's credibility was shattered when documents were discovered in October 2011 revealing that Holder had been sent briefing papers on Fast and Furious as early as July 2010. Holder continued to refuse to deliver the requested documents. Obama's involvement with Holder in the Fast and Furious scandal became permanent when he invoked executive privilege as the House Oversight Committee prepared to vote to hold AG Holder in "contempt of Congress" for his blatant refusal to provide the subpoenaed documents.

As these developments unfolded, House Speaker John Boehner issued a statement in which he charged that by claiming executive privilege[65] after his administration had refused to provide the subpoenaed documents, Obama as well as Holder was proven to be involved in a cover-up.

"The decision to invoke executive privilege is an admission that White House officials were involved in decisions that misled the Congress and have covered up the truth." Boehner said, and then asked, "So what is the Obama administration hiding in Fast and Furious?"[66]

Those who follow politics will remember that it was not the Watergate scandal but the cover-up that ended up forcing Richard Nixon to resign the office of president. Obama's decision to associate himself so closely with Holder's problems, which include his refusal to appoint a special prosecutor to investigate the high-profile national security leaks, has come as a surprise to many in Washington. With the House of Representatives voting to hold AG Holder in contempt of Congress, the 2012 election could be remembered as "Holder-gate."

During his initial days in office, Obama created a firestorm of criticism from conservatives and moderates (amid cries of jubilation from the far left) with executive orders and stated intentions in respect to intelligence gathering, confinement of terrorist prisoners, and their prosecution. He issued orders to close the Guantanamo Bay prison within a year,[67] to close overseas CIA prisons,[68] and to ban enhanced interrogation techniques that had been used on high-value known Islamic terrorist detainees in the aftermath of the 9/11 attacks.[69] The ACLU and its radical left-wing allies were elated. These left-wing crazies, in the name of "civil rights" of all things, wanted to make sure that these brutal mass murders were not subjected to even minimal pain. Keeping America safe and sparing future victims of their attacks from horrific deaths never seems to cross their minds.

Then a few months later came the bombshell that rocked the political and intelligence communities in the nation's capital. President Obama decided to release four highly classified memos written by Justice Department lawyers providing legal rationale for the enhanced interrogation techniques used on such high-value terrorist detainees. The harsh interrogation methods described in detail in these memos were deemed necessary to gain urgent timely information to prevent other planned attacks. Most knowledgeable political observers, regardless of political persuasion, would agree that making public these memos was a further concession by Obama to his far-left supporters. The damage to the CIA and other intelligence agencies may be almost irreparable. The detailed information provided to the Islamic terrorists is absolutely invaluable to them. What foreign intelligence organizations will ever again trust the United States to keep a secret?

I can remember President Roosevelt during World War II warning the American people that "loose lips sink ships." Perhaps most serious is the fact that the president has tied his own hands in the case of a potential urgent and imminent terrorist threat that could endanger hundreds of thousands, if not millions, of American lives. Even if he were to decide in the face of such a potential emergency to disregard his own directive, what techniques would be available that the terrorists had not prepared possible captives to overcome?

Four former directors of the CIA as well as Obama's own current director, Leon Panetta, strongly advised against releasing these memos. The people who held the most crucial positions of authority when such interrogations were being carried out testify to the extreme value of the information obtained to prevent other 9/11 type attacks. Some information in declassified documents reveal that Abu Zubaydah, an aide to Osama bin Laden, finally "coughed up" the name Ramzi bin al-Shibh after having been water-boarded numerous times. Similar harsh interrogation on al-Shibh led to the disclosure and capture of Khalid Sheik Mohammed (often referenced as "KSM"), the now self-confessed mastermind of the 9/11 attack.

Amid the shock of President Obama's announcement of the release of the CIA memos, political firestorms broke out over questions of whether government officials involved in such interrogation methods would be subject to potential prosecution and whether Congress had been adequately briefed about the program.

When President Obama initially made his surprise announcement to forbid such interrogations, he vowed to look forward and not to the past. He initially stated that CIA operatives and others involved in devising and carrying out such directives, which he believed to constitute torture in violation of the Geneva Conventions, would not be subject to potential prosecution. However, in subsequent statements, Obama refused to include the lawyers at the Justice Department who had been called upon to evaluate the use of such interrogation techniques among those who should not be subject to prosecution. He stated that "no one is above the law" and that Attorney General Eric Holder, as the nation's top law enforcement official, would have to decide if such lawyers should be held accountable.

Congressmen, senators, former CIA and Justice Department officials, and a host of political prognosticators cried out that any such prosecutions (or other punitive actions) would have a major chilling effect on future dedicated public service in the intelligence community. The United States had been attacked by an enemy that recognized no humane standards of conduct, and most importantly, the threats of additional terrorist attacks hung heavily over a shocked and grieving nation.

(Many agonizing months later, filled with needless acrimony—causing not only heartburn but urgent justifiable concerns throughout the entire intelligence community—Attorney General Holder reluctantly stated that no charges would be pursued.)

An Already Weakened CIA Is Further Demoralized

The public controversy over the CIA's use of "enhanced" interrogation techniques has had certain devastating consequences for the intelligence community. Its vital role in protecting our security in this dangerous world is indisputable. In the early 1970s, the "Church Commission" (named for former Sen. Frank Church [D-Idaho]) was convened after the Vietnam War and Watergate and began to tie the hands of the FBI, CIA, and other intelligence organizations. (There were certainly some abuses during this period. But in frequent congressional fashion, the cure was much worse for the country than the disease.)

Things had just begun to improve when during the Carter years the House Intelligence Committee, chaired by Rep. Otis Pike (D-NY) at the time leaked some classified material that resulted in the murder of a CIA station chief in Athens, Greece. This was followed by President Carter's appointment of Admiral Stansfield Turner as director of the CIA. Shortly after his appointment, Turner wiped out virtually all human intelligence when he abolished 820 operational positions in the infamous "Halloween Massacre." To be sure, recruiting moles is a messy and somewhat disgusting business. They are normally not nice people. They usually have criminal records and live on the dark side. But Sunday-school teachers are not likely to be able to infiltrate the KKK, much less some Islamist terrorist cell!

Many believe that the ability to gather high-value intelligence in a timely manner will emerge as one of the biggest problems for the Obama administration. A number of close calls in preventing additional Islamic terrorist attacks that would have resulted in massive human carnage will be referenced below and discussed in some detail in the next chapter.

Attorney General Holder made even larger headlines in November 2009 when he announced that Khalid Sheik Mohammed, the mastermind of the 9/11 attack, the highest ranking and highest-value al-Qaeda terrorist ever captured, would be tried in civilian court in New York City, within blocks of the cowardly attack. The ground on which the Twin Towers once stood is considered almost "sacred" because of the memory of the Americans who lost their lives in the first jihadist attack on American soil. The outcry of protest for such an irresponsible decision was loud, emotional, incredulous, and, most importantly, bipartisan.

Theories abound about Holder's motives in persuading President Obama to prosecute KSM and four other 9/11 co-conspirators in the federal courthouse at Foley Square, less than a mile from the site of the World Trade Center. Many insisted that trying the worst war criminals in human history as ordinary criminals in a civilian court was a travesty. They did not deserve the benefits of the humane American civilian justice system; they should be tried in military tribunals as despicable war criminals.

Holder's moderate and conservative critics would contend that he has become the face of the far-left political movement that exerts major influence on President Obama. Whatever Holder's political motives might have been, he took the initial steps to obtain the high-powered support of the political leaders necessary to move KSM's trial to civilian court. These included Secretary of Defense Robert Gates, Secretary of State Hillary Clinton, Secretary of Homeland Security Janet Napolitano, New York Governor David Paterson, New York City Mayor Michael Bloomberg, and New York's powerful, liberal senior senator, Chuck Schumer, among others.

Despite the carefully orchestrated plans by Holder and his assistants to circumvent the Bush administration's intentions to try these jihadist war criminals in a military tribunal at Gitmo,[70] they made one critical mistake. They failed to factor in the intensity of the hostile reaction by the American people and their elected officials. The hard left has massive financial and technical resources, but the American people are more resilient and informed than the elitist left realizes. As expected, strong objections were raised by conservatives. But moderates and traditional liberals also concluded that the Constitution was never intended to be a suicide pact. Concluding that Islamic terrorists are entitled to the protections of the U.S. Constitution and the Bill of Rights is outright folly.

Initial criticism centered on the prohibitive cost of providing security in New York City during the trial, the likelihood of provoking new terrorist attacks, the spectacle of providing KSM a platform to spew forth anti-America jihadist rhetoric, and even more seriously, the concern over revealing tons of sensitive classified intelligence material to terrorists during the discovery process and the cross examination of witnesses. All of these and additional concerns were heatedly debated in the context of the widespread concerns of granting hardened Islamic terrorists who recognize no humane or civilized standards of warfare the same legal rights as American citizens. These precious legal rights, bought with the blood of patriots, should not be squandered on those who would only view such a humane gesture as a sign of weakness.

After six weeks of intense debate over trying jihadists in civilian courts massive new fuel was poured on this raging fire when the so-called Christmas Day "underwear bomber" was read *his* Miranda rights according to Holder's instructions. Umar Farouk Abdulmutallab, the Nigerian who had received his terrorist training and explosives from al-Qaeda in Yemen, was interrogated for about 50 minutes by FBI agents under the "public-safety exception" to Miranda. Then, as Jane Mayer noted in *The New Yorker*, he was informed of his right to remain silent. She writes:

"He divulged time-sensitive intelligence: he had been trained in Yemen, by affiliates of Al-Qaeda, and had obtained explosives from them. After he received medical treatment, a Justice Department source said, he started to 'act like a jihadi and recite the Koran.' He stopped cooperating and demanded a lawyer, at which point authorities read him his rights. On 'Inside Washington,' Charles Krauthammer declared that it was 'almost criminal' that Holder had allowed Abdulmutallab access to an attorney. Rudy Giuliani, the former mayor of New York, appeared on ABC, saying, 'Why in God's name would you stop questioning a terrorist?'" [71]

Fortunately, the parents of this would-be bomber traveled to the U.S. and convinced their son to cooperate further with American authorities. The fact that this foreign terrorist remained silent for five weeks before his family convinced him to cooperate could have been disastrous. He could have been in possession of vital information about additional attacks being planned in Yemen by al-Qaeda during this five-week timeframe.

The already heated debate over holding the trial for KSM and his co-conspirators in New York got hotter. Prominent Democrats began to get off the ill-conceived New York trial train. The wheels began to fall off the week of Jan. 25, 2010, when Mayor Bloomberg changed his earlier position and demanded that the KSM trial be held somewhere other than New York City. Junior New York Senator Kristen Gillibrand and Congresswoman Nydia Velazquez (D-NY) came out almost immediately against holding the trial in NYC. On Jan. 29, the chairman of the Senate intelligence committee, Dianne Feinstein (D-Calif.), sent a letter to President Obama, stating, "Without getting into classified details, I believe we should view the attempted Christmas Day plot as a continuation, not an end, of plots to strike the United States by al-Qaeda and its affiliates." She continued, "Moreover, New York City has been a high-priority target since at least the first World Trade Center bombing in 1993. The trial of the most significant terrorist in custody would add to the threat." [72]

The same afternoon, senior New York Sen. Chuck Schumer issued a statement that it is "obvious" that the KSM trial must be moved from NYC. (It was also obvious that the same U.S. Congress that had refused to appropriate the funds to close down Guantanamo until a plan was in place to relocate the terrorist detainees somewhere other than the United States would not allocate the funds necessary to hold a trial of the terrorists in New York.)

Holder's determination to try Islamic terrorists as criminals in civil court rather than as enemy combatants in military tribunals reached a new peak of opposition when he ordered the Miranda rights read to the would be Times Square terrorist bomber, who was in fact a naturalized American citizen.

On Saturday, May 1, 2010, Faisal Shahzad parked his SUV filled with massive explosives in Times Square. An alert street vender noticed smoke oozing out of the back of the vehicle and immediately notified the police. Less than 54 hours later, authorities took Shahzad off an already loaded airliner bound for Dubai.

Immediately after the explosives-filled vehicle was discovered, Mayor Bloomberg cautioned against overreacting, saying this was probably the work of a lone wolf or deranged individual. Administration officials in Washington echoed similar sentiments. Certainly none of these people wanted to be so "politically incorrect" as to suggest this might be part of an organized Islamist terrorist attack. Once Shahzad's identity was revealed, *The Washington Post* him as a "down on his luck" fellow who had failed to pay his mortgage, resulting in foreclosure, and this was probably what motivated the attack.

The facts in this case, which will be discussed in more detail in Chapter 4, tell a very different story. Shahzad came from a prominent Pakistani family, married an American-born woman of Pakistani heritage, which enabled him to obtain American citizenship, and brought back large sums of money, including $80,000 on more than one occasion. He travelled back to Pakistan dozens of times during his 10-year stay in the United States. On his most recent trip to Pakistan, he had received six months of intensive terrorist training at a Taliban camp in North Waziristan. Fortunately, he did not remember enough to buy the right type of fertilizer, he failed to open the valve on the propane cylinder, and he was unable to successfully ignite these powerful explosives. Otherwise, we would have experienced another 9/11-type disaster at Times Square, most likely involving even more human carnage. House Republican Leader, John Boehner, aptly stated, "Yes we were lucky, but luck is not an effective strategy for fighting terrorism."

The politically correct types became obsessed with the question of when Shahzad had become radicalized. It is known that his family was made up of mostly moderate Muslims in Pakistan—some members of his mother's family were even adherents of the relatively small sect of Sufi mystics who are noted for their tolerance. Yet I have not noticed anyone of prominence mention that the radical Wahhabis run most of the madrassas in Pakistan, which are funded by Saudi oil money. It is highly likely that Shahzed was simply reverting back to the extremist Wahhabi teachings to which he had been exposed in his youth.

Attorney General Holder, in testimony before the House Judiciary Committee, was reluctant even to admit that "radical Islam" was "part of the cause" of this attempted attack and other recent attacks or attempted attacks. Congressman Lamar Smith (R-Texas), the ranking Republican on the committee, asked Holder "whether 'radical Islam' was behind the attempted car bombing, last year's so-called 'underpants bomber,' or the killings at Fort Hood in Texas," as reported in *The Washington Times*.[73] Holder told the committee: "There are a variety of reasons why people do these things. *Some of them are potentially religious*" (emphasis added).

Congressman Smith was incredulous in his response: "I don't know why the administration has such difficulty acknowledging the obvious, which is that radical Islam might have excited these individuals." He then astutely pointed out, "If you can't name the enemy, then you're going to have a hard time trying to respond to them."

Holder typifies an attitude of some in this administration that appears to reach to the highest level. They either are so committed to a policy of political correctness that ignores obvious facts, mistakenly believing this serves the interest of moderate Muslims, or they are totally ignorant of the clearly stated motivations and goals of global Islamic terrorism. It is increasingly obvious that they have no understanding of the divergent teachings of Islam; the varied history of Islam, which includes hundreds of years of Muslim conquest and attempted conquest of Christian lands; the multitude of Muslim revivalist movements that seek a return to "pure" or fundamentalist Islam; and the extensive statements of such modern-day jihadist leaders as the late Osama bin Laden.

Just two weeks after Holder's appearance before the House Judiciary Committee, John Brennan, President Obama's advisor on counterintelligence and homeland security matters at the National Security Council, addressed the Center for Strategic and International Studies. Listening to Brennan on C-SPAN convinced me and, I believe, anyone with even an elementary knowledge of Islam and Islamic history that a blind commitment to political correctness leads to naïveté on the subject.

For example, Brennan explained that this administration would no longer use the words "jihadist" or "Islamist" because "jihad is a holy struggle, a legitimate tenet of Islam, meaning to purify oneself or one's community." Yes, this is one meaning of *jihad*, perhaps even the earliest meaning. But numerous Muslim and non-Muslim scholars have cited many examples where *jihad* also was frequently used in a military context. Some scholars document as many as 114 occasions where *"jihad"* is used in the Koran in a clear military context. Volumes have been written by Islamic scholars and jurists over the years on the different requirements for Muslim men's participation in "offensive" and "defensive" jihadist military actions.

Brennan suggested in answer to one question that a study of behavioral sciences might be productive in determining the motivation of such terrorists. Apparently, he remains unimpressed with their own statements that they are carrying out Allah's will, emphasized by the usual last cry of the suicide bomber, *"Allahu Akbar!"*

Brennan further stated his opinion that there is "no single cause" for the attacks of homegrown or foreign terrorists and no defining "terrorist profile." He is certainly correct that that there is no consistent profile based on education, social standing or station in life. These terrorists are sometimes highly educated and sometimes illiterate, some are rich while others come from poverty, some are young while others are old, and the list goes on and on. If you rule out their religious convictions, then they cannot be profiled. The only "single cause" is their religious convictions.

Why is it so difficult for the leaders of this administration—and Brennan notes similar attitudes in the previous administration—to understand that realistically recognizing the jihadist fervor of our terrorist enemies is not a disservice to the vast majority of moderate or peaceful Muslims throughout the world. On the contrary, being honest is a service of respect to moderate Muslims. It offers them the opportunity to clearly separate themselves from—and to emphatically condemn—these sworn Islamic jihadists who they believe to be following teachings they consider illegitimate.

No responsible or recognized leader, no matter how far to the right or the left, has ever suggested that we are at war with Islam. We are at war with global Islamist terrorists who have declared war on America in the name of their religious beliefs.

Obama's 'Foreign Apology Tour' to Saudi Arabia and Egypt

In June 2009, President Obama embarked on his first official visit to the Arab World.

On June 3, the president and his party were in Saudi Arabia on the eve of his much-anticipated address to the Muslim world in Cairo. Obama was scheduled to meet Saudi King Abdullah, primarily on the subject of Palestinian-Israeli peace negotiations. On the same day, a study examining the official Saudi government textbooks used in the kingdom's schools was released in the United States. The textbooks had been smuggled out of Saudi Arabia and translated by the Institute for Gulf Affairs.

The study of seven Saudi textbooks used in grades 6 through 12 revealed that these books "teach children to hate Jews and Christians and to use violence against them." The study was released at a press conference by three Democrat congressmen—Anthony Weiner and Joseph Crowley of New York and Shelley Berkley of Nevada—who hoped to draw attention to the problem before the president's meeting with the Saudi monarch. Weiner also sent an urgent letter to Obama condemning the hate-filled teachings and urged him to discuss the matter with Saudi leaders.

There is not a shred of evidence that President Obama even raised the issue with the king or any other Saudi official. It's a sure bet that Obama also did not mention the total lack of religious freedom in Saudi Arabia and the country's disgraceful treatment of women to Abdullah. The White House released few details of the meeting, saying mainly that the two men were further developing their personal relationship. At this point, Obama is better known for bowing to King Abdullah at an earlier G-20 summit meeting in London than for discussing any substantive issues with the king.[74]

The stage was set for Obama's eagerly awaited maiden speech to the Muslim world. The site for the speech was historic Cairo University. The Muslim world was already excited because the president's middle name is "Hussein," he has a Muslim heritage on his father's side, and he is the first American president ever to deliver a major speech in Egypt.

Obama stated clearly that America's bond with Israel was unbreakable, but he also insisted that the plight of the Palestinians is "intolerable." He also stated that "The United States does not accept the legitimacy of continued Israeli settlements."

The day after the speech, Saudi Foreign Minister Prince Saud al-Faisal told *Newsweek's* Christopher Dickey that "He called Israeli settlements in the West Bank 'not legitimate'—and this is more important, and stronger, than 'not legal,' which has often been repeated." Israel's right-wing coalition, headed up by Prime Minister Benjamin Netanyahu, has consistently opposed a settlement freeze and a two-state solution, which is also advocated by Obama.

"I have come here to seek a new beginning between the United States and Muslims around the world; one based upon mutual interest and respect; and one based upon the truth that America and Islam are not exclusive, and need not be in competition. Instead, they overlap, and share common principles—principles of justice and progress; tolerance and the dignity of all human beings," Obama confidently declared in his opening remarks at Cairo University.

Obama then admits—reluctantly, one might suspect—that "No single speech can eradicate years of mistrust, nor can I answer in the time that I have all the complex questions that brought us to this point." (The implication seems to be that if he just had the time, he could answer these complex questions in ways that mere mortals might understand.)

Then President Obama says that as we move forward, we must "say openly the things we hold in our hearts and that too often are said only behind closed doors." A few sentences later, he makes this claim: "And throughout history, Islam has demonstrated through words and deeds the possibilities of religious tolerance and racial equality."

These words must have sounded as strange to Muslims as they do to Christians and Jews who have any familiarity with Islamic teachings and history. The concepts of "religious tolerance" and "racial equality," in the true sense of their meanings, are specifically forbidden in the Koran and the theological writings of Islamic scholars and clerics. As is documented throughout this book, religious tolerance in the Koran is not afforded to "those who have been given the Book, until they pay the tax in acknowledgement of superiority and they are in the state of subjection" (Koran 9:29). Christians have been treated better in some Muslim countries at one time or another, but they have never been considered religious equals, with a few rare exceptions—the best example would be during the Shah's rule in Iran.

The mere suggestion that Muslim authorities could recognize "racial equality" is totally contrary to Muslim history, unless women are not considered to be a part of a race. In all official Islamic teachings, Muslim women are always considered to have half the value of Muslim men. This is true when women are witnesses, receiving an inheritance, and in all other areas of human activity. They are to stay in their place and serve their Muslim husbands in total obedience. (This is not meant to suggest that all, or even most, Muslims accept their official teachings. We have no way of knowing what is in any religious believer's heart. Polls suggest that this is not the case for most Muslims in America, for example. But Obama was addressing Muslim leaders in his official capacity.)

Obama obviously felt that if he cataloged the highlights of Christian-Western mistakes—sins committed by inept leaders—this would reassure the Muslim world. They would then know that he understands what caused some Muslim extremists to react in such a violent (a word he would never use) fashion. Surely, Obama must have reasoned that such a heartfelt confession would inspire Muslim leaders of all stripes to follow his humane example! (Osama bin Laden, Iran's President Mahmoud Ahmadinejad, and Supreme Leader Ayatollah Ali Khamenei might even be moved to tears!)

In a totally unwarranted gesture to the brutal and oppressive Islamic Republic of Iran, Obama confesses that America once helped overthrow an Iranian government (that of Iranian Prime Minister Mohammad Mosaddegh, in 1953). Obama contrasted this CIA coup, which he apparently thought was a "sin," to those of Iran after the overthrow of the Shah in 1979 and the subsequent consolidation of power by Ayatollah Khomeini. Columnist Charles Krauthammer explains how Obama proceeds to mildly chide Iran, "while on the other hand 'Iran has played a role in acts of hostage-taking and violence against U.S. troops and civilians.' (Played a role?!) We have both sinned, let us bury the past and begin anew."[75]

Obama's "outreach" to Iran not only smacked of groveling, but it was so factually inaccurate that it is unbecoming to have been uttered by any American (educated or uneducated), much less by an American president. Many scholars—and not only conservative scholars—contend that the so-called "coup of 1953" is among the best things the CIA has ever done. Certainly, virtually all scholars, including most liberals, agree that the Islamic Republic of Iran, established by Ayatollah Khomeini, is among the most violent and oppressive governments in human history.[76] As Krauthammer points out, "our own State Department *calls* [Iran] the world's 'most active state sponsor of terrorism'" (emphasis Krauthammer's).

What an uninformed example of an American "sin"! The CIA restoring the Shah to power in 1953 resulted in a 26-year American-Iran relationship that played an important role in winning the Cold War. The Soviets would never have invaded Afghanistan while the Shah commanded the fourth largest and one of the best-equipped armies in the world. It was not until irresponsible American foreign-policy neglect resulted in the Shah's fall in 1979 that the Soviets were emboldened to attack an Arab country.

For President Obama to gloss over Iran's behavior since Ayatollah Khomeini's rise to power is nothing short of shocking. Could he possibly be unaware of the well-known facts? As most Americans will recall, during the overthrow of the Shah's government, a group of armed students occupied the American embassy. These students, many of whom were radical, fundamentalist "Twelver Shiites," took 66 American hostages. The new Supreme Leader Ayatollah Khomeini allowed 52 of these Americans, who were officials of the U.S. government, to remain in captivity for 444 days. They were finally released the day Ronald Reagan was sworn in as president.

At the time President Obama delivered his speech at Cairo University, the Islamic Republic of Iran had already established an almost 30-year record of brutality at home and terrorism abroad. Iran's citizens, especially women, regularly experienced cruel and inhumane treatment under strict enforcement of one of the most severe forms of *sharia* law in Muslim history. From the founding of Hezbollah in Lebanon to the massive support of the Shiite terrorist armies in Iraq, their exporting of terrorism is unparalleled in today's Muslim world. Iran's deceptive tactics and outright lies in their determined efforts to secure nuclear weapons for nearly two decades are unquestionable.

Let the reader decide whether this is a strong enough confrontation of Iran by a president of the United States, in Obama's own unfiltered words as delivered at Cairo University:

> "Since the Islamic Revolution, Iran has played a role in acts of hostage-taking and violence against U.S. troops and civilians. This history is well known. Rather than remain trapped in the past, I have made it clear to Iran's leaders and people that my country is prepared to move forward. The question, now, is not what Iran is against, but rather what future it wants to build.
>
> "It will be hard to overcome decades of mistrust, but we will proceed with courage, rectitude and resolve. There will be many issues to discuss between our two countries, and we are willing to move forward without preconditions on the basis of mutual respect. But it is clear to all concerned that when it comes to nuclear weapons, we have reached a decisive point. This is not simply about America's interests. It is about preventing a nuclear arms race in the Middle East that could lead this region and the world down a hugely dangerous path.
>
> "I understand those who protest that some countries have weapons that others do not. No single nation should pick and choose which nations hold nuclear weapons. That is why I strongly reaffirmed

America's commitment to seek a world in which no nations hold nuclear weapons. And any nation—including Iran—should have the right to access peaceful nuclear power if it complies with its responsibilities und the nuclear Non-Proliferation Treaty. That commitment is at the core of the Treaty, and it must be kept for all who fully abide by it. And I am hopeful that all countries in the region can share in this goal."[77]

Most critics of this Obama speech point to this denunciation of Iran's behavior since 1979 as a very meek and mild reprimand for the most rogue of all rogue nations—perhaps rivaled only by North Korea. (The holding of American embassy officers and support staff as hostages was a clear predictor of the evil intentions of this radical Shiite government. The U.S. was even complicit in their "revolution" by not coming to the Shah's defense in a timely manner.)

A number of conservative commentators and scholars—represented notably by Charles Krauthammer and Victor Davis Hanson—justifiably complain of Obama's misuse of historical facts as well as his ahistorical interpretations of certain events. Victor Davis Hanson, a classicist and historian at Stanford University's Hoover Institute, comments on Obama's apparent motives. In a commentary titled "Obama's history is off,"[78] he writes, "Mr. Obama, in elegant fashion, may casually invoke the means of politically correct history for the higher ends of contemporary reconciliation. But it is a bad habit. Eloquence and good intentions exempt no one from the truth of the past—Mr. Obama included."

After Obama lists Muslims' enduring contributions to society, such as algebra, the compass, and pens (which actually came from the Chinese and Babylonians), Hanson admits that "medieval Islamic culture was impressive and ensured the survival of a few classical texts—often through the agency of Arabic-speaking Christians—it had little to do with the European rediscovery of classical Greek and Latin values. Europeans, Chinese and Hindus, not Muslims, invented most of the breakthroughs Mr. Obama credited to Islamic innovation."[79]

Even if we grant Obama the luxury of historical license to exaggerate such minor items of history for the sake of a feel-good speech, it becomes much more serious when he rewrites Islamic history and the core teachings of Islam as recorded in its historical—and, in the minds of devout Muslims, sacred—documents.

Hanson and Krauthammer both refer to Obama's ignorance of historical facts in his commendation of Islam's history of religious tolerance. Hanson writes,

"Mr. Obama also insisted that 'Islam has a proud tradition of tolerance. We see it in the history of Andalusia and Cordoba during the Inquisition.' Yet the Spanish Inquisition began in 1478; by then, Cordoba had long been re-conquered by Spanish Christians and was governed as a staunchly Christian city."[80]

Krauthammer touches on the subject:

> "On religious tolerance, he gently references the Christians of
> Lebanon and Egypt, then lamented that the 'division between Sunni
> and Shia have led to tragic violence' (notice the use of the passive
> voice). He then criticized (in the active voice) Western religious
> intolerance for regulating the wearing of the hijab—after citing
> America for making it difficult for Muslims to give to charity."[81]

Krauthammer dismisses Obama's misleading characterization of America's
laws regulating charitable giving in terms that foreigners could easily
misunderstand. He writes that Obama is "disgracefully giving the impression to a
foreign audience not versed in our laws that there is active discrimination against
Muslims, when the only restriction, applied to all donors regardless of religion is
on funding charities that serve as fronts for terror."[82]

Obama's attempt to remake Islamic teachings and history in a politically
correct fashion is most evident when he discusses "women's rights," "religious
freedom," and Islam's "proud tradition of tolerance" in his Cairo speech.

Obama could have factually and honestly stated that the plight of women
in Arabia improved, if only slightly, after Mohammad's army conquered the
Arabian Bedouin tribes. He could have also noted that the treatment of women
further improved—significantly in some cases—in some Muslim countries ruled
by more secular Muslim rulers. He could have noted a dramatic improvement of
women's rights after the fall of the Ottoman Empire and Ataturk's establishment
of a secular government in Turkey. He correctly stated in his speech that in Turkey,
Pakistan, Bangladesh, and Indonesia, "we have seen [these] Muslim-majority
countries elect a woman to lead."

What an opportunity for a American president to challenge Saudi Arabia,
Iran, Sudan, and other such Muslim nations, where women are still treated like
chattel, to bring their countries into the modern world and treat their women as
first class citizens. These countries are still abusing women under a strict
interpretation of *sharia* law as taught in the Koran and the schools of Islamic
jurisprudence.

Instead of following such an opportune path, Obama chose to confess that
the question of "women's equality" is "by no means simply an issue for Islam." To
make himself clear to his audience in Cairo, Obama continues, "Meanwhile, the
struggle for women's equality continues in many aspects of American life...." For
President Obama to equate some employment inequities and perhaps a less than
equitable distribution of Title IX funds for women's college sports in America with
polygamy (for men only), forced child marriage for little girls, and stoning for
women accused of adultery (in extreme cases when a girl was raped) as practiced
in some Muslim countries is to take groveling to a previously unknown level.

In *Human Events*, [83] the controversial, sometimes strident, but always scholarly Ann Coulter makes some interesting comments on Obama's Cairo speech. Concerning Obama's confession that both Muslim countries and America have a ways to go on women's rights, Coulter writes: "So on the one hand, 12-year-old girls are stoned to death for the crime of being raped in Muslim countries. But on the other hand, we still don't have enough female firefighters here in America." Then she picks out Obama's reference to Muslim women's head coverings and writes:

> "Delusionally, Obama bragged about his multiculti worldview saying, 'I reject the view of some in the West that a woman who chooses to cover her hair is somehow less equal.' In Saudi Arabia, Iran, Afghanistan and other Muslim countries, women 'choose' to cover their heads on pain of losing them."[84]

The mainline press was so in the tank for President Obama at the time of this speech that there was little criticism on its part, but it has had little choice but at least to mention Iran's continuing human rights violations against their own citizens who dare to oppose, or even criticize, the edicts and actions of this oppressive Islamic theocracy. Some of these sources have done a reasonably good job of reporting on the controversy surrounding Iran's stubborn determination to produce nuclear weapons and the ability to launch them in the face of world opinion. They may have even done a better job of keeping the American public informed about the developing Muslim Brotherhood takeover of the government in Egypt. All of these developments in the Muslim world have illustrated that President Obama's apologies only emboldened the radical Islamist factions in these Muslim-ruled countries.

It was almost a year after the Cairo speech before some of Obama's liberal supporters began to become disillusioned with his presidency. The disenchantment on the left began with some of Obama's actions or perceived inactions. He compromised on the public option (the right to purchase or be given insurance directly from the government) in health-care reform legislation; he had not moved on immigration reform; he wasn't pushing the homosexual agenda with enough zeal; environmental issues were not being addressed fast enough; and the list went on.

But by 2011, Obama apparently remembered the hundreds of millions of dollars his hard-left supporters had sunk into his initial presidential campaign and realized that he had better start moving on their issues. Now with the 2012 election fast approaching, Obama has once again reversed course and has taken up issues of importance to his hard-left secularist supporters. For example, he pushed through the repeal of "don't ask, don't tell," put into place during the Clinton administration, to allow openly homosexual members to serve in the military. Then he announced that his administration would no longer defend the Defense of

Marriage Act (DOMA) before the Supreme Court. (Fortunately, Speaker John Boehner and his Republican colleagues have instructed the lawyers for the U.S. House of Representatives to defend this act passed into law by a previous Congress.)

During and after the heated debate this year in North Carolina over the ballot initiative to ban not only gay marriage, but also civil unions, Obama spoke out on the controversy. In spite of the fact that North Carolina voters easily passed this initiative in a record voter turnout for a primary election, Obama took the step of saying that his thinking had evolved to the point that he now supports gay marriage—not just civil unions.

Then, in a high-profile and extensively reported executive decision, the Obama administration mandated that Catholic and other church-run educational institutions and hospitals must provide their students and workers with free contraception coverage, including the "morning-after pill." This frontal assault on religious liberty will be discussed in detail in Chapter 7. LCMS President Matthew Harrison has become actively involved in the campaign to defend the cherished religious liberties bequeathed to us by our Founding Fathers. He is strongly urging LCMS members and other Christians to join in the fight to prevent the secularists from taking away our constitutionally guaranteed freedom of religion.

The newly installed Obama administration, suffering under the illusion that the voters in the 2008 election had given them a left-wing mandate,[85] hit the ground running in an effort to push a radical "clean- energy" agenda. Just over a year later, the developing Solyndra scandal caused them to rethink some of the risky investments they were making in the name of "clean energy." A *Washington Post* investigative article is instructive. Reporters Carol D. Leonnig and Joe Stephens summarize the initial ambitious clean-energy undertakings and why the administration slowed them down. After a brief look at this process, it will be shown how radical environmental programs have been revived in time for the election. Some of the early paragraphs of this article set this program in perspective and explain why it has created an election year controversy:

> "Sanjay Wagle was a venture capitalist and Barack Obama fundraiser in 2008, rallying support through a group he headed known as Clean Tech for Obama.
>
> "Shortly after Obama's election, he left his California firm to join the Energy Department, just as the administration embarked on a massive program to stimulate the economy with federal investments in clean-technology firms.
>
> "Follow an enduring Washington tradition Wagle shifted from the private sector, where his firm hoped to profit from federal investments, to an insider's seat in the administration's $80 billion clean-energy investment program. . . .

"During the next three years, the department provided $24 billion in public funding to clean-energy companies in which Wagle's former firm, Vantage Point Venture Partners, had invested, a Washington Post analysis found. Overall, the Post found that $3.9 billion in federal grants and financing flowed to 21 companies backed by firms with connections to five Obama administration staffers and advisors."

Then the *Post* reporters note the political controversy these actions have generated:

"Obama's program to invest federal funds in start-up companies—and the failure of some of those companies—is becoming a rallying cry for opponents in the presidential race. Mitt Romney has promised to focus on Obama's 'record' as a 'venture capitalist.' And in ads and speeches, conservative groups and the Republican candidates are zeroing in on the administration's decision to extend $535 million to the now-shuttered firm Solyndra and billions of dollars more to clean-tech start-ups backed by the president's political allies."[86]

The article continues to make connections between major Obama fundraisers and loans to so-called clean-energy firms. The multitude of political connections held by Solyndra (and mentioned in the *Post* article), a start-up energy firm in Silicon Valley that planned to make solar panels, are sure to become a major campaign issue. For openers, Solyndra is a client of the powerful Silicon Valley law firm, Wilson Sonsini Goodrich & Rosati. Wilson Sonsini is noted for handling loan applications for clean-energy firms, and such clients have "reaped $2.75 billion in Department of Energy grants and financing, the *Post* analysis found." "The firm's chief executive, John Roos, was a top bundler for Obama's 2008 campaign" and therefore they have their own White House connections, the *Post* article notes.

Some concerns had been expressed about Oklahoma billionaire George Kaiser who was a large investor in Solyndra and a major fundraiser for Obama. But the real controversy focused on the actions of wealthy energy investor and high-tech consultant Steven J. Spinner when the content of his emails concerning the Solyndra loan guarantee were aired Oct. 7, 2011, on ABC news.

Spinner raised $500,000 for Obama's 2008 campaign. He has promised another half-million or more for Obama's reelection efforts, according to the article in *The Washington Post*. Spinner had served as an advisor to Energy Secretary Steven Chu on energy loans as part of his responsibilities from April 2009 until September 2010. Further, Spinner's wife, Allison, is a partner at Wilson Sonsini, and Spinner had pledged in writing to play no active role in Solyndra's loan request. But the emails aired by ABC tell a different story. In one email prodding Department of Energy officials, he wrote: "How hard is this? What is he waiting for? I have OVP [the office of the vice president] and the WH [the White House] breathing down my neck on this." Matthew Mosk and Ronnie Greene for ABC noted:

> "Many of the emails were written just days after Spinner accepted a three-page ethics agreement in which he pledged he would 'not participate in any discussion regarding any application involving [his wife's law firm] Wilson [Sonsini Goodrich & Rosati]."[87]

The ABC story explains that during the days leading up to the announcement of the approval of Solyndra's loan application, "Spinner emerges as a key figure in advocating for getting the deal done." Many of Spinner's emails during this period dealt with preparations for Vice President Biden's planned trip to California to announce the loan approval. The ABC account continues:

> "Spinner also wrote an email two weeks before the Solyndra loan closed to an aide to Vice President Biden, identifying the private investors in the deal. He attached to the emails a bio from Forbes Magazine of George Kaiser, an Oklahoma billionaire who raised up to $100,000 for Obama's 2008 campaign."

What's more, the *Huffington Post* noted,

> "In one email, Spinner asks a DOE official whether the White House budget office has completed the review of the Solyndra loan. 'Any word on OMB? Solyndra's getting nervous,' he wrote, four minutes after receiving an email from Solyndra."[88]

So much for an ethics agreement! Some political wags have suggested that the Obama people take care of their large givers and fundraisers in a fashion that would make the Nixon folks seem like pikers. Some of such mega givers to Nixon's campaign ended up in jail for their excessive giving and the largess they received in return. Of course, they were Republicans.

But no lessons last long in the minds of those in charge of this administration. With the election heating up, Obama cannot afford to offend his left-wing contributors. So he has drawn a line in the sand over the construction of the "Keystone Pipeline" at the insistence of the radical, and totally uninformed, environmentalists. If this pipeline, which would go a long way toward decreasing our dependence on foreign oil that is costing us over a billion dollars a day, is stopped for political reasons, it will have sad consequences. Communist China will end up with the Canadian oil and we will continue to send untold billions to foreign countries—many of whom want to kill us.

In the earlier days of Obama's rule, the ineptness of his administration's response to the B.P. oil spill in the Gulf was the hot button that motivated some leftists to begin to abandon ship and join in the cries of Obama's conservative critics. As Jeffrey Kuhner, president of the Edmund Burke Institute, a Washington think tank, writes in a *Washington Times* column, liberals began to learn what conservatives already knew—that Obama is incompetent to run the government because of his total lack of "any executive experience."

Kuhner explains:

> "Mr. Obama's seminal flaw is that he lacks any executive experience. He is unable to govern effectively because he has never had to do so. He has never run a business, a town or a state. In fact, he has never run a lemonade stand. His entire adult life has been spent in the bureaucratic class—as a community organizer, radical professor or politician. He has been part of the nonproductive segments of society, the parasitical elements living off the wealth of the private sector."[89]

Kuhner describes a growing attitude among many liberals:

> "Like a leaking boat, even many of his most die-hard supporters are turning on him. Maureen Dowd, Chris Matthews, Rachel Maddow—these leftists are coming to realize, to their horror, that Mr. Obama is incompetent. Their political messiah is turning out be an imposter. Rather than leading America to the liberal promised land, he is crashing upon the rocks of reality."[90]

Kuhner offers a harsh criticism of Obama's policies and actions in these words: "Immersed in multicultural socialism and virulent anti-Americanism, he despises his country—its free-market system, its Judeo-Christian heritage, its historical exceptionalism—to its very core. He knows how to lecture, scold and apologize. In other words, he knows how to talk, but not how to govern."[91]

I would have chosen different words, but as we have seen, Obama comes from a radical background, his policies have been extreme, and Kuhner is not the first to accuse Obama of at least having socialist sentiments and a secularist approach to government. His Cairo speech certainly smacks of anti-Americanism.

I would use this analogy in comparing Obama's approach to government to that of his predecessor. George W. Bush liked to dance the straightforward "Texas two-step." Bush left no wiggle room when he told the world after the jihadist attacks on 9/11, "you are either with us or with them." Bush began his government dance in previous years with the attitude of "don't mess with Texas." When the cowardly Islamic terrorists launched an unprovoked surprise attack on the Twin Towers and the Pentagon, Bush swirled around with a "don't mess with the U.S." resolve that rapidly caused the global jihadist planners and perpetrators in Afghanistan to hear an unfamiliar tune. Bush continued to pursue an anti-terrorist two-step with such resolve that these same terrorist planners were unable to carry out another of their planned 9/11-type attacks on American soil throughout the remainder of Bush's presidency.

Obama's political dance might be described as the "Chicago two-step." This dance was designed by the radical socialist Saul Alinsky, who authored *Rules for Radicals,* which became the "bible" for Chicago's political machine. (Alinsky believed that a non-violent "socialist revolution" could be accomplished by organizing disenfranchised minorities—primarily blacks.) The mayor's office—usually run by men named Daley—refined this dance to the degree that it became virtually the only dance in town for those who desired a political career. It is difficult to morph the "Chicago two-step" into a "U.S. two-step" since the initial music of the former calls for redistribution of the wealth and a government that divides the spoils. This is a socialist tune that dreams of a welfare state.

In the dance with global Islamic terrorism, the music seems to make different sounds from time to time. Obama (and I think it is wrong and counterproductive to question his claim to be a Christian) has strong Islamic sympathies, which came about naturally. Barack Obama's father and step-father were Muslims who came from devout Muslim families. The music he heard for a number of years as a youngster seems to have influenced him to develop a politically correct understanding of Islam and its history.[92] Hopefully, there are enough remnants of the old Bush two-step around to keep us safe from another Islamic terrorist attack!

Frank Gaffney, the sometimes extreme but respected conservative columnist, wrote a somewhat inflammatory column titled, "America's first Muslim president? Obama aligns with the policies of Shariah-adherents."[93] Gaffney pulls statements from Obama's Cairo speech that he says indicate Obama has, at a minimum, strong Muslim sympathies. (Whether Obama harbors some deep-seated Islamic beliefs is something that only God knows. I choose to take him at his word that he considers himself a Christian. In any event, this question is basically irrelevant.)

Gaffney offers a Clinton analogy, noting that the white Bill Clinton became known as "America's first black president"—a title he earned by pushing issues of special importance to the black community. In a similar way, Gaffney suggests, Obama could become known as "America's first Muslim president" without actually being a Muslim.

In the Cairo speech, Obama referred to the "Holy Koran" four times. Gaffney contends that it is rare for non-Muslims—even of the politically correct variety—to use the term "holy" when referring to the Koran. Gaffney then highlights this statement in Obama's speech: "I have known Islam on three continents before coming to the region where it was first *revealed*" (emphasis added). Gaffney explains, "Again, 'revealed' is a depiction Muslims use to reflect their conviction that the Koran is the word of God, as dictated to Muhammad."

In fact, Muslims believe that Mohammad received God's final revelation, rendering all other previous—valid at the time—revelations from God obsolete. Those who believe that Mohammad received God's true revelation by definition should consider themselves Muslims. As documented in this book, the Koran specifically recognizes and explains the meaning of God's prior revelations in the Old and New Testaments as preparation for Allah's final revelation to Mohammad.

Frank Gaffney zeros in on the meaning of Obama's statement following his remarks that Israel must abandon its settlements on the West Bank and pursue a two-state solution. Obama made this emotional plea:

> "Too many tears have flowed. Too much blood has been shed. All of us have a responsibility to work for the day when the mothers of Israelis and Palestinians can see their children grow up without fear; when the Holy Land of three great faiths is the place of peace that God intended to be; when Jerusalem is a secure and lasting home for Jews and Christians and Muslims, and a place for all the children of Abraham to mingle peacefully together as in the story of Isra, when Moses, Jesus, and Mohammad (peace be upon them) joined in Prayer."

Gaffney insists that "no believing Christian" would ever make such a statement, especially if he understood "the ways of Islam" as Obama claims to do. He is certainly correct in this contention. Obama's reference to "all the children of Abraham" and his apocryphal story of Moses, Jesus, and Mohammad praying together is best understood in the light of Obama's rank universalism.

However, it is strange that Obama would mention Mohammad's much-disputed Night Journey (referred to by Obama as the "story of Isra") from Mecca to Jerusalem where Mohammad purportedly ascended into heaven.[94] The Koran says only that Mohammad was taken from the Sacred Mosque to the farthest Mosque, with no mention of Jerusalem or any exact location (Koran 17:1). The Hadith, which Muslims believe to contain the sayings and teachings of Mohammad, records considerable details of the Muslim traditions concerning this miraculous journey.

Ibn Ishaq, who wrote the earliest biography of Mohammad and is considered by Muslim scholars to be the most authoritative source, gives the miraculous details. They involve a white animal called a "Buraq"—half donkey and half mule—with wings on its sides that transported Mohammad to Syria and back to Mecca overnight. According to Muslim tradition, the prophet ascended to the different levels of heaven. At one level he met Adam. At another level he met Abraham, Moses, and Jesus. Ishaq then contends that Mohammad served as the "*imam in prayer*" for Moses and Jesus. Mohammad's most trusted and revered biographer writes that this story was so hard to believe when Mohammad recounted the details the following day to his followers that "many Muslims gave up their faith."[95] Since it took a caravan a month to make this trip each way, this was too much for them to believe. Robert Spencer notes that Mohammad seemed later to back off from his claim that this was a physical journey. Spencer references Ibn Isaq's quote of Mohammad's favorite wife, Aisha, that "The apostle's body remained where it was but God removed his spirit by night."[96]

Why Obama would use such a "story," which is totally unfamiliar to almost all non-Muslims and probably regarded as only a "spiritual" experience by most Muslims, is a mystery! Apparently, Mr. Obama felt this was a great ecumenical example with three noted "prophets" of Judaism, Christianity, and Islam praying together. Maybe some liberal, nominal Christians would be touched by such an example, but devout and informed Muslims would have seen nothing ecumenical in such a hypothetical scene. Those who have read the Koran—which Obama would lead one to believe includes him—would know that the Koran specifically identifies Moses, Jesus, and Abraham as pre-existent Muslims before the totality of Islam was revealed to Mohammad.

Equally alarming is Obama's use of "peace be upon him," which is obligatory for devout Muslims when they mention their Prophet Mohammad's name. Obama expands this blessing to include not only Moses, but even Jesus. Muslims have used this blessing for *"deceased holy men"* throughout their history. But Muslim scholars and theologians have always been explicit in their teachings that Mohammad is not divine and is not to be worshiped or even venerated. (Mohammad's family and closest confidants buried him secretly so that some of his followers would not turn his grave into some type of shrine.) Only Allah is divine and is to be worshiped, according to their teachings. Since the founding of the faith, orthodox Christians have always taught that Jesus Christ is the risen and living Son of God. Conferring the Muslim blessing of dead holy men upon Jesus is not only a major concession to the preeminent authority of Islam, but a stern repudiation of the risen Christ, whom Obama claims to worship!

Obama's consistent claim that there are nearly 7 million Muslims living in America[97] is probably hyperbole used to illustrate how multicultural American has become. (According to most polling data, including the prestigious Pew studies, the actual number of American Muslims is half that number or less.)

Gaffney further notes Obama's declaration in his speech, "I consider it part of my responsibility as president of the United States to fight against negative stereotypes of Islam wherever they appear." Gaffney considers this statement proof of Obama's intentions "to promote Islam in America."

My question would be: "Does Obama consider radical Wahhabism, which dominates Saudi Arabia, and the even more extreme Salafism, prevalent in Egypt—both taught in Muslim and many non-Muslim countries—to 'be negative stereotypes of Islam'?"

If the president really wants to rid Islam of "negative stereotypes," he could demand that Saudi Arabia forbid the Saudi Wahhabis from sponsoring schools (Madrassas) that teach a radical jihadist version of Islam in America, for example. There is one such Saudi Academy in Northern Virginia just a few miles from his White House residence. Such action would put to rest once and for all the harsh speculation that he is a closet Muslim. More importantly, by such action the president could send a clear message that his Muslim sympathies are only for the peaceful and tolerant brand of Islam.

Obama and Religious Faith

This brings us back to where we began this chapter. America's most arrogant president, as Obama has been described by many of his critics, not surprisingly has a view of religious faith that reeks of universalism.

The devil always knows which distortion fits the times. I believe that Satan has elevated this politically correct arrogance to the realm of religion as his chosen modern-day weapon of deception. The devil, tired of trying to convince Christians that Jesus never lived in Palestine, revealed Himself as the promised Messiah to His disciples, died on the cross, and rose from the dead. It is much easier to concede these truths as facts of history. The devil's approach now is to convince Christians that while this information is important, they shouldn't get too excited about their beliefs. After all, God deals in different ways with different people at different times in history, and there is nothing unique about your religion—it just enables you to live better and earn your way into heaven.

Finally, Satan is confident that many pastors or priests today don't want to be called bigots in an age of tolerance. Political correctness would find it absurd to insist on the authority of God's Word over the enlightened understanding of modern human beings.

When a Christian ceases to recognize the absolute authority of God's Word, he or she can rationalize any teaching he or she chooses to believe. Our tolerant and arrogant age rebels against the very concept of eternal truth. Such an attitude empowers Satan to have a field day in ridiculing traditional Christian teachings and subtly suggest how they should be modernized.

Best-selling religion writer Stephen Mansfield, author of *The Faith of Barack Obama,* makes some interesting observations about the president's religious history and beliefs. In an article published June 1, 2009, in *USA Today,* titled "Obama's faith fits our times," Mansfield begins with this revealing paragraph:

> "When Barack Obama entered the presidency this year, he became religiously the most unusual chief executive the American people have ever known. *He's the first president not born in a Christian home.* He has been exposed more broadly to the religions of the world than any man to hold the office. He's also the only president to have once practiced a non-Christian faith" (emphasis added). [98]

Mansfield then notes that Obama's "particular brand of Christianity [is a] theologically liberal, somewhat neo-orthodox kind of faith." He points out that Obama is not the first American president to hold unorthodox religious views, using Jefferson and Lincoln as prime examples. Thomas Jefferson, always at odds with the New England clergy, immersed "himself in the writings of Unitarians and the rationalists." Abraham Lincoln, on the other hand, rejected "revealed religion" as a younger man, but Mansfield contends that in his days as president, as evidenced in his second inaugural address, Lincoln found "a deep and transforming faith."

One of Mansfield's major points is that Jefferson, Lincoln, and a couple of other presidents with unorthodox religious views "were out of step with the prevailing faith of their times." These men "were skeptics in an age of Christian fundamentalism, religious seekers in a religiously certain age," Mansfield writes. He proceeds to make this somewhat frightening but mostly accurate comparison: "Obama is not. In fact, the president is nearly an ideal example of the religious direction of his times, and in this he is in keeping with the majority of men who have held his office."[99]

Mansfield is obviously correct, based on almost all polling data, that the majority of Americans do not regard Christianity as God's exclusive revelation. In this multicultural age of tolerance, it is considered broadminded and politically correct to concede that all religions may lead to heaven. I would argue that this is where a comparison of Obama's beliefs with those of most American Christians begins and ends. The polling data also reveal that most Americans still believe that this nation was founded upon Judeo-Christian principles. Former House Speaker Newt Gingrich contrasts Obama's contention that America is a "secular" nation with the still prevalent attitude of the American people in these words:

> "Describing America's promise as a 'secular country that is respectful of religious freedoms,' as Obama did last April, is an act of willful historical revisionism. *The United States was founded as an intensely religious country that believes our rights come from God, including the right to worship as our conscience dictates.* The Founding Fathers forbade the establishment of a national religion to protect individual rights of conscience but understood that public life would reflect the religious nature of the American people. *This understanding of America's promise is far more tolerant of religion in the public square than the secular purge that we have seen since the Supreme Court outlawed school prayer in 1963*" (emphasis added).[100]

The prevailing attitudes of the American people on moral issues such as abortion, embryonic stem cell research, and homosexuality, as well as on the beliefs of Christians on specific doctrines, are also strongly at odds with Obama's professed beliefs. After noting that Obama's liberal Christian beliefs were molded by the "Afro-centric worship" and Black Liberation theology taught by the Rev. Jeremiah Wright, Mansfield characterizes some of Obama's beliefs and approach to Christianity:

> "And so he became a Christian, but of a non-traditional theologically liberal kind. Obama believes in the divinity of Jesus, yes,

and in his resurrection and his grace. *But he is not as sure about the meaning of Scripture, and cannot comfort his daughter about the afterlife, as he tells us in 'The Audacity of Hope.'* Indeed, he feels free to lean to one Scripture verse over another, to approach gay rights, for example, from the loving words of Jesus in the Sermon on the Mount but not the bigotry of Paul in his letter to the Romans" (emphasis added).[101]

Mansfield then references Obama's approach to Holy Scripture, which I would contend sets him apart from all but the most liberal Christians. Mansfield writes: "Perhaps most important of all, he believes in a 'living word of God,' one that reveals and expands, that comes from unexpected sources." He offers an Obama quote that I believe might be embraced only by very liberal theologians:

> "When I read the Bible,' he has written, 'I do so with the belief that it is not a static text but the Living Word of God and that I must be continually open to new revelations—whether they come from a lesbian friend or a doctor opposed to abortion.'"[102]

Mansfield elaborates on Obama's extraordinary understanding of the revelations he believes he receives:

> "These 'new revelations' might come from a non-Christian religion as well, for Obama does not believe his Christianity is the final word. 'I am rooted in the Christian tradition,' he has said. But 'I believe there are many paths to the same place and that is a belief that there is a higher power, that we are connected as a people.'" [103]

Without trying to look into anyone's heart to determine what a person really believes—something only God can do—these statements seem to indicate that Obama is not a Christian in the traditional meaning of the word. (The most encouraging evidence I have found that Obama is a Christian in some sense is statements he made in the midst of the Rev. Wright scandal. He said that Wright brought him to Jesus and baptized him and his children. As Mansfield notes, Obama says he believes in the divinity and the resurrection of Jesus. But how a person can believe in Christ's resurrection and still harbor doubts about the afterlife is a mystery to me.)

President Obama's religious activities have received mixed reviews. He hosted a Passover Seder on April 9, 2009, the first Jewish religious meal ever held at the White House. He chose not to attend or participate in any formal event marking the National Day of Prayer during his first year in office, although he did sign and issue a proclamation honoring the National Day of Prayer. (The U.S. Congress had designated a day of prayer in 1952, which was signed into law by President Harry Truman. In 1988, Congress amended the law and President Reagan signed it, designating the first Thursday in May for the National Day of Prayer.)

Much of the criticism of Obama's failure to attend any public event was predicated upon what President George W. Bush had done during his presidency. For eight straight years, Bush had invited prominent Christian and Jewish leaders, and a number of distinguished guests, including members of the National Day of Prayer Committee, to the East Room of the White House. This was a tradition started by George W. Bush, but it was patterned after similar events hosted by Presidents Reagan and George H.W. Bush.

As to be expected, several prominent evangelicals were critical of Obama's failure to continue the Bush tradition at such difficult times in our country's history. In a *Washington Times* article, Julia Duin references the reaction of some evangelicals:

> "'For those of us who have our doubts about Obama's faith, no, we did not expect him to have the service,' said Wendy Wright, president of Concerned Women for America. 'But as president, he should put his own lack of faith aside and live up to the office.'
>
> "Referencing a remark the president made at a recent press conference in Turkey that Americans 'do not consider ourselves a Christian nation,' she added: 'That was projecting his own beliefs, but not reflecting what the majority of Americans feel. It's almost like Obama is trying to remake America into his own image. This is not a rejection of Shirley Dobson [chairwoman of the National Day of Prayer Committee and an attendee at all eight of the Bush events]; it's a rejection of the concept that America is a spiritual nation and it foundation is Judeo-Christian'
>
> "David Brody, White House correspondent for the Christian Broadcasting Network, said in a column that, 'within the conservative evangelical community, there was never any real expectation that the White House would hold an event.'"[104]

Other religious leaders defended Obama's decision not to publicly participate in the National Day of Prayer but expressed appreciation for his proclamation.

The controversy surrounding the National Day of Prayer the following year centered on the ruling of a Wisconsin federal judge. A group of atheists and agnostics in Madison, Wis., had filed a lawsuit against the Bush administration, claiming that recognition of a National Day of Prayer by the White House was a violation of the separation of church and state. The suit had been re-filed against the Obama administration when it assumed power. On April 15, 2010, Madison-based Judge Barbara Crabb ruled in favor of the plaintiffs. Within hours of this ruling, the White House announced that President Obama "intends to recognize a National Day of Prayer," as he had done the previous year. A week later, the Department of Justice also announced that it would appeal Judge Crabb's ruling.

An even more heated controversy developed when an invitation to the Rev. Franklin Graham to participate in the Pentagon's National Day of Prayer service was rescinded. Graham's much earlier contention that Islam is an "evil" religion because of the way it treats women and his personal belief that salvation comes only through Jesus Christ caused the Pentagon brass to have second thoughts. The National Day of Prayer Task Force pulled out of the service at the Pentagon, citing the military's politicizing of the event.

Graham, the honorary chairman of the 2010 National Day of Prayer Task Force, held a prayer service on the sidewalk outside the Pentagon early in the morning. He told reporters, "I have a son in Afghanistan and I came today to pray for our men and women that serve this nation. They risk their lives every day to protect our freedom. So my prayer was that God would watch over them." He also told reporters that he appreciated President Obama's proclamation and the Justice Department's appeal of the Wisconsin decision. Graham and his group then proceeded to the U.S. Capitol for a large celebration of the National Day of Prayer.

On April 3, 2010, the day before Easter, Obama's weekly address was titled by the White House Press, "President Obama Extends Holiday Greetings." Others identified Obama's remarks as an "Inclusive Easter Greetings." The *Christian Post* sums up President Obama's greetings:

> "The president made it clear that his family will be celebrating the resurrection of Jesus Christ on Easter Sunday, but made an effort to extend a Passover greeting to Jewish families and to address Hindus, Muslims and people of no faiths in his holiday message."[05]

Some have contrasted Obama's politically correct, generic, non-committal remarks, carefully crafted to be very inclusive, on the eve of Easter with his warm, compassionate, deferential, and highly complementary address to the Muslim world in his speech at Cairo University.

The White House press office described Obama's weekly address in these words: "In this week of faithful celebration, President Barack Obama used his address to offer his holiday greeting and to call on people of all faiths and nonbelievers to remember our shared spirit of humanity." Obama's actual words in the address read,

> "This is a week of faithful celebration. On Monday and Tuesday nights, Jewish families and friends in the United States and around the world gathered for a Seder to commemorate the Exodus from Egypt and the triumph of hope and perseverance over injustice and oppression. On Sunday, my family will join other Christians all over the world in marking the resurrection of Jesus Christ.
>
> "And while we worship in different ways, we also remember the shared spirit of humanity that inhabits us all—Jews and Christians, Muslims and Hindus, believers and unbelievers alike."[106]

Three days later, on the morning of April 6, 2010, when President Obama hosted an Easter Prayer Breakfast in the East Room of the White House, he sounded decidedly more Christian in his remarks. Who is to judge if this dramatic change is merely evidence of spiritual schizophrenia, unfortunately shared by many other modern-day Christians, or a reaction to criticism of his distortion of the traditional White House Easter message? President Obama amused his audience of Christian leaders and prominent laymen—and women—with the confession that there is nothing about Easter he could tell them "that you don't already know." Then the president made apparently heartfelt remarks that seem out of character from many of his previous—and a few subsequent—statements:

> "But what I can do is tell you what draws me to this holy day and what lesson I take from Christ's sacrifice and what inspires me about the story of the resurrection.
>
> "For even after the passage of 2,000 years, we can still picture in our mind's eye, the young man from Nazareth marched through Jerusalem, object of scorn and derision and abuse and torture by an empire. The agony of crucifixion and the cries of thieves. The discovery, just three days later, that would forever alter our world—that the Son of Man was not to be found in His tomb, that Jesus Christ had risen.
>
> "We are awed by the grace He showed even to those who would have killed Him. We are thankful for the sacrifice He gave for the sins of humanity. And we glory in the promise of the resurrection.
>
> "And such a promise is one of life's great blessings, because, as I am continually learning, we are, each of us, imperfect. Each of us errs—by accident or design. Each of us falls short of how we ought to live. And selfishness and pride are vices that afflict us all.
>
> "It is not easy to purge these afflictions, to achieve redemption. But as Christians, we believe that redemption can be delivered—by faith in Jesus Christ. And the possibility of redemption can make straight the crookedness of a character; make whole the incompleteness of a soul. Redemption makes life, however fleeting here on Earth, resound with eternal hope."[107]

Other than singling out the Roman "empire" as the source of Christ's ridicule and torture—rather than the Jewish religious leaders at the time—there is little in this statement with which orthodox Christians can disagree. In fact, it is a powerful statement of the beliefs of Christians regarding Christ's death and resurrection.

Dispute and debate over President Obama's faith—or perceived lack thereof—will undoubtedly continue as long as he is president of the United States. This question is important to many because they believe it affects the way he seeks to govern, especially in regard to the so-called "social" issues that are charged with moral and humanitarian concerns.

As far as the most widely debated and compelling moral concerns for Christians, such as the protection of human life, the future looks bleak at the present time. In one of his earliest actions, President Obama signed an executive order reversing the Bush policy of denying funds to overseas foreign government organizations that promote abortions. (Many Americans are questioning why we are sending any money overseas for population control in the middle of an economic recession and a spiraling national debt, for that matter, especially when it can be used to destroy unborn babies.)

President Obama, in a campaign speech to Planned Parenthood, had promised to sign the so-called Freedom of Choice Act when elected president if it were passed by Congress. As we all know, this act would make an abortion almost as easy to obtain as buying aspirin over the counter at the corner drug store. It would also require doctors to perform abortions against their religious convictions. Hospitals owned and operated by churches would be required to make abortions available, also contrary to their religious teachings.

Fortunately, the controversial and time-consuming legislative agenda pushed by the president and the Democrat-controlled Congress during Obama's first two years in office did not allow time to extensively debate such moral issues as abortion. Once the Republicans gained control of the House in the 2010 election, it would become almost certain that this administration could not push through any pro-abortion legislation. This does not mean that the cause of preserving human life has not suffered. President Obama issued an executive order shortly after becoming president countermanding President Bush's executive order limiting federal funds for embryonic stem cell research.

Christians in America who are concerned about protecting our traditional moral values as bequeathed to us by the Founding Fathers took some small comfort from President Obama's attempts to reach out to the Christian community, particularly Evangelicals, during the primary and the inauguration. Obama's Saddleback appearance with the Rev. Rick Warren at least partly explains the fact that he made some inroads among young Evangelicals during the campaign. He explained inviting Warren to offer the invocation at the Inaugural ceremony as an effort to be inclusive with people of faith.

President Obama's initial stated intention not only to retain, but to expand, President Bush's "faith-based" initiatives at the White House and extend them to the states sounded encouraging. Obama proposed to expand Bush's Office of Faith-Based and Community Initiatives into a larger 12-office operation renamed the "White House Council for Faith-Based and Neighborhood Partnerships."

If President Obama would have decided to use the extensive resources of all segments of our religious communities, he would have been building on the sound foundation of the Founders of our country. These organizations could be a major force in fighting poverty, hunger, disease, and other urgent problems in our society. If he would have decided not to attach restrictions that violate the teachings of these churches, church groups, or other faith-based organizations, he would have been following a precedent dating back to the earliest days of this Republic.

But once again, the devil was in the details. It soon became clear that the distinctive social concerns and hiring policies of the traditional Christian denominations were not going to be respected by this administration. As reelection politics became the dominant concern of this White House in 2012, the Obama administration took steps to appease its far-left social liberal and secular supporters. It had successfully maneuvered to lift the ban on openly homosexuals serving in the military. In addition, following the 2012 North Carolina primary vote to forbid civil unions as well as same-sex marriages, Obama had a conversion and stated that he now favors gay marriage. Much more serious and threatening to the religious liberties guaranteed to us by our Founders, Obama issued executive orders forcing church-run organizations to violate their beliefs in providing medical services.

These subjects will be discussed in some detail in the final chapter of this book. This chapter will deal with the citizenship responsibilities of Christians in general and Lutherans in particular. Former LCMS President Gerald Kieschnick and current LCMS President Matthew Harrison have demonstrated a modern-day understanding of Luther's theology of the "Two Kingdoms" at a crucial time in our history. They have and are setting examples of how God expects all of us to carry out our civic responsibilities.

Notes

[1] Former Speaker Newt Gingrich has many devout followers and many equally devout enemies. He is frequently praised and criticized. But neither friend nor foe has ever questioned his extraordinary intellect or his academic credentials. He is a recognized scholar in American history and is known for his research of religion in early America and the Founder's attitudes toward the role of religion and morality in the founding documents they produced. Having known him very well before and after his becoming speaker of the U.S. House of Representatives, I was privy to hearing how his Republican colleagues, who elected him as speaker, described him. The most frequently used characterization was that he may be too smart to be speaker because he comes up with more good ideas than we can digest, much less enact into law.

[2] The Inaugural Address of President Barack Obama, January 9, 2009. The full text is available at http://www.whitehouse.gov/blog/inaugural-address/.

[3] His point of view appears to be a radical version of the politically correct theories advanced by today's secular elitists. This will be shown in Chapter 6, "The Culture War Being Waged by the Radical Secularists," to be a total and deliberate distortion of the Founders' intents and beliefs.

The most prominent Founding Fathers will be extensively quoted and their theory of government will be explained in detail. There was such a minuscule number of people of other faiths at the time that the Founders were concerned only with keeping one Protestant Christian denomination from dominating the others or becoming an officially recognized federal church. Most states had an established denomination during this period. While Jefferson believed the states had such a right, he believed it was a bad practice and fought to disestablish the Anglican Church in Virginia.

[4] The survey, which incorporates the view of 35,000 individuals, builds on the work of several important similar studies. The Pew Forum reports are available online at http://religions.pewforum.org/.

[5] Obama's description of his religious beliefs will be discussed in more detail in the concluding pages of this chapter in a section titled "Obama and Religious Faith." *New York Times* bestselling author Steven Mansfield's book *The Faith of Barack Obama* will be used as an authoritative reference. Many of Obama's statements on

Islam and its history will also be stated in the following pages of this book.

[6] Chapter 6, "The Culture War Being Waged by the Radical Secularists," will include a detailed account of this subject. Madison's introduction of the article that would become the First Amendment to the Bill of Rights and its legislative history will be examined in detail. The words of the Founders in regard to religious freedom as well as those of Supreme Court Justice Joseph Story, who was appointed by President Madison, will be given. President Jefferson's intended meaning of the "wall of separation" metaphor in his letter to the Danbury Baptists will be documented. Justice Hugo Black's motives for his distortion of this phrase will also be laid out. This is in fact the "great lie" popularized by the secularists in their deliberate attempt to destroy the country's moral and religious foundations and to remake this country in their own image and imagination.

[7] I have chosen to use Corsi's book in this section for a few details that are sometimes disputed, because he gives the different scenarios and cites more references than other books I have read on this subject.

[8] Barack Obama, *The Audacity of Hope: Thoughts on Reclaiming the American Dream* (Crown Publishers, 2006), 202. These quotes also found in Corsi, *Obama Nation* (Threshold Editions, 2008), 184.

[9] Obama, 203.

[10] Obama, 204.

[11] Frantz Fanon's relatively short life yielded two potent and influential statements of anti-colonial revisionary thought, *Black Skin, White Masks* and *The Wretched of the Earth*. "In *The Wretched of the Earth*, Fanon develops the Manichean perspective implicit in *BSWM*. To overcome the binary system implicit in which black is bad and white is good, Fanon argues that an entirely new world must come into being. This utopian desire, to be absolutely free of the past, requires total revolution, 'absolute violence' (37). Violence purifies, destroying not only the category of white, but that of black too" (http://www.english.emory.edu/Bahri/Fanon.html).

[12] Roger Baldwin, the radical secularist, socialist, and communist sympathizer, was the principal founder of the American Civil Liberties Union in 1920. The ACLU has since led the fight in the cultural wars to secularize America and drive God from the public square. This organization and its activities will be discussed in detail in Chapter 6.

[13] "[Ralph] Ellison's emergence as a canonical writer came at a crucial moment in U.S. cultural history, when the Left aesthetic of the 1930s and 1940s was displaced by a triumphant ascendance of what Thomas Schaub has identified as the 'new liberalism.'" In "Boy on a Train," "the boy is initiated not only to the realities of racism, but also to a militant response to it. The boy's mother prays with her sons: 'Things is hard and we have to fight … O Lord, we have to fight!' (Ellison, 18). The boy, in confused response, thinks to himself that he must kill the 'something' (19) that is making his mother cry: 'Yes, I'll kill it. I'll make it cry. Even if it's God, I'll make God cry, he thought. I'll kill Him; I'll kill God and not be sorry!' (20) In his realistic rendering of the boy's confusion, in a situation that in some ways parallels that of Ellison's early life (his father died when Ellison was three, and he and his brother were raised by their widowed mother), Ellison metaphorically transforms a militant religious attitude into a secular militancy" (http://www.thefreelibrary.com/ Writer+on+the+Left%3A+Class+and+Race+in+Ellison's +Early+Fiction.-a0110963243).

[14] Langston Hughes wrote his most radical book, *The Ways of White Folks,* in 1934 after returning from two years in the Soviet Union. His work is steeped in racial pride and pessimism about race relations in America and its economic system.

[15] Corsi, 80.

[16] For an in-depth look at Frank Marshall Davis and his relationship with the Dunham family, see Corsi, 84 ff.

[17] Obama explains in *Dreams from My Father* how he eagerly listened to "Frank" expound on his philosophy as he and Obama's grandfather shared a bottle of Scotch.

[18] It is an interesting read about how Kellman inherited his political organization from the radical socialist Saul Alinsky, who authored *Rules for Radicals*. Alinsky believed that community organizers could bring about a "socialist revolution" by mobilizing the discontented and disenfranchised blacks. He was opposed to violence and believed that demonstrations accomplished little (Corsi, 128 ff.). Corsi's description of the racial struggles in Chicago's South Side is also very revealing, 127.

[19] Corsi, 153.

[20] Corsi, 154. Most of the details of Rezko's activities and his relationship to Obama are taken from Chapter 6 of *Obama Nation*, 152 ff.

[21] If anything, Dohrn was more radical than Ayers. She led the radical Weatherman faction in an SDS fight over the group becoming more radical and violent. She organized the Day of Rage riots in Chicago in October 1969. She and Ayers had helped found the Weather Underground after the death of three members of the

Weathermen in 1970 in Greenwich Village when the bombs they were making exploded. She was a principal signor of the "Declaration of a State of War" against the United States in 1970. In a Weather Underground magazine article in 1975 she wrote, "We are building a communist organization to be part of the forces which build a revolutionary communist party to lead the working class to seize power and build socialism. ... We must further the study of Marxism-Leninism, etc." See "Bernadine Dohrn" in Wikipedia contributors, "Bernardine Dohrn," *Wikipedia, The Free Encyclopedia,* http://en.wikipedia.org/wiki/Bernardine_Dohrn (accessed June 20, 2010).

[22] Corsi, 117.

[23] Corsi, 148.

[24] Corsi, 148.

[25] Dr. Anthony B. Bradley, associate professor of theology at The King's College in New York City and a research fellow at the Acton Institute, wrote an excellent article titled "The Marxist Roots of Black Liberation Theology," which is available on the Acton Institute Web site. Dr. Bradley, an African-American, wrote his Ph.D. dissertation on "Victimology in Black Liberation Theology."

[26] James Cone, *A Black Theology of Liberation*, 63-64. Quoted in "James Hal Cone" in *Wikipedia, The Free Encyclopedia*. Accessed June 20, 2010, at http://en.wikipedia.org/wiki/James_Hal_Cone.

[27] It is probably reasonable to assume that most clergymen other than the most dedicated theologians, such as seminary professors, did not pay much attention to Black Liberation Theology. Prior to the Jeremiah Wright revelations, I would have had little interest in this subject except for the relationships those advocating liberation theology had with radical communist insurgents and communist regimes in Latin America.

[28] The Rev. Jeremiah Wright had retired after 36 years as senior pastor of Trinity United Church of Christ, preaching his last sermon on Feb. 10, 2008. When Wright became Trinity's pastor on March 1, 1972, the congregation had a membership of around 250 and an average attendance of less than 100. When he retired, Trinity was a mega church with more than 8,500 members. Trinity's Web site (until recently somewhat revised) made it clear that Trinity was a black church dedicated to the needs and struggles of black people, encouraged black power, and taught Black Liberation Theology based primarily on the writings of James Hal Cone.

[29] Obviously, the number of people eligible to vote increases in each election as the population grows. The population increased by 8 percent between 2000 and 2008, while the turnout percentage of eligible voters increased by 25 percent in that period. But the turnout percentage of voters grew by almost twice the percentage between 2000 and 2004 than between 2004 and 2008.

[30] *Washington Post Magazine*, Jan. 18, 2009.

[31] Jann Wenner and Eric Bates, "Roundtable: The GOP Victory—and Obama's Next Steps," *Rolling Stone*, http://www.rollingstone.com/politics/news/roundtable-the-gop-victory-the-tea-party-ascendancy-and-obamas-next-steps-20101110 (Dec. 10, 2010).

[32] We will attempt to find preliminary answers to these questions as we look at roughly the first three and a half years of Obama's presidency. Gergen is certainly correct when he says that Obama believes he can make this a center-left country. Many would argue that he has lost sight of the center.

[33] Karl Rove, "History Favors Republicans in 2010," *The Wall Street Journal*, Nov. 13, 2008.

[34] A study of Obama's rapid and unlikely rise to political power is extraordinary to say the least. Twelve years after being elected to the state senate in Illinois at the age of 35, and just four years after being elected to the U.S. Senate, he was elected to the nation's highest office. Adding to the drama, Barack Obama was elected president of the United States just eight years after being soundly defeated in a Democrat primary for the U.S. House of Representatives by a former Black Panther named Bobby Rush. Each of his first two successful elections—for the state senate and the U.S. Senate—were made possible by series of unusual and unexpected developments. An ultra-liberal state senator, Alice Palmer, decided to run for a vacated U.S. House seat, and she handpicked Obama to replace her in the Illinois Senate. Alice lost this special primary for Congress and decided to run for reelection to her old state senate seat. Due to the shortness of time, she was barely able to collect the required number of signatures to qualify for the state senate primary ballot. Obama hired an attorney to successfully challenge enough signatures to keep the woman who had recruited him off the ballot. By this action, he won his first election to the Illinois Senate in a race he would have had little chance of winning had the incumbent survived the ballot challenge. Obama entered the Democrat primary for the 2004 U.S. Senate race in hopes of getting the nomination to run against popular Republican incumbent Senator Peter Fitzgerald. This initially appeared to be a suicide mission. First, in the Democrat primary he started out running well behind the well known Blair Hull, who was backed by the Illinois Democrat establishment. Then

totally out of the blue, Hull self-destructed in a sex scandal. This handed Obama the Democrat nomination no one thought he could win. Second, the very wealthy Senator Fitzgerald, who could have spent as many millions as he needed in his campaign, tangled with U.S. House Speaker Denny Hastert, also from Illinois, over some spending projects in the state and decided not to run for reelection. Third, Republicans had another strong, well-known candidate waiting in the wings to take on the still little-known state senator. Jack Ryan, who was also wealthy enough to spend massive sums of his own money in addition to expected large Republican fundraising efforts, dropped out of the race when his own sex scandal was exposed. Illinois Republicans were forced late in the campaign to import perennial candidate Alan Keyes as their standard bearer, which enabled Barack Obama to be elected with ease. Some political prognosticators would suggest that this unusually easy rise to the highest realms of political power for a man whose résumé included little other than being a lawyer in Chicago, a part-time law professor (or "senior lecturer," which was his official title) and fulltime community organizer was enough to give him a "messianic complex." Obama's even more spectacular long-shot bid that resulted in wresting the Democrat presidential nomination from the presumptive favorite, Sen. Hillary Clinton, and going on to win the November general election would certainly reinforce such messianic ambitions, if the thought had crossed his mind. For those interested in a more in-depth look at this conjecture can find relevant sections of Dr. Jerome R. Corsi's *Obama Nation* very interesting. *Game Change: Obama and the Clintons, McCain and Palin, and the Race of a Lifetime* by John Heilemann and Mark Halperin (Harper, 2010) offers some equally fascinating reading, even if some of the deep background and "off the record" quotes are considered questionable by some scholars.

[35] Vladimir Putin was once again elected president of Russia on May 7, 2012.

[36] I deliberately choose to use the word "liberal" in connection with the far left in this context since I know many of these operatives—a few quite well. I cannot believe they have not figured out Soros' ultimate game plan even if they have little personal contact with Soros himself. If and when a liberal Bill Buckley rises up in their midst, I would not be surprised to see many of them jump ship.

[37] David Horowitz and Richard Poe, *The Shadow Party: How George Soros, Hillary Clinton, and Sixties Radicals Seized Control of the Democratic Party* (Thomas Nelson, 2006), 181.

[38] David Horowitz's secular Jewish parents, both of whom taught high school in the Forest Hills area of New York City, were long-time members of the American Communist Party and outspoken supporters of Joseph Stalin. After receiving a B.A. from Columbia University and a master's degree in English literature at UC-Berkley, he spent some time in London. Now considering himself an intellectual authority on Marxism, Horowitz worked for the Bernard Russell Peace Foundation. When details of Nikita Khrushchev's 1956 "secret speech," in which he condemned "the crimes of the Stalin era," became known, David Horowitz followed his parents' example in breaking with Soviet communism. On his return to the U.S., David became editor of the New Left magazine, *Ramparts*, a position that enabled him to become close friends with Black Panther founder Huey Newton and other communist and far-left leaders.

[39] In 2006, the Board of Directors of the Center for the Study of Popular Culture (CSPC) decided to change the name to the David Horowitz Freedom Center. The CSPC was founded to establish a presence in Hollywood, to bring in conservative speakers for debate and discussion with the liberal community. The chairman of the board, Jess Morgan, said they changed the name for two reasons. "First, when the Center began, just as the Cold War was ending, we thought that the significant issue of our time would be the political radicalization of popular culture. The culture is still a battleground, but after 9/11, it is clear that freedom itself was under assault from the new totalitarianism of terror. Secondly, David Horowitz, the Center's founder, has become increasingly identified with issues of freedom at home and abroad. We wanted to honor him and also support the efforts he has undertaken. The name change does this and rededicates us to the mission at hand." One of the Center's purposes is the production of FrontPageMag.com, a conservative daily online magazine. Another is providing a database of left-wing agendas, activists, and causes under the name "Discover the Networks." It also operates the Individual Rights Foundation (IRF), composed of lawyers dedicated to preserving free speech and the freedom of association for conservative students and organizations that constantly are under attack by the politically correct liberals.

[40] David Horowitz and Jacob Laksin, *The New Leviathan: How the Left-Wing Money-Machine Shapes American Politics and Threatens America's Future* (Crown Forum, 2012), 6.

[41] Horowitz and Laksin, 6.

[42] Horowitz and Laksin, 8-9.

[43] As has been emphasized in this chapter, the two-decade struggle between conservatives and hard-right libertarians for control of the Republican Party was not only difficult but the outcome was not assured at certain times. Even today, the hard-right libertarians such as Glenn Beck and Dr. Ron Paul, while not nearly

strong enough to threaten a takeover of the party, could present a challenge to the election gains of conservative Republicans.

[44] A number of members of Congress who have extensively studied the government debt, including the recognized expert on the subject, Senator Tom Coburn (D-OK), question the accounting methods employed by the CBO and other government agencies. They insist that the government debt is considerably larger. Sen. Coburn, for example, has produced a document showing the government's unfunded mandates totaling $130 trillion—considerably more than the $45.8 trillion projected by the CBO.

[45] Wikipedia contributors, "United States public debt," *Wikipedia, The Free Encyclopedia*, http://en.wikipedia.org/wiki/United_States_public_debt (accessed Aug. 14, 2012). While not always considered authoritative on every subject, Wikipedia is noted for contributions by scholars on various sides of most issues. This article is 34 pages long, includes instructive charts, and is extensively documented. I have used it repeatedly as a source of numbers and facts in this section of the book. There is also a large number of other documents on the national debt. Of course, a number of books have been written on government debt. The best and most readable I have found is written by David M. Walker, the former comptroller general of the United States. His book, *Comeback America* (Random House, 2010), gets the reader's attention on the first page of Chapter 1, "Fiscal Crisis 101," when he points out that the average American household owes $483,000 of the *total* government debt.

[46] A few Republican and some of the remaining conservative Democrat congressmen might have initially realized the potential importance of President Obama's selection of Leon Panetta to serve as his CIA director. No MCs on either side of the political aisle had any personal objections to the well-liked and highly competent former member of Congress. Some worried that he didn't have any direct experience in the intelligence field. I suspected early on that he might become a major asset to our country in this role. When he was sworn in as a congressman from California in 1977, my friend and now partner, Stu Spencer, advised me to get to know him, as he believed he would become an important player over time. Stu had known him since his early involvement in politics as a Republican. Panetta had worked for a short period of time early in the Nixon administration.

It became obvious when you got to know him that Leon Panetta, the son of Italian immigrants, was very patriotic and filled with compassion for others. Since this was in the early days of the civil rights movement (which was not that popular among some Republicans at the time), he had some disagreements with a few of his superiors. He decided to leave the administration and move to New York City. When he returned to California, he decided to run for Congress as a Democrat. He won and served in the U.S. House of Representatives for 16 years before retiring to become the director of OMB in the Clinton administration. Panetta then served as President Clinton's White House chief of staff before taking another leave from politics. This background all becomes important, as it often does, when Obama asked him to head up the CIA. President Obama was able to place his confidence and trust in the judgment of this man.

[47] The Obama administration has been criticized harshly by many national security experts, such as Sen. John McCain, for its failure to persuade al-Maliki's government to allow American troops to remain in Iraq beyond 2011. Such talks broke down over their insistence that if American troops remained they must be subject to Iraqi law. Such critics noted that we have spent more than $800 billion and sacrificed 4,400 lives of American service members to oust a dictator, protect Iraq from al-Qaeda and other such radical Islamist terrorist organizations, and enable Iraqis to establish a fledgling democracy.

[48] Obviously his crowning achievement was his decision to allow the Navy SEALs to take out Osama bin Laden in Pakistan, as stated above.

[49] Jo Becker and Scott Shane, "Secret 'Kill List' Proves a Test of Obama's Principles and Will," *The New York Times*, May 29, 2012. Accessed Aug. 17, 2012 at http://www.nytimes.com/2012/05/29/world/obamas-leadership-in-war-on-al-qaeda.html?pagewanted=all.

[50] A more detailed analysis can be found in Wikipedia under the title "Taliban" (http://en.wikipedia.org/wiki/Taliban). A Council on Foreign Relations article titled "The Taliban in Afghanistan" is also instructive. See http://www.cfr.org/afghanistan/taliban-afghanistan/p10551.

[51] S. Yousafzai and R. Moreau, "The Doctor's Grim Reward," *Newsweek* (June 18, 2012), 20-22.

[52] However, many inexcusable leaks by CIA employees have occurred in recent times. Such leaks became more frequent after Watergate, the Church Commission hearings, and the "Halloween Massacre" during the Carter administration that decimated human intelligence gathering. This subject will be further explained later in this chapter.

[53] Former Secretary of Defense Donald Rumsfeld in a recent interview on Fox News emphasized what a vital ally Pakistan has been in the war on terrorism. He stressed that we must find a way to maintain a good relationship with Pakistan.

[54] North Korea's act of firing a torpedo from one of its submarines and sinking a South Korean warship, the Cheonan, on March 26, 2010, has heightened tensions dramatically. In a May 24, 2010, article, the Associated Press noted that this attack resulted in the "killing of 46 sailors in the South's worst military disaster since a truce ended the Korean War in 1953."

[55] Steven Nelson, "Holder says experiences of 'my people' not similar to contemporary voter intimidation," *The Daily Caller,* March 3, 2011. Accessed Aug. 15, 2012, at http://dailycaller.com/2011/03/03/holder-says-experiences-of-my-people-not-similar-to-contemporary-voter-intimidation/.

[56] Eric Holder, "Attorney General Eric Holder at the Department of Justice African American History Month Program, Wednesday, February 18, 2009, Remarks as prepared for delivery." Accessed Aug. 15, 2012, at http://www.justice.gov/ag/speeches/2009/ag-speech-090218.html?loc=interstitialskip.

[57] Gene Demby, "Eric Holder: Voter ID Laws Threaten Voting Rights," *The Huffington Post*, May 30, 2012. Accessed Aug. 17, 2012, at http://www.huffingtonpost.com/2012/05/30/eric-holder-voting-rights-cbc_n_1556955.html.

[58] Our Founders believed it is a God-given right for free men to choose their own government, and they considered each vote of these free men almost sacred. (Tragically, it took 82 years for of-age male former slaves to be granted that privilege. It took another 50 years for adult female citizens to gain this coveted right. We certainly were not a perfect republic at the time of our founding. But we were the best hope in human history.)

[59] The "Fast and Furious" operation will be explained in subsequent pages.

[60] These national security leaks focus primarily on two areas. One is the leaking of information about the use of "cyber warfare" to temporarily disable Iran's computers used in their efforts to produce nuclear weapons. Two, the leaks would reveal the "kill list" technique for targeting the Islamist terrorists for the week's drone strikes. But the revelation of the infiltration of al-Qaeda in Yemen with a double agent has added urgency to the already roaring congressional debate over the release of highly classified material. Some have charged that our national security is being sacrificed on the altar of political expediency. In the words of a highly regarded political commentator, they are trying to make Obama look like a "tough guy" as the 2012 election approaches. This subject will be discussed in more detail in the following pages.

[61] Josh Gerstein, "Eric Holder under siege," *Politico*, June 12, 2012. Accessed Aug. 17, 2012, at http://www.politico.com/news/stories/0612/77348.html.

[62] The U.S. and Israel jointly developed the Stuxnet computer virus that temporarily disrupted the Iranian nuclear computers—at least until we told them what was wrong with their computers.

[63] Senator Lieberman was elected to the U.S. Senate as an Independent. Since he caucuses with the Senate Democrats he serves as a full committee chairman based on seniority in the Senate. Lieberman, who was Al Gore's running mate on the 2000 Democrat ticket, is respected by his colleagues on both sides of the political aisle and is an expert in national security matters.

[64] For anyone interested in the details of the Plame-Libby controversy, there are many links on Wikipedia and other online sources giving details on the subject.

[65] By precedent and some court rulings, executive privilege can only be invoked when the president and his White House aides are involved in the deliberations contained in such subpoenaed documents.

[66] John Boehner, "On the Need for the Obama Administration to Quit Stonewalling & Provide All of the Facts on the Fast & Furious Operation," June 21, 2012. Accessed Aug. 20, 2012, at http://boehner.house.gov/news/documentsingle.aspx?DocumentID=300419.

[67] The major shock was that he set a timetable without a plan to relocate and prosecute the 241 detainees, the vast majority of whom are hard-core Islamic terrorists. Fortunately, the timetable keeps slipping because of opposition to bringing the worst of the worst to a prison on the American mainland.

[68] The executive order closed down only so-called CIA prisons (which critics have referred to as "black sites"), not what is sometimes identified as "safe houses." These safe houses are CIA facilities where CIA operatives can go to protect themselves. These facilities could be used to hold terrorist suspects for a short period while deciding whether to send them to the U.S. or other countries where they can be brought to trial. Some experts have speculated that when Obama received his first highly secret intelligence briefing, he concluded that he had better not go too far to please his "wing-nuts" but allow himself some leeway under certain compelling circumstances.

[69] In this executive order, Obama also decreed that the rules of interrogation would follow the *Army Field Manual*. This manual was actually written to instruct and protect corporals, sergeants, and other enlisted men who might of necessity become involved in prisoner interrogation. It can be read by the terrorists on the Internet, and anyone who might be captured will know exactly what to expect in their interrogation. At the

time this executive order was issued, one of Obama's lawyers explained that the president would appoint a commission to study whether any additional rules of interrogation were needed for intelligence officials. Some suggested that by this action he left himself some slight wiggle-room in the face of an extreme threat.

[70] Many recognized authorities contend that Holder was so obsessed with reversing the Bush policies that it clouded his judgment. The Bush administration can be properly criticized for not proceeding with such trials in a timely manner once such military tribunals were authorized by Congress. The fact that some trials were held in civilian courts before the U.S. Congress and the courts legitimized the military commissions is certainly no justification for such dangerous action.

[71] Jane Mayer, "The Trial: Eric Holder and the Battle over Khalid Sheikh Mohammed," *The New Yorker*, Feb. 15, 2010. Accessed Aug. 20, 2012, at http://www.newyorker.com/2010/02/15/100215fa_fact_mayer.

[72] Peter Finn, Carrie Johnson, and Anne E. Kornblut, "Trial of alleged Sept. 11 conspirators probably won't be held in Lower Manhattan," *The Washington Post*, Jan. 30, 2010. Accessed Aug. 20, 2012, at http://www.washingtonpost.com/wp-dyn/content/article/2010/01/29/AR2010012903213.html.

[73] Stephen Dinan, "Holder balks at blaming 'radical Islam,'" *The Washington Times*, May 14, 2010.

[74] President George W. Bush raised a few eyebrows and became the brunt of a few jokes when he held King Abdullah's hand while showing him around his ranch in Crawford, Texas. In the king's culture, men holding hands is a sign of friendship. However, bowing to the king has religious as well as political meaning. Since the king of Saudi Arabia is the ruler and therefore the protector of the two most holy cities for Muslims—Mecca and Medina—the gesture of bowing to him is a recognition of his spiritual authority. Non-Muslims are not allowed to set foot anywhere in these areas of the kingdom.

[75] Charles Krauthammer, "Obama Hovers from on High," *The Washington Post*, June 12, 2009.

[76] This subject will be discussed in considerable detail in Chapter 5.

[77] Barack Obama, "Remarks of the President on a New Beginning," The White House, speech delivered June 4, 2009, at Cairo University, Cairo, Egypt. Accessed Aug. 20, 2012, at http://www.whitehouse.gov/the-press-office/remarks-president-cairo-university-6-04-09.

[78] *The Washington Times,* June 14, 2009.

[79] Krauthammer, "Obama's history is off."

[80] Krauthammer, "Obama's history is off."

[81] Krauthammer, "Obama Hovers From on High."

[82] Krauthammer, "Obama Hovers From on High."

[83] Ann Coulter, "Obama's Cairo Speech: Funny, If It Weren't So Terrifying," *Human Events*, June 15, 2009, 5.

[84] Coulter, 5.

[85] In the early pages of this chapter a number of political experts from both parties, such as Peter Hart, David Gergen, and Karl Rove, were quoted in their assessments of what the voters were saying when they elected Barack Obama. They all agreed, based on their expert analysis, that this was still a center or center-right country and that if the Obama people misread the results and thought the country had moved to the left, or even center-left, they could lose the support of many of the people who had voted for Obama in 2008. Their warnings proved to be prophetic in the 2010 midterm elections.

[86] Carol D. Leonnig and Joe Stephens, "Federal funds flow to clean-energy firms with Obama administration ties," *The Washington Post*, Feb. 15, 2012. Accessed Aug. 20, 2012, at http://www.washingtonpost.com/politics/venture-capitalists-play-key-role-in-obamas-energy-department/2011/12/30/gIQA05raER_story.html.

[87] Matthew Mosk and Ronnie Greene, "Obama Fundraisers Tied to Green Firms That Got Federal Cash," ABC News, Sept. 29, 2011. Accessed Aug. 20, 2012, at http://abcnews.go.com/Blotter/obama-fundraisers-ties-green-firms-federal-cash/story?id=14592626#.UDJIvt3iakc.

[88] Matthew Daly, "Steve Spinner, Energy Department Adviser, Pushed Solyndra Loan, Emails Show," *Huffington Post*, Oct. 7, 2011. Accessed Aug. 20, 2012, at http://www.huffingtonpost.com/2011/10/07/obama-fundraiser-pushed-s_n_1000826.html.

[89] Jeffrey Kuhner, "Classless presidency: Obama brings down the boot," *The Washington Times*, June 11, 2010, Section B.

[90] Kuhner.

[91] Kuhner.

[92] The fact that Obama studied Islam in his grade school years in Indonesia should have made a difference in

his understanding of Islam. Throughout most of its history, Indonesia has been one of the most secular and tolerant Muslim countries. This should have enabled him to draw a distinction with the radical Wahhabism taught in Saudi Arabia and many other parts of the Muslim world.

[93] *The Washington Times,* June 9, 2009.

[94] This entire account is undoubtedly patterned after the biblical account of the transfiguration of Jesus recorded in Matthew 17 and Mark 9.

[95] Alfred Guillaume, *The Life of Muhammad: A Translation of Ibn Ishaq's Sirat Rasul Allah* (Oxford University Press, 1979), 181 ff.

[96] Robert Spencer, *The Truth about Muhammad* (Regnery Publishing, Inc., 2006), 83 ff.

[97] Gaffney notes that this is the number advanced by the radical Muslim Brotherhood.

[98] Stephen Mansfield, "Obama's faith fits our times," *USA Today,* June 1, 2009, 11A.

[99] Mansfield.

[100] Newt Gingrich, "A secular-socialist machine," *The Washington Post,* April 23, 2010, A19.

[101] Mansfield.

[102] Mansfield.

[103] Mansfield.

[105] Julia Duin, "Obama to be prayer day no-show," *The Washington Times,* May 6, 2009.

[105] Michelle A. Vu, "Obama Sends Out Inclusive Easter Greeting," *Christian Post,* April 3, 2010. Accessed Dec. 31, 2011, at http://www.christianpost.com/news/obama-sends-inclusive-easter-greeting-44600/.

[106] The White House, Office of the Press Secretary, "Weekly Address: President Obama Extends Holiday Greeting," April 3, 2010. Accessed Aug. 20, 2012, at http://www.whitehouse.gov/the-press-office/weekly-address-president-obama-extends-holiday-greeting.

[107] The White House, Office of the Press Secretary, "Remarks by the President at Easter Prayer Breakfast," April 6, 2010. Accessed Aug. 20, 2012, at http://www.whitehouse.gov/the-press-office/remarks-president-easter-prayer-breakfast.

4

Modern-Day Muslims: Two Radically Different Views of Islam

Certain historical events frequently leave indelible memories in a person's mind. The death of a loved one, the assassination of a president or some other prominent public figure, and an unprovoked attack on one's country are among the best examples. All of these events are permanently lodged in my memory.

I can remember, for example, exactly where, as an eight-year-old boy, I was standing on the screened-in porch at my grandparent's farm house—with my family huddled around an old, static-filled radio—as we listened to President Roosevelt announce that the Japanese had attacked Pearl Harbor. The fear and concern I felt as a young boy is still vivid. We may not have understood why this devastating surprise attack had occurred, but we had no doubt who our enemy was and what they intended to do to our country.

Likewise, every detail is all too vivid in my mind after the second plane hit the Twin Towers. Such a totally unprovoked attempt to slaughter masses of innocent civilians was unknown in civilized history. Like virtually every other rational person on earth, my immediate questions were *who?* and *why?*

The answer to the first question came quickly and, unfortunately, predictably: Islamist terrorists! Before the smoke had cleared, names well known to the intelligence communities and political leaders—Osama bin Laden and al-Qaeda in particular—hit the airwaves. Such names may have been only vaguely familiar to most citizens at the time, but they would soon become household words.

Sitting at my desk most work days since 9/11, 2001, with a spectacular view of the U.S. Capitol dome out the window—with "Freedom" standing proudly on its very top—I have asked myself the same questions over and over. What could possibly motivate any human beings, regardless of their religious ideology, to be filled with enough hate and rage to give their own lives to murder in cold blood thousands of innocent people—including some who were of their own religious persuasion?

It is instructive to analyze American foreign policy (especially since the Cold War ended) to see what has so inflamed Muslim extremists all over the world. Resentment of what many Muslims consider American debauchery and the attendant fear of its spread to Muslim societies via "modernization" efforts also cannot be ignored. But first it is essential to strive to understand the religious motivation of these terrorists. Dr. Bernard Lewis, ever cautious to be factually precise, describes Islamic terrorists as sometimes being at least partly motivated by other issues, "but religion is always a major, often *the* major element in defining the struggle" (emphasis included in text).[1]

To truly understand the deep religious convictions of radical Islamic terrorists and supporters, we need to understand how they contrast with or relate to mainline Islam. What beliefs do they share in common, and what are the sources of their disagreements? Politically correct "scholars" and certain politicians insist that the terrorists have hijacked or distorted a religion of peace and its history. They would have us believe there is no teaching of violence in the Koran, the actions of Mohammad, or Islam's history that would motivate a modern Muslim to commit terrorist activities.

In stark contrast, modern-day Islamist terrorists insist they are simply following the clear teachings of their religion and its history. They quote the Koran, Mohammad, and/or other recognized Islamic authorities to justify all of their terrorist activities. They piously claim they are only diligently carrying out Allah's will as clearly explained by Mohammed.

Some of the more hardcore anti-Islamic terrorist authors, in their justifiable zeal to protect America and her allies in this life and death struggle, tend to suggest that the terrorists are historically correct in their interpretation of Islam and its history. (In effect, they sometimes imply that *moderate* Muslims are hijacking a historic religion of conquest, violence, and intolerance in their efforts to make modern Islam look peaceful, tolerant, and respectable.)

Such conservative experts on Islam contend, certainly with some justification, that the terrorists are taking their religious devotion and game plan directly from the teachings and history of Islam. They point specifically to Mohammad's role as military leader in the conquest of Arabia and his instructions to his followers to conquer the mostly Christian lands surrounding Arabia following his death. In fairness, all such authors I have read are careful to point out that the Koran and Mohammad's teachings also contain teachings of peace and compassion.

In many of his writings, Lewis argues that in most cases Muslim conquests were not intended to force the inhabitants to convert to Islam but to make such conversion possible. Lewis frequently points out that Muslims were taught from the beginning that they must strive to share through *jihad* (or "holy war," which will be examined in detail in this book) the final revelation of the one true faith they had received, in order that others might be saved. He also explains that Muslims were not taught that the whole world must convert to Islam, but that *sharia*, or Islamic holy law, must be established throughout the world to achieve true justice and peace on earth.

In the Conclusion to his latest book, *Islam: The Religion and the People,* Lewis warns against trying to understand Islam based on what he considers two extreme interpretations. He writes that the intention of his book is

> "to present a picture of Islam as it really was and is—not the demonized version shared by the terrorists and their opponents, nor the apologists' sanitized version of a religion of love and peace throughout the ages, but rather the historic reality: Islam as it began, grew, developed and changed throughout the centuries, both in theory and in practice, in different parts of the world, from the beginning to the present day."[2]

In order to understand the nature and threat of the "holy war" declared on America and her allies by Osama bin Laden, it is essential to try to comprehend the ideological and theological split in today's Muslim world.

In perhaps overly simplified terms, the majority view has been described as "moderate, secularist, and peaceful Islam." Many prominent authorities contend that at least one billion of the world's 1.3 billion Muslims fall into this category. This group probably could correctly be referred to as part of a massive "silent majority" of present-day Muslims.

Prominent moderate Muslims will be referenced in this chapter as they urge other "moderates" to let their voices be heard in condemning the terrorists. Lewis warns of the potential consequences of the silence of influential moderates:

> "The distinctions between Islam and fundamentalism, and between fundamentalism and terrorism, are also obscured by the unwillingness of some Muslim communal leaders and religious dignitaries to condemn terrorist acts unequivocally. This unwillingness, and the popular mood to which it panders, have done and are doing great harm to the image of Islam among non-Muslim People."[3]

The second and much smaller group could accurately be referred to as "radical, fundamentalist, revivalist Islamists."[4] This group may well number about 300 million Muslims, as far as their convictions and support—financial and otherwise—are concerned.[5] Most authorities further estimate that, as part of this group, only 1 percent of the world's 1.3 billion Muslims—roughly 13 million—are active terrorists.

If we fail to comprehend the religious fervor (some call it fanaticism), dedication, and determinism of these fundamentalist Muslims, we cannot know the enemy we face.

An article in *The Washington Times* for Sept. 14, 2010, announced the release of a 177-page scholarly and extensively documented study written by a bipartisan blue-ribbon panel of 19 of America's foremost defense and counterterrorist experts ("Team B II").[6] This article, "Second opinion needed on Sharia: Our political establishment wears blinders and ignores the threat," was co-written by three of the most prestigious panel members.[7] The conclusions reached by these recognized experts seem to be a confirmation of all that I had already written in this book. It was comforting to realize that more than two years of research on my part had yielded accurate information on this potential threat to our very survival as a free and moral nation.

However, it was even more alarming to realize that my worst fears were true, that those in the highest levels of government, charged with providing for the security of this country, have no realistic understanding of the severity of the threat and the nature of our enemy.

At this point, it is important to learn and understand how these experts distinguish between genuine moderate Muslims and their Islamist counterparts.

Challenging the policies of administrations of both parties (which have been based on shallow assumptions about the severity of the threat we face and the nature of this totally ideologically driven enemy), they write:

> "We consequently have joined a group of security-policy practitioners and analysts in subjecting this ideology and its adherents to a new Team B study. Our assessment challenges bedrock assumptions of current American policy on combating (and minimizing) what the government calls 'extremism' and on engaging (and appeasing) Shariah proponents who claim to reject terrorism. These proponents are described, wrongly, as 'moderates' because they appear content to achieve their patently immoderate designs through political-influence operations, 'lawfare' and subversion. Participants in the study constitute a rich reservoir of national security experience drawn from military, intelligence, homeland security, law enforcement and academic backgrounds."

The authors then proceed to distinguish between the truly moderate Muslims and the fundamentalist Muslims, which they identify as "Islamists." Not surprisingly, the clear line of distinction is based on their attitudes toward *sharia* and subsequently *jihad*.

> "Shariah is the crucial fault line of Islam's internecine struggle. On one side of the divide are Muslim reformers and authentic

moderates—figures like Abdurrahman Wahid, the late president of Indonesia and leader of the world's largest liberal Muslim organization, Nahdlatul—who embrace the Enlightenment's veneration of reason, and in particular, its separation of the spiritual and secular realms. On that side of the divide, Shariah is defined as but a reference point for a Muslim's personal conduct, not a corpus to be imposed on the life of a pluralistic society.[8]

"The other side of the divide is dominated by 'Islamists,' who are Muslim supremacists. Like erstwhile proponents of communism and Nazism, these supremacists—some terrorists, others employing stealthier means—seek to impose a global theocratic and authoritarian regime, called a caliphate. On this side of the divide, Shariah is a compulsory system that Muslims are obliged to wage jihad to install and to which the rest of the world is required to submit.

"For these ideologues, Shariah is not a private matter. They see the West as an infidel enemy to be conquered, not a culture and civilization to be embraced or at least tolerated. It is impossible, they maintain, for alternative legal systems and forms of government like ours to coexist peacefully with the end-state they seek."[9]

As one would expect of former generals, U.S. attorneys, or former directors of the CIA, they readily confess that they are not theologians and make no judgment as to which of these two disparate views accurately reflects "true Islam." Their concern is that decision-makers understand that those who insist on imposition of *sharia* are "supremacists" intent on world domination.

(In the report, the authors quote the Koran and other authoritative Islamic theological sources to illustrate the foundation of Muslim supremacism. Then they proceed to examine statements of modern day Islamic leaders. For example, after quoting the Koran that Muslims are "the best of peoples" [3:110] and that non-Muslims are "the most vile of created beings" [98:6], they quote the words uttered in 1998 by Omar Ahmad, co-founder and board chairman of the Council on American Islamic Relations: "Islam isn't in America to be equal to any other faith, but to become dominant. The Koran should be the highest authority in America, and Islam the only religion on earth."[10])

Woolsey and the others insist that we must do everything we can "to empower Islam's authentic moderates and reformers." They wisely argue that we cannot promote a policy that "fictionalizes" Islam and its history in the vain hope that by striving not to offend Islamists, we will motivate them to finally come around to rational and peaceful behavior in spite of their firmly held ideology. In their words: "If we are to face down Shariah, however, we must understand what we are up against, not simply hope that dialogue and 'engagement' will make the challenge go away."

"The definition of 'moderation' needs to be reset, to bore in on the Shariah fault line. Only by identifying those Muslims who wish to impose Shariah can we succeed in marginalizing them," the authors point out.[11]

Lewis carefully identifies what he refers to as the "revivalist" Muslim clerics throughout Islamic history who have founded or promoted radical Sunni sects such as Wahhabism and Salafism. They always call for a return to "pure" Islam, which they claim goes back to Mohammad and the first four "rightly guided" caliphs. The emphasis is always on waging "holy war" with the intent of establishing "Islamic law" throughout the world. Osama bin Laden was raised in strict Wahhabi Sunni Islam, and over time seems also to have developed a fondness for the even more radical Salafism that has much in common with Wahhabism.

I rely heavily upon Lewis in this and the next chapter because he is so highly respected by Muslim and non-Muslim scholars alike. There is a widespread consensus among those in agreement with Lewis and those who are his critics that this man as a scholar leans over backwards to make sure that he treats Muslims and non-Muslims fairly.[12] Lewis wants to make sure that we understand the nature and severity of the Islamic terrorist threat without "demonizing" the religion of Islam and its people.

In the Introduction to this book, I offered an artfully crafted quote from Lewis, contrasting his role in British intelligent during World War II and his intellectual role in "the war on terrorism" (his lecture audiences include the defense and intelligence communities). To paraphrase his contrast between the two periods of time, Lewis says that during World War II we (the allies) knew who we were and who the enemy was and certainly understood how high the stakes were. Sadly, he would continue that in the life and death struggle with the Islamic terrorists, we (America and her free-world allies) aren't sure who we are and totally fail to understand our enemy and just how high the stakes are in this war.

In *Islam: The Religion and the People*, after succinctly describing the religion of Islam, its theology, history, ideology and divisions, Lewis concludes with a final chapter on "Radical Islam." The first paragraph of the Introduction gives a flavor of this must-read book and underlines the absolute necessity of understanding Islam if we are to understand our radical Islamic-terrorist enemy. He writes:

"The Koran is the Muslim Bible. The mosque is the Muslim church. The Mullah is the Muslim priest. Friday is the Muslim Sabbath. All these statements are true; all of them can be dangerously misleading. They reflect the resemblances, even the kinship, between the Christian and Muslim worlds—the many faceted affinity between these two religions and the religiously defined civilization to which they gave rise, which makes such comparisons plausible and, in some measure, accurate. But at the same time they conceal or obscure the real and sometimes profound differences between them".[13]

In a much earlier book, Lewis describes the Muslim "ethos" or "worldview" in an interesting way. Muslims view the coming of the Prophet Mohammad as the ushering in of the final phase of the long struggle between monotheism and polytheism. In explaining the word "Islam," Lewis writes, "For Muslims, strictly speaking, it denotes the one true faith which has existed since the creation of the world, and in this sense Adam, Moses, David, Jesus and others were all Muslims."[14]

Muslims believe that there are genuine revelations in the Old and New Testaments inasmuch as they point to the coming of Allah's final revelation, which made all previous revelations obsolete. The "Qur'an completes and supersedes all previous revelations" and "whatever truth they contained was now incorporated in his message."[15]

It is complicated, to say the least, to comprehend how the Muslim terrorist and the overwhelming majority of the world's moderate Muslims can reach such radically different conclusions on what their faith requires of them. The beliefs they hold in common are almost self-evident, since Muslims have no history of disagreements on basic doctrines of Islam.

The basic tenets of Islam are simple and are accepted by virtually all Muslims. The "five pillars" of Islam are well known to even the most elementary student of the subject. The defining creed and first pillar, which might be compared to the Apostle's Creed for Christians in terms of importance, is only two sentences: "I testify that there is no God but Allah. I testify that Muhammad is the Prophet of Allah."

Muslims understand that this simple confession commits them to the monolithic unity of God and the finality of the prophethood of Mohammad. The Koran makes it clear that Allah has no "son" or "associate," and to contend otherwise would be blasphemy. The Koran also repeatedly states that Mohammad is Allah's "final prophet" and there will not be another after him. He has received God's final revelation to man for all time.

Attendant doctrines dealing with heaven and hell, the last days, the resurrection of the dead, and the divine origin of the Koran will be examined in the next chapter. But Muslims have no history of disagreement on such matters.

The other four pillars (prayer, alms-giving, fasting, and, for those who can afford it, the mandatory once-in-a-lifetime pilgrimage to Mecca) have seen no serious dispute at any time in Islamic history, although diligence in carrying out such religious obligations has varied at least slightly from country to country and age to age.

The Biblical "higher-criticism" and "modernism" movements that have so plagued Christianity since the early 1900s would be totally foreign to Islamic thought. Christian fundamentalism, which arose in opposition to higher-criticism's attempts to discredit the authority and divine origins of Holy Scripture, would also sound strange to a devout Muslim's ears. Fundamentalism has a significantly different meaning in an Islamic context which will be repeatedly mentioned for the sake of clarity.

The differences in the religious beliefs of moderate and radical Muslims have little or nothing to do with basic doctrines. However, such agreement on the theological foundations of their faith can tend to obscure the issues on which radicals[16] and moderates have strong disagreements.

Two Major Differences

It would be accurate to say that there are two major religious differences separating fundamentalist Muslims from moderate Muslims. One, they have different understandings of the command to engage in *jihad* to spread the one true faith so that others might be saved; and two, the responsibility to establish *sharia* law so the world may experience a truly peaceful and just rule. But the differences are deeper and more complex.

All Muslims—fundamentalist, radicals, moderates, secularists, or however they describe themselves—accept the authority of the same Koran. They all have access to the same biographies of the life of Mohammad, especially the oldest and most revered, which was passed down from the devout Muslim Ibn Ishaq. The lengthy early collection of the traditions and sayings of Mohammad (called *Hadith*) are equally available to those who seek them. The Muslim conquest of the Byzantine Christian and Persian lands by the "four rightly-guided caliphs" in the first 100 years after Mohammad's death is well documented in history for all to see. The same is true of the caliphate dynasties that succeeded the early caliphs. (In common with all religions, particularly Christianity, Muslims disagree over details and interpretations of some of these teachings and actions.)

For example, most Muslims would believe that they have a divine obligation to spread the faith of Islam to offer salvation to unbelievers. The clear command in the Koran, which is extensively detailed in Islamic theology, to wage offensive "holy war" to advance the cause of Islam cannot be disputed by a devout Muslim. But how this "holy war" is to be waged causes major disagreements in the Muslim community. Offensive "holy war" applies only to the spread of Islam and does not always involve military action or violence—as a matter of fact it frequently indicates a preference for non-violent action.[17] Occasionally such actions may be as peaceful as an attempt to employ gentle persuasion.

Defensive "holy war" involves the defense of Muslim lands (which is defined as any land ever occupied by Muslims) and is obligatory for all able-bodied Muslim men. (The meaning of *jihad* is so complicated and important in understanding the difference between peaceful and violent Muslims that an entire section of the next chapter will be devoted to the subject.)

A related and even more complicated topic that gives rise to divisions among Muslims is "Islamic law" or *sharia*. Islamic law regulates every aspect of a Muslim's life—what we would call civic as well as religious behavior—including *jihad*. There are four historically recognized schools of jurisprudence in Sunni Islam and one in Shiite Islam. (A section in the next chapter also will be devoted to this subject.) Without some basic understanding of holy war and Islamic law (sometimes translated as "holy law"), as well as the different interpretations of Islamic history, we cannot understand Islamic terrorism.

The failure to realize how moderate and radical Muslims interpret *jihad* and *sharia* (as well as certain events in Islam's history) differently is the major source of such widespread confusion about who our terrorist enemies really are and what they believe. If we develop an understanding of what the terrorists believe in these areas, we can begin to realize why they hate America with such a passion. The jihadists understanding of "holy war," "holy law," and their interpretation of Islamic history are the foundation of such fanatically held religious convictions.

I am personally convinced that Lewis best explains how terrorist leaders, such as the late Osama bin Laden, can inspire such masses of Islamic terrorists to the degree that they eagerly seek suicide missions or martyrdom.[18]

The unique privilege of hearing a lecture by arguably the world's foremost authority on this subject was afforded me Oct. 25, 2007, in Washington, D.C.[19] The elderly, amazingly articulate Dr. Lewis addressed these questions about the motivation and beliefs of the Islamic terrorists for more than an hour. The event was in a large conference room, packed to overflowing, with a spellbound audience of intellectual and political leaders in the Nation's Capital. (I may well have been the most undistinguished person in the invited audience.)

Lewis confronted the most important question first as he explained why the title of his lecture, "The Challenge of Islam," had been chosen. He said that in his lifetime there had been three major "challenges" to the West that threatened "our very survival":

> "The first was Nazism of the Third Reich, the second was Bolshevism of the Soviet Union, and the third is the problem that we confront at the present time. And I would like to emphasize my belief that this threat is no less serious and in some ways is more serious than that presented by its two predecessors."

He was careful to explain in simple terms what he meant so as not to be misunderstood. For example, he pointed out that while it is technically correct to speak of the struggle against terrorists or terrorism, such a description is misleading. To illustrate, he noted that Winston Churchill would have been correct in a technical sense had he told the British people during World War II that they were threatened by bomber airplanes or submarines and that these were their enemies. But Churchill wisely explained to the people who the Nazis were so they could "understand" their enemy, what they believed, and how evil their intentions were.

Lewis then proceeded to explain meticulously what he means by "Islam." The word is difficult to understand because it has more than one meaning. By way of contrast, he pointed to differences in the meaning of "Christianity" and "Christendom." Whereas Christianity describes a religion with its belief structure and worship life, Christendom is the name of "a civilization" that developed under its influence but contained "many elements that are not Christian and some even are anti-Christian."

To emphasize a source of confusion, Lewis stressed that Muslims as well as non-Muslims use the word "Islam" as an equivalent in one sense to "Christianity" and in another sense as an equivalent to "Christendom." "No one, I think, could seriously dispute that Hitler and the Nazis came out of Christendom. But no one could seriously maintain that they came out of Christianity."

Explaining the lack of such a distinction in the historic Islamic world, Lewis notes that "secular" is "a word for which until very recently there was no equivalent in Arabic, Persian or Turkish. A word that was lacking because the notion was lacking." The Koran and the teaching of Mohammad made no distinction between religion and state since for them and for Islam they were one and the same. The failure to understand such a distinction not only has led us to misunderstand them, but also them to misunderstand us. In the next chapter, we will delve deeper into this subject.

(Using words such as "secular," "moderate," or "mainstream" in describing Muslims today is imprecise and must be constantly defined. Until Mustafa Kemal Ataturk established the Turkish Republic [as a secular dictator] and abolished the caliphate in 1924, after the fall of the Ottoman Empire, the word "secular' would have no meaning in the Muslim world, although some may have been aware of the word as a description of the infidel Western Countries.

(Ataturk is still an arch-enemy of Muslim radicals or militants for what they believe to be his attempts to "secularize" their religion. Using the word "moderate" to describe any group of Muslims is a convenient way to distinguish Muslims who are not radicals or extremists from those who are, but the word can be subject to many different interpretations. Fundamentalist or conservative Muslims have always viewed "modernization" as an attempt to distort the purity of their religion. Using the word "mainstream"[20] in describing Muslims is much more difficult to define than when ascribing the appellation to Christians.)

Lewis continued his lecture by briefly evaluating the similarities and differences between Christian and Muslim beliefs and their histories as he set the stage to explain how such history is viewed through Osama bin Laden's eyes. (At this point, it became obvious to me that if we ever hope to understand what radical Islamists believe about their religion and its history, we must also attempt, as best we can, to understand what non-radical Muslims believe.)

"Islam and Christianity, Islam and Christendom have a great deal in common. They are both religions of a certain specific type, and as far as I know they are the only religions of that type," Lewis stated. He then noted that these two religions are sometimes referred to by their detractors as "triumphalist religions."

This is because these two religions believe that "they are the fortunate recipients of God's final message to humanity, which is their duty not to keep selfishly to themselves, like the Jews and the Hindus and the Confucians, but to bring to the rest of humanity, removing whatever obstacles there may be on the way."

In *Islam: The Religion and the People,* Lewis emphasizes that the differences between the Islamic and Christian worlds are "more than merely verbal."

> "There are other differences, arising from the contrasting circumstances of their origins and early history. Jesus was crucified, and his followers were a persecuted minority for centuries before they obtained control of the state and were able to exercise authority. The life of Muhammad, the founder of Islam, was very different. Not he but his enemies were put to death, and during his lifetime he established a state of which he was sovereign.... In Islam, the prophet who brought the holy book and founded the faith also founded and headed the first Muslim state, and both promulgated and enforced the one all-embracing holy law. There is therefore an interpenetration of religion and politics, affecting government and law, identity and loyalty, to a degree without parallel in Judeo-Christian history."[21]

Before describing the Islamic "revivalist" movements and the Muslim clerics who led such revivals to restore Islam to its original "pure" form, Lewis offered his audience a view of Islam's theology and history as Osama bin Laden saw it.

In his lecture, Lewis referred to Osama bin Laden as "one of the more remarkable Muslim spokesmen of the present age." In the next chapter, a careful analysis of Osama bin Laden himself and al-Qaeda, the terrorist organization he founded, is essential. Examining Wahhabism, the radical sect of Sunni Islam practiced in the bin Laden home and preached in the mosques he attended while growing up, explains how Osama's radical philosophy developed.

As we discuss Osama bin Laden's life in more detail, we will learn how he was later influenced by other radical and "revivalist" schools of Sunni fundamentalism. Osama was first introduced in some depth to the teachings of Qutbism and Salafism during his college days at King Abdul Aziz University in Jeddah. These other radical, purist, or revivalist schools of Sunni Islam undoubtedly buttressed his extremist views. But such extremist convictions held by the man who declared war on America were molded by Wahhabi theology, which dominates Saudi Arabia.

Parenthetically, one of the most serious sources of the problems Pakistan faces today with controlling terrorism in its country is found in their educational system. In this traditionally poor country, the Wahhabis stepped forward years ago and agreed to build and run Pakistan's schools for them. They had plenty of Saudi oil money to provide an education for Pakistani youngsters that the government couldn't afford. So massive numbers of school children in Pakistan received indoctrination in the radical, fundamentalist teachings of Wahhabism. It is not difficult to figure out that this produced fertile ground for recruiting by al-Qaeda and the Taliban. (This type of Wahhabi indoctrination has happened—and still is happening all over the world. It is occurring even in parts of the United States.)

Osama bin Laden made a name for himself and gained his initial notoriety in the Muslim world as a result of his efforts in Afghanistan after the Soviet invasion. With the Soviets' "retreat, defeat and (the) collapse" of the Soviet Union, we viewed this as a major victory for America, President Ronald Reagan, and the free world. The long Cold War had been won! Osama saw these events from a totally different perspective.

Lewis in effect translates and interprets Osama's many written and spoken statements on his vision of world history. Lewis explains that for Osama bin Laden, the war in Afghanistan against the Soviets was merely an extension of the war between believers and unbelievers that had gone on for 14 centuries.

> "We in the West think of the defeat and collapse of the Soviet Union as a Western victory, or more specifically, as an American victory, or even more specifically, as President Reagan's victory. According to the point of view of Osama bin Laden and his many, many followers, it was nothing of the kind. It was not a Western victory in the Cold War; it was a Muslim victory in a Holy War. It was a triumph of Islam in a jihad against the infidels. Osama bin Laden is very clear and very explicit on this subject. This war between the true believers and the unbelievers has been going on for 14 centuries."

Obviously, Osama bin Laden believed—or at least his followers are convinced he believed—that Allah enabled the *mujahedeen* (or "holy warriors") to defeat the mighty Soviet Union. The massive American military assistance had nothing to do with the victory, in Osama's words.

Using Osama's statements—sometimes his exact words— Lewis carefully laid out bin Laden's view of history through his Islamic eyes. No one in the room understood this as a casual history lesson, because we realized that our terrorist enemies see the United States of America as the major obstacle to their ultimate victory. These terrorists believe they have a divine obligation to attack America in any and every way possible.

Osama believed that the war between Islam and Christianity had gone through several phases since Mohammad commanded the caliphs who succeeded him to conquer the lands surrounding Arabia. The first phase was "the first great Islamic expansion" that saw Muslim armies expand into Europe, conquering Spain, Portugal, and southern Italy. But the Christians belatedly fought back, driving the Muslims out by the reconquest of former Christian lands.

The second major expansion took place when the Ottoman Empire conquered the ancient Christian city of Constantinople and ultimately reached the gates of Vienna. The Muslim advances aimed at world domination (and subsequently the establishment of Islamic law) were halted when they were decisively defeated at the "second siege of Vienna."

Once again the Christian (European) forces eventually fought back. Then, as Lewis quotes Osama bin Laden's exact words, "came the final humiliation," when virtually all the lands of Islam were conquered and divided among the rival European empires. Even Istanbul (formerly Constantinople under Christian rule), which had become the seat of the caliphate, was occupied by infidel armies.

At some point, Osama must have reached the conclusion that he must take up the mantle and lead or inspire the jihadists to carry out what he believed to be the final phase of this 1,400 year struggle. (I assume, based on many readings on the subject, that Osama bin Laden became convinced that the role that had fallen on his shoulders in the Afghanistan conflict was preordained by Allah. Some contend that he believes he must become the new caliph and command the faithful.)

Lewis continued:

> "As Osama bin Laden put it, in this, the final phase of the ongoing holy war, 'we, the Muslims, have to fight against these two superpowers. In Afghanistan, we have defeated and destroyed the more deadly, the more dangerous of the two. Dealing with the soft, pampered and effeminate Americans will be easy. They lack the appetite or the capacity for the kind of war in which we shall now be engaged.'"

Lewis believes Osama was convinced by events in the 1980s and 1990s that he had accurately assessed America. The Islamic terrorists bombed American installations—embassies, military barracks, and even an American warship—all over the world. These acts of terror were met with harsh rhetoric but timid action. We removed our troops, bombed mostly uninhabited—or slightly inhabited—lands. When we bombed a pharmaceutical manufacturing facility (which some suggested might have been making biochemical weapons), we did so at night in order that no one would be killed, save possibly some unfortunate cleaning crews.

Bin Laden was emboldened by the Islamic successes in driving the infidels from Muslim lands: the Soviets from Afghanistan and the Americans from other parts of the Muslim world. Lewis said that Osama was especially encouraged by the fact that Islamic terrorist attacks on American troops in Mogadishu and Beirut were followed by an immediate withdrawal. Osama was convinced these withdrawals proved his dictum about Americans: "Hit them and they'll run."

Such weak responses to vicious attacks convinced Osama bin Laden it was time to begin the planning of a dramatic and devastating attack on the heartland of America in the latter half of the 1990s.[22]

We now know that the plans for the 9/11 attacks were agreed upon in 1998. The careful selection of the suicide terrorists and their intense training began in earnest at that time. They agonized over every detail, trying to avoid any mistakes.

(This gives rise to the questions that never completely go away: How could our government, with all of its sophisticated intelligence-gathering capacities, have not taken more seriously the threat that some such an attack was being planned?[23] There had been an abundance of warnings, including the bombing of the World Trade Center in New York in 1993, the attack on the U.S.S. Cole in October 2000 (just 10 months earlier), the bombing of embassies in North Africa, and other such terrorist activities.[24] America learned the hard way that 9/11 signaled an all-out Islamic terrorist war on American and her Western allies![25])

Lewis explained succinctly for his audience what 9/11 was about in the minds of Osama bin Laden and his fellow Islamic terrorist leaders:

> "This was the culmination of Phase I in driving the infidels out of the lands of Islam. It was the inauguration of Phase II, bring the Holy War into the heartland of the enemy to complete the final conquest of the world and its submission to the true faith, doing them the great service of paving their way toward heaven and all its delights."

Lewis wants to make sure that we understand the religious motivations of our terrorist enemies. Once we understand, he hopes we will make our voices heard on the subject. It is all too evident that most of our policymakers either do not have this knowledge or are not acting on such knowledge.

Lewis concluded his lecture and the Q&A session mainly by explaining certain events in Islam's theological history that inspired these terrorists. He refers in his books to the "revivalist" theologian who advocated a return to "pure" Islam and its puritanical practices. In this case, he mentions the one who is the most important in understanding today's Sunni Islamic terrorism, Muhammad ibn Abd al-Wahhab.

He notes that al-Wahhab would have been only a country preacher in a remote desert area of Arabia, unknown to history, except for two events. Unfortunately these two events would threaten world peace in modern times.

One, Najd, the remote village in which al-Wahhab lived, was on a main route used by Muslims for the annual pilgrimage to Mecca. The stories he heard from these Muslims was virtually his only source of information from the outside world. Al-Wahhab became convinced that the defeats being suffered by the Ottoman Empire in the late 18th century were not a result of their failure to modernize their military. The defeats were a result of having failed to wage holy war and to enforce strict holy law as required by pure Islamic teachings. They had lost the favor of Allah because of their lack of devotion.

Two, and most important of all, one of al-Wahhab's earliest converts was Muhammad ibn Saud, who ruled the province of Najd. This would lead to the "marriage of the House of Saud with Wahhabism." The victory of the House of Saud over the Hashemite dynasty in the mid 1920s gave the Saudi monarchy immediate prestige as custodian of the two Muslim holy cities, Mecca and Medina. This would also enable the Saudis to exert major influence over the entire Muslim world as millions of Muslims made the pilgrimage to Mecca each year.

Then the world changed dramatically with the discovery of oil in Saudi Arabia. This created wealth beyond the Saudi's wildest dreams. As Lewis noted:

> "This made Saudi Arabia a world power, first within Islam, and then within the larger world. And gave a global importance to a version of Islam which would otherwise have been an extremist fringe on the edge of a marginal country. It is no longer that now. And the Wahhabi element is of great and growing importance."

Lewis repeated his warning that the radical Wahhabi version of Sunni Islam is being spread around the world in Muslim schools, courtesy of Saudi oil money. In the Q&A session, Lewis raised the question of how long Americans and Westerners can afford to "turn a blind eye" to the Saudis' financing of the teaching of extremist Wahhabism worldwide. [26] He somberly concluded in his final statement of the lecture that he sees "only one real solution to the Wahhabi problem and that is to find a cheap and effective substitute for oil. I'm not joking."

To prevent a false impression of worldwide Islam, a few comments about Wahhabism should be made at this point and discussed in more detail in the next chapter. As Lewis stated in his closing comments, "the Wahhabi-dominated Sunni version of Islam" is not that of "the popular masses" of Sunnis. (He also says "the popular masses" of Shiites do not embrace the radical Shiite version of Islam upon which "the Iranian revolution" was based.) I would further point out that while virtually all fundamentalist Wahhabis in Saudi Arabia and other parts of the world accept a strict interpretation of holy war and holy law, the overwhelming majority of them certainly are not terrorists, and most do not support terrorism as a valid means to achieve their goals.

Recent polling data from Saudi Arabia indicates that two-thirds of the population, which is overwhelmingly Wahhabi, now holds an unfavorable opinion of al-Qaeda and Osama bin Laden.[27] They strongly reject the tactics of suicide bombings and the killing of other Muslims in al-Qaeda's terrorist activities. They also resent the fact that such terrorist activities have invited retaliation on Muslim countries and further defamed the name of Islam among non-Muslims.

The Saudi Arabia dilemma is by far the most important long-term key to future peace and tranquility between the Muslim and non-Muslim worlds. King Abdullah, as the monarch of the Kingdom of Saudi Arabia, is the custodian of the "Two Holy Mosques" and therefore has considerable influence throughout the Muslim world. A deal struck in 1750 between regional ruler Muhammad bin Saud and Islamic reformer Muhammad Ab al-Wahhab resulted ultimately in the establishment of the Saudi monarchy in 1932. A continuing result of this deal is that fundamentalist Sunni Wahhabism is the official religion of Saudi Arabia until this day. This marriage has resulted in a complicated and sometimes contradictory relationship. The vast majority of Wahhabis in Saudi Arabia, and in many other places, denounce the radical Islamists who engage in acts of terror. But many such terrorists find the justification for their acts of terror in the radical brand of Islam they teach.[28] Saudi rulers must keep the fundamentalist Wahhabi clerics happy—even when they insist on strict enforcement of *sharia* law, which always results in discriminatory and sometimes brutal treatment of women. If the powerful mullahs turn the masses against the fragile monarchy,[29] it could spell deep trouble for them.

As explained in Chapter 3, Saudi intelligence joined with our CIA to infiltrate al-Qaeda in Yemen with a double agent. The operative, posing as a suicide bomber, persuaded them to provide him with one of AQAP's new non-metallic bombs for such a mission on an airliner bound for America. The Saudis desperately need our protection from radical Islamist terrorists,[30] and we are heavily dependent on their oil.

Saudi Arabia has 25 percent of the world's known oil reserves and the capacity to produce 10 million barrels of oil a day. The Saudis can control the price of the crude oil we import from the Middle East based on how much they choose to produce. Compare the leverage they have today to what they will have when our energy demands increase by 45 percent in 23 years (by 2035) as experts predict. These facts help explain why we have been reluctant to lean on them for their human-rights violations. Perhaps this also sheds light on why our government never demands that they cease providing billions of dollars each year to their Wahhabi clerics so they can spread radical Wahhabism around the world.

There is a solution to this urgent problem if we listen to Bernard Lewis' warning that we will never solve "the Wahhabi problem" until we find a "cheap and effective substitute for oil." God has placed the vital natural resources necessary for such a "substitute" in our country. We certainly have the technology. All we need is the political will! There are many possible sources of energy that can help wean us off our excessive addiction to foreign crude oil. Some are not yet cost effective, and others may make a difference in the future but are not likely to make much of an impact in the near term. But our national security needs dictate that we concentrate on the obvious. No reputable expert denies that we have more natural gas than Saudi Arabia has oil. As a matter of fact, the available data indicate that we have enough natural gas to fill our needs for at least 100 years. (If God lets the world stand that long, we will have plenty of time to develop many other sources of energy.)

Fabled oil man and noted philanthropist T. Boone Pickens made a very compelling case on "Fox News Sunday" June 24, 2012, for natural gas as the timely solution to our oil problem. Pickens made the point that we have so much natural gas in this country that we are considering exporting much of what is being produced at present to China and other countries.

Always in command of pertinent facts, Pickens also noted that we now import 4.4 million barrels of oil a day from OPEC. He then pointed out that we have 250 million gasoline-burning vehicles on our roads today. Of those, only 8 million are heavy duty trucks ("18-wheelers"). But these big trucks burn 3 million of the 4.4 million barrels we import from OPEC each day. If we converted all of these to natural-gas-burning vehicles, our dependence on oil from Middle Eastern countries, many of which are our enemies, could be virtually ended. Then Pickens adds this kicker: There is a major environmental incentive because burning natural gas would be "30 percent cleaner than diesel."

In view of such uncontested facts, the logical question is why on earth has Congress not already moved to provide the incentives necessary to motivate owners of large trucks to retrofit their old trucks and buy new ones that burn natural gas? As some political wags have suggested, this is a solution way too easy for a sufficient majority in Congress to agree upon. Obviously, the full answer is more complex, but the lack of congressional action is certainly shortsighted. Some farsighted major corporations, such as FedEx, UPS, and Waste Management, have undertaken a major program of conversion to natural gas.

Boone Pickens astutely contended that the conversion to natural gas as our primary source of fuel for our vehicles has to happen. There will be no choice in the not-too-distant future. But if we fail to add conversion incentives, it could take 10 to 15 years. Meanwhile, we will send trillions of dollars overseas, much of which will end up in the hands of Islamist terrorists, and we will continue needlessly to pollute our environment. And even more serious, we will compromise the urgent energy needs for our military in the event of a national security crisis involving some of the countries we depend on for our oil supplies.

Once again we ask, why is Washington so slow to act on such an important matter? One reason given by some is that Congress should not pick "winners and losers." This may be a result of the fact that the multi-billions of dollars spent on ethanol subsidies has made very little impact on our need for foreign oil. The government's massive subsidy of solar energy has likely produced more scandals than energy. But the totally beneficial use of natural gas for fueling vehicles, especially large diesel-burning trucks, is beyond debate. Natural gas is much cheaper than diesel, much more environmentally friendly, and is abundantly available.

Undoubtedly the major reason Congress has not acted is the large, well-funded chemical and fertilizer lobby. (Those who produce chemicals and fertilizer use large amounts of natural gas in this process. Therefore, when the price of natural gas is almost literally dirt cheap, they make windfall profits.) This lobby not only passes out sizable campaign checks to their supporters—not that unusual for most industries—but they are also sometimes noted for threatening to pour major resources into the campaigns of the opponents of those who vote to expand the use of our vast natural gas deposits even for reasons of national security.

It is undoubtedly true that the price of natural gas will reach a profitable level once it is in more demand for vehicles. But most experts contend that it will hit a peak and still run $1.50 a gallon less than diesel. This is certainly an incentive for big trucks to transition to natural gas. But it costs $60,000 or more to retrofit or purchase a large truck that uses natural gas. This is why there must be an incentive such as a tax credit in order to get these heavy diesel-burning trucks off our roads in a timely manner.

The stakes could not be much higher. It should get our attention when no less of an authority than Lewis warns that the only way he believes we can stop the worldwide spread of radical Wahhabism, which breeds much of today's terrorism, is to find a "cheap and effective substitute" for Saudi oil.

Does Our Government Understand?

Confusion about Islam, Islamic history, and the sources of the deep-seated religious convictions of the Islamic terrorists (as we have illustrated) can at least partially explain—certainly not excuse—the failure of most of our government leaders and policymakers to understand our enemy in the so-called "war on terrorism." But the failure to comprehend the religious underpinnings of radical Islamic terrorists has placed this country in grave danger. Such a lack of understanding has led to questionable, if not dangerous, foreign policy decisions. The American people must strive to understand and insist that our government leaders understand what motivates our terrorist enemies.

The extremely urgent and serious nature of this problem is evidenced when our government officials—reaching at times to the highest level—issue statements that indicate they either do not understand the motivation of the radical Islamic terrorists or are deliberately playing down their intentions for some misguided foreign policy considerations.

I will attempt to document in the following pages the bipartisan nature of the problem. What do the Islamic terrorists conclude when an American president says that "an ancient religion of peace" has been hijacked by a bunch of terrorists, as did George W. Bush? Osama bin Laden and his fellow terrorist leaders logically would conclude that America's leaders have little or no knowledge of Islam or Islamic history. Many of our leaders certainly give evidence that they completely underestimate the depth of the religious appeal these terrorist leaders have to potential terrorists.

Everyone seems to agree—even liberal apologists—that the poor and uneducated are more susceptible to the call to become jihadists even at the expense of their own lives *because they believe it will gain Allah's favor in the hereafter*. But the best known and most recent Islamist terrorist attacks—and attempted terrorist attacks—on American soil, as well as that of our European allies, involved mostly highly educated men from privileged backgrounds. A few of the most notorious of these jihadist efforts will be analyzed in this chapter. The fact that in each case their devotion to Islamist *jihad* inspired their terrorist actions will become irrefutably self-evident.

The self-professed obvious ignorance of the religious nature of this war evidenced by American policymakers also is valuable to the terrorist hierarchy for reaching out to the hundreds of millions of fundamentalist Muslims who will never become active terrorists.[31] The terrorist leaders seek clandestine financial support[32] from such Muslims and the tacit respectability that comes from an occasional mention of the nobility of their goals—or, if nothing else, just the failure of these Muslims to publically condemn their terrorist activities.

The Obama Administration wasted little time making it clear that they don't see this struggle as a "global" conflict or a "war on terrorism." They chose simply to describe the Islamic terrorist threat in a more "politically correct" manner as "overseas contingency operations." Such words must have been beautiful music to the ears of the terrorist masterminds. It was not until Jan. 7, 2010, just a few days before the first anniversary of his swearing in as president, that President Obama finally admitted that we were at least at war with al-Qaeda. The global Islamic terrorist threat is much larger than al-Qaeda. But there is no question that al-Qaeda and its former leader, Osama bin Laden, was the engine driving the jihadist train.

Dr. Ayman al-Zawahri, long considered to be the "brains" of al-Qaeda, took control of the organization after bin Laden's death. Al-Zawahri, a devout follower of Qutbism, is even more radical (if that is possible) than bin Laden and is certainly more daring. Al-Qaeda, like the Taliban, has been weakened by U.S. efforts, but al-Zawahri is making every effort to get this train back on its dangerous track. We must pray and be eternally vigilant to prevent him from getting his hands on a nuclear weapon or some type of a biological weapon.

As noted in the previous chapter, President Obama initially attempted to play down the Christmas Day 2009 would-be Nigerian underwear bomber's unsuccessful attempt to bring an airliner down over Detroit by contending it was the work of "an isolated extremist." Once the security report was evaluated and released 14 days later, however, Obama's understanding of the Islamic terrorist threat may have changed dramatically. The late liberal political writer, David Broder, who had a reputation for being fair and balanced, wrote a column printed in *The Washington Post* Jan. 8, 2010, titled "Obama's wake-up call." He makes the case that this event may turn out to be as significant for President Obama as 9/11 was for President Bush.

Exactly a week earlier, on Jan. 1, an op-ed piece in the *Post*, "War? What war?," written by conservative columnist Charles Krauthammer, was highly critical of Obama's belated initial response to this terrorist attack that almost cost 288 people in the air their lives. Had it not been for the heroic action of some passengers—especially one Dutch citizen—and a faulty detonator, it is difficult to speculate on how much additional carnage might have occurred on the ground.

The Islamic suicide bomber had planned for the explosion to occur not simply anywhere along the route, but over the city of Detroit. Krauthammer contends:

> "From the beginning, President Obama has relentlessly tried to play down and deny the nature of the terrorist threat we continue to face. Napolitano renames terrorism 'man-caused disasters.' Obama goes abroad and pledges to cleanse America of its post-9/11 counterterrorist sins. Hence, Guantanamo will close, CIA interrogators will face a special prosecutor and Khalid Sheik Mohammed will bask in a civilian trial in New York—a trifecta of political correctness and image management."[33]

Krauthammer says that Obama's tendency to play down a jihadist conspiracy in the attempted Detroit airline bombing follows the same pattern he set when cautioning "against jumping to conclusions" about "Nidal Hasan's Islamist ideology" when Major Hasan on Nov. 5, 2009, murdered 13 in the Fort Hood shooting spree.

In his Jan. 1 article, Krauthammer complained that Obama's refusal even to refer to the "war on terror" was giving the impression that the president thought the war was over, if it ever existed. Unfortunately, warned Krauthammer, al-Qaeda certainly does not think this war is over.

A week later, Obama had received the intelligence report revealing all the evidence available to our intelligence agencies about the Nigerian terrorist's father trying to warn about his son's demeanor, the one-way plane ticket paid for in cash, and his having no luggage on a trip to Detroit in the middle of the winter. More importantly, President Obama was given details about Umar Farouk Abdulmutallab's leaving Nigeria for a considerable stay in Yemen, where he met with al-Qaeda operatives who ultimately provided him with the explosives. The Nigerian's contacts and probable meetings with the radical imam Anwar Aulaqi,[34] and all the rest may have opened President Obama's eyes to the severity and urgency of the threat posed by al-Qaeda globally.

In response to such detailed intelligence, President Obama for the first time said we are at war with al-Qaeda and that "we will do whatever it takes to defeat them." David Broder senses that this episode had a major impact on the president:

> "The Christmas plot appears to have shaken Obama like nothing else that has happened in the first year. When he allowed the White House to quote his warning to his Cabinet colleagues that another 'screw up' like that could not be tolerated, he seemed to signal that his benign leadership style has reached its limits."[35]

If Broder is correct that this blatant al-Qaeda terrorist plot has incensed Obama to the degree that the 9/11 attack infuriated Bush, our country will be safer for it.[36] Bush determined that those responsible must pay the price. The result was that no Islamic terrorist attack took place on American soil for the remainder of George W. Bush's presidency.

We can only hope that what Broder calls "Obama's wake-up call" will be loud enough to motivate him to stand up to the hard left-wingers who helped elect him—at least in this war with the Islamic terrorists.[37] One example undoubtedly typifies the pressure Obama will be under from such hard left-wingers. Just two days after Broder's reasonable interpretation of President Obama's forceful response—once he had all the facts at his disposal—to this latest al-Qaeda directed terrorist plot, a member of the hard-left press responded. Dana Milbank, to whom some refer as part of the "irresponsible left" rather than simply the "hard left," penned a column for The Washington Post's Jan. 10, 2010, "Sunday Opinion" section titled, "Was that al-Qaeda's best shot?"

Once Milbank finishes his jokes about "Jihad Jockeys" and "Fruit of the Boom," he tries to make a case for how amateurish al-Qaeda is—or has become—and how minimal the terrorist threat is that they pose to America and her allies. My first reaction was that this column is so absurd that it doesn't deserve any rational refutation. But then I realized that the hard left—certainly not honest liberals—is adept at using such diversionary tactics. The hard left in the media or academia, like their counterparts in the political world and the ACLU, have never been inclined to let the security interest of our citizens get in the way of their hard-core agenda.

Surely Milbank realizes how devastating this well-planned suicide attack could have been but for this young Nigerian's failure to properly detonate these explosives and the swift and heroic action of certain passengers and crew. All intelligence experts concluded that he had more than enough explosives to have blown a massive hole in the aircraft.

Maybe Milbank didn't follow the lengthy and sophisticated plot that al-Qaeda and its Taliban co-conspirators hatched and that claimed the lives of seven brave—and virtually irreplaceable—CIA operatives in Afghanistan. Two lengthy front page articles as well as an article in the "Outlook" section titled "Al-Qaeda's New Grand Strategy"[38] in the same edition of The Washington Post as Milbank's column document the truth about the growing and alarming al-Qaeda terrorist threat. However, far left elitists steer clear of knowledgeable authorities who would present facts that contradict their preconceived ideas of how they want things to be.

A front-page story headlined "Tape reveals close links among 3 terrorist groups," written primarily by Post special correspondent Haq Nawaz Khan in Pakistan, states the severity of the threat. Referencing a videotape released after Jordanian doctor Humam Khalil Abu-Mulal al-Balawi's suicide bombing of a CIA outpost in Afghanistan, Khan wrote this chilling account:

> "The videotape confirmed the Pakistani Taliban's central role
> in the bombing and exposed its close links with al-Qaeda and with the

Afghan Taliban. It suggested an unexpected degree of coordination, capability and shared ambition among the three movements that some experts here said may force the United States to reassess its regional and even global counter-terrorism strategy."[39]

Charles Krauthammer, in a *Washington Post* op-ed a week after his highly critical column, commends Obama for taking certain initiatives such as "high-level special screening for passengers from 14 countries, the vast majority of which are Muslim with significant Islamist elements." He further praises the president's decision not to transfer any prisoners from Guantanamo to Yemen.

Still the biggest mistake as far as Krauthammer is concerned is to treat the would-be Nigerian bomber, Umar Farouk Abdulmutallab, as a common criminal and afford him a trial in an American court. He is not an American citizen, he was trained and equipped with explosives by al-Qaeda, and he is clearly an enemy combatant. Krauthammer says that if he is held in a military prison, he can be interrogated about al-Qaeda in the Arabian Peninsula and its plans for additional attacks on America and her allies.

Ilan Berman, vice president of the American Foreign Policy Council, obviously believes that our leaders know more than some of their statements would indicate: "In practice, however, both the United States and its adversaries understand full well the objective of the current struggle: to confront and defeat the forces of radical Islamic extremism."[40] This does not totally reassure me that such leaders truly recognize the religious nature of this "war."

The next high-profile Islamic terrorist attempt to inflict massive human carnage on Americans occurred at New York's Times Square on May 1, 2010. Attorney General Holder's determination to try Islamic terrorists as criminals in civil court rather than as enemy combatants in military tribunals reached a new peak of opposition when he ordered the Miranda rights read to the would-be Times Square terrorist bomber, who was in fact a naturalized American citizen. On Saturday, May 1, 2010, Faisal Shahzad parked his recently purchased used sports utility vehicle, filled with massive explosives, next to Viacom at Times Square. An alert street vender noticed smoke oozing out of the back of the vehicle and immediately notified the police. Less than 54 hours later, authorities took Shahzad off an already loaded airliner bound for Dubai.

Immediately after the explosives-filled vehicle was discovered, New York Mayor Michael Bloomberg cautioned against overreacting, saying this was probably the work of a lone wolf or a deranged individual. Administration officials in Washington echoed similar sentiments. Certainly none of these people wanted to be so "politically incorrect" as to suggest this might be part of an organized Islamic terrorist attack. Once his identity was revealed, Shahzad was described by *The Washington Post* as a "down on his luck" fellow who had failed to pay his mortgage, resulting in foreclosure, and that this was probably what motivated the attack after his chance at the American Dream failed.

The facts in this case turned out to be a very different story. Shahzad came from a prominent wealthy and well-educated Pakistani family; he received a B.A from the University of Bridgeport in 2002; and in 2004, he married an American-born woman of Pakistani heritage in an arranged marriage. (Her Pakistani parents lived in Colorado when she was born, while her father was earning two master's degrees in petroleum engineering and economics at the Colorado School of Mines. He is a recognized expert in his field, and the family now lives in Saudi Arabia.)

His marriage enabled him to obtain American citizenship, and he brought back large sums of money—$80,000 on more than one occasion. He travelled back to Pakistan dozens of times during his 10-year stay in the U.S.

On his most recent trip to Pakistan, he had received six months of intensive terrorist training at a Taliban camp in North Waziristan. Fortunately, he did not remember enough of such training to buy the right type of fertilizer; he failed to open the valve on the propane cylinder and was unable to successfully ignite these powerful explosives. Otherwise, we would have experienced another 9/11 type disaster, most likely involving even more human carnage, at Times Square. Luck was on our side again. House Republican Leader John Boehner aptly stated, "Yes we were lucky, but luck is not an effective strategy for fighting terrorism."

All the politically correct types became obsessed with the question of when Shahzad became radicalized. It is known that his family was made up of mostly moderate Muslims in Pakistan—some members of his mother's family even were adherents of the relatively small sect of Sufi mystics who are noted for their tolerance.

At the time, I did not notice anyone of prominence mention the fact that the radical Wahhabis run most of the madrassas in Pakistan, which are funded by Saudi oil money. As a matter of fact, if the politically correct types who were trying to play down any jihadist motivation would have taken the time to check, they would have discovered that he actually attended primary school in Saudi Arabia before finishing his middle-school and high-school education in Pakistan. It is highly likely that he was simply reverting back to the extremist Wahhabi teachings he had been exposed to in his youth.

The "down on his luck" description didn't carry much weight when it became evident that the enthusiastic, would-be Times Square bomber had become increasingly immersed in Islamic theology as far back as 2006 and had subsequently lost interest in his professional career. His marriage came on hard times in 2009 when he insisted that his University of Colorado-educated wife start wearing a *hijab* and move with their two young children to Pakistan while he sought a job in a Muslim-ruled country. He didn't pay his mortgage, which resulted in a foreclosure, because he no longer wanted to live in the United States, which he now considered to be evil because it was killing Muslims.

After being indicted by a federal grand jury in June on 10 counts of terrorism and weapons charges, he pleaded guilty to all charges in the U.S. District Court in

Manhattan. Shahzad defiantly identified himself in court as a "Muslim soldier" and threatened continued Islamic holy war against America.

Attorney General Holder, in testimony before the House Judiciary Committee on May 13, 2010,was reluctant even to admit that "radical Islam" was "part of the cause" of this attempted attack and other recent such attacks or attempted attacks. In the hearing, Congressman Lamar Smith (R-Tex), the ranking Republican on the committee, asked Holder "whether 'radical Islam' was behind the attempted car bombing, last year's so-called 'underpants bomber' or the killings at Fort Hood in Texas," as reported in *The Washington Times*.[41] Holder told the committee: "There are a variety of reasons why people do these things. Some of them are potentially religious." Congressman Smith was incredulous in his response: "I don't know why the administration has such difficulty acknowledging the obvious, which is that radical Islam might have excited these individuals." He then astutely pointed out, "If you can't name the enemy, then you're going to have a hard time trying to respond to them."

Holder's attitude toward possible terrorist threats to our country unfortunately is typical of many of the highest officials in the Obama administration. They either are so committed to a policy of political correctness that ignores obvious facts (apparently mistakenly believe this serves the interest of the majority of moderate Muslims), or they are totally ignorant of the clearly stated motivations and goals of global Islamic terrorism. It is becoming clear that they have no understanding of the divergent teachings of Islam; the varied history of Islam, which includes hundreds of years of Muslim conquest and attempted conquest of Christian lands; the multitude of Muslim revivalist movements intended to bring about a return to "pure" or fundamentalist Islam; and the extensive statements of a multitude of modern-day jihadist leaders such as Osama bin Laden.

Just two weeks after Holder's appearance before the House Judiciary Committee, John Brennan, President Obama's advisor on counterintelligence and homeland security matters at the National Security Council, addressed the Center for Strategic and International Studies. The purpose of the address was to offer CSIS members and members of the press a review of the administration's new National Security report, to be released the following day. Listening to Brennan's remarks and answers during the Q&A period on C-SPAN convinced me (and I believe anyone with even an elementary knowledge of Islam and Islamic history) that a blind commitment to political correctness leads to naïveté on the subject.

For example, Brennan explained that this administration would no longer use the words "jihadist" or "Islamist," because "jihad is a holy struggle, a legitimate tenet of Islam, meaning to purify oneself or one's community." As is extensively documented in this book, this is one meaning of "*jihad*" as used in the Koran and the subsequent schools of Islamic jurisprudence. Many scholars contend this was the earliest meaning of "*jihad*" during the Meccan period when Mohammed and his followers had no political and military power. Numerous Muslim and non-Muslim scholars—including Dr. Bernard Lewis—have referenced many examples where *"jihad"* was frequently used also in a military context—some scholars document as many as 114 occasions where *"jihad"* was used in the Koran in a clear military context. Volumes have been written by Islamic scholars and jurists over the years on the different requirements for Muslim men's participation in "offensive" and "defensive" jihadist military actions.

Brennan suggested in answer to one question that a study of behavioral sciences might be productive in determining the motivation of such terrorists. Apparently he remains unimpressed with their own statements that they are carrying out Allah's will, as emphasized by the usual last cry of the suicide bomber, *"Allahu Akbar!"* Brennan further stated his opinion that there is "no single cause" for the attacks of homegrown or foreign terrorists and no defining "terrorist profile." He is certainly correct that that there is no consistent profile based on education, social standing, or station in life. These terrorists are sometimes highly educated and sometimes illiterate, some are rich while others come from poverty, some are young while others are old, and the list goes on and on. If one rules out their religious convictions, then they cannot be profiled. Certainly, some terrorists are inspired to a jihadist act by a particular event in the Muslim world, for example, but the only "single cause" is their religious convictions.

To make himself perfectly clear in a June interview with *The Washington Times,* Brennan actually told reporters that he disagrees that "there is an Islamic dimension to terrorism."[42] Astonishing!

Why is it so difficult for the leaders of this administration—and Brennan calls on similar attitudes of leaders of the previous administration—to understand that realistically recognizing the jihadist fervor of our terrorist enemies is not a disservice to the vast majority of moderate or peaceful Muslims throughout the world? On the contrary, being honest is a service of respect to moderate Muslims. It offers them the opportunity to separate themselves clearly from—and to emphatically condemn—these sworn Islamic jihadists whom they believe to be following teachings of their religion they consider illegitimate. No responsible or recognized leader—no matter how far to the right or the left—has ever suggested that we are at war with Islam. But we are at war with global Islamic terrorists who have declared such a war on America in the name of their religious beliefs.

White House counterterrorism advisor Brennan did indicate that the new National Security report recognizes that we are still involved in a war with al-Qaeda and its worldwide affiliates. He also indicated awareness that these terrorist organizations are actively recruiting more terrorists, including American citizens, all over the globe. He pointed out that in addition to many other means, they are also extensively using the Internet for such recruitment.

As far as I am concerned, the most flagrant example of a total lack of understanding of the motivation and beliefs of the Islamic terrorists was written by

Vice President Joe Biden during the 2008 political campaign.[43] Then-Senator Joe Biden wrote an op-ed piece for the *Wall Street Journal* titled "Republicans and Our Enemies."[44] Biden's article illustrates an apparent lack of understanding that exists even among the highest levels of our political leaders about the nature of the threat we face from the radical Islamic terrorists. This misunderstanding is chilling. The purpose of the Biden article was to respond to an op-ed a few days earlier by Senator Joe Lieberman, who argued that Democrats had forsaken the foreign policy of such prominent Democrat presidents as FDR, Harry Truman, and JFK.

Senator Biden first criticized the foreign policies of President Bush and Senator John McCain, especially as they related to Iran. Biden proceeded to criticize President Bush for ignoring more serious international threats because of his "obsession with the 'war on terrorism.'" (What could possibly be more important than stopping the terrorists who are constantly attempting to kill Americans? Obviously, the Iranian threat is very serious, because Iran is determined to produce nuclear weapons. But an American president should have the competence to deal with more than one threat at a time.)

At that point, Biden makes arguably the most uninformed statement ever uttered by a Western leader: "But to compare terrorism with an all-encompassing ideology like communism and fascism is evidence of profound confusion." Even the slightest study of the history of Islam, the Muslim wars of conquest, especially under the "rightly guided caliphs" in the seventh and eighth centuries, and the statements in the Koran and the teachings of Mohammad concerning *jihad* and Islamic law would reveal the sources of the "all-encompassing ideology" of the Islamic terrorists. No "ism" in human history, including Hitler's Nazism, has ever been so "all-encompassing"!

"Moderate" Muslims may interpret these matters in a different way, or even privately reject some evidence to the contrary that is hard to explain, but Islamic terrorists claim such teachings and examples not only as justification for their actions but as divine commands they dare not ignore. Osama bin Laden, Ayman al Zawahiri, the founders of the Muslim Brotherhood, Hamas, Hezbollah, the Taliban and the hundreds or perhaps thousands of other Islamic terrorist organizations and their adherents clearly and repeatedly justify their behavior as obedience to Allah's commands.

In late 2008, Robert Spencer released his eighth book on Islam and *jihad* with the title *Stealth Jihad: How Radical Islam Is Subverting America without Guns or Bombs.* He makes the following astute point in response to a University of North Carolina professor's bemoaning the fact that little positive is said about the image of Islam in Europe and America. This blatant Islamic apologist on the UNC faculty offers his theory that westerners are projecting their negative feeling about themselves on others as they criticize Islam. Spencer responds:

> "Projection? So we are to believe that the September 11 attacks in New York and Washington, the 2005 attacks in London, the

Madrid subway bombing, the attacks on a school in Beslan and a theatre in Moscow, the 2002 and 2005 Bali bombings, the murder of Theo van Gogh in the streets of Amsterdam, the beheadings of Nicholas Berg and Daniel Pearl, the murder of scores of Buddhists in southern Thailand, and over ten thousand other jihadist terror attacks around the world since September 11—all committed by Muslims and in the name of Islam—have nothing to do with Islam's negative image in the West? (emphasis added).[45]

Biden tries to justify his outrageous statement by arguing that terrorism "is a means, not an end"[46] and references the difference between the Shiites and Sunnis as well as the different Persian and Arabian backgrounds. He is right that Persians and Arabs don't especially like each other because of past history. It is also true that the Sunni-Shiite split, which arose in the early days after Mohammad's death, has been long and bloody. However, their disagreements relate to questions of the legitimate successors to Mohammad and ritualistic concerns about holy places, holy days, and saints. There has never been any serious disagreement about *jihad* and *sharia*.

What terrorists could Joe Biden possibly have had in mind who did not have an "all-encompassing ideology" like the communists and fascists? Could he have possibly thought that some of these terrorists were Hindus or Buddhists? Certainly he could not have been referring to the Islamic terrorists who declared "holy war" on America and her allies and dramatically demonstrated their sincerity in the 9/11 attack.   It was often said of atheistic communism and godless fascism that they carried out their oppressive, murderous, and evil regimes with religious zealotry. Islamic terrorists take their zealotry to a new level—because they believe with all their heart that they are carrying out Allah's will.

As already mentioned, this total lack of understanding of the nature of our enemy is not partisan, as illustrated by some of the compromises made by the Bush administration so as not to offend Islamic sensitivities as they carried out the "war on terrorism." However, in spite of certain statements by Bush that indicated an apparent failure to understand what really motivates our enemies, this may not have been the case. The Bush administration carried out the "war" so effectively for more than seven years, none of the above-mentioned 10,000 terrorist attacks after 9/11 occurred on American soil.

But for the future, the bottom line remains: You cannot win a war if you fail to understand the nature and goals of your enemy. America's enemy is not Islam or the hundreds of millions of peace-loving Muslims around the world. Our enemy is the radical or fundamentalist Islamist who employs terrorism as a weapon of *jihad* to conquer the world and establish *sharia* law throughout the earth.

This same President Bush, who popularized the statement that an "ancient religion of peace" had been "hijacked" by a bunch of terrorists, announced to the world boldly and repeatedly after 9/11, "You're either with the terrorists, or you're with us." He certainly realized this was going to be a long and difficult struggle that would affect future generations and would determine the type of world in which they would live.

Bush's bold and forceful responses, which entailed hitting the terrorists where it hurt the most, on their own turf, showed that he understood the magnitude of the "holy war" declared by Osama bin Laden on behalf of global jihadists.

Bush also had a firm grasp of recent history. He knew that in the 1980s and 90s there had been numerous attacks by Islamic radicals on American installations and forces all over the world, with only limited and ineffectual American responses. To the total surprise of some bleeding-heart liberals, as well as of certain of our allies—and especially to Osama bin Laden—such an anemic response was not going to be repeated on his watch. Osama's insistence to his fellow terrorists that America was so soft and pampered that if you "hit them they'll run" was not part of this Texas "cowboy's" makeup.

So, what motivated George W. Bush to so unequivocally characterize Islam as an ancient religion of peace? No one who knows George Bush would suggest he was motivated by some sudden desire to be "politically correct." If this were to be so, it would be the only example of such behavior that immediately comes to mind. The answer is that his remark probably came from some advisors who had made no independent study of Islam or Islamic history in the modern world or throughout its history. (It certainly would not have been Vice President Dick Chaney!) They most likely argued that this would be the diplomatic approach, which might reassure some of the rulers of moderate Muslim countries that he was not criticizing Islam as a legitimate major religion.

Bush's statement seems in total conformity with those of other prominent leaders, who may have had similar advisors. In his book *Religion of Peace? Islam's War against the World*, Dr. Gregory M. Davis quotes President Bill Clinton in 1998, First Lady Hillary Clinton in 1999, UN Secretary Kofi Annan on Sept. 14, 2001, British Prime Minister Tony Blair in 2004, and CIA Director George Tenet in 2002, all extolling "the universal values that are embodied in Islam"; describing Islam as "a religion of peace"; claiming, "The doctrine and teachings of Islam are those of peace and harmony"; and asserting, "Our foes are literally 'the fringe of the fringe' in the Muslim world." He adds another Bush statement in 2005: "Whatever we choose to call this enemy, we must recognize that this ideology is very different from the tenets of the great religion of Islam."[47]

The actual effect of these statements may well have been to strengthen the hand of the radicals and further tie the hands of the moderate Muslims who know all too well the dual elements of Islamic teachings and history. The radicals rejoice that the most powerful world leaders are underestimating their true power, since they all seem to know little or nothing of Islam's teachings or history. Virtually every statement uttered by the leaders of the Islamic terrorist organizations is referenced by quotes from the Koran or the teachings of Mohammad or revered Islamic scholars and religious leaders throughout their 1,400-year history. Even the youngest of suicide bombers almost inevitably cry out *"Allahu Akhbar"* as their last words.

President Reagan's Example

Many reasons have been given to explain President Ronald Reagan's successful efforts to lead America and the free world to victory in the Cold War. Reagan's vision, determination, and trust in the unique abilities of the American people, and his personal leadership qualities are among the attributes most frequently cited. These personal traits—and many other such attributes—were indispensible to his success in leading us to victory in this long hard-fought war. No man deserves more credit for his efforts to influence the world's future at such a crucial time in world history.

However, the indispensible element in such a history-changing accomplishment was made possible because no leader of the free world ever understood Marxist Communism and its history better than Ronald Wilson Reagan. (Winston Churchill and perhaps Margret Thatcher would be his only serious rivals for possessing such knowledge.) Partially due to his responsibilities at the General Electric Theater, Reagan had spent a major part of his adult life studying Marx, Engels, Stalin, and Mao in addition to other communist leaders and theoreticians.

Reagan understood the motivations, nuances, and differences in interpretation among the Marxists better than most so-called scholars on Marxism. He knew, for example, that the masses of ordinary communists[48] were looking for a better life and hoped that a redistribution of wealth could be accomplished by peaceful means. He understood that they had been sold a bill of goods about the evils of capitalism, private property, and the goal of establishing a "utopia on earth."

More importantly, President Reagan's diligence in studying the origins and goals of Marxism, as well as the diversity of tactics advocated, enabled him to understand their leaders. Since Marxism was only some 100 years old, he carefully analyzed their previous actions, especially during and after World War II. He clearly understood that for devout communists—as for devout jihadists—the end always justified the means. Reagan knew the strengths and weaknesses of his peers in communist countries, especially in the Soviet Union and communist China.

Put simply in terms of today's struggle with Islamic terrorism, President Reagan understood the enemy we faced at the time and therefore what action had to be taken to win the Cold War. Reagan also had total faith in the American people's willingness to rise to the challenge when the severity of the threat was properly explained and they were adequately motivated.

Reagan had become convinced that the threat posed by the Soviet Union and its communist allies was a life and death struggle for the existence of freedom in the world. He obviously was aware that America had to take the lead in defeating this totalitarian ideological threat that threatened to enslave the entire world. I believe that as his political career evolved, with all its ups and downs, he came to realize that only a strong and determined American leader could marshal the resources to defeat such an enemy. It is my further belief that he reluctantly concluded that it might be his destiny to be that man. (I came to this conclusion based on having followed his career very closely from the time I first heard his address on national TV in the waning days of the 1964 Goldwater campaign. The speech was titled "A Time for Choosing," and the television fundraising appeal following the address raised more money than any previous such political appeal. Having had the privilege of getting to know him personally, even in a limited capacity, confirmed my original convictions.)

Due in a major way to his previous knowledge and convictions concerning the Soviet threat, Ronald Reagan enthusiastically studied the first Team B report commissioned by CIA Director George H.W. Bush in 1976. Former CIA Director James Woolsey and his co-authors of the Team B II report summarize the findings and Reagan's reaction to the original Team B report in these words:

> "The conclusions of this experimental Team B study differed sharply from the government's regnant theory. The skeptics found that, pursuant to its communist ideology, the Soviet Union was determined to secure the defeat of the United States and the West and to tyrannize the globe. Thus, not only was détente unlikely to succeed, but national-security policies undertaken in its pursuit exposed the nation to grave danger. The study was particularly persuasive to former California Gov. Ronald Reagan, who would use it not only to challenge the detentist policies of the Ford and Carter administrations but to build the strategy that ultimately brought down the "Evil Empire.""[49]

Bill Gertz, in his *Washington Times* articles, makes this observation:

> "The group of experts (Team B II) was modeled after the official CIA Team B, whose 1976 contrary analysis said U.S. intelligence assessments had underestimated Soviet nuclear forces. That Team B report led to the military buildup under the Reagan administration."[50]

(I played a role in this Reagan effort due to my involvement with the American Security Council [ASC].[51] The American Security Council had adopted the slogan "Peace through Strength" to define an effective U. S. strategy to win the Cold War. Our goal was to put together a national coalition for Peace through Strength with a strong congressional outreach. We launched the effort at the Freedom Study Center in Boston, Virginia, in 1978 with the cooperation of many similar national organizations and a blue ribbon congressional component. My job was to direct the effort to forge together a bi-partisan group of senators and congressmen to lead the congressional effort. Peace through Strength planks were included in both the 1980 and 1984 platforms at the respective Republican National Conventions.[52]

Reagan would adopt "Peace through Strength" as a meaningful slogan for his 1980 campaign for the presidency. While a student at Princeton University, my oldest son, Herb, spent a summer internship with the American Security Council researching the military and national security policies and defense spending of the Carter administration as compared to previous administrations. He produced a comparative analysis of Soviet spending on their military, new weapon systems, and nuclear capacity. Herb's in-depth analysis documenting the downsizing of our military forces and capacities and/or canceling or postponing the development of new weapons systems was widely used by Richard Allen in the 1980 campaign. The highly acclaimed national security expert was a top security and defense policy advisor to Reagan's 1980 presidential campaign. Allen would then serve at a crucial time as President Reagan's first National Security Advisor.]

Bill Gertz makes the salient point:

> "The administration's failure to understand the Islamist nature of the terrorist threat is 'inviting more violent jihad against this country,' Mr. Gaffney said.
>
> "The report calls for a campaign against radical Islamists following the model used against communist ideology and activities during the Cold War, infiltrating foreign-supported jihad groups by the FBI and other aggressive security measures.
>
> "'Today, the United States faces what is, if anything, an even more insidious ideological threat: the totalitarian socio-political doctrine that Islam calls Shariah,' the report says."[53]

The report clearly leaves the unmistakable conclusion: *If we are to win the global war being waged by the Islamists—with weapons that include terrorism as well as more "peaceful" means, such as infiltration—we must elect another U.S. president of Ronald Reagan's stature, knowledge, vision, and courage!*

As has been illustrated here, most of our present-day leaders and policy-makers do not demonstrate an adequate understanding of the nature of our terrorist enemies. They seem to especially fail to comprehend the devout nature of our enemies' religious motivation. I would hope that none of such leaders underestimate the resolve of the American people when the nature and severity of the threat is properly explained.[54] Certainly, the heroic actions of the brave men and women fighting Islamic terrorists on foreign fields at this very moment (in spite of frequent evidence of confusion in Washington) testify to the fact that the American spirit is alive and well.

I detect that some of the most far left Islamic apologists just do not want to confront the *facts* that Bernard Lewis lays out in his books about the clear teachings of Islam and the actual account of Islamic history. Their agenda requires that they present Islam as only a religion of peace and tolerance—far superior to all Western religions, including Christianity.

This is not to say that some conservatives do not also approach this subject with an agenda of their own. The same confusion in grasping certain aspects and nuances of Islam is evidenced not only by moderate and "politically correct" scholars, but also by some conservative scholars.[55] Islam's theology and history is complex. Like most religious teachings and histories, it is subject to more than one interpretation.

The thesis of this book—based on the conclusions of world-renowned authorities on Islam such as Lewis—is that the motivation of the Islamic terrorists is their understanding of the theology and history of Islam. Such terrorists may be infuriated by what they believe American foreign policy does to the Islamic world and appalled by what they perceive as America's moral decay, as some conservative writers maintain, but they are moved to action by what they believe their religion requires of them.

The New York Times bestselling author Michael Scheuer, the former CIA agent who founded and ran the CIA's Bin Laden Unit, is bipartisan and blunt in his criticisms of most of America's recent leaders and policymakers, with the possible exception of Ronald Reagan. Basing many of his accounts on personal experience, Scheuer contends that our foreign policy strategies developed during and after the Cold War have gotten us in "on both sides" of a "religious war"— "Muslim versus Jew," in the Middle East—" in which there was no imaginable solution."[56]

Scheuer's critics have accused him of almost everything except striving to be "politically correct" in any area. They say he is anti-Semitic, anti-Arab (especially anti-Saudi Arabia and the rest of the oil cartel), an isolationist, anti-Clinton, anti-Bush (both of them), and doesn't always show the proper respect for superiors in the intelligence community. In his book, he refutes these charges and insists that one must let blame fall where it belongs. I believe it would be accurate to characterize his attitude this way: those who have the responsibility to make decisions must bear the responsibility for those decisions. If they let political concerns or politically correct considerations color those decisions, they should be held accountable.

Scheuer, now an adjunct professor of security studies at Georgetown University and a Senior Fellow at the Jamestown Foundation, also will be referenced in the next chapter as we examine the causes, successes, and failures in the war on terror.[57] At this point, we will note a few foreign policy mistakes that Scheuer believes were made by American officials because they did not understand our terrorist enemies and the nature of the war they declared on America.

Scheuer argues that the motivation for the Islamists' terrorist attacks on America is rooted primarily in two Cold War foreign policy decisions. On the one hand, American foreign policy has become totally subservient to the interests of Israel and her "right" to exist. On the other hand, we have propped up "Muslim police states" and become involved in "entangling alliances" with Muslim dictators (especially in the case of Saudi Arabia) because they are our "oil masters."[58]

Scheuer insists that American foreign policy must always put America's interest ahead of all other concerns. (Why was Reagan Scheuer's favorite president? "Reagan left the constant impression that he was out to protect America, first, last and always.") Scheuer scoffs at the contention that any nation has a "right" to exist. This is a claim America has never made even for itself. Nations survive because of the way they conduct their affairs and make the necessary preparations for their survival.

That these two foreign policy initiatives had been in place for a long time severely tied President George W. Bush's hands after the 9/11 attack, according to Scheuer. George H.W. Bush and his advisors are criticized for answering their "oil master's" call in Saudi Arabia to drive Saddam's troops from Kuwait and then not destroying the military that kept the dictator in power. This would have made the future invasion of Iraq after 9/11 unnecessary and saved many American lives. (I would argue that if Saddam's army would have been destroyed, this would have led to an Iranian style Shiite theocracy in Iraq and created a very serious Iran-Iraq threat to peace in this part of the world. I am also not endorsing all of Scheuer's criticism and suggestions but offering them for the reader's consideration.)

The Saudis are harshly criticized by Scheuer as ingrates and duplicitous allies. They not only tolerate a harsh system of *sharia* law that especially mistreats women, but they provide billions of dollars for the spread of the radical Wahhabi version of Islam throughout the world. Scheuer says one of the first things he did upon establishing the CIA's Bin Laden Unit was to request information from the Saudi government that they had on bin Laden and al-Qaeda. Since that request had not been fulfilled when al-Qaeda carried out the 9/11 attacks five years later, the request was urgently resubmitted. The request still had not been honored when he retired from the CIA in 2004.

America's leaders mistakenly believed that the end of the Cold War ushered in an era of world peace when America could use its moral influence and resources to engage in nation-building activities, Scheuer opines. He contends the exact opposite was the case. The struggles, threats, and détente practiced by the "Super Powers" had the practical effect of keeping in check the smaller rogue nations, especially Muslim nations, with radical pent-up aspirations. Whereas the "captive nations" would long for the freedom of a Western-style democracy, as they shared a common European heritage, this would not be true of the Muslim countries. Muslims even in oppressive countries saw a secular government as contrary to their Islamic religion, Scheuer points out.

Once at war following the Islamic terrorist attack, the American leaders still operated on "Cold War time," Scheuer says. Responses to Cold War threats rarely necessitated an immediate response, but in the war being waged by Islamic terrorists, response time might be limited to months, days, or, on some occasions, hours. If you missed an opportunity to destroy a terrorist target or a key terrorist, you might not get another chance. The Cold War doctrine of Mutual Assured Destruction had no meaning for terrorists who had no state sponsors, Scheuer explains.

Scheuer is especially critical of President Clinton and his national security team for their failure to kill Osama bin Laden when they had the opportunity on at least 10 occasions. He takes serious issue with their claims that the intelligence pinpointing bin Laden's location was not "good enough"[59] or, on one occasion, that the room in which he was to sleep was too close to a mosque.[60]

In most cases, the Clinton administration's reluctance to try to kill bin Laden was motivated by a fear of harming Israel or offending some Muslim ruler, as Scheuer sees it. In 2000, when Islamic terrorists blew a hole in the USS Cole killing 17 American sailors, Richard Clarke decided against bombing al-Qaeda terrorist training camps in Afghanistan. Clarke, who was the head of counterterrorism for the CIA at the time, failed to recommend such a retaliatory strike because the Israeli-Palestine peace talks were at a crucial stage and time was running out for the Clinton administration.[61] As we know now, some of the 9/11 hijackers were undoubtedly training in these camps at the time.

Professor Scheuer chides the George W. Bush administration for wasting valuable time after the decision had been made to invade Afghanistan by trying to build coalitions instead of inflicting massive losses on the Taliban and al-Qaeda before they could fully disperse.[62] He also blames Bush and his security advisors for their failure to kill bin Laden at Tora Bora in December 2001 because of a flawed strategy.[63] They relied on the Cold War tactic of using proxies and placed tactical constraints on the elite forces charged with killing Osama, which made possible bin Laden's escape down the Pakistani side of the mountain.

But Scheuer reserves his harshest criticism for CIA Director George Tenet's duplicity in severely attacking Bush's botched attempt to kill bin Laden. Tenet claims in his memoirs about his CIA days that after we first learned in February 2001 that Osama bin Laden had been trying to acquire nuclear weapons, Bush had "to do whatever was necessary" to eliminate bin Laden and minimize such a threat. Scheuer counters that documents submitted to the 9/11 Commission "show irrefutably" that a Nigerian named Jamal Ahmad al-Fadl provided this information already in 1996. Al-Fadl had walked into the American embassy in Nigeria in 1996 and told them that "as far back as 1993, he helped bin Laden try to obtain uranium in Sudan to be used in some type of nuclear device."[64] So, this information had been available to President Clinton and his National Security Council since 1996, and there was not even a possibility the director of the CIA had not known of its existence. Scheuer indicates that Tenet was trying to cover his and his friend[65] Bill Clinton's backside if al-Qaeda ever exploded a nuclear device in America. On at least 10 occasions, with excellent intelligence available on bin Laden's whereabouts, they had never attempted to kill him, even once, even with all this information available to them.

As Scheuer documents the 10 confirmable opportunities the Clinton administration had to kill or capture Osama bin Laden, as well as George W. Bush's one opportunity to do so, he contends that al-Qaeda remains the number-one threat. Explaining the loss of memory the American people experienced concerning the terrorist threat during the two-year obsession with the 2008 presidential campaign, he explains:

> "Americans may have been reassured by the almost-always-wrong social scientists and so-called expert journalists who argue that al-Qaeda is dead and only 'home-grown' Islamic militants warrant attention. . . . They will find that the influence of bin Laden and al-Qaeda is spreading, the Salafist sect to which they belong also is 'gaining in numbers and influence across the Middle East,' and that the organization itself remains the single most dangerous threat to the continental United States. Indeed, al-Qaeda remains the most likely perpetrator of a nuclear attack on America" (emphasis added).[66]

This seems to be a slightly different emphasis than Ilan Berman's previously referenced contention in *Winning the Long War* that al-Qaeda has become more of a loose-knit franchise organization and:

> "Osama bin Laden, experts say, has transitioned from being the head of a unitary terrorist organization to being the ideological leader of a 'jihadist' movement comprising many new groups that operate without direct support or direction from him or his deputy, Ayman al-Zawahiri."[67]

Each emphasis probably contains different sides of the same truth.[68]

Scheuer's words in the "Introduction to the Paperback Edition" of *Marching Toward Hell*, written in early 2009, sounded prophetic when President Obama decided to send some 30,000 additional American troops to Afghanistan in what I refer to as the "surge" in Afghanistan. But Scheuer warns:

> "Americans will also find that because Osama bin Laden was not killed by Bill Clinton (who as president had ten chances to do so from May 1998 to May 1999) or George Bush (who had one chance, in December 2001) the tall Saudi has steadied, rebuilt, and expanded his organization after it was whacked hard by the U.S.-led coalition in 2001-2002. He also has facilitated the growing military capabilities of

the Taliban and its Afghan allies, who now have the military initiative in Afghanistan against NATO forces, the impact of which appears to be crumbling the resolve of the alliance's leaders."[69]

Scheuer is now convinced that the war in Afghanistan is lost because of our preoccupation with "nation-building" rather than with utterly destroying the Taliban. Our strategy in fighting the Taliban was flawed from the beginning by the Cold War hangover of "finding proxies ... to do America's dirty work." (Initially Pakistan president Pervez Musharraf was recruited.)

This is an alarming conclusion in my mind since in the body of his book, first published in 2008, he indicates that Afghanistan is a war we must fight because it provides a sanctuary for Osama and al-Qaeda. In the last chapter he writes, "The bottom line for America is that this war against bin Laden, al-Qaeda, and their allies was and is one that we must fight. As Abdel Bari Atwan[70] has written, 'We ignore al-Qaeda at our own risk. It is not going to go away.'"[71] Let's hope that his assessment of the difficult war in Afghanistan is overly pessimistic.

Scheuer is certainly correct that we must not lose the nuclear-armed Pakistan to al-Qaeda, the Taliban, or any other Islamic terrorists. (The initial resolve by the Pakistan government to root out Taliban and al-Qaida strongholds, coupled with the increasing use of precision unmanned drone strikes, definitely enhanced the stability of the government. But the turmoil resulting from not informing the Pakistani government in advance of the Navy SEAL raid on bin Laden's compound reopened old wounds. The situation was made worse when 24 Pakistani troops were accidentally killed in a drone strike in the terrorist infested area of North Waziristan in November 2011. An apology by Secretary Clinton on July 7, 2012, has resulted in the reopening of NATO supply routes into Afghanistan. It is obviously difficult to deal with a government heavily infiltrated by radical Islamists.)

Scheuer expresses a serious concern about how the Obama administration, with Democrats then controlling both houses of Congress, would begin to advance "the old saw about how terrorism is caused by poverty, unemployment, bad health, illiteracy, and hopelessness and how a huge, taxpayer-funded 'New Deal' for the Muslim world will solve the problem." Scheuer undoubtedly would not deny that the Islamic terrorist leaders have had considerable success in recruiting suicide bombers and other religiously motivated terrorists from the ranks of the underprivileged—young Palestinians who have spent most of their lives in refugee camps is a good example. But this certainly is not the typical profile of the best known jihadists. Scheuer explains from years of first-hand knowledge:

> "The Islamist enemies are not irrational, illiterate, and fanatic nihilists with bad teeth. They are pious, rational, patient, adaptable, and Internet-loving men who are motivated by what the United States government has done in the Muslim world for more than thirty-five

years, and not by what Americans believe and how they live and behave at home."[72]

As 2009 came to an end, the accuracy of this profile of an Islamic terrorist[73] was once again clearly illustrated by the terrorist massacre at Fort Hood, Texas, the failed Christmas Day bombing attempt over Detroit, and the suicide bombing that killed seven CIA operatives in Afghanistan. Faisal Shahzad, who in 2010 attempted to cause massive devastation in Times Square by blowing up his sports utility vehicle, is another terrorist who fits Scheuer's profile. All of these attacks were perpetuated by men of varying degrees of privilege.

Terrorists and Men of Privilege

Army Major Nidal Malik Hasan is an American citizen born of Palestinian parents in Arlington, Va. He graduated from high school in Roanoke, Va., where his parents opened a restaurant. Upon finishing high school, he followed his uncle and cousins in joining the army. During his eight years as an enlisted soldier, he received a bachelor's degree from Virginia Tech and then attended medical school at the Uniformed Services University of Health Science. With his M.D. in hand (received in 2003), he completed his residency in psychiatry at Walter Reed Army Medical Center.

Hasan was promoted from captain to major (in spite of questionable performance reports) before being transferred to Fort Hood to prepare for deployment to Afghanistan. Just about four months after arriving in Texas, Hasan walked into Fort Hood's Soldiers Readiness Center, where some 300 soldiers were being vaccinated and having their eyes tested in preparation for overseas deployment. Hasan open fire with two pistols, shouting "*Allahu Akbar.*" He killed 13 (actually 14, since one of the female soldiers was carrying a child) and wounded 43 others.

As the investigation unfolded, it became clear that red flags were all over the place in Hasan's career, especially after he began his medical studies and became a psychiatrist. In retrospect, Hasan's increasing radicalization and acceptance of the jihadist interpretation of Islam should have been evident.[74] Most significant in the months before his terrorist attack were some 18 e-mails with the radical imam Anwar al-Awlaqi (also spelled al-Aulaki). Al-Awlaqi is sometime described as the "bin Laden of the Internet" because of his Facebook page and blog.

Al-Awlaqi is now in Yemen where intelligence sources insist he has a leadership role with al-Qaeda in addition to serving as one of their spiritual leaders. Al-Awlaqi was identified on CBS News Dec. 30, 2009, as s senior talent recruiter and motivator "for al-Qaeda and all of its franchises." Many counter-terrorism experts claim that al-Awlaqi's main task now in Yemen's al-Qaeda is to convince enthusiastic jihadists of the rewards of martyrdom as suicide bombers.

The Aug. 25, 2010, edition of *USA Today* featured a front-page picture of al-Awlaqi with very revealing captions. The centerfold screamed out in large bold print: *"WANTED:* 'Bin Laden of Internet.'"[75] The Subheads "What makes cleric al-Awlaki so dangerous" and "Terrorist wears mask of scholar, knows his foe" were equally revealing. The article, written by Aamer Madhani, states:

> "Al-Awlaki, 39, who is an American citizen, has clearly gone beyond mild criticism of his country, according to the Obama administration, which in naming him a global terrorist has made him a target for assassination by U.S, forces or CIA drones. The designation was a recognition that al-Awlaki has risen in the ranks of anti-Western Islamic extremism and become a mortal enemy, a danger to America's national security on a par with 9/11 mastermind Osama bin Laden."

The author then makes this meaningful comparison of bin-Laden and al-Awlaqi:

> "Although both seek the same aim of a world ruled by Islamic law brought about violently if needed, the two take quite different approaches. Where bin Laden keeps a low profile, al-Awlaki has hundreds of sermons on the Internet. Bin Laden's past statements issue threats and orders to Muslims to kill; al-Awlaki's sermons explain to potential followers why the West is evil and are pocked with references to pop culture given in disarming American English."

Anwar al-Awlaqi, who had become recognized as the most influential motivator for al Qaeda recruits and suicide murderers, met his fate in Yemen Sept. 30, 2011, as the result of a hellfire missile fired from an American drone. Some have suggested that the missile that killed him was aptly named since he had inspired so many murdering terrorists, including some of those involved in the 9/11 attacks. President Obama deserves credit for authorizing the drone strikes that killed al-Awlaqi and many other radical Islamist terrorists. However, Obama's accolades have been diminished by the controversy over national security leaks from the Situation Room giving details of the process he uses in personally selecting the drone terrorist targets of the week.

The *USA Today* author specifically notes al-Awlaqi influence on Major Hassan; Abdulmutallah, the would-be underwear bomber; and Shahzad, who tried to explode his vehicle at Times Square, as well as his preaching to some of the 9/11 bombers. He further references CIA Director Leon Panetta's June 2010 TV interview when he says, "Mr. Awlaki is a terrorist who's declared war on the United States" and "He's trying to encourage others to attack this country."

While in medical school, Nidal Hasan began attending the Dar al-Hijrah mosque in Falls Church, Va., where Anwar al-Awlaqi served as the imam. (The New Mexico born al-Awlaqi, whose parents emigrated to the United States from Yemen, has been identified as the "spiritual advisor" of at least two of the 9/11 hijackers. The two, identified as Napa al-Hazmi and Hani Hanjour, also attended this Falls Church mosque.)

Al-Awlaqi praised Hasan's murderous rampage, calling him a "hero," and urged other Muslims serving in the American military to "follow in the footsteps of men like Hasan." The radical imam insists that he did not pressure Hasan to seek martyrdom as he killed American soldiers. However, he contends Hasan's attack was justified as a proper expression of *jihad*, since the West began the conflict with the Muslims.

A Pentagon review headed up by former Secretary of the Army Togo D. West and retired Admiral Vernon Clark, a former chief of naval operations, released on Jan. 9, 2010, questioned the failure of several officers, who should have reviewed his records, to intervene. Hasan's poor performance history and evidences of his religious radicalization should have raised serious questions to his superiors, the review reported.

Answering questions upon the release of the "Pentagon review of the Ft. Hood shootings," Admiral Mike Mullen, chairman of the Joint Chiefs of Staff, told reporters, "I think the issue of self-radicalization is one that we have really got to focus on because there is clearly more and more of that going on." The army secretary under President Clinton, Togo West, who enjoyed considerable bipartisan respect, also told reporters that we must strive for a delicate balance in keeping an eye out for troubled soldiers while not becoming too intrusive in their lives. He continued:

> "Do we want commanders in the mosque? No.... What we want is commanders' awareness of what's going on in their units.... Sometimes there are warning signs that need to be paid attention to and passed along the chain of command." [76]

In a statement that defies politically correct logic, Togo West also said that such radicalization "was not rooted in Islam." West could not have reached this conclusion based on a personal study of the Koran and the teachings of Mohammad and Islamic history. He must have been relying on some extremist "politically correct" Islamic "scholar." Such an assertion by West would have been strongly denied by Major Hasan, Imam al-Awlaqi, Osama bin Laden, or any other Islamic terrorist leader or any of their millions of followers. They would insist with total conviction that they are following pure Islam. It would have been perfectly correct—politically and otherwise—to say that the vast majority of modern-day Muslims do not advocate or personally condone this fundamentalist interpretation of Islamic teachings and its history.

(Islamic militancy did not just appear out of the blue when the radical Shiite jihadists overthrew the Shah of Iran and established an oppressive Shiite Islamic theocracy in Iran in the late 1970s. The predominantly Sunni mujahidin who drove the Soviet Union out of Afghanistan in the late 1980s—albeit with massive assistance from the U.S. and her allies—and then set their sights on the "Great Satan" under Osama bin Laden's leadership wasn't an aberration in Islamic history. What we refer to as Islamic extremism or radical *jihad* has been a part of Islam since the very beginning. Examples of such Islamic behavior throughout its history will be documented and examined in some detail in the next chapter.

(At times and places in Muslim history, the radical fundamentalists were dominant, and at times they were fighting what they believed were non-Islamic Muslim governments or rulers, as well as infidels. The radical and extremist schools of Islam, such as Salafism and Wahhabism, inspired by what Lewis calls Muslim revivalists, arose in earlier periods of Muslim history but are still very active today. They all advocate a return to what they believe is "pure" Islam, which entails the practice of *jihad* and the establishment of strict *sharia* law. When these jihadists are not in control of Muslim governments—this has been the case in most instances, especially since the fall of the Ottoman empire—they start terrorist organizations, such as al-Qaeda, to enable them to strive to carry out Allah's will as they believe they are commanded to do.)

It is very important for us to understand that these Islamist terrorists who have declared war on us and have repeatedly attacked us and our facilities and installations throughout the world certainly do not represent the vast majority of Muslims in the world. But if we are to understand the enemy we face, it is essential for us to know without doubt that *they* believe that they are devout Muslims following true Islam.

The Nigerian would-be "Christmas Day underwear bomber" was a member of one of the most prominent and wealthiest banking families in Nigeria. Umar Farouk Abdulmutallab not only did not become a potential suicide bomber because of poverty and illiteracy, he in fact grew up in luxury and was well educated. He certainly did not accept what he considered his mission to be a martyr because he was down-trodden and had no hope for a comfortable life in this world.

Abdulmutallab's intense studies of Islam had led him to believe that the jihadists were following pure Islam. His own father had approached the American embassy in Nigeria to warn them that his son seemed to have become radicalized. Abdulmutallab was obviously further convinced by al-Qaeda operatives in Yemen, particularly this same radical imam, Anwar al-Awlaqi, that martyrdom would curry Allah's favor and result in his enjoying all the pleasures of paradise.

Dr. Human Khalil Abu-Mulal al-Balawi, the Jordanian who turned out to be an al-Qaeda double-agent and strapped on the suicide belt that resulted in the death of seven of our most important CIA operatives in Afghanistan (and the wounding of at least six others) fits the same profile. An ambitious 32-year-old doctor from middle-class, English-speaking Jordanian parents, with a wife and two small children, was responsible for one of the most devastating attacks in CIA history.

Jordan is almost universally considered to be the Muslim country in the Middle East, if not the entire Muslim world, with the most moderate and peaceful brand of Islam. Jordan, having been plagued by terrorist attacks itself, also is America's strongest ally among Muslim countries.

This bloody suicide bombing of a fortified CIA installation illustrates two important points:

One, al-Qaeda, the Taliban, and their terrorist allies have become very flexible, patient, and technologically competent in carrying out their terrorist acts. Also, in spite of the successful attacks that have killed many key Taliban and al-Qaeda operatives in Pakistan and Afghanistan, these terrorist groups are still strong.

Two, the fanatical religious dedication of jihadists has little or nothing to do with a suicide bomber's station in life.

Shortly after arriving in Afghanistan in 2009, al-Balawi was interviewed by the Vanguards of Khurasan, a key al-Qaeda Internet site, and was asked about martyrdom. He reveals the depth of his firmly held jihadist faith in this interview, which was released after his suicide death. He had this to say:

> "When you ponder the verses and hadiths that speak about jihad and its graciousness, and then you let your imagination run wild to fly with what Allah has prepared for martyrs, your life become [sic] cheap for its purpose, and the extravagant houses and expensive cars and all the decoration of life become very distasteful in your eyes."[77]

How did al-Balawi, who grew up in the moderate Muslim country of Jordan, and journalist Defne Bayrak, al-Balawi's wife, who spent her formative years in the even more moderate Islamic country of Turkey, become so radicalized?

How did Umar Farouk Abdulmutallab, who grew up in a wealthy and moderate Muslim home in Nigeria and attended University College London, become so radicalized?

How did Army Major Nidal Hasan, who was born in Arlington, graduated from Virginia Tech, and did his psychiatric residency at Walter Reed Army Hospital, become so radicalized?

What about the intended Times Square bomber, Faisal Shahzad, a naturalized American citizen who had emigrated from Pakistan? He had a wife and two small children and had recently quit his job as a financial analyst after having previously received a B.A. and M.B.A. from the University of Bridgeport. Shahzad's family was wealthy enough to provide him servants, chauffeurs, and even armed protection when it was considered necessary as he was growing up. His father was a celebrated fighter pilot who had retired at the equivalent rank of a two-star general in Pakistan. Shahzad's family was made up mostly of moderate or even secular Muslims.

The same question could reasonably be asked about imam Anwar al-Awlaqi, who was born in New Mexico while his father was studying at New Mexico State

University. He went with the family back to Yemen when he was nine and returned to the U.S. at 20 to earn degrees from Colorado State University and San Diego State University and pursue his doctorate at George Washington University.

The educated and privileged al-Awlaqi did spend his teenage years in Yemen where Wahhabism, Salafism, and other radical schools of Islam are commonly taught. Even the supposedly enlightened governments of Jordon and Turkey do little—or are unable to do much—to control the teaching of the more extreme forms of Islam in the mosques and other Muslim organizations in their countries.

The Muslim extremists and terrorists named above have many characteristics in common. None was ever poor or downtrodden. All were well educated. None ever lived in repressive societies, such as Iran or Saddam's Iraq. None ever lived in a country where any strict or harsh form of *sharia* law was enforced, such as it is in Saudi Arabia. They all lived in at least relatively free societies.

But most importantly, they all shared a devout fundamentalist Islamic faith that they did not believe was an extremist distortion of the religion of Islam. They all believed they were following pure Islam taught by Mohammad as revealed by Allah. We must try to understand what they believe—*not what we think they believe*—and how their beliefs differ from moderate or mainline Muslims. Otherwise, we will never understand our enemy and what motivates their extremist actions.

When these recent terrorists who have become so prominent in the news—and many others like them who have not gained such notoriety—are investigated, they all have left a similar trail of warning. When friends, neighbors, fellow workers, family members, and other acquaintances are asked if they have recently noticed any change in their behavior, there is *always* one common thread. They have all become more religious and diligent about their observances required by Islamic teachings.

Major Hasan's co-workers observed that he had become more strident in discussing Islam and spent more time at the mosque. The "underwear bomber's" own father made mention of his son's recent obsession with Islam (the family had not been very devout and practicing Muslims). The Jordanian doctor was widely considered by many of his peers to be obsessed with the Islamic religion. Those who had known Shahzad during his college days noted that at some point in 2006 he became noticeably more vocal about the Muslim faith and diligent about praying fine times a day at the local mosques. This list could be greatly expanded without a single exception of which I am aware.

It would seem logical that even the most devout of the politically correct would recognize that those who engage in terrorist acts always show signs of obsessive religious devotion prior to their terrorist attempts. Surely this should reveal the true motivation of such Islamic terrorists. This pattern is always the same whether the terrorist in question is from Jordan, Yemen, Pakistan, Somalia, or the

United States. How can anyone—including the elitists—continue to ignore the blatant facts?

Such jihadist recruits from moderate Muslim and Western countries seem in important ways to be essential ingredients of Dr. Bruce Hoffman's description of "Al-Qaeda's New Grand Strategy." Al-Qaeda's new *death by a thousand cuts* strategy involves motivating rational and successful up-scale people to offer up their own lives in bloody terrorist attacks. Their successes in such efforts once again underline the power of their strong religious appeal.

Anne Applebaum identifies such educated and accomplished terrorists, frequently recruited on the Internet, as "jihadi elites." She raises questions about how they can be reached and dissuaded from signing up for—or engaging in—such terrorist attacks. My initial response would be that if you are going to convince anyone to abandon a strongly held opinion, you had better understand thoroughly the subject to be debated. This is especially the case if such an opinion is based on a deeply ingrained religious belief or perceived religious obligation.

Certainly as, if not more, important than identifying such jihadists to prevent them from inflicting their terrorist acts on innocent people is to understand what they believe in order to stop them from adding to their ranks. We must find a way to motivate truly moderate Muslims to join in a massive public effort to convince potential extremist recruits that this is not the type of Islam that the vast majority of modern Muslims practice today. There must be a united voice of Muslims and non-Muslims condemning all acts of Islamic terrorism. If there are genuine and legitimate grievances that some Muslims hold against America and her allies, we must find peaceful ways to address them.

There was a small sign of hope when concerned Muslims demonstrated in front of the courthouse in Detroit when the Christmas Day would-be suicide bomber was arraigned. A significant group of Detroit Muslims demonstrated to condemn the intended actions of this jihadist as anti-Islamic and a distortion of their religion. They wanted the world to know that they are Muslims but they also are Americans. They condemned his intended act in strongest terms. Their numbers were not large, and, irresponsibly, the mainline media gave them little coverage. This gesture should have been given headlines and built upon; certainly not ignored! Those elitists striving to be so "politically correct" just don't seem to get it. To reemphasize the obvious, they are not protecting moderate or mainline Muslims by such actions—or lack thereof—but are unwittingly furthering the goals of the terrorists.

It is certainly not in the interest of the honest, sincere, hard working, law abiding, peaceful, and devout Muslims in this country or around the world to gloss over the motivation and ideological self-identification of these terrorists who are carrying out such horrible acts in the name of their religion. Is it not time for moderate Muslim leaders, scholars, and theologians to challenge the claims of the radicals that they are simply following the true teachings of Islam? When Osama bin Laden or any of his ilk quoted the Koran, the sayings of Mohammad, or the teachings of highly respected Islamic authorities throughout their history to justify their violent action and goals, the response of such moderates in challenging their claims should be swift and detailed.

The deafening silence of the overwhelming majority of modern day "moderate" Muslim scholars—with a few notable exceptions—to condemn Islamic terrorism can only be explained by an almost total lack of understanding of the teachings of Islamic fundamentalists throughout Islam's history on the part of "politically correct" Americans. When such "politically correct" Americans include not only "scholars" from America's finest colleges and universities but what appears to be the majority of America's political leaders, reaching to the highest levels of government, the problem becomes even more severe.

At the risk of being redundant, it is not difficult to understand the reluctance of moderate Muslim leaders to risk their reputations—and possibly their lives—to explain the total religious devotion (as distorted and unguided as they may believe it to be) of an "enemy" we do not appear to be trying to understand. Still, there are some brave Muslims, who believe these jihadists or Islamic terrorists are distorting their faith by their violent acts, who have spoken out even in the face of grave danger.

There are undoubtedly legions of other seriously concerned Muslims who are also willing to stand up and be counted. They need the assurance that non-Muslims who share their concerns will appreciate their honesty and join with them in their efforts to save the world from the future devastations of this war being waged by Islamic terrorists. As they risk reputation and life, they do not need to be looking over their shoulders as the Western "politically correct Islamists apologists" accuse them (as Muslims) of being Islamophobes or something worse.

Dr. Tawfik Hamid knows about the "something worse" from personal experience, since he has been assaulted and had his life threatened several times.

Hamid, a one-time member of a violent Islamic terrorist organization in Egypt, attempts in his book *The Roots of Jihad (An Insider's View of Islamic Violence)* to answer what he considers to be the most important questions facing the world today. He warns in his Preface:

> "Any attempt to connect violence among Muslims to any reason other than the religious teachings itself will end in catastrophe for human civilization as it will totally miss the real cause, and thus the decision-makers will postulate totally wrong solutions. I hope that by the end of this book the reader will be able to determine if Islam is really hijacked by some people, or if the Muslims have been hijacked by Islamic teaching.... In short, Islamic terrorism is a real threat to humanity and civilization, and understanding its very deep roots is the most fundamental step toward finding the solution.[78]

Hamid explains that he was raised in a secular Muslim home in Cairo and did not develop a serious interest in religion until he was 16 years old. He then began to study the Koran and the teaching of Mohammad and some other Islamic theologians. Hamid also engaged in some study of the Bible so that he could adequately debate his Christian friends.

When Tawfik Hamid entered medical school, his interest in the Islamic religion had become so keen that he joined the *Jamaha Islameia* (JI), an even more radical Islamic organization than the Muslim Brotherhood with which it was affiliated. JI, which has since been banned by the Egyptian government, was headed up by Dr. Ayman al-Zawahiri. Al-Zawahiri is today the number-two man in al-Qaeda under Osama bin Laden and is believed by many to be the "brains" of this radical terrorist organization. Hamid attended medical school with al-Zawahiri, prayed with him, and listened to his lectures. Perhaps Hamid's early observation of the terrorist mentality from a man who would become one of the world's most dangerous terrorists enabled him years later to be the only person to predict the Islamic terrorist attack on the Twin Towers as well as their bloody attacks in Madrid and London.

Some 25 years ago, Hamid began to question some of the intolerant and harsh teachings of radical Islam. As he says in a recent video, "In the Red Chair," distributed by the Ethics and Public Policy Center, he became convinced that the Koran doesn't teach that apostates from Islam should be killed or that women should be stoned for adultery, but that it does teach that there should be no "compulsion" in religion. He gradually became further convinced that there was a compelling need for a reformation in Islam based on the peaceful interpretation of classical core texts. Hamid then spent almost 20 years preaching in mosques and other venues in Egypt calling for such a reformation based on peace and tolerance.[79]

After some physical attacks and frequent threats on his life, Hamid emigrated from Egypt to the United States. In the aftermath of 9/11, he decided to accept what he considered his obligation to speak out in the print media, broadcast media, and public forums to warn against the severity of the Islamic terrorist threat. In an opinion article in the *Wall Street Journal*, April 3, 2007, Hamid writes, "Without confronting the ideological roots of radical Islam it will be impossible to combat it." He then warns,

> "It is vital to grasp that traditional and even mainstream Islamic teaching accepts and promotes violence. Shariah, for example, allows apostates to be killed, permits the beating of women to discipline them.... Yet it is ironic and discouraging that many non-Muslim, Western intellectuals—who unceasingly claim to support human rights—have become obstacles to reforming Islam.... What incentive is there for Muslims to demand reform when Western 'progressives' pave the way for Islamic barbarity?"[80]

Hamid ends the article with what amounts to a plea to these Western "progressives" to take an objective look at Muslim violence throughout its history and the persecution of Christians in some Muslim lands today. He makes the point, a theme of this book, that the politically-correct Islamic apologists are, perhaps inadvertently, performing a disservice to moderate Muslims as well as non-Muslims. Hamid notes:

> "All of this makes the efforts of Muslim reformers more difficult. When Westerners make politically-correct excuses for Islamism, it actually endangers the lives of reformers and in many cases has the effect of suppressing their voices. Tolerance does not mean toleration of atrocities under the umbrella of relativism. It is time for all of us in the free world to face the reality of Salifi Islam[81] or the reality of radical Islam will continue to face us."

Their numbers are not large, but there are other prominent truly moderate and patriotic Muslim leaders living in this country who are bravely willing to speak out against radical Islamic teachings. In an open forum at the State Department on Jan. 7, 1999, Sheikh Muhammad Hisham Kabbani[82] told his audience that 80 percent of American mosques are controlled by Islamic extremists. Sheikh Kabbani explained that he had personally visited 114 mosques across the United States and found that in 90 of them, the worshippers were exposed to radical Islamic theology. Kabbani stated clearly, "I cannot speak on behalf of all Muslims, as many nonprofit organizations in America do." However, Sheikh Kabbani is the head of the "Islamic Supreme Council of America," an organization with more than 8,000 contributors and participants that runs 23 Islamic study and meeting centers.

Kabbani was immediately condemned and threatened by radical American Muslims. A group of nine Muslim organizations in the United States immediately issued a press release viciously attacking his testimony. One would hope that after 9/11, 2001, Sheikh Kabbani's warnings would be taken more seriously.[83]

As we turn to a somewhat detailed look at Islam's founding and history in the next chapter, I hope that this analysis of the deeply religious beliefs of the Islamic terrorists who have declared war on America (and how they differ from the beliefs of moderate Muslims) will be helpful for understanding this subject.

As a postscript to this chapter, it might be instructive to take a brief look at the controversy surrounding the proposed building of the so-called "Ground Zero" mosque and Islamic center in New York in view of its effect on Muslim and non-Muslim relations in America. The controversial imam heading up the project, Feisal Abdul Rauf, who claims to be a moderate interested in building better relations with the Muslim world but has made statements that indicate some sympathies with the terrorist's cause, has tried to frame the debate on the First Amendment's guarantee of freedom of religion.

Rauf has garnered some political support from the likes of Mayor Bloomberg and Manhattan Borough President Scott Stringer, as well as from an off and on endorsement by President Obama. There has been corresponding opposition from key senators such as John McCain (R-Ariz.), Joe Lieberman (D-Conn.), Harry Reid (D-Nev.), and Olympia Snowe (R-Maine) and a considerable number of congressman and other elected officials—mostly Republicans. All of the polling data indicate that more than two-thirds of the American people and some 70 percent of New Yorkers are opposed to building a mosque so close to Ground Zero, on a location that was actually damaged by debris from the 9/11 explosion.

The families of those murdered by Islamic terrorists on 9/11 are overwhelmingly against building a mosque so close to ground that is considered sacred because of the brave, innocent men and women who lost their lives during this terrorist attack. Many of the bodies will be buried on this spot until judgment day.

No one of any substance has suggested that Muslims, like Christians, Jews, or any other religion, do not have the right to erect a house of worship anywhere in the U.S. if they meet all legal requirements, such as zoning regulations. This privilege is afforded them in the land of liberty in spite of the fact that in some Muslim countries, Christians have difficulties building churches or even repairing existing churches. In Saudi Arabia, not a single church—or any other non-Muslim house of worship—is allowed. Bigotry and religious intolerance are so severe that an American soldier temporarily stationed in the kingdom to defend their country cannot even have a Holy Bible in his own quarters. But this is not an issue for Muslims in the land of liberty.

The primary issue dominating the debate to this point has focused on the question of respecting the sensitivities of those still grieving—and who will continue to do so for the rest of their lives –over their tragic losses This debate has included the questions of who will be allowed to provide financing for this $100 million structure. Will countries supporting Islamist terrorism, such as Iran, be allowed to participate? Will Saudi Arabia be able to buy a seat at the table for the radical Wahhabi sect of Islam? Will radical imams[84] be allowed to proclaim the virtues of holy war and Islamic law within eyesight of the location of the most devastating attack on American soil by terrorists who believed they were carrying out Allah's will? These are certainly legitimate questions.

Perhaps more important is the symbolism involved in constructing a mosque inside a 15-story Islamic cultural center at this location. It is certain to be a distraction to the commemorative monuments being constructed on Ground Zero and might discourage visitors from visiting this site. It will also be a constant reminder that the perpetrators were involved in an act of Islamic *jihad*. It seems logical that the vast majority of moderate and peaceful Muslims would not want an Islamic cultural center in the background for fear that it might suggest that they had something to do with an act they condemn.

Even more seriously, such symbolism might also be identified with the ancient Islamic practice—started by Mohammed himself—of building a mosque on the holiest site of the ground in the country or city they had conquered. To be fair, it is probably reasonable to assume that the average Muslim has no more in-depth knowledge of Islamic history than the typical Christian does of Christian history. But it is beyond question that all Islamic clerics and terrorist leaders will recognize the significance of such an act. The terrorist leaders, under the direction of Osama bin Laden, will loudly boast that they have planted their flag at the site of their most successful attack on American soil. Such symbols were intended to celebrate significant Muslim victories and declare the superiority of Muslims.

The history of such symbolism began in 630 A.D. when Mohammad led his conquering army into Mecca and proceeded to the Kaaba, which had the sacred "Black Stone" imbedded in one of its walls.[85] The Kaaba housed icons of hundreds of pagan gods and had been the destination of pilgrimages for centuries for the pagan tribes. Muslim history records that there were 360 icons to various gods in the temple and that Mohammad cast all of them out, except for an icon of Jesus and Mary. Mohammad then is reputed to have told the crowds that had gathered that Mecca was made holy when God created the world and that the Kaaba would be the "holy of holies until resurrection day."

The second caliph, Umar, conquered Syria in 636 and Jerusalem in 638. In just 50 years, construction was begun on the Dome of the Rock Mosque on the original site of Solomon's Temple. In 705, an ancient Christian church, dedicated to John the Baptist, in Damascus was converted to the Grand Mosque of Damascus.

When the Muslim armies were finally able to conquer Christian Spain in 784, after several earlier bloody attempts, Emir Abd ar-Rahman I almost immediately seized the beautiful Christian Visigothic church of St. Vincent and turned it into a mosque. The Great Mosque of Cordoba, which was remodeled several times over the years, was known for its ornate beauty and was the most prominent structure for the Islamic community in the capital city of Cordoba for some 300 years. It stood triumphantly as the symbol of Islamic superiority and conquest in the Muslim world. When King Ferdinand III of Castile re-conquered Cordoba in 1236, the Great Mosque was restored as Roman Catholic cathedral.

Cordoba House may have been chosen as the name for the Islamic center intended to be built two blocks from Ground Zero since there is a somewhat exaggerated claim that Jews and Christians were treated in a tolerant manner as *dhimmi* (people of the Book) during the Muslim rule in Spain. Whereas their treatment was better than in most other Muslim-controlled lands, it was far from as good as some politically correct historians would have their readers believe. This subject will be further addressed in the next chapter.

The first Christian emperor of the Holy Roman Empire, Constantine the Great, founded the city of Constantinople, to which he referred as "the New

Rome." One of his first undertakings in the new city was to begin construction in 360 on the Great Church. Constantine's church was destroyed in 404 and rebuilt by his son and Emperor Theodosius II, with construction starting in 405. After the second church was also destroyed in 536, Emperor Justinian ordered the building of a much larger church, which became known as the Hagia Sophia, or the Church of the Holy Wisdom of God.

The Hagia Sophia would remain one of the crown jewels of the Christian empire for about 900 years until Constantinople was conquered by the Ottoman Turks. After a series of relentless failed attacks on Constantinople, the Turks finally subdued the capital of the Byzantine Christian empire and changed its name to Istanbul. The Ottomans not only moved the seat of the caliphate to Istanbul, but they also converted Hagia Sophia into the Ayasofya Mosque. This was a bold statement of Islamic supremacy to the world as far as the Ottomans were concerned. The site remained an active mosque until 1935, when Turkish president Kemal Ataturk, who had abolished the caliphate and established a secular Turkish state in 1923, turned Hagia Sophia into the Ayasofya Museum.

The Muslim practice of turning holy sites into mosques as a sign of superiority stretched into modern times when Libya's president Muammar Qaddafi in the 1970s turned 78 Jewish synagogues into mosques in Libya.

It appears to me that it would be a remarkable gesture of good will if moderate Muslims would rise up and demand that the sensitivities of the grieving families be recognized and the Cordoba House be located somewhere else in New York City.

Canadian Muslim journalist and author Raheel Raza has been an outspoken critic of terrorist acts committed in the name of Islam. Raza has risked her reputation—as well as her life—to write the book *Their Jihad, Not My Jihad: A Muslim Canadian Woman Speaks Out* and by her tireless efforts condemning the refusal of most Muslims to grant equality to Muslim women. In regard to the Ground Zero Islamic Center, or Cordoba House, controversy, Raza and fellow Muslim writer and board member of the Muslim Canadian Congress, Tarek Fatah, summed up the true goals of those Muslims pushing the mosque in such close proximity to Ground Zero in these bold words:

> "We Muslims know the ... mosque is meant to be a deliberate provocation, to thumb our noses at the infidel. The proposal has been made in bad faith, ... as 'Fina,' meaning 'mischief-making' that is clearly forbidden in the Koran .... As Muslims we are dismayed that our co-religionists have such little consideration for their fellow citizens, and wish to rub salt in their wounds and pretend they are applying a balm to sooth the pain."[86]

Notes

[1] Bernard Lewis, *What Went Wrong?: The Clash Between Islam and Modernity in the Middle East* (Harper Perennial, 2003), 164.

[2] Bernard Lewis and Buntzie Ellis Churchill, *Islam: The Religion and the People* (Pearson Prentice Hall, 2008), 167.

[3] Lewis and Churchill, 163.

[4] As will be emphasized in this chapter, neither of these two groups is monolithic and could perhaps more accurately be divided into numerous sub-groups. For example, the vast majority of the peaceful Muslims would fall into the category of what I call the "silent majority." On the other hand, the vast majority of those described as radical Islamists may support jihad but refrain from participating in violent terrorism.

[5] Ilan Berman, author of *Winning the Long War: Retaking the Offensive against Radical Islam*, says in an op-ed in *The Washington Times* (Oct. 18, 2009) that there is "a mass of 'undecided' Muslim voters whom we need to convince to sit out this fight."

[6] The Team B II report is titled "Shariah: The Threat to America." This section from the Preface explains the origin of the blue ribbon panel's name and the purpose of its product: "This study is the result of months of analysis, discussion and drafting by a group of top security policy experts concerned with the preeminent totalitarian threat of our time: the legal – political – military doctrine known within Islam as 'Shariah.' It is designed to provide a comprehensive and articulate 'second opinion' on the official characterizations and assessments of this threat as put forth by the United States government. The authors, under the sponsorship of the Center for Security Policy, have modeled this work on an earlier 'exercise in competitive analysis' which came to be known as the 'Team B' Report. That 1976 document challenged the then-prevailing official U.S. government intelligence estimates of the intentions and offensive capabilities of the Soviet Union and the policy known as 'détente' that such estimates ostensibly justified. This study challenges the assumptions underpinning the official line in the conflict with today's totalitarian threat, which is currently euphemistically described as 'violent extremism.' And the policies of co-existence, accommodation and submission that are rooted in those assumptions." The original Team B report, which was authorized by then-CIA Director George H.W. Bush, will be further examined later in this chapter as we discuss how President Reagan essentially won the Cold War.

[7] The article was written by James Woolsey, CIA director under President Clinton; Andrew C McCarthy, assistant U.S. attorney in New York during the Clinton administration, who prosecuted the first World Trade Center bombing suspects; and General Ed Soyster, who served as director of the Defense Intelligence Agency under Presidents Reagan and George H.W. Bush. The article is available online at http://www.washingtontimes.com/news/2010/sep/14/needed-a-second-opinion-on-shariah/?page=all.

[8] It is plausible to speculate that one of the reasons President Obama has such a politically correct, idealized or fictionalized view of Islam is his having spent many of his grade-school years in Indonesia. Indonesia, home to the world's largest Muslim population, is the only country that converted to Islam without having been conquered by Muslim invaders. This religiously pluralistic country was converted to Islam by Muslim traders, not invaders. As a result, many elements of their native religious traditions were incorporated into their brand of Islam. Therefore, a more tolerant version of the Islamic religion has always been taught in Indonesian schools. This would represent a stark contrast to the fundamentalist, revivalist brand of Islam taught in the madrassas in Saudi Arabia, Pakistan, and Afghanistan, for example. Living with his mother and stepfather in Indonesia, Obama was exposed to a much more moderate type of Islam in the public schools than is taught in most of the Muslim world. When Indonesia was granted independence by the Dutch in 1949, a freedom of religion provision even was included in their constitution. This does not mean that some of the 33 provinces in Indonesia do not try to enforce sharia law, however, as will be discussed in the section of this book dealing with Christians living in Muslim countries.

[9] Woolsey, McCarthy, and Soyster.

[10] William G. Boykin and Harry Edward Soyster (team leaders), *Shariah: The Threat to America: An Exercise in Competitive Analysis (Report of Team B II)* (The World Security Network, 2010), 30.

[11] The Team B II report will be valuable in discussing *sharia* and *jihad* in the next chapter.

[12] Even the Preface to the Arabic translation by the radical Muslim Brotherhood of Lewis' *The Middle East and the West*, has this to say: "It is clear the author is one of two things; either a candid friend or an honorable enemy. And, in either case, he is one who disdains to distort the truth." Lewis' attempts to be immensely fair have earned him some criticism from certain more conservative Western scholars on Islam but has earned him respect from many in the Muslim world and better access to certain Islamic documents.

[13] Lewis and Churchill, *Islam: The Religion and the People*, 1.

[14] Bernard Lewis, *The Middle East and the West* (Harpercollins College Div., 1968), 229.

[15] Lewis, *The Middle East and the West*, 219.

[16] I have chosen to use the word "radicals" in certain contexts to distinguish them from the hundreds of millions of "fundamentalist" Muslims who do not participate in terrorism. It is basically correct to say that all terrorists are fundamentalists, but certainly not all fundamentalists are terrorists. Such distinctions should become more understandable as we discuss these matters throughout this book.

[17] Robert Spencer points out that *jihad* is used in a military context more than a hundred times in the Koran. Dr. Bernard Lewis states that on numerous occasions, the context in which *jihad* is used in the Koran can be interpreted only in military terms.

[18] I have not lost sight of the fact that Islamic terrorism is a global war and takes different shapes and forms in various parts of the world. For example, the Islamic Republic of Iran sponsors Shi'a terrorism at least with massive financial support. Shiites comprise only 15 percent of the world's Muslims, but they are the strong majority sect in Iran and Iraq. Shiites also have significant minorities in other troubled Islamic countries. Iran's unabated efforts to develop nuclear weapons magnify this threat greatly. Ilan Berman's excellent book, *Winning the Long War: Retaking the Offensive against Radical Islam* (Rowman & Littlefield Publishers, 2009), addresses the many threats from radical Islam and will be discussed in more detail later in this book. At this point, Lewis is discussing the rationale used by the late Osama bin Laden and his allies for justifying their terrorist attacks and why the "Great Satin" must be destroyed.

[19] The event was hosted by former Senator Rick Santorum of Pennsylvania and the "Ethics and Public Policy Center." I took some of my own notes, but a transcript of the taped speech was later provided.

[20] An anecdote from a book-signing event I attended Oct. 6, 2009, offers a lighthearted but meaningful illustration of how difficult it is to be precise in using such descriptions in defining Muslims. Senator Kit Bond (R-MO) and noted foreign correspondent and writer Lew Simons were advancing their new book, *The Next Front*. This book deals with the 250 million Muslims in Southeast Asia who share in common many characteristics with other Muslims worldwide but also exhibit many significant differences. This book offers some significant insights on this sometimes almost forgotten large bloc of Muslims. Senator Bond was asked to explain "mainstream" Muslims. Without missing a beat, Bond replied, "Those Muslims who don't hate us!" (I was tempted to add "or don't hate us as much.")

[21] Lewis and Churchill, *Islam: The Religion and the People*, 5.

[22] Lewis would note that Osama and other Islamic leaders were "shocked" by the initial, forceful response of the new American president, George W. Bush. It even prompted some "reconsideration on their part." Calling on personal experience at a joint OIC-EU meeting in Istanbul shortly after Bush's "axis of evil" speech, Lewis detected fear on the part of certain leaders of Islamic countries. As time passed, however, such Muslim leaders, not understanding this "to-and-fro" debate of a democratic society, were convinced they saw "weakness, fear and indecision" among the Americans. He advised that American leaders should be careful with what they say publicly.

[23] The National Commission on Terrorist Attacks upon the United States was created by the U.S. Congress and President Bush in 2002. The 9/11 Commission was to thoroughly examine these questions. The commission was to be composed of five prominent Republicans and five prominent Democrats. Virtually all of those selected are considered moderates in their respective parties. The commission and its "Report," which took almost two years to prepare (it was first released July 22, 2004) will be discussed in detail in this book.

[24] You could go back even to 1983, when a suicide bombing killed 241 U.S. Marines in Beirut, Lebanon. Of course, the Islamic terrorists involved in this attack were Shiites who were motivated, if not directed, by the radical Ayatollah Khomeini in Iran. The radical Sunni terrorists were preoccupied with fighting the Russians in Afghanistan in the 1980s, but they did raise their heads in other parts of the world from time to time. Osama bin Laden started an organization called the "Office of Services" in 1982 in Afghanistan that would morph into al-Qaeda in 1988.

[25] Osama bin Laden had issued a *fatwa* in October 1998 declaring war on America.

[26] By some reliable estimates, the government of Saudi Arabia has provided some $4 billion a year for more than two decades to support the Wahhabi educational efforts. See Berman, *Winning the Long War*, 47.

[27] This trend is evidenced in other parts of the Muslim world. A Pew Center poll showed that between 2003 and 2007, support for Osama bin Laden fell from 59 percent to 20 percent in Jordon and from 59 percent to 41 percent in Indonesia. See Berman, 14. Berman also notes that by 2006, "*three-quarters of al-Qaeda's pre-September 11 leadership was estimated to have been killed or captured*" (p.5, n.7). This certainly does not mean

that al-Qaeda has become less dangerous. Berman and other scholars contend that al-Qaeda, in Berman's words, experienced a *"metamorphosis from a terrorist group into a global ideological movement."* It is now a more loose-knit franchise operation all over the world. But they still take orders from the Supreme Terrorist Commander.

[28] Wahhabism, Salafism, and Qutbism or some combination of the three most often provide the theological foundation for Sunni terrorism. These reform schools of Islamic teaching all state a desire to return to "pure Islam." They will be further explained in the next chapter.

[29] King Abdullah is now 89 years old and reportedly in failing health. The 81-year-old crown prince, who was Abdullah's half brother, passed in October 2011. Abdullah's full brother was then named crown prince, but he died June 16, 2012. The current crown prince is another brother, Prince Salman, who was 76 years old at the time of his selection.

[30] Saudi Arabia's porous borders are shared by Shiite-dominated Iraq, whose bordering neighbors include the violent Shiite theocracy in Iran and al-Qaeda-infested Yemen on the south. Only the Red Sea separates Saudi Arabia from Muslim Brotherhood-run Egypt. The Saudis need our protection now more than ever before.

[31] Even the ultra-liberal Islamic apologist, John Esposito, concedes that 7 percent of the 1.3 billion Muslims in the world "subscribe to most—if not all—of bin Laden's extremist worldview." See Berman, p.5. Esposito's percentages would total almost a hundred million. Berman notes, "More sober assessments, meanwhile, put the number of Muslims sympathetic to at least certain parts of the radical Islamic agenda much higher: at as much as 36 percent of the world Muslim population." The number I have seen used by most scholars is that at least 1 billion of the 1.3 billion Muslims in the world are "peaceful" Muslims.

[32] Sunni terrorist organizations, such as al-Qaeda, the Taliban, the Muslim Brotherhood, etc., have no state sponsorship and must depend on individuals or groups (frequently so-called charitable organizations) for their funds. Shiite terrorist organizations can depend on the Islamic Republic of Iran for their basic financial needs. How the Brotherhood's control of the government of Egypt will change the equation is an open question at this time. Some authorities fear that Egypt could become a state supporter of Sunni terrorism at some point if the Muslim Brotherhood ever gains total control. The best hope under the circumstances is that the Egyptian military keeps the radical elements of the Brotherhood under some control.

[33] Charles Krauthammer, "A terrorist war Obama has denied," *The Washington Post*, Jan. 1, 2012. Accessed Sept. 3, 2012, at http://www.washingtonpost.com/wp-dyn/content/article/ 2009/12/31/ AR2009123101744.html.

[34] The American-born Aulaqi, whose parents were from Yemen, was the imam at a mosque in Falls Church, Va. Many known terrorists, including at least two of the 9/11 suicide bombers and the Fort Hood mass murder, Major Hasan, attended the Falls Church mosque. It is reliably reported that since moving back to Yemen, Aulaqi's major responsibility with al-Qaeda there is to recruit and motivate suicide bombers from the ranks of the dedicated jihadists. Abdulnutallab was undoubtedly one of his star recruits.

[35] David Broder, "Obama's wake-up call," *The Washington Post*, Jan. 8, 2012. This article is available online as "Failed Christmas bomb plot will likely alter Obama's agenda," at http://www.washingtonpost.com/wp-dyn/content/article/2010/01/07/AR2010010703241.html.

[36] President Obama's record has been mixed since he said "we will do whatever it takes to defeat them." He did allow an expanded use of drones against al-Qaeda and Taliban targets and approved the plan to go after bin Laden. But he has also approved an accelerated and dangerous troop withdrawal schedule from Iran and Afghanistan. In addition, the Obama administration is experiencing one of the most serious and dangerous series of national security leaks in the country's history.

[37] President Obama obviously approved Holder's decision to read this Nigerian, who certainly was not an American citizen, the Miranda rights under the American criminal system. At that point, the "underwear bomber" clammed up after having given valuable information to his interrogators prior to being offered such rights, intended for American citizens. On the possible positive side, Holder indicated in congressional testimony that they may seek a "public safety" exemption in Miranda when there is a reasonable concern about an imminent attack. Obama's "wake-up call" may not have been as clear as Broder had hoped, judging from his response in the Times Square scare, which will be discussed in the following pages.

[38] Bruce Hoffman, professor of security studies at Georgetown University and senior fellow at the U.S. Military Academy Combating Terrorism Center, writes an authoritative article on al-Qaeda's growing threat as it adopted a new and sophisticated strategy. Hoffman points out that while many experts, in and out of the intelligence community, spent much of 2008 and 2009 touting al-Qaeda's demise, the terrorist group was engaged in developing a new and innovative strategy. "In contrast to its plan on Sept. 11, which was to deliver a

knock-out blow to the United States, al-Qaeda's leadership has now adopted a 'death by a thousand cuts' approach." When the intelligence community finishes putting the dots together, they will likely find that this new strategy is well demonstrated by the Christmas underwear bomber, the Jordan doctor, and probably Major Hasan through his continued email correspondence with imam Aulaqi. These all were undoubtedly al-Qaeda-inspired and -directed attacks.

[39] Pamela Constable and Haq Nawaz Khan, "Tape reveals close links among 3 terrorist groups," The Washington Post, Jan. 10, 2010. The article is available online as "CIA bomber calls for attacks on U.S. in video" at http://www.washingtonpost.com/wp-dyn/content/article/2010/01/09/AR2010010900508.html.

[40] Berman, xv.

[41] Dinan, "Holder balks at blaming 'radical Islam.'"

[42] Quoted in Bill Gertz, "Shariah a danger to U.S., security pros say," The Washington Times, Sept. 14, 2010.

[43] Biden's motives were obviously purely political, but even a feigned lack of understanding was extremely dangerous.

[44] Joseph Biden Jr., "Republicans and Our Enemies," The Wall Street Journal, May 23, 2008.

[45] Robert Spencer, Stealth Jihad (Regnery Publishing, 2008), 232-233. Spencer notes that a complete listing of these terrorist attacks can be found at http://www.thereligionofpeace.com. The thesis of this book will be discussed in some detail in the section of Chapter 5 dealing with "jihad" and "sharia."

[46] By definition, terrorism is a means used by the Islamist or Jihadist to accomplish the end of killing Americans to promote their "holy war" in order to establish sharia law around the world. The five American Muslims, who attended the same mosque in Northern Virginia, captured in Pakistan at the end of 2009 said they had come to Pakistan to join the Taliban or al-Qaeda in killing Americans. They insisted they were not terrorists because jihad is not terrorism since it is commanded in the Koran. Biden could technically refer to those who accept this "all-encompassing ideology" as Jihadists, Islamists, Islamic radicals, or some other such term. The important thing is that he realize that those who practice such acts of terrorism are solely motivated by their understanding of Islamic theology and Islamic history.

[47] Dr. Davis' book is a short, easily readable work in understandable language that extensively documents the radical elements in Islam from its founding to the present day. He makes little attempt to examine the peaceful and tolerant elements also found in this religion and even mildly criticizes the more moderate scholars on Islam such as Dr. Bernard Lewis. However, he clearly presents the severity of the threat by the radical Islamic terrorists in today's world and the need to understand the nature of the enemy we face. It is a worthwhile read not only for non-Muslims but even for Muslims who might question why these terrorists believe they are following the true teachings of pure Islam.

[48] "Communism" means Marxist communism in this context.

[49] Woolsey, et. al., "Second opinion needed on Sharia: Our political establishment wears blinders and ignores the threat."

[50] Gertz, "Shariah a danger to U.S., security pros say."

[51] I worked full time for the ASC for more than two years before moving to Washington in 1971 to take a job as executive assistant to the chairman of the House Committee on Internal Security. In that position and in my subsequent employment at The Tobacco Institute, I continued to work part-time on the Peace Through Strength initiative. I had such a close personal relationship with John Fisher, president of ASC, that he sub-leased me space at a very reasonable rate when I started my own lobbying firm. John Fisher is one of the true unsung heroes in helping to win the Cold War.

[52] Following Reagan's election, I continued and intensified my efforts to pass a Peace Through Strength resolution in the U.S. Senate, making sure that it was bi-partisan.

[53] Gertz, "Shariah a danger to U.S., security pros say."

[54] The jihadist understanding of Islamic theology and history drives their every action.

[55] In reading some of the critiques of Lewis' most recent books by "experts" and others, I often question whether we have read the same book. Lewis notes that there is evidence of some such confusion among Muslims of all stripes about various aspects of their religion. Lewis' meticulous scholarship and devotion to accuracy in all conclusions is evidenced by the fact that his praise extends from Al Abram, Cairo, described as the most influential Arab world newspaper (which contends that "Bernard Lewis has no living rival in his field") to National Review's blanket assertion, "When it comes to Islamic studies, Bernard Lewis is the father of us all. With brilliance, integrity, and extraordinary mastery of languages and sources, he has led the way for... investigators seeking to understand the Muslim world." Taken from "Praise for Bernard Lewis" in Islam: The Religion and the People.

[56] Michael Scheuer, *Marching Toward Hell: America and Islam after Iraq* (Free Press, 2008), 42.

[57] The themes advanced by Scheuer in these sections are all taken from *Marching Toward Hell*.

[58] Truman's decision to establish the state of Israel as a buffer against Soviet expansion among the weak Islamic countries in the Middle East was the origin of such policy. The Yom Kippur War in 1973 and Nixon's all-out support for Israel, resulting in Saudi King Faisal's subsequent oil embargo, cast such a policy in stone.

[59] Sheuer, p.61. Scheuer points out that this was the reason "Mr. Clinton and his colleagues told the Hamilton-Kean 9/11 Commission" that they did not go after bin Laden on the 10 opportunities they had in one year from May 1998 to May 1999. Scheuer, who was responsible for such intelligence gathering at the time, refutes Tenet's claim that they wanted such intelligence from more than one source by insisting that this was not the case and "the information was about as good as it gets." See pp. 90-91.

[60] Sheuer, 83.

[61] Sheuer, 34.

[62] Sheuer, 11.

[63] Sheuer, 106.

[64] Sheuer, 17.

[65] After the 1992 presidential election, Tenet joined President-elect Clinton's national security transition team. President Clinton subsequently appointed him to three positions with the CIA, the third as director.

[66] Sheuer, xi.

[67] Berman, 2.

[68] Both Scheuer and Berman would undoubtedly agree with Dr. Bruce Hoffman's contention in a January 2010 *Washington Post* article that al-Qaeda has adopted a new strategy. Hoffman persuasively contends that al-Qaeda's leadership has abandoned the 9/11 strategy of a "knock-out" blow in favor of a "death by a thousand cuts" approach. Of course, this may only be a temporary strategy.

[69] Sheuer, xii.

[70] The Palestine-born Atwan has lived for more than 30 years in London, where he is editor-in-chief of *Al-Quds al-Arabi*, frequently referenced as the most influential Arab-language newspaper in the West. Atwan is the only Western journalist to have spent time with Osama bin Laden at his Tora Bora hideout.

[71] Scheuer, 250.

[72] Sheuer, xix.

[73] Most Western scholars on Islam would agree with Scheuer's contention that American foreign policies and their results have motivated the jihadists to action much more than America's perceived moral debauchery. But as Dr. Bernard Lewis has so carefully documented, the Islamic terrorists' violent reaction to American foreign policy comes from their deeply held Islamic beliefs, which they believe compel them to engage in "holy war." Even if we changed most of our foreign policies, "the Great Satan" would still stand in their way for spreading *sharia* law throughout the world. To understand our enemy, we must understand their theological beliefs and their worldview, which they believe comes directly from the Koran and the teachings of Mohammad.

[74] Some of Hasan's classmates at the Army medical school have come forward to say that they warned their superiors of his strident Islamic views at the time. It has been documented that he claimed that "the war on terrorism is a war on Islam" and that "Sharia law should trump the Constitution." Others claim that he also argued that suicide attacks were justified under *jihad*. This all happened during the time frame in which Hasan was attending the Falls Church mosque where Aulaqi was imam.

[75] An updated version of the article is available online at http://www.usatoday.com/news/nation/2010-08-25-1A_Awlaki25_CV_N.htm.

[76] This story was reported in the Jan. 16, 2010, edition of *The Washington Post* by Craig Whitlock. All would agree that we do not want our commanders snooping around in mosques attended by soldiers under their command. But we must find some way to identify which mosques attended by American Muslim soldiers have radical imams preaching and encouraging jihadist terrorism.

[77] Quoted in Robert Windrem and Richard Engel, "Al-Qaida double-agent killed CIA officers," NBC News. Accessed Sept. 3, 2012, at http://www.msnbc.msn.com/id/34687312/ns/world_news-south_and_central_asia/t/al-qaida-double-agent-killed-cia-officers/#.UERvio3iakc.

[78] Tawfik Hamid, *The Roots of Jihad* (Top Executive Media, 2006), ix.

[79] Considering his statement above about Muslims being "hijacked by Islamic teaching," he apparently believes there is a strain of peaceful teachings in the Koran that can be used by "moderate Muslims" to counter the

more radical teachings of the fundamentalist Muslims in their history and today.

[80] Tawfik Hamid, "The Trouble with Islam," *The Wall Street Journal*, April 3, 2007. Available online at http://online.wsj.com/article/SB117556869968257964.html.

[81] Salafi Islam will be discussed under Islamic revivalist movements in the next chapter.

[82] Sheikh Kabbani, a native of Lebanon, is an internationally recognized Islamic scholar who comes from a family of Islamic scholars who trace their linage directly back to Mohammad. They have led the muftiate of Lebanon for more than 150 years. Kabbani, who believes that radical Wahhabi theology has perverted the peaceful and tolerant teachings of classical Islam, will be discussed in more detail later in the book.

[83] See Steven Emerson, *American Jihad: The Terrorists Living Among Us*, (Free Press, 2003), 159-161.

[84] Imam Rauf told Ed Bradley on "60 Minutes," two weeks after the 9/11 attack, that Osama bin Laden was "made in the USA" and that U.S. foreign policy was an "accessory to the crime" of 9/11. He also has said that America should be "Sharia compliant." As will be documented in the section on "*sharia*" in the next chapter, virtually all traditional interpretations of Islamic law clearly teach Muslim superiority and the inferiority of women. Rauf also has refused to denounce Hamas as a terrorist organization.

[85] The history of the Kaaba, which will include some Muslim traditions of Abraham's visit to see his son Ishmael, will be discussed in detail in the next chapter. An account of Mohammad's conquest of Mecca and details of his visit to the Kaaba will also be discussed at that point.

[86] Raheel Raza and Tarek Fatah, "Mischief in Manhattan," *Ottawa Citizen*, Aug. 9, 2010. Quoted in *Wikipedia, The Free Encyclopedia*. Accessed Oct. 10, 2010, at http://en.wikipedia.org/wiki/Raheel_Raza. An accomplished public lecturer, Raheel Raza received a standing ovation after delivering an address to the members of Parliament and international diplomats in the House of Commons in Canada. The title of her address was "Celebrating our Differences."

5

The Threat of Islamic Terrorists: A War We Dare Not Lose

"Jihad is sometimes presented as the Muslim equivalent of the Crusade, and the two are seen as more or less equivalent. In a sense this is true—both were proclaimed and waged as holy wars for the true faith against an infidel enemy. But there is a difference. *The Crusade is a late development in Christian history* and, in a sense, marks a radical departure from basic Christian values as expressed in the Gospels. Christendom had been under attack since the seventh century, and had lost vast territories to Muslim rule; the concept of holy war, more commonly, a just war, was familiar since antiquity. *Yet in the long struggle between Islam and Christendom, the Crusade was late, limited, and of relatively brief duration. Jihad is present from the beginning of Islamic history—in scripture, in the life of the Prophet, and in the actions of his companions and immediate successors. It has continued throughout Islamic history and retains its appeal to the present day*" (emphasis added).[1]

Dr. Bernard Lewis
The Crisis of Islam: Holy War and Unholy Terror

When one undertakes the difficult task of trying to understand the complicated history of the founding, spread, teachings, and goals of Islam, it seems essential to start with the Muslim "ethos" or worldview. All the scholars I have read present a consistent picture of how Muslims view the world. Lewis, for example, writes that Muslims understand the coming of the Prophet Mohammad as ushering in the final phase of the long struggle between monotheism and polytheism.

(Before I continue, please permit me an aside on Dr. Bernard Lewis. The stature and respect Dr. Lewis commands, not only among Western scholars on Islam but also among their counterparts in the Muslim world, sets him apart from all the rest. At 94 years of age, Dr. Lewis is Cleveland E. Dodge Professor of Near

Eastern Studies Emeritus at Princeton University. Lewis has published more than 30 books on the subject of Islam and the Middle East, has served as editor for a number of larger publications, and has written hundreds of articles. Lewis is highly respected for his scholarship and balanced approach to sensitive issues of Islamic theology and history by authorities from all areas of the ideological spectrum in the West as well as in Muslim countries. When Lewis is quoted, there can be disagreement only from either the hardcore politically correct Islam apologists or hard-right Islamic antagonists. This is why after 9/11 the Bush administration used Lewis extensively to brief intelligence and military agencies.)

Of the word "Islam," Lewis explains: "For Muslims, strictly speaking, it denotes the one true faith which has existed since the creation of the world, and in this sense Adam, Moses, David, Jesus, and others were all Muslims."[2] Muslims believe there were genuine revelations in Old and New Testament times inasmuch as they pointed to the coming of Allah's final revelation, which made all previous revelations obsolete. The "Qur'an completes and supersedes all previous revelations" and "whatever truth they contained was now incorporated in his message."[3]

When Muslim clerics or scholars call for a discussion of the commonality of the Abrahamic faiths of Jews, Christians, and Muslims, we must understand what they mean. Surah 3:67 of the Koran reads: "Ibrahim (Abraham) was not a Jew nor a Christian but he was (an) upright (man), a Muslim, and he was not one of the polytheists." This clear and explicit passage, especially in the light of equally clear Muslim teachings, becomes extremely important in discussing, for example, the controversy caused by Pope Benedict XVI's lecture at the University of Regensburg, which will be discussed in section 15 of this chapter. Following the pope's speech, 138 Muslim scholars called for dialogue with Christians. The "Yale letter" signed by more than 300 Christian "leaders" in response to the Muslims' open letter is especially telling. Apparently, none on the faculty of the Yale Divinity School or any of the Christian "leaders" were aware of these Islamic teachings.

An integral part of the Muslim worldview involves the divine command to spread Islam throughout the world until the entire world either has accepted Islam or at least has submitted to Muslim rule. One of the means by which the Islamic faith is to be spread is by *jihad*, or holy war, in the name of Allah. This will be discussed in detail in section 5 of this chapter.

Why should Lutherans, especially Lutheran clergymen, care enough about the threat from Islamic terrorists to try to understand the origin, nature, and goals of those who have declared this war? Well, we would all agree that we have a citizenship responsibility to do our part to protect and defend our native land against all threats, foreign and domestic. That would be a responsible and patriotic answer. But in this case, I believe our responsibilities go much deeper. Unlike all past terrorist threats, which were always political in nature, the threat posed by the radical Islamic terrorists is deeply religious in nature. These terrorists believe they have a divine duty to destroy us by any and all means necessary.

Is this the beginning of the final struggle between the world's two largest religions? We would be loath to reach such a dramatic and alarming conclusion. But the Islamic terrorists see this struggle in just such stark terms!

The worldwide Islamic terrorist network, inspired and directed by the late Osama bin Laden and a legion of like-minded radical terrorist leaders, views this as not merely another clash of cultures that has now spanned almost a millennium and a half, but the definitive conflict that will finally end in the Islamic conquest of the world. They believe that Allah has commanded such a holy war against the infidels and that he is on their side. They also believe that time is on their side and that once the Great Satan, which now is America, falls, their task will be easier and the results will be inevitable.

Is this just a fantasy in the minds of some crazy men hiding in caves, or is it an outgrowth of the deep-seated teachings and history of the Islamic religion? It seems to me that it is incumbent on us to seek to answer. A religion that commands the allegiance of some 1.3 billion adherents today and has had such a major impact on 1,400 years of world history cannot be taken lightly. Is this perhaps a perversion of the teachings of Islam? Certainly, a majority of today's Muslims do not agree with bin Laden and other like-minded extremists.

Let's take a look at the history and teachings of Islam. As we do, it will be helpful at times to make comparisons with the teachings and history of Christianity. These two historic monotheistic religions together claim—with varying degrees of devotion—the allegiance of 55 percent of the world's population.

The Prophet Mohammad and the Religion He Founded

It goes without saying that one who does not have a command of the Arabic language or the history of Arab culture must rely on those who do. (In my seminary days, I had a short-lived dream of becoming an Old Testament scholar, inasmuch as biblical Hebrew had been fairly easy for me. A one-quarter course in beginning Arabic cured me of that dream.) I have therefore studied the works of many western Islamic scholars and will reference a number of them in this chapter. In this section, I rely most heavily on the works of Dr. Robert Bernard Lewis, Dr. Robert Spencer, and Dr. Serge Trifkovic.

One valuable lesson I learned at the seminary and tried to pass on to my students when I taught philosophy for a few years was always to evaluate carefully the primary sources being used by the author of a secondary source document.

I have already introduced Dr. Bernard Lewis. His works are too numerous for a definitive listing, but I would suggest you begin with his rather short book, *The Crisis of Islam*, and proceed from there. In a lecture I heard Lewis deliver, he stressed the importance of trying to think as the Muslim thinks in order to fully understand Muslim culture, teachings, and history.

Robert Spencer is director of Jihad Watch, a program of the David Horowitz Freedom Center, and author of *The Politically Incorrect Guide to Islam (and the*

Crusades) and four other books on Islam and Islamic terrorism. Spencer's most recent book (2006), *The Truth about Muhammad: Founder of the World's Most Intolerant Religion,* fills a major void in understanding Mohammad's life and teaching. Very few biographies of Islam's prophet are available in English. Spencer uses only Muslim sources, since no other early documents exist. The first source is obviously the Koran. The second is the Hadith (the traditions and sayings of Mohammad), which has equal authority to the Koran for Muslims. The third is the Sira, which comprises the three earliest Muslim biographies of Mohammad, the first of which was written just over 100 years after his death. The earliest copy of this biography is a redacted manuscript produced by Ibn Ishaq less than 60 years after the original author's death. Spencer is so careful to document his use of the most ancient primary Islamic sources that he writes 13 pages explaining these documents, which are the most respected by Muslims scholars.

Spencer did not write this book without considerable thought, since the author now lives under protection at an undisclosed location. Even though all the events in the book about Mohammad's life, actions, and teachings are taken from Islamic sources, Muslims would consider some of the conclusions to defame their prophet and are therefore blasphemous. The punishment for blasphemy in Islamic *sharia* law is death in most cases. This book is a must read for those seeking to understand Mohammad and his teachings.

Politically correct Western "scholars" as well as Muslims will tell you that the best English biography of Mohammad is Martin Lings' *Muhammad: His Life Based on the Earliest Sources.* Lings, a Muslim convert and recognized Islamic scholar, uses three of the primary sources also used by Spencer and all other serious biographers of Mohammad. Lings uses Ibn Ishaq's *Sirat Rasul Allah (Biography of the Prophet of Allah)* as his primary source. The value of reading Lings' biography is that you receive a picture of Mohammad's life, teachings, and actions as Muslims believe and wish us to believe.

There are certainly two ways of understanding Mohammad based on a study of the Koran and other early Islamic sources. Lings' book is true enough to the earliest Islamic sources that you will be able to discern both views of Mohammad. We would hope that all Muslims would perceive Mohammad as a man of peace and tolerance, yet it defies logic to understand how they could miss the teachings of holy war, intolerance, and the necessity of Islam ruling the world under strict Islamic *sharia* law. Of course, not all Muslims get around these teachings. Osama bin Laden and the worldwide Islamic terrorist network—and the millions of fanatical terrorists they inspire—accept these teachings in a deadly serious way.

If you have the appetite to wade through Arabic genealogies and develop a basic understanding of early Islamic history, you can get your information about the life of Mohammad from a translated version of the earliest and most widely accepted biography of Islam's prophet. Ibn Ishaq wrote the first known biography probably just over 100 years after Mohammad's death. He obviously had collected the most trusted oral traditions passed down from the prophet's close companions, wives, and followers. Certainly some of these oral traditions came from people who had known people who actually knew Mohammad. Ibn Ishaq, a devout Muslim, intended to present Mohammad in the best of all possible lights.

Unfortunately, no copy of Ibn Ishaq's original biography has been preserved. Rather, we have a redacted version (still some 700 pages) by Ibn Hisham, who died just 61 years after Ibn Ishaq. Ibn Hisham says he left out some things for the sake of brevity, some that didn't mention "the apostle and about which the Quran says nothing" and "things which it is disgraceful to discuss."[4] This work was translated in 1955 by Alfred Guillaume and is available in a 2002 edition published by Oxford University Press. Most scholars believe this book to be essential in understanding the context of the Koran and Mohammad's life in a source that Muslims would not dispute.

Serge Trifkovic has pursued a career in broadcasting and journalism since receiving his Ph.D. at the University of Southampton and is a distinguished author. Two of his books, *The Sword of the Prophet: Islam; History, Theology, Impact on the World* and *Defeating Jihad: How the War on Terror May Yet Be Won, in Spite of Ourselves*, are excellent sources on Islam and the threats its radical terrorist adherents pose to Western civilization.

To understand the life, teachings, and actions of Mohammad, it is important to remember that these events took place in the 6th and 7th centuries A.D., a time in which the world was a far different place than the one in which we live today. Throughout antiquity, empires rose and fell with regularity. Wars raged in most parts of the world. Brutality, such as beheadings, the slaughter of entire populations, and destruction of cities, at times was evident. Slavery was the rule, not the exception. Women were treated as chattel in many parts of the world. Child marriages were not uncommon, and infanticide raised its ugly head from time to time.

The barren and harsh deserts of Arabia created unusually difficult living conditions. The Bedouin tribes there were no model of civilized behavior, but they had their codes of morality and standards of behavior. As Trifkovic points out, some of Mohammad's actions would certainly be abhorrent and criminal by today's standards, but they would be dubious even in the context of 7th century Arabia.[5] Let's take a look.

Most traditions hold that Mohammad (Spencer records his full name as Muhammad ibn Abdallah ibn Abd al-Muttalib) was born in 570 or 571 A.D. in Mecca, a small oasis town in western Arabia, in a region known as the *Hejaz*. (This region, which also includes Medina in today's Saudi Arabia, is considered so holy to Muslims that a non-Muslim is forbidden to set foot on the ground in the area.)

Mohammad was a member of a nomadic Arab tribe, the Quraysh, which like other Arabic tribes was pagan and polytheistic and worshiped a number of gods and goddesses. Trifkovic believes it is likely that the Quraysh were influenced by their monotheistic neighbors in the fourth and fifth centuries, and they probably recognized "Allah," a name for God known elsewhere in that part of the world, as the most powerful moon god. He contends that the ancestry of the indigenous population of Arabia stems from two roots, both with Old Testament origins:

> "Many Arabs believed that they were descended from Ishmael, the son of Abraham; they were known as Moaddites. Muhammad's ancestors belonged to this group. Others claimed their ancestry to the uplands of the southwestern corner of the Arabian Peninsula, in today's Yemen. It has been suggested that they are descended from another Old Testament patriarch, Joktan (Gen. 10:25-26), and that there is in fact a local tradition of an ancestor named Qahtan." [6]

The Quraysh tribe was custodian of the Kaaba (Ka'ba), meaning "cube," a rectangular building with the sacred "Black Stone" embedded in one of its walls. The structure was filled with images of the most popular pagan gods. Pilgrimages to worship the Black Stone had been occurring among pagans for centuries. As custodians, the Quraysh were held in esteem by the other Bedouin tribes, and it was a steady source of revenue. There is a tradition, referenced by Trifkovic, that holds the Arabs were descendents of Abraham through Ishmael, Abraham's son with his Egyptian slave, Hagar. The extended myth teaches that Hagar traveled to Mecca and the Kaaba with the young child after Sarah expelled her from her home. The story holds that when Hagar laid the baby Ishmael on the ground close to the Kaaba, he became so thirsty that he was kicking the ground. To save Hagar and her baby, the angel Gabriel opened the well of Zamzam, which is still there today, to provide water. Other fables hold that Abraham came to visit Hagar and Ishmael and rebuilt the walls surrounding the Black Stone. The Quraysh custodianship of the Kaaba becomes important when Mohammad tries to convert them and rid the holy place of all gods but Allah.

Lings begins his biography with an elaborate and detailed description of how Hagar and Ishmael ended up in Becca (or Mecca, as it would be subsequently known), where they were visited frequently by Abraham. Lings' hypothesis is that God fulfilled his promise to Abraham by establishing two great nations whose descendants would be as numerous as the stars in the heavens. He writes:

> "Not one but two great nations were to look to Abraham as their father—two great nations, that is, two guided powers, two instruments to work the Will of Heaven, for God does not promise as a blessing that which is profane, nor is there any greatness before God except greatness in the Spirit. Abraham was thus the fountainhead of two spiritual streams, which must not flow together....Two spiritual streams, two religions, two worlds for God; two circles, therefore two centers." [7]

Lings continues to explain how God commanded Abraham and Ishmael to build the Ka'bah (his spelling) and how an angel provided the sacred black stone. He also contends that Isaac and his descendents initially recognized this holy temple raised by Abraham until the Quraysh of the Hollow, as Lings refers to Mohammad's tribe, grew so large that they could no longer remain in the valley of Mecca. Then the pagan tribes took control of the Kaaba and turned it into a pagan shrine.[8]

Most tradition holds that after Mohammad captured Mecca in 630 A.D. that he threw out icons of all the pagan gods, which by then numbered 365, and reclaimed the Kaaba for worship of Allah alone. There is a tradition that Mohammad actually left icons of Mary and Jesus in the Kaaba.

Albert Hourani in *A History of the Arab Peoples* suggests that the idea of Mohammad being a descendant of Ishmael arose of necessity after Mohammad had fled to Medina. He speculates that the Jewish tribes in Medina could not conceive of accepting Mohammad as a prophet apart from a common ancestry. If the Ishmael link could be established, this would establish a "spiritual descent" from Abraham.[9] In any event, Muslims believe that Mohammad's Quraysh tribe were descendents of Abraham though his son Ishmael.

Mohammed's father died when Mohammed was two years old, and he was orphaned at the age of six. He was raised for a few years by his grandfather, Abdel Muttalib, who was purportedly the keeper of the Kaaba. However, his grandfather died when Mohammad was nine. Mohammad was then taken in by an uncle who made him a camel driver. This enabled the teenaged Mohammad to visit Syria and Palestine. Sitting around the camp fires on these journeys he would be exposed to many conversations with different people, including Christians and Jews. What's more, Mecca was on a caravan route between the Mediterranean and the East, which also enabled Mohammad for many years to have considerable interchange with Christians and Jews who were traveling in the caravans. The orphaned child grew into manhood poor and with no special status among the tribe. Power and money were defining issues for his tribe and he logically had some resentment, which would make it easier for him to destroy many of them in later years.

Trifkovic describes what he considers to be a defining moment in Mohammad's early life. In 595, when Mohammad was only 15 or 16 years old, the Ethiopians were threatening to invade Mecca. As his uncle was assembling an army to fight the Ethiopians, the young Mohammad ran away and would as a result have to endure considerable criticism from his family. At about the age of 25, he took a job as a shepherd and then was hired by a traveling cloth merchant. This turned out to be a good move for Mohammad, since the job took him to Hayacha, a market town south of Mecca. It was here he met his first wife, a wealthy widow named Khadija.[10] Khadija, who was 15 years older than Mohammad, would provide him with financial means. About 15 years later, in 610, she would be the first to hear of what Mohammad described as a revelation from Allah through the angel Gabriel when Mohammad was about 40 years old. Khadija would subsequently become the prophet's first convert to Islam.

Spencer suggests that without Khadija's encouragement, Mohammad might never have become a prophet. After three years of receiving new revelations, he began to preach his new religion to the Quraysh and other inhabitants of Mecca. Over the course of some nine years, he gained some converts, but hostilities became so heated that he and his followers were forced to flee in 622 to Medina. There he received additional revelations, the Koran (Qur'an) was completed, he gained many converts, and he assumed political authority and leadership.

Lewis considers Mohammad's arrival in Medina to be the beginning of the Islam era.

The devout Muslim who penned Mohammad's first biography, Ibn Ishaq, describes the preparations Allah made for Mohammad before giving him permission to flee Mecca. Under the title "The Apostle Receives the Order to Fight," Ishaq explains:

> "The apostle had not been given permission to fight or allowed to shed blood before the second 'Aqaba. He had simply been ordered to call men to God and to endure insult and forgive the ignorant. The Quraysh had persecuted his followers, seducing some from their religion, and exiling others from the country. They had to choose whether to give up their religion, be maltreated at home, or to flee the country, some to Abyssinia, other to Medina. When Quraysh became insolent towards God and rejected His gracious purpose, accused His prophet of lying, and ill treated and exiled those who served Him and proclaimed His unity, believed in His prophet, and held fast to His religion... He gave permission to His apostle to fight and to protect himself against those who wronged them and treated them badly."[11]

The Medinan period in Mohammad's life deserves some special consideration since it was here he gained political and military power as the Prophet of Islam and planned and executed the battles to force all of the Arabian tribes into submission to the Islamic faith. By 615, only two years after Mohammad had begun publicly preaching Islam in Mecca, some of his earliest converts had fled the persecution in Mecca and took their new religion with them. Some ended up in Medina (known at the time as Yathrib), where they spread the Muslim faith.

Hearing of the intensifying persecution of Muslims, and of especially Islam's prophet, 75 men professing Islam traveled the distance of about 200 miles south from Medina to Mecca to meet with Mohammad. They offered to protect him and arrange his escape from Mecca if he would come and live with them in Yathrib. Mohammad had just received the above-mentioned revelation allowing him to fight those in Mecca and others who opposed him. He and 70 of his most loyal followers joined these men on their return journey to Yathrib.

On Sept. 24, 622, the group arrived in Yathrib. As Lewis, Trifkovic names this date the "beginning of the history of Islam." The Arabic phrase meaning "the city of the prophet" was shortened to the word "Medina" as the new name for ancient Yathrib. In about a year and a half, with a victory in battle under his belt, Mohammed solidified his power base in Medina. Three years later he would become the "absolute ruler of Medina."[12] It was time for Mohammad and his followers to conquer Arabia.

There were a number of Jewish tribes in Medina, three of which were most prominent and exerted some degree of economic and political influence in the city. They were the Banu Qaynuqa, the Banu Nadir, and the Banu Qurayzah. Spencer describes Mohammad's early relationship with these tribes in these words:

> "From nearly the beginning of his prophetic career Muhammad was strongly influenced by Judaism—situating himself within the roster of Jewish prophets, forbidding pork for his followers, and adapting for the Muslims the practice of several daily prayers and other aspects of Jewish ritual. Now he began to try to gain their acceptance of his prophetic status. For the first year and a half after the Muslims' arrival in Medina he even had them face Jerusalem for their prayers."[13]

One of the most significant acts by Mohammad during these early years in Medina was the negotiation of a pact with the three Jewish tribes. As Spencer records it, the pact would be regarded by Muslims as the "world's first constitution." Ibn Ishaq called it a "friendly agreement" between Muslims and Jews.

The pact clearly distinguishes the rights of the "believers" and "unbelievers" as they live together under Islamic rule. The unbelievers are always subservient, but not as severely under this agreement as in subsequent conditions offered to the *Dhimmi*. The *Dhimmi* are the people of the Book, originally only Jews and Christians, who would be offered the option of living under Muslim protection in conquered lands if they agree to accept very strict conditions. (This subject will be examined in some detail in section 4 of this chapter.) The conditions became more severe in the latter case as Mohammad would receive additional revelations on the subject.[14]

In any event, Mohammad will break the agreement in 624 when he orders some of the Jews killed and banishes the others from Medina.[15]

Violence in the name of Islam began with a vengeance in 624 when Mohammad, now with a dedicated military force of Muslim warriors, led raids on caravans and camp sites of his own Quraysh tribe. The Muslims attacked even at night, which would involve killing women and children in addition to their armed rivals. Taking booty became a motive in addition to revenge and the ultimate goal of conquering all the tribes of Arabia in the name of Islam.

At the same time, the situation with the Jewish leaders in Medina continued to deteriorate. Frequent arguments broke out over religious teachings. One example recorded in the first biography of Mohammad arose over the question of the punishment for adultery. Mohammad asked what was taught in the Torah about such punishment. Was it not stoning? One Jewish leader answered, "We announce the crime and lash them." Mohammad then demanded that the relevant portions of the Torah be read. When the Jewish leader tried to omit the verse that mandated stoning for adultery, Mohammad cried out, "Woe to you Jews! What has induced you to abandon the judgment of God which you hold in your hand?" He continued, according to the biography, "'I am the first to revive the order of God and His Book and to practice it.' Mohammad would command the stoning to begin and one eyewitness would later confess that 'I saw the man leaning over the woman to shelter her from the stones.'"[16]

Islam's greatest early *jihad* victory, according to Spencer and virtually all scholars on Islam, was the Battle of Badr. That the Jews in Medina were not accepting Mohammad as God's final prophet and converting to Islam caused him great consternation. Mohammad decided it was time to begin the conquest of the Arabian tribes in what he believed to be Allah's command to him to spread the Islamic faith. He selected as his first target his own Quraysh tribe because of their prominence and the fact that they had rejected him as Allah's prophet in Mecca.

The Hijra and the Battle of Badr are absolutely integral to the establishment and defining of Islam over the years. They are both frequently referenced by Islamic scholars, reformers, radicals and fundamentalists throughout the Islamic era. From the founders of Salafism, Wahhabism, and Qutbism to Osama bin Laden and the current General Guide of the Muslim Brotherhood, Dr. Muhammad Badi, these are recurring themes. The Battle of Badr is prominently referenced in the Koran as evidence of the power of Allah when *jihad* is waged according to Allah's commands.

To summarize the sequence of events that led to the establishment of Islam: In 622, Mohammad and his followers took a journey, known as the Hijra, from Mecca to Medina. The Muslim era dates from the beginning of the Arabic year in which the Hijra[17] took place, according to Dr. Lewis. Shortly after the Hijra, Mohammad received Allah's permission to shed the blood of infidels by waging *jihad* or holy war. By 624, Mohammad had become the most prominent leader in Medina—he was the de facto ruler of the town. By this time, Mohammad had assembled a fighting force numbering more than 300 men. Badr would define Islamist *jihad* when it occurred through Islam's history.

Mohammad determined that the time was right and planned the first major and most significant attack involving his Muslim warriors. This famous battle became commonly known as the Battle of Badr and still serves as a rallying cry for Islamic terrorists until this very day. Robert Spencer, and many other non-politically correct scholars on Islam, as well as such respected moderates as Dr. Lewis, indicate that to truly understand the rise and spread of Islam in its founding days; the reason the Crusades were called some 400 years later; and the persistence of Islamic extremism throughout its history, it is necessary to be familiar with the Battle of Badr.

Some of Mohammad's followers were reluctant to attack the Quraysh caravan that was to travel through the town of Badr, just some 80 miles from Medina. Many of them, like Mohammad, were members of the Quraysh tribe and knew of their fighting abilities. Mohammad claimed to have had a revelation that Allah would give them the victory and the booty, which was considerable. This first major jihadist victory against overwhelming odds—Mohammad's biographers record 300 or fewer Muslims against 1,000 experienced Quraysh troops—is heralded in all of Mohammad's biographers and most importantly in the Koran. Ibn Ishaq devotes 25 pages in *The Life of Muhammad* to the Battle of Badr as well as numerous other references to this extraordinary attack.

Surah 3 of the Koran states:

"And Allah did certainly assist you at Badr when you were weak: be careful of (your duty to) Allah then, that you may give thanks.

When you said to the believers: Does it not suffice you that your Lord should assist you with three thousand of the angels sent down?

Yea! If you remain patient and are on your guard, and they come upon you in headlong manner, your Lord will assist you with five thousand of the havoc-making angels.

And Allah did not make it but a good news for you, and that your hearts might be at ease thereby, and victory is only from Allah, the Mighty, the Wise" (Koran 3:123-126).

The Koran goes even further and gives Allah credit for the slayings in chapter 8:

"So you did not slay them, but it was Allah Who slew them, and you did not smite when you smote (the enemy), but it was Allah Who smote, and that He might confer upon the believers a good gift from Himself: surely Allah is Hearing, Knowing" (Koran 8:17).

This certainly explains why Muslims, beginning with the first caliph and persisting unabated to the modern day Islamist terrorists, are so anxious to cite the Battle of Badr as their example and justification.

Egypt's General Guide of the Muslim Brotherhood, Dr. Muhammad Badi, in a February 2011 sermon, emphasizes the absolutely essential role the Hijra and the Battle of Badr played in the founding and continuing history of Islam. In a Friday sermon in 2010, Dr. Badi had claimed that the United States "was on the threshold of collapse and would soon fall, like other immoral societies before it." Badi, as the supreme leader of the Brotherhood worldwide today, states why he is so confident that the Islamists will be victorious over today's infidels in these words, which I quote again for emphasis:

"Allah said: The hosts will be routed and will turn and flee [Koran 54:45]. This verse is a promise to the believers that they shall defeat their enemies, and [that their enemies] shall withdraw. The Companions of the Prophet received the Koranic promise in Mecca, whey they were weak ... and a little more than nine years after the Hijra, Allah fulfilled his promise in the Battle of Badr...."

Dr. Badi's firebrand rhetoric certainly explains the fear evidenced by the Christian minority in Egypt as well as the secularists and moderate Muslims about the control of the Egyptian government the Brotherhood now claims after the 2012 election. It must be remembered why Hassan al-Banna founded the Muslim Brotherhood in 1928. First the Ottoman forces had been soundly defeated in 1923. Then in 1924 Kemal Ataturk abolished the caliphate and turned Turkey into a Western-style secular country. This was the ultimate humiliation to the faithful, such as al-Banna and hundreds of millions of fundamentalist Muslims throughout the former Ottoman Empire, which was now divided into 50 different nation states. Dr. Lewis, also a linguistic authority, notes that there was no equivalent to the English word "secular" in Arabic, Farsi, or Persian at the time of Ataturk. Al-Banna insisted that the caliphate must be restored and that Muslim-ruled countries must be governed by strict *sharia* law. The Muslim Brotherhood is capable of making tactical "conversions," but their goals never change.

In any event, Dr. Badi's words should also encourage eternal vigilance when evaluating the role of the Muslim Brotherhood in any country—certainly including the United States.

The theological implications of the victory at Badr were that, with Allah on their side, numbers of warriors didn't matter. The outcome of this first major battle in Islam's holy war struck fear in the hearts of the tribes throughout Arabia and emboldened Mohammad.

Meanwhile, Mohammad's troubles with the Jews in Medina intensified and his forces lost a battle in the mountains near Mecca in a Quraysh counter-attack with an army of 3,000 men against the Muslim army of only 1,000.

Mohammad broke his treaty with the Jewish tribes in Medina and expelled two of the three most prominent tribes from the city. This caused great concern among the largest and strongest tribe remaining in Medina. Their concern led to the greatest threat to the survival of Mohammad's Muslim army and his very position as the absolute ruler of the Islamic state. Mohammad's own Quarysh tribe had assembled its largest force yet and convinced another large Arabian tribe to join forces with them to undertake a massive assault on Medina. When Mohammad found out about the planned attack, he decided to build a large trench in front of Medina. This would become well known in Islamic history as the "Battle of the Trench."

When the invading Arab tribes tried to storm Medina, the trench prevented them from entering the city. As the battle continued to be fought indecisively for several weeks, the leaders of the Jewish tribe from Medina secretly sent emissaries to meet with the Quarysh and present a plan to trap Mohammad and his men. The Jewish tribe would raise their forces to attack the Muslim army from the rear when the Quraysh and their allies leveled a major assault on Mohammad's troops.

This plan might have been fatal for Mohammad, but he had a spy in the Jewish ranks. This recent Jewish convert to Islam managed to secretly meet with both sides and sow discord amongst Mohammad's two assembled enemies. When the Jews refused to join the battle on the Sabbath and the weather took a terrible turn for the worse, the plan faltered. The Arab tribes gathered their scattered tents and animals and withdrew. Thus Mohammad survived another battle that could have ended his movement.

One event that would define early Muslim history happened while Mohammad was helping to prepare for the attack by digging in the trench. Mohammad claimed to have received a revelation to conquer Byzantine Christian lands west of Arabia and Persian lands in the east.

Mohammad was furious with the Jewish tribe in Medina for their secret cooperation with the Quraysh during the Battle of the Trench. He considered them traitors and ordered their strongholds in Medina attacked. After 25 days of attacks, the Jewish tribal leaders chose to surrender. Mohammad told one of his trusted aides to determine what to do with this tribe, the Banu Qurayzah. When the aide recommended that their warriors be killed and their women and children enslaved, Mohammad took his advice. Spencer points out that ancient sources report that between 600 and 900 men were massacred, most of them beheaded.

"The massacre of the Banu Qurayzah has been understandably a source of embarrassment to Muslims," Spencer writes. He further explains that Islamic apologists' efforts to explain this massacre have ranged from outright denial to contending that it was not such uncommon behavior in the 7th century.[18] What amazes me about any attempt to deny that these events happed is that they are taken from the earliest authoritative Islamic sources (see Ibn Ishaq, p. 464).

By 627, Mohammad had total control of Medina, and over the next three or four years he would become the undisputed master of all Arabia.

Apparently unwilling to submit to Muslim rule without a fight, another Arab tribe (Banu Mustaliq) related to Mohammad's tribe began preparations to attack the Muslims. Learning their intentions, Mohammad had a revelation from Allah to kill the men and take their women and children, along with their possessions, as booty. Some of the Muslim warriors who had been separated from their wives for some time during these ongoing battles asked if they could have sexual relations with these women. Mohammad's answer was yes, as long as they did not intend to keep them as slaves with the intention of collecting ransom money for them. They could not have them for sexual pleasure and booty at the same time. Spencer makes the point that treating women as "war prizes," even in 7th century Arabia, must have called into question Mohammad's status as a model of behavior to be emulated.[19]

Mohammad himself even gained another new wife during this settlement after the victorious battle.

In 628, Mohammad surprised and generated some opposition from certain of his followers when he agreed to a 10-year truce with the Quraysh. Mohammad had received a revelation about making the ancient and popular pagan pilgrimage to Mecca a mandatory tradition of Islam. An initial Muslim pilgrimage had not been possible since his own tribe, the Quraysh, had fortified Mecca. Some of his key associates believed that the time had come to attack Mecca and take control of the city, but Mohammad must have thought that the time was not yet right and that such an attack would involve bloodshed he intended to avoid in a couple of years. In any event, he and the Quraysh signed The Treaty of Hudayhiyya, which mandated the 10-year truce along with other provisions. It turned out to be nothing but a stalling tactic for Mohammad, since the treaty would be violated two years later, in 630, when the Muslims made their triumphant march into Mecca.

Perhaps it was to quell the dissatisfaction over the treaty that led to the decision to raid the oasis at Khaybar for additional booty. This oasis was inhabited by certain Jewish tribes, including some that had been exiled from Medina, and it contained considerable wealth. The invading Muslims received considerable resistance, and both sides suffered a large number of casualties, but the Muslims prevailed.

Mohammad decided to let the Jews go into exile and take with them only the possessions they could carry. Some wanted to stay, and he agreed to allow them to do so under strict conditions. But when Mohammad discovered they had tried to hide some of their most valuable treasures, he was furious. He demanded that their warriors be killed, their women and children be taken as slaves, and their lands confiscated. Mohammad ended up with another wife and survived an attempt to be poisoned. This was all justified based primarily on their attempts to deceive.[20]

There is some debate over which party was the first to violate the 10-year truce prohibiting violence, but in 630 Mohammad believed it was time to conquer Mecca. The size of the Muslim army (some estimate its size at 10,000 men) marching toward Mecca must have convinced the tribal leaders defending the city not to offer any resistance. Spencer quotes Ibn Sa'd, one of the earliest Muslim biographers of the prophet, as saying that when Mohammad's troops entered the city, "the people embraced Islam willingly or unwillingly."[21] There was a short list of apostates from Islam and some who had especially insulted Mohammad to be executed, but there was no resistance and, therefore, no violence.

Mohammad, his close associates, and a horde of followers proceeded to the Ka'bah (or Kaaba), where he cleansed the pagan shrine of its idols. Spencer puts the number of icons in this temple at 360. He quotes the first of Mohammad's Islamic biographers, Ibn Ishaq, writing that Islam's prophet proceeded to remove every icon but those of Mary and Jesus.[22] Mohammad then spared the lives of the Quraysh leaders.

Spencer then makes this salient statement:

"The people of Mecca now gathered to pay homage to Muhammad. It was the crowning moment of his prophetic career; eight years before he had been exiled from his home city, and now it lay at his feet. One of his chief companions, Umar, made all the men promise to obey Allah and Muhammad, as the Prophet looked on."[23]

Mohammad made statements that Allah had made Mecca holy when he created the world and that it is to be the "holy of holies until resurrection day." He then gave the keys to the caretaker of the Kaaba.

There would be one more battle before Mohammad would have total control over all of Arabia.

There was a warlike Arabian tribe in a city south of Mecca that had been historic rivals of Mohammad's own Quraysh tribe. They had rejected Mohammad's prophetic claims years earlier and they were not now going to become Muslims without a fight. Mohammad took no chances, assembling a 12,000-man army to march south to their city, Ta'if. The men of Ta'if surprised him, though, by taking a fortified position in a dry river bed just south of Mecca, which afforded them a tactical advantage.

When the Muslims first encountered the army of Ta'if, the Muslim troops fell into disarray and started to flee in large numbers. After some period of exhorting and commanding his troops to reassemble and defeat this enemy in Allah's name, Mohammad finally restored order and won the hard-fought battle. After success in this battle, taking the city of Ta'if was no challenge.[24]

Arabia was now conquered by the fierce warrior and prophet of Islam. There were still a few scattered tribes in Arabia who had not submitted to Islam, but they would all "convert" by the following year, 631, either out of conviction or fear.

With Arabia totally subdued, Mohammad turned his attention to the Byzantine and Persian empires surrounding Arabia. He wrote letters to their rulers urging them to convert to his new faith. When they refused, he urged his followers to wage *jihad*, or holy war, to conquer these infidel lands and establish Allah's reign.

That Mohammad personally led the first Muslim army to conquer a Christian land in 631 has been explained in the Introduction to this book. Lings, a devout Muslim convert, in his English biography of Mohammad makes the strange claim that Mohammad decided to conquer the Christian city of Tabuk because he had been warned that some of the Byzantine Christian rulers were planning an invasion of Arabia. This defies reason in many ways. First of all, some early Christian rulers may have done some dumb things, but to consider invading an oasis in the middle of a desert defended by nomadic tribesmen with 7th-century modes of transportation would give dumbness a really bad name. Second, Mohammad had explained in some depth the visions he had received about conquering Byzantine Christian countries when he was helping dig the trench in preparation for the Battle of the Trench. As previously pointed out, Mohammad intended to set an example for his followers in carrying out the command to conquer Christian lands.

After Mohammad returned from Tabuk, he made one last pilgrimage to Mecca. During this pilgrimage, he set the rules for the *hajj,* the pilgrimage to Mecca that all Muslims are expected to make at least once in their lifetimes. He also had much to say about the rights of women and the *dhimmis* (a pact with the people of the Book, i.e., Christians and Jews, establishing how they can live in Muslim-controlled lands as second-class citizens), which will be discussed elsewhere. Mohammad also gave unbelievers—pagan Arabs—the option of submitting to Allah or, if they did not leave Arabia within four months, death.[25]

After this last pilgrimage to Mecca, Mohammad returned to Medina. He died there a short time later, on June 8, 632, at the age of 63.

In concluding this section on the life of Mohammad, I would offer quotes from two scholars on Islam to underline the importance of understanding the life of Islam's prophet. Spencer cites an example of a Muslim actually questioning Mohammad to his face about whether he was being just:

> "The Prophet of Islam was incredulous. "If justice is not to be found with me then where will you find it?" ... Indeed, Muslims ever after have found justice in Muhammad, and only in him. His words and deeds exemplify their highest pattern of conduct, forming the only absolute standard within Islam: anything sanctioned by the example of the Prophet, with the sole exception of incidents such as that of the Satanic verses, in which he was repentant, is good."[26]

Holy Books

Christians and Muslims each have a holy book they believe is God's final revelation to man. The Christian Scriptures, the Holy Bible, consist of 66 books, written over many years, which Christians believe is the divinely inspired Word of God. Lewis writes:

> "The Qur'an, for Muslims, is a single book promulgated at one time by one man, the Prophet Muhammad. After a lively debate in the first centuries of Islam, the doctrine was adopted that the Qur'an itself is uncreated and eternal, divine and immutable. This has become a central tenet of the faith."[27]

Mohammad wrote the surahs (verses) of the Qur'an (or dictated the messages he received) over a period of some 20 years. Spencer states:

> "The suras of the Qur'an are not arranged chronologically, but according to length. Islamic theology divides the Qur'an into 'Meccan'

and 'Medinan' suras. The Meccan ones come from the segment of Muhammad's career as a prophet, when he simply called the Meccans to Islam. Later, after he had fled to Medina, his positioned hardened. The Medinan suras are less poetic and generally much longer than those from Mecca: they're also filled with matters of law and ritual— and exhortations to jihad warfare against unbelievers." [28]

This distinction becomes important in considering the more peaceful and violent verses, as Spencer points out. He also makes the point that in the Islamic doctrine of abrogation (*naskh*), Allah can change his mind:

"This is the idea that Allah can change or cancel what he tells Muslims: 'None of Our revelations do we abrogate or cause to be forgotten, but We substitute something better or similar: knowest thou not that Allah Hath power over all things?'(Qur'an 2:106)" [29]

Serge Trifkovic describes the process by which the Koran reached its final written form in these words:

"Starting in 610, at increasingly frequent intervals until his death, Muhammad received 'revelations,' or verbal messages that he believed came directly from Allah. Some of them Muhammad and his followers kept in memory and sometimes they were written down. Around 650 A.D. they were collected and written in the Kuran, the sacred scriptures of Islam, and eventually codified in the form that has endured till today. Muslims believe the Kuran is divine revelation, written in the words of Allah himself." [30]

The fact that Mohammad wrote different verses in the two periods and that Allah can change his instructions has made for some interesting disputes and radical disagreements among Islamic as well as non-Islamic scholars over the years.

The contacts Mohammad had with Jews and Christians in Mecca and on his travels would help serve his purposes in writing the Koran. He misquotes the Old Testament in several places but not as severely as he distorts the New Testament. Some of Mohammad's strange New Testament references undoubtedly reflect the fact that many—probably most—of the Christians with whom he had come into contact in Arabia were considered heretics by the orthodox Byzantine Christians: Gnostics, who weren't interested in the resurrection of the body since they believed that all physical matter was evil; Nestorians, who refused to accept the unity of the two natures of Jesus; and some Monophysites, who denied the two natures of Christ, teaching that the human nature of Christ had been absorbed by His divine nature. Members of these heretical groups had fled Byzantine lands to escape persecution and had landed in various parts of Arabia.

Since Mohammad intended to teach that Islam was the final fulfillment of the religion of the Old and New Testaments, he made efforts to show that the coming of the last prophet—Mohammad himself—was prophesied in the Jewish and Christian Scriptures.

Some of the teachings about Jesus in the Koran are totally bizarre. Mohammad most likely heard some of these stories and myths in the conversations he had with the various heretical Christian sects. A few examples should be of interest to the readers.

Robert Spencer writes in *The Truth about Muhammad*: "The Jesus of the Qur'an, although not divine, is a powerful miracle worker. He even speaks in His cradle: 'He shall preach to men in his cradle and in the prime of manhood, and shall lead a righteous life' (Qur'an 3:46)." Mary knew that some who came to visit her under the palm tree, according to the Koran, might question her chastity, so she instructed them to ask the baby Jesus. He, of course, defends his mother.

Spencer speculates also that Mohammad's denial in the Koran that Jesus was crucified but taken directly to heaven without tasting death most likely came from heretical Christian groups. The Jews only thought they had killed Jesus, but it would have been wrong for Allah to allow one of his prophets to die in shame and humiliation. Spencer thinks Gnostic stories may have led Mohammad to believe that God made Judas look like Jesus and that the Jews nailed him to the cross thinking it was Jesus.[31]

Radically Different Views of Religion and State

One of the defining differences in Christian and Islamic thought involves the relationship between religion and government.

Jesus taught His disciples that "my kingdom is not of this world" and instructed them to "render unto Caesar the things which are Caesar's and unto God the things that are God's." A tiny persecuted minority of apostles, disciples, and their followers spread God's Gospel of salvation in the crucified Christ throughout a hostile Roman empire against all odds. They changed a mighty empire and ultimately transformed world history with only the power of God's Word.

In stark contrast, the mighty warrior Mohammad established, as Lewis emphasizes, a political and religious community of Muslims, with the Prophet as head of state during his own lifetime. To use a Christian metaphor, there could be no "separation of Church and State," because they were one and the same.

Lewis concisely explains the founding of Islam:

> "For the formative first generation of Muslims, whose adventures are the sacred history of Islam, there was no protracted testing by persecution, no tradition of resistance to hostile state power. On the contrary, the state that ruled them was that of Islam, and God's approval of their cause was made clear to them in the forms of victory and empire in this world. In pagan Rome, Caesar was God. For Christians, there is a choice between God and Caesar, and endless

generations of Christians have been ensnared in that choice. In the universal Islamic polity as conceived by Muslims, there is no Caesar but only God, who is the sole sovereign and the source of law. Muhammad was His Prophet, who during his lifetime both taught and ruled on God's behalf. When Muhammad died in 632 C.E., his spiritual and prophetic mission, to bring God's book to mankind, was completed. What remained was the religious task of spreading God's revelation until finally all the world accepted it. This was to be achieved by extending the authority and thus also the membership of the community which embraced the true faith and upheld God's law. To provide the necessary cohesion and leadership for this task, a deputy or successor of the Prophet was required. The Arabic word kbalifa was the title adopted by the Prophet's father-in-law and first successor, Abu Bakr, whose accession to the headship of the Islamic community marked the foundation of the great historic institution of the caliphate."[32] [The caliphate will be discussed in the following section.]

Mohammad's Charge to Conquer and Convert

Mohammad announced to his followers, when he was helping to dig the trench in preparation for the Battle of the Trench, that Allah had revealed to him that the lands to the east and the west of Arabia must be conquered. Islam's Prophet had set the example for his followers by leading the successful invasion of the Byzantine Christian enclave of Tabuk himself in 631 A.D. Mohammad had also sent messages to the Byzantine emperor, Heraclius, and other rulers of neighboring lands, offering them the opportunity "to embrace Islam and you will be safe." When they refused to convert, they were no longer safe.[33]

Abu Bakr, Mohammad's constant companion and father-in-law, was selected as the first caliph after considerable debate. Abu Bakr's major challenge was to bring together the divergent tribes and individuals that constituted Islam in Arabia. Many had converted out of expediency or just in order to survive under the new rule. The "Wars of Apostasy" with which the first caliph was forced to deal during his brief reign were proof that many had accepted the new faith in merely a nominal way with little understanding of the basic teachings. Once Mohammad died, some of the Arab tribes disavowed Islam.

The first caliph was so preoccupied with internal strife that he initiated only a few major battles. However, the battles against the apostate tribes in Arabia and with those living on the borders of Arabia were extremely violent and bloody. Apparently, Abu Bakr intended to set an example concerning the consequences of apostasy and strike fear in the hearts of those they intended to invade. (Abd El Schafi's *Behind the Veil: Unmasking Islam* deals with these subjects in some detail.[34])

Abu Bakr did have the foresight to select Umar, another of Mohammad's companions and fathers-in-law, as his successor. Umar's 10-year reign as the second caliph from 634 to 644 would be marked by major Islamic conquest. He apparently had the organizational skills and leadership qualities to mobilize his fighting forces for conquest, and he certainly believed he had the authority to do so based on the revelations of Allah in the Koran. When Mohammad was having his troubles convincing the residents of Medina to convert, he claimed that Allah gave him this revelation:

> "Fight those who do not believe in Allah, nor in the latter day, nor do they prohibit what Allah and His Apostle have prohibited, nor follow the religion of truth, out of those who have been given the Book, until they pay the tax in acknowledgement of superiority and they are in a state of subjection. And the Jews say: Uzair [Ezra] is the son of Allah; and the Christians say: The Messiah is the son of Allah; these are the words of their mouths; they imitate the saying of those who disbelieved before; may Allah destroy them; how they are turned away!" (Koran 9:30, 31).

Trifkovic points out that a few raids on the borderlands of Byzantium and Persia had convinced Umar that they were both weak. These two empires had been involved in so many battles over the years they had drained many of their resources.[35]

Umar was emboldened to call for the first major *jihad* or holy war since Mohammad's death. Dr. Bernard Lewis describes *jihad* as it relates to the spread of Islam in these words: "The object of jihad is to bring the whole world under Islamic law. It is not to convert by force, but to remove obstacles to conversion."[36] Regardless of whether the populations converted or were just subjugated, the blitzkrieg employed by Umar in conquering Christian and Zoroastrian lands would have been envied by Alexander the Great, as well as Adolph Hitler.

Most of the works I have read by non-Muslim scholars, with the obvious exception of the most avid politically correct elitists, agree that the Muslim conquests, some of which will be briefly enumerated, were totally unprovoked military actions for the sole purpose of spreading a religion. Spencer and Trifkovic implicitly bemoan the fact that most of the people in the western world are so historically illiterate that they believe the fighting between Muslims and Christians began during the Crusades. The sometimes extremely violent and bloody early Muslim conquest of Christian lands took place some 400 years before the First Crusade was even considered.[37]

In 636, Caliph Umar won a decisive battle against the Byzantine Christian forces at the battle of Yarmuk, where some report that as many as 30,000 of Heraclius' most veteran troops were killed.[38] Damascus had already fallen the previous year, and after such a costly defeat, all of Syria would soon fall under Islamic rule. Jerusalem was conquered in 638 and Palestine had a new master.

Some of the early Muslim conquests may have be made easier since many people of Arabic origin had previously immigrated to certain areas of the Middle East. Others contend that many of the heretical Christians living in the Byzantine Empire would welcome a conqueror who would not persecute them because of their view of the doctrine of Christ. Spencer provides specific evidence that refutes such attempts to justify hostile invasions waged to spread the new religion. The Muslim invasion of Egypt began in December 639 and ran into such stiff opposition that Egypt was not conquered until November 642, when Alexandria finally fell. Spencer writes that accounts of the slaughtering of innocent civilians, including women and children, the taking of large numbers of slaves, the plunder of valuables, and the desecration of churches abound.[39]

While conceding that the Abbasid caliphate (which ruled for some 500 years from 750 to 1258) ruled in a relatively tolerant manner most of the time, Trifkovic has this to say about the early Muslim conquest:

> "Slaughters did occur in the initial wave of conquest: during the Muslim invasion of Syria in 634, thousands of Christians were massacred; in Mesopotamia between 635 and 642, monasteries were ransacked and the monks and villagers slain; in Egypt the towns of Behnesa, Fayum, Nikiu and Aboit were put to the sword.... In North Africa, Tripoli was pillaged in 643 by Amr, who forced the Jews and Christians to hand over their women and children as slaves to the Arab army."[40]

The first four caliphs, which would include Uthman and Ali (both sons-in-law of Mohammad) as well as Abu Bakr and Umar, are universally referred to by Muslims as "the rightly guided ones." They presided over the early conquest of Christian lands not only in the West, but also when the Persian Empire in the East, which also included many Christians, was conquered in 641. Three of these four caliphs were assassinated by their own people (Umar was murdered by one of his disgruntled Christian slaves from Iraq). Ali's murder would lead to the Sunni-Shiite split.

The caliphs who came after the first four would push further into Europe. After earlier, unsuccessful attempts, the Muslims finally conquered Spain in 715. Spain would remain under Islamic rule until 1492, when Christian forces finally reclaimed this previously Christian nation, which had remained under Muslim control for more than 700 years.

On numerous occasions during the late 7th century and 8th century, Muslim attempts to penetrate deeper into Europe (especially into France and Italy) would result in the loss of booty and the taking of Christians as slaves. Europe could have been lost for Christianity had the Franks under General Charles Martel not defeated them in 732 in the battle of Tours.

They did not quit trying to place the entire Christian empire under Allah's rule. They unsuccessfully invaded France in 792 and 843. In 846, the Muslim armies actually reached Rome and held Sicily until 1091. They did not forget about the Christian stronghold in the East and attacked Constantinople in 668 and 717. Sadly, this great center of eastern Christianity would fall a few centuries later to the Ottomans, in 1453.

Lewis offers a rather concise account of the Muslim conquest of Christian lands from Caliph Umar's first decisive victory against the Byzantine forces in 636 to the peak of the Ottoman Empire in the 16th and 17th centuries:

> "In the course of the seventh century, Muslim armies advancing from Arabia conquered Syria, Palestine, Egypt, and North Africa, all until then part of Christendom... In the eighth century, from their bases in North Africa, Arab Muslim forces, now joined by Berber converts, conquered Spain and Portugal and invaded France; in the ninth century they conquered Sicily and invaded the Italian mainland. In 846 a naval expedition from Sicily even entered the River Tiber, and Arab forces sacked Ostia and Rome. This provoked the first attempts to organize an effective Christian counterattack... In the East, between 1237 and 1240, the Tatars of the Golden Horde, conquered Russia; in 1252 the Khan of the Golden Horde and his people were converted to Islam. Russia, with much of Eastern Europe, was subject to Muslim rule, and it was not until the late fifteenth century that the Russians finally freed their country from what they called the 'Tartar yoke.' In the meantime a third wave of Muslim attacks had begun, that of the Ottoman Turks, who conquered Anatolia, captured the ancient Christian city of Constantinople, invaded and colonized the Balkan peninsula, and threatened the very heart of Europe, twice reaching as far as Vienna."[41]

We should remember that the above is a list of unprovoked attacks on Christian lands, many of which also included a considerable number of Jewish residents. During much of this time period, the Muslim conquerors were also invading the Persian Empire, which included a significant number of Christians and some Jews, as well as India and other countries. These Muslim caliphs, military leaders, and warriors were taking Mohammad's command from Allah to wage offensive "holy war" to spread the rule and faith of Islam throughout the world with total dedication. Today's Islamic terrorists take not only their examples but what they believe to be their divine obligations to wage *jihad* in today's world from such Muslim history.

By 750, with more than two-thirds of the land that previously comprised the Byzantine Christian Empire now under Muslim control, the so-called "Golden Age of Islam" had its beginnings. Some Islamic scholars date the Golden Age from the 8th to the 13th century, when the caliphate was located primarily in Bagdad. This group of scholars writes about the "Islamic Renaissance" during this period of time when Europe was in the dark ages. They usually further contend that the Ottoman Empire rose from the ashes of the Golden Age when Osman I declared himself ruler of the Seljuk empire in 1299. Others simply consider the Golden Age to have existed in some form from the 7th century to the 16th or early 17th century, when the Ottoman Empire reached the pinnacle of its political and military power. One thing that seems to be consistent in most sources is that the Islamic empire was rarely united and totally peaceful internally (due partly but not exclusively to the Sunni-Shiite split) during the best years of the earlier caliphs or during the Ottoman reign.

One example used in Lewis' *What Went Wrong* is not only instructive but may well have been providential in saving Christendom. The new Safavi dynasty in the old Persian Empire, the Ottoman Empire's neighbor to the East, had brought what now is known as Iran together with Shi'ism as the official religion. With such a hostile and powerful Muslim neighbor, the Ottoman sultan was unable to engage in an all-out assault on the Holy Roman Empire. Lewis quotes the imperial ambassador in Istanbul as saying "that it was only the threat from Persia that saved Europe from imminent conquest by the Turks."[42]

The understanding of Golden Age of Islam and the rise and fall of the Ottoman Empire is not easy to sort out for those who are not students of Islamic history. In my opinion, the best somewhat detailed single source is *The Middle East* by Bernard Lewis. It is relatively easy reading and is filled with interesting anecdotes and comparisons. The defeat of the last Ottoman sultanate in 1918 forms the backdrop to the Introduction of Lewis' *The Crisis of Islam* and will be discussed later in the context of al-Qaeda and Osama bin Laden.

Two important elements in understanding the rise and 1,400-year history of Islam are the treatment of the *dhimmis* and the extensive use of slaves.

The fact that Mohammad believed himself to be the final prophet in the line of the Old Testament prophets and Jesus in the New Testament necessitated a different way of dealing with the "people of the Book." The Koran clearly teaches that the Jews and the Christians received valid revelation in the Abrahamic tradition. It further teaches that they distorted this revelation and failed to recognize the finality of the prophethood of Mohammad. They were however monotheists and were to be treated differently under Islamic rule than the pagan polytheists.

Outright pagans, such as the polytheistic members of the Arabian tribes, had a simple choice to either submit to Islam or face the sword (Koran 9:5). In fact, many of them, as well as the subsequently conquered polytheists and atheists of other countries, became slaves of the Muslims as a third choice. After Mohammad conquered Mecca and "cleansed" the Kaaba, he issued one last call for conversion to the pagan tribes in Arabia who had refused to accept Islam. Those who continued to resist conversion, in an apparent gesture of good will and according to Allah's revelations, were given a four-month grace period in which they could leave Arabia as an option to death or slavery (Koran 9:1-3).

The Jews and Christians as people of the Book became known as the *dhimma*, an Arabic word meaning both "protected" and "guilty." Those who refused to convert could live in Muslim-ruled lands in a subservient condition and pay a special tax. The status of Jews and Christians is spelled out in Koran 9:29: "Fight those who do not believe in Allah ... nor follow the religion of truth, out of those who have been given the Book, until they pay the tax in acknowledgement of superiority and they are in a state of subjection."

It is very important to understand the status of the *dhimmis* living in Muslims lands since it has existed in one form or other from the time the first Byzantine Christian country was captured until this very day. By Islamic definition, those who submitted to Allah were superior to nonbelievers, who could never be treated as absolute equals in a Muslim state. They were "guilty" because they had refused to accept Allah's final revelation, but they could be a "protected" minority in a Muslim land if they accepted subservient conditions. They could even practice their religions under certain restricted conditions.

The *dhimmi* must accept social, legal, political, and religious inferiority and pay the *jizya*, or special tax. Conditions varied from place to place in terms of severity and enforcement, but there were some conditions that were virtually universal. Christians could not seek to convert Muslims or make open displays of their faith, such as placing crosses on their churches or ringing church bells. Non-Muslim men could never marry a Muslim woman because she would be in a position of being under the authority of a man who was an unbeliever. Muslim men could always marry chaste non-Muslim women. Many Christians converted, especially in the early years, because of the difficulties of living under such oppressive conditions as non Muslims. There were also numerous forced conversions, especially in North Africa and Spain.

In *The Middle East*, Lewis discusses the roles of the *dhimmi*, whom he calls "tolerated unbelievers," as compared with slaves and women. He points out that treatment varied from time to time and from ruler to ruler and makes this point:

> "Dhimmis remained, however, inferior, and were not allowed
> to forget their inferiority. They could not testify before Muslim courts,
> and like slaves and women, they counted for less than Muslims in
> matters of compensation for injury. They were not free to marry
> Muslim women under pain of death, though Muslim men were free to
> marry Christian or Jewish women."[43]

(Robert Spencer devotes a chapter of *The Politically Incorrect Guide to Islam* to a discussion of the *dhimma*.[44] Additional references to the restrictions of the *dhimmi* will be made during the discussion of *sharia* [Islamic law].)

Slavery also had a role in the founding and development of Islam. Sadly, human slavery is almost as old as history itself and was widely practiced by most of the great empires of antiquity. The Babylonian, Egyptian, Greek, and Roman empires especially come to mind. It is probably not widely known that the Muslim empires took this practice to new heights.

My guess is that few Americans have any knowledge of the Muslim trans-Sahara slave trade between roughly the 9th and 14th centuries that some estimate resulted in the movement of close to 10 million African slaves to the regions around the Mediterranean, Red Sea, and the Indian Ocean. Even fewer know that North African Muslims, primarily around the Barbary Coast, took nearly a million European Christian slaves between 1500 and 1800. These Christian slaves came heavily from Italy but also from France, Spain, Holland, and Great Britain, as well as some from the Americas and even Iceland. The majority of these slaves were forced to work in galley crews, among the most strenuous of human tasks. The only advantage they had over African slaves was that if they survived for a few years, there was a chance they might eventually be allowed to go back home.

I must admit that I had no idea such slavery ever existed until my research on slavery led me to a book by Dr. Robert C. Davis, professor of Italian social history at Ohio State University. Davis' book, *Christian Slaves, Muslim Masters: White Slavery in the Mediterranean, the Barbary Coast, and Italy, 1500-1800*, is extensively documented but not an unusually difficult read for those interested in this subject. One especially interesting point is made by Davis in the Introduction. He speculates that whereas the Muslims obviously hoped to make a profit, they have been even more motivated by an element of revenge "for the wrongs of 1492 [when the Christians reclaimed Spain], for the centuries of crusading violence that had proceeded them, and for the ongoing religious struggle between Christian and Muslim that has continued to roil the Mediterranean world well into modern times." He continues that with vengeance as their motive, they were more successful than their Christian counterparts. "By all indications, as this study attempts to show, Mediterranean slaving out-produced the trans-Atlantic trade during the sixteenth and into the seventeenth centuries, and this only in terms of the Barbary Coast."[45]

The Muslim use of slaves, especially military slaves, in their initial period served them well in their founding days—most of the time. During the raids and conquest led by Mohammad in Arabia, he and his followers took many slaves. A large number of these slaves would swell the ranks of the invading Muslim armies under Caliph Umar I and his successors during their initial conquests. Since *offensive* holy war to spread Islam was a communal responsibility of the *umma* (community of believers), the use of slaves and even mercenaries was very common for such purposes.

The practice of training young captive boys from childhood as military slaves became so prevalent that they were given a special name: *mamluk*. This designation, which simply meant "owned," would afford them a higher rank than the ordinary economic and domestic slaves. This system became very extensive by the ninth century, when the Muslims started capturing Turks. The Turkish slaves were especially suited for military purposes and provided the Muslims with a mighty army. They may have been too adept at the work, since on some occasions Turkish military slaves took over as commanders of certain military forces and even ruled some countries. Lewis further explains:

> "As the military caste became predominantly Turkish, and as the regimes of Islam became predominately military, the Turks established a domination that lasted for a thousand years. As early as 868, the first independent dynasty in Muslim Egypt was founded by a Turkish military slave, and most subsequent regimes in Egypt were of similar origin."[46]

Jihad Then and Now: Islam's Holy War

Every one who studies Islam knows there are five clearly stated pillars of faith in the Koran. Many scholars on Islamic teaching recognize *jihad* as the virtual sixth pillar. Islamic apologists like to point out that *jihad* meant "spiritual striving" before it meant "holy war." The preeminent Islamic scholar, who is always careful to be historically precise in order not to give needless offense, Dr. Bernard Lewis, describes *jihad*:

> "The term 'jihad', conventionally translated 'holy war', has the literal meaning of striving, more specifically, in the Qur'anic phrase 'striving in the path of God'. ...The overwhelming majority of early authorities, however, citing relevant passages in the Qur'an and in tradition, discuss jihad in military terms."[47]

It is interesting to note the somewhat detailed discussion of *jihad* in the book by Abdel Bari Atwan, *The Secret History of Al Qaeda*. Atwan, a Muslim who was born in Palestine, is editor-in-chief of an Arabic publication in London, where he has lived for the last 30 or so years. He is the only Western-based journalist ever to have spent time with Osama bin Laden in his hideout in Tora Bora. Atwan's book is especially instructive in understanding the "holy war" that Osama and his al-Qaeda allies declared on America. Some conservative scholars contend that on a few occasions, Atwan's Muslim bias in interpreting historical events and Islamic teachings is evident. Even so, he can also be quite frank:

> "It is a completely alien cultural concept for many in the West that a religion might not only sanction killing but enjoin its followers to kill as a religious duty. In certain circumstances Islam does just this. ... According to the Qur'an, Allah gave the Muslims permission for

jihad in the second year of hijraxl[48] to defend themselves and deter their enemies from attacking them. The Qur'an clearly states: 'Fight in the cause of Allah those who fight you and do not transgress, for Allah loves not the aggressors' (2:109)."[49]

He continues by making the distinction between offensive and defensive *jihad*.

Offensive *jihad* is the responsibility of the *umma* (the Muslim community) and can only be called by the *caliph* as the head of the *umma*. I assume he intends to imply that the caliph as Mohammad's successor had the same authority as Islam's prophet in calling a *jihad* to convert the unbelievers. Since offensive holy war is a communal obligation, there are different ways in which individual Muslims can support the effort, such as providing financial or moral support in recruiting warriors and taking care of their families.

Defensive *jihad* on the other hand is an absolute obligation on every able-bodied Muslim man and can include attacks on those who not only occupy Muslim lands but even station troops in such lands. These distinctions become very important in understanding the nature of the enemy we face in today's radical Islamic terrorists.[50]

Hopefully it will become clear as we quote a few of the best non-Muslim Islamic scholars that the fundamentalist Muslims, from the days of Mohammad until the present time, take very seriously their perceived responsibilities to wage both offensive and defensive *jihad* until the world is conquered for Allah. It is difficult to understand how any Muslim apologist, based on a study of the Koran and the earliest universally accepted Islamic traditions, could seriously argue that Allah commanded them to wage offensive holy war in order to protect themselves. The tensions and hostilities between Mohammad and his own Arabic tribe developed over the rejection of the prophetic claims he made in Mecca. The tribes in Arabia had no interest in conquering Mohammad and his followers; they simply were refusing to submit to his new religion. Certainly the Byzantine and Persian empires had no hostile designs to invade a few oases in the Arabian Desert.

The fact was that when those in Medina continued to reject the Prophet Mohammad's calls to conversion, offensive holy war was ordered to spread Islam. "The Muslim jihad ... was perceived as unlimited, as a religious obligation that would continue until all the world had either adopted the Muslim faith or submitted to Muslim rule," Lewis writes in *The Middle East*.[51]

In *The Politically Incorrect Guide to Islam*, Spencer states:

> "There are over a hundred verses in the Qur'an that exhort believers to wage jihad against unbelievers. 'O Prophet! Strive hard against the unbelievers and the hypocrites, and be firm against them. Their abode is Hell and evil refuge indeed' (Qur'an 9:73). 'Strive hard' in Arabic is jihadi, a verbal form of the noun jihad. This striving was

to be on the battlefield: 'When you meet the unbelievers in the battlefield, strike off their heads and, when you have laid them low, bind you captives firmly' (Qur'an 47:4)."[52]

Spencer describes how *jihad* is the "highest duty of Muslims" and how they believe they are doing the right thing for unbelievers since if such unbelievers fail to submit to Allah they will end up in hell. After analyzing the pertinent verses in the Koran commanding *jihad*, Spencer examines the uses of *jihad* by Mohammad and his followers from the early caliphs until today's terrorists."[53] These chapters are very informative for a more in-depth understanding of the subject. Trifkovic includes a nine-page chapter in *Defeating Jihad* that sheds additional light on this very important subject.[54]

Some of the more flagrant examples of Allah's commands in the Koran to wage *jihad* include these verses:

> "Fight those who do not believe in Allah, nor in the latter day, nor do they prohibit what Allah and His Apostle have prohibited, nor follow the religion of truth, ... out of those who have been given the book [i.e., Jews and Christians], until they pay the tax in acknowledgement of superiority and they are in a state of subjection." (Koran 9:29).

Perhaps the best known verse in the Koran urging Muslims to wage *jihad* against unbelievers is frequently referred to as the "Verse of the Sword." Allah commands his followers to slay those who refuse to submit in these words:

> "So when the sacred months have passed away, then slay the idolaters wherever you find them, and take them captives and besiege them and lie in wait for them in every ambush, then if they repent and keep up prayer and pay the poor-rate, leave their way free to them, surely Allah is Forgiving, Merciful...."(Koran 9:5).

Allah assures them that they will make the unbelievers fear them:

> "When your Lord revealed to the angels, I am with you, therefore make firm those who believe. I will strike terror into the hearts of those who disbelieve. Therefore strike off their heads and strike off every fingertip of them" (Koran 8:12).

Allah concedes that they may not want to fight, but it is necessary to subdue the unbelievers:

> "Fighting is enjoined on you, and it is an object of dislike to you; and it may be that you dislike a thing while it is food for you, and it may be that you love a thing while it is evil for you, and Allah knows, while you do not know" (Koran 2:216).

Muslims must smite the unbelievers in battle, but the Muslims who die in battle will be rewarded:

> "So when you meet in battle those who disbelieve, then smite the necks until when you have overcome them, then make (them) prisoners, and afterwards either set them free as a favor or let them ransom (themselves) until the war terminates. That (shall be so); and if Allah is pleased He would certainly have exacted what is due from them, but that He may try some of you by means of others; and (as for) those who are slain in the way of Allah, He will by no means allow their deeds to perish" (Koran 47:4).

Dr. Walid Phares and Dr. Fawaz Gerges, both born and raised as Christians in Lebanon, offer valuable and unique insights into modern-day Islamic jihadism from entirely different points of view.[55] Dr. Phares' *Future Jihad: Terrorist Strategies against the West* and Dr. Gerges' *Journey of the Jihadist: Inside Muslim Militancy* are very interesting reads. Since both men personally knew Muslims who had become involved in the Islamic jihadist movement, they bring more to the table than their impeccable academic credentials. Their own life experiences may have caused each of them to come away with a different perspective, but they offer valuable information about today's Islamist terrorists.

Phares succinctly, and in a most interesting and instructive way, describes "The Jihad Divide" that developed after the abolition of the caliphate and that brought into question how *jihad* could be called and waged in order to establish *sharia* law, as fundamentalist Muslims believed Allah had commanded them. He explains that the Muslim world was split between "Top-Down Jihad," advocated by the Wahhabi Saudis, and the "Bottom-Up Jihad" espoused by the Muslim Brotherhood. *The Wahhabi Saudis refined Top-Down Jihad*:

> "In the long run, the Wahhabi Saudis, endowed by nature with some of the world's greatest oil resources (known since the 1950s), opted from a top down approach. Their regime would organize the various stages that would make jihad viable over half a century....
>
> "The Wahhabi state logic was perhaps the most perfect one: Float with the world, release the teachings without violence, let the teachings plant the seeds, wait for their growth, irrigate them with money, and make sure to mollify any abrupt reaction from the other side. The rich oil state maximized its advantages to the highest: oil and religious proselytizing.
>
> "This smooth strategy of 'selling' the doctrine within the Muslim world, school after school and country after country, needed internal backing from within the kingdom. A historic deal was cut between the emirs on the one hand and the radical clerics on the other.

The monarchy would manage the finances and political power, including diplomacy, while the scholars would be in charge of the souls, especially the young ones. The other component of the equation, the Salafi clerics, roamed the world preaching Wahhabism with state funding and encouragement. The Saudi model of jihadism was endorsed by the rulers and funded by oil. The spread of Islamic fundamentalism was backed by the economic superpower of the Wahhabi Saudis. In this environment, many future jihadists would choose the path of war against the infidels. The Saudi state generated an immense pool of Islamic fundamentalists inside the kingdom and worldwide, but ultimately it was not able to keep all these 'students' under check of the 'teacher.' One of those students, a model to others, was Osama bin Laden." [56]

The other approach, *"Bottom-up Jihad," was perfected by the Brotherhood*. In general terms, these two schools of *jihad* have molded and encompass the Islamic terrorist threats confronting the world today. Phares details the Muslim Brotherhood's brand of Islamist terrorism in these words:

"With almost the same ideology, the Muslim Brotherhood of Egypt chose a different approach to spread its ideas and political influence: from the bottom up. Not trusting the rulers but willing to work with them the Ikhwan strategy is as patient as the Wahhabi but articulated differently. The Brotherhood of Hassan al Banna, one of the scions of modern-day jihadists, aimed to spread at the grassroots level outside the control of the government. When weak, the network lies low and expands slowly. When strong, or when events favor it, the group accelerates its activities and pursues its goals mercilessly. The 'brothers' are keen to inculcate deep ideological teachings before engaging in the political struggle—but when they do, they are ruthless. They are neither intimidated by oppression nor swayed by causes greater than theirs. They wait for the moment in history, unimpressed by what the dominant political culture wants or calls for.

"During World War II, the Brotherhood hoped the Nazis would win. After Israel was established, the Brotherhood, unlike most Arab regimes, preferred to gain support within the Arab world rather than to support what it perceived as a coalition of failing Arab regimes. To the Brotherhood, the war against the Jews and Israel cannot be won with un-Islamic (or not sufficiently Islamic) governments. During the cold war, their priority—like the Wahhabis'—was to fight and defeat communism first before facing off with the capitalists. The Ikhwan (MB) opened chapters in most Arab and Middle Eastern countries as well as within émigré communities in the West. Competing with the

Wahhabis, they would become the backbone of most Islamist and jihadist organizations of the future. Behind the dominant and most extremist organizations of the 1980s and the 1990s lies the shadow, if not the umbilical link, of the Brotherhood. This rock-solid network generated waves of militants, one decade after another. Over generations they came to penetrate and influence the complex educational system in the region, as well as its religious and media apparatuses. Above all, they would eventually provide masterminds of terrorism to jihadist movements, including al-Qaeda's number two man, Ayman Thawahiri (Zawahiri).

"The Wahhabis and the Brotherhood are the pillars of Sunni Salafism. They intertwined, merging at times but competing fiercely at other times. They both produced offshoots, including leading jihad groups from Algeria to the Philippines. But the shattering of the caliphate not only released subcurrents among the Sunni radicals: it also allowed non-Sunni Muslims (i.e. The Shiites in Iran, Lebanon and other places) to emerge for the first time in history as a jihadi power."[57]

Islamic Sharia Law

In a manner similar to *jihad*, some occasionally identify *sharia* law as the seventh pillar of Islam. Since *sharia* falls into the category of practical theology—how Muslims are expected to live their lives—it is not defined as thoroughly and precisely in the Koran as the five pillars of faith (new situations would arise after the Koran was written).

It is sometimes difficult for Christians to understand *sharia*, or Islam's holy law, because the Bible uses the word "law" in different ways. Christians believe in "natural law," which God wrote in the hearts of Adam and Eve. As a result of the fall, this natural law became blurred. Therefore, God revealed His divine Law in both the Old and New Testaments, most dramatically in the Ten Commandments. Christians are expected to live in accordance with God's moral law. Because of original sin, we cannot keep God's law perfectly, but Christ has fulfilled the law for us. In addition, Christians are to live in society under civil law as good citizens. We are expected to "render unto Caesar the things that are Caesar's" and draw the line only in cases where government might require us to do something that is contrary to God's law. In such a case, we would be required to insist that we "ought to obey God rather than man." Fortunately for those of us who live in the United States, we are rarely, if ever, faced with such a dilemma.

In the case of Muslims, the Koran and Islamic tradition teach that there is only one law revealed by Allah. There is no distinction between religion and state according to Islamic teachings. *Sharia* seeks to regulate virtually every area of life, from dietary habits to dress codes. Consumption of alcoholic beverages can result in floggings and imprisonment. Women not properly covered or traveling unescorted by a male family member can be beaten by Islamic police or imprisoned in some Islamic countries. The Koran makes it clear that men are superior to women and husbands have the responsibility to discipline disobedient wives and "beat" them if necessary (Koran 4:34).

Islamic law also sets penalties for theft, adultery, blasphemy, apostasy, and murder. It regulates marriage and divorce. A Muslim man can have as many as four wives. (This restriction apparently did not apply to Mohammad, who had at least nine and possibly as many as 15 wives, depending on which Islamic scholars you read. Other exceptions were also made throughout Islam's history.) Muslim men can marry non-Muslim women, but the reverse is forbidden. It takes two Muslim women to equal one Muslim man in a legal setting. Non-Muslims (*dhimmis*) living in Muslim lands have no legal or political rights.

Stoning for adultery is clearly taught in the Koran and is still allowed in some Muslim countries—though the burden of proof is high. Mohammad's favorite wife Aisha, whom he married when she was six or seven years old, was accused of being unfaithful. This obviously distressed Mohammad. Allah, according to Mohammad, gave a revelation saying if the accusers could not provide four witnesses, then they were liars (Koran 24:13). So to this day, Islamic law requires four male witnesses before a man or woman can be stoned to death for adultery.

For the first 200 years or so after Mohammad's death, there was debate, discussion, and disagreement among Muslim legal scholars over some—not all— laws that regulate virtually every area of a devout Muslim's life. The debate was mostly about matters not specifically covered in the Koran or the traditions of Mohammad or having to do with the penalties for disobedience. A number of schools of Islamic jurisprudence arose in Islamic lands, but by the end of the ninth century, four had gained prominence and authority among Sunni Muslims and exist until the present. The are the Hanafi, the Shafi'i, the Maliki, and the Hanbali schools.

Lewis indicates that by the year 900, most felt in all schools that the "consensus of the believers" had been reached and that all basic laws had been decided, at least among the Sunnis. This does not mean that some differences did not exist, but they were mostly of the ritualistic variety. The Shiites have their own separate school of law known as the Ja'fari, which is often more severe and can still evolve. This is a complicated subject and I name three brief resources for those who have an interest in more detail. Chapter 12, "Religion and Law," in Lewis' *The Middle East* provides a 24-page scholarly but easy to read analysis.[58] In *The Sword of the Prophet,* Trifkovic includes a chapter ("The Fruits") that describes *sharia* especially as it relates to apostasy, women, slavery, and other matters.[59] Spencer covers the subject of Islamic law in *The Politically Incorrect Guide to Islam (and the Crusades)* in two chapters ("Islam: Religion of War" and "Islam: Religion of Intolerance").[60]

According to strict Islamic teachings, the ruler of a Muslim land is not to interpret Islamic holy law but merely to enforce it. In practice, the strict interpretation of *sharia* law and the prescribed punishments have varied from time to time and country to country. There have been some more benevolent Muslim rulers who governed in a more secular manner, which resulted in "better" treatment of Christians and Jews, for example. But it is extremely rare to find a place or time when non-Muslims received anywhere close to the same treatment as Muslims. When this did happen, the ruling authorities had to contend with various types of uprisings and threats from fundamentalist Muslims living in their lands.

Some contend that the Ottoman Turks came very close to granting equal rights for non-Muslims during the waning days of the 19th century and the early days of the 20th century. Most contend that this happened because they needed the help of the British to defend themselves from the Egyptians and Russians. Probably two of the best examples in modern times are Iran under the Shah and to some degree Egypt.[61]

Among the most inflammatory charges the Ayatollah Khomeini used to stir up opposition against the Shah was that he was not governing under *sharia* law. He was allowing complete freedom of religion for Christians and Jews—including the right for Muslims to convert. Equally as humiliating, the Shah was granting such non-Muslims equal political and legal rights. These were among the primary charges that led to the overthrow of the Shah's regime.

Anwar al Sadat, who was President of Egypt from 1970 until his assassination in 1981, tried to govern as a secular ruler. In 1977, the Egyptian State Assembly, described as Egypt's highest judicial authority, passed a law requiring death for apostasy after the offender was given 30 days to repent. Sadat never enforced this law. However, in 1986, five years after Sadat's assassination, eight young Egyptians were arrested on charges of converting to Christianity. These "apostates" were never sentenced to death, but they did remain in jail for eight months until public outcries from around the world caused them to be released. Even more interesting is an article from *al-Tahrir* ("Liberation"), a weekly Islamic magazine published in New York, apparently justifying the assassination of Sadat. A 1983 quote from this Muslim youth magazine defines their understanding of apostasy and is quite revealing:

> "The apostate is not only the person who relinquishes Islam and embraces another religion, but the symptoms of apostasy are many, and those who practice them deserve to be killed. The symptoms of apostasy are: when the ruler does not govern by God's law (most Muslim rulers do that), or when the ruler derides some aspect of the religion or one of the Islamic laws as the ex-president of Egypt, al-Sadat, did when he said that the dress of the Muslim women is like a tent."[62]

One recent event involving three liberal and well educated Muslims highlights the confusion about the application of Islamic law today. Former Senator Rick Santorum relates an event that happened after he made a speech addressing religious freedom and Islamic intolerance before a group of students at Harvard University. After the speech, three students at Harvard who were Muslims (two females and one male) came down to talk to him. They told him that he had totally misunderstood Islam and that it was a religion of peace and tolerance. Here is Santorum's account of the rest of the conversation:

> "So I asked them a question: Should apostates—Muslims who convert to another religion—be subject to execution?
>
> "One of the women quickly said no. She insisted that she was free to leave Islam if she wanted to, and that she knew other people who had done so without a problem - in the United States.
>
> "I said I wasn't talking about her and others' freedom of religion in this country. What if they lived in a Muslim-majority country?
>
> "Silence. Eventually, the young man blurted out, 'That's different.'
>
> Why? I asked. I recall him saying, 'Because in Muslim countries, Islam and the government are one, and converting from Islam is the equivalent of treason against the government, punishable by death.' The two women agreed.[63]

There are still many Muslim countries in the world where Islamic law requires death for apostasy. How frequently they are enforced is another question, but harassment and persecution is almost universal.

It strikes me as amazing how countries can become politically correct, just like the elites in these countries. Saudi Arabia not only enforces the death penalty for apostasy, but it also does not allow Bibles in the country. Christians or people of other religions stationed in Saudi Arabia or working in the country cannot practice their religion or even speak about it. There are certain areas around Mecca and Medina in which non-Muslims are totally forbidden. The Saudis justify this based on the fact that Mohammad was born, raised, lived, and died in Arabia and that the Kaaba is the holiest place on earth for Muslims. Their final justification is that the Prophet Mohammad said, "Let there not be two religions in Arabia."

Those of us who believe in religious freedom certainly believe that Muslims should be totally free to practice their religion as they see fit as long as they do not infringe on the rights of others. Jews claim that Palestine is the "Promised Land" given to them by Yahweh and so have a divine right to occupy it forever. Christians can claim valid rights to the "Promise Land" because we believe in the promised Jewish Messiah, who was born in Bethlehem and was crucified and rose from the dead in Jerusalem. Therefore, these are the holiest places on earth for us. Does this mean that we have the right to claim these places for our own use only and forbid all others to practice their religion in the Christian Holy Land?

It is an undisputable fact that the Holy Land was under Byzantine Christian rule when it was invaded and conquered by Arab Muslims during their unprovoked and bloody military campaigns in the seventh century. Since powerful Christian countries in modern times all believe in the separation of church and state, there have been no military campaigns to reconquer the Holy Land since the Crusaders failed to do so. This could have been easily accomplished by the British, Germans, or even the French in the latter part of the 19th century. I am sure we would all agree that it would not have been the right thing to do. This entire discussion underlines the fact that Islam makes no distinction between religion and state. For a strict Muslim, he is defined by his faith rather than his race or nationality. The problems this creates in dealing with the radical Islamic terrorist threat in today's world should be obvious

Dr. Fawaz Gerges, who is always politically correct and sometimes accused of being an Islamic apologist, offers a frank assessment of the difficulty of bringing the Islamic fundamentalists into the modern world:

> "Islamists and jihadists are not born-again democrats and will never be. They are deeply patriarchal, seeing themselves as the guardians of faith, tradition, and authenticity. Their rhetoric remains soggy with anti-Western diatribe. Even mainstream Islamists oppose women's rights and empowerment, or freedom of expression for critics and artists. In Kuwait and Saudi Arabia, Islamists have vehemently opposed efforts to give women the right to vote or drive cars. In Egypt, Morocco, Jordan, Tunisia, Algeria, Pakistan, and other Muslim countries, they denounce any legislation that would enable women to divorce abusive husbands, travel without male permission, or achieve full representation in parliaments and state bureaucracies."[64]

Gerges could have added death for apostasy and blasphemy to his list. But even a non-Muslim scholar of Arabic origin who tries to put the best face on Islam offers this evaluation that he is not willing to sweep under the rug.

The Push for America and Europe to Become "Sharia Compliant"

Imam Rauf, best known for his efforts to build the "Ground Zero" mosque and Islamic Center just blocks from the site of the Islamist terrorist attacks on the World Trade Center, somehow became recognized as a moderate Islamic authority by both the Bush and Obama administrations. It may be true that Rauf is sincere in his desire for peace and tolerance among Muslims and Jews and Christians in America. But Imam Rauf told Ed Bradley on *60 Minutes*, two weeks after the 9/11 attacks, that Osama bin-Laden was "made in the USA" and that U.S. foreign policy was an "accessory to the crime" of 9/11. He also said that America should be "Sharia compliant." This seems to have become a crusade for him.

Rauf wrote in *The Washington Post*, "Policymakers must recognize that, more often than not, the terrorists the world should fear are motivated by political and socioeconomic—not religious—concerns."[65] (This may well be a fond hope in Rauf's mind, but it flies in the face of the facts of what virtually all Islamist terrorists clearly state in their own words.)

Rauf identifies five so-called myths about Muslims. The fifth is that "American Muslims want to bring sharia law to the United States." Rauf writes:

> "In Islam, sharia is the divine ideal of justice and compassion, similar to the concept of natural law in the Western tradition. Though radicals exist on the fringes of Islam, as in every religion, most Muslim jurists agree on the principal objectives of sharia: the protection and promotion of life, religion, intellect, property, family and dignity. None of this includes turning the United States into a caliphate."[66]

Once again, this is a nice, non-threatening list of principles Rauf claims as the essence of *sharia* law. But the four recognized Sunni Muslim schools of Islamic jurisprudence certainly do not emphasize such principles as the essence of *sharia*. They all begin with the absolute superiority of male Muslims and offer severe penalties for apostasy, blasphemy, adultery, homosexuality, and many other crimes.

The one dominant school of Shiite jurisprudence does leave room for revisions of some *sharia* requirements at different times. But this is the school establishing law in Iran today and there is no evidence of modern day compassion in their interpretation of *sharia*. For example, the story of a 32-year-old Iranian Christian pastor, Youcef Nadarkhani, being sentenced to death for refusing to denounce the Christian faith to which he converted from Islam as a teenager, has filled the news media. Our State Department facilitated his release from an Iranian prison after 1,000 days of detention, but he is still under a death sentence and must return to court in September. In the process, the Iranian civil-rights attorney who dared to represent the pastor has been sentenced to nine years in prison for "crimes against the state."

The situation in Europe, where Muslims have not assimilated to the culture to the same degree as their coreligionists in the U.S., is spinning out of control. In February 2008, Archbishop of Canterbury Rowan Williams shocked the Western world by proposing in a BBC radio interview that Sharia law be formally introduced in Great Britain. Author Bruce Bawer, perhaps best known for *While Europe Slept*, writes in *Surrender: Appeasing Islam, Sacrificing Freedom* about Imam Rauf's reaction to Williams' proposal:

> "[T]he Washington Post's response to Williams' speech was to run a piece on its Web site by Feisal Abdul Rauf headlined 'Archbishop of Canterbury Was Right.' 'It is time for Britain to integrate aspects of Islamic law,' wrote Rauf, author of a book entitled What's Right with

Islam: A New Vision for Muslims and the West. Among his arguments was that 'the integration of Sharia law would provide some modicum of equilibrium among Jewish law, Christian law and Islamic law,' thus providing 'an aggregated legal framework that represents all three Abrahamic traditions, Jewish, Christian and Muslim. By doing so, Britain would ensure that Muslims stay engaged, not isolated or estranged, and assume active ownership in civic participatory duties and responsibilities.' In other words, Muslims in the West don't want to live under secular democratic law, so give them sharia—whose integration into Western jurisprudence would only be fair anyway, since it would balance out the Judeo-Christian influence. . . . Rauf swept the horrors of sharia totally under the rug—and did so with the imprimatur of one of the nation's most respected newspapers." [67]

The Wahhabi Sect

The rise of Wahhabism and its marriage to the House of Saud in about the middle of the 18th century would in many ways define the world in which we live today. The importance of this subject is so essential in understanding today's Islamist terrorist threat that Dr. Bernard Lewis devotes an entire chapter of *The Crisis of Islam* to the subject.[68]

As Lewis explains, Muhammad ibn 'Abd al-Wahhab was a theologian who lived in a remote area of Arabia called the Najd from his birth in 1703 until his death in 1792. As he grew up and became an Islamic theologian, his knowledge of what was happening in the outside world was gleaned primarily from those making the annual pilgrimage to Mecca. He learned that the Islamic armies were suffering a series of defeats, causing the Ottoman Empire to lose much of its territories. Al-Wahhab became convinced that the infidels were defeating the Muslims not because of their superior modern warfare, but because the Muslims had forgotten their heritage and forsaken the pure form of Islam. These Muslim rulers must return to a pure teaching of Islamic holy war (*jihad*) and a strict enforcement of Islam's holy law (*sharia*) if they were to regain their former prominence.

Lewis states that one of al-Wahhab's early converts to this "puritanical version of Islam" was Muhammad ibn Saud, who ruled the province of Najd where Wahhab lived and taught. Lewis describes the relationship in an unusual way when he writes that "the House of Sa'ud" was "inspired by a religious revivalist movement, the Wahhabis."[69]

Abdel Bari Atwan in *The Secret History of Al-Qaeda* emphasizes the role that *jihad* played in this alliance from its inception. Ibn Saud and al-Wahhab agreed to declare holy war against "deviant Muslims" as well as non-Muslims. "In 1745 the two men swore an oath that together they would conquer the peninsula (then part of the Ottoman Empire) and establish a Wahhabi-based kingdom there."[70] Atwan stresses the total interdependence of this powerful Islamic state and this radical sect of Sunni theology when he writes, "The Saudi regime as well as Saudi society is underpinned and legitimized by Wahhabi doctrine," and "This complex interdependence of the Al Saud and Wahhabism has its roots in the very foundation of Saudi Arabia as a nation-state."[71]

The Saudi forces with their new religious zeal set out to conquer and purify Muslim leaders who had gone astray. They even conquered and occupied the holy cities of Mecca and Medina, which they intended to "cleanse." The Ottoman Empire was able to subdue the Saudis in 1818 and occupy their capital, but the Wahhabi doctrine survived.[72]

The alliance between the House of Saud and the Wahhabis would reappear in the early years of the 20th century and result in total control of Saudi Arabia by the mid to late 1920s. Lewis explained in his Washington, D.C., lecture that the Saudi monarchy was formed in the area of the Najd where the tribal chiefs were of the House of Saud. They were virtually all converts to Wahhabis. Their military strength grew to the point that they were able to defeat the Hashemite dynasty that controlled most of the rest of Arabia, including Mecca and Medina, in 1920. These events would change the history of the Islamic world and have major consequences for our world today. The Saudi monarchy would rapidly become one of the major forces among Islamic countries, and Wahhabism was on its way to becoming the most powerful theology in Sunni Islam. (Sunnis make up about 85 percent of the world's 1.3 billion Muslims.)

Lewis explained in his lecture how the influence of the House of Saud and the Wahhabi teachings spread so rapidly and continue to exert such a pervasive influence on the entire Muslim world as well as on radical Islamist terrorism. The creation of a Saudi kingdom in charge of Mecca and Medina would become increasingly significant: "As the custodian of the Holy cities," the Saudi ruler "now had tremendous prestige" and "enormous standing in the Islamic world as a whole. As the controller of the pilgrimage, he had enormous influence over the millions of Muslims who came every year from all over the Muslim world to the cities which he ruled." Then something unexpected happened that would immensely magnify his prestige and influence. The discovery of oil placed tremendous wealth beyond anyone's wildest dreams at his disposal. Lewis continued,

> "This made Saudi Arabia a world power, first within Islam, and then within the larger world. And gave a global importance to a version of Islam which would otherwise have been an extremist fringe on the edge of a marginal country. It is no longer that now. And the Wahhabi element is of great and growing importance."[73]

In his lecture and in *The Crisis of Islam*, Lewis discusses a few examples of how the Wahhabis with almost unlimited Saudi oil money now virtually dominate Islamic education all over the world, especially through the *madrassas* they finance and run. In the first place, the Wahhabis have unfettered access to millions of

Muslim pilgrims in their country every year. Wahhabism's influence "as the official, state-enforced doctrine" of Saudi Arabia and the "custodian of the two holiest places of Islam, the host of the annual pilgrimage, which brings millions of Muslims from every part of the world to share in its rites and rituals," is clearly unrivaled in the Muslim world.[74] The opportunities this affords the Wahhabi religious leaders to spread their fundamentalist philosophy of Islamic holy war (*jihad*) and the obligations of Muslims not only to live by, but insist on the enforcement of strict *sharia* law are not only vast but frightening. Their teachings of hatred for the Great Satan (America), Israel, and all of America's western allies underscore the likelihood of continuing threats from radical Islamic terrorists.

In addition to opportunities to indoctrinate pilgrims on their annual visits to Mecca, the teachers and preachers of Wahhabism have "at their disposal immense financial resources, which they use to promote and spread their version of Islam," Lewis writes. After explaining the traditional meaning of the word "*madrasa*" as an institution of higher education and scholarship, he addresses its meaning today. "In modern usage the word madrasa has acquired a negative meaning; it has come to denote a center for indoctrination in bigotry and violence."[75] He discusses the tens of thousands of madrassas run by the Wahhabis in Muslim lands such as Pakistan and Saudi Arabia and even a growing number in America and Europe. There is even a Wahhabi-run madrasa in Fairfax County, Virginia. Lewis points that out that in Western countries where the public schools are good, they take a different approach:

> "[W]here public educational systems are good, Wahhabi indoctrination centers may be the only form of Islamic education available to new converts and to Muslim parents who wish to give their children some grounding in their own inherited religious and cultural tradition. This indoctrination is provided in private schools, religious seminars, mosque schools, holiday camps and, increasingly, prisons."[76]

On the other hand, in some Muslim countries, "the Wahhabi-sponsored schools and colleges represent for many young Muslims the only education available."[77]

Atwan addresses the same efforts by the Saudi government after the discovery of oil. He writes that they "started a program of exporting Wahhabism throughout the Muslim world and even to Muslim populations in the West. ... Wahhabi-sponsored schools, colleges and university posts proliferated. It is worth remembering that in many Muslim countries there is little state-funded education, and these Saudi-funded schools, or madrassas, provide the only education available." He concludes this point with an interesting observation: "However, with the curriculum dominated by the Wahhabi interpretation of Islam, some of these madrassas—particularly in Pakistan and Saudi Arabia—have produced exactly the type of jihadis who now, ironically, represent the most serious threat to its survival the Saudi regime has encountered."[78]

It is exactly this radical Wahhabi theology that molded Osama bin Laden and motivates his activities until this day, as we shall see.[79]

The Founding and Development of Al-Qaeda

Jesus warned of "wars and rumors of wars." Much of history has been defined by war. Many, if not most, wars through the centuries have been characterized by religious motives. But one might have thought that when the Ottoman Empire fell in 1924 and Kemal Ataturk, the founder of modern Turkey, agreed to divide the Muslim countries into 50 different nation states that wars based on religious beliefs and motivations would cease in the "enlightened" 20th century.

Shortly after the beginning of the 20th century, the world was embroiled in World War I, described by President Woodrow Wilson as the "war to end all wars." Only about two decades later, the United States again was called upon to lead efforts on behalf of the free world to end the threat of Nazism, fascism, and communism in World War II, and then the Cold War. But before the 21st century was a year old, we were dramatically and sadly reminded that radical, fundamentalist Islamists will never abandon the "holy war," *jihad*, they believe Allah has commanded them to wage.

Granted it is difficult for anyone living in the modern Western world to comprehend that there are legions of Islamist leaders and tens, if not hundreds, of millions of followers who believe with all their hearts that they are divinely commanded to wage a religious war in the cause of Allah. In a consistent historical fashion, the politically correct elitists[80] are in a typical state of denial about the intentions and severity of the threat posed by the Islamic jihadists. Muslim editor and scholar Abdel Atwan, who was trusted by Osama bin Laden although he did not accept his goals, is very intuitive about Western attitudes. He astutely analyzes the politically correct blind spot when he writes in *The Secret History of Al-Qaeda*: "It is a completely alien cultural concept for many in the West that a religion might not only sanction killing but enjoin its followers to kill as a religious duty."[81]

It is not reasonable to assume that obviously brilliant men have never read the Koran or the earliest Muslim-written biography of Mohammad or that they never studied Islam's long history of bloody conquest. Surely some of them have studied al-Banna's founding of the radical Muslim Brotherhood and have read Sayyid Qutb's works, which further radicalized the Brotherhood. They must have read as well the writings and statements of Ayman al-Zawahiri and Osama bin Laden. In most instances, the failure to accept the totally religious nature of the "holy war" being waged against America by the Islamic jihadists has to be a case of academic arrogance so common and destructive among politicians and theologians. Those of us who have followed both disciplines have always felt alarm when we see opinion leaders in either field become convinced that they know more than anyone else.

There are numerous Islamist terrorist organizations around the world that were either founded by or grew out of the Muslim Brotherhood. But if we are to understand the nature and severity of the terrorist threats we face from radical Islamists, we must understand al-Qaeda and the late Osama bin Laden, the man who founded this violent organization. There are millions of ordinary radical terrorists—including untold numbers of suicide bombers—around the world who have sworn revenge on "The Great Satan" for what they consider to be their hero's assassination.

It is also essential that we understand that bin Laden and other terrorist leaders do not speak for the Islamic religion or the hundreds of millions of peaceful Muslims around the world.[82] Nor do these Islamist terrorist organizations speak officially for any Muslim government, even though they might receive some support and encouragement from a few of the more radical Islamic countries, such as Syria or Iran.

(Since it is a virtual Shiite theocracy, Iran would not support Sunni terrorist organizations such as al Qaeda. Iran does support such Shiite terrorist organizations as Hezbollah in Lebanon and al Sadr's *Mahdi* army in Iraq. The situation in Iran continues to become more dangerous by the day as the Iranian government blatantly strives to produce deliverable nuclear weapons. Almost as threatening is Iran's not-too-veiled desire to "help" establish a Shiite theocracy in neighboring Iraq, which is now virtually defenseless after the withdrawal of the American troops.)

It is equally important to state that no Muslim nation has declared war on America. No official *fatwa* calling for *jihad* against America has been issued by worldwide Islam. There is no longer a caliph or even titular head of Islam since the Turks abolished the caliphate in 1924. Some had speculated that bin Laden himself "had aspirations to the caliphate."[83] In any event, this one man, Osama bin Laden, while the emir or leader of al-Qaeda, called for *jihad* against America and her allies. Thus bin Laden became the first terrorist to declare a religious holy war on America. He insisted that every devout Muslim has a divine obligation to wage holy war against America, whom he called the Great Satan.

Bin Laden's total justification for *jihad* is based on the life and teachings of Mohammad. No one can reasonably question the depth of the religious convictions that motivated the terrorist acts of bin Laden and his followers. To do so was at one's own peril. Osama's own dedication to such a cause was so strong that he gave up a life of luxury as a billionaire to live on the run in caves without modern conveniences. (Some of bin Laden's most loyal supporters might have been slightly disillusioned to learn that he spent the last years of his life in a luxury complex in Pakistan. But the overwhelming number of the masses who idolized bin Laden will never learn such details.)

Before taking a closer look at Osama the man, his beliefs and goals and the terrorist organization he founded to carry out his plans, let us look at what led to the timing of his attacks on America.

In his lecture in Washington, Dr. Bernard Lewis briefly summarized Islam from its founding by the prophet Mohammad until the present time. He discussed the Muslim conquest, expansion, and defeats in terms of their belief that it is the sacred duty of Muslims to promote the faith to the infidels in order to offer them the opportunity of salvation. Lewis mentioned how this history had gone through several phases and interpretations. He then offered us "the presentation of this history, as seen by one of the more remarkable Muslim spokesman of the present time—a man called Osama bin Laden."

Since Lewis has carefully studied the statements made by bin Laden, he is able to explain the nuances of his thinking in a fascinating way. The defeat of the Soviets in Afghanistan and the collapse of the Soviet Union had nothing to do with the Cold War, as far as bin Laden was concerned. Lewis says that bin Laden saw this not as "a western victory in the Cold War; it was a Muslim victory in the Holy War." Bin Laden is very explicit on the subject, according to Lewis: "This war between true believers and the unbelievers had been going on for 14 centuries."[84]

The first two phases of this war occurred when the early caliphs conquered significant lands and built an Islamic empire. This empire suffered major losses, and the Golden Age of Islam began to fade. Then the Ottoman Empire expanded Islamic rule to an even greater extent. Finally, in the 18th and 19th centuries, the Ottoman Empire began to suffer defeats. The ultimate humiliation of Islam occurred when the European powers divided up the Ottoman lands into their colonial empires in the early 1920s.

The powers prohibiting the spread of Islam throughout the world had changed from Christian Europe in the previous generations to the superpowers—the Soviet Union and the United States. Lewis again quotes bin Laden's statements on what he believes to be the final phase of the ongoing holy war:

> "[W]e, the Muslims, have to fight against these two superpowers. In Afghanistan we have defeated and destroyed the more deadly, the most dangerous of the two. Dealing with the soft, pampered, effeminate Americans will be easy. They lack the appetite or the capacity for the kind of war in which we shall now be engaged."[85]

Lewis enumerates some of the terrorist plans and actual attacks carried out by al-Qaeda and other terrorists under Osama bin Laden's control during the 1980s and 1990s, emphasizing the bloody attacks in Mogadishu and Beirut. America's response to these attacks caused bin Laden to boast, "Hit them and they'll run." Then he asserts that this helps us understand what 9/11 was about since it was "bringing the Holy War into the heartland of the enemy to complete the final conquest of the world and its submission to the true faith, doing them the great service of paying their way toward heaven and all its delights."[86]

Lewis concludes that President Bush's strong response was a major surprise to Osama and his associates. They regrouped and tried to assist the Taliban and al-Qaeda in Afghanistan. The invasion of Iraq was also unexpected by bin Laden and his associates. Their reaction would be to infiltrate al-Qaeda operatives into Iraq and help fan the flames of decades of sectarian violence between the Sunnis and Shiites. They would even join with their Shiite enemies to kill Americans. If there is an upside to the Iraq war other than to rid the country of a brutal dictator, it is that the al-Qaeda terrorists were diverted from carrying out additional terrorist attacks on U.S. soil.

There are a number of informative books on al-Qaeda and bin Laden's life and actions that I will list below and use occasionally.[87] I intend to use *The Secret History of Al Qaeda* as my primary source for two reasons. One, the fact that Abdel Bari Atwan spent more time with bin Laden than any other Western-based journalist offers some unique insights. Two, the fact that Atwan is a Muslim assures me that what he writes about al-Qaeda and bin Laden might have a slight bias but does not exaggerate any of the events. As is the case with all terrorists, it is much more important to understand what they believe the Prophet Mohammad taught rather than what moderate Muslims believe he taught.

In 1957, Osama bin Laden was born in Riyadh, Saudi Arabia, of a Syrian mother, Aliyah, who had become the fourth wife of Muhammad Awad bin Laden in 1956. (Aliyah takes on a little intrigue since she was apparently very close to her only son, Osama. Abdel Atwan writes that the Saudi government flew Osama's mother by private jet in 1998 to "Afghanistan in the hope that she might dissuade her son from pursuing jihad and talk him into returning to Saudi Arabia."[88])

Muhammad bin Laden had emigrated from southern Yemen to Riyadh seeking a job as a construction worker. Six months after Osama's birth, the family moved to the Hejaz, the area of Saudi Arabia where Mecca and Medina are located. This would afford Osama ample opportunities to visit the Muslim holy cities when he was growing up. Atwan says that Muhammad bin Laden was known for the hospitality he showed to the pilgrims traveling to Mecca each year. This practice would be continued by two of the older bin Laden brothers after their father's untimely death in 1967.

Among those visiting the bin Laden household each year would be some prominent Islamic theologians from whom Osama would be able to learn. Muhammad bin Laden was a simple construction worker when he first arrived in his adopted country, but through his ability to establish political connections at the highest levels with the royal family and his astute business skills, he started his own construction company and rapidly became prominent and wealthy. When the royal family selected his company to remodel the mosques in Mecca and Medina, the bin Laden construction company was well on its way to becoming the largest and wealthiest construction company in the Arab world.

Atwan illustrates the close bonds between the bin Laden family and the royal family with reference to an event that took place when Muhammad bin Laden died in a plane crash: "[W]hen Muhammad bin Laden was killed in a crash in 1967, King Faisal told the fifty-four orphans they were all his children now."[89]

Like other affluent children in Saudi Arabia, Osama experienced the changing and turbulent times of the late 1960s and the 1970s. The sudden wealth caused by the oil boom resulted in increasing contacts with westerners and their traditions. The wars in the Middle East had an influence on all inhabitants in the area. As a young rich teenager, Osama had made some trips to Beirut where he apparently experienced some drinking sprees and womanizing. The outbreak of the Lebanese civil war in 1975 ended these trips. In 1974, at the age of 17, Osama married for the first time, to a Syrian cousin, and attended King Abdul Aziz University in Jeddah from 1974 to 1978.[90]

Osama had been raised in the strict and puritanical tradition of Sunni Wahhabi theology. The Wahhabi theologians contended that the civil war in Lebanon was Allah's punishment for their forsaking Islamic holy law for the immoral habits of western society. With Jeddah, a port city, becoming more open to the western lifestyles because of the oil boom, the university became a haven for radical Islamic teachings. As a student, Osama bin Laden was already immersing himself in his Wahhabi training when he came under the influence of the man who arguably would exert the greatest influence on his life and terrorist activities. Sheikh Abdullah Azzam came to lecture at King Abdul Aziz University and Osama became his student. This professor-student relationship would extend well beyond Osama's college years.

Sheikh Azzam started out as a Palestinian radical who attended Sharia College of Damascus University, from which he received a B.A. degree in *sharia* law in 1966. The following year, Israel captured Azzam's hometown in the Six Day War. He managed to escape to Jordan and join the *jihad* against Israel. As the war was winding down, he went to Egypt and received his M.A. in *sharia* and in 1973 his Ph.D. in "the Principles of Islamic Jurisprudence" at the "prestigious al-Azhar University."[91]

At al-Azhar University, Azzam was introduced to the teachings of Sayyid Qutb, the radical Egyptian who was widely recognized as the foremost intellectual of the Egyptian Muslim Brotherhood in the 1950s and 1960s. An educator by profession, Qutb studied in the U.S. from 1948 to 1950 and left the country violently anti American because of what he believed to be our moral decadence. He became an extreme advocate of *sharia* law and global Islamic *jihad* against the infidel. He was a prolific writer and wrote many documents, including *Milestones* and *In the Shades of the Qur'an*, which have motivated modern-day radical Islamic terrorism. The man who is sometimes referred to as "the spiritual father of radical Islam," Sayyid Qutb is also widely recognized as the writer "whose ideas shaped al-Qaeda." Perhaps it was Sayyid Qutb's teaching of the inevitability of the "conflict of cultures" between the true Muslims and the unbelievers that would influence Osama bin Laden the most.

Osama believed that the present-day struggle was the final stage in the long conflict to spread Islam worldwide and subdue the infidel. Qutb taught that Muslim rulers who failed to create a truly Islamic society, which included the strict enforcement of Islamic law and a commitment to *jihad* against the infidel, should be opposed as un-Islamic. Qutb was arrested in 1954 in connection with the attempted assassination of Egyptian President Gamal Abdel Nasser and wrote most of his books in prison prior to his execution in 1966. Radical Islamic terrorists regard him as a martyr. His school of Islamic teachings is called Qutbism.

These names are very important in our attempt to understand the terrorist threats we face from radical Islamists because these are the men who motivate today's radicals. Azzam studied Qutb's writings in Egypt, and Osama bin Laden was instructed in Qutbism at the University in Jeddah. Sayyid Qutb's brother, Muhammad, also lectured at the university where bin Laden attended his classes. He not only had the intellectual capacity to assimilate the radical theology of such men but he had the financial capacity to fund the terrorist network to implement them once Azzam motivated bin Laden to action.

Sheikh Azzam had broken with the Palestine Liberation Organization in the mid 1970s because of its nationalist character and the Marxist orientation of the struggle since they were supported by the Soviet Union. Azzam reasoned that Palestine should be liberated because the infidel should be driven out of Islamic lands based on global *jihad*. Some believe he played a role in the founding of Hamas. After receiving his Ph.D., Azzam taught at the University of Jordan, where his radical jihadist views were not well received. He packed his bags and headed to Saudi Arabia where he was offered a position as lecturer at King Abdul Aziz University in Jeddah. This move would end up serving Azzam's purposes, since he would meet the bright young, enthusiastic, and wealthy student, Osama bin Laden. This spell-binding orator would arguably exert more influence than anyone else on the beliefs and actions of this student who would become the world's best-known terrorist.

There would be a few bumps in the road before the joint terrorist movement founded by these two men took off in a major way.

In January 1979, Islamic fanatics inspired by the radical Ayatollah Khomeini overthrew the Shah of Iran and established an Islamic theocracy. Most likely inspired by this successful revolution, a group of fundamentalist Muslims on Nov. 30, 1979, seized and occupied the Grand Mosque in Mecca. They were apparently upset with what they viewed as un-Islamic policies of the Saudi government and thought they would spark a country-wide revolution. The violent and bloody conclusion to the seizure of the Mosque led to major repression by the government of Saudi Arabia. One of the consequences was the expulsion of Islamic professors, such as Abdullah Azzam, suspected of teaching fundamentalist tenets of Islamic theology. However, Sheikh Azzam had barely unpacked his bags in Pakistan before the Soviets invaded Afghanistan on Christmas Day.

Azzam eagerly involved himself in the struggle against the infidel Soviet Union who had invaded Afghanistan. He even issued his own *fatwa* urging Muslims throughout the world to accept their divine obligations to join in the holy war triggered by this invasion. After establishing his base of operation in Peshawar, Pakistan, on the Afghan border, he reached out for help from his jihadist contacts, especially to his brightest and wealthiest student (and now disciple) in Jeddah. Osama bin Laden enthusiastically responded to his mentor and offered his help.

Azzam arranged several secret trips for bin Laden to Peshawar and Afghanistan, where he met several leaders of the "holy war." Atwan writes that bin Laden told him that he more or less moved to Afghanistan "full time" in 1982.[92] Azzam and bin Laden set up an organization called the Office of Services (identified in various documents by slightly different Arabic spellings), which would eventually morph into al-Qaeda. This Office of Services would be used to recruit volunteers for this *jihad* effort and raise funds to finance the efforts of the *mujahedin*. Bin Laden's money was the early source of funds for plane tickets, visas, and major fundraising efforts and other expenses.

Partly through bin Laden's efforts, the Saudi government became strong supporters of the *mujahedin* in Afghanistan. Thousands of men volunteered to fight and millions of dollars were raised by Saudi citizens. (As has been pointed out earlier in this book, the billion or more dollars clandestinely contributed by the U.S. government was matched or exceeded by the Saudi government.)

In a slightly different account of bin Laden's activities in Afghanistan from other sources, Atwan explains:

> "In 1984, bin Laden founded Bayt al-Ansar (House of the Supporters) in Peshawar. His mission was to provide a station where newly arrived volunteers for jihad could be received before being sent for training .... By 1986 bin Laden had set up his own training camps in various parts of Afghanistan. In 1988 he established an office to record the names of the mujahedin and inform the families of those who were killed. The name of the register was 'al-Qaeda ('the base' or 'foundation'), and that is how the organization got its name. Most Islamist sources say that the embryonic al Qaeda network was established at this point."[93]

A fact that all agree upon is that Osama bin Laden returned home to Saudi Arabia as a widely acclaimed hero in 1989, shortly after the final Soviet troops were withdrawn. This hero status would be short lived as far as the government of Saudi Arabia was concerned, since bin Laden was placed under house arrest in the mid 1990s for reasons that will be explained shortly. Two weeks after bin Laden returned home in 1989, his mentor, long-time jihadist associate in Afghanistan, and "co-founder" of al-Qaeda was assassinated in Peshawar. Conspiracy theories abound explaining Sheikh Abdullah Azzam's assassination.

These conspiracy theories relating to involvement in Azzam's assassination range from the CIA to Osama bin Laden himself, neither of which make any sense as far as I am concerned. It is an apparent fact that bin Laden and Azzam had parted ways on the future of al-Qaeda as the war in Afghanistan was winding down. This ideological divide was accentuated after bin Laden developed a close working relationship with Dr. Ayman al-Zawahiri, who was universally recognized as number two in command of al-Qaeda until he assumed control after bin Laden's death. It might be instructive to take a brief look at what brought about the bin Laden—Azzam split and what al-Zawahiri brought to the table both ideologically and organizationally as we seek to better understand the al-Qaeda terrorist threat.

Most authorities on modern-day Islamic terrorism seem to agree that the disagreement between bin Laden and Azzam arose over the future role of al-Qaeda in the Islamist holy war after the Soviets were forced to leave Afghanistan. Sheik Azzam was reportedly opposed to fighting Muslim governments, even if they had become secular and corrupt. He felt this would create disunity among Muslims among whom they hoped to inspire defensive *jihad* to drive the infidels from Muslim lands. Azzam wanted the emphasis to be on driving unbelievers, including rulers, from Islamic lands. His first target obviously would be to drive such unbelievers out of his home country of Palestine by declaring *jihad* against Israel.

At the same time, bin Laden had become increasingly concerned that the ruling family in Saudi Arabia was tolerating secular western behavior and was too close to America whom he believed to be the Great Satan. His attitudes toward the future role of al-Qaeda in continuing jihadist activities would be greatly influenced by his relationship with Ayman al-Zawahiri. Atwan writes, "Although the two men did not officially join forces under al-Qaeda's banner until 1998, they certainly met and exerted increasing influence on each other throughout the preceding decade."[94]

Al-Zawahiri came from a prominent middle-class Egyptian family, many of whom were involved in the medical community. They were not very political, with the exception of one uncle who was a student of Sayyid Qutb and became an avid follower of this radical Islamic thinker. At 14 years old, obviously having been influenced by his uncle, al-Zawahiri joined the Muslim Brotherhood. The following year, Qutb was executed for his role in the attempted assassination of Nasser. At such a young age, al-Zawahiri and a group of fellow students formed an underground cell determined to overthrow the Egyptian government and replace it with a true Islamic state. This radical organization would eventually merge with similar groups to form Egyptian Islamic Jihad.

After completing his medical education, al-Zawahiri would become "emir" or the leader of Egyptian Islamic Jihad (EIJ) and is believed to have planned and organized the assassination of President Sadat in 1981. Having been arrested a few months before the actual assassination took place, he spent some time in jail.

After being released from prison, al-Zawahiri spent a year practicing medicine in 1985 in Jeddah, Saudi Arabia. He left there for Peshawar to provide medical care for *mujahedeen* wounded in the Afghan war. It was here, in about 1986, that he developed a lasting relationship with Osama bin Laden bin Laden. Al-Zawahiri would begin the process of influencing bin Laden's position on post-Afghanistan war *jihad*. At the same time he would be competing with Sheik Azzam for bin Laden's financial support for the Egyptian Islamic Jihad activities.

The relationship between bin Laden and al-Zawahiri would grow closer and closer over the years. They jointly ran the most radical and dangerous terrorist organization the world has ever seen until bin Laden's death in 2011. Al-Zawahiri is now in control as he attempts to revitalize al-Qaeda and return it to its première role in the world of Islamist terrorism.

Osama bin Laden did not even enjoy a year as a war hero in Saudi Arabia before he alarmed and irritated the Saudi government. In *The Secret History of Al-Qaeda*, Abdel Atwan describes bin Laden's activities in Saudi Arabia:

> "In a nation where criticism is tantamount to treason, bin Laden began questioning the Saudi regime. In a 1989 letter addressed to King Fahd, bin Laden urged reform and a more faithful application of shari'ah law in the kingdom. He also warned of the imminent danger posed by Saudi Arabia's neighbor, Iraq. The 'greedy and aggressive' Saddam Hussein, he claimed, had his eye on Kuwait and, ultimately the kingdom's own oil fields. He further upset the Saudi authorities by openly denouncing Saddam as a kafir."[95]

Calling Saddam a "*kafir*" or apostate caused the ruling family to fear retaliation from the Iraqi dictator. They warned Osama that he would be punished if he continued to engage in politics and took away his passport. Bin Laden fired off another strong letter to the king warning against an appeal for American help after Hussein invaded Kuwait in August 1990. He offered to recruit and train holy warriors who had been involved in the fighting in Afghanistan to defend Saudi Arabia. Osama's offer was rebuffed by the government and he was once again warned to stay out of politics.

Bin Laden's outcry against the Saudi state for inviting half a million American troops onto Saudi soil and America's response would serve as his justification for *jihad* against America. He called Saudi Arabia "an American colony" and continued, "We believe that America has committed the greatest mistake in entering a peninsula which no religion from the non-Muslim nations has entered for fourteen centuries."[96i] Osama's defiance caused the Saudi authorities to place him under house arrest.

In 1992, Osama bin Laden slipped out of the country and established a new location for al-Qaeda operations in Khartoum, Sudan. "In what were to be al-Qaeda's first attacks, it bombed US soldiers in transit at the Goldmohur Hotel in

Aden, Yemen, in 1992, killing three people and wounding five, and in 1993 two Black Hawk helicopters were brought down in attacks in Mogadishu," and the "US swiftly withdrew its troops from Somalia," Atwan writes.[97]

Bin Laden reportedly financed the Egyptian Islamic Jihad's unsuccessful 1995 attempt, under the leadership of al-Zawahiri, to assassinate Egyptian President Hosni Mubarak. To round out Bin Laden's major targets at the time, Atwan writes that he "launched his first attack on his other great enemy—the Saudi regime—in 1995 when an al-Qaeda cell in the kingdom bombed a housing compound for foreign workers in Riyadh."[98]

1996 was an eventful year for Osama bin Laden and al-Qaeda. The government of Sudan yielded to persistent pressure from Saudi Arabia, Egypt, and the United States and expelled bin Laden and his followers from Sudan. The al-Qaeda headquarters was moved to Afghanistan where Osama reestablished his close relationship with the Taliban, which was finally consolidating its control of Afghanistan. This move would provide al-Qaeda a safe haven to operate its terrorist training camps. In June 1996, al-Qaeda operatives in Saudi Arabia bombed the American base at Khobar Towers, killing 19 American soldiers and wounding another 500 people.

In August 1996, Osama bin Laden issued his own *fatwa* personally declaring war on America. The "Declaration of Jihad against the Americans Occupying the Land of the Two Sacred Places" was signed only by Osama bin Laden. He apparently now believed that he had the religious authority to issue his own *fatwa* calling for "defensive *jihad*" against the Americans.

"Defensive jihad is the absolute religious duty of every able-bodied Muslim man, and if asked to participate by a 'just and pious leader' he must not refuse," writes Abdel Atwan. He continues, "The emphasis on the caliber of leadership here is very important, and gives some insight into why bin Laden is so careful about his image. His piety and austere lifestyle have become legendary in the Muslim world." But "offensive jihad can only be called by the caliph, the head of the umma."[99]

Offensive *jihad* to spread the Islamic faith can be called only by the caliph as, the head of the umma or body of true Muslims. On the other hand, *defensive jihad* to wage holy war against infidels occupying or threatening Muslims lands can be called by a recognized spiritual leader. Bin laden must have believed that he already qualified as a recognized Islamic religious leader capable of calling for defensive *jihad*. There is some debate as to whether he perceived himself to be the one who would become the new caliph, although the caliphate was *de facto* abolished by Kemal Ataturk in 1924.

Atwan writes, "The absence of a caliph is seen by some Muslims as a violation of the shari'ah, and restoring it a crucial first step in reversing their fortunes. One of al-Qaeda's declared aims is to restore the caliphate and, by implication, the former glory of the umma."[100]

Osama bin Laden was referred to by Abu Musab al-Zarqawi (the leader of al-Qaeda in Iraq until he was killed in 2006) as "'the Sheikh of the Holy Warriors' and it is the iconic (some of his followers have even used the word 'messianic') status of bin Laden that confirms al-Qaeda's identity and ensures its continued existence and growth."[101] Bin Laden had indicated on several occasions that he desired martyrdom and inspired such desires among his followers, including a glorification of suicide missions. According to his radical belief martyrdom is a certain guarantee to paradise.

Even the politically correct Lebanese-born Christian scholar on Islam, Dr. Fawaz Gerges, documents that Osama bin Laden used the *Hijra* of Mohammad and his followers when they fled to Medina and the Battle of Badr when they attacked and defeated the much stronger Quraysh from Medina to justify his role in Islamic history. Gerges explained that bin Laden had seen his forced exodus from Saudi Arabia to Sudan and then to Afghanistan as the 21st century version of Mohammad's *Hijra* to Medina in 622. Osama bin Laden further believed that the victory Allah gave to Mohammad at Badr proved that such a Muslim victory could happen again under his leadership. Many of his followers undoubtedly cling to such a dream, even after the Navy SEALs ended bin Laden's own evil designs.

On Feb. 23, 1998, Osama bin Laden and Ayman al-Zawahiri issued a joint statement announcing the formation of the "International Islamic Front against the Jews and Crusaders." They intended to bring together under one large umbrella al-Qaeda, Egyptian Islamic Jihad, and other militant Islamic groups in order to wage global *jihad*. In this statement, which was faxed to Atwan in his London office, "they call upon 'every Muslim who believes in Allah to do Allah's will by killing Americans and stealing their money wherever and whenever possible.'"[102] Shortly thereafter, they bombed the U.S. embassies in the East African countries of Kenya and Tanzania, killing a total of 224 people, including 11 Americans. It was during this timeframe that al-Zawahiri sold bin Laden on his strategy that America must be hit on its homeland. Thus began the planning for what would result in the 9/11 terrorist attacks on the Twin Towers of the World Trade Center and on the Pentagon. These attacks resulted in massive human carnage of civilians, including a few Muslims. The war being waged by these Islamic terrorists would have no ground rules or moral constraints.

Al-Qaeda would become an international terrorist organization dependent on no political state, but a worldwide group of cells communicating, organizing, and implementing terrorist acts via the Internet and other high-tech means of communication. In effect, it became a franchise operation of loosely organized cells capable of inflicting terror all over the globe. Many attempted terrorist attacks have been thwarted in the U.S., but they have claimed numerous human lives (almost all civilians) in London, Madrid, Karachi, Bali, Mombasa, Riyadh, Casablanca, Istanbul, Khobar, Amman, and all over Iraq. All of this is done in the name of what they believe their religion requires. Certainly moderate Muslims around the world are embarrassed and horrified by such actions. But these radical fundamentalist Islamist terrorists believe they are carrying out Allah's will. We must seek to understand these terrorists and their motives if we are to successfully defeat them.

The fact that American Muslims are much better integrated into American society than they are in Europe is very encouraging. This makes it much more difficult for al-Qaeda to establish "cells" in this country, but they can slip in terrorists as they did prior to 9/11. At the same time, on the few occasions when al-Qaeda operatives have been able to recruit Muslim American citizens to become active terrorists, the results have been heartrending and disastrous. On other occasions, the acts of American Muslim terrorists, recruited by al-Qaeda, would have been catastrophic had they not failed due to Divine Providence or good luck.

The American-born imam, Anwaral al-Awlaki, whose parents were from Yemen, is the best example. He was the spiritual advisor to some of the 9/11 suicide bombers; he inspired the radical American-born Major Nidal Hasan (whose parents were from Palestine), who murdered 12 soldiers and an unborn baby and wounded many others in the Fort Hood massacre; and he became known as al-Qaeda's number-one recruiter and motivator for suicide attackers.

Then there is the would-be Times Square bomber, who was born in Pakistan but had been an American citizen for a number of years. Fortunately, he was not smart enough to buy the right type of fertilizer. It was even more fortunate that a New York street vender was astute enough to immediately report smoke oozing from the bomber's rental vehicle. Had these two events not occurred, there would have been more human carnage resulting from his location in proximity to Times Square than resulted from the attacks on the Twin Towers. In each of these cases, as well as others, these Islamist attacks could have been prevented with the necessary surveillance.

We must learn two indispensible facts before it is too late. One, we are in a war declared by radical Islamist jihadists. Unlike classical Islam, which had rules of war even in their most violent days, these fanatical jihadists recognize no civilized rules of war. Any type of deception, suicide attacks, or anything else (including killing civilians, women, and children—even Muslims) is permissible if it furthers what they believe is Allah's command for them to wage "holy war." Two, our wise Founders never remotely intended for our Constitution to be a "Suicide Pact."

There are numerous factors that come into play for a person in search of an understanding of how the United States has reached the point we are at today in our efforts to defend against the multi-faceted Islamist terrorist threats. The inroads of the Muslim Brotherhood in America, the front groups that support terrorism in the United States, the individuals who work in these groups, the so-called Muslim Mafia, and the dominance of politically correct vocabulary—among academia, the press, and the government—in public discussion of this looming threat have impeded our ability to keep this country safe. Towards the goal of aiding the reader in understanding the connections between these elements, I intend to address each of them in some detail.

In spite of the fact that Muslims are so much more assimilated in the U.S. culture than in any other non-Muslim country, it is surprising and frustrating to see the statements by leaders of some of the self-professed moderate Islamic organizations who claim to represent the millions of peaceful and peace-loving Muslims all over the world. Shortly after Arab immigration, which included a significant number of college students, began in the early 1960s, the Muslim Brotherhood moved quickly to establish a foothold in this country. The Muslim Brotherhood is known as the "mother" of all modern-day radical Islamist organizations, whether their method of operation is to infiltrate by peaceful and stealth means or to employ all the violent forms of jihadist terrorism.

The Muslim Brotherhood founded the Muslim Student Association in 1963 as the first of a large group of future fronts or subsidiaries in America. Ten years later, with the continued growth of Muslims in America, the North American Islamic Trust (NAIT) formed an investment vehicle for the Brotherhood to buy title to more than 300 mosques and madrassas (Islamic schools) in the U.S. These were brilliant and well thought out moves on their part. One, they knew that the educated young Muslims would provide a pool of Muslim Brotherhood leaders in the future if they developed an early relationship with them. Two, they wanted to make sure they were taught "pure Islam," which they believed was the essence of fundamentalist Wahhabism as taught in Saudi Arabia.[103] The Muslim Brotherhood has preyed on the young since its founding and unfortunately it always seems to have worked.

When we discuss the modern phenomenon of Muslim immigration to non-Muslim lands, we will examine extensive polling data on the attitudes of Muslims in their adopted homelands. One such poll, by the prestigious Pew polling firm, proves the effectiveness of the Brotherhood's youth strategy in this country. A 2007 Pew poll found that the "under 30" group of American Muslims is much more religious than their elders. The 18- to 29-year-old Muslims were more likely to identify themselves as "Muslims first" rather than "Americans first" by a 60 percent to 25 percent margin. Of more concern was that 26 percent of the under-30 Muslims in America agreed that "suicide attacks were justified under some circumstances," compared to only 13 percent of all American Muslims.

In any effort to advance their long-term goals in America and worldwide, the Muslim Brotherhood proceeded to establish a subsidiary for each of their top priorities. The Brotherhood has founded or exercised major control over at least 18 Muslim organizations in America.

The Rise of the "Muslim Mafia" in America

There is no rival to *Muslim Mafia: Inside the Secret Underworld that's Conspiring to Islamize America* by David Gaubatz[104] and Paul Sperry (WND

Books, 2009) in presenting the history of the Muslim Brotherhood in America in such meticulously fascinating detail. These two relentless investigators have much in common and complement one another. One is a hard-nosed investigative journalist and media fellow at Stanford University's Hoover Institute. The other is an experienced terrorist investigator and counterterrorism expert who had a distinguished military career in intelligence. He speaks fluent Arabic and was deployed to Saudi Arabia and several other Middle Eastern countries. The writers of this book possessed recently declassified Brotherhood documents and other FBI evidence of terrorist activities involving some Muslim organizations and individuals.

They also had hard evidence that no one else could possibly have. David Gaubatz's son Chris had been, in their words, lodged in the "belly of the beast." Chris had managed to fake a Muslim conversion and under an assumed name, landed a strategic internship with the Council on American-Islamic Relations (CAIR) that lasted for several months.

David Marshall (Chris' new name) had been so diligent in his preparation that he not only fooled his superiors in the CAIR structure for whom he worked but also became a favorite of one of the top leaders in the office. Ibrahim Hooper, CAIR's communications director, became so fond of "David" (Chris) that he even offered to arrange a marriage for him with one of the girls at the mosque he attended.

Unbelievably, he ended up being trusted to perform the menial task of shredding untold boxes of sensitive material in CAIR's strategic Washington, D.C., office. These boxes turned out to be a treasure trove of material that had accumulated over the roughly 15 years of CAIR's existence at the time. At that time, the Bush administration's "war on terrorism" was resulting in increasing FBI investigations and unannounced searches and seizures of the files of Muslim organizations. Therefore, a decision was made to destroy such material in this CAIR office. As "David" threw himself into this thankless job, he was able cart off untold numbers of such boxes. The material he took (after shredding tons of worthless materials) ended up containing "12,000 pages of compelling internal documents and video surveillance" exposing "the criminal conspiracy" of CAIR and other Muslim Brotherhood-associated organizations.

To alert readers to the serious nature of the material contained in this book, the Muslim Brotherhood's creed is printed in bold red letters at the top of the back cover of the book: "Allah is our goal, the Prophet is our guide, the Quran is our constitution, jihad is our way, and death for the glory of Allah is our greatest ambition."

There is an abundance of evidence in *Muslim Mafia* that virtually all of the leaders in the Brotherhood and the organizations it has founded or helped to found support stealth efforts to further the cause of Islam and the spread of *sharia* law in America. Most of them understand that this is going to be a long process that will involve laborious efforts by Muslims to infiltrate the American political systems and its various government entities.

It may well be the case that some conservative American authorities and authors assume that it is so difficult to get the attention of the American public that they must employ the "shock treatment." On the other hand, a softer and less strident approach would make it more difficult for the politically correct Islamic apologists to dismiss the evidence presented by these authorities by name calling. Discounting carefully documented evidence by calling the presenters of such evidence "Islamophobes," "racists," or "bigots" may be wearing thin on a public not as dumb as the politically correct consider them to be. A Pew Research Center poll released Aug. 30, 2011, which very extensively examined the attitudes of American Muslims, will be looked at in some detail. But one finding that is most significant and will bear repeating is this:

> "Many Muslims fault their own leaders for failing to challenge Islamic extremists. Nearly half (48%) say that Muslim leaders in the United States have not done enough to speak out against Islamic extremists; only about a third (34%) say Muslim leaders have done enough in challenging extremists. At the same time, 68% say that Muslim Americans themselves are cooperating as much as they should with law enforcement."[105]

An earlier book by Paul Sperry (*Infiltration: How Muslim Spies and Subversives Have Penetrated Washington* [Thomas Nelson, 2008]) includes a short chapter on "The Muslim Mafia." This book offers a few details on how Muslims, under the leadership of Abdurahman Alamoudi, had infiltrated the Clinton administration and the Congress. Sperry devotes most of this book to how Grover Norquist orchestrated an extensive—and successful—Muslim outreach program in Bush's 2000 presidential campaign. Most of this book deals with how this effort was translated into influence in the Bush administration before and after 9/11. This book will be extensively referenced in the section discussing the campaign and the key Muslim players that surfaced due to Norquist's efforts. Sperry notes that some FBI agents and others involved in the Islamic terrorist investigations on several occasions had begun to refer to a "Muslim mafia."

In summary, the Sperry and Gaubatz book *Muslim Mafia* will uncover evidence that this "mafia" is run by the Muslim Brotherhood and financed primarily by the Saudis with some help from the Emirates. The movement is deeply motivated by the radical Wahhabi sect of Islam, which strives to establish such radical Wahhabi teachings in mosques and Muslim schools throughout America. Further, the anti-Israel cause of Palestinian terrorists is the major rallying cry that the Brotherhood uses to inspire their members and expand their membership. Like the Sicilian crime mob, which is also a terrorist society, they make their decisions and conduct most of their activities in strict secrecy. Any public statements they release are carefully choreographed so as not to discourage the faithful while concealing their true intentions in language intended to sound very moderate and broadminded. They are very skilled at the ancient art of "*Al-Taqiya*," perfected by the initial Muslim caliphs, which is considered to be morally acceptable "deception" when it is used to further the cause of Allah. Each new Brotherhood front was started with a specific purpose in furthering the goals of the Brotherhood. Eighteen such organizations are singled out in the book about the Muslim mafia.

In Chapter 14 of Muslim Mafia ("The 'Ikhwan Mafia'"), the authors write:

> "For that matter, the Brotherhood is known within Islamic circles as the 'Ikhwan mafia,' (Ikhwan is the Arabic word for brother) because of its highly organized structure, centralized control, and covert operations. Like the mob, it has its own internal bylaws, security and military infrastructure. A network of front groups, cutouts, and shell companies shield its criminal activities from the authorities." [106]

Based on information contained in the documents they obtained and information from FBI agents who have investigated the Brotherhood, they contend its structure is almost the mirror image of the mob. It is run by a "shura council" composed of "crime centers" run by "godfathers" and "is led by a supreme don called a general 'masul.'" They further explain:

> "The council directs regional underbosses, or 'masuls,' who in turn give orders to capo-like figures known as 'naquibs.' The 'naquibs' control the front groups, and train the field commanders, or ikhwans, who are sworn members, according to Brotherhood documents declassified by the government." [107]

It is eerie and frightening that their own documents reveal how they patterned their organization in this way because of the successes crime families have had in gaming the American system. Before identifying the four main wings of the Brotherhood's mafia, the authors make an interesting observation about why the Brotherhood has been so successful over the years. The Brotherhood has always aggressively reached out to young Muslims in order to assure the future of the movement. Sperry and Gaubatz note, "Mohammed (KSM), the mastermind of the 9/11 attacks, was drawn to violent jihad in Kuwait after joining the Brotherhood at age sixteen and attending its desert youth camps." They had just mentioned that the organization makes a point of reaching out to college students and encouraging them to attend an "Ikhwan camp" where they "conduct jihadist training activities" for potential "young soldiers."

The writers identify four key wings of the "Ikhwan Mafia":

1. *The Palestine Committee* is the Hamas wing that operates chiefly out of California, Texas, Illinois, and Washington, D.C. "Prosecutors [in the Holy Land Foundation trial] believe CAIR is its mouthpiece and

its lobbying arm in North America. With the Holy Land Foundation under multiple indictments, most investigators believe that CAIR is now the premier player in this group and that Omar Ahmad, CAIR's founding chairman, is now the "masul" or the "supreme don."

2. *The Safa Committee* "is the Saudi wing made up of more than one hundred business and charitable front groups operating mainly out of Northern Virginia (along the so-called Wahhabi Corridor, just outside D.C.), as well as Georgia. Before he was sent to prison, Alamoudi controlled the group, along with Jamal Barzinji,[108] who remains at the helm. Safa provides financial and intellectual capital for the cause, while also controlling a vast real estate portfolio. (Large sums of Saudi money flows to Safa.)

3. *Islamic Circle of North America* "is the Pakistani wing based out of New York." The writers note that ICNA recently merged with the Muslim American Society (MSA) located in Alexandria, Va. This group runs such things as "prayer and youth camps" at mosques run by the Brotherhood. They provide ideological indoctrination and sometimes advocate *jihad* and martyrdom "and the creation of Islamic states in the 'evil' West.".

4. *Islamic Society of North America* (ISNA) "is the founding 'nucleus' of the movement in North America, declassified Brotherhood documents confirm." ISNA and the Islamic Association for Palestine (IAP) are the two oldest non-education related Brotherhood fronts founded in America Both were established in 1981. Based in Indiana and Washington, D.C., ISNA "controls campus recruitment, evangelism, banking and investments, and the dispensing of *fatwahs* for the Brotherhood. Through a subsidiary trust, it also owns and controls the lion's share of the major mosques in America." The four purported godfathers in this wing are prominent imams, including the Pakistani born imam Muzammil Siddiqi of the Islamic Society of Orange County mosque.[109]

The Brotherhood requires the same discipline and loyalty as the mob. They are sworn to secrecy and swear allegiance to the Muslim Brotherhood creed affirming that they are lifetime "slaves" to Allah. There are a few differences between the Sicilian mafia and the Brotherhood mafia. The Brotherhood family frequently meets in religious sanctuaries instead of topless bars and butcher shops, but there is not a long list of differences on many of their cold-blooded methods of operation. The American Brotherhood's actual killings are most often associated with the support of terrorist organizations such as Hamas—and then the money is funneled through one of their fronts so as to protect their "moderate" image. They have been accused of being responsible for motivating and training some young American Muslims who have turned up in war zones in Pakistan and

Afghanistan, for example. But so far they have avoided being listed by the federal government as a terrorist organization and, therefore, it is not a crime to be a member of the American branch of the Muslim Brotherhood.

The Story behind CAIR's Founding

The Muslim Brotherhood's comprehensive and successful method of operation is described in vivid detail in "Fronting For Hamas," Chapter 3 of *Muslim Mafia*. It details the Brotherhood's essential role in the founding of the Council on American-Islamic Relations, best known as CAIR. The authors quote a line from a brief prepared by Assistant U.S. Attorney Gordon D. Kromberg for a case before the U.S. Court of Appeals for the Fourth Circuit in December 2007: "From its founding by Muslim Brotherhood leaders, CAIR conspired with other affiliates of the Muslim Brotherhood to support terrorists."[110]

The trial of the now-defunct Holy Land Foundation, formerly the largest Islamic charity in the United States, on charges of funding terrorist organizations began in 2007. In a report on the trial, *The Dallas Morning News* reported that FBI agent Lara Burns *"took the stand to go over wiretap transcripts from a secret 1993 Philadelphia meeting held by Hamas leaders in America."* The Hamas leaders were explaining that the organization created to represent their concerns in America, the Islamic Association for Palestine (IAP), had gotten a bad name and its efforts were not generating the funds Hamas needs to carry out its mission in Palestine. One of the federal prosecutors asks FBI agent Burns if such an organization had been established since the 1993 meeting? She responded without hesitation "CAIR!"[111]

As noted earlier, IAP was one of the earliest fronts established in America by the Muslim Brotherhood. It was incorporated in Chicago in November 1981. The registered agents listed on the incorporation papers included Sami Al-Arian. Al-Arian is the radical Islamist college professor in Florida who would later help to found and run Palestinian Islamic Jihad—and almost single handedly deliver the crucial Muslim vote for George W. Bush. Another agent listed on the incorporating papers was Mousa Abu Marzook, who in addition to being an IAP founder was deputy political bureau chief of Hamas. Marzook also led the Brotherhood's Palestine Committee before he was deported to Jordon. He now lives in Syria.

> "IAP was named in a May 1991 Muslim Brotherhood document—titled 'An Explanatory Memorandum on the General Strategic Goal for the Groups in North America"— one of the Brotherhood's 29 likeminded 'organizations of our friends' that share the common goal of destroying America and turning it into a Muslim nation. These 'friends' were identified by the Brotherhood as groups that could help teach Muslims 'that their work in America is a kind of grand Jihad in eliminating and destroying the Western civilization from within and "sabotaging" its miserable house by their hands . . . so

that . . . God's religion [Islam] is made victorious over all other religions."[112]

These are straightforward goals stated in the written words of the Muslim Brotherhood in an internal document never intended to be released. Among the other 28 "likeminded organizations of our friends"—a politically correct way of saying our "fronts"—are some well-known organizations in the Brotherhood's "mafia." The next name on the list is the Islamic Society of North America (ISNA), since it also was established in 1981, the same year as IPA. Also on the list is the Muslim Students Association of the U.S. & Canada, which grew out of the Muslim Students Association, the very first Muslim Brotherhood front officially established in America. They also list the "Occupied Land Fund," which became known as the Holy Land Foundation—they are very adept at choosing meaningful names for their organizations.

The stage had been set since IPA had become increasingly known as an organization that supported Palestinian *jihad* against Israel. During 1992 urgent appeals from Hamas, financial help had increased. One appeal letter from a Hamas member in the Gaza Strip introduced by the government in the Holy Land trial was handwritten in Arabic. Excerpts from the letter pleaded, "Provide us with what helps of funds and weapons" . . . "Weapons, weapons, our brothers." The letter went on to explain "Jihad in Palestine is different from any jihad" and emphasized with emotion: "The meaning of killing a Jew for the liberation of Palestine cannot be compared to any jihad on earth."[113]

The meeting, which ended up being wiretapped by the FBI, was called by Omar Ahmad, the president of IPA, for October 1993 at a Marriott Courtyard hotel in Philadelphia. The key leaders of the Brotherhood, IAP, and the Holy Land foundation had gathered to make an urgent decision about what should be done. Sperry writes, "The IAP and Holy Land officials worried, however, that the Hamas infrastructure in America was insufficiently equipped to launch a convincing propaganda campaign." They needed a media operation that was savvy enough to "deceive" the media and the government while "they advanced their radical agenda of supporting violent jihad abroad while slowly institutionalizing a Shariah theocracy at home," according to Sperry and Gaubatz.[114] (The writers note that the records of the wiretapping revealed that they talked directly about "deception"—once again, *Taqiya* is an ancient orthodox teaching of Islam.) Shukri Abu Baker, the president of the Holy Land Foundation, was caught on tape saying that they need words that would give their agenda a "media twinkle."[115] (Abu Baker is now serving a 65-year federal sentence, having been found guilty of funneling millions of dollars to Islamic terrorist organizations.)

Very important attendees at the meeting were the IAP president, Omar Ahmad, and public-relations director, Nihad Awad. The two had been born and raised in the same Palestinian refugee camp, and not surprisingly, they both "burned with hatred toward Israel as well as their adopted country for supporting the Jewish nation economically and militarily."

As a result of this meeting, the Muslim Brotherhood's oldest child gave birth to a new and much more powerful Brotherhood child, or more accurately, "front." The Council on American-Islamic Relations (CAIR), which now bills itself as "America's largest Muslim civil liberties advocacy organization," was born. The organization would have an amazingly strong family resemblance, if not an identical statement of purpose, because CAIR's first president was Omar Ahmad and its first secretary-treasurer was Nihad Awad. The writers of *Muslim Mafia* remark on the significance of this development as it relates to the ongoing Islamic terrorism, especially in the Middle East:

> "CAIR is first mentioned by name in Brotherhood documents as part of the July 30, 1994, agenda of the Palestine Committee. This is the smoking gun linking CAIR directly to the Hamas network inside America. Minutes reveal the purpose of the meeting was to discuss 'suggestions to develop (the) work of CAIR' and its 'coordination' with the Hamas triumvirate of IAP, Holy Land (which shared its Dallas offices with IAP), and the Washington-based United Association for Studies and Research, or UASR. Along with IAP, UASR was co-founded by the deputy chief of Hamas's political operations, Mousa Abu Marzook, who led the Brotherhood's Palestine Committee in America before being designated a terrorist by the U.S. He is now considered a fugitive living in Syria.[116]

Muslim Mafia provides a wealth of information, carefully documented, concerning the role the Muslim Brotherhood and its affiliates or fronts in America have played in supporting violent terrorism in various parts of the world and their enduring threat. The book also adds tremendous insight into "stealth jihad" in all of its manifestations. Those who seek to Islamize America a little bit at a time have a plan—carefully thought out and deliberately flexible—to infiltrate all facets of American society in an effort to advance the cause of Islam and promote *sharia* law in this country. We must endeavor to understand the severity of this threat, of which the last three American presidents and most of those who serve or served them at the highest levels seem to have little knowledge.

President Bush Reaches Out to Islam

President George W. Bush should be commended, not criticized, for his foresight in letting the American people and the world know that we had been attacked by Islamic terrorists—not by the religion of Islam. He also should not be severely criticized for not having become at least somewhat expert on the teachings of Islam and its history.

The Islamist threat was clearly on the horizon. Terrorists had bombed American embassies in Africa, the barracks housing American troops in Saudi Arabia, the World Trade center in 1993, and the USS Cole less than a year earlier, on Oct. 12, 2000. Al-Qaeda was emerging as a major threat to world peace. Osama bin Laden had declared war on America and the Taliban controlled most of Afghanistan.

It's true that in view of such a looming threat from Islamic terrorists, a case could be made that even a busy presidential candidate should have found time to delve at least slightly into the subject. For example, he could have found time to read the Koran and review a few books on the actual teachings and history of Islam, written by a recognized and balanced scholar like Dr. Bernard Lewis. Even though President Bush's statements about the religion of Islam after 9/11 were obviously weighted for political consumption, such a cursory study would have prevented him from expressing himself in the vocabulary used by the most blatant politically correct Islamic apologists.

But few, if any, other American presidents understood the nature of the threat posed by an American enemy as Reagan understood the Soviet Union's intentions to spread communism throughout the world. Even Reagan himself was so consumed by the necessity of winning the Cold War that he paid only sporadic attention and reacted in a mixed fashion to the growing threat from Islamic terrorists.

In 1983, when a suicide bomber, recruited by Islamic Jihad, bombed the American Marine barracks in Beirut, Lebanon, killing 241 American servicemen, President Reagan promptly brought home the remaining American troops. By contrast, when Libyan dictator Muammar Gaddafi in April 1986 ordered his terrorist operatives to bomb a discotheque in Berlin, in which 19 were killed and 229 injured, Reagan struck back quickly. He ordered Gaddafi's compound in Libya bombed. The Muslim ruler just barely escaped the attack. So that he would not be misunderstood, President Reagan publically warned Gaddafi that if he continued to train and deploy terrorists, he "would do it again." By then he was paying more attention. This reaction also got Gaddafi's attention strongly enough that he would eventually abandon his ambitions to obtain nuclear weapons—a policy to which he adhered until he was killed.

President Bill Clinton never demonstrated any understanding of radical Islam or any realization as to how serious such a threat might become if not forcefully addressed. Paul Sperry in Chapter 2 ("Politically Correct Suicide") of *Infiltration* offers a transcript of President Clinton's remarks at a White House briefing Nov. 15, 1994, that reveals his utter ignorance of Islamic terrorism:

> "I tried to do a lot as I have traveled the world—and I did this when I was in Jordan speaking to the Jordanian parliament—to say to the American people and to the West generally that even though we

have had problems with terrorism coming out of the Middle East, it is not inherently related to Islam—not to religion, not to the culture. And the tradition of Islam in Indonesia, I think, makes that point very graphically. It's something our people in America need to know, it's something people in the West—need to know" (emphasis added). [117]

How could any educated person, much less a Rhodes Scholar, who happened to be president of the United States make such an uninformed claim that would make most politically correct apologists blush? How could a reasonable person deny with a straight face that such terrorism is all about religion? (Even if some terrorists are inspired to *jihad* because of America's policy toward Israel or infidels occupying or "colonizing" Muslim lands, it is because they believe that once Muslims have ruled a country, Allah has given it to them forever!) It should be remembered that Clinton had 10 opportunities to kill or capture Osama bin Laden during his presidency.[118] Had Clinton acted on sound and reliable intelligence, bin Laden would never have lived to plan the dastardly 9/11 attacks. But politically correct political considerations allowed the most destructive attack on American soil since Pearl Harbor to occur.

Sperry notes that the president always "sets the tone throughout government" in such matters. Therefore, Clinton's remarks at the National Museum of Women in the Arts, just after the first attack on the World Trade Center in 1993, set the tone. He complained that "so many people" are unfairly identifying "the forces of radicalism and terrorism with Islam." (I cannot help but wonder whether Clinton thought the "*blind sheik*" and all of his radical followers were Buddhist or Hindus! Political correctness has become the most important ally to radical Islam since the Mongols converted to their faith.) The tone was that Islam was above reproach and must always be treated with respect and that Muslims were never to be associated with terrorism.

Paul Sperry goes on to write that "President Bush, who considers Islam a 'great religion,' has carried on the tradition, and then some." In an effort to prove his point, Sperry notes that Bush was the first American ever to mention mosques in his Inaugural Address along with "churches and synagogues." Sperry would emphasize Bush's early promise to "Muslim leaders [that] he will refrain from using the word Islamic to describe terrorist, as in 'Islamic terrorism.'" I would add that this was a major concession to the Muslim Brotherhood and their fronts, affiliates, and associates and their teams of Washington lobbyists. It had to be a surprise and an occasion for celebration behind closed doors in radical Muslim circles. This meant that their carefully orchestrated plan of infiltration and deception was working. (The earliest caliphs, following Mohammad's instructions they would insist, perfected the doctrine of *Taqiya,* or *al-Taqiya,* in their first 40 years of conquest of Christian and Persian lands. This technique of morally sanctioned "deception" has never been more perfected than by the Muslim Brotherhood from its founding until this very day.) This decision was at least a mixed blessing for the Islamic terrorists. They could step-up their recruitment efforts in the mosques and other Islamic venues without undue surveillance or interference and boast to their followers about the gullibility of America's leaders. *The losers in this decision were the truly moderate Muslims hoping to rid their religion of such terrorists and the countries earmarked for the terrorists' attacks._*

Sperry notes that a week after the 9/11 attacks, in a press conference following his visit to a Washington mosque, Bush pleaded with the American people to respect Muslims and Islam's teachings of "peace." When making this statement, the President was standing next to CAIR Executive Director Nihad Awad,[119] whom he invited to sit near the first lady for his 9/11 speech to Congress. (Awad's radical ties should have been well known to at least some of Bush's advisors.) President Bush would also host the "first-ever *iftar* dinner at the White House" during Ramadan just two months after the 9/11 arracks. Sperry adds to the list:

> "Then on the eve of the first anniversary of 9/11, he praised Islam as a loving faith that no American should fear. 'All Americans must recognize that the face of terror is not the true face of Islam,' He said. 'Islam is a faith based upon love, not hate.'"
>
> "A month later, he outdid himself by proclaiming, 'Islam is a vibrant faith. We respect the faith. We honor its traditions. Our enemy does not. Our enemy don't [sic] follow the great traditions of Islam. They've hijacked a great religion. . . . Islam is a faith that brings comfort to people. It inspires them to lead lives based on honesty, and justice, and compassion.'"[120]
>
> "Visiting the resort island of Bali a year after Islamic terrorists tied to al-Qaeda blew up two nightclubs packed with Americans and other foreign tourists, the president had more praise for Islam, gushing, 'Islam is fully compatible with liberty and tolerance.'"[121]

The question we should explore is, Who was primarily responsible for giving President Bush advice in his outreach to the American Muslim community in the days immediately following 9/11? In a Nov. 11, 2001, article in *The New Republic*,[122] author Franklin Foer identifies Grover Norquist as the person most responsible for Bush's outreach efforts. Foer uses the respected Arab-American pollster John Zogby as his primary source for this claim in his article, "Grover Norquist's Strange Alliance With Radical Islam." After explaining that Norquist was successful in "bringing American Muslims into the Republican Party," as had been his record as "one of the right's most influential activists," Foer writes:

> "According to several sources, Norquist helped orchestrate various post-September 11 events that brought together Muslim leaders and administration officials. 'He worked with Muslim leaders

to engineer [Bush's] prominent visit to the Mosque,' says the Arab-American pollster John Zogby, referring to the president's September 17 trip to the Islamic Center of Washington. Says Zogby, who counts Norquist among his clients, 'Absolutely, he's central to the White House outreach'" (emphasis added).[123]

Foer begins his five-page article with a reference to the Sept. 26, 2001, convening of *"15 prominent Muslim—and Arab—Americans"* at the White House by President Bush. Bush had begun the meeting by contending that "the teachings of Islam are teachings of peace and good." Obviously the president expected these Muslim leaders to condemn unequivocally the terrorists for committing such acts of terrorism in the name of Islam. Foer explains:

> "Unfortunately, many of the leaders present hadn't unambiguously rejected it. To the president's left sat Dr. Yahya Basha, president of the American Muslim Council, an organization whose leaders have repeatedly called Hamas 'freedom fighters.' Also in attendance was Salam Al-Marayati, executive director of the Muslim Public Affairs Council, who on the afternoon of September 11 told a Los Angeles public radio audience that 'we should put the State of Israel on the suspect list.' And sitting right next to President Bush was Muzammil Siddiqi, president of the Islamic Society of North America, who last fall told a Washington crowd chanting pro-Hezbollah slogans, 'America has to learn if you remain on the side of injustice, the wrath of God will come.' Days later, after a conservative activists confronted Karl Rove with dossiers about some of Bush's new friends, Rove replied, according to the activist, 'I wish I had known before the event took place.'"

In his article, Foer carefully avoids accusing Norquist of personally defending Islamic terrorism. He writes, "While nobody suggests that Norquist himself is soft on terrorism, his lobbying has helped provide radical Islamic groups—and their causes—a degree of legitimacy and access they assuredly do not deserve."

Foer specifically questions Norquist's judgment—or lack thereof—in selecting the Muslim leaders or activists he recommends for Bush's outreach efforts. One of the most glaring examples was the prominent inclusion one of the founders and executive director of CAIR, Nihad Awad. Awad, a self-professed Hamas supporter, has such a questionable record of association with Islamic radicals that he certainly was not the public face that should have been standing next to President Bush at the Sept. 17, 2001, event outside the Washington mosque. CAIR, the organization Awad represents, has an even worse record of support for Hamas worldwide.

Foer quotes the respected professor of Islamic studies at Harvard, Ali Asani, as making this comment: "There is general concern among Muslim intellectuals about how not only CAIR but some of these other organizations are claiming to speak in the name of the Muslim community, and how they're coming to be recognized by the government as spokespeople for the Muslim community in the U.S."

The previously quoted Pew polling data clearly reveal that the estimated 2.75 million Muslims living in America today (an increase of almost half a million since 2007) are among the most moderate Muslims in the world. The more radical Muslim organizations created by the Muslim Brotherhood, such as CAIR, clearly do not represent the majority of American Muslims. It is certainly a disservice to truly moderate Muslims to make them the face of the Muslim community appearing with American leaders—especially when it's the president of the United States.

Foer references some of Norquist's fellow right-wing activist friends who have confronted him on his judgment concerning the Muslim "leaders" he recommended to President Bush. For example, Norquist's ties to CAIR and the American Muslim Council (founded by Abdurrahman Alamoudi, who is now serving 23 years in prison for terrorist-related activities) caused Paul Weyrich to confront him over such concerns. Foer quotes Weyrich as saying: "I have on at least one occasion [confronted him] and he assured me that he knew what he was doing and I shouldn't have any concerns." Later, Foer quotes Weyrich as saying, "I'm afraid Grover's woefully naïve."

We have without question one of the best intelligence-gathering operations and the best-prepared military in the world. But if we fail to understand our enemy, the U.S. military and our intelligence operatives will not be able to protect Americans from Islamist terrorist attacks.

Rumsfeld Admits the Administration's Failure

Former Secretary of Defense Donald Rumsfeld, in a Sept., 11, 2011, interview with Fareed Zakaria on CNN's "Fareed Zakaria GPS," sheds light on the confusion in the Bush administration over defining our Islamic enemy. In a special edition of Zakaria's program on the 10th anniversary of the 9/11 attacks, Rumsfeld was his guest. In the course of the interview, Zakaria asked the man who was in the Pentagon when the terrorists crashed the plane into the building whether, looking back, he has any regrets. Secretary Rumsfeld responded:

> "I'll give you one example, I think we've done a not very good job of—we've put a lot of pressure on terrorist networks, but for whatever reason, Americans are very reluctant to talk about radical Islamism or Islamists. We don't want to be seen as against a religion.
>
> "And so, the Bush administration didn't do a good job. We were careful and words were always sensitive. And we never—you can't win a battle of ideas, a competition of ideas unless you describe the enemy,

say who it is, say what's wrong with it, say what we do and why that's what's right.

"We did that in the Cold War. We defeated communism. And we were tongue tied over this.

"And the Obama administration is much worse. They won't even use the word in their hearings. The attorney general doesn't want to even discuss it."[124]

The often controversial Donald Rumsfeld has served more American presidents and probably has been involved in thwarting more threats over the years to America's security than any man alive today. The reason Rumsfeld has generated so much controversy is because he tells it like it is and has no desire to be a politically correct elitist. In the CNN interview, he justifiably mentions the positive things done to put a 90-country coalition together and disrupt terrorist networks, for example. But he astutely confesses that we (meaning the Bush administration) didn't do a good job defining the enemy. He said, "Americans are reluctant to talk about radical Islamism or Islamists. We don't want to be seen as against a religion." This is significant! Who had Bush's ear on this subject? Under a best-case scenario, it was someone who wanted to be "politically correct."

This subject is of such importance in understanding the mistakes made by the Bush administration and compounded many times over by the Obama administration that it needs to be examined in some detail. This will not be an attack by innuendo on the motives of American lobbyists who represent Muslim governments, Muslim-owned businesses, or Muslim organizations. It will be a rational attempt to separate the truly moderate American Muslim leaders from those controlled by the Muslim Brotherhood. This will entail an analysis of the American Muslim "leaders" with whom Norquist and others are closely associated, including Alamoudi, al-Arian, Kahled Saffuri, and Suhail Khan, just to name a few of the best-known Muslim operatives in the U.S.

* * * * *

Another Excursus on Lobbying

As I noted in my discussion of lobbying in Chapter 1, those who live, work, or do business in this country have a right to be represented before the U.S. government as long as they respect and abide by our laws. Winston Churchill is often remembered for saying that democracy is a terrible form of government but far superior to any other system ever devised by any previous civilization. The system of government bequeathed to us by our wise Founding Fathers is not perfect but it certainly is superior to any that has endured in the history of man. The freedoms of religion, of speech, of peaceful assembly, and of the press are widely praised as uniquely enlightened guarantees from 18th-century men. But what is truly unique in the First Amendment is the guarantee of the people's right *"to petition the Government for redress of grievances."*

America's elected leaders have no divine right to rule and are expected to govern according to the will of the people, who preserved for themselves the right to petition (or "lobby," in modern parlance) the government on matters of importance to them. In a way similar to how we expanded freedom of religion to include those of faiths other than Christian, the privilege to petition or lobby the government also expanded during America's history. Corporations, all types of businesses, labor unions, various special-interest groups, and eventually even foreign corporations and foreign governments were afforded the privilege of being represented before the various branches of the American government.

Hundreds, probably thousands, of foreign corporations and governments have had, and still have, Washington representation. Certainly thousands of Washington lobbyists have represented foreign governments and foreign corporations for many years. There are more foreign registered lobbyists today than at any time in our history. In the interest of full disclosure, I will note that Hecht, Spencer and Associates has had foreign clients over the years. We still represent a foreign government that is a strategic American ally today.

Among other foreign governments and corporations, we have represented two that were involved in controversy at the time. But in every case, we made sure that we never did anything that was contrary to the best interests of our own country. As matter of fact, our decisions to represent the P. W. Botha government in South Africa in the early 1980s and the government of Panama during Eric Delvalle's presidency in the late 1980s were not made without in-depth discussions with key Reagan administration officials. We wanted to be careful not to get involved in any representation that might involve being asked to promote policies that were in potential conflict with policies of our own government.

This is not the place for a full discussion of the representation of South Africa or Panama. But a few cursory details will shed light on how Stu Spencer and I felt that American lobbyists always have a civic responsibility to use careful and sound judgment in agreeing to represent a foreign government. (This, of course, would involve frank discussions with the potential client.) Actually, in both cases cited here, it turned out that there were compelling reasons for us to become involved as American representatives of these two governments.

In the case of South Africa, P.W. Botha is best known as the apartheid-era president of the South African government[125] that had grown out of the so-called Anglo-Boer wars almost a century earlier. The "Boers" were descendents of Dutch farmers ("boer" is Dutch for "farmer") who had ultimately won independence from the British. They were commonly referred to as Afrikaners for more than a century. The controversy was over the country's longtime apartheid policies. South Africa had a system of racial segregation at least as severe as the old Jim Crow laws in this country. Many scholars on the subject note that during his long reign as prime minister and president, Botha went back and forth between upholding and reforming the apartheid laws. (Some of the key reforms took place during our short tenure of representing him.)

By far the most important consideration in taking this client was the strategic importance of South Africa in the very hot Cold War at the time. Mineral rich South Africa had some of the world's largest gold mines among its abundant resources. However, South Africa was surrounded by countries with communist rulers or communist insurgent movements. The best examples are the government of Angola, which was under virtual communist control, and Namibia, whose government was administered by South Africa (it was confronted with a violent communist-dominated insurgency called SWAPO [South West Africa People's Organization].)

Just to sketch the situation that existed in the 1980s:[126] The Soviets were pouring billions of dollars into support of the Angolan government. There were as many as 40,000 Cuban troops in Angola, as well as a few thousand Russian and East German military combatants (not just advisors).[127] There was a SWAPO headquarters and extensive military training camps in Angola. They were training communist insurgents to infiltrate Namibia and conduct sabotage and other deadly attacks. Also in Angola was the National Union for the Total Independence of Angola (UNITA), the pro-American true freedom fighters under the leadership of Jonas Savimbi. UNITA was in constant conflict with the Angolan government troops, primarily under the Soviet and Cuban-run ANC (African National Congress) military umbrella. UNITA was covertly supported by South Africa with significant U.S. assistance. Such assistance predated the Reagan administration but took on new urgency after President Reagan took office.

In plain language, the Soviets, with unlimited Cuban military personnel, intended to consolidate absolute control of Angola, create a "peoples revolution" to drive South Africa out of Namibia, and ultimately spur an uprising in South Africa leading to a "war of national liberation." The Soviets knew that the only thing preventing them from virtual control of the African continent were the powerful South African Defense Forces. They also were totally confident that if a successful revolution took place in South Africa, the new president would not be Nelson Mandela. The new leader would be a Castro-type of their choosing. (The communists had already established strong footholds or control in the other surrounding countries.)

Obviously, it was in the interest of America and its free-world allies for the Botha government to survive in the face of the looming communist threat. It also would make it easier for Reagan and a few other Western leaders to continue their support of the Botha regime if he engaged in some significant reforms of apartheid. Our task was fairly simple. We endeavored in our regular meetings with the South African ambassador to the United States to stress the importance of some reforms as soon as possible and an indication that more would take place in the near term. On our trips to South Africa we offered the same advice to high-level government officials, and on a few occasions to P.W. Botha himself. Some meaningful reforms were enacted during our representation and other more dramatic reforms reached the planning stages.

The problem unfortunately was simple once again: The survival of the Botha government was not threatened by liberals on the left who wanted to do away with apartheid. Botha's ability to stay in power was under constant threat from the even more hard-line Afrikaners on the right who wanted to strengthen the apartheid laws. Botha faced periodic elections,[128] and if he did not stay in power he could do nothing.

Another benefit of our representation of South Africa was that we were able on occasion to bring back (very discretely and, obviously, with the consent of our client) to the proper American officials firsthand accounts of the situation on the ground in Angola, Namibia, and other countries in the region. (Sometimes it was more firsthand than I might have desired. I never really enjoyed the tree-top flights into remote parts or Angola and some other countries in the region.) On several occasions, I took congressmen and senators on trips to South Africa for personal inspection of the country and meetings with government officials. (An interesting fact of the time was that no government publically admitted to any involvement in Angola—not the Soviets, the Cubans, the South Africans, or the Americans. This ended up sparing me from a few unique but possibly frightening experiences. On a few occasions some of the congressmen and senators requested to visit Savimbi's UNITA headquarters or one of his camps. On the first such occasion, as we landed on an airstrip at the tip of South African territory to board another plane to fly to a Savimbi camp, I jumped out of the South African plane to accompany the MCs (members of Congress) to visit Savimbi. I was abruptly called back and told I could not accompany them. On the flight to a friendly native village on the South African border, they explained to me why I could not go with the MCs. Since I was employed by the South African government, if I got killed or captured it would be impossible for them to deny their involvement. I guess a similar fate by one or all of the MCs could just be speculated on by the press. In any event, I thoroughly enjoyed my two-hour-plus visit with this totally Christian tribe before we returned to pick up the MCs.)

To my point of responsible representation: After the 1984 reelection of President Reagan, Stu flew back to D.C. in order for the two of us to discuss our continuing representation of South Africa. It was his opinion that since the press knew of his close personal relationship with President Reagan, it might be a disservice to the government of South Africa for us to continue to represent them. The press would likely begin to speculate that President Reagan remained so firm in his support of the Botha government mainly due to our influence. While not true, such potential stories could be bad for us as well as for South Africa. We did terminate our representation, and no such story ever surfaced in the press until many years later.[129]

I believe our representation of South Africa was valuable to them and possibly to the future of that region of the world. President Botha managed to retain control of the South African government until the Cold War was coming to an end, and his successor was able to peacefully relinquish control of the government to the overwhelmingly black population. The man most revered by the native population, Nelson Mandela, was elected president. I came to form an opinion of the universally regarded hardnosed President Botha in two private meetings (the only ones I had without MCs present) that differs from most I have read. I am relatively sure that like many of our own most famous senators, congressmen, and other government leaders until fairly recent times, Botha believed that some type of racial segregation was ordained by God. But he was obviously a brilliant man and he knew that absolute white control of the overwhelmingly black population of South Africa was going to end at some point. It is my opinion that he hoped to prevent massive violence and allow the white indigenous population who had been there for generations to live in relative peace. I was further convinced that he, like the other whites who had lived there all their lives, loved his country and always wanted to call South Africa home. I have finally concluded that he accomplished that goal as well or better than any other person could have done.

Our decision to represent Panama was less complicated but was surrounded by some controversy. Panama was of great strategic importance to the United States because it controlled the canal that provided the timeliest (by thousands of sea miles) ship travel between the two great oceans.

When we were approached to represent Panama, the president was Eric Arturo Delvalle. Delvalle was a good man whose family heritage was that of one of the oldest and most respected Jewish families in Panamanian history. (His uncle had been the first Jewish president in Latin America.) The controversy was generated by the fact that General Manuel Noriega was the de facto military ruler of the country. Noriega was accused of using heavy-handed tactics to put down internal rebellions that threatened his control. Such accusations had gained international attention. (Rumors of harsh interrogations involving torture and assassinations abounded.)

Our two tasks were simple. One, our understood goal was to help strengthen Delvalle's government. President Delvalle took his job of running the government of Panama with the utmost seriousness. Two, our unstated goal was to establish a relationship with General Noriega and gain his trust. The ultimate goal was to convince him to turn over the responsibilities of the civil government to the president and concentrate on leading the Panamanian Defense Forces.[130]

We knew that no one in the Reagan administration would oppose our representing the government of Panama. But we wanted to make sure that we didn't get ourselves into a situation we would be better off avoiding. (This would happen anyway, as will be explained.)

There was only one person with whom we needed to visit in the administration: Bill Casey, director of the CIA. Casey, who had been the campaign manager for the Reagan presidential campaign, was our close friend. We quickly set up a meeting with the director. After brief pleasantries, I immediately summed up the purpose of our meeting.[131] I told Director Casey that we had been offered a contract to represent Panama. I further explained that we obviously had not come to him seeking any classified information or to seek any assurances of help from him. We just wanted to ask him as a friend if his inclination was that we could better spend our time in other endeavors. Without hesitation or any reservation, he allowed that he thought this would be a good opportunity for us. He probably thought that we might be of help to him in some way.[132]

We helped President Delvalle as we played a role in securing some much needed U.S. assistance.[133] We did our job so well in developing a relationship with and gaining the trust of the duplicitous General Noriega that it almost ended our careers for good. Noriega obviously studied Stu's and my background and knew all about us. He had some of his top assistants spend time with us before he invited us for drinks and dinner. He came to the accurate conclusion that we were sincere and had no ulterior motives. We simply wanted to play a role in strengthening the relationship between our country and a strategic ally. We hoped to respectfully influence him to let the elected civilian government run the government. Our hemisphere and the free world needed a stable Panama. Noriega needed to understand that the world was suspicious of military dictatorships. In any event, we were able to gain his confidence to the point that Stu and I were two of a handful of Americans ever to be invited to Noriega's hideaway located on a breathtaking spot on the ocean. (The security was incredible.) Then the unexpected happened without our knowledge.

During this period, there was a clandestine operation taking place that would become well known as the "Iran-Contra affair." This undertaking was so secretive that very few government officials at the highest levels knew about it. (Certainly we knew nothing about this undertaking. As it turned out, President Reagan also knew nothing about the second part of this operation now known as the "Nicaraguan-Contra" affair. CIA Director Casey had to know but he obviously could not tell us.) This entire operation (certainly the second part) was being run by a well-meaning, bright, but overly ambitious Marine colonel named Oliver North. North had been assigned to the National Security Council at the White House as deputy director of political-military.

The initial operation, which President Reagan had to have approved, involved selling guns to Iran in return for the release of American hostages. The second and even more secretive part of the operation, which even President Reagan did not know about, involved using the money from the sale of weapons to Iran to arm the contras in Nicaragua fighting the radical communist government in that country.[134]

The last trip Stu and I took to Panama was our longest and most enjoyable. We had a security detail to drive us around and "protect" us. This security detail was so large that it seemed to get into our way at times. We met with President Delvalle and many of his advisors every day—most often more than once a day. The only thing that was strange was that we never met with Noriega on any occasion during the trip. It was not until after the U.S. invaded Panama in 1989 to capture the drug smuggler who had consolidated control of the government that we learned the "rest of the story." Documents uncovered after the U.S. military took control read like a horror story. Colonel North had become so concerned about our developing a close relationship with Noriega, who was essential to his contra gunrunning operation, that he decided he better take action. He was afraid that Noriega would try to impress us by telling us about the role he was playing in the Nicaraguan contra operation. North did know enough about us that he was aware that Stu frequently visited with Reagan and on some occasions had a private dinner with Ron and Nancy. He was very concerned that Stu would mention this to Reagan and his operation would be shut down.

So Ollie North's solution to his dilemma was to tell Noriega that Stu and I were "double agents" and that he better not trust us. (This obviously infuriated a man of Noriega's temperament.) Translation: While those attentive security guys were driving us through areas of Panama City we had never seen before, they were waiting on orders from the boss to knock us off. Fortunately, Noriega ultimately decided on a less severe course of action. He told President Delvalle not to renew our contract, which was due to expire in a few months. (One of the purposes of our visit was to discuss contract renewal with President Delvalle.) It came with some surprise when we were notified a few weeks later that our services were no longer needed. This notification seemed odd at the time in view of the quality meetings we had just had with the president and his top people. But we had plenty to do, anyway. After the documents were analyzed, we learned from a friend, who had access to this material, "the rest of the story." It was never particularly funny to Stu and me to hear that for about a week we were "dead men walking." Politics is sometimes a contact sport!

But to the point: It is not a question of whether or not peaceful governments with which the United States has diplomatic relations deserve Washington representation. They do! Responsibility is on the backs of American lobbyists. They must always make sure they take no action that will in any way endanger their country and its citizens.

* * * * *

The Norquist Effect

Grover Norquist is a longtime powerful political figure in conservative and Republican circles. His interest and involvement in Muslim issues appears to have developed in the mid to late 1990s. His efforts during and after the 2000 election afforded American Muslims access to the highest levels of the Republican power structure and the government they established after that election. Norquist's actions have generated substantial scrutiny and much debate, which subsided only temporarily when the Democrats regained the White House in 2008.

More recently, this debate has centered on Norquist's persistent efforts to influence conservative foreign policy (with the help of many libertarians) and by extension to influence Republican foreign policy toward a dangerous form of isolationism. (Such efforts not only encourage the Islamic terrorists but strengthen the hand of American Muslim leaders who want to advance the cause of Islam in America by making this country more "*sharia* compliant.") These efforts by such non-mainstream players in the Republican Party as Congressman Ron Paul, who seems to treat Islamist terrorists no differently than any other enemy of America, are mostly ignored as an inevitable libertarian bump in the road. Such "bumps" had to be overcome throughout the history of the Goldwater-Reagan revolution. (Some of the more hard-core members of the John Birch Society and other extreme libertarians are the best examples of the challenges the leaders of this genuine Goldwater-Reagan conservative movement had to deal with.) But today's threat from a respected and even sometimes feared "movement conservative" such as Norquist (albeit one with libertarian tendencies) cannot be ignored.

This is probably a good time to offer a disclaimer about overly broad generalizations, which are a shorthand method of expression that frees the writer from lengthy and wordy explanations (and which I sometimes employ myself).

For example, those who espouse the basic tenets of libertarianism are no more a monolithic entity in their views than those of us who are committed to what I call classical or traditional conservatism. In each case, some of those who are devotees of each of these politically charged ideological schools are more extreme (or in some cases fanatical) in their views than people who might be described as more mainstream. Some authorities on libertarianism refer to the three legs of its ideological stool. Many followers cling to two legs of this stool and are ambivalent about the third leg or outright reject it. Almost all of those who consider themselves to be libertarians are devoted to its "fiscal" leg, which advocates limited government, lower taxes, and less spending. Most libertarians cling to what I call its "left leg," which stands for an isolationist or non-interventionist foreign policy. (This description is used since I believe the "left leg" has much more in common with the far left than the far right. It may simply mark the point in the ideological circle where the two extremes meet.) There is more disagreement in the movement about the third leg, which I have named the "religious leg," or more accurately, the "anti-religious leg," which has to do with the government's role—or lack thereof—in regulating moral behavior. (I will elaborate further on this in the section on the Cultural Wars. The Founding Fathers had much to say on this subject.) Libertarians, like conservatives, are clearly not a monolithic group!

In a similar fashion, Islamists and Islamist organizations, which range from radical terrorist groups such as Hamas and al-Qaeda to the more self-professed non-violent organizations such as CAIR and MSA, also are not monolithic in all their views. All of these groups, and most of those like them, grew out of the Muslim Brotherhood network and represent its dual identity from its founding.

Such Muslim organizations disagree as much or more than American political organizations over methods of operation and tactics and certainly cannot be identified as monolithic. However, these Muslim organizations and their followers are much more monolithic in their goals and objectives because they are solely based on what they believe to be the unchanging divine obligations placed on them by Allah and his prophet Mohammad. (Hassan al-Banna started the Muslim Brotherhood specifically to combat secularism by returning to "pure" Islam, by reestablishing the caliphate, and by establishing Muslim governments that would enforce strict *sharia* law until all people in the world lived under Allah's laws.)

I have no knowledge about Grover Norquist's religious beliefs and will leave speculation to others. Those who appear to question the depth of his patriotism are engaging in harsh and unworthy tactics in my opinion. Not that Norquist is any stranger to harsh tactics and accusations. When a politician, candidate, or elected official dares to disagree with Norquist's self-perceived infallibility on tax matters, he calls him or her everything but a gentleman or an educated female. Perhaps the only trait possessed by Norquist that overshadows his intellect is his arrogance. But my concern is the lack of judgment Norquist may have used in giving President Bush advice about which Muslim leaders to reach out to and which ones to avoid at a traumatic time in our history. Such advice may have been passed along personally by Norquist or through one of his surrogates.

Before describing some of the supposedly "moderate" Muslim leaders (who turned out to have connections with radical Islam) that Bush invited to the White House or appeared with in public, it is important to understand how Norquist's Muslim connections developed. In 1997, Grover Norquist founded a lobbying firm with David Safavian named the Merritt Group, which was renamed Janus Merritt Strategies and is sometimes known just as "Janus Merritt." In addition to such clients as BP America, the Saginaw Chippewa Indian tribe, and the National Indian Gaming Commission, they also represented some foreign clients such as the governments of Pakistan and Gabon. Norquist, out of conviction that I am sure was based on his background, had represented Jonas Savimbi's UNITA in Angola. Frank Gaffney says that Abdurrahman Alamoudi gave the firm $50,000 because of his interest in Muslim issues, such as the use of "secret information" (i.e., classified information) in deportation proceedings.[135] (The rise and fall of the Ethiopian-born Alamoudi, who currently is serving a 23-year sentence for his role in financing Muslim terrorist organizations and a plot to assassinate a Saudi prince, will be further discussed because of his prominence in the American political scene for more than a decade.)

In 1998, Norquist co-founded the Islamic Free Market Institute with Khaled Saffuri, a Palestinian who had grown up in exile in Kuwait before coming to the U.S. to attend college. Saffuri was working as a lobbyist and deputy director or the American Muslim Council (AMC), which had been founded by and was headed up by Abdurrahman Alamoudi before he joined Norquist in founding the Islamic

Free Market Institute. Norquist's bright young Muslim "conservative star," Suhail Khan, was named to the Institute's board of directors. Another co-founder of the Institute was an old Muslim friend of George W. Bush from his oil days in Texas named Talat Othman. Othman was a Palestinian-American who emigrated to this country with his family in 1947, when he was 11 years old. He and the younger Bush had served together on the board of Harken Energy.

Samah Alrayyes, a Muslim described in Wikipedia as "a Kuwaiti PR specialist,"[136] was a director of the Institute before she became a specialist for Muslim countries at the Bureau of Legislative and Public Affairs at USAID. Samah and Grover were married in 2005. The Islamic Institute, the name it became known by, was initially partially underwritten by the prominent politically connected Muslim Alamoudi. Many observers began to refer to the Islamic Institute, which shared space in the Americans for Tax Reform offices, as the "nerve center for Muslim lobbying."

At some point, Norquist and Saffuri had agreed to represent the country of Qatar. In his previously quoted Nov. 11, 2001, *New Republic* article, Franklin Foer questions the Muslim organizations represented in meetings with President Bush and makes this point:

> "And Norquist hasn't only developed ties to American groups that apologize for terror. He has also flacked for at least one Middle Eastern autocracy: Qatar. Eager to improve relations with the United States, Qatar worked with Norquist and Saffuri to help portray itself as a liberal outpost in the Islamic world. In April, Saffuri sponsored the 'First Annual Conference on Free Trade and Democracy' in the Qatari capital of Doha, for which the Islamic Institute received over $150.000 in payments from the Qatar Embassy's Ministry of Foreign Affairs Account. (Saffuri says these were reimbursements for the travel expenses of congressional delegates.) A lobbyist at Norquist's firm, Janus-Merritt, had solicited pro-Qatari op-eds from at least one conservative pundit. When the emir of Qatar came to Washington, Saffuri hosted a Capitol Hill luncheon in his honor. And just three weeks after September 11, Norquist wrote an op-ed in The Washington Times in which he claimed that 'Qatar has taken great strides to enshrine values of universal suffrage, a free press, and human rights.' He continued, 'She really means it on being a reliable ally.'
>
> "... Two days after Norquist's op-ed, The Washington Post reported Qatar refusal to support a widening of the war on terrorism to include Islamic Jihad, Hamas, or Hezbollah. And, just two weeks later, the foreign minister of Qatar—our 'reliable ally'—announced that '[t]he] attacks against Afghanistan are unacceptable and we have condemned them. It is our clear position.'"[137]

It doesn't strike me as unusual that the eccentric but politically astute Norquist would target Muslims as Republican voter opportunities, just as he had Hispanics and Indian Americans. (Norquist serves on the boards of the Hispanic Leadership Fund and the Indian-American Republican Caucus.)

In 1997, according to Paul Sperry, while Governor Bush was pondering whether or not to become a candidate for president in 2000, Norquist traveled to Texas to meet with Karl Rove. Norquist had no trouble convincing the Republican political guru—or "boy wonder," as Bush frequently called him—of the value of a major Muslim outreach program for the presidential race. *The initial decision that came out of this meeting may well have ended up changing American history*, as Sperry documents in Chapter 27 of *Infiltration,* which is titled "Undue Influence At The White House." At the least, his use of post-election polling data makes a compelling case for how this outreach decided the election.

When Norquist co-founded the Islamic Free Market Institute, or "Islamic Institute," he intended for this non-profit organization eventually to serve as the Muslim outreach arm of the Bush campaign. Norquist had recruited many of the top Muslim leaders in America's political world to become personally and professionally involved in the Institute. Their lobbying focus was on issues most important to the majority of American Muslims. (There are some lobbying restrictions on non-profit organizations, but Norquist still had his Janus-Merritt Strategies lobbying firm, which certainly was very profitable.) All they had to do was to secure Bush's support for these issues of burning importance to Muslims and they could deliver the overwhelming majority of the Muslim vote. The major issues were clear and emotional: The use of "secret evidence" in deportation cases and racial profiling at airports. (Khan's former boss, Republican Congressman Tom Campbell of California, was a co-sponsor of a bill called "the Secret Evidence Repeal Act"; Sen. Spencer Abraham of Michigan, a close friend of Saffuri, sponsored the same bill in the Senate.)

Reportedly, Norquist, in his conversation with Rove, used the Council on American-Islamic Relations' greatly exaggerated estimate of the number of Muslims living in America. CAIR estimated the Muslim population in America to be about 6 million, a number that is coincidently a little larger than the size of the Jewish population. (It is highly doubtful that the growing Muslim population in America is even close to the 6 million claimed by CAIR and other Muslim organizations. Even they admit that their number is based mostly on anecdotal evidence. CAIR said it counted the number of American mosques and multiplied by an average attendance.) Perhaps the most accurate estimate of the Muslim population is just under 2.5 million, according to the most recent poll taken by the Pew Foundation. Others estimate the number at between 1.5 million and 4.1 million. Still, any of these numbers suggest a lot of potential voters.

Since the Jewish vote usually goes overwhelmingly for Democrats, the Muslim vote could be a counterbalance. Norquist would make the point, which

Rove probably already knew, that American Muslims, like Hispanics, are social conservatives and should be inclined toward the Republican philosophy. In addition, American Muslims were better off financially than most other groups of Americans and should be drawn to the Republicans' support for a free-market economy. They could be decisive in a state with a large Muslim population, such as Michigan, though that did not turn out to be the case.

But then there was Florida.

The majority of Muslims are very moral, socially conservative people who appreciate the opportunity to compete in a market-driven economy—very compatible with Republican principles. But as the 2000 election was unfolding, they had other issues on their minds. The use of "secret evidence" (classified material) in deportation cases and racial profiling at airports would drive their political decisions. Rove and Norquist agreed, and they convinced Bush.

Saffuri arranged for candidate Bush to meet with Alamoudi and ask for his support. On a campaign trip to Tampa, Saffuri made sure that Bush met with al-Arian and pose for a picture with him and his family.[138] (Both Alamoudi and al-Arian have served time in prison—Alamoudi is still serving a long sentence—on charges of aiding terrorists.) Bush condemned the use of secret evidence and racial profiling at airports in campaign speeches and even asked his old pal Talat Othman to give a prayer at the Republican National Convention—the first time a Muslim ever offered a prayer at the national convention of either party. The effort to drive up the Muslim turnout and increase the Republican percentage of that vote worked. Arguably, the Muslim vote tipped the presidential election for George W. Bush.

Sperry offers a convincing case that the Muslim vote in Florida made the difference in who won Florida and therefore determined who would be the next president of the United States. The Bush campaign strategy turned out to be brilliant! Sperry writes in *Infiltration*:

> "Al-Arian was credited with delivering the Muslim vote for Bush in Florida, which in effect provided him the margin of victory in that hotly contested race. A great many of the Muslims in Florida cast ballots for the first time; and all told, Muslims favored Bush over Gore by twenty to one. 'The margin of victory for Bush over Gore in the Muslim vote was 46,200—many times greater than his statewide margin of victory,' Norquist noted after the election. 'The Muslim vote won Florida for Bush,' and thus the national election."[139]

Norquist is certainly correct that had Muslims in Florida voted as they had in past elections (with a Democrat preference) and all other groups also voted the same as they had, then Gore would have won Florida and been sworn in as the 43rd president of the United States. Some political analysts might argue that without the Muslim outreach in Florida (especially with al-Arian, who was suspected of harboring Islamic terrorist sympathies), some other groups might have voted more heavily for Bush. But such an argument would not hold much water since probably few non-Muslim Floridians even knew al-Arian was involved.

Anyone who has been involved in political elections or follows elections closely understands that the candidate and those running his campaign must get the candidate to the brink before a small group can push them over the finish line. Evidence from the polling data indicates that is exactly what happened in this case. I believe I can fairly characterize Sperry's conclusion by saying that he would concede that the Muslim outreach strategy was brilliant but that the price paid for this Muslim support was excessive and dangerous in the face of the Islamist threat.

(I cannot believe that Sperry or any of Bush's other conservative critics would argue, though, that the country would be safer had Al Gore been elected president. Since my office is across the street from the Democrat Club, I frequently walk past it—and stop in some time—on my way to one of the House office buildings or the Capitol Hill Club. In the initial months after the recount and the Supreme Court decision declaring Bush the winner, I would hear snide remarks from some of my Democrat friends, including Democrat members of Congress, about how we stole the election. There was some genuine bitterness evident in their remarks. In stark contrast, making this same trip in the months after the 9/11 attacks, most of these same Democrat friends walked up close enough to me not to be overheard and whispered something like "Thank God George Bush is president!")

Sperry explains in his book how Norquist was able to use this Muslim support in the election to "infiltrate" the top tier of our government (including the White House) with his Muslim cronies. Sperry specifically notes that "Norquist's group managed to place one of its staffers, Suhail Khan, inside the White House as the official gatekeeper for Muslims." He further explains, "Once Khan was inside the gates of the White House, he and Norquist put together a blanket list of no less than eighty-three Muslim activists whom they wanted Rove to invite to White House outreach events. The list, submitted in 2001 to the Secret Service for security clearance, reads like a who's who of hard-line Islamists and Wahhabists, some of whom are known terrorist sympathizers and supporters under federal investigation, such as Jamal Barzinji of the Safa group. Norquist's name tops the list, a copy of which I have obtained."[140]

Like him or not, it would be difficult for anyone to deny that Paul Sperry is a top-notch investigative journalist. In the footnote for the above quote, Sperry mentions that David Hossein Safavian, another associate in Norquist's lobbying firm, was Number 79 on the list. Safavian would also land a job at the White House. Khaled Saffuri, who had been named as the official point man for Muslim outreach in the Bush campaign by Karl Rove, obviously had carte blanch access to the White House. Without a doubt, Norquist and his Muslim White House insiders greatly influenced the selection of, or even hand picked, the Muslim leaders Bush would invite to the White House or appear with in public after 9/11.

Unfortunately, this would lead to the selection of Muslim leaders who represented organizations that were at least tolerant of certain types of terrorism, such as that practiced by Hamas and Hezbollah. In addition, virtually all of them were committed to the Muslim Brotherhood's goals of moving America in an Islamic direction by making it a more *"sharia* compliant" society.

Norquist's *philosophy of government* has been consistently libertarian throughout his career, based on all the information I have found. He shares with conservatives a belief in limited government, low taxes, and a fear of European socialism and the threat of a cradle to grave welfare state. But he may take his philosophy to extremes that conflict with the more practical approach of traditional conservatism. As William F. Buckley noted in his mature years, there is often a fine line between libertarianism and anarchy. Buckley also pointed out that "conservatism has a certain affinity for reality." Though there should be limits, there are certain things that government must provide for its citizens, especially in a country with a population of more than 300 million people and a world so interconnected.

Grover Norquist is best known for founding—at President Reagan's request in 1985—and running Americans for Tax Reform, an organization that states it is against all tax increases. This would make sense for an organization with a basically libertarian that really doesn't believe in government.

Norquist even more strongly sides with libertarianism (and the far left) against conservatism in the area of *moral and traditional values.* Libertarianism insists that government can limit individual liberties only to prevent an individual from physically harming another person. (Talk about ignoring the Founding Fathers, who almost to a man insisted, in John Adams' words, that our form of government is suited only "for a moral and religious people.") One notable example is that Norquist is a member of GOPride and strongly supports allowing gays to serve in the military. If Norquist harbors any Islamic tendencies, they certainly are not reflected in this position.

Norquist's *current isolationist foreign policy position* is totally consistent with libertarians as well as the hard left and the overwhelming majority of American Muslim leaders. Former senator and Republican presidential candidate Rick Santorum recently explained what an isolationist foreign policy would mean. In discussing libertarian and fellow candidate Ron Paul's position on foreign policy, Santorum eloquently explained the dangers of such a position. He said that Paul wants to build a wall around America and pull out of world affairs. If the most powerful country in the world exited the world stage, Santorum explained, this would create a vacuum that others would try to fill. Obviously, this would be an opening that the Islamic jihadists would strive to enter. Communist China, who has undertaken an ambitious program to further build its military might, could take the opportunity to spread its influence. I would add that Russia has starting making some noise about reasserting itself in world affairs. In any event, Norquist has "announced his plan to assemble a center-right coalition to discuss pulling out of Afghanistan to save hundreds of billions of dollars."[141] If such a premature effort were to be successful, the brutal Taliban would rejoice for the opportunity to start training Islamist terrorists again without interference. Also they could expand their inhuman treatment of women under *sharia* law without opposition.

Suhail Khan: Norquist's Right-Hand Man

We should evaluate some of the men who may have influenced President Bush's choices of Muslim leaders to be invited to the post-9/11 events and then look at the backgrounds of some of those who were invited.

The most obvious and perhaps the most important, at least in the long term, is *Suhail Khan*, who was a White House staffer at the time of the 9/11 attacks and is still very active in Republican and conservative groups—much to the chagrin of many leading conservatives, I might add! When asked at the 2011 CPAC (Conservative Political Action Committee) convention about the Muslim Brotherhood, Khan answered point blank, "There is no Muslim Brotherhood in the United States."[142] This answer was greeted with shock and disbelief by many in the audience. Suhail Khan's family has had close relations with the Muslim Brotherhood since it founded its first front in America in 1963.

Suhail Khan was born of southern Indian Muslim immigrants in Boulder, Colo., and grew up in California. He received a B.A. in political science from the University of California and a J.D. in 1995 from the University of Iowa. He began his political career as the policy director and press secretary for Congressman Tom Campbell, a liberal Republican from California who had become a champion of Muslim causes. While serving in that position, Khan caught the eye of Grover Norquist, who invited him to join him at the Islamic Institute. After Campbell gave up his House seat for an unsuccessful run for the U.S. Senate in 1998, Khan joined Norquist at the Institute. Shortly thereafter he would become actively involved in the 2000 Bush presidential campaign, primarily working in Muslim and Asian outreach programs.

After George W. Bush was elected president, Khan landed a job, with Norquist's assistance, in the Bush White House Office of Public Liaison. In this role, he was involved heavily in outreach to the Asian-American community. He would logically be considered somewhat of an expert on Islam (and at least knowledgeable about Islamist terrorism) since he was a lifelong Muslim from a very active Muslim family. Khan had been honored by such Muslim organizations as Alamoudi's American Muslim Council (AMC) and the Islamic Society of North America (ISNA), which he addressed on more than one occasion. After the Islamist terrorist attacks of 9/11 and the subsequent uproar over some of the Muslim leaders to whom President Bush reached out, Khan was rapidly transferred to the Department of Transportation.

Suhail Khan serves on the Board of Directors of the American Conservative Union and the Indian American Republican Council and is the "Senior Fellow for Christian-Muslim Understanding" at the Institute for Global Engagement (IGE), a very liberal "Christian" organization that espouses a politically correct view of Islam. One prominent member of its Board of Directors is Georgetown professor John Esposito, who heads an institute at Georgetown University that is intended to promote understanding of Islam and is liberally funded by a Saudi prince. Imam Feisal Abdul Rauf, the mastermind behind building the "Ground Zero" mosque and Islamic center, is another member of the IGE Board of Directors.

Mahboob Khan, Suhail Khan's father, was a founder and the first vice president of the Muslim Student Association (MSA). The MSA was established in 1963 as the first global Muslim Brotherhood front in America. Mahboob Khan was also involved in the founding of three *sharia*-adherent mosques in California. One of the three, the Islamic Society of Orange County, hosted a fundraiser held by Sheikh Omar Abdel Rahman (better known as "the blind Sheikh") in December 1992. Just two months later, "the blind Sheikh" was identified as the mastermind of the first attack on the World Trade Center.

In *Penetrating the White House*, Sperry describes Suhail's father in these words:

> "It turns out his late father is one Mahboob Khan, the legendary leader of a San Francisco-area mosque that raised thousands of dollars for Osama bin Laden's second in command—not once but twice—in the 1990s. Dr. Ayman al-Zawahiri bought satellite phones with the funds. The large Wahhabi mosque also routinely raised money for the Holy Land Foundation, a large Dallas-based charity which is under federal indictment [five of its organizers were convicted in 2008] for funding Hamas suicide bombers and their families. Guest speakers at the elder Kahn's mosque, known as the Muslim Community Association, have included the head of Pakistan's militant Islamic Party, who has praised Chechen and Palestinian terrorists.

> "In fact, Suhail Khan's father left quite a legacy of extremism before his death in 1999. Among other things, he was:
> - "one of the founding members of the Saudi-backed Muslim Student Association and Islamic Society of North America, major players in the Wahhabi lobby;
> - "founder of Santa Clara, California-based American Muslims for Global Peace and Justice, whose chairman defended the Taliban even after 9/11;
> - "co-founder of the Wahhabi mosque in Orange County, which converted al-Qaeda suspect Adam Gadahn, whose face is now plastered on FBI wanted posters the world over."[143]

Of Suhail Khan's mother, Frank Gaffney writes, "It is instructive that Suhail's mother, Malika Khan, is also active with a prominent Muslim Brotherhood front. She still serves on the board of directors of the California chapter of the Council on America Islamic Relations, an organization the federal government has tied to Hamas and that was an unindicted co-conspirator in the trial of the Holy Land Foundation conspiracy."[144]

As the oldest child in a devout *sharia*-practicing Muslim family, Suhail Khan would never have been shielded from the beliefs of his parents. As a matter of fact, the first son of such an active Muslim father would be expected to carry on the religious traditions of the family. It would be grossly unfair even to suggest that Suhail's father would have supported or in any way condoned Islamic terrorist acts in the United States. It would be equally naïve to suggest that a man actively involved in Muslim Brotherhood fronts since his college days would not endeavor to pursue Muslim Brotherhood goals in America through non-violent means. The question of support for Hamas or Hezbollah is a sticker question. Members of these organizations do not define violent acts to "defend" occupied Muslim countries (i.e., Palestine and Lebanon) as terrorism.

(I must at least note at this point that when some critics raise questions about Suhail Khan's background, he tends to accuse the critics practicing "guilt by association" rather than address the concerns that are raised. And parents are sometimes closely associated with their children!)

Suhail Khan seemed to express his own personal opinion at the Islamic Society of North America (ISNA) convention in 1999:

> "This is our determination. This is the fierce determination we must resolve to bear in every facet of our lives. This is the mark of the Muslim. The earliest defenders of Islam would defeat their more numerous and better equipped oppressors, because the early Muslims loved death, dying for the sake of almighty Allah more than the oppressors of Muslims loved life. This must be the case where we— when we are fighting life's other battles...."[145]

The major concern is that Suhail Khan's connections with various conservative organizations, other conservatives, and especially key Republican staffers—facilitated by his being perceived as Grover Norquist's best friend—put him in a position to exercise major influence. An article posted on *FrontPageMag.com* by Paul Sperry notes:

> "Mr. Khan is now a spokesman for the Congressional Muslim Staff Association, working with a Muslim convert named Jihad Saleh Williams (of all Arabic names he could have picked, he chose Jihad). Mr. Khan spends a lot of time on the Hill. He's briefed GOP leadership staff on various issues and has now cozied up to some of

House Speaker John Boehner's people. He's even gained the trust of key staffers running the Republican Study Committee, the caucus for conservatives in the House."[146]

The organizations founded by or affiliated with the Muslim Brotherhood are relentless in their efforts to influence or threaten American politicians. During the 2008 presidential campaign, Muneer Fareed, then secretary general of the Islamic Society of North America (ISNA), demanded that Sen. John McCain, the Republican presidential nominee, stop using the word "Islamic" when he spoke of the terrorist threats to America. Fareed, speaking on the behalf of a coalition of American Muslim groups, said that the use of the adjective "Islamic" when describing "terrorists and extremist enemies of the United States" is offensive to the Muslim community. He suggested that McCain just call them criminals "because that is what they are."[147] Fortunately, the McCain campaign responded in the article that "the reality is, the hateful ideology which underpins bin Ladenism is properly described as radical Islamic extremism. Senator McCain refers to it that way because that is what it is."

Fareed is an Islamic scholar and one would have to assume that he had carefully read the statements by bin Laden and al-Zawahiri expressing their own ideology or speaking on behalf of al-Qaeda. Bin Laden, al-Zawahiri, and their associates always quoted the Koran, the actions and teachings of Mohammad, and Islamic history to justify their holy war and its terrorist actions. What these "moderate" Muslim leaders should be doing is denouncing al-Qaeda and other Islamic terrorist organizations that are promoting *jihad* and terrorist activity as the real embarrassment to what they believe to be true Islam.[148] They should also be condemning the teachings of the radical fundamentalist strain of Wahhabi Islam in the madrassas from Saudi Arabia and Pakistan, throughout Europe, and even in California and Virginia. We have mentioned a few truly moderate Muslim scholars who have tried to condemn radical Islamic teachings and actions. It is informative to see the kind of treatment these brave souls received from their peers.

For a more in-depth understanding of the activities of al-Qaeda and other Islamic terrorist organization in the United States, read Steven Emerson's *American Jihad: The Terrorists Living Among Us* (Free Press, 2003). This relatively short book is an easy read and is very informative.

For liberal journalists or moderate Muslims to try to deny or cover up the absolute religious motivation of these Islamic terrorists is not only counterproductive but dangerous. It certainly does not promote better relations between Muslims and Christians or between Muslims and non-Muslims in general. If mainline Muslims are saying that the fundamentalist followers of the late Osama bin Laden are distorting the true teachings of Islam, they are to be commended and supported. This is the source of true dialogue which can be very productive. It is dishonest to deny that members of al-Qaeda and other Islamic terrorist organizations believe that they are following the true teachings of Allah as revealed through Mohammad. They may be totally wrong in their beliefs about these teachings, but they are certainly among the world's most dedicated believers.

The Sunni-Shiite Violent Split

Islam's most divisive and violent division has endured through the ages and plays a major role in the terrorist war being waged by Islamic radicals today.[149]

The Muslim Prophet Muhammad died in 633 without designating a successor (caliph) to lead Islam. Many in the early Muslim community believed that Ali, a cousin whom Muhammad had raised from a small child and who later married one of Muhammad's daughters, should be named caliph. But a majority in the community decided that Abu Bakr, Muhammad's closest confident and father-in-law, should assume the mantle of the Prophet.

To prevent a similar dispute after his own death, Abu Bakr designated Umar, a member of the Quraysh, the old aristocratic clan of Mecca, to succeed him. After a 10 year reign, Umar was murdered, and Uthman of the Umayyad clan within the Quraysh was named the third caliph. Scattered groups of Muslims were so upset of Ali's being passed over yet again that they started referring to themselves as *Shia Ali*, followers of Ali. Uthman ruled for 12 years when supporters of Ali became so distraught they literally hacked Uthman to death. After a period of anarchy following the murder, Ali finally emerged as the fourth caliph.

But another period of bitter struggle ensued as Muhammad's favorite wife, Aisha, was so determined to return the caliphate to the Quraysh aristocracy that she raised an army, which Ali was forced to defeat in the "Battle of the Camel." The turmoil in Islam among the Sunnis, the Shiites, and an even smaller egalitarian group, the Kharijites, raged unabated during the fewer than five years of Ali's reign as caliph. The struggle became so heated that Ali was murdered by an irate Kharijite. He was buried in Najaf, which along with Karbala—both are in Iraq—is one of the two holiest sites for Shiites. (It was in this holy Shiite city, Najaf, a center of Shiite study of theology, that Ayatollah Khomeini would spend 13 years after being exiled from Iran by the Shah in 1964.)

Ali's murder would lead to another stormy period in Islam's early history. It came to a head when Ali's second son, Hussein (or Husayn), took up the cause in 680 of restoring the caliphate to the Prophet's blood relatives. His attempt was to fail, but it ended up firmly establishing Shia Islam as a major sect in the Muslim religion.

Preferring death to compromise, Husayn led his 72 followers, including women and children, in a suicide mission against the powerful Umayyad army. They were slaughtered in the Battle of Karbala. In *The Shia Revival*, Vali Nasr explains that this tiny band fought heroically for six days against a Syrian army of thousands until all but two were killed and beheaded. The survivors were Zaynab, Husayn's sister, and Husayn's son, Ali. The sister accompanied her brother's head to Damascus and successfully pleaded for the life of Ali. This heroic act on her part would save the only remaining male member of the family, ensuring the continuity of Shiism, as Ali would become the fourth Shia imam.[150]

The battle of Karbala transformed the Shia Ali from a group of scattered devotees to a separate sect in Islam obsessed with martyrdom. They proceeded to establish the imamate. Shiism teaches that there were to be 12 legitimate imams, starting with Ali, his sons Hasan and Husayn. According to their tradition, the 12th imam, known as the "Hidden Imam," was hidden away as a young boy to protect his life and still exists in some type of occult state. They further believe that he is the *Mahdi*, or messiah, and will return to usher in the age of perfect justice and ultimate judgment. Nasr explains:

> "The Shia believe that God hid the Twelfth Imam from physical access in order to preserve his life. The return of this Mahdi or Hidden Imam will herald the end of time and the advent of perfect divine justice—a messianic view very similar to those among Jews and Christians. During his occultation, the Twelfth Imam is the unseen Lord of the Age (imam al-zaman), the permanent imam until the Day of Judgment. With his 'second coming' there will be a reign of justice until the return of Jesus, at which time the world will end. The events surrounding the return of the Twelfth Imam closely parallel Judeo-Christian prophecies about the end of time and the Battle of Armageddon. Historians have suggested that Shia messianism bears traces of Zoroastrian and Judeo-Christian influence, though Shias believe that their messianic doctrine was mandated by God and any similarity it may have to that of other religions is proof of its validity, reflecting the divine plan for humanity."[151]

Sunnis totally reject this Shiite teaching, and the battle over choosing Muhammad's temporal successor caused a major rift in Islam that continues to this day.

Kenneth Pollack notes that the Shia Ali rejected "the reigning system of choosing leadership by consensus" and believed "that the caliph must come out of the Prophet's house, for it was only Muhammad's descendants who possessed the knowledge and wisdom of the Prophet. In contradiction, those who became known as Sunnis believed that any man within the Meccan aristocracy could assume the leadership of Islam through the process of consensus among Muhammad's early converts."[152]

Pollack explains further:

> "The concept of the imamate is important because it contributes to another key difference between Sunni and Shi'ah. In its simplest form, the Sunni faith maintains that God has given mankind everything we need to live our lives properly in the form of the Quran

and the sayings and histories of the Prophet, the proper interpretations of which were finalized in the ninth and tenth centuries. Shi'ahs believe that the imams were themselves divinely guided, and so it fell to them to lead the community in righteous fashion, which they did by definition. The loss of the twelfth imam consequently posed a problem for the Shi'ah: Who was going to lead them? This problem led eventually to a reliance upon men called mujtahids—those capable of practicing ijtihad (the ability to interpret the holy scriptures). These were religious leaders responsible for guiding the community in the absence of the imam."[153]

Nasr makes a comparison between differing beliefs within Christianity and Islam that might help the Western mind understand the behavior patterns of the radical Shiites in Iran, Iraq, Lebanon, and other countries where they have a significant presence. He describes what he believes to be a similar approach of orthodox Sunnis and "low church Protestants" to religious authority and access to God. The majority Sunnis believe that Muhammad was Allah's prophet and that his teachings, especially in the Koran, provide them with all the knowledge of and access to God that they need. The word "*Sunni*" is short for the Arabic phrase that means "people of tradition and consensus." The Prophet's successor "was succeeding only to his role as leader of the Islamic community and not to his special relationship with God or prophetic calling." They could select Abu Bakr and his successors by majority consensus of the Muslim community. Similarly, Protestant Christians teach that Jesus is their Savior, that He left them all the teaching they need in the Bible, and "that all believers are capable of understanding religious truth in a way and to a degree that tenders special intermediaries between man and God unnecessary."[154]

Shiites, on the other hand, believe that Muhammad chose Ali to be his successor. Nasr writes:

> "Shias believe that the Prophet possessed special spiritual qualities, was immaculate from sin ... and could penetrate to the hidden meaning of religious teachings. Shias further believe that Ali and his descendants had these special spiritual qualities too. They bore the light of Muhammad. They were his 'trustees' and were privy to his esoteric and religious knowledge. They could understand and interpret the inner meaning of Islam, as opposed to merely implementing its outward manifestations."[155]

Nasr explains, "The early sufferings of the Shia shaped their approach to religion. They revered their imams as specially blessed by God and immaculate from sin. They also included in this group Muhammad and his daughter, Fatima and refer to them as 'Fourteen Immaculate from Sin' (Sahara ma'sum)."[156] This he compares to the Catholic hierarchy and the need for a priest to intercede for the people.

Obviously, one cannot equate Christian and Islamic beliefs, but devout Catholics do believe that the Pope is infallible in matters of faith. Fundamentalist Shiites blindly follow the teachings of the imams and the representative of the 12th Imam in all matters of faith and conduct. This helps to understand their willingness to murder and suffer martyrdom when told to do so by the recognized religious authorities.

Nasr states his belief that the Shiite festival of Ashoura, which commemorates the battle of Karbala and the slaying of Husayn, has many similarities to the Christian observance of Holy Week and the passion of Christ. The ceremonies of Ashoura over the years have involved major pilgrimages of millions of Shiites who weep, mutilate themselves, pray over and over, and cry out for revenge for the death of Husayn. This has led to a cult of martyrdom that in recent times has spread from Iran to Lebanon and throughout the Middle East and manifests itself in "suicide bombers" and other "martyrdom missions." The human bombers so prevalent in Iraq and other parts of the world are "a predominantly Shia phenomenon, tied to the myths of Karbala and the Twelfth Imam."[157] (In recent years, however, al-Qaeda, a Sunni organization, has adopted similar tactics in Iraq, Pakistan, Afghanistan, and elsewhere.)

Twelver Shiism, the predominant branch of the sect, believes that the Twelve Imams were infallible. In the 19th century, they added the most authoritative religious title in Shiism, *marja-e-taqlid,* the deputy of the 12th Imam until his return from his occult state. Shiites have a fairly well developed religious hierarchy. The top of the order is ayatollah ("sign of God") and grand ayatollah ("greatest sign of God"). This helps to explain Ayatollah Khomeini's unchallenged authority in the minds of the faithful after the revolution in 1979. Nasr writes:

> "After Khomeini assumed power, his titles became loftier still. He was referred to as Na'eb Imam (Deputy to the Twelfth Imam). On one occasion a parliamentary deputy asked him if he was the 'promised Mahdi.' Khomeini did not answer. Fearing that Khomeini had not heard, the MP repeated the question. Khomeini still did answer, astutely neither claiming nor denying that he was the Twelfth Imam."[158]

Khomeini's vindictiveness and brutality was justified, they would believe, because his cause in creating a pure Islamic theocracy was part of their history. However, the element in this system that would pose the greatest threat to the civilized world was the fanaticism it bred, and the preoccupation with martyrdom.

Stephen Kinzer writes in *All the Shah's Men* that in a Shiite world shaped by Zoroastrian tradition, Ali and Hussein became their heroes. He continues:

"They are believed to have sacrificed themselves, as the truly pious must, on the altar of evil. By doing so, they embraced a pattern that still shapes Iran's consciousness. They bequeathed to Shiites a legacy of religious zeal, a willingness and even an eagerness to embrace martyrdom at the hands of Allah's enemies. Ali remains the most perfect soul and the most enlightened leader who ever lived, excepting only the Prophet himself; Shiites pore over his speeches and memorize his thousands of proverbs and aphorisms. Hussein epitomizes the self-sacrifice that is the inevitable fate of all who truly love Islam and humanity. His martyrdom is considered even more significant than that of Ali because it was inflicted by government soldiers rather than by a lone fanatic. Grasping the depth of this passion is essential to any understanding of modern Iran."[159]

This belief would reach its first peak in Iranian history when Ismail established the Safavid dynasty in 1501. His first act after assuming the throne was to declare Shiism the official state religion. As Kinzer describes him, "The Savid leader, Ismail was a militant Shiite who sent his warriors into battle crying: 'We are Hussein's men, and this is our epoch! In devotion we are slaves of the Imam! Our name is Zealot and our title is Martyr!'"[160]

This type of religious fanaticism would reach its pinnacle with Khomeini six centuries later. Iran's president today, Mahmoud Ahmadinejad, is a fundamentalist Twelver Shiite. How frightening it is even to conceive of him having nuclear weapons when he might consider hastening the return of the "hidden Imam," or *Mahdi*.

The Fall of Iran: America's Most Costly Foreign Policy Mistake[161]

Muhammad Reza Shah, the second of the Pahlavi dynasty, ascended to the monarchy in 1941. Reza Shah, the Shah's father, had ruled Iran since 1925. A strong and decisive ruler who is often given credit for creating the modern state of Iran, Reza Shah was forced to abdicate the throne to his son when the Allies occupied Iran in 1941. Although he had tried to stay neutral in World War II, he was suspected of having Nazi sympathies because of his admiration for Hitler's strong rule in Germany and because he had a strong dislike for the communist government in neighboring Russia.

When it became obvious that the Allies were going to occupy Iran, Reza Shah voluntarily abdicated because, as he explained to his son, he "couldn't take orders from an English captain."

During the Allied occupation, from 1941 to 1946, the Shah did what he was told. The three Allied powers had agreed to leave Iran six months after the war ended, but when the time came for departure, Stalin balked. Iran's first political party, Tudeh (Masses), which was started in 1942, initially included communists among other groups, but by 1944, the Marxists had taken control. This proved to be a very tempting target for Stalin, and he refused to withdraw his troops.

The Shah appealed to the United States to help liberate his country. The U.S. responded affirmatively, with the request that Iran serve as a buffer against Soviet expansionism in the region. After a confrontation between Truman and Stalin, Stalin backed down in what many historians consider the first crisis of what would become known as the Cold War. Thus began a productive, fruitful, and sometimes rocky relationship with Iran and her Shah that would last for more than 30 years. Mistakes were made by all the parties involved, but the Shah's rule managed to keep the Soviets out of Arabic territories and radical Shiite leaders at bay until 1979.

Shortly after an assassination attempt on the Shah in 1949, his popularity hit a high point. The Shah used this new-found popularity to urge the Majlis, the Iranian parliament, to make some significant changes in the way the government was run. The one that would have a lasting effect was the way in which the prime minister was chosen. Under the old system, the Majlis selected a prime minister and the Shah was to confirm or reject their choice. Under a change proposed by the Shah and approved by the Majlis, the Shah now would propose a candidate and the Majlis would confirm.

A long list of weak prime ministers had posed no significant threat to the power of the throne until the charismatic and very popular Dr. Mohammad Mosaddegh accepted the position in 1951. This would lead to a crisis that in turn resulted in a successful CIA-sponsored coup in 1953, which became one of the defining points in the long history of Iran.

Although probably not unusual for the time in history, a 100-year period of British colonial influence in Iran had ravaged the country's resources and ignored the needs of the Iranian people. After discovering oil in 1908, the Anglo-Persian Oil Company was established and an Anglo-Persian Agreement was signed that was overwhelmingly favorable to the British. The working conditions were terrible, the Iranian workers lived in squalid quarters, and Iran received only a pittance from the profits.

The conditions of the agreement were modified in 1933 under Reza Shah, and the company name was changed at his insistence to the Anglo-Iranian Oil Co. Only minor improvement was made, however, and the issue exploded again in 1949 when the Shah was unable to get the Majlis to approve a Supplemental Agreement. The issue came to a head in 1951 when the Shah was forced to appoint Mossadegh as prime minister due to the overwhelming popularity of his nationalist movement and the insistent demands of demonstrators. Everything reached the boiling point when the newly elected prime minister had the Majlis vote to nationalize the oil company.

The Anglo-Iranian Oil Company was by far the major financial profit center in the entire British colonial empire, and the British had consistently refused all efforts to compromise. The situation became so severe that President Truman was told in a meeting of the National Security Council that the AIOC, which had been the world's fourth-largest oil exporter and supplied 90 percent of Europe's petroleum, was evacuating its employees and that a complete shutdown of the facilities was a real possibility. Kinzer writes, "British warships were patrolling ominously offshore. Middle East experts on the National Security Council staff warned in a report that if the oil conflict could not be resolved, 'the loss of Iran to the free world is a distinct possibility.' Their report asserted that the British were seriously considering invading Iran and warned that such an invasion 'might split the free world, would produce a chaotic situation in Iran, and might cause the Iranian Government to turn to the Soviet Union for help.'"[163]

As the crisis intensified, the British appealed to Truman to consider an overthrow of the Mossadegh government. But Truman wanted no part of a coup. The President appeared to have major sympathy for the plight of the Iranians, and on this occasion, he and his advisors might have been right—if the prime minister had been a different type of leader. History will continue to question whether the totally non-pragmatic Mossadegh could have been led to a compromise that might have resulted in some type of an Iranian democracy. He was a fire-brand visionary, consumed with a nationalistic zeal for improving the conditions of the people and ridding the country of foreign domination.

Mossadegh made no effort to control the communist movement, Tudeh, allowing many communists to serve in the Majlis. When he took control of the War Ministry in 1951 as a condition of accepting the position as prime minister, only 110 military officers were members of Tudeh. By 1953, this number of officers had swelled to 640.[164] Mossadegh also spurned all attempts at compromise with the British and the United States. Many foreign policy experts contend that had his rule been left unchallenged, a Soviet takeover was inevitable. And, any unilateral action on our part at the time would have shattered our relationship with the intransigent British.

General Dwight D. Eisenhower was elected president in 1952. As the threat in Iran grew, the strategy changed. Ike was reluctant to see the U.S. government become involved in an attempt to overthrow a foreign government, but under the influence of the ardent anti-communist Dulles brothers, he reluctantly accepted their plan. Secretary of State John Foster Dulles and his younger brother, Allen, director of the CIA, recruited Kermit Roosevelt to undertake a brash and risky operation. The hope of having an island of stability and a bulwark against Soviet expansionism in the region was considered well worth the risk.

Kinzer in *All the Shah's Men* tells the fascinating story of how this fearless young man, Kermit Roosevelt, accomplished the impossible by using the CIA, which was less than six years old at the time, to overthrow a popular leader of a foreign government. The project, code-named "Operation Ajax," was coordinated with the British covert agency, the SIS (also known as MI6), which provided potential Iranian undercover agents to the CIA. After many years in Iran, the British knew where to find the moles and those who could be recruited for assistance, either by cash, royalist convictions, or both.

An initial coup attempt failed, and Roosevelt was urged by his superiors to flee the country. The determined operative ignored the advice and decided to make one last attempt in the next few days. A second cable, which was delayed a couple of days by an ineffective communications system, ordered him to leave the country for his own safety and to avoid potential embarrassment to the U.S. government. By the time Roosevelt received this message, Mossadegh already had surrendered to the Imperial Guard, and the Shah was on his way back to Iran from a brief exile to assume total rule.

The CIA's involvement in, much less total control of, this operation was denied for many years. Regardless of the circumstances, the U.S. government and the Shah embarked on a 26-year relationship that would play a major role in winning the Cold War with the Soviets. The abrupt ending of the relationship in 1979 would start the next major struggle between the free world and Islamic radicalism—the "war on terror."

By 1958, the Shah's Iran, with the help of a billion dollars in loans and grants from the U.S. government, had amassed an American-trained and -equipped army of 200,000 men. This was deemed necessary, even essential, since Iran shared a 1,200-mile border with the Soviet Union. This build up was continued during the Kennedy presidency, but JFK, influenced by a team he considered to be "the best and the brightest" and driven in part by uprisings elsewhere in the region, decided to be proactive in Iran. He pressured the Shah into undertaking a series of reforms that the Shah already was considering.

The Shah envisioned himself as a progressive monarch with a genuine desire to improve the lives of his people. So, he undertook these reforms, known as the "White Revolution," with only minor hesitation. In fact, the Shah had been working on a series of reforms since about 1958. He was a little hesitant to move too fast, however, because the country over which he took total control in 1953 was a third-world country, deeply in debt because of Mossadegh's oil fiasco, and only semi-literate. In *Answers to History*, the Shah dedicates an entire chapter to the White Revolution, which he justifiably viewed with much pride. The first two reforms the Shah undertook in 1963 involved the distribution of public and privately held land to the peasants and the emancipation of women.

These reforms drew the immediate ire of Khomeini, who launched into a campaign against the Shah, accusing him of usurping the powers of the clergy and attacking the Shiite religion. Khomeini's activity started some riots and minor uprisings among the most fanatic Shiites, but his views were not embraced by the masses of the Iranian people.

The Shah made many reform efforts over the years, but JFK and his eggheads didn't understand that this developing country was not ready for too many major reforms in a short period of time. As Ali Ansari points out in *Confronting Iran*, this country had been propelled from the economy of the camel and donkey to the early jet age in a very few years.[165] As the Shah gave land and equipment to the peasants, the tractors sat rusting in unplowed fields because the peasants did not have the spare parts or know how to fix them. The Shah in his book wrote that he was expected to bring his country from the Middle Ages to the technological age in just a few years. He had intended to do just that.

In 1950, he issued a decree to give more than 2,000 hamlets and villages that belonged to the Crown to some of the peasantry. Prime Minister Mossadegh objected, because being a large land owner himself, he didn't want the land system changed. After Mossadegh's fall in 1953, the Shah started a program to redistribute the Crown lands. By the end of 1958, he writes, "more than 500,000 acres of Crown lands were shared among more than 25,000 farmers."[166] When he began in 1963 to divide up public and private land held by the "landed gentry," many of them politicians, and by the clergy, it is easy to see how such a program could create enemies.

The initial action of the second step in the White Revolution was to give women basic human rights to vote and participate in society as somewhat equal to men. This enhanced Khomeini's demagogic platform, because his Islamic beliefs gave women no rights. One can easily understand the wave of religious fanaticism the Family Protection Act of 1975, which the Shah convinced the Majlis to pass, would spark some dozen years later.

The real source of discontent started in December 1963, when LBJ pressured the Shah into having a law passed to grant legal immunity to U.S. government personnel in Iran. In 1964, when the Shah forced the Majlis to pass the "Status of Forces Agreement," the protests, inspired by Khomeini's fire-breathing rhetoric, began to get out of hand. The Iranian people, wearied by many years of foreign occupation and yearning for the national sovereignty that befitted a nation with such a glorious history, were more than willing to hear the Ayatollah's calls for the Shah's ouster. (An earlier system giving foreign occupiers immunity from Iranian law had been dismantled by the Shah's father, Reza Shah.)

The Shah then made what some consider the biggest mistake of his 38-year reign. He failed to listen when, I have been told, the CIA, SAVAK (the Iranian intelligence and security organization), and many of his cabinet and personal advisors urged him to rid the world of this trouble-making fanatic, Khomeini. (The question of justification for political assassinations or the lack thereof, even for treason, is above my pay grade.)

Various conjectures for the Shah's hesitancy to have Khomeini permanently removed have been offered. Among these is that he felt Khomeini, as a revered mullah, was too poplar and that his death would spark a revolution. However, it has been pointed out that other revered opposition leaders had died of unexplained natural causes or simply had been assassinated with only a short-lived outcry. It's further suggested that the military and various police organizations were simply too strong at the time for a serious rebellion to be successful. Maybe the Shah's Islamic faith deterred him from ordering the murder of a Shiite "holy man" of Khomeini's stature. But had the Shah decided to take drastic action, he could have found a wealth of justification in Islamic history, dating back to Mohammad himself.

Two things I have learned from books written by the Shah and his twin sister bear consideration.

Princess Ashraf makes a meaningful observation about Khomeini's capture stirring up the people and causing bloody riots:

> "When he was apprehended, another clergyman, Ayatollah Kazem Shariat Madari (now Khomeini's strongest rival) interceded on his behalf with General Hassan Pakravan of SAVAK, pleading that Khomeini be given the designation of 'ayatollah,' which would give him immunity from the most severe penalties under the law for his treasonous activities. This was done, and Khomeini was merely asked to leave the country. (When Khomeini took power in 1979, he repaid his benefactor, General Pakravan, by having him executed, thus conveniently eliminating the man who knew that Khomeini himself had had ties in the past to SAVAK.)"[167]

Therefore, under Iranian law he could not be executed for treason. It would have required some clandestine action to rid the world of this mad man, which the Shah chose not to do for reasons known only to himself.

Second, and perhaps more important, the Shah professes in *Answer to History* to be a man of strong faith. I take a man's expressions of his convictions seriously when he is staring his own mortality in the face. He was working around the clock to finish this book, knowing that his own death was eminent. He passed within weeks after completing his "autobiography."

The Shah confesses that his religious beliefs molded his reign as monarch:

> "My faith has always dictated my behavior as a man and as a head of state, and I believe that I have never ceased to be the defender of our faith. An atheist civilization is not truly civilized and I have always taken care that the White Revolution to which I have dedicated so many years of my reign should, on all points, conform to the principles of Islam.... I believe that the essence of Islam is justice, and that I followed holy Koran when I decreed and organized a national communal solidarity, when our White Revolution abolished privilege and redistributed wealth and income more equitably."[168]

He even argues that except for a few "Moslem extremists," who were obviously motivated by Khomeini, the "clerical mainstream" stayed with him, even in the mid 1970s, because of his commitment to Islam:

"When I became Shah, I swore an oath to uphold the constitution and to defend the faith, the Shiite religion of the Twelve Imams. In turn, the clergy recognized me as sovereign and as Defender of the Faith. I am a religious man, a believer; I follow the precepts of the sacred Book of Islam, precepts of balance, justice, and moderation."[169]

Not to be cynical about clerical sincerity, but I wouldn't be surprised if the Shah would not agree that the wholesale loss of clerical support might have been at least partly motivated by the ending of stipends to the mullahs in 1977. The Shah says that he has no direct knowledge of CIA support of the mullahs, but some Western sources allege that the CIA was spending between $400 and $450 million a year on the Iranian clergy until Carter ordered that this assistance cease in 1977. On the other hand, he admits:

"For some time my government had been providing our clergy with substantial support. In 1977 due to the exigencies of our economy, Prime Minister Amouzegar was forced to eliminate these payments. Western analysts have theorized that these actions precipitated an organized rebellion of the clergy."[170]

In spite of all these noble theories, it is most likely the Shah simply underestimated this man he considered a raving fanatic and felt that banishing Khomeini would solve the problem. In 1964, Ayatollah Khomeini was forced into exile. The exile began with a short stay in Turkey. After a few months he moved to Najaf, Iraq, where a Shiite shrine for Ali is built; it is a Shiite center of study and a hotbed of Shiite fanaticism. Khomeini would study and write for 13 years in Najaf. Most of his documents consistently called for the violent overthrow of the Shah's government. He was as effective in disseminating his anti-shah propaganda from this Shiite holy city as he would have been in Iran, due to proximity and the steady flow back and forth of Shiites from Iran. In 1978, when the revolutionary fervor began to flame, the Shah prevailed on Saddam Hussein to send Khomeini to France, but the damage had long since been done. And, living near the French capital would provide Khomeini with a worldwide media base.

With Khomeini in exile, the Shah continued his military build-up under LBJ and greatly increased it under Nixon. When Nixon assumed office in 1969, the United States was bogged down in the war in Vietnam, and he rapidly developed his policy, the "Nixon Doctrine," of finding regional allies to control the spread of communism. With Henry Kissinger's urging, Nixon designated the Shah as the prime defender of the Persian Gulf and the surrounding areas—with some minor assistance from Saudi Arabia, as Iran is not an Arab country—from the threat of Soviet expansionism. Nixon, again with Kissinger's strong encouragement, gave the Shah virtual free reign to buy as much U.S. military hardware as he desired.

The Nixon administration would later be criticized for allowing him to spend too much money on the military and not enough on the domestic economy over the years.

By 1972, Iran had a defense budget of more than $3 billion and so was able to amass the fourth largest army in the world. The Shah had become a respected and essential ally in the free world's struggle against communism.

The Shah had done virtually everything we asked of him (though he had raised oil prices against our wishes, going so far as to quadruple the price in 1973). His country experienced several periods of prosperity and development, especially in the early 1970s. However, constant internal threats from the Soviet-backed communist Left and the radical Shiite clerics and their fanatical followers were an ever-present source of concern.

The Shah knew he needed reliable intelligence and loyal security forces to contain the blind ideological threats of the dedicated communists and the Shiite Islamic fundamentalists. The intelligence role was to be carried out by SAVAK, an organization later referred to by the Shah's enemies as the "Shah's secret police." SAVAK was reorganized in 1957 with the help of the CIA, the British MI6, and, some believe, with some assistance from Israel's MOSAD. All seem to agree that the U.S. played the lead role in establishing the agency and training the agents. The U.S. was undoubtedly eager to establish such an agency in order to monitor Soviet plans, movements, and activities—especially the missiles the Soviets were testing from Iran's adjoining border.

One of the first things SAVAK accomplished was uncovering significant communist infiltration into the Iranian army, which if left unchecked could have led to a Soviet-backed coup attempt. The Shah realized that threats included a religious ideology that was absolute and uncompromising as well as threats from the Soviets.

The CIA's close relationship with SAVAK allowed the agency to constantly monitor the pulse of Iranian society and to influence many of SAVAK's activities. This close relationship probably started to abate after Watergate and the Church Commission hearings, which devastated our intelligence community. Congressman Otis Pike, heading up an intelligence committee in the House, continued the assault under Ford, and the revealing of classified information became a serious threat to all of our covert operations. A CIA station chief in Athens, for example, was murdered soon after his identity was leaked.

Shortly after Carter appointed Admiral Stansfield Turner to be director of the CIA, the new director wiped out virtually all human intelligence operations around the world, eliminating 820 operational positions in what is generally referred to as the "Halloween Massacre." As a result, Carter's intelligence regarding the rising threat of a revolution in Iran would be severely limited.

By the time Carter became president, Ayatollah Khomeini's popularity and influence among the Shiite community had reached epidemic proportions. The

Tudeks, typical of communists around the world, would join any uprising, believing they would be able to take over any revolution at the right time. The uninformed nationalists, many of whom had seen their wealth diminish with some of the Shah's reforms, were convinced that a revolution and forcing the Shah from power would ultimately end up with some type of secular government elected by the people. President Carter, who had specifically challenged Iran's human rights violations during the presidential campaign, started out his relations with the Shah in much the same way as his five immediate predecessors.

The Shah had spent $3 billion on military procurement in 1973, $5 billion on arms and materiel in 1975, and would spend $9.4 billion on his military and security operations in 1977. He not only was our bulwark against Soviet expansionism in the Persian Gulf region, but he was our largest customer for military procurements in the world. Carter not only continued to supply him with his military needs, he also invited the Shah for a state visit in November 1977 and accepted the Shah's invitation to spend New Year's with him in Iran a little over a month later. This is when Carter offered his frequently quoted New Year's Eve toast to the Shah: "Iran under the great leadership of the shah is an island of stability in one of the more troubled areas of the world. This is a great tribute to you, Your Majesty, and to your leadership, and to the respect, admiration, and love which your people give to you."[171]

This toast, like so many statements made by political figures, would have the unintended consequences of inflaming the already burning anti-American sentiments in Iran. Kenneth M. Pollack, author of *The Persian Puzzle*, feels so strongly about Carter's New Year's toast that he asserts in his book:

> "It was Carter's unintentionally offensive remarks in Tehran that set into motion the chain of events that became the Iranian Revolution. Immediately afterward, Khomeini blasted Carter for being a hypocrite, promoting human rights only when it was convenient for the United States because it had no military or commercial interests. On January 7, the regime responded with a misstep of its own, placing an anonymous editorial in the newspaper Ettela'at that blamed all of the recent protests on 'Red and Black' reactionaries (meaning Communists and Islamic extremists). For good measure, the piece insinuated that Khomeini was a foreigner, an agent of the British, a drunkard, and a closet homosexual. The next day, there were many massive demonstrations in Qom, Iran's religious center, to which the shah's police responded with violence, killing several people (including mullahs) and wounding many more."[172]

This observation seems significant because the scholarly Pollack is a well-educated liberal Democrat who worked in the Clinton administration as director for Gulf affairs at the National Security Council and is now at the Brookings

Institution. He counts as his friends such people as Stanfield Turner and Henry Kissinger. I point this out to indicate that Pollack is not a Republican critic of Carter but an authority on the Iranian situation.

Carter was not alone among prominent Democrats who praised the Shah over the years. JFK was highly complimentary of the Shah's undertaking the White Revolution. LBJ in 1967 told the Shah, "The changes in Iran represent very genuine progress. Through your White Revolution, Iran has risen to the challenge of new times and new generations ... without violence, and without bloodshed."[173] And the Shah writes that Senator Ted Kennedy, speaking at Teheran University in the spring of 1975, "praised us for our remarkable achievements in the Middle East."[174]

There were as many as 45,000 American citizens living in Iran at the time of Carter's New Year's remarks. Carter even approved additional sales of military weapons to the Shah in March 1978.

How does one explain what caused the situation to get out of control so rapidly? One thing on which all agree is that both the Shah and President Jimmy Carter greatly underestimated Ayatollah Khomeini and his influence on the turbulent situation that was unfolding. The Shah, as was often the case, was ignoring advice from his Iranian advisors, and the Americans weren't giving him any of the right kind of advice.

The Carter administration in non-public forums never seemed to miss the opportunity to lecture the Shah on human rights violations and the steps that should be taken to calm the people down. The fact of the matter probably was that so much was going on to change the economic and social structure of the country that it bred discontent. The Shah's reforms, which had been going on since the early 1960s, were intensified in the mid 1970s.

These continuing reforms would stir up the clergy even more, create opposition from the privileged class, and cause the communists to see opportunities amid the discontent. Nasr argues in his book that what happened in Iran to the Shah caused Indonesia and Egypt to re-evaluate the operations of their governments: "The stark contrast that the Shah had allowed to appear between the Islamic values of the opposition and his own regime's assertive secularism seemed an especially noteworthy source of weakness to avoid."[175] Sadly, a misguided U.S. foreign policy was pushing him in the direction of even more secular reforms.

The Shah would replace the Prime Minister of 12 years with a younger progressive man with extensive foreign policy experience. He announced plans for new elections, as he wanted to establish

> "a true democracy designed to foster my country's real interest. But my opponents were not interested in that approach. As a result, the more I liberalized the worse the situation inside Iran became. Every initiative I took was seen as proof of my own weakness and that of my government." [176]

The Shah's twin sister believes that the final rift with the mullahs came when the government subsidies were stopped in 1977. She believes that these payments were nothing but a form of bribery.

> "But this decision came at a high price politically: anti-Shah sermons were preached from then on in 11,000 mosques throughout the land. Curiously, SAVAK, the Shah's secret police--the supposedly all-knowing intelligence source--made no reports on the extent and manner in which the mullahs were now using the sanctity of the pulpit to undermine the throne."[177]

Pollack tries to refute the frequently held view that an "intelligence failure" caused by CIA Director Turner's gutting the clandestine services caused a deeply divided Carter administration to fail to take any meaningful action until it was too late. He does point out that Brzezinski admits that he did "not consider Iran a crisis until early November" 1978.[178] One can possibly understand why he was so out of touch since the CIA "spooks" had issued the report *Iran in the 1980s,* in which Carter's covert agents surmised, "Iran is not in a revolution or even a 'pre-Revolutionary' situation." One thing is for sure: Neither Carter nor the Shah seemed to recognize the seriousness of the threat until no solution was viable except military control of the country.

The embassy diplomats were of no help, since most of them seemed to sympathize with the concerns of the protestors who wanted an overthrow of the Shah's government. The Shah was convinced that there were those in the State Department, especially "the McGovernites in the second echelon of the State Department, who were anxious to see his government fall."[179]

Three groups would be vying for control in Iran: 1) the well organized Marxists, 2) the dedicated Shiites, under complete control of the Ayatollah, and 3) the "liberals," as they were called. The latter were a much smaller unstructured group of nationalists and anti-imperialists who wanted a secular government free of foreign influence.

One would have thought that seasoned diplomats, even those with a liberal and idealistic philosophy, could have figured out who would end up controlling any new government. The "liberals" who hoped for a secular, semi-democratic government had no chance for long-term control. The Marxists weren't going to take control of a new government without Soviet intervention, and even Carter would not allow that to happen. If the diplomats would have taken the time to even casually study the history of the Shiite Muslim religion, especially as it was practiced in Iran, they would have known what type of government a successful revolution would bring. Khomeini had already selected the Revolutionary Council members when he was in France.

Ali Ansari points out in *The Persian Puzzle* that the Shah's vacillation between tolerance and oppression of dissenting views was disturbing his allies at home and abroad. The Shah had cultivated the image of a monarch who had inherited the throne of the mighty Persian king, Cyrus the Great, and could control the destiny of his people, but he seemed incapable of any consistent forceful action. As early as April 1978, General Pakravan, a former deputy head of SAVAK, was telling U.S. diplomats that the United States must become proactive before it was too late, since the Shah would not listen to any of his Iranian advisors.[180] This sage advice fell on the deaf ears of diplomats who either weren't smart enough to understand the seriousness of the situation or didn't care if the Shah fell.

When President Carter finally realized that absent some dramatic military action, he was going to go down in history as the president who lost this strategic ally for the free world—either to an eventual communist dictatorship or, worse yet, to a fanatical Shiite theocracy that would spread terrorism around the world—he knew he must try to take some action. Having had U.S. diplomats previously advise the Shah against a military crackdown that would embarrass the U.S., Carter now was having belated second thoughts. The President instructed Brzezinski to call the Shah and tell him that although the U.S. still favored a peaceful solution, we would support him in whatever course of action he deemed necessary.

The Shah's top generals asked him to allow them to take charge of the crisis by military rule and absolve him of the responsibility for the bloodshed that would certainly result. He toyed with the idea and made one feeble attempt, which he promptly retracted. To his credit, the Shah "genuinely did not want to be the author of a vast new bloodbath."[181]

Wikipedia has a summary of Brzezinski's biography with an interesting account of the National Security Advisor's response to the imminent fall of the Shah's regime.[182] Brzezinski, realizing the potential catastrophic consequences of the loss of Iran and joined by Secretary of Energy James Schlesinger, had advocated U.S. military assistance to the Shah. On the other side of the argument, high level officials in Cyrus Vance's State Department argued that the Shah must go, regardless of who replaced him. When the matter reached the crisis stage in November 1978, Brzezinski called for a U.S. military invasion to stabilize the situation. Carter was indecisive but did send the "Constellation" aircraft carrier to the Indian Ocean. Having more second thoughts, he almost immediately countermanded his original order.

Brzezinski was on solid ground because the "bilateral agreement signed on March 5, 1959, by the U.S. and Iran" provided that the U.S. would provide military assistance to Iran if needed.[183] A swift and massive U.S. invasion and temporary occupation would logically have reduced the bloodshed since there would have been no resistance from the Iranian military. One wonders if a Soviet warning in *Pravda* for the U.S. and the West to stay out of the internal affairs of Iran played a role in the decision. The time frame in late November corresponds almost exactly. In reality this had to be Soviet bluster, since they would not have dared take on the U.S. forces and the Shah's 700,000 man army.[184]

The compromise "solution" within the administration was to try to cut a deal with the Iranian generals to support a moderate government after the Shah's government fell. Sandra Mackey says that as the Shah's "pompous military commanders, arrogant cabinet," and other privilege elite, complained that the Shah was "instinctively weak" and "lacked the killer instinct of his father," but he made a difficult decision and this time was decisive: "Before the new year of 1979, the shah concluded that he could not survive politically. To his credit, Muhammad Reza Shah refused to sit on a throne floating in the blood of his own people."

The Shah says in his book that he realized the blood that would have been shed had he ordered a military takeover would have paled in comparison to the slaughter that was taking place under Khomeini as he was writing in 1980, but this did not alter his personal convictions:

> "But even that fact does not resolve my fundamental dilemma—a sovereign may not save his throne by shedding his countrymen's blood. A dictator can, for he acts in the name of an ideology and believes it must triumph no matter what the cost. But a sovereign is not a dictator. He cannot break the alliance that exists between him and his people. A dictator has nothing to bestow for power resides in him alone. A sovereign is given a crown and must bequeath it to the next generation. This was my intention. Under my rule, Iran had reached a certain cultural, industrial, agricultural, and technological level. I still hoped to raise these levels before abdicating, so my son, Crown Prince Reza, could reign over a nation, strong industrially, militarily, and culturally, with a growing nuclear industry and no longer as dependent on oil."[185]

The Shah's human rights record was far from perfect, but he was fighting a communist insurgency and a fanatical group of Shiite clerics and their equally fanatical followers, who were taking their orders from the biggest fanatic of all, Ayatollah Khomeini. Those who might have been "tortured" were Soviet agents or radical Shiite revolutionaries and terrorists who started fires in public facilities, set off bombs, or engaged in other violent acts. Their intentions were the overthrow of his government. The claims of those trying to stir up a revolution started out with a modest set of numbers that were then greatly exaggerated by any multiples that the left-wing press would print: "Now in *Chronicles of the Repression,* a clandestine paper printed in Iran and used by the opposition against SAVAK, it was specified that between 1968 and 1977, that is over nine years, the number of people *arrested* for political reasons was exactly 3,164."[186]

This supposed detailed record compiled by the Shah's enemies of 3,164 political prisoners who simply had been arrested would soon grow into claims that 25,000 or 100,000 had been tortured or executed. The liberal Western press seemed anxious to print any charges without the slightest thought of verification.

By the time of the revolution, there were only a few hundred left in prison, since the Shah had pardoned some 1,500 revolutionaries as a part of his liberalization program advocated by the U.S. government. Most of them were immediately put to death by Khomeini's people since they were primarily Soviet agents.

The Shah further explains the actual operation of the government in regards to SAVAK:

> "Our Prime Minister was directly responsible for the day-to-day operations of SAVAK. As head of state, I could only intervene at the request of the Minister of Justice to exercise the Right of Pardon over condemned men. However, when I learned that torture and abuse existed, as a matter of policy I ordered it stopped. I was deeply moved when I heard that before being tortured and assassinated, Mr. Hoveyda, the former Prime Minister, and the former heads of SAVAK, Generals Pakravan, Nassiri, and Moghadam had insisted that they had never received an order whatsoever from me with regard to a suspect, an accused man, or a condemned one."[187]

How many of the charges of brutality leveled by the Shah's enemies are true is a debatable question. The authors I have read have differing opinions. All are aware that all the previous Persian/Iranian monarchs had their methods of dealing with those who sought to overthrow their empire. Even the most enlightened ruler realizes that he could not provide a just rule for the masses of his people if he were no longer on the throne. It should be remembered that the Persian/Iranian people had been ruled over for more than 2,500 years by monarchs or foreign conquerors. They had never known any other form of government.

My belief that the stories of the Shah's alleged atrocities are greatly exaggerated by his enemies is based on two impressions.

First of all, I had the opportunity in the early 1980s to get to know a number of Iranians who had fled Khomeini's reign of terror. I came to know two of the Shah's distant cousins, who happened to be Iranian Christians, fairly well. They, of course, had known many of their Muslim neighbors very well and knew—or knew of—many of the trouble makers they suspected of having communist leanings. They knew the Shah as a person who was somewhat "tender hearted" and disliked any kind of brutality. To be sure, I knew they were not disinterested bystanders. They never disputed that he had felt it necessary to take some actions that he was not happy about. But, they were totally convinced that the stories of torture and executions pushed by his enemies were blown way out of proportion.

Second, I was struck by an account in Stephen Kinzer's book. Kinzer, a veteran *New York Times* foreign correspondent is certainly not an apologist for the Shah. But in *All the Shah's Men,* he relates an interesting story about one of the Shah's strongest supporters. Colonel Nasiri, who commanded the Imperial Guard in 1953, was one of the first persons contacted by Kermit Roosevelt when he plotted the coup that year. Nasiri was a total royalist and he immediately accepted his assignment. The Shah's first official act after reclaiming his throne with absolute power following the successful coup was to make Nasiri a General. In 1965, the Shah placed him in charge of SAVAK. The Shah removed him from that post in the late 1970s to placate the rioters amid charges of torture by the agency. The Shah expressed shock over the allegations that SAVAK was using torture against his enemies.

Did the Shah throw his most dedicated supporter and perhaps the man he owed more to than anyone, except Roosevelt, for regaining his power without good reason? Or, was he genuinely enraged to learn of the tactics Nasiri was using at SAVAK? After learning as much as I have about Mohammad Reza Shah, it's difficult for me to believe that he would throw such a man to the wolves without probable cause!

The Shah's government, by the way, was pro-American, friendly to Israel, and had brought its people into the modern world. Women, for one good example, could be educated, drive cars, hold jobs, and live like first-class citizens. The reports of human rights violations were disputed by many, as I have pointed out, and under the worst case scenario were minor in comparison to other countries in that part of the world. The government that replaced the Shah showed the world how to take human rights violations to extremes that would compete with Hitler and Mao as the worst in human history.

Ansari makes this observation about Khomeini's revolution:

> "Although some initially conjectured that he would soon be regarded as a saint, as the brutality of the revolution took shape on our television screens and religious nationalism overtook secular liberalism and the Left, Khomeini easily filled the void vacated so ignominiously by the Shah. The Shah was now seen as a paper dictator, a humble precursor to the real thing: Khomeini was a medieval theocrat, irrationality personified."[188]

Some have conjectured that within a few months of Khomeini's return to Iran in February 1979, by far more people had been murdered than in the Shah's entire 38-year reign. But now those who were tortured, imprisoned, and often killed were pro-American, pro-Israel, pro-Western of any variety, or just nationalists who simply wanted a just secular government. Any criticism of Khomeini or the mullahs running the country under his direction could result in the death sentence. Any act considered to be "un-Islamic" would be considered deserving of death.

Pollack has a chapter titled "American Held Hostage" in his book *The Persian Puzzle* about how Khomeini ran Iran after his return from France that deserves careful reading.[189] In my opinion, this chapter gives valuable insight into the type of Islamic fanatics we continue to face in Iran, Iraq, Lebanon, and other trouble spots around the world. Just a few highlights on what he says. He believes that, "No one knew what role Khomeini would play in the future government, nor was there universal agreement that he was the undisputed leader of the revolution." He does point out that Khomeini was the most popular figure in Iran and that 3 million people lined the streets for his return to Tehran on February 1, 1979. He continues:

> "When he retired to Qom after two weeks in the capital, the general expectation was that he would perform a purely supervisory role as 'Imam,' providing legitimacy to the new regime and little more. At that time, he gave no impression that he wanted to play a direct role in the management of the nation. But it very quickly became clear that he would.... Whatever his intentions, Khomeini quickly became the arbiter of post revolutionary Iran."[190]

After a discussion of his view of God as "a harsh and vengeful deity—full of fury, demanding the eye and the tooth of retribution for human transgressions of divine law," he points out how this molded Khomeini's view of the proper government. The Ayatollah would opt for a "theocratic philosopher-king—a man so learned in Islamic law that all of his peers and all of his countrymen would recognize that only he could provide 'right-minded' guidance." He makes the point that not all the mullahs initially agreed, because it ran contrary to orthodox Shiite theology.

> "Although most foreigners tend to see Khomeini as the very embodiment of dogmatic Shi'i Islamic theology, in actuality, this notion ran directly contrary to the mainstream tradition in Shi'i Islam, which held that all governments were illegitimate as long as the twelfth imam remained in hiding, and therefore it was unseemly for mullahs to involve themselves in politics. Khomeini insisted on precisely the opposite."[191]

He then discusses the Revolutionary Council, the *komitehs* "committees," the "revolutionary tribunals," among others who took the law into their own hands and passed out "justice" with no fairness and no mercy.

It is certainly not fair to blame Carter and his administration for all the mistakes that have been made in Iran by previous administrations, but they made the fatal policy mistakes that cost us the best ally we ever had in that part of the world. The investments the U.S. had made over the previous 30-plus years were too great and the stakes too high to lose such a strategic ally in such a volatile part of the world. Whether the loss of Iran resulted from neglect, indecisiveness, or just plain liberal incompetence is beside the point. This foreign policy failure is inexcusable, and our children and grandchildren are likely to pay for this mistake for years to come as the war on terrorism rages on. It is not difficult to understand why General Alexander Haig resigned his position as Supreme Allied Commander of NATO in 1979 to protest this major foreign policy blunder. This whole situation is so disturbing to me that I take little comfort from the fact that the fall of the Shah and the hostage taking that followed played a major role in Reagan's election.

When the Shah fell and Ayatollah Khomeini gained total power, a violent Islamic movement, begun in the 7th century, took on global dimensions. Having consolidated this power into a totally Islamic theocracy by slaughtering tens of thousands of the perceived enemies of the government (those who were "un-Islamic"), these Islamists turned to worldwide terrorism. They trained and supported Hezbollah to terrorize Lebanon. The bombing of the Marine barracks in Beirut in 1983 would claim the lives of 240 Marines, for example. They have been the largest financial supporter of Hamas and its oppressive rule in Palestine. They train and give financial rewards to the families of suicide bombers who terrorize Israel and Iraq.

There were reports earlier in the Iraqi war that Shiite Iran was harboring, training, and supporting al-Qaeda operatives. If true, this would have been strange since al-Qaeda is a radical Sunni organization dominated by Wahhabi fundamentalists. Perhaps when it came to fighting the Great Satan, they may have put their theological differences aside for a short time. The Sunnis, who make up 85 to 90 percent of the world's Muslim population (over 1 billion adherents), and the Shiites, who number possibly as many as 150 million, have fought each other since shortly after Mohammad's death, as we noted earlier.

The overwhelming majority of Muslims in Iran are Shiites, mostly "Twelver Shiites." The Shiites are the majority group also in Iraq and have significant populations in Palestine and Lebanon. The fear that the fall of Saddam Hussein would ultimately result in the establishment of another Iranian-style radical Shiite theocracy in Iraq is a legitimate concern. Such a concern was not shared only by the United States, Israel, and much of Europe, but by the rulers of the Sunni-dominated Islamic countries. The possibility of two adjoining oil-rich countries engaging in "state-sponsored" Islamic terrorism of the Shiite variety is alarming indeed. The fact that Iraq also shares a border with Syria adds additional fears. While Syria is a majority-Sunni country, its president, Bashar al-Assad, is a member of the minority Alawite sect, a Shiite group. Assad is married to a Sunni Muslim and is accused of supporting terrorist organizations run by Sunnis and Shiites alike. Assad has especially been criticized for Syria's role in the carnage in Lebanon.

In fairness, it should be pointed out that much of the terrorism in the Middle East in modern times has revolved around the existence of Israel. No fair-minded person would claim that Israel is without blame. Just as Christians must accept their share of responsibilities for misdeeds in past conflicts with Muslims, so must Israel shoulder its responsibilities in today's conflicts.

In any event, those in Khomeini's new government showed their appreciation for the U.S. role in allowing their revolution to succeed by permitting a group of armed students to occupy the American embassy and take 66 hostages. Fifty-two of them would spend 444 days in captivity until Ronald Reagan was sworn in as president. With the Shah's military might out of the way, the Soviets invaded Afghanistan on Dec. 25, 1979. I believe that Carter's role in the fall of the Shah's government of Iran will go down in history as one of the two biggest foreign-policy blunders in American history. The other obviously would be at Yalta in 1945, when FDR gave away Eastern Europe to Soviet slavery that would not begin to come to an end until Ronald Reagan was president.

Three Events that Saved Christian Europe (and ultimately America) and a Fourth that Preserved What the First Three Had Accomplished

Without any of these three historic events, there is reasonable certainty that students today would be studying the Koran instead of the Bible—not only at Oxford, but also at Yale (improbable as it might be that either place would exist in an Islamic world):

1.   The Battle of Tours (Poitiers).
2.   Charlemagne's coronation as the first emperor of the Holy Roman Empire and the idea of a Christian "holy war" to thwart the Muslim conquerors.
3.   The long-overdue Crusades.
4.   And the fourth that preserved what those three had accomplished: The Battle of Vienna in 1683, which ended Islam's attempts to conquer Europe.

Conquering Muslim armies swept into the Middle East shortly after Mohammad's death, conquering Jerusalem, Syria, Egypt, and parts of North Africa. They also subdued the Persian Empire to the east, including some Christian lands in that area. By 750 A.D., the Muslims had conquered Spain, Portugal, and other Byzantine holdings. The fierce Muslim warriors now controlled almost two-thirds of previously held Christian lands.

In 732, almost exactly 100 years after Mohammad's death, the Muslim armies had invaded parts of southern Italy and southern France. Then a battle occurred that would save Europe from Muslim domination. The celebrated Moorish general Abd al-Rahman and his seemingly invincible Muslim army were determined to march on to Paris and take all of France. But they ran into a hammer that was harder than they had expected. At Poitiers, they met a French army commanded by a general named Charles Martel, affectionately known as "The Hammer." The victorious French army and their famous general changed the history of the world, as Edward Gibbon bluntly states in *The Decline and Fall of the Roman Empire*. If Martel would not have won the Battle of Poitiers, also called the Battle of Tours, the rest of Europe would have fallen like dominos.[192]

The Christian world could well have been threatened with collapse once again had Charlemagne not been crowned the first emperor of the Holy Roman

Empire in 800 A.D. and advocated a Christian "holy war" to thwart the Muslim conquerors. Had a lesser man than Charlemagne assumed his role in history, we all might know the Koran by heart!

It is of the utmost importance that we understand why the First Crusade was called and what the Crusades actually accomplished in spite of some bad behavior displayed in a number of the Crusades. Such an understanding takes on new urgency in view of the fact that many liberals in academia, the press—and politicians—today tend to call up the Crusades as some justification for today's Islamist terrorism.

Stop and think about it for a minute. What brought about the Crusades?[193] The Muslims were not provoked by Jerusalem or Syria or Spain or France or any other nation. They were absolute aggressors who were determined to spread their religion by conquest. It raises questions about the scholarship, if not the motives, of politically correct "scholars," and even some "church leaders," who insist that Christians must repeatedly apologize for the Crusades. The worst thing about the Crusades is that they came too late. (If the Crusades would have occurred earlier, it is reasonable to speculate that less blood would have been shed, and it is almost certain that so much of the once-Christian empire would not have been lost to the Muslims.) The Christian world had turned the other cheek to the point that it had almost no cheek left. The Byzantine Christian Empire had virtually nothing left of its once vast empire except Greece by the time the call came for the First Crusade.

What motivated Pope Urban II to call the First Crusade? Let us look at the circumstances that prompted this call.

The church in the East and the church in the West had fought theologically for hundreds of years over the authority of the pope in Rome. But with the Christian empire of Byzantium on the verge of collapse, the new Byzantine emperor overcame his pride and appealed to his theological adversaries for help. Pope Urban II, who "called for the First Crusade at the Council of Clermont in 1095, was calling for a defensive action—one that was long overdue."[194] Had the call come sooner, there would have been more of the Byzantine Empire to protect.

Dr. Rodney Stark,[195] in the Introduction to his book *God's Battalions*, summarizes a few of the stated beliefs of politically correct "scholars" and Islamic apologists in these words: "To sum up the prevailing wisdom: during the Crusades, an expansionist, imperialistic Christendom brutalized, looted, and colonized a tolerant and peaceful Islam." He then includes a statement I believe substantiates my long-held belief that the politically correct view of Islamic history was developed during the early days of the "Cultural Wars":

> "Finally, claims that Muslims have been harboring bitter resentment about the Crusades for a millennium are nonsense: Muslim antagonism about the Crusades did not appear until about 1900, in reaction against the decline of the Ottoman Empire and the

onset of actual European colonialism in the Middle East. And anti-crusade feelings did not become intense until after the founding of the state of Israel. These are principal themes of the chapters that follow."[196]

The Eastern and Western branches of Christianity had squabbled over doctrine and the primacy of the pope for centuries. It might not have been easy for Emperor Comnenus to make such a desperate appeal to the pope for help in light of such a tumultuous history. But certainly Pope Urban II had to be magnanimous to respond favorably to his plea. They must have both realized that the fate of Christianity hung in the balance. (Although it turned out that Comnenus' motives were not as pure as those of Urban II.) I would contend that God had intervened in the decision in spite of the fact that He knew that the revengeful actions of sinful men would spin out of control on certain occasions. However, the Church of Jesus Christ on earth must survive!

The Byzantine emperor explained to the pope that the Seljuk Turks, who had recently converted to Islam, had again captured Jerusalem (which previously had been reclaimed by the Christians) and had moved to within 100 miles of Constantinople. Stark explains,

> "In his letter, the emperor detailed gruesome tortures of Christian pilgrims to the Holy Land and vile desecrations of churches, altars, and baptismal fonts. Should Constantinople fall to the Turks, not only would thousands more Christians be murdered, tortured, and raped, but also 'the most holy relics of the Saviour,' gathered over the centuries would be lost. 'Therefore in the name of God ... we implore you to bring this city all the faithful soldiers of Christ .... [I]n your coming you will find your reward in heaven, and if you do not come, God will condemn you.'"[197]

There is no doubt in my mind that it was no accident that the pope at the time came out of monastic life. Urban II was much more of a spiritual leader than the secular leader some of his predecessors had been. The more worldly popes may not have called for the Crusades, and if they did, they might not have been able to raise the money and troops necessary. Emperor Comnenus, in spite of his passionate plea to the pope, turned out to be duplicitous, and such duplicity led to most of the atrocities that occurred during the Crusades.

Christian forces did wage some counter-attacks in Christian-held lands that were conquered by Muslim invaders, but as Dr. Bernard Lewis notes, the First Crusade marked the first organized effort by Christian leaders to fight back after 400 years of Muslim attacks and conquest. He also explains that the word "crusade" "derives of course from the cross and originally denoted a holy war for Christianity," but it has long since been used in entirely different contexts, such as "morally driven causes." He then points out, "The one context in which the word 'crusade' is not used nowadays is precisely the original religious one. The word 'Jihad' too is used in a variety of ways, but unlike "crusade" it has retained its original, primary meaning."[198]

Without the Crusades, Greece would surely have fallen eventually, and the Muslim armies would have set their sights on Rome. The Roman Empire was viewed as the major obstacle that stood in the way of the Muslims' divine command to wage holy war to conquer the world for Allah. Battles had been waged between the Muslim and Byzantine armies during the eighth, ninth, and 10th centuries. The Muslims were relentless in their efforts to conquer the world for Allah one battle at a time. Faced with the threat of losing all their lands, Christians finally fought back and even attempted to reclaim some of their fallen territory.

In Islamic theology, Allah's command to conquer the world teaches that once a land is conquered and belongs to the House of Islam it is Islam's forever. If the infidel retakes any country previously conquered by Muslims, this imposes a divine obligation on all Muslims, regardless of where they live, to wage defensive *jihad*, or holy war, to drive them out of "their" country.

To make the point as to why the First Crusade was so vital to the very survival of Christianity, we must look at the situation in the Middle East in the 10th and 11th centuries. In the second half of the 10th century, in response to increasing Muslim persecution of Christians, especially in the Holy Land, the Byzantine Christians moved from a strictly defensive position to an offensive position and tried to recapture some of their lost territories. The Byzantine armies were so successful in reclaiming such places as Crete, Cilicia, Cyprus, and parts of Syria, including the ancient Christian city of Antioch, that the Muslims decided drastic action was necessary. The caliph in Baghdad declared *jihad* and Muslims from as far away as Central Asia gladly responded to join their Muslim brothers in this holy war to take back these previously held Christian lands in the Middle East.

The Byzantine Christians appealed for no similar help from their Roman Christian brothers at the time. We can only dream of what the world would be like today if such a call would have been issued and a positive response would have followed much earlier in history. We might even have peace in the Middle East! But no such plea for help was issued until the Byzantines had suffered defeat after defeat during most of the 11th century and had virtually retreated to Greece as their last stronghold.

It is almost universally accepted as fact that the massacre of Muslims and Jews in Jerusalem in 1099, after a bitter five-week siege by the Christian troops, is perhaps the ugliest day in Christian history.[199] This view of the capture of Jerusalem by the Crusaders, based on conventional wisdom, is so rarely challenged that I, like many others with a cursory knowledge of the subject, at one time pretty much accepted this conclusion uncritically.

Then I picked up *The Politically Incorrect Guide to Islam (and the Crusades)* by Robert Spencer (Regnery Publishing, 2005). I was particularly attracted to this book because it had been so violently attacked by the politically correct Islamist apologists. Reading the seven-page chapter titled "PC Myth: The capture of Jerusalem was unique in medieval history and caused Muslim mistrust of the West" led me to a renewed interest in the Crusades. Today's politically correct culture had become so pervasive that PC adherents in effect were justifying Islamist jihadism as a belated response to the "horrors" of the Crusades. This tactic was playing a major role in confusing our leaders' response to the Islamist threat, which is in fact totally rooted in what the Islamist terrorists believe to be Allah's command to wage *jihad* until the world is ruled by *sharia*.

My eyes were really opened when I ordered a copy of Rodney Stark's *God's Battalions*, referenced earlier. Stark was the ideal person to research and write this book, as he had absolutely no ax to grind—his unbiased scholarly credentials are impeccable, and although raised in a Lutheran home in North Dakota, he once admitted to having become "personally incapable of religious faith." (He has given recent indications, though, that he may have regained a basic Christian faith.) He undertook a study of the Crusades out of academic curiosity and a scholarly search for historical accuracy. He frankly notes in a discussion of the purported massacre of Jews during the siege of Jerusalem, that when he wrote about anti-Semitic acts in earlier works, he had uncritically used now-disputed references. He writes:

> "Caution should especially be applied to the claim that when the Jewish residents of Jerusalem fled to their major synagogue, they all died when angry crusaders burned the building down around them. This is a favorite example of those determined to condemn the Crusades and one I repeated in an earlier study of anti-Semitic outbursts. On the face of it, the story is plausible. As reported in several previous chapters, Jews frequently sided with the Muslims against the Christians in the holy land. In this instance, there were Jews in Ifitkhar's regular forces as well as in the city militias. Hence, there is no reason to assume that the Jews would have received special treatment; people inside synagogues were as endangered as those inside mosques. Nor can there be any doubt that there were substantial traits of anti-Semitism among the crusaders."[200]

Neither Stark nor Spencer—certainly not Lewis nor any other author I have read—would make any attempt to contend that the behavior of the Christian crusaders in reclaiming Jerusalem was in keeping with the teachings of the Lord they claimed to serve. And the sad fact is that the First Crusade is now remembered almost universally in history for the unacceptable behavior of the crusaders because of the purported massacre of many Muslims and Jews. But this was not the characterization of the Christian victory in Jerusalem when it happened, because conquering the city followed the generally accepted rules of war at the time. (At this time in history, if a city's defense forces or army refused to surrender to an invading military force, the losing side could expect massive killings or slavery or both. The victorious army knew it could almost always expect major causalities among its troops were there to be a battle. Therefore, the invaders would try to discourage such resistance by demanding surrender or slaughter! [The Christian crusaders suffered heavy losses in the initial stages of the siege of Jerusalem.] What's more, the victorious forces didn't want to take the risk that their vanquished foes could easily reassemble and strike back. Finally, they wanted to set an example for future foes to consider before deciding to resist an invasion. Because of the teachings of Jesus, Christians should not have accepted such rules of battle. Unfortunately, in some cases they did adopt such wartime behavior.)

The Muslims in 1099 were alarmed because they had lost the key city in the Holy Land—they were not outraged because they believed a large numbers of Muslims or Jews had been killed. There also is evidence that the number of those actually killed has been greatly exaggerated. Stark writes:

> "Even so, there is very credible evidence that most of the Jews were spared and that the story that all the Jews were burned alive may be false! Some of the Christian accounts report that the Jews were taken captive and later forced to clear the corpses out of the city, which is what the Israeli historian Moshe Gil believes happened. Indeed, one of the famous Genza letters discovered in Cairo in 1952 was written in Hebrew by Jewish community leaders seeking funds to ransom Jews taken captive at the fall of Jerusalem. It is possible, too, that some Jews died when their synagogue was burned while most Jews in Jerusalem did not take shelter in a synagogue and were taken captive."[201]

For Muslims to have complained at the time of the fall of Jerusalem about the brutality in this battle would have contradicted their common behavior in most of their conquests. Stark writes that "dozens of Muslim massacres of whole cities have been reported in previous chapters, and the crusaders knew of such occurrences."[202] During the Muslim invasion of Syria just five or six years after Mohammad's death, the Muslim forces slaughtered 30,000 Byzantine Christian troops helplessly trapped in a valley surrounded by a lake. Once again, such slaughters can be at least partly explained by the brutality that characterized this period of history. Much more serious at the time for the future of the Crusades was the reaction of many Christians when word spread back home about the behavior of some of the crusaders. This clearly represented behavior Christ had forbidden His followers!

Stark makes it clear beyond reasonable debate that this tragically bloody conquest would never have occurred had Emperor Comnenus been a man of his word. Comnenus' treachery is without question the major cause of this indelible blot on Christian history.[203]

A summary timeline of the First Crusade puts events in perspective. Stark explains that when Pope Urban II took the platform in the French city of Clermont on Nov. 27, 1095, he delivered "a speech that changed history." In calling for the First Crusade, the pope had set a departure date of Aug. 15, 1096. He chose this date because the crops would have been harvested by then and the crusaders would have to live off the land since they could only take limited supplies with them. Most supplies would of necessity consist of armaments needed for battle. They were required to take the money necessary to purchase the food and other supplies they needed along the way.

Some groups of crusaders left earlier than the chosen departure date. Walter the Penniless, a leader of "The People's Crusade," actually arrived in Constantinople on July 20, 1096, after traveling for 102 days. Peter the Hermit left Cologne with his followers on April 19 and arrived in Constantinople on Aug. 1, 14 days before many of the contingents left on their eastward journey. By the pope's chosen date, approximately 130,000[204] Europeans had left for Constantinople.

The European crusaders had been promised that they would be joined in the Byzantine capital by a large number of seasoned, battle-experienced troops under the command of Emperor Comnenus. Had this been the case, a march through Asia Minor, with Comnenus leading the troops, would have been relatively easy. Most of the cities on the way, which had recently been taken from the Byzantines by the Seljuk Turks, would have offered only minor resistance when confronted with such a powerful military force. Under such circumstances, the Muslim ruler would have been ready to lay out a surrender plan by the time they reached the gates of Jerusalem. (The second part of the agreement was that the Byzantine forces would maintain a sufficient presence in Jerusalem to keep it under Christian control once it was recaptured. As would be discovered later, Comnenus had never intended to keep this promise. Jerusalem was not of enough strategic importance to his empire to justify the cost and manpower of such an undertaking. He certainly was not concerned about the safety or treatment of Latin Christian pilgrims.)

Emperor Comnenus had welcomed Walter the Penniless and Peter the Hermit with their forces. These leaders and the people they brought with them were the type of crusaders the emperor had expected. Comnenus even gave Peter a large amount of gold and asked him to lead the contingent when the other forces arrived to begin their march to regain the lost areas in Asia Minor. But when the many other contingents from the Latin countries began to reach Constantinople, Comnenus' paranoia and his obsessive fear of Roman imperial desires consumed him.

Comnenus had made sure that the original agreement granted him ultimate control of the Latin troops. They were to swear allegiance to him in this undertaking. Such an agreement had relieved his initial fears because he believed that the crusaders to be sent by those who responded to the pope's appeal would be primarily peasants and mercenaries. Comnenus initially thought that European nobility certainly would not become personally involved in such a time-consuming and difficult undertaking. But when new and larger delegations of the crusaders arrived, Comnenus panicked. These contingents included princes, thousands of nobles and knights, as well as many more thousands of trained troops. Stark notes the distinguished nature of these princes and their successes in previous battles. For example, Bohemond of Taranto and his father had fought, "and usually won, a number of battles against Byzantine armies led by Emperor Alexius Comnenus himself." Bohemond's arrival in Constantinople "followed by his large army of veteran Norman knights" must have convinced Comnenus that his worst fears had materialized.[205]

When the entire cast of highly motivated and dedicated leaders of this Crusade and the crusaders that would follow them had finally been assembled, they were ready to travel what would turn out to be the bloody roads to Jerusalem. Stark explains the stalemate that developed:

> "For when the time came to attack the Turks, Alexius did not take command. Nor did he merge his army with the crusaders. Instead, he sent a small contingent to accompany the crusaders in Asia Minor only as far as needed to recover recently lost Byzantine territory; he interpreted the oath sworn to him by leading crusaders as giving him full and exclusive rights to all these recovered cities and areas. Once the Western knights had accomplished that goal, Alexis seems not to have intended that even a token Byzantine army go any further. His position was that if the crusaders wanted to push on to the Holy Land, that was their own concern, but that 'Jerusalem was strategically irrelevant to the empire.'" [206]

Never mind Emperor Comnenus' passionate plea to Pope Urban II about the torture and murder of Christian pilgrims or the desecration of the Church of the Holy Sepulcher. Comnenus was now showing his colors and his true concerns: the preservation of the Byzantine Christian Empire. If the Roman Christians were concerned about the treatment of their pilgrims and the destruction of Christian holy sites, they could take care of it themselves.

When the armies of the crusaders undertook the 25-mile journey to Nicaea, Comnenus sent only "a small detachment of Byzantine engineers, with siege machines" to accompany them. The siege of Nicaea began on May 14, 1097, when the crusaders surrounded the city. Their numbers had already dwindled by almost two thirds.[207] However, they still had a trained fighting force of almost 40,000. They were having little difficulty repelling the attacks by the Muslim forces inside the city. However, before they were able to enter Nicaea, they were faced with a counter attack from a large Muslim force commanded by the feared Sultan Arslan. After an entire day of fierce fighting, the highly touted, massive Muslim army fled in disarray. The Muslims learned in this first battle that "man for man" they were "no match for the well-armed westerners on open ground," as Stark notes. But the Christians also suffered serious casualties. The following day when the crusaders were staged to storm the city, they were surprised to see the flag of surrender. (It would unfold in the near term that more of Comnenus' treachery was involved. He had secretly negotiated the surrender in return for some concessions that would only cause more problems for the crusaders in the future.)

After only a short rest, the crusaders were back on the road to Jerusalem, which would of necessity lead through Antioch. They encountered two severe attacks from the Muslim Turks before reaching Iconium. The Christian troops repelled the two well-planned Muslim attacks but not without sustaining costly losses. In the second attack, the crusaders once again soundly defeated Arslan's celebrated troops and foiled his attempt to even the score. This second humiliation caused Arslan to seek revenge in retreat by employing a scorched earth policy. His soldiers were ordered to destroy all crops and every vestige of food and water. This presented the crusaders a major challenge while travelling through this barren area of Asia Minor. Due to the unbearable summer heat and the lack of food and water, the Western Christian forces lost most of their horses and large numbers of their forces died of starvation or thirst before they reach Iconium in a fertile valley filled with orchards and running streams. The time for a few days of rest and relaxation in Iconium, which they took without opposition, was truly a blessing of God.

Their traveling historian contended that the remainder of the trip to Antioch was the most difficult of all. This was not so much because of military threats, since most Muslim forces fled when they threatened to attack, but the very steep mountain pass they chose to cross as they approached Antioch took a heaver toll than their bloody battles. But finally, with fewer beasts of burden, fewer combatants, and many fewer armaments (which they were forced to leave in that difficult mountain pass), they arrived at the gates of Antioch June 9, 1098. It had been a year since they had conquered Nicaea and two since they had left the comforts of home. Unfortunately for these weary warriors, it would be almost exactly another year before they beheld the gates of Jerusalem on June 7, 1099. Once again, there was not a single Byzantine soldier to greet them.

Using virtually every reliable source available, including some ignored by scholars with an agenda, Stark explains what really happened when the crusaders captured Jerusalem. Equally as important, he further explains why it happened as it did. The situation was extremely challenging under a best-case scenario. Undoubtedly it was very depressing under a more realistic evaluation.

Stark quotes the noted historian on the Crusades, Sir Steven Runciman, to establish what the crusaders faced: "According to Steven Runciman, 'The city of Jerusalem was one of the great fortresses of the medieval world.... The walls were in good condition and [it was manned by] a strong garrison of Arab and Sudanese troops."[208] Stark makes it clear that the troops now defending Jerusalem were not

Turkish. The Fatimids of Egypt had defeated the Turks a year earlier after the western Christians had routed them at Antioch.

Stark describes the battle and travel-weary crusaders in these words; "The crusader force that gathered to attack Jerusalem consisted of only about thirteen hundred knights and perhaps ten thousand infantry, having been reduced by about two-thirds from the crusader army that besieged Nicaea two years previously."[209] As the crusader forces were approaching Jerusalem, the Muslim ruler of the city had ordered the livestock driven away, the wells around the city polluted, and had expelled the Christian population. (This was a smart move since Christians were the largest part of the population of Jerusalem at the time. He feared that they would defect to the Christian invaders once the siege of the city began.)

When the Christian forces launched their initial attack on June 13, they had little trouble subduing the Muslims defending the outer perimeters of the city. But it was obvious that they could not scale the walls of the city due to their lack of equipment such as ladders and siege machines. Then God intervened! As Stark explains: "At this critical moment six Christian ships—two from Genoa and four from England—arrived at Jaffa, about twenty-five miles away." As it turned out, this totally unexpected event turned the tide and enabled the crusaders to accomplish their primary goal of restoring Jerusalem to Christian control. As Stark further notes, "All six [ships]carried food, but the Genoese ships also had cargoes of ropes, nails and bolts needed for making siege machines."[210]

Stark lays out the case in clear and simple terms, with extensive documentation, that Comnenus' repeated treachery drove the atrocities that occurred during the Crusades. (It is a fair question to ask if the emperor had reason for some concern based on past history. But he had appealed for Roman help.) Again, had the powerful crusader forces been joined by the battle-tested Byzantine army, the road to Jerusalem would have been relatively clear. With such powerful forces approaching them, the Turkish armies along the route would have fled. The rulers of Nicaea and Antioch as well as the other cities along the way would have commanded their forces to stand down while they negotiated the most favorable terms of surrender. The ruler in Jerusalem would have opened his gates for a peaceful entry of the Christian troops. Had Comnenus honored what the pope believed was an agreement to leave a large enough force behind to assure the stability of Jerusalem, peace might have endured for many years. (Some Muslim caliph eventually would have called for a holy war to recapture the holy city of Jerusalem. But with trained Byzantine troops stationed in Jerusalem and in the key cities along the way in Asia Minor, Roman rulers could send reinforcement troops in a much shorter period of time. Actually, if the pope in Rome and the emperor in Constantinople could have reached a binding truce based on Christian honor, there would have been an abundance of Roman Christian knights and other trained soldiers anxious to volunteer for long deployments in the city so holy to Christians. With such a powerful combined force of Romans and Greeks serving side by side, most Muslim rulers would have been extremely hesitant to risk their honor and troops. But all men are sinful and the devil would never let such a thing happen as long as he could possibly tempt them to do otherwise.)

But the worst-case scenario played out and even under the least exaggerated version of what happened in the siege of Jerusalem (keeping in mind that no one suggested it violated the rules of war at the time), it still turned into a Christian tragedy of great magnitude. Perhaps even worse, the Byzantine treachery, which cost the crusaders so dearly in lives and treasure, was the direct cause of the sack of Constantinople during the Fourth Crusade. There would never have been a Fourth Crusade, which pitted Christian against Christian, had Comnenus not reneged on so many promises.[211]

In any case, the Christians should have known better: our God would never have condoned, much less commanded, such behavior. All these concerns aside, the fact is that had the Roman army not come to the aid of their beleaguered Byzantine brothers, we might all be reading the Koran in our native Arabic language.

In the final chapter of God's Battalions, titled "Mission Abandoned," Stark leaves his readers with some final thoughts that relate to America's present struggle with radical Islamism. As the years went by, the European Christians began to lose enthusiasm and support for the Crusades. They were too expensive. Too many of their young men were being taken away from their families, large numbers of whom would never return. Did conflicts on the other side of the continent make them more secure? Stark contends that "a medieval version of the antiwar movement eventually prevailed: after two centuries of support, the kingdoms in the Holy Land were abandoned." Pacifism and isolationism replaced patriotism and zeal to defend their religion. Some will remember Osama bin Laden's contentions that Americans don't have a stomach for war and will not stay the course if the faithful are committed to wage jihad for as long as it takes. Stark's warnings certainly should give us food for thought.

The state-sponsored threats of Muslim armies invading Europe did not disappear until the Christian army won a decisive victory at the second Battle of Vienna in 1683. Following this defeat, the Ottomans lost one province after another until their empire virtually evaporated. Then, in the words of Osama bin Laden, "came the final humiliation"[212]—when the lands of Islam were divided up and occupied by rival European empires.

The Muslim goal of world domination did not disappear, but they were forced to change their tactics dramatically.

A Modern Phenomenon: Muslim Immigration to Non-Muslim Lands

Lewis makes a telling point about today's challenge by pointing out that significant Muslim immigration to lands being ruled by non-Muslims is a totally modern phenomenon.

Since Mohammad taught that Islam as a religion and Islam as a state are one and the same, such immigration sounds strange indeed. Traditionally, devout Muslims by definition desire to live under an Islamic theocracy. Their migration developed initially in modern times mostly out of necessity. Obviously, such immigration raises serious problems of assimilation for Western countries. This complex problem begs further exploration.

In his lecture, "The Challenge of Islam," delivered Oct. 25, 2007, at the Hotel Washington in Washington, D.C., Dr. Bernard Lewis kept his audience spellbound for an hour as he spoke nonstop without a note. When he turned to the modern practice of Muslim immigration, he said:

> "We now have a phenomenon which we never had before, that is Muslim migration to non-Muslim countries. In the past, it was regarded as a disaster for Muslims to be ruled by non-Muslims. This was something unacceptable. There were even discussions among the Jewish whether Muslims may stay if their country is conquered by the infidels, or must they leave? In the earlier period, the general view was that they must leave, and later, the problem reached such dimensions that that was no longer possible. In our own time, we have the opposite: Muslims migrating to the West and there are now large and growing Muslim communities in Europe, in North America, and in other places. If you are a Muslim living in Hamburg, or Berlin, or Los Angeles, or Detroit, or wherever it may be, it is very natural that you should want to give your children some grounding in your religion and in your culture. And what do you do? You look around for the normal places where that could be arranged—evening classes, holiday camps, etc.—there are lots of these in Europe and America. And overwhelmingly, they are owned, operated and run by Wahhabis. So what they get in these is the full Wahhabi blast and this fanatical, extremist, and radical version of Islam."[213]

After giving several examples of how these Wahhabi-run schools and other religious activities breed Islamic fundamentalism and therefore terrorism, Lewis makes this very important disclaimer: "As I tried to suggest before, the dominant spirit, both of the Iranian Revolution and of the Wahhabi-dominated Sunni version of Islam, are *not those of the popular masses*" (emphasis added). This is the good news and offers the hope that honest dialogue might be possible. It should be instructive to compare Muslims living in America to those living in Europe.

In *America Alone*, author Mark Steyn lays out the worldwide Islamic threat in an interesting, somewhat funny, and occasionally slightly vulgar manner.[214] This book is a must read for those who have an interest in the rapidly increasing number of Muslims living in the Western world, once referred to as the "Christian world." After you read through the first 30 or 40 pages dealing with patterns of population growth, which are important now but will reach a crucial stage 15 or 20 years down the road, it is difficult to put the book down.[215] He comes up with so many interesting, and sometimes frightening, examples of Muslim activities and behavior in western countries that you seldom read about in the American press. They range from Muslim demands in England that non-Muslim school teachers be required to wear head scarves in class so as not to offend Muslim students to the extensive drain on already overburdened welfare programs.

Steyn documents the spiraling Muslim influence in Europe with this example: "Brussels has a mayor, Freedy Thielemans, who presided over a ruling Socialist Party caucus of 17 other members." After listing their names he continues, "Ten out of eighteen members of the ruling caucus of Brussels are Muslim, right now. That's to say, the capital city of the European Union already has a Muslim-majority governing party."[216]

Steyn uncovers the underlying problem in most of Europe. The Europeans have lost their heritage by abandoning their Christian foundations and are increasingly incapable of dealing with a movement steeped in a deeply religious motivation. He writes:

"Almost by definition, secularism cannot be a future: it's a present-tense culture that over time disconnects a society from cross-generational purpose. Which is why there are no examples of sustained atheist civilizations. 'Atheist Humanism' became inhumanism in the hand of the Fascists and Communists and, in its less malign form in today's European Union, a kind of dehumanism in which a present-tense culture amuses itself to extinction. Post-Christian European culture is already post-cultural and, with its surging Muslim population, will soon be post-European."[217]

The Europeans have even less grasp of the problem they are facing than do we Americans.[218] There are some in Germany who have suggested that declaring an official "Muslim Holiday" will somehow appease the radical Islamists! If we in the U.S. would just have thought of that before 9/11!

One account mentioned in Steyn's book, the prosecution of a well-known British imam or mullah named Abu Hamza, is very interesting and revealing. Abu Hamza was being tried on nine counts of soliciting to murder and various other charges for his activities in the mosque where he taught and led prayers for young British Muslims. His lawyer came up with a telling defense that the imam was just teaching his interpretation of the Koran that imposed an obligation on Muslims to engage in *jihad* and fight in the defense of their religion. The counsel for Abu Hamza said, "It is said he was preaching murder, but he was actually preaching from the Koran itself." If you do not already have a copy of Steyn's book, it will be well worth your time and effort to purchase one.

For the most part, the assimilation into American society of Muslims who have immigrated to America is so superior to that of their European counterparts that we are in a position to set an example for living together in peace and harmony.[219]

Political Correctness from Muslim and Western Perspectives

A major difference between Christianity and Islam from their founding days is the question of debate and disagreement over the essential doctrines of the two religions. Historical circumstances surrounding the founding of each religion partly—but not completely—explain the different responses of each.

Christ's disciples and apostles strongly condemned false teachings as the work of the devil, but they had no power to physically restrain those who taught false doctrine, even had they desired to do so. On the other hand, Mohammad's disciples, especially the early caliphs who succeeded Islam's Prophet, inherited a powerful army capable of eliminating dissenters from their ranks. Mohammad's initial successor as the first caliph, Abu Bakr, spent much of his reign fighting the "Wars of Apostasy" to rid the new religion of those who were not true believers but had converted out of fear or convenience.

Saints Paul and Peter warned the earliest Christians about "false prophets" in their midst who would attempt to lead the faithful astray. The earliest church councils condemned teachings that distorted basic biblical doctrines, as well as those who taught them, and warned of eternal damnation for those who taught and believed such heresies. Verbal condemnation was the only weapon in their arsenal until the Roman Emperor Constantine converted to Christianity.

As the Christian Church gained political, and, as a result, military, power, its methods of operation would change over a period of time. There are few, if any, definitive examples of attempted "forced conversions" as a result of military conquest. There are many examples of abuse of non-Christians living in Christian lands. There are even more examples of persecution of heretics and those accused of heresy. There are frequent examples of Christian heretics questioning even the most basic and essential Christian doctrines: the deity of Christ, the virgin birth, the bodily resurrection of Jesus Christ, the doctrine of the Holy Trinity, and other such fundamental doctrines.

In various periods of Christian history, true heretics and even those merely "accused of heresy" were persecuted, burned at the stake, stoned, or just banished from their homelands. Well-known examples range from the Spanish Inquisition to the pre-Reformation burning at the stake of reformer John Huss. The use of force to enforce religious beliefs or conformity is always wrong and uncivilized. Christianity does not come to the table for dialogue with Islam or any other religion with clean hands.

There is no such history of debate over and the challenging of basic doctrines in Islamic history. Even the long and bitter Sunni-Shiite split did not involve any questioning of the "five pillars of faith" in Islam. Orthodox Sunnis condemned the Shiites throughout their existence for "innovations" and pagan practices of venerating their "saints," especially Hussein and Ali. These charges have resulted in major persecution and much bloodshed. But no Shiite cleric or religious authority has ever questioned the monolithic unity of Allah and the finality of the prophethood of Mohammad. By definition, Muslims believe without question that "There is no God but Allah and Mohammad is His Prophet."

The authority and divine origin of the Koran is not a topic for discussion among Muslims. It must be accepted without question. Strict enforcement of such beliefs has been a trademark in Muslim-ruled lands during their entire history. (Even in lands ruled by secular or moderate Muslim rulers, criticism of basic Islamic doctrines is never permitted.) Any deviation from such confessions is considered to be apostasy and is severely punished, frequently by death.

In our "politically correct" modern world, the historic patterns for Muslim and Christian theological behavior have changed very little, if at all. (The obvious exception is that in so-called Christian lands today, not only are Christian heretics not persecuted, they are rarely even stigmatized.)

In America, we have gone through the modernist-fundamentalist struggle in the early days of the 20th century; the so-called "higher-criticism" of the Bible; the "God is dead" fad; and the loss of any absolute truth based on sound biblical teaching in most mainline Protestant denominations. The Roman Catholic Church is even split between "traditionalists" and varying types of "reformers." There has been a corresponding significant increase of "evangelical" Christians, but some insist that the United States, like Europe, is living in the post-Christian age.

In any event, political correctness dominates religion as well as politics in the United States. In 2003, author Dan Brown published a novel titled *The Da Vinci Code*. This book, billed as a mystery/detective novel, is a cheap-shot blatant attack on historic Christianity based on no recognized or reliable historical sources but rather on stories manufactured in the author's mind. Yet, the politically correct immediately seized on these startlingly new "facts" that can revolutionize our understanding of "historic" Christianity. Then Columbia Pictures released "The Da Vinci Code" as a movie in 2006. If such a thing would have happened in a majority-Muslim country involving Mohammad or Islam, irate Muslims would most likely still be demonstrating and burning things down.

In stark contrast, a Mel Gibson film, "The Passion of the Christ," received exactly the opposite response from these same politically correct elites. This movie, based squarely on biblical accounts and early Christian sources, was denounced as "intolerant" and "divisive." It should come as no surprise that politically correct Christian "scholars," "historians," and some church "leaders" who revel in apologizing for past Christian behavior, take a different attitude when discussing Islam. The same men and women who do not hesitate to challenge Christian teachings are careful not to criticize Islam in order not to offend Muslim sensitivities.

If any genuine dialogue is ever to take place, it is unrealistic to expect that any Muslim cleric, religious scholar, or leader will in any way criticize or even question any basic beliefs of Islam. Their core Islamic beliefs, like historic orthodox Christian beliefs, are believed to be exclusive and final and cannot be negotiated, compromised, or even questioned.

Fortunately, it is not necessary for Muslim scholars or leaders to question any of their essential beliefs for meaningful discussions to take place and, one would hope, to succeed.

Muslim theologians and jurists have from the beginning experienced disagreements on *jihad* and *sharia*. These two non-essential theological concepts are the sources of the terrorist threats of the radical Islamists. It has been repeatedly pointed out that the masses of mainline orthodox Sunnis do not agree with the fundamentalist interpretations of *jihad* and *sharia* taught in the radical Salafi and Wahhabi sects. Common grounds can be found for Muslims to live peacefully in majority-Christian lands and Christians to be afforded the same opportunities in Muslim-ruled lands. Such a basic understanding could be of great value in defeating the Islamic terrorists. If Muslim leaders sincerely believe that the terrorists are distorting the true teachings of Islam, the first step in stopping the terrorists is to say so.

"A Common Word" and the "Yale Letter"

On Sept. 12, 2006, Pope Benedict XVI presented a lecture at the University of Regensburg in Germany.[221] This lecture resulted in an enormous controversy over a quote about Islam from a 14th-century Byzantine emperor. This ongoing controversy clearly illustrates the urgent need for honest Muslim-Christian dialogue, and it shows the difficulties involved in such an undertaking. Virtually all the key players became involved. Muslim extremists in various parts of the world burned some Christian churches, killed a nun among others, and threatened a terrorist attack on the Vatican.

A month later, 38 Islamic scholars sent an "Open Letter" to the pope pointing out "some errors" in his lecture and calling for a theological dialogue. The Vatican issued a statement containing sort of an apology if the pope's remarks had inadvertently given offense and expressed a willingness to meet to discuss Christian-Islamic relations. This response didn't satisfy the Muslim scholars.

A year later, on Oct. 13, 2007, 138 Muslim scholars sent a second open letter, titled "A Common Word between Us and You," to the pope and Christian church leaders throughout the world that called for a dialogue on their shared "Abrahamic faith" and other theological issues held in common.

The Vatican response (to be discussed in some detail shortly) was measured and appeared to be unwilling to compromise basic Christian doctrines. This response insisted on the discussion of human rights and mutual respect for the religious liberties of each other. This was not what these Muslim scholars wanted to "dialogue" about.

What is almost unbelievable is the response generated by Christians at the Yale Center for Faith and Culture in what generally is referred to as the "Yale Statement" or the "Yale Letter." On Oct. 18, 2007, just a month and five days after the second open letter issued by the Muslim scholars, a full-page advertisement appeared in the *The New York Times* with a response that had been drafted by the Yale faculty members and signed by some 300 Christian leaders. Their response, "Loving God and Neighbor Together: A Christian Response to 'A Common Word between Us and You,'" proves to be religious political correctness personified.

The pope's 2006 lecture at the University of Regensburg was titled "Faith, Reason and the University—Memories and Reflections."[221] Its major focus was the relationship between faith and reason. The pope referenced a treatise written by Manuel II Paleologus, one of the last Christian Byzantine emperors, just prior to the fall of Constantinople to the Ottoman Turks. The emperor had recorded a dialogue he had had with an "educated Persian," probably in 1391. The pope speculates that the emperor recorded these dialogues sometime during the siege of Constantinople, which lasted from 1394 to 1402. (It probably wasn't difficult for the emperor to be concerned about forced conversion during this Muslim siege.)

Benedict quotes Paleologus as arguing that spreading the faith through violence is unreasonable and that violence "is incompatible with the nature of God and the nature of the soul." He further refers to the emperor's argument: "The decisive statement in this argument against violent conversion is this: not to act in accordance with reason is contrary to God's nature." These references were all used by the pope to explain a quote by the emperor: "Show me just what Muhammad brought that was new and there you will find things only evil and inhuman, such as his command to spread by the sword the faith he preached."

Immediately after Pope Benedict's speech, cries for an apology or a retraction were heard from Muslim leaders and government officials in Muslim-ruled countries. The Vatican put out information clarifying the English translation of the German, explaining that the pope never indicated that he agreed with the Byzantine emperor's more inflammatory opinions.

On Sept. 16, 2006, a *New York Times* headline read "Pope Apologizes for Uproar Over His Remarks." On that same day, the secretary of state of the Holy See, Tarcisio Cardinal Bertone, issued a statement insisting that the pope was offering "certain reflections on the theme of the relationship between religion and violence in general, and to conclude with a *clear and radical rejection of the religious motivation for violence, from whatever side it may come.*" He added that the pope "sincerely regrets that certain passages of his address could have sounded offensive to the sensitivities of the Muslim faithful and should have be interpreted in a manner that in no way corresponds to his intentions."[222]

Morocco recalled its ambassador to the Holy See, Pakistan's parliament passed a resolution condemning the pope, Turkey's prime minister demanded a "retraction," and Malaysia demanded an apology. Muslim clerics and scholars attacked the pope's lack of understanding of Islamic teachings, and many called for a dialogue. The violent protests and condemnations apparently motivated 38 of these clerics and scholars to send an "Open Letter to His Holiness Pope Benedict XVI." This letter was somewhat moderate by Muslim standards, but it included the traditional Islamic approach in discussing theology.

The 2006 letter discusses a number of Islamic teachings, then includes a paragraph with the heading "Something New?" There the Muslim authors write, "You mention the emperor's assertion that 'anything new' brought by the Prophet was 'evil and inhuman, such as his alleged command to spread by the sword the faith he preached.' What the emperor failed to realize—aside from the fact … that no such command has ever existed in Islam—is that the Prophet never claimed to be bringing anything fundamentally new."[223]

Muslims clearly teach that Allah's revelations came in stages that included genuine revelations to the "people of the Book"; that Allah's prophets included Adam, Abraham, Moses, and Jesus; and that the revelations they received pointed to the final revelation given to Mohammad. Muslims further teach that the revelations recorded in the Old Testament and the New Testament became corrupted over the years, with the result that most failed to recognize Mohammad as Allah's final prophet. Thus Muslims say that Mohammad brought nothing "fundamentally new" other than the final revelation. The writers close this section of the open letter, "According to Islamic belief, all the true prophets preached the same truth to different peoples at different time. The laws may be different, but the truth is unchanging."

The Muslim clerics concluded their appeal to the pope with a call to discuss "what we have in common with our shared Abrahamic traditions." As we have seen, the Koran clearly states that "Abraham was a Muslim," albeit one who had not received Allah's final revelation. The Koran also teaches that Jesus was a servant of Allah, who has "no son" or "no associate" but who made Jesus a prophet.

The "Open Letter" (2006) signed by the 38 Muslim clerics did contain a new approach that some feel might signal a change in Muslim strategy and that becomes even more evident in the second letter, "A Common Word between Us and You" (2007). They actually quoted some verses from the Bible, even if they were taken out of context. The traditional Islamic position had always been that everything that anyone needed to know about Judaism or Christianity could be found in the Koran.

In any event, the Vatican didn't fall for a dialogue on the commonality of the Abrahamic faiths and shared traditions. (Obviously, the Vatican knew the Islamic teachings on these subjects, unlike the Protestants who drafted and endorsed the Yale letter.) Instead, the Vatican suggested a dialogue on religious freedom and mutual respect for each other's right to freely practice and proclaim their faith without fear of persecution or discrimination. This was not what these 38 Muslim scholars had in mind. As a result, their failure to bring about direct talks with the Vatican on their terms led a year later (Oct. 13, 2007) to 138 Muslim leaders sending a new letter—"A Common Word between Us and You—to the pope and Christian "leaders" around the world.

The wording of "A Common Word between Us and You" can be placed in context by examining certain verses in the Koran used in the letter. For those who cannot read Arabic, it is important to use an English translation written by a recognized Muslim scholar and sanctioned by the Muslim community.[224] At the same time, those of us who have attended a Christian theological seminary and studied Old Testament Hebrew and New Testament Greek know it is sometimes difficult to find an exact English translation of every word or phrase in the Bible.

One subsection, "Come to a Common Word!," quotes Jesus as saying, "He who is not with me, is against me" (Matt. 12:30); "For he who is not against us is on our side" (Mark 9:40); and "... for he who is not against us is on our side" (Luke 9:50). The Muslim letter says these statements are not contrary to each other in Christian tradition because the first refers to demons and the other two refer to "people who recognized Jesus but were not Christians." The Muslim scholars say that they "recognize" Jesus, quoting part of a verse from the Koran as support: "Muslims recognize Jesus Christ as the Messiah, not in the same way Christians do (but Christians themselves anyway have never all agreed with each other on Jesus Christ's nature), but in the following way: '... the Messiah Jesus son of Mary is a Messenger of God and His Word which he cast unto Mary and a Spirit from Him ...' (Al Nisa', 4:171)." This statement concludes, "We therefore invite Christians to consider Muslims *not against* and thus *with them*, in accordance with Jesus Christ's words here."

It is arrogant enough that the writers of "A Common Word" would reference heretical Christians who reject orthodox teachings about Christ's nature when supposedly reaching out to mainline Christians. But compare the words of the entire verse in the Koran to the partial line they have extracted from this verse:

> "O followers of the Book! Do not exceed the limits in your religion, and do not speak (lies) against Allah, but (speak) the truth: the Messiah, Isa son of Marium is only an apostle of Allah; and His Word which He communicated to Marium and a spirit from Him; believe therefore in Allah and His apostles, *and say not, Three. Deist, it is better for you; Allah is only one God: far be it from His glory that He should have a son; whatever is in the heavens and whatever is in the earth is His; and Allah is sufficient for a Protector*" (Koran 4:171, emphasis added).

In the final lines of the letter, a call is made to put differences aside and seek to "live in sincere peace, harmony and mutual goodwill," as they claim "God says in the Holy Quran in 5:48." This is so blatant they must realize that Christians aren't proficient in the Koran since three verses later, in 5:51, the Koran reads: "O you who believe! Do not take the Jews and Christians for friends; they are friends of each other; and whoever amongst you takes them for a friend, then surely he is one of them; surely Allah does not guide the unjust people."

The Protestant and Orthodox response in the "Yale Letter" was an almost immediate, totally knee-jerk reaction driven by Christian "scholars" who do not appear to have even a minimal understanding of Islamic theology. They certainly have no grasp of the subtleties of Islamic terminology used by Muslim scholars.

Shockingly, most of those involved in the production and promotion of the "Yale Letter" are various types of Evangelicals. They seem to be so driven by the desire to be politically correct that they are oblivious to the facts. Certainly, many of them are motivated by a sincere desire to have a dialogue with Muslims, but such a dialogue will not only be meaningless but counterproductive if one begins by sacrificing basic Christian teachings. Those on the other side began the debate by stating their basic Islamic teachings in bold terms.

The Barnabas Fund, an international Christian aid organization that supports persecuted Christians, prepared an analysis of "A Common Word" and the "Yale Letter" response.[225] This was not a diversion or academic exercise for them but involves the very reason the organization exists. They spend their lives trying to find ways to assist Christians who are persecuted by Muslims in such places as Pakistan, Afghanistan, parts of Indonesia, and especially in Nigeria, Sudan, and Somalia. The Barnabas Fund issued an initial analysis of the Yale statement 10 days after it was published. A further response was published in January 2008."[226]

An informed analysis of the Muslim open letter reveals the prominence of the traditional *da'wa* (call to convert and submit to Islam), *tawhid* (the monolithic unity of God), and the finality of the prophethood of Mohammad. *Da'wa* has always been offered historically to non-Muslims prior to the declaration of *jihad*. *Tawhid*, by definition, rules out the possibility of the deity of Jesus Christ as well as the doctrine of the Trinity. The Barnabas Fund analysis of "A Common Word" concludes that the document "in reality turns out to be a missionary pamphlet extolling Islam and denigrating the very heart of Christianity. It seems likely that the Muslim authors assumed that Muslim readers would understand the veiled intentions while Christian readers not conversant with Muslim traditions would fail to understand."

The authors of the Yale Letter[227] were careful not to offend the sensitivities of the Muslims they addressed. They mentioned Jesus Christ but never used the words "Lord" or "Savior." They made no reference to the centrality of the Trinity in the Christian doctrine of God. Compared with the tone of the Muslims' "A

Common Word," its authors would have to view this is as a major concession by the Christians who signed the Yale Letter.

The Yale Letter authors took the meaning of "political correctness" in a religious context to new extremes when they wrote, "we want to begin by acknowledging that in the past (e.g. in the Crusades) and the present (e.g. in excesses of the 'war on terror') many Christians have been guilty of sinning against our Muslim neighbors." Did the 138 Muslim clerics who signed the "A Common Word" even hint at an apology for the 400 years of Muslim conquest of Christian lands that made the First Crusade necessary? Was there a word of apology or even of sympathy from the Muslim authors for the victims of the 9/11 terrorist attacks carried out in the name of their religion? Christian church leaders must understand that groveling does not lend itself to constructive dialogue. Even more serious is the possibility that the expression of such "corporate" Christian guilt for the Crusades and the Iraq war might embolden some Muslim nations in their perceived justification for the persecution of Christians in their lands.

Dr. Patrick Soohkdeo, international director of the Barnabas Fund, believes that the authors and signers of the Yale Letter fall into different categories. Some may have accepted a liberal ecumenical interpretation of Christian theology and no longer feel it necessary to defend our fundamental doctrines. Others, certainly including some Evangelicals, are so anxious to improve the conditions of Christians living in Muslim lands and so desperately want to share the Gospel with Muslims that they are willing to make unreasonable concessions. Still others just don't have any grasp of Islamic teachings and actions.

A few individual reactions to the Muslim initiatives by different Church leaders are informative.

The metropolitan of an ethnic Eastern Orthodox body in New York was encouraged that these Muslim clerics referred to "Jesus as the Messiah."[228] He apparently didn't know that the Koran uses the term but with the meaning of an early prophet.

ELCA Presiding Bishop Mark Hanson, president of the Lutheran World Federation, was grateful for the Muslim authors' emphasis on a common heritage in the "sacred texts of the Abrahamic faiths."[229] He must have missed the statements in the Koran that all previous revelations were superseded by Allah's final revelation and that Surah 3:67 states that Abraham was not a Jew or a Christian but he "was an upright man, a Muslim and he was not one of the polytheists."

The Barnabas Fund analysis quotes the Anglican bishop of London, Richard Chartres, in regard to the Muslim letter: "This is a substantial letter which speaks of the unity of God from a Muslim perspective. It demands a substantial response which approaches the same theme from a Christian perspective." The analysis then makes this very astute observation about the Chartres remarks:

> "The Yale authors would have done well to heed his recommendation. The Muslim letter indeed calls for a response which

clarifies the Christian orthodox position on these themes. Only from such a clear statement of Christian positions can progress be made in dialogue towards a reconciliation that fully accepts the right of the other to be different without suffering any disadvantage for it."

The Barnabas Fund response sums up the substance of "A Common Word" from the 139 Muslim clerics and the "Yale Letter" signed by some 300 Christian clerics in these clear words:

> "The Muslim scholars in their opening letter respectfully call Muhammad 'the Prophet Muhammad,' adding the compulsory PBUH (Peace Be Upon Him) after every mention of his name, placing him immediately after God in the opening invocation: 'In the Name of God, the Compassionate, the Merciful, And may peace and blessings be upon the Prophet Muhammad,' as well as quoting the shahada: 'There is no god but God, Muhammad is the messenger of God' in which Muhammad is again mentioned immediately after God. The Christian scholars on the other hand, have denigrated and marginalized the person of our Lord and Savior Jesus Christ, merely referring to Him as 'Jesus Christ' as the Muslim scholars have done, as though he were just a mere human being with no special status for Christians. There is no allusion to his deity and lordship. There is no exaltation of his person and rank. It would seem he is not even a prophet with the status Muhammad has for Muslims. They have thus inadvertently confirmed the Muslim view of the superiority of Muhammad over Jesus."

The Barnabas Fund response also includes a report on the Roman Catholic response to "A Common Word":

> "The Vatican was rather slow to respond officially to the Muslim initiative. It seemed not so much interested in pure theological dialogue as in a more practical exchange that discussed the realities on the ground of Christians living in Muslim countries. Following a correspondence between the Vatican Secretary of State, Tarcisio Bertone, on behalf of the Pope, and the Jordanian Prince, Ghazi bin Muhammad bin Talal, clarifying the issues between the two sides, the way was opened for a summit meeting. The Pope stressed that he wanted to discuss respect for the dignity of all human beings, awareness of the other's religion, and a common commitment to promoting mutual tolerance among the younger generation. In other words, the Pope would not accept the limits set by the Muslim leaders of only discussing the theological implications of their statements on love of God and the neighbour, but wanted it expanded to include

practical implementations in the Muslim world, including discussion of human rights and equality for non-Muslims. The Pope also stressed that the common ground between Muslims and Christians is their belief in One God who is creator and judge, rather than accept the Muslim letter`s spurious definition of common ground between the two faiths as love for God and neighbour. The Jordanian prince insisted that the dialogue be limited to theological and spiritual themes."

The result of this response is a "Catholic-Muslim Forum," which has met twice—in November 2008 and November 2011. After the latest session, an article in *The Tablet*, a British Catholic weekly, reports, in part:

> "Five years after Pope Benedict XVI's Regensburg address that ignited protests around the Islamic world, the Catholic-Muslim Forum established to improve interfaith relations has said that what began as formal dialogue has become increasingly characterised by friendship.
>
> "The forum, which grew out of Muslim dissatisfaction with comments in Pope Benedict's 2006 Regensburg speech, held its second round of theological consultations in Jordan last week. The fate of Middle Eastern Christian minorities amid the Arab Spring's Islamist renaissance provided a sombre background to the meeting, much as perceived Christian misunderstandings about Islam preceded the first session of the forum at the Vatican in November 2008. But increasing contacts between Catholic officials and Muslim scholars of the Common Word initiative, the 2007 Islamic dialogue appeal to Pope Benedict, have created bonds that helped both sides tackle sensitive issues."[230]

This Catholic-Muslim Forum could become important in determining how well Christians and Muslims can live together in Muslim-ruled countries, as well as in secular countries with large Christian majorities.

The Way to Dialogue and Better Relations

The two basic problems in developing better Muslim-Christian dialogue and ultimately better relations is the same as winning the war being waged by radical Islamic terrorists:

1. Moderate Muslims—who are certainly in the majority, if not the overwhelming majority, in most places in the world—must be encouraged to speak out against terrorism perpetuated in the name of Islam and other Islamic extremism.

2. Those who illustrate a type of religious devotion to political correctness in regard to Islam must understand the damage they are doing to moderate Muslims and the encouragement they are providing

to radical Islamic terrorists. They are also obscuring the facts we need to know in order to understand the nature of our terrorist enemies.

A study of Islamic history demonstrates that any criticism of Muslim doctrines is not allowed and any deviation from this rule is subject to severe punishment. Apostasy, blasphemy, and even questioning of religious authority could result in beatings, imprisonment, or death. There certainly were similar periods in Christian history. However, in modern times, certainly as far back as the beginning of the 20th century, Christians have been free to publicly question even the most fundamental Christian doctrines without fear of reprisal. They might be threatened with hell-fire in the afterlife if they don't change their ways, but not physical punishment on earth. It would be ideal if all religions respected such freedom of conscience. But this really is not the question.

It is not necessary for modern or moderate Muslims to question the core teachings of their religion to fight terrorist acts committed in the name of their religion. There can be no reasonable debate that members of al-Qaeda and other Islamic terrorist organizations believe they are carrying out Allah's commands. During the American presence in Iraq, Sunni Muslims there increasingly turned against the Sunni Wahhabi al-Qaeda terrorists, charging that they were distorting and abusing Mohammad's teachings in the Koran. They were literally risking their lives on a daily basis by denouncing the indiscriminate murders of fellow Muslims and the enforcement of an oppressive form of *sharia* law as a distortion of Islam. However, since the American pullout and the crackdown on Sunnis by Prime Minister Maliki, new al-Qaeda-type bombings have reappeared.

Survey data indicate that while Muslims in America are moderates, they seem to be overwhelmingly reluctant to condemn Islamic terrorism. There are some notable exceptions, and these people should be recognized as true Muslim heroes. (One example noted in the previous chapter, Sheikh Muhammad Hisham Kabbani, head of the Islamic Supreme Council of America, proves his point. Recall that Sheikh Kabbani appeared before a forum at the U.S. State Department in 1999 and warned that 80 percent of the mosques and Muslim charitable organizations in America had been taken over by Muslim extremists. So-called moderate Muslim organizations protested and our government ignored his warnings. Had our leaders paid adequate attention, the Twin Towers might still be standing.) Steven Emerson sheds further light on this subject in his book *American Jihad: The Terrorists Living Among Us*. In Chapter 8, "Fighting Back, A Story of Unsung Heroes," he makes the point that in spite of "militant Islamist voices" heard in mosques all over the country, "militant Islamic views are confined to a relatively small slice of all American Muslims."[231]

Ironically, while writing this section, I glimpsed at an interview of a spokesman for CAIR (Council on American-Islamic Relations). The news commentator repeatedly listed well-known Islamic terrorist organizations such as Hamas and Hezbollah and asked the CAIR spokesman if he condemned them as terrorist organizations. The only answer he would give each time was that he "condemned terrorist acts by whoever they were committed."

A number American Muslim groups, such as the American Islamic Congress, have been started to condemn radical Muslims who commit terrorist acts in the name of their religion, but they don't seem to attract large numbers of followers. They also seem incapable of generating much media attention.

One of the major obstacles preventing the American people—and America's leaders—from understanding the nature and severity of the threat posed by radical Islamic terrorism today is the disinformation being disseminated by the politically correct Western elite "scholars" and opinion makers. (They also undoubtedly remove much sense of urgency for moderate Muslims to join in an effort to discredit Islamic extremists.)

These elitists, who are willing, and even apparently eager, to criticize Christianity and to disparage "Christian" or "American" values, are so sensitive not to offend Muslims that they sometimes appear to be Islamic apologists. This group seems so obsessed with proving how tolerant, broad-minded, multi-cultural, and politically correct they are that they become oblivious to the facts. As unbelievable as it sounds, some of them become so blinded by their desire to be recognized as unbiased "scholars" that they even search for ways to excuse those who attack us by blaming something in our behavior. If we have done something they don't like, then surely we can understand why they kill innocent civilians, including women and children!

Those of us who are in a position to make a difference by helping to inform the American people about the nature of the threats we face are confronted with an awesome responsibility. We must not be alarmists who might unintentionally spread hate and fear and tread upon some of the liberties we hold so dear in this great free country. Rather, we must be realists who seek to clearly understand the nature of our enemy and their history, which has motivated them to declare war on the free world.

If we are not thoroughly informed ourselves, we cannot properly inform those we hope to reach with our message. We are not at war with the Islamic religion and certainly not with the great majority of the law-abiding citizens who choose to practice this religion. We Christians hold strongly different religious beliefs (which we should be able to discuss in a peaceful manner) with those who practice the Muslim religion.

On the other hand, we do a great disservice to our people if we sugarcoat the threats from those who clearly state in their own words and demonstrate with their actions that they believe that they have a divine command to destroy the infidels (i.e., the Christians and the Jews).

In 2007, PBS introduced a documentary series titled "America at a Crossroads," dealing with the Islamic terrorist threat. I saw the first episode, in which they introduced the Islamic "authorities" who advised on the content. As they were interviewed, they spoke of this "noble and peaceful" ancient religion that was being totally distorted by the extremists. They "explained" that *jihad* means "struggle" rather than "holy war," that Islam means "peace" before "submission," and that Islam justifies war only in "self-defense." I couldn't help but question how men of such apparent intellectual ability could be so naïve.

A short time later, Frank Gaffney and Martin Burke of ABG Films came out with another documentary, "Islam vs. Islamists," which had been produced for the "America at a Crossroads" series with a sizable grant from the Corporation for Public Broadcasting. But PBS refused to air it as part of the series. They felt it might offend American Muslims. Fortunately, Fox News stepped in and ran the documentary on more than one occasion.

I am totally convinced, after many years of study, that liberals (and I know the pitfalls of generalizing) are incapable of dealing with a totalitarian philosophy. They don't believe in original sin and cannot bear to believe that all men are not basically good and reasonable and just want a good and peaceful life like the rest of us. Whether it's fascism, Nazism, communism, or radical Islamism, they can't grasp the fanaticism and the total lack of any moral values and compassion in these evil totalitarian systems.

From one "ism" to the next, the liberals continue to believe that if you will just be nice to them, reason with them, and treat them as we would like to be treated, then their evil desires will go away and everybody will just live happily ever after. Liberals seem to be totally incapable of learning that all efforts at "appeasement" are viewed by totalitarian regimes as signs of weakness.

Neville Chamberlain and his French counterparts thought they could appease Hitler, and millions of Jews paid the price with their lives. Attempts to appease Stalin and Soviet communism resulted in the enslavement of Eastern Europe for decades. It took a Herculean effort by Winston Churchill and the tragic attack on Pearl Harbor to awaken FDR before it was too late to the fact that the threats posed by Hitler and his allies were real and serious. Roosevelt turned right around and fell under the spell of Stalin—"Uncle Joe," as Franklin referred to the murderous and compassionless tyrant.

It took Ronald Reagan to understand the evil in the Soviet communist system, to bring this "evil empire" to its knees, and to win the Cold War. We need such leadership today if we are to survive the threats posed by the radical and dedicated Islamist terrorists.

Notes

[1] Bernard Lewis, *The Crisis Of Islam: Holy War and Unholy Terror* (Random House Trade Paperbacks, 2004), 38.

[2] Bernard Lewis, *The Middle East: A Brief History of the Last 2,000 Years* (Scribner, 1997), 229.

[3] Lewis, *The Middle East*, 219.

[4] Alfred Guillaume, *The Life of Muhammad: A Translation of Ibn Ishaq's Sirat Rasul Allah* (Oxford University Press, 2002), 691.

[5] Serge Trifkovic, *Defeating Jihad* (Regina Orthodox Press, 2006), 29.

[6] Serge Trifkovic, *The Sword of the Prophet* (Regina Orthodox Press, 2007), 14. He discusses the Kaaba and the previous uses of Allah in pre-Islamic times in more detail on 21 and 22.

[7] Martin Lings, *Muhammad: His Life Based on the Earliest Sources* (Inner Traditions, 2006), 1–2.

[8] Lings, 2-6.

[9] Albert Hourani, *A History of the Arab Peoples* (Belknap Press, 2010), 18.

[10] Trifkovic, *The Sword of the Prophet*, 25–26.

[11] Guillaume, 212.

[12] Trivkovic, *Defeating Jihad*, 23–24.

[13] Robert Spencer, *The Truth About Muhammad* (Regnery Publishing, 2007), 90. Spencer details all significant interactions and battles with the Arab and Jewish tribes during Mohammad's conquest of Arabia in this book. I will try to pick out some of the more significant and interesting details for a short summary. To understand militant Islam today, it is essential to understand not only the Prophet's instructions to his followers but also his actions as their political and military leader.

[14] Spencer, 90–92.

[15] It should be noted that Ishaq and other Muslim writers always contend that Mohammad took all of his actions in accord with Allah's instructions. Ishaq includes such acts under defensive warfare (*jihad*) following the above quote. Spencer, 212–213.

[16] Spencer, 102.

[17] The Hijra is also used by Muslims to describe the holy province in Arabia that includes Mecca and Medina.

[18] Spencer, 128–132.

[19] Spencer, 133–134.

[20] Spencer, 138–143.

[21] Spencer, 147.

[22] Spencer, 149.

[23] Spencer, 149.

[24] Spencer, 150–151.

[25] Spencer, 160–162.

[26] Spencer, 151–152.

[27] Bernard Lewis, *The Crisis of Islam: Holy War and Unholy Terror* (Random House Trade Paperbacks, 2004), 8.

[28] Robert Spencer, *The Politically Incorrect Guide to Islam (and the Crusades)* (Regnery Publishing, 2005), 24.

[29] Spencer, *The Politically Incorrect Guide to Islam (and the Crusades)*, 24.

[30] Trifkovic, *Defeating Jihad*, 22.

[31] See Spencer, *The Politically Incorrect Guide to Islam (and the Crusades)*, 53 ff., where he also discusses certain Old Testament misquotations in the Koran.

[32] Lewis, *The Crisis of Islam: Holy War and Unholy Terror*, 6-7.

[33] Spencer, *The Politically Incorrect Guide to Islam (and the Crusades)*, 108. This book and Serge Trifkovic's *The Sword of the Prophet* will be used extensively in this section on the first caliphs and the early Muslim conquests. Dr. Bernard Lewis will be another source and will be noted at the time.

[34] Abd El Schafi, *Behind the Veil: Unmasking Islam* (Pioneer Book Company, 2002). See pp. 11–73.

[35] Trifkovic, *Defeating Jihad*, 91.

[36] Lewis, *The Middle East*, 234.

[37] For a brief scholarly discussion of the conquest of Umar and his successors, see Spencer, *The Politically Incorrect Guide to Islam (and the Crusades)*, 107-117, and Trifikovic, *Defeating Jihad*, 87ff.

[38] David L. Lewis, *God's Crucible: Islam and the Making of Europe, 570-1215* (W.W. Norton & Company, 2009), 72.

[39] Spencer, *The Politically Incorrect Guide to Islam (and the Crusades)*, 109–110.

[40] Trifkovic, *Defeating Jihad*, 95.

[41] Bernard Lewis, *What Went Wrong?: The Clash Between Islam and Modernity in the Middle East* (Harper Perennial, 2003), 4-6.

[42] Lewis, *What Went Wrong?*, 8–9.

[43] Lewis, *What Went Wrong?*, 210–211.

[44] Spencer, *The Politically Incorrect Guide to Islam (and the Crusades)*, 47–63.

[45] Robert C. Davis, *Christian Slaves, Muslim Masters: White Slavery in the Mediterranean, the Barbary Coast, and*

Italy, 1500-1800 (Palgrave Macmillan, 2003), xxv-xxvi.

[46] Lewis, *What Went Wrong?*, 87–88.

[47] Lewis, *What Went Wrong?*, 233.

[48] Lewis explains the *Hijra* in *The Middle East*: "The migration of the Prophet and his followers from Mecca to Yathrib (later Medina) is known in Arabic as the *Hijra*, literally the migration and is regarded by Muslims as the decisive moment in Muhammad's apostolate," 52-53.

[49] Abdel Bari Atwan, *The Secret History of Al Qaeda* (University of California Press, 2006), 68–69.

[50] Atwan's understanding of *jihad* is developed on pp. 67-70 in *The Secret History of Al Qaeda*.

[51] Lewis, *What Went Wrong?*, 233.

[52] Spencer, p.19.

[53] Spencer, 33–45.

[54] Trifkovic, *Defeating Jihad*, 39–47.

[55] These two recognized scholars on Islam and Islamist terrorism offer unique insights into Islamic jihadism partly because of the similarity of their backgrounds. Dr. Walid Phares was born and raised in Beirut, Lebanon. Dr. Fawaz Gerges grew up in the village of Tal Abbas in the Akkar valley in northern Lebanon. They both grew up in neighborhoods inhabited by Muslims and Christians and both spoke and read Arabic. They both have extensive and impressive academic backgrounds. Phares' degrees include a master's degree in international law from the Universite de Lyons in France and a Ph. D. in international relations and strategic studies from the University of Miami. Gerges' academic achievements include a Ph.D. from Oxford University and a M.Sc. from the London School of Economics and Political Science.

A comparison of their backgrounds is important because Dr. Phares is heavily criticized by the politically correct elitists for his hard-line criticism of Islamists and jihadists. Dr. Gerges, on the other hand, is challenged by conservative scholars because of his politically correct approach to Islam and his sometimes-apparent efforts as an Islamic apologist. Since they both lived through the bloody civil war in Lebanon, why the differences in their approaches and emphasizes regarding Islamic terrorism? The answer to this question perhaps offers another important piece to the puzzle of truly understanding our terrorist enemies. It is important to note that Phares and his family are Maronite Christians, while Gerges comes from a family of Greek Orthodox Christians. Since the Maronites are part of the Roman Catholic communion and the Greek Orthodox are descendants of the Byzantine Christian Empire, the ancient Christian split is still in existence at least to some degree in Lebanon. The Roman or Latin division between the Greek or Byzantine branch of Christianity, so evident at the time of the Crusades, is still divisive in the Middle East. Sadly, there is more to the story in this case. Fawaz Gerges' older brother, "a colonel in the Lebanese army, was killed in 1990 by the Lebanese Forces," he notes in his book. The Lebanese Forces was a Christian militia, made up mostly of Maronite Christians, organized to fight the PLO and the Syrians occupying Lebanon during the war. This somewhat detailed background seems necessary in appreciating the "unique insights" into Islamic militancy these two men bring to the table.

Dr. Phares is an authority on the Arabic language and Arabic history in addition to a sometimes first-hand appreciation of Islamic terrorism. Phares practiced law in Beirut for a few years before emigrating to America in 1990. His explanation of "Bottom Up Jihad" as perfected by the Muslim Brotherhood in contrast to the "Top Down Jihad" practiced by the Wahhabis in Saudi Arabia is especially instructive.

[56] Walid Phares, *Future Jihad: Terrorist Strategies Against The West* (Palgrave Macmillan, 2006), 72 – 73.

[57] Phares, 65.

[58] Lewis, *The Middle East,* 218-243.

[59] Trifkovic, *The Sword of the Prophet,* 143-181.

[60] Spencer, *The Politically Incorrect Guide to Islam (and the Crusades),* 33-46 and 47-63.

[61] The ouster of Hosni Mubarak after 30 years in power and the first election in history of a Muslim Brotherhood Islamist has set Egypt on a new and dangerous course. Mubarak, like his predecessor, Anwar al Sadat, ruled Egypt mostly as a secular head of state. One of the reasons for the fall of both was the religious toleration of Christians and Jews. Their regimes became noted more for the persecution of Islamist radicals who threatened their secular governments. Now the Coptic Christians, as well as members of other religions and secularists, are justifiably fearful of persecution.

[62] Quoted in Schafi, *Behind the Veil,* 16.

[63] Rick Santorum, "The Elephant in the Room: A war of ideas within Islam," *Philly.com,* Feb. 22, 2012. Accessed Aug. 29, 2012, at http://www.philly.com/philly/columnists/rick_santorum/20091105_ The_Elephant_in_the_Room__A_war_of_ideas_within_Islam.html?c=r.

[64] Fawaz A. Gerges, *Journey of the Jihadist: Inside Muslim Militancy* (Houghton Mifflin Harcourt, 2006), 16.

[65] Feisal Abdul Rauf, "Five myths about Muslims in America," *The Washington Post*, April 1, 2011. Accessed Aug. 29, 2012 at http://www.washingtonpost.com/opinions/five-myths-about-muslims-in-america/2011/03/30/AFePWOIC_story.html.

[66] *Ibid.*

[67] Bruce Bawer, *Surrender: Appeasing Islam, Sacrificing Freedom* (Doubleday, 2009), 263-264. Bawer continues in this book to give frightening examples of how parts of Europe are buying into toleration of *sharia*. A judge in Frankfurt, Germany, ruled against a young Moroccan-German woman's plea for an expedited divorce based on her husband's brutality. The judge argued "that the wife should have been prepared for such treatment given that her husband's religion granted him the 'right to use corporal punishment.'" Another "horrific" decision was to treat "honor killings as manslaughter rather than murder" based on *sharia* law. Some courts in Norway have followed suit, since such killings according to their native customs are not crimes at all (see pp. 264 ff).

[68] Lewis, *The Crisis of Islam,* 120-136. Lewis also makes important references in *The Middle East* and his lecture I attended, referenced earlier. These sources emphasize the importance of this subject.

[69] Lewis, *The Middle East,* 202.

[70] Atwan, 154.

[71] *Ibid.*

[72] Lewis, *The Crisis of Islam,* 121.

[73] Bernard Lewis, Washington, D.C., lecture, Oct 25, 2007, author's notes.

[74] Lewis, *The Crisis of Islam,* 128.

[75] Lewis *The Crisis of Islam,* 129.

[76] Lewis *The Crisis of Islam,* 128.

[77] Lewis, *The Crisis of Islam,* 129.

[78] Atwan, 157.

[79] To quote two overused axioms: 1) Politics makes strange bedfellows, and 2) politics is not an exact science. These expressions are doubly true when it comes to diplomacy. With this in mind, I recommend two *New York Times* bestsellers written by a former CIA operative, Robert Baer, relating to U.S. relations with Saudi Arabia: *Sleeping with the Devil: How Washington Sold Our Soul for Saudi Crude* and *See No Evil: The True Story of a Ground Soldier in the CIA's War on Terrorism.*

[80] Those who follow history will remember that the non-interventionists or isolationist elitists contended that Germany and Japan posed no threat to the United States prior to Pearl Harbor. Likewise, those dubbed the politically correct "Ivy-League" elitists, such as McNamara and Kissinger, never accepted the fact that the Marxists really believed they could establish an utopia on earth. It took a Ronald Reagan to understand that the Soviet Communists actually intended to conquer the world.

[81] Atwan, 68, 69.

[82] We must be constantly reminded that almost all scholars on Islam recognize that at least one billion of the world's 1.3 billion or so Muslims are moderate and peace-loving Muslims. Such moderate Muslims have as much to fear from this still very large number of radical Muslims as do non-Muslims.

[83] Lewis, *Ibid.,* xvii-xviii.

[84] This section is taken largely from Dr. Lewis' lecture, based on my notes and the transcript that was provided to the participants.

[85] *Ibid.*

[86] *Ibid.*

[87] Two are by Steven Emerson: *Jihad Incorporated: A Guide to Militant Islam in the U.S.* (2006) and *American Jihad: The Terrorists Living Among Us* (2003). Another is *Bin Laden: The Man Who Declared War on America* (2001) by Yossef Bodansky.

[88] Atwan, *The Secret History of Al Qaeda,* 42. Atwan says that Aliyah was Muhammad's fourth wife and Osama was one of 54 children, the 21st of 29 brothers. Other sources contend that Aliyah was Muhammad bin Laden's 10th wife (of 22) and that Osama was the 16th child. I suspect that Atwan is closer to being accurate since he personally interviewed Osama and at least two of his brothers. In any case, he is telling the story as Osama wanted it told.

[89] Atwan, 160.

[90] Some scholars on Islam report that his college years were from 1976 to 1981. As we discuss some events in Osama's life and al-Qaeda, the reader should keep in mind there is some scholarly disagreement on certain details. It appears that modern Muslim history, like its ancient history, is not as precise as Western history.

[91] Yossef Bodansky, *Bin Laden: The Man Who Declared War on America* (Prima Lifestyles, 2001), p.11.

[92] Atwan, 43.

[93] Atwan, 44.

[94] Atwan, 75.

[95] Atwan, 161.

[96] Atwan, 162.

[97] Atwan, 48.

[98] Atwan, 78.

[99] Atwan, 70.

[100] Atwan, 70.

[101] Atwan, 88.

[102] Atwan, 79.

[103] As previously explained, Hasan al-Banna founded the Muslim Brotherhood on the radical fundamentalist theology of Salafism and Wahhabism. Sayyid Qutb further justified violent *jihad* against non-Islamic Muslim rulers as well as the infidels, typified by America.

[104] The Islamic apologists and politically correct liberal elitists have tried to discredit this long and extensively documented book by attacking the character of David Gaubatz, calling him an Islamophobe, among harsher descriptions. The Arabic-speaking Gaubatz has spent so much time in counterintelligence stationed in Muslim-ruled countries that he has apparently become convinced that the majority moderate Muslims in the world have hijacked a violent religion. In some of his personal statements (not recorded in this book), he has failed to distinguish Islam from Islamist jihadists. (The book is 422 pages long, including a 52-page Appendix that provides copies of Muslim Brotherhood and Council on American-Islamic Relations [CAIR] documents, as well as documents from other Islamic organizations in America. This section is followed by 43 pages of footnotes.) CAIR filed a lawsuit against Gaubatz for stealing their documents when his son brought many of the documents home rather than destroying them as instructed. *Politico*, a widely read bipartisan D.C. weekday newspaper and blog (www.politico.com), published a story Nov. 2, 2009, describing the lawsuit, which was dismissed by the court. They made this telling remark: "In an interesting twist, despite the book's harsh claims that CAIR is part of a 'jihadist network,' the suit does not allege libel or defamation." In any event, the book was written by the highly respected journalist and author Paul Sperry. Sperry primarily used the CAIR documents, unclassified FBI material, and other such documentation in preparation for writing the book, with some obvious input from Gaubatz.

[105] Pew Research Center for the People & the Press, "Muslim Americans: No Signs of Growth in Alienation or Support for Extremism: Mainstream and Moderate Attitudes," Aug. 30, 2011. Accessed Aug. 30, 2012, from http://www.people-press.org/2011/08/30/muslim-americans-no-signs-of-growth-in-alienation-or-support-for-extremism/.

[106] David Gaubatz and Paul Sperry, *Muslim Mafia: Inside the Secret Underworld that's Conspiring to Islamize America* (WND Books, 2009), 236

[107] Gaubatz and Sperry, 235-236.

[108] Barzinji was one of the original co-founders of the Muslim Student Association.

[109] Gaubatz and Sperry, 237-238.

[110] Gaubatz and Sperry, 42. This seven-page chapter, 42-49, explains in shocking detail why CAIR was founded and the role the Muslim Brotherhood played in its founding.

[111] Jason Trahan, "FBI: CAIR is a front group, and Holy Land Foundation tapped Hamas clerics for fundraisers," *The Dallas Morning News,* Oct. 7, 2008. Accessed Aug. 30, 2012, from http://crimeblog.dallasnews.com/2008/10/fbi-cair-is-a-front-group-and.html/.

[112] DiscoverTheNetworks.org, "Islamic Association for Palestine (IAP)." Accessed Aug. 30, 2012, at http://www.discoverthenetworks.org/printgroupProfile.asp?grpid=6215..

[113] Gaubatz and Sperry, 43.

[114] Gaubatz and Sperry, 43. The preparation for *sharia* theocracies may sound prophetic 20 years later with the victory of the Muslim Brotherhood in the Egyptian election. The only thing that stands between the Muslim Brotherhood's desire to establish such an Islamist theocracy in Egypt today is the Egyptian military. Hopefully the Military leaders will not shrink from preventing such a development that could have disastrous consequences in the entire region and the world, as well as in Egypt.

[115] Gaubatz and Sperry, 44.

[116] Gaubatz and Sperry. This quote and those immediately preceding it are taken from pp. 42-49.

[117] Paul Sperry, *Infiltration: How Muslim Spies and Subversives Have Penetrated Washington* (Thomas Nelson,

2008), 16.

[118] These opportunities are documented by former CIA agent Michael Scheuer, who started and ran the CIA's "Bin Laden Unit," in his book *Marching Toward Hell: America and Islam After Iraq* (Free Press, 2008).

[119] We noted earlier Nihad Awad's role in the founding of CAIR in 1993 to replace the Islamic Association for Palestine (IPA) to raise funds for Hamas.

[120] Sperry, 16-17.

[121] Sperry, 16-17.

[122] *The New Republic* has been a weekly publication on politics and the arts since its founding in 1914. It is known as basically liberal on fiscal and social issues while moderate to conservative on foreign policy or defense issues. It tended to support the Democratic Leadership Council and the "New Democrats" as typified by Bill Clinton and Joe Lieberman.

[123] Franklin Foer, "Grover Norquist's Strange Alliance With Radical Islam," *The New Republic*, Nov. 11, 2001. Accessed Aug. 30, 2012, at http://www.freerepublic.com/focus/fr/561786/posts.

[124] Interview with Donald Rumsfeld, "Fareed Zakaria GPS" (Sept. 11, 2011), Transcript. Accessed Aug. 31, 2012 at http://transcripts.cnn.com/TRANSCRIPTS/1109/11/fzgps.01.html.

[125] Botha served six years as prime minister when that was the most powerful position in the government. He was elected president in 1984 when executive power was transferred to that office. He served as president of South Africa for five years.

[126] This is a subject on which few scholarly works have been written. What has been written mostly comes from politically correct authors who give little evidence that they know what the Cold War was all about.

[127] I had good reason to ignore politically correct denials of such fighting forces since I saw Russian, East German, and many Cuban POWs in Angola.

[128] During Botha's time heading up the government as prime minister, a major uproar in Parliament could cause him to be replaced. He was always under fire from the most extreme supporters of apartheid.

[129] It was a difficult occasion when I scheduled a dinner with the elderly South African ambassador to the U.S. at the Georgetown Club. He knew nothing of the decision Stu and I had reached. The kindly Christian gentleman actually broke into tears when I explained our decision. (He had other American lobbyists he had inherited, but we were his find. Stu always insisted I could handle such meetings best one on one. "Thanks a lot" was my response.) I shed a few tears myself, especially when he explained that he had come authorized to raise our retainer significantly. Unfortunately, it didn't matter.

[130] It should be noted that Panama already had some very good Democrat lobbyists. They knew and worked well with Delvalle and at least one of them had developed a close relationship with Noriega. They had recommended Hecht, Spencer and Associates because of our relationships with the administration and Republican members of Congress.

[131] Stu always wanted me to take the lead in such meetings, and he would correct me if I said something wrong or with which he disagreed. He probably knew I was going to talk anyway. He always said I was a better lobbyist than he since I could deal with congressional "BS" better than he could.

[132] As a matter of fact, there was one notable meeting. I happened to have an early morning meeting with the CIA director just hours after a ship loaded with guns and ammunition headed for a communist country was seized in the Panama Canal. The first thing I did was to ask Mr. Casey about the ship now in custody. His immediate response was, "How long have you known about that ship?" When I said for several hours, he blurted out: "Hell, I have only known about it for less than an hour. Your intelligence sources are better than mine!" Needless to say, we had a short meeting since he was anxious to find out why he didn't know about the event sooner.

[133] Delvalle always tried to do the right thing for Panama. He had a good relationship with Noriega and remained a loyal ally until Noriega was indicted by the U.S. on charges of drug smuggling in 1988. At that time he tried to remove Noriega as head of the Panamanian Defense Forces, and Noriega ended up having him replaced as president. Fortunately, we had long ceased to represent Panama by that time.

[134] This was actually a brilliant plan in my opinion. These contras were pro-American freedom fighters opposing a brutal regime that was headed up by a Castro puppet. The only problem was that it was illegal. After the Vietnam War ended, the "Boland Amendment," which forbade American involvement in such conflicts, was passed into law. The president could not be informed since he would be duty bound to bring such an undertaking to an immediate end. If North, like Noriega, would have been smart enough to study our backgrounds, he would have learned of my anti-communist background and my hawkish military and national security inclinations. I would have been an ally.

[135] Frank Gaffney Jr., "A Troubling Influence," *FrontPageMagazine.com*, Dec. 9, 2003. Accessed Aug. 31, 2012, at http://archive.frontpagemag.com/readArticle.aspx?ARTID=15084.

[136] Wikipedia contributors, "Grover Norquist," *Wikipedia, The Free Encyclopedia*, http://en.wikipedia.org/wiki/Grover_Norquist (accessed Sept. 4, 2012).

[137] See http://www.freerepublic.com/focus/fr/561786/posts.

[138] Sperry, *Infiltration*, 279. Many publications give details about the Muslim involvement in the 2000 campaign but Sperry's is the most interesting and detailed. He notes, for example, "At the time, counterterrorism agents at the FBI's field office in Tampa were investigating al-Arian, a Palestinian American who in speeches had referred to Jews as 'monkeys and pigs' and shouted 'Death to Israel!' while raising money for Palestinian jihadists."

[139] Sperry, *Infiltration*, 281. As noted in the Introduction, Bush won Florida by 537 votes.

[140] Sperry, *Infiltration*, 281-282.

[141] Ted Balaker, "Where Has the Antiwar Movement Gone?," *The Huffington Post*, Jan. 27, 2011. Accessed Sept. 3, 2012, at http://www.huffingtonpost.com/ted-balaker/where-has-the-antiwar-mov_b_815073.html.

[142] For a video of Khan making this statement, see http://www.youtube.com/watch?v=5lnIla7twYc.

[143] Sperry, *Infiltration*, 308-309.

[144] Frank Gaffney, "Memorandum for Members of the Board of Directors of the American Conservative Union," Jan. 14, 2011. Accessed Sept. 3, 2012, at http://suhailkhanexposed.com/wp-content/uploads/2011/01/20110121_Memo_to_the_ACU_Board_115.pdf.

[145] Sperry, *Infiltration*, 2-3. It is difficult to determine what period in Islam's history Khan might have had in mind. In the very beginning in Mecca, Mohammad's own tribe rejected his claim to be a prophet and he and his followers were forced to relocate to Medina. Mohammad had no army in Mecca and there was no fighting. Once Mohammad established his army in Medina, he did attack a caravan of his own tribe and defeated a large superior force in the well-known Battle of Badr. On most other occasions, Mohammad commanded the largest army. The earliest caliphs were always the aggressors when they invaded the Christian lands. They were never invaded and lived under no oppressors for the first 400 years, unless a few lived in lands the Muslims had not conquered.

[146] Paul Sperry, "Who Is Suhail Khan?," *FrontPageMag.com*, Jan. 20, 2011. Accessed Sept. 4, 2012, at http://frontpagemag.com/2011/paul-sperry/who-is-suhail-khan/.

[147] This account is based on a front page story in *The Washington Times*, "Muslims press McCain on 'Islamic' terror label," April 21, 2008. The article, with the title "McCain pressed on 'Islamic' terror label," also is available online at http://www.washingtontimes.com/news/2008/apr/21/mccain-pressed-on-islamic-terror-label/?page=all.

[148] Dick Morris and Eileen McGann in their book *Fleeced* (Harper, 2008) show how the Society of Professional Journalists has taken political correctness to new extremes. In Chapter 2, "How the Liberal Media Downplay Terrorism," pp. 45-76, they discuss "diversity guidelines" proposed at the National Convention of the Society of Professional Journalists in Seattle Oct. 6, 2007. Among other things, the Society urges journalists to avoid words such as "Islamic terrorist" or "Muslim extremist." The book makes a strong case for how liberal or "politically correct" journalists not only are downplaying the religious motivation of such terrorists but are minimizing the severity of such terrorists threats themselves.

[149] My understanding of Persian history, Zoroastrianism, the Islamic invasion, and the rise and teachings of the Shiite sect is based primarily on four sources: Vali Nasr, *The Shia Revival: How Conflicts within Islam Will Shape the Future* (W.W. Norton & Company, 2007); Sandra Mackey, *The Iranians: Persia, Islam and the Soul of a Nation* (Plume, 1998); Kenneth M. Polack, *The Persian Puzzle: The Conflict Between Iran and America* (Random House Trade Paperbacks, 2005); and Stephen Kinzer, *All the Shah's Men: An American Coup and the Roots of Middle East Terror Second*(Wiley, 2008). I will attempt to give appropriate credit and point out some of their disagreements in additional footnotes.

[150] Nasr, 41-42.

[151] Nasr, 67-68.

[152] Sandra Mackey, *The Iranians,* 50.

[153] Pollack, 12.

[154] Nasr, 38.

[155] Nasr, 37-39.

[156] Nasr, 54.

[157] Nasr, 133.

[158] Nasr, 131.

[159] Kinzer, 22-23.

[160] Kinzer, 25.

[161] In addition to the sources mentioned above regarding the Sunni-Shiite split, the British and U.S. involvement

in Persia/Iran, the coup of 1953, U.S. foreign policy decisions over the 37-year reign of Mohammad Reza Pahlavi, and the revolution of 1978-79, which resulted in the Shah's fall, I have relied heavily on the following primary sources: Mark Bowden, *Guests of the Ayatollah: The Iran Hostage Crisis: The First Battle in America's War with Militant Islam* (Grove Press, 2007); Hamilton Jordon, *Crisis* (Berkley, 1983); Ali M. Ansari, *Confronting Iran: The Failure of American Foreign Policy and the Next Great Crisis in the Middle East* (Basic Books, 2007); Mohammad Reza Pahlavi, *Answer to History* (Stein & Day, 1982); and Princess Ashraf Pahlavi, *Faces in a Mirror: Memoirs from Exile* (Prentice Hall, 1980). Once again, I intend to try to give adequate credit to these interesting sources and others.

[162] M. Pahlavi, 67.

[163] Kinzer, 97.

[164] M. Pahlavi, 91.

[165] Ansari, 45.

[166] M. Pahlavi, 102.

[167] A. Pahlavi, 167.

[168] M. Pahlavi, 60.

[169] M. Pahlavi, 148.

[170] M. Pahlavi, 154.

[171] Mackey, 208.

[172] Pollack, 127.

[173] M. Pahlavi, 102.

[174] M. Pahlavi, 203.

[175] Nasr, 149.

[176] M. Pahlavi, 149.

[177] A. Pahlavi, 195.

[178] Pollack, 132 ff, incl. footnotes.

[179] M. Pahlavi, 23.

[180] Ansari, 79.

[181] Pollack, 132-133.

[182] Wikipedia contributors, "Zbigniew Brzezinski," *Wikipedia, The Free Encyclopedia*, http://en.wikipedia.org/wiki/Zbigniew_Brzezinski (accessed Sept. 6, 2012).

[183] M. Pahlavi, 150.

[184] Mackey, 282.

[185] M. Pahlavi, 167.

[186] M. Pahlavi, 158.

[187] M. Pahlavi, 148.

[188] Ansari, 83.

[189] Pollack, 141-180.

[190] Pollack, 143.

[191] Pollack, 144.

[192] Described briefly in Mark Steyn, *America Alone: The End of the World As We Know It* (Regnery Publishing, 2008), 123.

[193] In 2005, the noted historian and scholar on Islam, Robert Spencer, wrote *The Politically Incorrect Guide to Islam (and the Crusades)*, which challenges the myths propagated by the "politically correct" concerning the Crusades. In Part II, "The Crusades," he includes five short chapters with titles that reveal their importance: Chapter 10, "Why the Crusades Were Called" (pp. 121-132); Chapter 11, "The Crusades: Myth and Reality" (pp. 133-145); Chapter 12, "What the Crusades Accomplished – And What They Didn't" (pp. 147-157); Chapter 13, "What if the Crusades Had Never happened?" (pp.159-169); and Chapter 14, "Islam and Christianity: Equivalent Traditions?" (pp. 171-179). Much of my knowledge of the Crusades was gleaned from or confirmed by reading these chapters.

[194] Mark Steyn, *America Alone: The End of the World As We Know It* (Regnery Publishing, 2008), 125.

[195] Dr. Rodney Stark, for 32 years a professor of sociology and comparative religion at the University of Washington before becoming co-director of the Institute for Studies of Religion at Baylor University in 2004, has published 28 books and 144 articles, mostly in the fields of sociology, the sociology of religion, and the history of religious movements. After graduating from college, Stark served in the U.S. Army and worked as a

journalist for the *Oakland Tribune* before entering graduate school. He received his M.A. and Ph.D. from The University of California at Berkeley. One of his earlier books, an introductory college sociology text book, is in its tenth edition. I cite his background because I believe that his 2009 book, *God's Battalions*, is the most authoritative, comprehensive, and balanced book available on the history of the Crusades and the reasons they were waged. (The book has two descriptive subtitles: "The Case for the Crusades" and "The Truth about the Christian Crusades and Muslim Jihad.") This book is essential reading for anyone who is trying to understand today's threat from Islamic terrorism.

[196] Rodney Stark, *God's Battalions* (HarperOne, 2009), 8-9.

[197] Stark, 2.

[198] Lewis, *The Crisis Of Islam: Holy War and Unholy Terror,* 38.

[199] Spencer quotes an early 12th-century Christian bishop who wrote a history of Jerusalem as having written that the Crusaders "killed between twenty and thirty thousand people in the city." He also references a Muslim author, writing 100 years after the event, as claiming that the "Crusaders 'killed more than seventy thousand Muslims' in Jerusalem," 136.

[200] Stark, 159.

[201] Stark, 159.

[203] I must reemphasize that any Christian pastor or layman who desires to obtain a better understanding of why the Crusades took place and what they did and did not accomplish must read Stark's *God's Battalions*. This fair and balanced work discusses opposing views and includes an extensive bibliography for readers seeking more information or seeking to substantiate his references.

[204] Stark notes that sources for an exact number of crusaders on the First Crusade are sketchy at best. For example, Fulcher of Chartres claimed that there were 6 million, of which 600,000 made it to Jerusalem. Stark points out that this is impossible since the entire population of France was only 5 million. The most reliable scholars try to determine how many left from the various countries. Stark states: "The best modern estimates are that around 130,000 set out for the Holy Land, of which about 13,000 were nobles and knights accompanied by perhaps 50,000 trained infantrymen and 15,000 to 20,000 noncombatants, including clergy, servants, and the usual camp followers."

[206] Stark, 137.

[207] Such attrition was due partly to military skirmishes along the way and to outbreaks of disease. But most attrition was due to the fact that many had just turned around and headed back home. They had just decided the journey was too difficult, and many of them had little military value in any case.

[208] Stark, 155.

[209] *Ibid.*

[210] Stark, 156.

[211] Stark's descriptions of the other four Crusades make for interesting reading.

[212] Dr. Bernard Lewis quotes this phrase in various places (including in his lecture referenced in a number of places) as a major motivation of Osama bin Laden and other Islamic terrorists.

[213] Dr. Lewis' rather lengthy quote is recorded here because he is such a universally recognized authority on the subject and packs a wealth of information and challenges into this statement. The quote is taken from an early transcript of the lecture, which was not edited by Lewis and could contain minor grammatical errors.

[214] Mark Steyn, *America Alone: The End of the World As We Know It* (Regnery Publishing, 2008).

[215] Steyn's birthrate statistics should be taken seriously. He gives this example: "Scroll way down to the bottom of the Hot One Hundred top breeders and you'll eventually find the United States, hovering just at replacement rate with 2.11 births per woman. New Zealand's just below; Ireland's at 1.9; Australia, 1.7. But Canada's fertility rate is down to 1.5, well below replacement rate; Germany and Austria are at 1.3, the brink of the death spiral; Russia and Italy are at 1.2; Spain, 1.1—about half replacement rate. So Spain's population is halving with every generation",10.

[216] Steyn, xi-xii.

[217] Steyn, 98. Steyn discusses secularism in Europe in pp. 96-98, 100-102, and 110.

[218] A book released in 2006 by an American-born author who now lives in Norway, Bruce Bawer, *While Europe Slept: How Radical Islam Is Destroying the West from Within* (Anchor, 2007), is a worthwhile read. Bawer apparently is a libertarian, since one of his strong criticisms of Islam relates to the treatment of homosexuals. However, since he now lives in Scandinavia and has traveled extensively throughout Europe, he offers some important insights to this discussion.

[219] For an informative take on what happens when the Muslim population reaches certain percentages of a country's overall population, see "What Islam Isn't," an adaptation from *Slavery, Terrorism & Islam: The Historical Roots and Contemporary Threat* by the Rev. Dr. Peter Hammond (Christian Liberty Books, 2005), at http://archive.frontpagemag.com/readArticle.aspx?ARTID=30675.

[220] Benedict was a professor of theology at the University of Regensburg in Regensburg, Bavaria, Germany, from 1969-1977. He resigned his professorship when he became a cardinal and was named archbishop of Munich.

[221] The text of the lecture is available online at http://www.vatican.va/holy_father/benedict_xvi/speeches /2006/september/documents/hf_ben-xvi_spe_20060912_university-regensburg_en.html.

[222] "Statement by Card. Tarcisio Bertone, Secretary of State," Sept. 16, 2006. Accessed Sept. 5, 2012, at http://www.vatican.va/roman_curia/secretariat_state/card-bertone/2006/documents/rc_seg-st_20060916_dichiarazione_en.html.

[223] "Open Letter to His Holiness Pope Benedict XVI," Oct. 12, 2006, 3. Accessed Sept. 5, 2012 at http://www.sis.gov.eg/PDF/En/Arts&Culture/0726070000000000010001.pdf.

[224] The copy of the Koran I have used for this book was translated by M.H. Shakir and distributed by Tahrike Tarsile Qur'an, Inc., which describes itself as "a nonprofit religious organization ... devoted to the dissemination of authentic knowledge concerning Islam through the sale and free distribution of copies of the Holy Qur'an and its translation."

[225] The international director of the Barnabas Fund is the Rev. Dr. Patrick Sookhdeo, who was born into a Muslim family in Guyana. When he was in his teens, his family immigrated to England, where he was first exposed to Christianity. At the age of 22, he converted to Christianity and began his studies to become an Anglican priest. He earned a Ph.D. in Islamic Studies at the University of London. In 1989, he created the London-based "Institute for the Study of Islam and Christianity." Dr. Sookhdeo spends most of his time directing the Barnabas Fund, but he is also a senior visiting fellow at the Defense Academy of the United Kingdom and a visiting fellow at Cranfield University, also in the U.K. He is an expert in analyzing the intricacies of Islamic terminology.

[226] The Barnabas Fund analysis can be retrieved at http://barnabasfund.org/US/News/Archives/Barnabas-Fund-Response-to-the-Yale-Center-for-Faith-and-Culture-Statement.html.

[227] The "Yale Letter" (formally, "Loving God and Neighbor Together: A Christian Response to A Common Word Between [sic] Us and You") is available online at http://www.yale.edu/divinity/news/ 071118_news _nytimes.pdf.

[228] See http://www.acommonword.com/index.php?page=responses&item=46.

[229] See http://www.acommonword.com/index.php?page=responses&item=2.

[230] Tom Heneghan, "Tauran hails friendship with Muslims," *The Tablet*, Dec. 3, 2011. Accessed Sept. 5, 2012, at http://thetablet.co.uk/article/162067.

[231] Steven Emerson, *American Jihad: The Terrorists Living Among Us* (Free Press, 2003), 159.

6

The Cultural War Being Waged by the Radical Secularists

The secular war that threatens our nation today is referred to popularly as the "Cultural War," "Culture War," or even "Culture *Wars*." (Stephen Carter notes a 1991 book by sociologist James Davison Hunter with the title *Culture Wars*. In the book, Hunter "quotes a 1981 address in which the president of Yale University told incoming freshmen that politically active Christian evangelicals were 'peddlers of coercion.'"[1] The "Culture Wars" title, or something akin to it, for the cultural struggle in our country has taken on a life of its own.)

The Cultural War is more difficult to define than the war we face with the radical Islamic terrorists. It is insidious, and it often cloaks itself in the vocabularies of patriotism or individual rights. This war has been well planned. It is purposefully so multifaceted that even the most well intentioned God-fearing citizens fail to realize that a struggle for the very soul of this country is raging.

We would do well as informed citizens to carefully consider such questions as these: *Who is waging this war, and what are their goals? What is at stake? When did this war begin? What role did religious faith play for our nation's Founding Fathers and for our Republic's first citizens? What responsibilities do we have as Lutheran Christians, especially those among the Lutheran clergy, to become involved in this cultural struggle?*

These are among the questions I intend to explore in this chapter and the next.

Some would argue that we had a strong radical secularist element among the early Founders and that this element wanted to establish a government devoid of all moral and religious (especially Christian) values. Except for Ethan Allen and Thomas Paine (and maybe a handful of others few have ever heard of), the facts do not bear out such a conclusion. In fact, even the least orthodox (in Christian terms) of the best-known Founders clearly recognized the vital importance of the role of religion in the founding of this country.

As the country moved into the 20th century, there were a few early communists, socialists, anarchists, and atheists who resented capitalism and any moral restrictions on one's behavior and who wanted to destroy or change our system of government. But I believe that war on the moral and religious foundations of the American Republic was declared in earnest in 1920 with the founding of the American Civil Liberties Union, or ACLU.

While the numbers of organizations attacking America's moral foundations are legion in today's society, the ACLU is the oldest, largest, best financed, and most dangerous of them all. Since Roger Baldwin and a few others founded the ACLU, it has taken the lead in organizing, planning, and implementing the attacks on the moral and religious values of America. Baldwin and his inner circle took seriously one of the best known sayings of Karl Marx: "A people without a heritage are easily persuaded."

Knowing that they could not destroy the strong moral and religious foundations of such a great nation rapidly without a violent revolution (and even their early communist allies would soon reluctantly realize that this was not going to happen), they took a more gradual approach. They could damage the foundations a little at a time and relegate religion to a purely private matter with no place in the debate on public morality and behavior. They would take on moral issues one at a time as each opportunity arose. The planned efforts by the left-wing secularist organizations to infiltrate academia, law, the media, some elements of government, and other disciplines that controlled public opinion would take time to germinate and grow. The liberal elites in the various disciplines would be used either wittingly or unwittingly to advance their causes.

The ACLU and its growing number of allies had only limited success until their first major breakthrough came in the form of a U.S. Supreme Court decision in 1947. Justice Hugo Black, a former U.S. senator from Alabama with a checkered past, orchestrated the debate and wrote the majority opinion in *Everson v. The Board of Education,* a case involving Catholic parochial school children being reimbursed by New Jersey taxpayers for bus fares to school, just as public-school children were. In a decision that ironically allowed the Catholic-school children to receive bus fares, the historically anti-Catholic Black wrote in the majority opinion that the "First Amendment has erected a wall between church and state. That wall must be kept high and impregnable."

Black ignored the history surrounding the First Amendment, including James Madison's clear reservations and statements, the congressional debate, and the explicit intentions of the Congress that drafted and passed the First Amendment. He further misused Jefferson's "wall" metaphor and gave the impression that Jefferson had something to do with drafting and passing the First Amendment, in spite of the fact that Jefferson was out of the country as minister to France at the time. In fact, Black's interpretation of "wall of separation" would make many of the actions and statements of Jefferson and Madison during their presidencies flagrant violations of the law.

Perhaps most telling as regards Black's lack of serious scholarship in preparing his interpretation of the First Amendment is his apparent failure even to consult Justice Joseph Story's *Commentaries on the Constitution*. Joseph Story served 34 years on the Supreme Court, from 1811 to 1845. He was appointed by President Madison (who is credited with being the primary author of the First Amendment) and was a professor at Harvard Law School during most of these years. Former Chief Justice William Rehnquist characterizes Story's *Commentaries* as "by far the most comprehensive treatise on the United States Constitution that had then appeared."[2]

With Black's majority opinion in the *Everson* decision, *judicial activism* burst on the scene as a major weapon in the radical secularists' cultural war on America's traditional values. The date of the *Everson* decision is comparable to the 9/11 date forever to be associated with the attack on our country by radical Islamist terrorists.

In the next chapter, we will examine the life of Justice Hugo LaFayette Black in an attempt to understand his revolutionary decision concerning "the wall of separation between church and state." (It is remarkable that for almost 150 years after the founding of this nation, the Judeo-Christian moral values upon which this country was founded existed virtually unchallenged. This is especially remarkable considering that during this period of time we went through the bloodiest war in our history, with both the North and the South claiming that the God of the Bible was on their side.)

When Thomas Jefferson wrote about a "wall of separation" between church and state in his letter to the Danbury (Connecticut) Baptist Association, it was the only time he ever used this metaphor in a religious context. This "wall of separation between church and state" was so important to Jefferson that he never referred to it in any of his other writings, before or after the Danbury letter! Recently reconstructed hand-written notes in the margins of the draft letter to the Danbury Baptists—made possible by new technology in the FBI lab—cast major light on Jefferson's intended audience and his purpose for writing the letter. The controversy over this letter and Jefferson's beliefs about the proper relationship of church and state will be examined later in this chapter. It will become evident that if Jefferson did want to build a wall of separation between church and state, it would have been a very low wall. It would need to be low enough for him to step over two days after writing his letter to the Danbury Baptists, when he attended a Christian worship service in the U.S. House of Representatives—a practice he followed almost every Sunday during the remaining seven years of his tenure as president. (Incidentally, Madison often followed the same practice when he was president.)

When we examine the faith of our Founders and their attitudes toward the importance of religion in the country they founded, the evidence dispels the liberal-secularist myths about how irreligious they were and how they wanted to protect the government from Christian influence.

Using the lowest reasonable measurement, we would be compelled to bestow the title of "Founding Father" on at least 204 men.[3] This would include those who were delegates to the Continental Congresses, the signers of the Founding documents, and members of the first U.S. Congress. The overwhelming majority of these men were Trinitarian Christians, and most were known for deep religious convictions. They were properly representative of their constituents, because this young country was inhabited by a strong majority of deeply religious people.

While it is true that a few of the most famous Founders held less than orthodox Christian beliefs, a closer look at what they actually believed flies in the face of much of the conventional wisdom spouted by many of the hardcore secularists who long for a society governed without any moral constraints. Statements made by some "scholars" that the majority of the Founders were deists are based either on wishful thinking or on lack of scholarship. (Benjamin Franklin was a self-confessed deist, but certainly not of the variety who believed that God is an "absentee landlord." When Franklin's laudatory remarks about the Christian religion are considered, it is easy to understand why some refer to him as a "Christian deist.")

George Washington's actions following his first inauguration speak volumes regarding the attitude toward religion in the country at the time. After Washington took the first presidential oath at Federal Hall in New York City on April 30, 1789, he improvised "so help me, God" at the conclusion of the oath and then kissed the Bible. After the ceremonies, President Washington and his party, which evidently included all the members of the First Congress, attended a worship service at St. Paul's Chapel in New York City.[4]

Some of the radical secularist "scholars" make a big deal out of the fact that God is not mentioned in the Constitution. It makes me question what they have been doing. They certainly have not been studying the controversies surrounding the drafting and adoption of a "federal" constitution. The states were so reluctant to give up power to a federal government that the drafters certainly were not going to bring religion into the mix. Any religious questions were reserved solely for the states.

Six of the 13 states had some type of established church. All had some religious regulations. Eleven of the 13 states had a religious test for holding office (most required belief in the deity of Jesus Christ); a number of the states had such a test for establishing eligibility to vote. The climate was so tense surrounding the Constitutional Convention that Patrick Henry even refused to attend, saying that he "smelt a rat." The final draft of the Constitution was never voted on by the Convention delegates. Once 39 of the 55 delegates had signed the Constitution, the document was sent to the states for ratification without a vote. (The delegates did feel compelled to ban a religious test for holding federal office and virtually established the sanctity of Sunday, "the Christian Sabbath," as a federal day of rest.)

In 1740, the Anglicans, Congregationalists, and Quakers were by far the largest churches in the colonies. Then the Great Awakening took place between 1735 and 1745, and many settlers began to flock to the more evangelical churches. Anglican priests and Congregationalist ministers would go back to England and other places in Europe and complain about the sad state of affairs of religion in America. It was not that the American settlers were forsaking the Christian religion; they were abandoning traditional denominationalism. By 1800, the largest denominations in America were the Baptists, Presbyterians, and Methodists (who didn't have their first meeting in America until 1766).[5]

Was America a Christian nation at the time of its founding? The evidence is clear that the Founders certainly did not want a federally established national church. There should, however, be no reasonable question that at the time of our founding, America was a nation of Christians. Richard John Neuhaus, in making the case that the contention that America is a secular society is a relatively new idea, quotes interesting language from two 20th century Supreme Court decisions. In a 1931 Supreme Court decision relating to whether a conscientious objector could become a citizen, a sentence reads: "We are a Christian people, according to one another the equal right of religious freedom, and acknowledging with reverence the duty of obedience to God." Neuhaus then quotes from a 1951 decision by Justice William O. Douglas, who was not known as a deeply religious man, but who writes: "We are a religious people whose institutions presuppose a Supreme Being" (*Zorach v. Clauson*).[6] Father Neuhaus then notes that more recent Supreme Court decisions seem to shy away from such language.

Alexis de Tocqueville spent nine months in the United States in 1831 and returned to his native France to publish his first volume of *Democracy in America* in 1835. As we examine a few of his impressions of religion in America, we will understand why he believed that there was no other country on earth where the Christian religion had more influence over its people. In a brief discussion of how visitors to our country often notice features that we tend to take for granted, Richard John Neuhaus makes another interesting observation. After pointing out that we usually quote Tocqueville as an early foreign observer of religion in 19th-century America, he quotes another source from a different part of the globe:

> "The Austrian journalist Francis Grund wrote in 1837: 'The religious habits of the Americans form not only the basis of their private and public morals, but have become so thoroughly interwoven with their whole course of legislation that *it would be impossible to change them without affecting the very essence of their government...*'" (emphasis added).[7]

My research on this subject indicates there can be no reasonable doubt that this is an accurate description of how our government functioned from the time of our founding until the cultural bomb that was dropped in 1947 shattered the moral foundations of our government so carefully crafted by our wise Founders.

Following on the precedents set by the *Everson* decision, the ACLU and its allies won Supreme Court decisions banning prayer in public schools in 1962 and 1963. In 1964, the Supreme Court overturned a conviction based on an Ohio obscenity law. In 1968, the Court struck down an Arkansas law prohibiting the teaching of evolution in public schools.

The once-simmering war on American cultural values was now burning bright, and it burned out of control once again in 1973. The *Roe v. Wade* decision overturned state abortion laws and granted abortion virtually on demand. (There was a companion case, *Doe v. Bolton*, decided at the same time with the same results that has not received as much notoriety.) This decision took the question of judicial activism to a new high and reshaped national politics. The convoluted reasoning of the seven unelected justices who took a matter of such great moral importance out of the hands of the people and their elected representatives will be discussed below. Suffice it to say at this point that more than 40 million babies have lost their lives, child abuse cases have quadrupled, and the number of births to unmarried women has more than tripled. The most telling fact may be that the two women involved in *Wade* and *Bolton* are now strongly pro-life and are doing everything they can to stop the atrocious acts being performed in their names.

Republics and democracies historically have been few in number in comparison to totalitarian forms of governments and are all too frequently short lived. The demise and eventual fall of such governments ruled indirectly by the people have usually resulted from internal moral decay due to the loss of religious convictions. In *The Naked Public Square*, Neuhaus makes this sobering and penetrating observation about the major struggles in the 20th century:

> "The case can be made that the great social and political devastations of our century have been perpetrated by regimes of *militant secularism*, notably those of Hitler, Stalin and Mao. This is true, and it suggests the naked public square is a dangerous place. When religious transcendence is excluded, when the public square has been swept clean of divisive sectarianism, the space is opened to seven demons aspiring to transcendent authority. As with a person so also with a society, the last condition is worse than the first" (emphasis added).[8]

Benjamin Franklin, arguably the least religious of the well-known Founders as far as profession of faith and the frailties of his personal behavior are concerned, believed very strongly that encouragement of religion is essential for the survival of this government. Franklin's fear that Americans might lose their religious devotion perhaps helps to explain his response to a lady at the conclusion of the Constitutional Convention when she asked: *"Well, Doctor, what have we got—a*

Republic or a Monarchy?" To which he responded: *"A Republic, if you can keep it."*[9] Franklin, like Abraham Lincoln after him, was concerned about how long a nation that derived its power from the consent of the governed could survive.

This is a question that must be seriously considered by every generation, and it must not be taken lightly. As we were taught—at least in my high-school history classes—*"eternal vigilance is the price of liberty."*

The Adoption of our Founding Documents

The Declaration of Independence

To better understand what the Founders who drafted and adopted our major historical documents intended, let us take a closer look at the historical climate and the circumstances that existed at the time they were creating these documents.

On June 7, 1776, Richard Henry Lee of Virginia introduced a resolution before the Second Continental Congress, which first convened May 10, 1775, stating that "these colonies are, and of a right ought to be, free and independent states." This resolution was quickly seconded by John Adams. The Congress then appointed a five-man committee—John Adams of Massachusetts, Benjamin Franklin of Pennsylvania, Robert R. Livingston of New York, Roger Sherman of Connecticut, and Thomas Jefferson of Virginia—to draft a Declaration of Independence. Adams, who believed that Jefferson wrote ten times better than any man in Congress, recommended to the committee that Jefferson be chosen as the draftsman.[10] The committee agreed unanimously. Jefferson considered all the best ideas that had been floated and then prepared the draft document. Adams took the lead in the debates, as Jefferson was never known to be a good speaker or debater. As Adams would later recall, Jefferson sat "silently and sullenly" as the delegates debated and revised his language. Some 55 delegates, who would also be known as Founding Fathers, representing 12 of the 13 states (Georgia had not participated in the First Continental Congress but sent delegates to the 2nd Congress who arrived in Philadelphia on July 20, 1776), took part in the process of perfecting and adopting The Declaration of Independence. Jefferson is properly known as the author of the Declaration, but he certainly did not act alone.

The Constitution and the Bill of Rights

In a similar fashion, there were 55 Founding Fathers representing 12 of the 13 states (Rhode Island sent no delegates) at the Constitutional Convention in 1787. They debated the various drafts of the Constitution, and when 39 had signed the final draft, they sent it to the states for ratification.[11] The Constitution was, of course, a difficult sell since the states were very reluctant to give up power to a federal government. Some delegates refused to sign, and a few delegates simply left the convention.

Likewise, there were 91 Founding Fathers who were members of the First United States Congress. Of these, 19, including James Madison and Alexander

Hamilton, had been delegates to the Constitutional Convention. As vice president, John Adams was president of the Senate. This Congress, which convened March 4, 1789, was composed of 26 senators and 65 members of the House of Representatives. The overwhelming majority of these 91 Founders participated in the congressional debates, cast votes on various amendments, and ultimately voted on final passage of the final text of the First Amendment. They obviously played the same role in the adoption of the other amendments that would become known as the Bill of Rights. I say the "overwhelming majority," since New York, North Carolina, and Rhode Island were the last states to ratify the Constitution, and five senators and none of the representatives were not seated until later in the session.[12]

James Madison Jr. of Virginia played a key role in both assemblies and is sometimes referred to as the father of the Constitution (even though Governor Morris of Pennsylvania wrote most of the Constitution[13]) and the author of the Bill of Rights. These titles testify to Madison's prominence in the wording and passage of these founding documents, but in reality, he was but one of many Founders who were of great importance in this process.

It is of major significance that Thomas Jefferson played no part in the writing or passing of the Constitution or the Bill of Rights. Jefferson was minister to France from 1785 to 1789 and was not even in the country during either process. Jefferson's understanding of the First Amendment would of necessity (just as anyone else who was not present in the First Congress for the debate) have been based on a study of the drafts, the amendments, the discussions, the amended language that was voted on, and the compromises made to achieve the final language. He was in no better position to have a definitive understanding of the "establishment clause" than any of the other Founders. The fact that he shared a close friendship with James Madison, and the fact that Madison was considered by some to be Jefferson's disciple, offers no special insight. *The fact of the matter is that if the language Madison had originally proposed would have been adopted without change, Jefferson's figure of speech about the "wall of separation" would have made absolutely no sense!*

Jefferson's Letter to the Danbury Baptists[14]

It should be obvious to all that we must try to ascertain the circumstances surrounding Jefferson's letter to the Danbury Baptist Association in order to better understand why he wrote the letter and what message he actually intended to convey. On Oct. 7, 1801, the Danbury Baptists wrote a courtesy letter to President Thomas Jefferson "congratulating him on his appointment to the chief Magistracy in the United States." The Danbury Baptist Association, organized in 1790, was made up of 26 churches located mostly in the Connecticut Valley. They had appointed a committee to write this letter in which they took the opportunity to thank him for his past and present service to the country.

"Sir, when we reflect on your past services, and see a glow of philanthropy and good will shining forth in a course of more than thirty years we have reason to believe that America's God has raised you up to fill the chair of State out of that good will which he bears to Millions which you preside over."[15]

Then to assure him of their continuing support and prayers for him as he faced the difficult job that lay ahead, they concluded:

"May God strengthen you for the arduous task which providence and the voice of the people have cal'd you to sustain and support you in your Administration against all the predetermin'd opposition of those who wish to rise to wealth and importance on the poverty and subjection of the people."[16]

As good Republicans, they had expressed in the letter that they knew he could not control the laws and actions of the state governments. They knew Jefferson would be sympathetic to their plight since most of them lived in Connecticut where the government was controlled by the Federalists and the Congregationalist Church was the official state religion. They complained that their religious liberties were not treated as "inalienable rights" but only "favors granted" by the Congregationalist-Federalist establishment and these "favors" were always subject to withdrawal by the civil state. They were grateful that Jefferson had been their champion two decades earlier when they were suffering under the yoke of the established church in Virginia, the Episcopal Church. They did not ask for a public proclamation or anything else. They just wanted Jefferson to understand their plight and probably by implication, they wanted him to know that they breathed a little easier knowing that while he was president he would not let Congress establish a national church.

This somewhat detailed background becomes quite important in light of some relatively new discoveries surrounding the process Jefferson followed in drafting his letter to the Danbury Baptists. It had been almost universally assumed by everyone, including the most eminent scholars on all sides of the "wall of separation" issue, that Jefferson's letter was just a hastily drafted courtesy note to a group of his supporters. Included would be Chief Justice William Rehnquist, who is universally regarded as one of the foremost authorities on the First Amendment. Rehnquist refers to Jefferson's letter as a "short note of courtesy, written 14 years after the Amendments were passed by Congress." These opinions are no longer substantiated by the historical evidence, however, as a result of James Hutson's efforts to have inked-out portions of Jefferson's notes on his draft letter restored, using new FBI techniques, cast new light on Jefferson's purposes and meaning. This discovery will be discussed in the following pages.

First, let us look at the historical background. In order to understand the true purpose of Jefferson's letter and the audience he intended to reach, we must realize it was written in the context of the presidential election of 1800, which was still on Jefferson's mind. This presidential election was the early "father" of negative political campaigns. This campaign was not only negative, but it was personal, since many of the attacks were aimed at Jefferson himself. In his previously referenced essay, Dr. Daniel Dreisbach points out that *"Jefferson's religion or the alleged lack thereof, emerged as a critical issue in the campaign"* (emphasis added).[17] A brief look at the 1796 campaign (and its outcome) might help us better appreciate the climate of the 1800 campaign. The presidential election of 1796 pitted Vice President John Adams and Gov. Thomas Pinckney of South Carolina as the candidates of the Federalist Party against former Secretary of State Thomas Jefferson of Virginia and Sen. Aaron Burr of New York running on the Democrat-Republican ticket (most often referred to as the Republican Party at the time).[18] Many Federalists would have preferred the more radical Alexander Hamilton as their candidate, and they probably only reluctantly supported Adams as the lesser of two evils. Partly because of this split in the Federalist ranks, Adams eked out only a narrow 71 to 68 electoral majority over Jefferson, who then was selected as vice president.

The Adams administration was marked by turmoil and infighting. The British and French were at war. Adams and the Federalists favored Britain; Jefferson and the Republicans favored France. The Federalists, who controlled Congress, passed the contentious Alien and Sedition Acts, installed a standing army, built war ships, and as a result, raised taxes. These and many more issues that sparked strong disagreement and political fights set the stage for the bitter campaign for president in 1800.[19]

The two tickets for the 1800 presidential campaign were John Adams and his running mate, Charles Cotesworth Pinckney, for the Federalist Party and Thomas Jefferson and Aaron Burr for the Republican Party. With George Washington's death in 1799, the only man who could unite and motivate the Federalist Party was gone. Hamilton was the leader of the "High Federalists," who did not trust Adams. A scheme devised by Hamilton and his Federalist co-conspirators to enable Pinckney to get more electoral votes than Adams ultimately doomed his chances for reelection. Under the system in place at the time, if Pinckney got the most electoral votes, he would become president. This scheme ended up working to the advantage of the Republican candidates.[20]

A worse fear for the Federalists was that Jefferson might get elected. That is where religion was injected into the campaign. The Federalists realized that America was a very religious nation and overwhelmingly Christian of one creed or another. They further realized that their best hope was to make "Jefferson's religion" or "lack thereof" the dominant issue against him in the campaign. (The tradition at the time was that the candidates did not campaign, but the party members did the campaigning.)

Jefferson was attacked as an infidel devoid of moral values. The charge was made that Jefferson had become so intoxicated with the religious and political extremism of the French Revolution that he was unfit to serve as president of the United States. When Jefferson served as Minister to France from 1785 to 1789, seeds of the French Revolution had begun to germinate, but by the time of the election of 1800 it was in full bloom. The French Revolution had turned violently anti-religious in general and angrily anti-Christian in particular. The "Goddess of Reason" had been enthroned on the high altar at the cathedral of Notre Dame, and the goal was to destroy every vestige of Christianity. When the not particularly religious Alexander Hamilton lamented to his friend Lafayette of the horrors of the "massacres" and "the doctrines of Atheism openly advanced" to the apparent approval of the masses, you know it was bad. He further wrote that the differences between the American and French Revolutions were "the difference between liberty and licentiousness."[21]

The two revolutions were diametrical opposites with the American Revolution being grounded on strong religious faith and based on Christian traditions, with some elements of rebellion against "Papists doctrines and superstitions." Therefore Jefferson, who still supported the French Revolution believing that early excesses would be moderated in time, was called a *libertine* and an *atheist*.[22] Jefferson, who probably had already converted from Deist to Unitarian at this stage in his life, was certainly not anti-religious, and he resented these charges.

(Incidentally, Adams lost the election with 63 votes in the Electoral College, with Jefferson and Burr ending up tied with 73 each. Since this was prior to passage of the 12th Amendment, the House of Representatives had to choose the president because Burr refused to withdraw from consideration. On the 36th ballot, a Federalist congressman from New Jersey turned in a blank ballot, and Jefferson became the third president of the United States. By this time, Alexander Hamilton had become convinced that Jefferson was the lesser of two evils, and he convinced the New Jersey Congressman to break the stalemate.[23])

During the year that Jefferson served as president before receiving the Danbury letter, he had steadfastly refused to follow the tradition of Presidents George Washington and John Adams in designating national days of public fasting and thanksgiving. (Calling for days of prayer, fasting, and thanksgiving to God was a routine practice by virtually all of the state chief executives. Jefferson had done so himself as governor of Virginia in 1779 when he issued a proclamation appointing "a day of publick and solemn thanksgiving and prayer to Almighty God."[24]) The Federalist press continued to condemn Jefferson as immoral and irreligious because of his refusal to designate a national day of prayer and thanksgiving in view of the peace treaty between France and England.[25] These relentless attacks infuriated

President Jefferson as low blows by his political enemies. They could result in future political problems if not addressed. Furthermore, the questioning of his moral character hurt him deeply. The truth of this description of his reaction is borne out by his frequent discussion of "his" religious faith and dependence on a benevolent God in his later actions and letters.

Once again we ask who, then, was the real audience Jefferson intended to reach in his letter to the Danbury Baptists? Dating back to the 1950s, a few scholars had suggested that his intended audience was his Federalist tormentors— his Baptist supporters afforded him the opportunity to take on his enemies. These scholars didn't have much evidence to support this theory other than educated speculation based on the situation in Federalist New England at the time. The evidence changed radically in 1998 when a draft of Jefferson's now-famous letter with suggested changes noted in the margins was released. Parts of this document had been considered illegible until the FBI lab had restored the text using some very modern techniques.

James Hutson, who as chief of the Manuscript Division of the Library of Congress requested the FBI's assistance, concludes that this document gives us insight into Jefferson's intended audience.[26] He contends that the Danbury letter served both to soothe Jefferson's allies and frustrate his enemies. It was a political statement written to reassure Jefferson's Baptist constituents in New England of his continuing commitment to their religious rights. It also was used to strike back at the Federalist-Congregationalist establishment in Connecticut for vilifying him as an "infidel" and "atheist" in the rancorous presidential campaign of 1800. These attacks had never subsided and had recently intensified.

Contrary to the previous belief that this was a hastily drafted note to his Baptist supporters in Connecticut, Jefferson actually sent a draft of the letter to Attorney General Levi Lincoln, a Massachusetts Republican, and Postmaster General Gideon Granger, a Connecticut Republican, for their consideration and input. Jefferson wanted to know how these New Englanders thought it would play in the North. They were his chief political advisors in that area of the country. Jefferson confessed in a note to his advisors that the letter as presently drafted is "seasoned to Southern taste only," and they should feel free to make suggestions that might make it play better in their area of the country. At Levi Lincoln's suggestion, an entire section (dealing with the declaring of days of thanksgiving and prayers) in Jefferson's original draft is omitted in the final letter and the phrase "*eternal* wall of separation" is revised to read "wall of separation." He was advised to be careful not to sound too antireligious to the pious ears of his New England supporters. There is no question that the letter to the Danbury Baptists was for pure political consumption—"a political manifesto, nothing more."[27] The political scheme worked perfectly since the Danbury letter was published in the Republican press in just a matter of days.[28]

Madison and the First Amendment

James Madison believed that no additional amendments to the Constitution were necessary. He engaged in heated debate over this very subject with Patrick Henry and others during Virginia's ratifying convention. Henry and his supporters were insisting that some revisions to the Constitution (such as the Bill of Rights) must be made before ratification.

Henry lost this battle but was successful in persuading the Virginia legislature not to select Madison as one of the state's first senators. Henry, Richard Henry Lee, and James Monroe even had the congressional-district lines drawn in an attempt to deny the popular Madison a seat in the First Congress. Madison did get elected to the U.S. House of Representatives—he defeated James Monroe 1,308 to 972—but not until after he was forced to commit to consider amendments to the Constitution.[29]

Initially, Madison had "adamantly maintained that a specific bill of rights remained unnecessary because the Constitution itself was a bill of rights." Madison had three main objections to a specific bill of rights: (a) it was unnecessary, since it purported to protect against powers that the federal government had not been granted; (b) it was dangerous, since enumeration of some rights might be taken to imply the absence of other rights; and (c) at the state level, bills of rights had proven to be useless paper barriers against government power.[30]

It is interesting to note, as Stephen Mansfield points out in *Ten Tortured Words*, that the primary opposition to the Bill of Rights was based on the view that such amendments were unnecessary because the Constitution had given the federal government no authority over, for example, guns, religion, or the press. How could the federal government encroach on areas where it had been granted no authority? Hamilton argued in *The Federalist* that a "Bill of Rights" *was not only unnecessary but "would even be dangerous.... For why declare that things shall not be done which there is no power to do."*[31]

Jefferson had been unable to persuade Madison of the necessity for of a Bill of Rights. In a letter to Madison from France in 1787, Jefferson expressed his concerns about the Constitution:

> "I will now add what I do not like. First, the omission of the Bill of Rights providing clearly and without the aid of sophisms for freedom of religion, freedom of the press, protection against standing armies, restrictions against monopolies, the eternal and unremitting force of habeas corpus laws and trial by jury."[32]

Always willing to listen to reason and anxious to have as much unity as possible among the states, Madison finally listened as the U.S. House of Representatives prepared to organize in 1789.[33] As Chief Justice Rehnquist points out in his dissenting opinion in a 1985 Alabama school prayer case (*Wallace v. Jaffree*), five of the 11 colonies that had ratified the Constitution also had proposed amendments guaranteeing individual liberty by early 1789. Three—New Hampshire, New York, and Virginia—wanted a declaration of religious freedom. Rhode Island and North Carolina

> "flatly refused to ratify the Constitution in the absence of amendments in the nature of a Bill of Rights. Virginia and North Carolina proposed identical guarantees of religious freedom: 'All men have an equal, natural and unalienable right to the free exercise of religion, according to the dictates of conscience, and no particular religious sect or society ought to be favored or established, by law, in preference to others.'"[34]

* * * * *

Justice Rehnquist's scholarly and thorough analysis of Black's opinion in *Everson* regarding the "establishment clause" is used extensively in this paper. This powerful 23-page dissent, along with Mansfield's *Ten Tortured Words* and Hutson's numerous publications, are among the best sources available for the layman.[35]

James Hutson is the curator of manuscript at the Library of Congress. His scholarship in the field of founding history has few, if any rivals, especially as it relates to the original documents. Hutson's *Religion and the Founding of the American Republic* (1998), the companion piece for a Library of Congress exhibit, is the ultimate authority on how religion influenced the Founders. I will refer to this book extensively as we examine early American religious habits and the beliefs of the Founders.

Hutson's previously referenced article, "A Wall of Separation: FBI Helps Restore Jefferson's Obliterated Draft," gives invaluable new insight to Jefferson's well-known letter. *Religion and the New Republic: Faith in the Founding of America* (2000), edited by Hutson, also is an important work. One of his most recent books, *Forgotten Features of the Founding: The Recovery of Religious Themes in the Early American Republic,* will be of special interest to those with a theological interest and background. If there is any question left in anyone's mind whether Dr. Hutson has read more original documents on the subject than anyone else and is the foremost authority on religion in America, another of his books, published in 2008, will put that question to rest. *Church and State in America: The First Two Centuries* justifies the contention by some scholars that he knows so much about the religion of the Founders that he virtually qualifies as an original source himself.

Dr. Daniel Dreisbach of American University is an eminent scholar whose books are not difficult to read but that seem to target the scholarly community. His previously referenced *Thomas Jefferson and the Wall of Separation between Church and State* is a recognized authoritative work on this complex subject. This 283-page book includes 153 pages of appendices and voluminous reference notes. It is difficult to argue with his methodology in reaching his conclusions.

Philip Hamburger's 514-page book, *Separation of Church and State*, is long but perhaps the definitive work on this important subject. It is also not a difficult read for those who have a sufficient interest in the issues relating to church and state.

David Barton, the founder of WallBuilders, has published a 25-page booklet, "Separation of Church & State: What the Founders Meant." This is an easy source, filled with pertinent quotes from the Founders, and has a number of examples of moral decay evident in our society as a result of ignoring the moral principles of our Founders. A larger book, *Original Intent: The Courts, the Constitution & Religion* (2008), is an excellent resource that contains Founding documents, biographical sketches of the Founders, and a wealth of material on revisionism and judicial activism.

I have listed these books and refer to others throughout this book as resources chiefly because of my conviction that the plan of the liberal secularist elites has been working: They have so infiltrated academia with liberal secularists that they not only write the textbooks used in our schools, but they also produced the vast majority of scholarly works on the Founding period and Founding documents. Until rather recently, Americans interested in learning more about the relationship between church and state have had few resources other than those that perpetuate the same secularist bias. (It took 400 years of Muslim conquest of Christian-held lands for Christians to finally fight back in the Crusades. It is somewhat encouraging that it took only a little over 50 years for conservative Christian scholars to launch a counter attack against secularists who had initiated a well-organized campaign to undermine the moral and religious foundation so carefully laid down by our wise Founding Fathers.)

Dreisbach, while speaking specifically about the policy of the so-called "separation" of church and state, describes this problem correctly:

> "No phrase in American letters has more profoundly influenced discourse and policy on church-state relations than Jefferson's 'wall of separation.'...The bibliography at the end of this volume confirms that enough books and articles to fill a small library have been written on the 'wall' metaphor. So why another book on the subject? Because, prior to my 1997 article in the 'Journal of Church and State,' very little had been written that examined in detail the text and political content of the Danbury letters, which contains Jefferson's trope.... Instead, most books and articles on the 'wall' simply *presume that the First Amendment erected a 'wall of separation'* and make that presumption their point of departure for discussing the Supreme Court's church-state jurisprudence. The extensive and continuing reliance of courts on the metaphor invites further scrutiny of Jefferson's imaginative phrase" (emphasis added).[36]

* * * * *

Now comfortable with his compromise, Madison rose on the day the new Congress convened, March 3, 1789, to announce his intention to introduce amendments to the Constitution. He was concerned that Rhode Island and North Carolina had not yet ratified the Constitution, but he doesn't seem to have been in any great hurry to introduce the amendments. It was on June 8, a little more than three months later, that Madison introduced nine amendments composed largely of suggestions from the various ratifying conventions. Madison's original language for what ultimately became the Religion Clause of the First Amendment read, "The civil rights of none shall be abridged on account of religious belief or worship, nor shall any *national* religion be established, nor shall the full and equal rights of conscience be in any manner, or any pretext, infringed" (emphasis added).[37]

The states had spoken and must be assured that Congress would not establish any national church. Having experienced the horrors of British troops killing colonial parsons, burning Bibles and hymnals, and turning captured churches into stables and whorehouses during the Revolutionary War, they knew firsthand that they wanted nothing of an "English-style State Church."[38]

In typical legislative fashion, Madison's amendments were referred to a "Committee of the Whole on the State of the Union," which did nothing for six weeks. On July 21, the amendments were assigned to a Select Committee of the House, composed of Madison and 10 others, which after a week reported out new wording that very succinctly read: "No religion shall be established by law, nor shall the equal rights of conscience be infringed."[39]

The House of Representatives finally began debate on the First Amendment Aug. 15, 1789. It is of the utmost importance for us to analyze the debate in the House to determine what James Madison and the other members of Congress actually intended for the Religion Clause in the First Amendment to mean. Sadly, this is a task that Hugo Black either failed to undertake or abandoned when he discovered that such an undertaking would negate his preconceived and intended results.

Only the most hardcore secularists could deny that the moral fiber of our nation would be much stronger today if Black would have exercised the intellectual honesty to find out what those who adopted the First Amendment actually intended. It strikes me as bizarre that Black did read and did refer frequently to Madison's "Detached Memorandum"[40] in his efforts to determine the Founder's intended meaning. This document was written some 34 years later by Madison, who was now in his 70s and in retirement on his tobacco plantation. It is an interesting historical document if you are curious about how dramatically the elderly Madison had changed his mind since he retired from the active political arena.

The "Memorandum" makes it clear that Madison *now* believed that religious proclamations by the president and the hiring of chaplains in the military and the Congress, as a few pertinent examples, should be forbidden by the First Amendment. These opinions must strike anyone as odd in view of Madison's own actions as a congressman and president of the United States. Just some 20 years after the Bill of Rights was passed by Congress and ratified by the states, President Madison proclaimed public days of thanksgiving and prayer. Without any recorded word of opposition or concern expressed in any existing document, he allowed the branches of the military to hire and pay their chaplains from tax-payer dollars throughout his presidency. Even more contradictory is that Madison actually sat on the House committee that set salaries for the House Chaplain during the very time that the First Amendment was debated and passed.[41]

It has always seemed to be more than coincidental that Madison's previously unknown "Detached Memorandum" was first discovered among some very old files at William and Mary College in 1946. Interestingly enough, the discovery took place just a year before Black's revolutionary decision. I cannot help but believe that Justice Black's reading of this recently discovered text was the trigger that ended up causing so many of the moral and ethical problems we are experiencing in our country today. This is in spite of the fact that the document had so little impact at the time of its writing or that no one even knew it existed over the 120 some-odd years before it turned up at William and Mary! This is not the time to try to figure out why Madison changed his mind so dramatically in his old age and flagrantly contradicted his actions and opinions in his earlier active political life. The facts, however, speak for themselves, and we will momentarily shed some light on what he intended to accomplish when the First Amendment was adopted.

A quick look at some of the debate in Congress on the First Amendment should be quite revealing.

On Aug. 15, the Select Committee appointed a month earlier reported to House floor a revised version of Madison's original amendment: "No religion shall be established by law, nor shall the equal rights of conscience be infringed."[42] Congressman Peter Sylvester of New York immediately objected to the amendment on grounds that such wording "might be thought to have tendency to abolish religion altogether." Congressman John Vining of Delaware suggested the two phrases be transposed. Roger Sherman of Connecticut opposed the passage of any amendment, since Congress had no delegated authority to "make religious establishments." Representative Samuel Livermore of New Hampshire proposed that the amendment read: "Congress shall make no laws touching religion, or infringing on the rights of conscience." Some liked this wording, but Madison, who eventually would rise to his feet to take issue with this amendment and defend his original language, did not. This was a fortunate development because this would give Madison the opportunity to explain exactly what he understood the purposes of the amendment to be:

"Mr. Madison said, he apprehended the meaning of the words to be, *that Congress should not establish a religion, enforce the legal observance of it by law, nor compel men to worship God in any manner contrary to their conscience.* Whether the words are necessary or not, he did not mean to say, but they had been required by some of the State Conventions, who seemed to entertain an opinion that under the clause of the constitution, which gave power to Congress to make all laws necessary and proper to carry into execution the constitution, and the laws made under it, enabled them to make laws of such a nature as might infringe the rights of conscience, and establish a *national* religion; to prevent these effects he presumed the amendment was intended, and he thought it as well expressed as the nature of the language would admit" (emphasis added).[43]

Although Madison's statement seems perfectly clear, debate continued on the floor of the House. Madison suggested that insertion of "national" before "religion" would answer the objections to the Standing Committee's language. He pointed out that he believed that the people feared that one sect might get the upper hand, or two might join together to establish a religion and compel others to conform. He thought the insertion of the word "national" would specifically prohibit such a possibility.

Congressman Gerry of Massachusetts objected to the word "national" because we were a federal government, not a national government. New Hampshire Congressman Samuel Livermore moved to change the committee language to read, "Congress shall make no laws touching religion, or infringing the rights of conscience." Livermore's amendment was passed by a vote of 31 to 20 over Madison's objection, primarily because of the failure to include "national" before religion.

The following week, without any apparent debate, the House voted to alter the language of the Religion Clause to read "Congress shall make no law establishing religion, or to prevent the free exercise thereof, or to infringe the rights of conscience." Since the Senate debate was secret at the time, we don't have as clear a picture of their deliberations. We do know that on Sept. 3, 1789, the first United States Senate considered several different wordings of the Religion Clause and finally decided on this language: "Congress shall make no law establishing articles of faith or a mode of worship, or prohibiting the free exercise of religion." The Senate then sent this language to the House. The House refused to accept this exact wording and requested a conference with the Senate. The House and Senate conferees ultimately agreed on the language that made its way into the Constitution as a part of the First Amendment: "Congress shall make no law respecting an establishment of religion, or prohibiting the free exercise thereof."

Mansfield makes a strong case for the genius of Congress' final wording of the Religion Clause:

> "The language is important. The new law did not simply forbid Congress to erect a State Church or establish an official religion. This goal would have been achieved by most of the proposed amendments we have seen above. Instead, the new law was actually broadened beyond what had been proposed. Congress was not only forbidden to establish an official religion, but it was forbidden to make a law that even dealt with the issue of an establishment of religion. Here we see the states protecting their prerogatives, their authority to establish religion if they chose to. Congress was forbidden to make a law that even touched or treated—this is the meaning of the word respecting in context—the matter of an establishment of religion. Therefore, the states' authority to establish religion was protected while Congress's authority to establish religion was cut off. The law was a double-edged sword, but only for Congress and the federal government."[44]

There was not one word spoken in the entire debate that would have even suggested the establishment of a secular nation free from religious influence. There was not a hint that the federal government could not support religion, as long as it did not favor one sect over another. On the contrary, several members expressed the concern that they not do anything that would allow the federal government to harm religion. It is ludicrous to even think that any member of Congress would have mentioned "a wall of separation" between church and state. Such a member's words would have most likely been "taken down," and he might well have been tarred and feathered on his return home.

The metaphor of a "wall of separation" between church and state was already fairly well known at the time. The metaphor was first used by the Anglican divine Richard Hooker, by the Scottish intellectual James Burgh (a man highly admired by Jefferson as he recommended to his son-in-law that he read Burgh's works), and by the firebrand Baptist preacher and dissenter Roger Williams, founder of the Rhode Island Plantation Colony. Madison's words and actions in passing the Religion Clause of the First Amendment do not bear the slightest resemblance to the attitudes expressed in his "Detached Memorandum" written well over 30 years later.

It is worth mentioning a few other actions taken by this same Congress that would have violated the First Amendment it had just passed if Black's revisionist view of the Religion Clause would have been in effect.

One day after Congress adopted the final language of the Religion Clause, Elias Boudinot, a congressman from New Jersey, proposed a resolution asking

President George Washington for a Thanksgiving Day Proclamation. Boudinot stated that he

> "could not think of letting the session pass over without offering an opportunity to all the citizens of the United States of joining with one voice, in returning to Almighty God their sincere thanks for the many blessings he had poured down upon them."[45]

A few members objected for various reasons, but none on grounds concerning any violation of mixing church and state. Two congressmen from South Carolina, Aedanas Burke and Thomas Tucker, questioned whether this was a wise move. Burke said he did not like "this mimicking of European customs." Tucker thought that such religious matters should be left to the States. Representative Roger Sherman, a Pro-Administration[46] member from Connecticut, strongly supported the resolution,

> "not only as a laudable one in itself, but as warranted by a number of precedents in Holy Writ: for instance, the solemn thanksgiving and rejoicings which took place at the time of Solomon, after the building of the temple, was a case in point. This example, he thought, worthy of Christian imitation on the present occasion..."[47]

Boudinot's resolution passed in the House of Representatives on Sept. 25, 1789.

Two weeks later, George Washington issued the presidential proclamation designating "Thursday, the 26th day of November next, to be devoted by the people of these States to the service of that great and glorious Being who is the beneficent author of all the good that was, that is, or that will be." After listing His blessings before we became a nation and after our nationhood, Washington asked that "we may then unite in most humbly offering our prayers and supplications to the great Lord and Ruler of Nations, and beseech Him to pardon our national and other transgressions;" and finally *"to promote the knowledge and practice of true religion and virtue*, and the increase of science among them and us; and, generally, to grant unto all mankind such a degree of temporal prosperity as He alone knows to be best" (emphasis added).[48]

We should never forget Washington's Thanksgiving Proclamation or Boudinot's resolution in the First Congress requesting such a Proclamation as we celebrate Thanksgiving Day with our families. I am sure Black's secular followers believe he could have prevented such joyous celebrations if he had only been alive at the time!

Most scholars evaluating the founding of the United States would agree that the most important piece of legislation passed by the Continental Congress other than the Declaration of Independence was the Northwest Ordinance. Mansfield points out that this far-reaching ordinance not only established the process by which Western territories might become states, but it also was such an enlightened document for this particular time in history. The Northwest Ordinance forbade slavery in those regions, assured basic liberties, established territorial governments, and even attempted to safeguard the rights of Native Americans. Also for our purposes, it gives us a bright look at the attitude of the Founders toward the role of religion in establishing this country.

In a provision for establishing schools, the ordinance reads: "Religion, morality, and knowledge, being necessary to good government and the happiness of mankind, schools and the means of education shall forever be encouraged."[49]

That religion, morality, and education are essential to good government were just common-sense beliefs for most of the Founders. The schools that were to be built were all private and religious. This was the era before the rise of public schools. As Rehnquist reminds us, it was not until 1845 that Congress limited land grants in the new states and territories to nonsectarian schools.[50] The Northwest Ordinance was about to expire. On the very day in 1789 that Madison introduced his proposed amendments (which became the Bill of Rights), Congress brought up for consideration its reenactment. How could a sane person argue that the same Congress that reenacted the Northwest Ordinance of 1787, which authorized and funded joint efforts between the federal government and the churches, would enact a First Amendment that would make their current actions unconstitutional? Such an argument defies common sense.

Those serving on the Supreme Court shortly after the Bill of Rights became a part of the Constitution seem to have had no trouble understanding what the drafters meant. Perhaps the best case in point is Joseph Story, who was an associate justice of the United States Supreme Court from 1811 until 1845. During much of that time he also served as a professor at Harvard Law School, and his *Commentaries on the Constitution* were the reference of record among early American lawyers. Rehnquist says that his *Commentaries* were "by far the most comprehensive treatise on the United States Constitution that had then appeared." Mansfield writes that since "he helped to shape the nation's jurisprudence for nearly a half century, his understanding of the meaning of the First Amendment should be taken as definitive."

As we read Justice Story's words in Volume 2 of his *Commentaries*, where he discusses the "Establishment Clause" of the First Amendment, let us bear in mind that Justice Story not only knew James Madison but was *appointed to the Supreme Court by President James Madison*:

"Probably at the time of the adoption of the Constitution, and of the amendment to it now under consideration [First Amendment], the general if not the universal sentiment in America was, that Christianity ought to receive encouragement from the State so far as was not incompatible with the private rights of conscience and the freedom of religious worship. An attempt to level all religions, and to make it a matter of state policy to hold all in utter indifference, would have created universal disapprobation, if not indignation....

"The real object of the First Amendment was not to countenance, much less to advance, Mahometanism, or Judaism, or infidelity, by prostrating Christianity; but to exclude all rivalry among Christian sects, and to prevent any national ecclesiastical establishment which should give to a hierarchy the exclusive patronage of the national government. It thus cut off the means of religious persecution (the vice and pest of former ages), and of the subversion of the rights of conscience in matters of religion, which had been trampled upon almost from the days of the Apostles to the present age...."[51]

Remember once again that these words were written by a man living in the early 1800s (just a little over 25 years after the First Amendment was adopted) and appointed to the Supreme Court by Madison himself. Based on this somewhat extensive evaluation of the circumstances and actions surrounding the adoption of the First Amendment, it seems beyond doubt that this Amendment was designed for two purposes: (1) to prevent the federal Congress from establishing a national church and to further prevent the Congress from denying any American citizens their religious liberties, and (2) to assure the states that the federal Congress would not take away any authority from the states not specifically granted to the federal government in the Constitution. The fact that Justice Black would further rule in his opinion that the 14th Amendment makes the First Amendment applicable to the states is beyond comprehension. *Black makes this decision in the face of the original intent of Congress, the subsequent congressional history both before and after ratification of the 14th Amendment, and consistent Supreme Court rulings to the contrary for the first 80 or so years after the 14th Amendment was ratified.*

The question of whether or not the 14th Amendment would make the First Amendment applicable to the states was actually raised shortly after its ratification in 1868. In 1875, Congressman James Blaine of Maine attempted to resolve the issue legislatively by quoting the Establishment Clause almost verbatim and making it binding on the states. The Congress soundly defeated the Blaine bill. This is especially significant since 23 congressmen who voted on the Blaine bill had been members of the Congress that passed the 14th Amendment. They knew what they meant when the Amendment was originally passed.

In the 80 years between 1870 and 1950, Congress defeated the Blaine Amendment or similar proposals *25 times*. Talk about legislative intent! In similar fashion, the Supreme Court had rejected all attempts to apply the Bill of Rights to the states under the application of the 14th Amendment. These Supreme Court decisions included the famous "Slaughterhouse Cases" of 1872 and *Hurtado v. California* in 1884. These decisions were consistent with the 1833 opinion of

Supreme Court Chief Justice John Marshall in the landmark case *Barron v. Baltimore*. In speaking for a united court, the Chief Justice wrote, "The Constitution was ordained and established by the people of the United States for themselves, for their own government and not for the government of the individual States." Therefore, he continued, the Bill of Rights "contains no expression indicating an intention to apply them to the state governments."[52]

Black's opinion is the classic example of just how far activist judges will go in revising and rewriting history and making law rather than fulfilling their obligations to determine the constitutionally of laws passed by the people or their chosen representatives in Congress.

Jefferson and His Metaphorical Wall

If, however, Jefferson did want to erect a "wall" of separation between church and state, he must have built a very low wall. This would have been necessary because two days after he wrote his letter to the Danbury Baptists, he stepped over this "wall" to attend a church service held in the U.S. House of Representatives. The sermon was delivered by the firebrand Baptist farmer turned preacher, John Leland, a member of the Danbury Baptist Association. Hutson speculates that Jefferson felt comfortable attending church on federal-government property because one of the most intense fighters against the established state churches was to be the preacher.[53] Hutson adds that many scholars believe Jefferson had developed a more favorable view of Christianity in the 1790s than he held in his deist days of the late 1770s and 1780s. This changing religious attitude had "led him to endorse the position of his fellow Founders that religion was necessary for the welfare of a republican government, that it was, as Washington proclaimed in his Farewell Address, indispensable for the happiness and prosperity of the people. Jefferson had, in fact, said as much in his First Inaugural Address."[54]

Attending worship services in the Capitol was a practice Jefferson would continue to observe virtually every Sunday during the remaining seven years of his presidency. He even had the Marine Band play for these services on some occasions. Jefferson may not have believed the messages delivered in these services by evangelists and preachers of the more traditional denominations, but he was there in the Capital nearly every Sunday to set his example. He firmly understood the importance of religion in the founding and preservation of this Republic and wanted to encourage its practice—even in federal government structures.

Jefferson also unabashedly called upon God for guidance and blessing in difficult times. He won reelection in 1804 easily, but he knew the country was still divided and the threat of war hung heavily over the nation. (Fortunately for Jefferson and America, the War of 1812 didn't erupt until Madison was commander in chief.) Whatever one might say about any of Jefferson's particular religious beliefs, there is little dispute about his dependence on divine Providence. He stated it very clearly in his second inaugural address:

"I shall need, too, the favor of that Being in whose hands we are, who led our fathers, as Israel of old, from their native land and planted them in a country flowing with all the necessaries and comforts of life; who has covered our infancy with His providence and our riper years with His wisdom and power, and to whose goodness I ask you to join in supplications with me that He will so enlighten the minds of your servants, guide their councils, and prosper their measures that whatsoever they do shall result in your good, and shall secure to you the peace, friendship, and approbation of all nations."[55]

In an article titled "The Wall Jefferson Almost Built," Heritage Foundation Fellow Joseph LoConte writes that Jefferson saw no conflict between the First Amendment and the availability of public property and public facilities for religious services. He points out that Jefferson opened many federal buildings, including the Treasury, the War Office, and the Supreme Court on Sundays for religious services. After lengthy discussions with James Hutson about Jefferson's attitude toward the use of public facilities for worship services, LoConte quotes Hutson: "It is no exaggeration to say that, on Sundays in Washington during Thomas Jefferson's presidency, the state became the church ...."[56]

Before turning to a detailed look at the role religion played in our founding, the religious climate in our founding period, the religious affiliations and convictions of the larger group of Founders, and what we know about the religious affiliations and attitudes of the best known Founding Fathers, we will examine the progress of the Cultural War since Black's infamous decision.

Faith of Our Founders

For almost 100 years after America's founding, only a handful of individuals would have seriously questioned whether this country was founded on strong Judeo-Christian religious principles. Just as liberal secularists today claim that "of course" we are a secular society, virtually everyone during this period would have said "of course" we are a Christian Society. What was obvious, though, was that America wanted no national established church and took steps to keep this from happening. This was the basic reason for the establishment clause in the First Amendment.[57]

In the late 19th century, an anti-immigrant and anti-Catholic bias began to dominate public opinion. A strong, perhaps overwhelming, case can be made that such a bias totally motivated Hugo Black's 1947 *Everson* opinion. Yale Law School professor Stephen Carter dates this anti-Catholic hysteria even earlier:

"In the middle of the nineteenth century, voters in several states turned to the unabashedly anti-Catholic Know-Nothing Party, which controlled both houses of the Massachusetts legislature and elected some seventy five members to the House of Representatives. Those who joined the party had to swear never to vote for anyone not born in the United States or anyone who was a Catholic. This was quite a horrific moment in our history, and not as large an aberration as we might like to pretend. There has long been a vigorous anti-Catholic strain in American public life, as Al Smith discovered during his 1928 presidential campaign and, a few decades later, John Kennedy nearly did. It is not dead yet."[58]

These attitudes so prevalent in the second half of the 19th century carried over into the 20th century. This provided fertile ground for those determined to radically alter, if not totally destroy, the moral and religious foundations of this nation. The Industrial Revolution and the creation of the factory system resulted in social inequities that would be blamed on unbridled capitalism. The "October" or "Bolshevik" Revolution in 1917 would vault Lenin to be the First Premier of the Soviet Union. This event would inspire and motivate American communists, socialists, atheists and other secularists in their dream to remake the American system of government. World War I, the Great Depression, and World War II would round out the first half of the 20th century. This was the environment in which the likes of Roger Baldwin worked to eventually develop a class of secular elites who would be motivated to demolish the religious foundations of America.

The cultural wars in modern times, especially after *Roe v Wade*, will be discussed in the next chapter. A look at the efforts (certainly not always coordinated) of secularist leaders to infiltrate the disciplines that mold public opinion should shed some light on the problems we face

As we examine the religious beliefs of the Founding Fathers and the people they represented, it is important to understand what modern-day Americans know about these subjects. It would be accurate to say that most Americans know very little—and much of what they know is wrong! Why do our citizens know so little about such a vital aspect of our heritage? Perhaps the bigger question is why so many Americans seem to buy myths perpetuated by the secular elites about the role of religion—or lack thereof—in the founding of the country. Why is there not at least enough intellectual curiosity to examine the sources relied on by these liberals? A number of recent scientific surveys clearly indicate that the more educated the country becomes, the less many of these educated Americans seem to know about early American history.

It is not difficult to make the case that until the last decade or so of the 20th century, the intellectual liberals wrote most of the textbooks on American history, as well as the majority of scholarly works. It is just as easy to make the case that students don't seem to reading them anyway.

The Intercollegiate Studies Institute (ISI), working with the University of Connecticut's Department of Public Policy, selected 50 colleges and universities throughout America to test literacy on constitutional and governmental history and policies. One study was conducted in 2005 and a second in 2006. In each case, 25 colleges were selected from the most elite and expensive, such as Harvard, Yale, Duke, the University of California at Berkley, and UVA. The other 25 were selected on a random basis.

Researchers asked 60 questions of roughly 140 freshmen and 140 seniors at each institution. The multiple-choice questions ranged from "Who wrote the Declaration of Independence?" to a definition of the "Monroe Doctrine." The averages for the two surveys were very similar. In the 2005 study, college freshmen averaged 51.7 percent and college seniors 53.2 percent. In 2006, the freshman scored 50.4 percent and the seniors 54.2 percent. The randomly selected schools averaged lower scores for their entering classes, but in most cases the "value added" in the next three years was considerably higher. For example, in 2006, Yale had the highest entering scores at 68.94 percent, but seniors showed a drop of 3.09 percent, scoring 65.85 percent. The randomly selected Concordia University Nebraska, Seward, freshmen scored 46.29 percent, but the seniors were at 55.28 percent—a gain of 8.99 percent.

In any event, all had failing scores, with no school scoring higher than a D+. Fewer than half of the college seniors, 47.9 percent, knew that "we hold these truths to be self evident, that all men are created equal" came from the Declaration of Independence. Also, fewer than half knew that the First Amendment prohibits the establishment of a national church; that Yorktown was the decisive battle of the American Revolution; or that NATO had been founded to resist Soviet expansion.

Not only are our grade schools and high schools failing to teach children about how our country was founded, but the finest colleges and universities are doing no better. No wonder we don't know who we are! We are losing all appreciation of our glorious American heritage. We need to be reminded again that Karl Marx boasted, "A people without a heritage are easily persuaded."

If there is a bright side to such a bleak picture, it might be that the best and brightest of our young people certainly are not overdosing on the works of liberal secular elites. They just don't know much about anything when it comes to our heritage. (The constant barrage of sophisticated public relations campaigns about sex, pornography, homosexuality, and the pleasures of an amoral, if not an immoral, society is an increasing threat to our young people. There has never been a greater need to help build a solid moral foundation for their lives.)

There may be another ray of light. There is an apparent proliferation of new books on the founding period that relate to our religious heritage, the question of religion in the public square, and what separation of church and state meant in the early days of this republic. Increasingly over the last five or six years (maybe eight or 10 years), bookstores have installed sections filled with new and recent books on these subjects. Political books are selling. This may partly be the result of conservative churches (primarily Evangelicals) getting more involved in politics since the Reagan Revolution.

Seeing their politically correct turf threatened, the liberals seem to be fighting back. This is creating a crucial dialogue in which Christians *must* get involved. Christians from all walks of life—church leaders, teachers, scholars or just interested citizens—cannot avoid the responsibilities of citizenship. As Martin Luther would remind us in his theology of the "two kingdoms," God expects us to be responsible members of both the Kingdom of the Right (church) and the Kingdom of the Left (state). We are needed in the public square now more than ever! If people of faith abandon the public square, the morals of our society are certain to decay. The secularists who recognize no absolute truths or transcendent moral values rely on relative mores that change with the whims of a frequently self-indulgent society.

Over the last few years, a number of books by liberal writers have argued that some of the most prominent Founding Fathers were not Christian, and therefore would favor not allowing religious speech in the public square. One such book is *Moral Minority: Our Skeptical Founding Fathers* by Brooke Allen. I don't think this sudden interest in the religious faith of our Founders results from a nagging question they have wondered about for many years. It appears to be just another effort of such liberals to make America a totally secular state, devoid of all religious speech and the Judeo-Christian values upon which most Americans believe our value system was founded.

None of these secularist writers, including Allen, have made any startling discovery by reporting that such famous and influential members of the Founding Fathers as Franklin, Washington, Adams, Jefferson, Madison, and Hamilton might not have been orthodox Christians. I don't think you can reasonably define Christianity in broad enough terms to include Franklin, Adams and Jefferson in the traditional Christian fold, based on their own discussions of their religious beliefs. I wish this were not the case because I would very much like to meet them in heaven. And, we really do not know what Washington or Madison believed in their hearts, because they do not discuss their personal faith in any known, existing document. We are left to speculate about what these two believed based on their actions, statements they made about religion in general, or what someone else recorded about conversations they had with each of them. We will look at such information shortly. As for Hamilton, he attended church with his family the day before his duel with Aaron Burr. In his final hours, after being mortally wounded by Burr, he sought and finally received Holy Communion from an Episcopal priest. Hamilton certainly confessed his traditional Christian faith when he was staring death in the face. There is evidence that he had become more devout in his Christian faith after the similar death of his son in a duel just three years earlier.

At this point, I believe it is fair to assume that the renewed liberal interest in the religious beliefs of certain Founding Fathers and the role of religion in the colonies at that time is a response to a considerable number of scholarly works written by conservative scholars in recent years. During most of the 1940s, 50s,

60s and 70s, the liberal secularists had the field pretty much to themselves. There certainly has not been a sea change in the 1980s, 90s and the 21st century, but we have seen an increasing number of conservatives ("traditionalists" might be a better word) in all disciplines rise up to proclaim that we are not going to lose our moral and spiritual heritage without a fight. Our forefathers paid much too great of a price to sustain the American dream for us to allow the very foundation upon which this great free nation was built to be destroyed. When freedom is threatened, free men and women must rise up to defend that freedom as dedicated men and women have done throughout our history.

A rising number of conservative scholars in the last 20 or so years have picked up the torch of laboring through the original documents of the Founders, trying to understand the context in which our founding documents were actually drafted and ratified. They have not simply accepted the "conventional wisdom" passed along for years by a multitude of liberal scholars with an agenda who sought no critical evaluation of the "evidence." The liberal scholars who dominated the debate for so many years were willing to pick and choose statements (frequently out of context) from the dozen or so best known Founders while virtually ignoring the hundreds of lesser known Founding Fathers. These lesser known Founders were much too committed to their traditional Christian beliefs for the liberal taste and goals.

It seems strange that none of these liberal historians—or at least those who just accepted conventional wisdom uncritically—seemed to have paid much attention to the writings of Alexis de Tocqueville. Stephen Carter, in *The Culture of Disbelief*, makes this observation:

> "When Alexis de Tocqueville visited the United States early in the nineteenth century, he wrote, in Democracy in America, that the young nation's 'religious atmosphere was the first thing that struck me on arrival in the United States.' Indeed, Tocqueville claimed, America was 'the place where the Christian religion kept the greatest power over men's souls.' In Tocqueville's view, this meant that liberty was tempered by a common morality: 'Thus, while the law allows the American people to do everything, there are things which religion prevents them from imagining and forbids them to dare.' Put simply, as political scientist Roger M. Smith has noted, Tocqueville 'believed that the support given by religion to virtuous standards of behavior was indispensable for the preservation of liberty'"[59]

I have referred to several of the best of these conservative scholars, but the one who stands out as the man who has changed the debate in a positive direction is Dr. James H. Hutson. After receiving his Ph.D. in history from Yale University, he was a member of the history departments at Yale and William and Mary before becoming the chief of the Manuscript Division at the Library of Congress, a position he has now held for 25 years. Dr. Hutson is not only an eminent scholar but also a prolific writer. He has authored numerous scholarly articles and served as editor of many volumes as well as authoring several of his own books. Patricia Bomoni, the well-known author of *Under the Cope of Heaven* describes him well in critiquing his *Religion and the Founding of the American Republic*: "Hutson has done a stunning job in synthesizing a huge amount of material in elegant and vigorous prose. He has been everywhere and read everything. This is a *tour de force.*"[60]

This masterpiece is essential reading to understand the impact of religion in the founding of this American Republic. A later book by Hutson, *Forgotten Features of the Founding: The Recovery of Religious Themes in the Early American Republic*, adds another dimension to the role of religion in our founding. After carefully reading these two books, one would find it difficult, if not impossible, to disagree with Tocqueville in his assessment of religion in America. After his nine-month visit to America in 1831, Alexis De Tocqueville, as referenced by Carter, returned to France where he would write, "There is no country in the whole world in which the Christian religion retains greater influence over the souls of men than in America." Tocqueville was very impressed with the way in which the Christian religion, including Catholicism, flourished in "the most democratic country in the world." He saw things firsthand as he traveled throughout the country that the 20th century liberals failed to uncover in their research. Let us examine some of Hutson's examples from the original sources as we look at the religious beliefs of some of the Founding Fathers in light of the religious climate in America at the time.

Was America Founded as a Christian Nation?

There were undoubtedly a few individuals scattered throughout the colonies who might have dreamed of a federal theocracy with an established national church of their own choosing. However, they would have been few indeed. Certainly none of the most prominent Founders wanted any part of a nation dominated by any Christian denomination. They knew enough about the problems in Christian Europe when the church dominated the state. They also knew a good deal about the state dominating the church.

For the *structure* of our government, we are heavily indebted to John Locke and owe a sizable debt of appreciation also to the Magna Carta.[61] The *moral foundation* of this nation and the system of values that has endured over the years is another question. The Judeo-Christian foundation of moral values seems to me to be self-evident from our founding documents and the early history of this country. I use the word "Judeo-Christian" with full knowledge that the early settlers of this land were overwhelmingly Christian,[62] as our citizens have been throughout our history.

The question as to whether America was considered to be a "Christian nation" during its founding period is a topic of considerable debate to this day.

Some of the best known Founders most likely would have shied away from such a description. Jefferson, Franklin, Adams, and probably Madison and Washington would fall into this category.[63] But the vast majority of the several hundred lesser-known Founders and the overwhelming majority of the population would not have had such a problem. Most of them would have said "of course" we are a Christian nation. The evidence in support of such a description is overwhelming. In many ways, the Christian religion dominated first the colonies and then the states.

Nine of the original colonies had some type of established church during the colonial period. Only Pennsylvania, Delaware, New Jersey, and Rhode Island never had an established church. (Parts of New York also apparently recognized no established church.) Jefferson and Madison fought consistently to disestablish the Anglican Church in Virginia, but they never denied the right of a majority of the people in the colonies (or states) to do so. By the time of the ratification of the First Amendment in 1791, or shortly thereafter, nine of 11 states that ratified the First Amendment[64] had ceased to provide direct financial support to an established state church.

It seems evident that colonial, then state, requirements for mandatory church attendance and tax support for the clergy, anti-blasphemy laws, and Sabbath regulations (even recognized in Article 1:6 of the Constitution) argue strongly that most Americans believed America to be a Christian nation, at least in a broad sense of the term. After the adoption of the Declaration of Independence in 1776, the new states (former colonies) needed to draft state constitutions. In 1777, Thomas Jefferson wrote *five* bills that he wanted included in the new Virginia statutes regarding religion. Unfortunately, most people are only aware of the most famous, "A Bill for Establishing Religious Freedom." The other four dealt with preserving the property and contents previously owned by the Church of England for the Episcopal Church; punishment for "Disturbers of Religious Worship and Sabbath Breakers"; "A Bill for Appointing Days of Public Fasting and Thanksgiving"; and "A Bill Annulling Marriages Prohibited by the Levitical Law and Appointing the Mode of Solemnizing Lawful Marriage."[65] These bills would never have been drafted by someone who was trying to ban religion from the public square.

The U.S. Constitution, Article 6, Section C,[66] specifically prohibits a religious test for holding federal office. This is the only time religion is specifically mentioned in the U.S. Constitution, and for good reason. The 55 men assembled at the "Philadelphia Convention" or "Constitutional Convention" knew how difficult it would be to entice the states to give up any authority to the "federal" government. The states so jealously guarded their rights in religious matters that any mention of the subject could jeopardize the entire document. However, the drafters felt strongly that they must prohibit a "religious test" for holding federal office, especially since nearly all the states had their own "religious tests." These state religious tests were not uniform, as shall be pointed out. Not only did it make sense to ban a federal "religious test," but it would have been impossible to craft one that the nine states necessary for ratification could agree upon. The delegates did acknowledge the sanctity of Sunday (Article 1:7) and made a point to spell the date "in the year of our Lord one thousand seven hundred and eighty seven" (Article 7).

An analysis of the denominational preferences of the 55 delegates in Philadelphia is interesting and revealing. There certainly was no anti-religion or secular bias, because virtually all 55 delegates to the convention were members of a Christian denomination. There was only one deist, Benjamin Franklin, unless you can make that label stick on Washington as well. None were Unitarians. (Thomas Jefferson and John Adams weren't delegates, as they were abroad in Europe at the time.) Thirty were Episcopalian/Anglican; 16 were Presbyterian; and eight were Congregationalist. There were three Quakers, two Catholics, two Methodists, two Lutherans and two Dutch Reformed—and one self-professed deist. This adds up to more than 55, since a few of them changed denominations and both are listed. Alexander Hamilton, for example, was born of Huguenot ancestry, became a Presbyterian and ultimately an Episcopalian. Tom Mifflin of Pennsylvania was a Quaker who became a Lutheran.[67]

But of the original 13 colonies/states, only New York and Virginia had no religious test for holding public office. Hutson makes the point that most of the churches and clergy supported acts requiring such religious tests. He contends that "twelve of the thirteen revolutionary state governments" adopted such "test acts."[68] Noting that Baptists were most opposed to churches receiving financial support to pay their clergy, he makes this observation about religious tests:

> "The most restrictive of these acts, which required office holders
> to profess a belief in the divine inspiration of the Old and New
> Testaments, were passed in Pennsylvania and Delaware, states where
> Baptists had a strong presence."[69]

Under William Penn's leadership, Pennsylvania was the first state to officially allow Catholics to hold public office. Penn made the right to hold office dependent on a belief in the deity of Christ and the inspiration of the Old and New Testaments. In a change in the state constitution, Pennsylvania extended this right to Jews in 1790. Pennsylvania probably also was the first state to take such official action. Georgia, Massachusetts, North Carolina, New Hampshire, New Jersey, South Carolina, and Rhode Island limited the holding of political office to Protestant Christians. Delaware, Pennsylvania, Maryland, and Vermont allowed Trinitarian Christians to hold office.[70]

Many of the states who entered the Union at a later date, exemplified by Arkansas, Tennessee, and Texas, also included in their constitutions a religious test for holding public office. They all required belief in a Supreme Being. The constitutions of newer states to join the Union and the revised constitutions of the original states over time would limit the religious tests to a belief in God or a

Supreme Being. They were basically monotheistic and Christian only by implication. The Bill of Rights in the Texas Constitution of 1876 is a good example:

> No religious test shall ever be required as a qualification to any office on account of his religious sentiments, provided he acknowledge the existence of a Supreme Being."[71]

It is interesting to note that the Texas' original constitution upon becoming a state in 1845 had a prohibition of a religious test in Section 3 of Article 1 of the Bill of Rights, quoting the exact language in the U.S. Constitution: "No religious test shall ever be required as qualification to any office or public trust in this State." This leads to the question as to why such religious "test acts" were instituted in the first place. It seems obvious that these test acts initially were intended to preserve the Christian character of America—in many cases the Protestant Christian character. By the time Tennessee, Arkansas, and Texas included basic "test acts" simply requiring a belief in God, most of the original states had either removed or modified their requirements in a similar fashion. It seems equally obvious that the states' desires to promote sectarian concerns may have diminished, but the desire to preserve a moral nation built upon sound religious principles was as strong as ever.

While most state religious tests had been removed by the turn of the 19th century, some of these religious tests existed in one form or another until 1961, when in *Torcaso v. Watkins* the Supreme Court disallowed the application of Maryland's "belief in God" statute. Actually, they were not all totally abolished until the U.S. Supreme Court in 1978 struck down the Maryland and Tennessee restrictions as unconstitutional.

The *Torcaso v. Watkins* decision was handed down by a unanimous Court of nine very liberal justices. The Warren Court arguably was the most liberal in U.S. history. This decision rises to the level of concern for conservatives or traditionalists primarily because it is another flagrant example of unelected activist judges disregarding states rights. (The concerns of the most avid and famous Republican leader at the time of the founding were realized once again. Thomas Jefferson had worried about and warned about judges who would reach for power never granted to them. Jefferson also firmly believed that the powers not specifically delegated by the states to the federal government were reserved to the states in perpetuity. Perhaps the major disagreement that Jefferson and Madison had with Washington and Adams during their presidencies was over the appointment of activist Federalist judges. They complained that these judges weren't sticking to their responsibility to interpret the Constitution instead of trying to make laws as they saw fit.)

Few would argue with the right of the people of the states to elect agnostics or atheists if they choose to do so. But to deny the rights of the people to express their preference through their elected representatives that positions of public trust be filled by those who at a minimum believe in the existence of God is to flaunt the will of the people. This is especially true for an appointed position. (A case can be made that people have the right to elect an atheist by a popular vote. For the first time in U.S. history a publicly professed atheist is serving in the U.S. House of Representatives.)

The intrigue to at least take a close look at the majority opinion in *Torcaso* is that it was written by none other than Justice Hugo Black.

Article 37 of the revised Maryland Constitution simply stated, "That no religious test ought ever to be required as a qualification for any office of profit or trust in this State, *other than a declaration of belief in the existence of God*; nor shall the Legislature prescribe any other oath of office than the oath prescribed by this Constitution" (emphasis added).

Roy Torcaso was appointed by the governor of Maryland as a notary public in the early 1960s. When he, as an atheist, refused to declare his belief in God, the appointment was refused. Torcaso brought suit and was rebuffed by the Maryland Circuit Court and the Maryland State Court of Appeals. The Supreme Court agreed to hear the case. Oral arguments were heard April 24, 1961, and a decision was rendered June 19, 1961.

In writing the majority opinion, Justice Black stated, "This Maryland test for public office cannot be enforced against appellant, because it unconstitutionally invaded his freedom of belief and religion guaranteed by the First Amendment and protected by the Fourteenth Amendment for infringement by the States."[72]

Black once again was successful in leading his judicial colleagues to conclude that they knew more about the meaning of the 14th Amendment than the Congress that had drafted the amendment and the states that had ratified it. It should not be forgotten that only six years after the 14th Amendment was adopted by Congress, the Blaine bill was defeated. The Blaine bill would have made some provisions of the Bill of Rights, including the First Amendment, binding on the states. Over the roughly 75 years that had intervened before the 1947 *Everson* decision, Congress had defeated the Blaine bill or some variation of it another 24 times. It was absolutely clear that all of the U.S. Congresses that convened from 1789 to 1947 knew that the Bill of Rights was intended solely to limit the power of the federal government and protect the rights of the states.[73]

The only positive thing to come out of the majority opinion in *Torcaso* was that Black, either in a rare moment of honesty or a slip of the pen, recognized "Secular Humanism" as a religion in Footnote 11. He wrote: "Among the religions in this country which do not teach what would generally be considered a belief in the existence of God are Buddhism, Taoism, Ethical Culture, Secular Humanism, and others."

The careful scholar, but always eminently fair, Yale Law School Professor Stephen Carter offers some interesting insights in his brief reference to Black's reasoning in the *Torcaso* decision. In *God's Name in Vain*, Carter begins: "Recognizing that we are a religious nation is not the same as creating an official religion." He discusses how religious "test-oaths" have been used throughout history even to divide Eastern Orthodox and Western Christians. Carter then quotes Oliver Ellsworth, a delegate to the Constitutional Convention, who was later quoted by Black. Ellsworth said:

> "In short, test-laws are utterly ineffectual; they are no security at all; because men of loose principle will, by an external compliance, evade them. If they exclude any persons, it will be honest men, men of principle, who will rather suffer an injury, than act contrary to the dictates of their consciences." [74]

Carter then evaluates Black's use of the Ellsworth statement in his majority opinion in these words:

> "Of course, an oath that God exists is not the kind of oath that scared the Framers. They were worried about using the test-oath to separate Christians from Christians, not to separate Christians from non-Christians. I am not suggesting that their values should be our values; I am suggesting the serious limits of a rhetoric that puts into the mouths of the Framers values that we have developed for ourselves. If we think—and I hope we do—that it is wrong to discriminate, in the voting booth, say, between Christians and non-Christians, the reason is not that the Framers were worried about it. They were not. The reason is that history has taught us to be wary of it. If we are irritated at, or frightened by, groups who, today, seem willing to re-impose test-oaths, let the reason for anger be stated clearly: not that the Constitution is against it, but that history is." [75]

Comparing Black's written opinions in *Everson* (1947) and *Torcaso* (1961) leads to the inevitable conclusion that Justice Hugo Black was a total charlatan. Black either never read a word of the extensive congressional debate surround the "Religion Clause" in the First Amendment, or if he read such debate he totally ignored it. Madison's own words in this debate would have prevented his distorted use of the "wall" metaphor. Then he takes Ellsworth's words in the "test-act" debate totally out of context because they suit his purposes in the *Torcaso* decision.

Another interesting and somewhat strange fact is that when the U.S. Constitution was adopted, seven states had a prohibition of clergymen holding political offices. They were Delaware, Georgia, Maryland, New York, North Carolina, Virginia, and South Carolina. This seems strange because these were very religious states and all of them except Delaware had some type of established church. The role the clergy played in calling for and defending American independence also make this prohibition seem odd. We can be absolute sure, though, that they were not concerned about any kind of separation between church and state. The most powerful explanation is that there was such a concern for the need to have the Gospel proclaimed and such a shortage of preachers.

A brief article, "The Exclusion of Clergy from Political Office in American States: An Oddity in Church-State Relations," by William Silverman examines the options for this exclusion.[76] The anti-Catholic argument seems weak since significant Catholic immigration did not occur until the middle of the 18th century, long after most of these state exclusions of the clergy for holding public office had been enacted. The anti-Anglican or "Patriotism" hypothesis makes some sense in certain cases. The bulk of the "Loyalist" clergy who opposed the American Revolution were members of the Church of England. These clergymen had sworn allegiance to the King in their ordination vows. Most of the seven original states who forbad clergymen from holding political office had a significant Anglican/Episcopal population.

However, the most persuasive motive for such clergy-exclusion is the one I had reached before reading this article. The importance of the work of the ministry and the shortage of clergymen at the time is the compelling argument. The New York State Constitution, as Silverman points out, stated that such a provision was included so as not to distract the clergy from their "great duties."[77] South Carolina, Mississippi, Tennessee, and Texas included similar wording to New York's in their constitutions. The Missouri Constitution of 1820 simply excluded the clergy along with duelists, those convicted of perjury, bribery, or "other infamous crimes" from holding public office.[78] Strange!

The prohibitions against clergy holding political office were removed in most states by the latter part of the 19th century, but the Tennessee and Maryland exclusions did not officially end until 1978.

Religion in America in the Founding Period

Brooke Allen in *Moral Minority* describes the religious beliefs of the most famous Founders in terms of the conventional wisdom of the typical liberal writers. Before examining what we can know for sure about their beliefs (and not only what liberals expect us to believe, just because they wrote it) we should briefly try to determine what the religious beliefs and practices of the population in general were in America at the time of our founding.

Hutson carefully dispels some of the self-perpetuating liberal myths about religion in America in the 18th century.[79] There was a somewhat widespread belief in England that Christianity was on the wane and at a low ebb in the colonies at the time. Nothing could have been further from the truth. Where would such an erroneous opinion have come from? Strangely enough, it probably came from the established clergy. The Anglican and Congregationalist ministers would return to England from America and complain about religious attitudes and church attendance in the colonies. Why? Because especially after the "Great Awakening," from about 1735 to 1745, the established churches were on the decline and the evangelical movement was growing by leaps and bounds. Probably the most famous evangelist during this period was George Whitefield, who was actually an Anglican priest turned evangelical. He drew crowds in the thousands, and there were numerous stories about people traveling for days to hear him preach. In 1740, the big three churches in America were the Anglicans, Quakers, and Congregationalists. By the turn of the century, the largest denominations in America were the Baptists, Presbyterians, and Methodists. Preachers were hard to come by, and laymen sometimes became lay preachers. Stories abound about settlers in frontier areas building churches hoping to attract a preacher—any kind of preacher, as long as he was a Christian.

Liberal historians have added to the *myth* of religious indifference during the founding period based on the fact that attendance at Holy Communion was low indeed. James Hutson's Chapter 4 on "The Christian Nation Question" in *Forgotten Features of the Founding* comprehensively addresses the reasons for such small numbers receiving Holy Communion. In the case of the Anglican churches, there were no bishops in America to administer confirmation, the rite that made members eligible to receive the sacrament. Devout Anglicans would not flaunt church dogma and attend communion without having been confirmed. (Interestingly enough, this could help explain why Washington took Holy Communion regularly before the Revolutionary War and did not do so after the war. Maybe he did not want to set himself apart from the people. This will be discussed when we examine the faith of George Washington.)

Hutson describes the Presbyterians:

> "Many dedicated Presbyterians rejected communion for reasons peculiar to that denomination. During the colonial period Presbyterian congregations conducted, once a year, marathon 'communion seasons,' lasting from three to five days, which often resembled religious revivals...."[80]

Apparently the great awakenings and evangelists such as Jonathan Edwards had so alarmed the people about God's wrath that they were sorely afraid of "eating and drinking damnation" to themselves. Many obviously were aware of 1 Cor. 11:29-30 and were fearful that they would not be properly prepared to receive the sacrament. Hutson stresses that the Congregationalists in New England had low, 10 to 25 percent, communion rates since they were also aware of Paul's warning about unworthy communicants. He then uses a Lutheran example:

> "Among colonial Lutherans the awesomeness of communion also dissuaded many from participating in the sacrament. Collin, the Swedish Lutheran minister in New Jersey, reported that at a service in 1783 only two people came forward for communion. One, a man of 60, stopped

short of the altar and said that 'the sacredness of the action frightened him and that he was perfectly powerless' to proceed. Martin Luther had a similar experience at the feast of Corpus Christi in Eisleben."[81]

Hutson makes a strong case that infrequent attendance at Holy Communion did not indicate that the country was without religious fervor. Exactly the contrary is the case, according to this eminent scholar:

> "Far from being prostrated by a religious depression, Christianity in America flourished after 1776... During and after the war this area boiled with evangelical energy. Methodists, Baptists and Presbyterians conducted what seemed to be a series of nonstop revivals...One scholar who has studied the exponential growth of Baptists, Methodists and Presbyterians in the period after independence asserts 'that it is more accurate to characterize the years from 1775 to 1790 as a Revolutionary revival' than a spiritual stupor." [82]

Once again we are reminded of just how correct Tocqueville was in 1831, when he stated that there was no "country in the whole world where the Christian religion retains greater influence over the souls of men than in America." The same statement would have been equally true in 1776, 1788, 1791, or any other year during that period. In *Democracy in America*, Tocqueville describes the Christian Sabbath in terms that must have sounded strange to all Europeans and especially unusual to French ears:

> "In the United States on the seventh day of the week, trade and industry seem suspended throughout the nation; all noise ceases. A deep peace, or rather a sort of solemn contemplation, takes its place. The soul regains its own domain and devotes itself to meditation."[83]

He goes on to explain how children are taken to church with their parents and hear speech strange to their little ears about evils caused by pride and covetousness and happiness that results from virtue. They then come home and the father opens the Holy Scriptures and talks about the goodness of the Creator and His promise of eternal life. (I'm sure that Tocqueville would have found during his nine-month stay in the United States that although such behavior was not universal, it was typical in many cases.) Tocqueville then makes an extremely important point about the country our Founders created for us:

> "Elsewhere in this book I have pointed out the causes which buttress the maintenance of American political institutions, and religion appears to be one of the most important... Americans show in practice that they feel it necessary to instill morality into democracy by means of religion."[84]

(As previously mentioned, some scholars make a palatable case that the sanctity of Sunday as the Christian Sabbath is implied if not mandated in Article 1, Section 7 of the Constitution. In making the point that the president has 10 days in which to act on a bill passed by Congress before it becomes law without his signature, Sundays are specifically excluded. Why? Obviously that is the day on which Christians take time off from their labors to worship God. [For those who might read this paper and are not theologically inclined, it should be noted that Sunday is the first day of the week, not the seventh. The early Christians chose the First day of the week for their worship services because that is the day on which Jesus rose from the dead.])

In view of the strong religious convictions of the majority of those in the American colonies, it should come as no surprise that our first government as a free country spent an inordinate amount of time encouraging the practice of religion. Hutson reminds his readers in *Religion and the Founding of the American Republic* (subsequently referred to as *Religion*) that the Continental-Confederation Congress that functioned from 1774 to 1789 was the first national government of the United States. (It was replaced in 1789 by the new federal government established by the Constitution.) It is remarkable that this early Congress with such a small membership accomplished so much.

When it first met in Carpenter's Hall in Philadelphia in 1774, there were only 55 members representing 12 of 13 colonies (Georgia was not present) who were constantly plagued by "no shows." They had no permanent home and very little power. Yet they defeated the greatest military power in the world, concluded the most successful peace treaty in American history, and survived unbelievable economic and other hardships to create the world's first constitutional republic. During all their difficulties, they never forgot their God and the role that religion must play in making a democracy work. They had their disputes, disagreements (sometimes violent arguments), and failures, but they never lost sight of their mission to create a free country.[85]

The First Fight: Prayer to Open the Continental Convention

Their very first fight was over religion. During the inaugural session of the Congress, convened Tuesday, Sept. 6, 1774, a lawyer from Boston named Thomas Cushing rose and moved that the delegates begin their session with a prayer. Two devout and orthodox Episcopalians, John Jay of New York and John Rutledge of South Carolina, objected to Cushing's motion. John Adams would record the event in a letter to his wife, Abigail, saying that "because we were so divided in religious sentiment"—Episcopalians, Congregationalists, Presbyterians, and others—"we could not join in the same act of worship." He would imply that Jay and Rutledge feared that an act of public prayer would elevate these other denominations and sects to the same level of dignity and legitimacy as their established churches. The vote could have gone either way. But Samuel Adams, a former tax collector from Massachusetts and a Congregationalist of the Puritan variety (who were not known for their religious tolerance), rose to save the day. John Adams explains in his letter to his wife:

> "Mr. S. Adams arose and said he was no bigot, and could hear a prayer from a gentleman of piety and virtue who was at the same time a friend to his country. He was a stranger in Philadelphia, but had heard that Mr. Duche' (Dushay they pronounced it) deserved that character, and therefore he moved that Mr. Duche', an Episcopal clergyman, might be desired to read prayers to the Congress tomorrow morning."

The two prominent Episcopal laymen could hardly object to such a suggestion. Adams, a Congregationalist, who became a Unitarian later, continues in his letter to his wife:

> "As it happened, the psalm assigned to be read that day by Episcopalians was the Thirty-fifth. In the hall, the priest read: 'Plead my cause, O Lord, with them that strive with me: fight against them that fight against me. Take hold of shield and buckler, and stand up for mine held.'"

Adams told Abigail, "I never saw a greater effect upon an audience." He continued, "It seemed as if Heaven had ordained that Psalm to be read on that morning."[86]

Jon Meacham, former editor of *Newsweek*, in his book *American Gospel*, seems to make an honest attempt to bridge the gap between the liberal and conservative views on the role of religion in the founding of this nation. It could be argued that he gives a little too much credence to the liberal bias, but you can judge for yourself. The late William F. Buckley Jr., founder of *National Review*, gives this evaluation: "This book is a great poultice on the simmering antagonism between the ultra-separationists... and those who plead co-existence... Meacham's invaluable book serves as a lodestar for original thought on the American Gospel."[87]

The ultimate story of the outstanding Anglican priest, Rev. Jacob Duche', has a sad ending, but it illustrates how God often uses weak and frail men to accomplish His purposes. Looking at the frailties of great men reminds one of Elijah, arguably the greatest prophet of all times. Elijah had rebuked the most powerful kings of his day when they disobeyed God, had been visited by angels, had performed miracles and heard God's voice, yet he had his weak moments. He got discouraged and went into the wilderness, sat under the juniper tree and prayed, "It is enough; now, O Lord, take away my life; for I am no better than my fathers" (1 Kings 20:4). (Never mind the fact that "his fathers" included some of the greatest men who ever lived.) Even after the angel came and ministered to him and provided food and drink, he still tried to hide in a cave. "And behold, the word of the Lord came to him, and he said unto him, What doest thou here, Elijah?" Elijah tries to justify his actions by reminding God that the children of Israel have forsaken His covenants, torn down His altars, slain His prophets "and I, even I only am left; and they seek my life, to take it away" (1 Kings 20:9-10). God had to remind even Elijah that he was merely human and not quite as smart as he thought he was: "Yet I have left me seven thousand in Israel, all the knees which have not bowed unto Baal" (1 Kings 20:18).

Back to Duche', who provided such important spiritual guidance to the members of the First Continental Congress in an unofficial capacity until his appointment as the body's first official chaplain on July 9, 1776. Hutson points out in *Religion* that the priest knew the piety of his audience and writes of a sermon he preached to the delegates in July 1775: "'Go on, ye chosen band of Christians,' he urged the members. Go on they did, frequently acting like a committee of lay ministers, preaching to the people of the United States as a national congregation, urging them to confess their sins, to repent and to bear the fruits that befit repentance."[88]

Hutson underlines the religious orientation of this Congress: "Congress's first charge to its constituents was the resolution of July 12, 1775, setting a national day of 'public humiliation, fasting and prayer' five weeks later on July 20." Congress then forwarded this resolution to the state authorities and the churches.[89] Sadly, Duche' defected to the British in 1777. One can only speculate that once the fighting was in full force, the Rev. Mr. Duche' came to the conclusion that he was conscience-bound to honor the ordination vows he had taken in the Church of England.

The Clergy and the War of Independence

All sources indicate that overwhelming numbers of clergymen in America were strong supporters of American independence. The evangelicals were especially fervent in their conviction that we had a God-given right to be a free nation. Virtually the only exception to the rule of the clergy supporting independence was that of a few of the Anglican priests, mostly in the northern part of the country. Large numbers of American clergy from all denominations (probably with the exception of the Anglicans) and sects were propelled "into the conflict with Britain" because of "a perceived threat to its institutional status, a threat posed by fears that piggy-backing on British reforms was a plan to impose Anglican bishops on America."[90]

A number of scholars contend (possibly with some justification) that the evangelical movement that grew out of "the Great Awakening" was the "engine" that drove the revolution. Hutson doubts this case can be made with any certainty. He points out that large numbers of theologically liberal preachers were among the strongest in defending our right to fight for our independence. The best example may be Pastor Jonathan Mayhew of West Church in Boston, "who combined extreme liberalism in theology with radicalism in politics." Mayhew would bellow out that "resistance to a tyrant was a 'glorious' Christian duty."[91]

We had a few well-known lawyers, political philosophers, and other patriots who certainly influenced some of the masses of the need for independence. But if there was an intellectual class in revolutionary America, it was the clergy. They could quote Locke and Montesquieu with the best of the political philosophers (e.g., Paine, Jay, and Hamilton), but it was the biblical examples of how God's people rose up to fight the oppressors that really moved the people. The reason that Thomas Paine's *Common Sense* had such an impact was his extensive use of "the Bible to prove that the British monarchy was illegitimate, that it could not be 'defended on the authority of Scripture; for the will of the Almighty, as declared by Gideon and the prophet Samuel expressly disapproves of government of kings.'"[92]

Examples of firebrand preachers proclaiming that Christians had a duty to resist tyrants abounded throughout the country. One of the most noteworthy examples of clerical involvement was the Presbyterian giant John Witherspoon. While serving as president of Princeton, he had attended the Continental Congress and signed the Declaration of Independence. Witherspoon was accused by his enemies of turning Princeton into a "seminary of sedition."

The foremost Lutheran example of clerical involvement was the Rev. Peter Muhlenberg, who in January 1776 threw off his clerical robes at the conclusion of his sermon in Woodstock, Va., and displayed the uniform of an officer in the Virginia militia. Peter Muhlenberg, the son of the famous American Lutheran patriarch, Henry Melchior Muhlenberg, became known as the "fighting parson" and retired from his distinguished military career as a major general. He was especially recognized for his bravery and military leadership at the decisive battle of Yorktown.[93]

The Number of Christians in America, Including Slaves

The men who represented the American people in the early Congresses during our founding years were not only extraordinary people who accomplished the impossible, but they were a good fit for their constituents. They were for the most part moral men with strong religious convictions. The same was true of the people they represented.

In the census year of 1790, the total population of the United States was 3,929,214. Of this number, there were 697,681 slaves and 59,527 free blacks, which would mean there were roughly 3.2 million whites. Probably no more than a couple of thousand were Jews. In 1654, the first Jewish migration of any size was made up of a shipload of Jews fleeing religious persecution in Brazil. They landed in New Amsterdam (which later became New York City), where the Dutch governor initially made it difficult for them to practice their religion. Hutson relates that they had weathered the initial resentment by the following year. He continues, "British conquest of New Amsterdam in 1664 improved the lot of the Jews and by the late colonial period small numbers were thriving in various colonial seaports."[94] There was probably a small sprinkling of Muslims (called "Mahometans" by the Founders), but they played no role in our founding. The politically correct nonsense about large numbers of African slaves bringing their Islamic faith with them to the New World holds no water. Unfortunately, slavery and the transporting and trading of slaves were a worldwide phenomenon that existed from antiquity.

> "Although white slavery, both in ancient and more modern times, is a provable fact, Africa has the dubious distinction of being the continent from which more slaves have been taken than any other continent. In antiquity, all the major civilizations have taken their share of slaves from Africa. In more modern times Arab slave traders carried on a brisk traffic in black slaves during the days of the Trans-Sahara slave trade. From the ninth century until the advent of the Trans-Atlantic slave trade, around the middle of the fourteenth century, Arab Moslem slave traders were responsible for an estimated ten million slaves taken from Sub-Sahara Africa. Most of these slaves were transported to areas around the Mediterranean Sea, the Red Sea and the Indian Ocean."[95]

The reason for this digression is to make the point that when the Portuguese and the British took over this lucrative African slave trade business from the Arab Muslim slave traders, they were engaging in an established business. You can rest assured that the Muslims were not taking their slaves from the Islamic tribes and countries in Africa. The fact is that in many cases, the Arab Muslims were involved in the business of having the African Muslim tribes capture slaves from the non-Muslim tribes.[96]

In any event, approximately 12 million Africans were shipped to the Americas from the 16th to the 19th centuries. Of these 12 million, 5.4 percent or 645,000 were sold in what is now the United States. Almost all of the African slaves who ended up in the United States were animists or the followers of some tribal religion. The one saving grace of this horrid system (if there is such a thing) was that the slave owners introduced their slaves to Christianity.

The indisputable fact is that of the almost 4 million inhabitants of the colonies (be they whites, free blacks, or black slaves), nearly all were Christians of one denomination or sect or another. Obviously, some were Christian in only the generic sense of the word. Perhaps some of the notables were "Christian" deists or "Christian" Unitarians, as we shall discuss. With only a handful of exceptions they believed in divine providence and the importance of Christian morality and the furtherance of the Christian religion for the successful creation and continuation of the American Republic. They may not have wanted to create a Christian nation, certainly not a nation with an established church, but America at the time of our founding was a nation of Christians.

Religious Beliefs of the Prominent Founders

The make-up and character of the men who served in these early Congresses and the religious faith of those who chose to reveal their personal beliefs is truly remarkable. In the chapter 4 of *Religion*, "Religion and the Congress of the Confederation, 1774–89," Hutson singles out several members of these Congresses who exemplified extraordinary Christian commitment. Most of these men fall into the category of those I refer to as the "forgotten Founders."

How often have you heard the name Charles Thomson? Charles' father immigrated to the British colonies in 1737 from Northern Ireland when Charles was only eight years old. One reason the father came to this country was to be able to freely practice his Calvinist faith. Unfortunately, the father died shortly after arriving in Philadelphia, leaving young Charles orphaned. Charles overcame his difficulties and grew up to become a successful Philadelphia merchant and politician. He served as secretary of the Continental Congress through its entirety (1774–1789). During these 15 years, he saw many congressional delegates come and go as he recorded the debates and decisions, thus providing tremendous continuity and influence. Hutson calls him "the soul of Congress." Charles retired from public life to translate the Scriptures from Greek to English.

John Dickinson, known as the "Pennsylvania Farmer," who wrote the first draft of the Articles of Confederation, also retired from Congress to devote himself to religious scholarship. In addition to other Christian documents, he wrote a commentary on the Gospel of Matthew.

Elias Boudinot, another important Founder who is less than a household name, was a descendent of French Huguenots who fled to this country to avoid religious persecution. Boudinot, a wealthy lawyer and leader of the Presbyterian Church in New Jersey, was known for his devout Christian faith and his service as president of the Continental Congress during 1782 and 1783. As a member of the First U.S. Congress, he introduced the resolution asking President Washington to issue a proclamation for a day of Thanksgiving for the new constitutional republic. Boudinot later retired in 1805 as director of the U.S. Mint to devote himself to writing Christian tracts. A year later, he would become the first president of the American Bible Society.

Perhaps a slightly better known Founding Father was John Jay, who served as president of Congress in 1778–79. Jay, who served his country in many official capacities, is best known as the first chief justice of the U.S. Supreme Court. Jay typified the religious devotion of so many of the Founders by becoming president of the American Bible Society when he retired from public life in 1821.

A fact that is not widely recognized but should be of interest especially to Lutherans is that the first Speaker of the U.S. House of Representatives was a Lutheran minister. The Rev. Frederick A.C. Muhlenberg, a congressman from Pennsylvania, was elected Speaker by his fellow congressmen when they first organized the U.S. House in 1789.

These few examples just touch the tip of the iceberg of the religious devotion of the majority of the Founding Fathers. Our Founding Fathers overwhelmingly represented the religious as well as the political beliefs of the population they served.

James Hutson in *Religion* gives us a flavor of the climate prevailing during these early Congresses and the religious attitudes of the men who served in them as he describes some of their earlier actions. Of particular note:

> "Congress's first charge to its constituents was its resolution of June 12, 1775, setting a national day of 'public humiliation, fasting and prayer' five weeks later on July 20.... The 'Continental fast' of July 20 did not disappoint those like John Adams, who predicted that 'Millions will be on their Knees at once before their great Creator, imploring His Forgiveness and Blessings, His Smiles on American Councils and Arms.' On the appointed day, Congress attended services and heard sermons in the morning at Duche's Anglican Church and in the afternoon at Francis Alison's Presbyterian meeting, being careful, as it was throughout the war, not to patronize exclusively any one denomination, lest it be accused of religious favoritism. Later, Congress worshipped en masse at Philadelphia's 'Roman Chapel,' July 4, 1779, and at the 'Dutch Lutheran Church,' October 24, 1781. In an additional effort to appear evenhanded in religious matters, Congress, after the Duche' debacle, appointed joint chaplains of different denominations."[97]

Anyone who questions the religious convictions of the 200-plus Founding Fathers who served in the earliest Congresses is simply ignoring the facts. Another "Congressional Fast Day Proclamation," signed by John Hancock as president of the Congress, set Friday, May 17, 1776, as a "day of Humiliation, Fasting and Prayer" throughout the colonies. Virtually all such proclamations contained Christian language, but this particular proclamation specified that such prayers be asked through the "merits and mediation of Jesus Christ."[98]

What do we know about the religious beliefs of the more prominent Founders? I have read enough of the statements of our most famous Founders to know that you can find a quote from each of them on most of the issues of the day. Frequently, you can find quotes on different sides of the same issue. Like most human beings, they would address the same issue in different contexts. Maybe they would change their minds on an issue, possibly more than once. (Look at the example we have previously discussed of Madison's changing views in old age.)

As previously noted, Madison and Washington left us no record of their personal religious faith. With the exception of Jefferson, the other big-name Founders didn't discuss their faith in much detail. We are pretty much dependent upon what they said about religion in general to piece together what they personally believed.

For example, as noted in the Introduction, I know of no example where any of the "Big Six" (Franklin, Washington, Adams, Jefferson, Madison, and Hamilton) had anything but ridicule for Thomas Paine's tract, "The Age of Reason," with its strong attack on biblical Christianity. Benjamin Franklin, probably the least religious Founder, advised Paine not to publish the tract since the "consequence of printing this piece will be a great deal of odium drawn upon yourself, mischief to you, and no benefit to others." John Adams, who some contend was no more personally religious than Franklin, wrote of the strongly anti-Christian tract, "The Christian religion is, above all the religions that ever prevailed or existed in ancient or modern times, the religion of wisdom, virtue, equity and humanity, let the Blackguard (scoundrel, rogue) Paine say what he will."

Adams, who had become a Unitarian, wrote in his Diary, "Suppose a nation in some distant region should take the Bible for their only law book, and every member should regulate his conduct by the precepts there exhibited! ... What a Utopia, what a Paradise would this region be." Adams recognized the Bible's value for the moral foundation of a nation.

Other well-known practicing Christian Founders such as Samuel Adams, Patrick Henry, and John Jay were even more harshly critical of Paine. Sadly, when Paine died in the United States, having been invited back into the country from France by a compassionate President Jefferson, he was buried in a field in New York, since no cemetery would take him. Only six mourners came to his funeral.

The Religion of Thomas Jefferson

Thomas Jefferson was raised in the Church of England at a time when it was the established church in Virginia and the only denomination funded by Virginia tax money. Prior to the revolution, Jefferson served as a vestryman in his local church. Avery Cardinal Dulles, a leading Roman Catholic theologian and authority on the religious beliefs of the Founding Fathers, has this to say of Jefferson's religious beliefs:

> "In his college years at William and Mary he came to admire Francis Bacon, Isaac Newton, and John Locke as three great paragons of wisdom. Under the influence of several professors he converted to the deist philosophy."

Dulles then concludes:

> "In summary, then, Jefferson was a deist because he believed in one God, in divine providence, in the divine moral law, and in rewards and punishments after death; but he did not believe in supernatural revelation. He was a Christian deist because he saw Christianity as the highest expression of natural religion and Jesus as an incomparably

great moral teacher. He was not an orthodox Christian because he rejected, among other things, the doctrines that Jesus was the promised Messiah and the incarnate Son of God. Jefferson's religion is fairly typical of the American form of deism in his day."[99]

Jefferson was certainly a "Christian" deist during the 1770s and most of the 1780s when he wrote the Declaration of Independence, served as governor of Virginia and minister to France. By the time he came to Washington, D.C., to be Adams' vice president in 1797, he had known and read the works of the dissenting English clergyman, Joseph Priestly. Priestly, who was raised a strict Calvinist, had gone through an infatuation with several ancient Christian heresies, the latest being Arianism, and had settled on a form of Unitarianism. His basic argument was that only revealed religious truths that conform to the truth of the natural world should be accepted. This appealed to Jefferson. Based on a letter he wrote to Priestly, he apparently became what might be called a "Christian" Unitarian.

As we have noted, Jefferson was so incensed by the Federalists' attacks on him as an atheist and infidel during the 1800 campaign that he defended his personal religious beliefs in many of his writings—such as the Jan. 9, 1816, letter to Charles Thomson. Recall from the Introduction that in this letter, Jefferson maintains that his "cut-and-paste" version of the Bible, which omitted the miraculous, yet is "proof that I am a real Christian, that is to say, a disciple of the doctrines of Jesus, very different from the Platonists, who call me infidel and themselves Christians and preachers of the gospel, while they draw all their characteristic dogmas from what its author never said nor saw."

One thing that must irritate the radical separationists and the fanatical secularists beyond description was President Jefferson's regularity in church attendance (usually on federal property).

President Jefferson first attended church in Washington at a Protestant Episcopal Church "at the foot of Capitol-hill." These services at Christ Church were held in a converted tobacco shed since there were no church buildings in D.C. at the time. It was not until January 1802 that Jefferson began regularly attending worship services in the chamber of the U.S. House of Representatives. At these services in the U.S. Capitol, President Jefferson heard sermons delivered by Baptists, Episcopalians, Methodists, Presbyterians, Congregationalists, and a variety of evangelists. He may well have listened to a sermon given by a Lutheran, although I have been unable to document such an occasion.

He most likely did not hear a Catholic priest preach because the first documented Roman Catholic preacher was Bishop John England of Charleston, S.C. Bishop England preached in the "Hall of the House of Representatives" on Jan. 8, 1826.

Jefferson did, however, with Vice President Aaron Burr, hear a sermon delivered in the U.S. House by the first female evangelist ever to speak in the House.

Hutson concludes that she was probably the first woman ever to speak officially in Congress in any capacity.[100]

Dorothy Ripley, an evangelist who was said to have crossed the Atlantic 19 times from England to preach to American audiences, was conducting an evangelistic tour in the southern states in 1805. Believing she had a God-given message to share with America's political leaders, she had friends approach the Speaker of the House, Nathaniel Macon of North Carolina, to ask permission for her to preach in the U.S. House. Macon, a Baptist, granted the request for her to preach in December 1805, and another piece of American history was made. If women were not even allowed to vote at the time, it must have seemed extraordinary for a woman to deliver a sermon from the Speaker's podium in the House!

An oft-repeated story most likely explains Jefferson's regular church attendance. The account is recorded in hand-written notes by the Rev. Ethan Allen of Maryland (apparently not related to Ethan Allen of Vermont), who had succeeded Andrew McCormick as rector of Christ Church in 1823. (McCormick was rector of Christ Church when President Jefferson had attended his church services in the converted tobacco shed and was reported to be a close friend of the president. He undoubtedly related the following story, which Allen recorded.) Jefferson was reported to be walking to church (it is unclear whether to Christ Church or the Capitol)

> "... with his large red prayer book under his arm when a friend querying him after their mutual good morning said which way are you walking Mr. Jefferson. To which he replied to Church Sir. You going to Church Mr. J. You do not believe a word in it. Sir said Mr. J. No nation has ever yet existed or been governed without religion. Nor can it be. The Christian religion is the best religion that has been given to man and I as Chief Magistrate of this nation am bound to give it the sanction of my example. Good morning Sir."[101]

Jefferson may not have believed all that was said in church, but he knew he had a duty to set an example for the people he served.

The Religion of Benjamin Franklin

Benjamin Franklin was not a very religious man himself, but he was a champion of religion and its value for the success of the American republic. Franklin's parents had hoped that he would have a career in the church; but, after discovering deism, he became, by his own admission, disillusioned with organized religion. In spite of his lack of an orthodox personal faith, Franklin would become an avid promoter of religion, especially of the Christian variety. John Adams once noted that Franklin was a mirror in which people saw their own religion. Adams wrote:

"The Catholics thought him almost a Catholic. The Church of England claimed him as one of them. The Presbyterians thought him half a Presbyterian, and the Friends believed him a wet Quaker."[102]

Franklin famously wrote to Thomas Paine, "If men are so wicked as we now see them with religion what would they be if without it?" In 1790, only about a month before he died, in answer to a question about his opinion of religion, he wrote a letter to the Rev. Ezra Stiles, president of Yale. In this frank, somewhat humorous, but also sad statement for those of us who are Bible-believing Christians, he stated:

> "As to Jesus of Nazareth, my Opinion of whom you particularly desire, I think the System of Morals and Religion, as he left them to us, the best the world ever saw or is likely to see; but I apprehend it has received various corrupt changes, and I have, with most of the present Dissenters in England, some Doubts as to his divinity; tho' it is a question I do not dogmatize upon, having never studied it, and I think it needless to busy myself with it now, when I expect soon an Opportunity of knowing the Truth with less Trouble ...."[103]

I guess we must concede to the liberals that Ben Franklin was a deist, albeit more accurately a "Christian" deist.

We would be remiss if we failed to make a brief reference to Ben Franklin's famous words at the Constitutional Convention in Philadelphia in 1788. It is easy to understand why the framers steered clear of any discussion of religion in the Constitution, as we have discussed in some detail. On the other hand, it is somewhat difficult to explain the apparent lack of personal piety that had characterized the previous Congresses and those that would follow with the establishment of the U.S. Congress. It is ironic but perhaps predictable that the one member among the 55 delegates who was a self-professed deist tried to call the other 54 to task. (Every delegate except Ben Franklin was a member of a Trinitarian Christian denomination. This assumes that two of the three Quakers fall under this definition. One of the Quakers had converted to Lutheranism, either before or shortly after the Philadelphia Convention.)

Once the secrecy of the Convention proceedings had been lifted, we now have the benefit of some of the debates:

> "Franklin reproved his fellow delegates for forgetting God, that 'powerful Friend' who guided America to victory over the mighty British Empire. I have lived 'a long time,' Franklin explained, 'and the longer I live, the more convincing proofs I see of the Truth—that God governs in the *Affairs of Men*... We have been assured, Sir, in the Sacred Writings, that "except the Lord build the House, they labor in vain that build it." I firmly believe this; and I also believe, that, without his

concurring Aid, we shall succeed in this political Building no better than the Builders of Babel.'"

Franklin would then move that that "Prayers, imploring the Assistance of Heaven, and its Blessing on our Deliberations, be held in this Assembly every morning." Franklin's motion was debated and voted down, "ostensibly because the Convention had no funds to pay local clergymen to act as chaplains."[104]

It comes as no surprise that the secularist liberal elites gloat over this incident as proof that the Founders lacked religious devotion. But they haven't been able to move less than a year down the road to consider the actions of the first United States Congress. This Congress, you will remember, authorized and set salaries for Christian chaplains; reauthorized the Northwest Ordinance, which urged the spread of the Christian religion; called for days of prayer and Thanksgiving; and attended Christian worship services en mass from time to time as examples of their Christian commitment.

The Religion of John Adams

When John Adams entered Harvard College at age 15, his father expected him to become a Congregationalist minister. After graduating from Harvard in 1755, Adams taught school for a few years before deciding to go to law school. In 1764, he married Abigail Smith, the daughter of a Congregationalist minister. She had so much influence on him and some of the decisions made during the founding that some scholars recognize her as the most prominent female Founder.

Adams is also regarded by liberal scholars as a deist, but the claim is difficult if not impossible to justify. In 1796, Adams denounced the deism of political opponent Thomas Paine in the above-quoted words attacking Paine's criticism of Christianity. Hutson says that deism is of interest to so many scholars not because of its numbers, since it was at best a "minority within a minority," nor because of the influence it may have exerted on the founding of a small new denomination referred to as Unitarianism. Rather, deism is of interest to liberal scholars because of the few prominent Founders branded with its label.

Adams, like many of his friends in and around Boston, did become a Unitarian. (Hutson references the joke about Unitarianism, that the Unitarians believed "in the Fatherhood of God, the Brotherhood of man, and the Neighborhood of Boston."[105]) Adams may have been influenced in his rejection of traditional Christianity, in favor of the more liberal theological tenants of Unitarianism, by his perceived view of the overreaching authority of the Roman Catholic Church. Because of his profound respect for the teachings of the Bible and his strong belief in life after death, he probably would be more comfortable being recognized as a "Christian" Unitarian. Adams contended that if one rejects the belief in life after death, "you might be ashamed of your Maker."

The Religion of Alexander Hamilton

Alexander Hamilton, who was born out of wedlock and had a reputation for being a ladies' man, doesn't leave us much information about his religious convictions. He denounced the excesses of the French Revolution in regard to religion, strongly advocated the support and encouragement of the Christian religion for the good of the Republic, and vigorously criticized Thomas Paine's degradation of Christianity in "The Age of Reason." In 1779, when Hamilton wrote to a friend in South Carolina asking help in finding a suitable wife, he listed some of the attributes he would find desirable. "As to religion a moderate stock will satisfy me," he wrote. But when Hamilton found his own Elizabeth, she was an extremely religious woman, and he described her as "best of wives and best of women."

He died an Episcopalian. On his death bed, he initially had trouble finding an Episcopal priest to give him Holy Communion because of the church's opposition to dueling. Hamilton confessed his sins, and one of his last acts on earth was to receive the body and blood of his Lord and Savior. The liberals will have a lot of trouble with honesty if they try to brand him as a deist.

The Religion of James Madison

James Madison, who wrote about almost everything else, left us no written record of his personal religious beliefs. When the liberals smugly include him in their list of the Founders' deist camp, they are just guessing. That is a poor guess; I believe a careful evaluation of the evidence will indicate it not to be so.

We do know that Madison grew up in the Church of England, the state religion of Virginia at the time. (We all know that the theology of the Anglican Church [Episcopal Church in America after the revolution] is a mixture of Lutheranism and Calvinism.) A young James Madison went off to college at the College of New Jersey (now Princeton), which was run by Presbyterian clergy. Madison immediately fell under the influence of the college president, Rev. John Witherspoon, a strict Calvinist and a highly regarded evangelical preacher. Witherspoon, as previously noted, would go on to become a signer of the Declaration of Independence and a leading clerical advocate of the American Revolution. Witherspoon not only had an influence on the young Madison's political philosophy but on his religious convictions as well.

After completing the four-year course at Princeton in two years, Madison stayed on for a year of "graduate school." One of the main reasons James Madison earned the title of Princeton's first graduate student was his desire to stay on at the college while he decided whether or not to enter the ministry. In 1773, Madison wrote a letter to a college friend, William Bradford, in which he revealed some of his struggles in deciding a future course for his life. He agonized over whether he should spend his life "as a fervent advocate in the cause of Christ" or choose to work in some secular profession. Two months later, Madison decided against his spiritual course of study and entered law school.[106]

Was Madison throughout his adult life and at the time of his death an Episcopalian, a Presbyterian, or a deist? (I think we can reasonably rule out Episcopalian, since in a letter written in 1819 he seems to relish the fact that the elaborate Episcopal churches built at public expense were being deserted "by their flocks to other worships." He also has some praise for the evangelical flocks who worship in "Meeting Houses of the plainest and cheapest sort."[107]

In honesty, we really don't know what religious beliefs he professed. Maybe the liberal historians who claim him as a deist had some way of divining the answer, or perhaps they just made it up. We do know he discussed religion in his public statements. Some reputable scholars contend he was still a Calvinist in the mid and late 1780s, based on statements of a few of his associates. This could explain how he was able to secure the crucial support of the Presbyterians in Virginia to defeat Patrick Henry's general assessment bill for all denominations, which was supported by George Washington among others.

Hutson documents the fact that Madison followed Jefferson's example of attending Sunday worship services in the Capitol, especially during the War of 1812. Hutson also reminds us that Madison designated national days of thanksgiving on four occasions between 1812 and 1815. Jefferson certainly showed his respect for Madison's religious scholarship by asking his friend in 1824 to compile a list of theological works for the library at the University of Virginia. Hutson concludes his discussion of Madison's religious beliefs in his usual scholarly way about matters that cannot be precisely documented:

> "Although there is no evidence that Madison was a closet evangelical, it seems apparent that, late in life, he retained substantial sympathy for the doctrine of the new birth and for its social consequences that he had learned long ago at Princeton."[108]

The Religion of George Washington

Now we turn to the most important Founder of them all, His Excellency George Washington.

In his writings and public statements, Washington is no more helpful than Madison in revealing to us his own religious beliefs. His public behavior and his public statements about the role and place of religion in the new American republic are all we have to consider.

To judge from Washington's public behavior, he was a loyal Episcopalian. He was baptized into the Church of England, which was to become the Protestant Episcopal Church after the revolution. In 1765, Washington began service on the vestry of his local church, playing an active role for many years. At least two prominent Episcopal churches in Northern Virginia until this day detail the roles President Washington played in the founding and sustaining of their congregations in their earliest days.

Washington's step-granddaughter (and informally adopted daughter), Nelly Custis Lewis, leaves us one piece of informative information. She stated:

> "I have heard her [Nelly's mother, Eleanor Calvert Custis, who resided at Mount Vernon for two years] say that General Washington always received the sacrament with my grandmother [Martha Washington] before the revolution."[109]

There apparently is no record of Washington taking communion after the revolution. Nelly's letter to Jared Sparks also indicates that after the revolution, Washington frequently attended Christian worship services with Martha, but their custom was to leave before Holy Communion was served. There is an account of Washington being confronted by an Episcopal priest concerning his lack of receiving the sacrament. This account holds that he stopped attending the church served by this particular priest. We do know that Washington did not request communion on his death bed. Evidently, he also never asked for a visit from the minister who waited in another part of the residence at Mount Vernon.

After Washington took the first presidential oath at Federal Hall, New York City, on April 30, 1789, he improvised "so help me, God" at the conclusion of the oath. He then kissed the Bible. After the ceremonies, President Washington and his party, which evidently included all the members of the First Congress, attend a worship service at St Paul's Chapel in New York City. The Rev. Samuel Provoost, Episcopal bishop of New York, officiated at the service. Provoost was then appointed as one of the two mandated congressional chaplains the following day.[110]

Washington certainly believed in divine providence and an Almighty Creator who ruled the universe, and he urged all Americans to repent of their sins and give thanks to the Almighty for all His many blessings. All of Washington's important public proclamations testify to his beliefs in this regard. There is also an abundance of Washington's statements indicating his firm belief in religious liberty and tolerance.

Perhaps once President Washington became the undisputed leader and most prominent figure of this young republic, he did not want to be seen as imposing his own personal Christian beliefs on the American people. If this were to be the case, I would refer to such an attitude as erring on the side of caution. Martha's decision to destroy his numerous personal letters to her after his death may well have resulted in depriving us of the first president's personal views on his religious faith, as well as on many other personal matters.[111]

One thing is for sure: when the liberal historians confidently assure us that Washington was a deist, they are divining or just guessing. Washington was an avid Mason and it is reasonable to assume that Masonic teachings were a major part of his religious beliefs. The Masons, certainly at that time, did not believe that God was an absentee "Landlord" who was not involved in human affairs.

The Religion of Aaron Burr

Not to ignore one of the better known Founders, we might look briefly at the religious orientation of Aaron Burr. Some liberal historians would add Burr to their list of prominent American Founders whom they count as a deist. Burr, like Washington and Madison, apparently didn't leave us much of a record of his personal religious beliefs. Aaron Burr was born in Newark, New Jersey to the Rev. Aaron Burr, Sr., a prominent Presbyterian minister and the second president of the College of New Jersey, now Princeton. Burr's mother, Esther Edwards, was the daughter of Jonathan Edwards, who arguably was the most famous Calvinist theologian in early America.

Aaron Burr received his A.B. degree in religion at Princeton in 1772, but two years later he decided to pursue a career in law. After a varied and unusual life that included a distinguished military career, Burr served as a U.S. senator from New York (he defeated Philip Schuyler, New York's first senator and Alexander Hamilton's father-in-law) and as the third vice president of the United States. He had a few entanglements with the law; he was charged with treason and engaged in a duel in which he killed Alexander Hamilton.

Burr traveled all over the world and died in 1836 at the age of 80. He was buried in Princeton Cemetery near his famous father and more famous grandfather. I have found no evidence that he strayed from his Calvinist beliefs and became a deist.

Deism

From my research, the conclusion can easily be reached that the word "deism" meant different things to different people in the early days of our republic, and it certainly had a different meaning than it does today. Of the "Big Six," I am willing to concede Franklin by his own declaration. Certainly, Thomas Paine and Ethan Allen confessed their deist convictions.

Adams and Jefferson acknowledged their Unitarian beliefs. However, the early Unitarians in this country had radically different beliefs prior to being taken over during the late 1830s by the likes of Ralph Waldo Emerson, who turned this "religion" into a philosophical and ethical debating society "tolerant" of all religions as well as those espousing no religion. During the days of Jefferson and Adams, the Unitarians accepted most of the teachings of the Bible; they simply rejected creeds and church doctrine. (Some also rejected most or all of the miracles recorded in the Bible.)

American Religion

For a new perspective on the religious attitudes of the Founders, be they the best-known or lesser-known Founding Fathers, James Hutson's *Forgotten Features of the Founding: The Rediscovery of Religious Themes in the Early American Republic,* is a fascinating read. This extensively documented book examines the importance of the Founders' belief in a "future state of rewards and punishment" and acceptance of the Old Testament concept of "nursing fathers" as a model for the church-state relationship. Hutson's arguments for such universally agreed upon principles makes it less important as to whether a Founder's personal religious beliefs were based in the theology of the more traditional Christian denominations or were of the deist or Unitarian variety. They all believed that the nation must have a solid religious foundation.

Jon Meacham leans toward the liberal historians' views of the religious beliefs of the Founders. But he makes a somewhat similar point in his *American Gospel: God, the Founding Fathers, and the Making of a Nation*. Meacham, who strongly recognizes the Founders' commitment to religious liberty, also recognizes the Founding Fathers' belief that such a free nation could survive only if it was based on a solid religious foundation. He sums up his thesis in the Introduction:

> "The great good news about America—the American gospel, if you will—is that religion shapes the life of the nation without strangling it. Belief in God is central to the country's experience, yet for the broad center, faith is a matter of choice, not coercion, and the legacy of the Founding is that the sensible center holds. It does so because the Founders believed themselves at work in the service of both God and man, not just one or the other. Driven by a sense of providence and an acute appreciation of the fallibility of humankind, they created a nation in which religion should not be singled out for special help or particular harm. The balance between the promise of the Declaration of Independence, with its evocation of divine origins and destiny, and the practicalities of the Constitution, with its checks on extremism, remains perhaps the most brilliant American success."[112]

Meacham continues as he points out that the Founders were struggling with "how to make a diverse nation survive and thrive by cherishing freedom and protecting faith," and concludes this discussion with a very interesting observation: "If the Lord himself chose not to force obedience from those He created, then who are men to try?"[113]

To adequately comprehend the threat of today's cultural war, it is important to understand how deeply religion—specifically the Judeo-Christian religion— was involved in every step of the founding of this great moral and generous nation. The self-appointed intellectual secular elites expect us to accept their "politically correct" reconstruction of American history simply because they believe this is the way it should have been. They must ask themselves, how can we be multicultural, inclusive, and intellectually tolerant if we insist on interpreting the history of this country as it actually occurred?

We should never doubt the seriousness of this struggle, since our very American heritage is at stake. Conservative Lutherans and other Bible-believing

Christians have much to offer in this struggle, which will determine what type of country we leave to our children and their children. I believe we are facing a call from God we dare not ignore!

Notes

[1] Stephen L. Carter, *The Culture of Disbelief: How American Law and Politics Trivialize Religious Devotion* (Basic Books, 1993), 58.

[2] William Rehnquist, "United States Supreme Court Justice Rehnquist's Dissent in *Wallace v. Jaffree*" (1985). I will use Chief Justice Rehnquist's dissent extensively in discussing Black's majority opinion and the question of the separation of church and state. The Rehnquist dissent is available online at http://www.belcherfoundation.org/wallace_v_jaffree_dissent.htm.

[3] From my extensive readings of scholars on the subject, I have determined that at least 250 men would deserve to be called Founders. But no one can argue with the 204 who meet these described criteria.

[4] Jon Meacham, *American Gospel: God, the Founding Fathers, and the Making of a Nation* (Random House, 2007), 15, 78.

[5] The subject of religion in the founding period will be discussed in some detail in this chapter. Two of Dr. James Hutson's books, *Religion and the Founding of the American Republic* (Library of Congress, 1998) and *Forgotten Features of the Founding, The Recovery of Religious Themes in the Early Republic* (Lexington Books, 2003) are two of the most authoritative sources on this subject. Hutson is the chief of the Manuscript Division at the Library of Congress and will be referred to frequently in the course of this chapter.

[6] Richard John Neuhaus, *The Naked Public Square: Religion and Democracy in America* (Wm. B. Eerdmans Publishing Company, 1996), 80.

[7] Neuhaus, 202-203.

[8] Neuhaus, 8-9.

[9] This exchange is taken from the notes of a delegate to the convention from Maryland, Dr. James McHenry. Some scholars dispute its authenticity, but it sounds like Franklin from what I have read about him. He was a brilliant and complex man and I will explore his statements on religion later in this chapter.

[10] From John Adams' notes, quoted in "Digital History" (n.d.). Accessed Dec. 31, 2011, at http://www.digitalhistory.uh.edu/learning_history/revolution/revolution_declaringindependence.cfm. Jefferson in turn praised Adams as "The Colossus of that Congress—the great pillar of support to the Declaration of Independence, and its ablest advocate and champion on the floor of the House" (Thomas Jefferson, *The Works of Thomas Jefferson*, Federal Edition [G.P. Putnam's Sons, 1904-5], Vol. 11).

[11] Neuhaus, 6.

[12] Neuhaus, 3.

[13] For history buffs, Richard Brookhiser's *Gentleman Revolutionary: Gouverneur Morris, the Rake Who Wrote the Constitution* (Free Press, 2004) is an interesting and informative read. In this book, one of the least known Founders is presented in a colorful way, but his importance in the founding of this country should not be overlooked.

[14] Daniel Dreisbach's lengthy essay "Thomas Jefferson, a Mammoth Cheese, and the 'Wall of Separation Between Church and State,'" in *Religion and the New Republic: Faith in the Founding of America*, (Rowman & Littlefield Publishers, 1999), 65-114, edited by James H. Hutson, is the primary source for this discussion. This 49-page article includes 24 pages of 172 reference notes including virtually every reliable source. This article should be read in its entirety by those interested discovering Jefferson's intended meaning. Philip Hamburger in his previously referenced book devotes Chapter 7, "Jefferson and the Baptist: Separation Proposed and Ignored as a Constitutional Principle" (pp. 144-189), which is another excellent source.

[15] Dreisbach, 70.

[16] Dreisbach, 70.

[17] Dreisbach, 69.

[18] Wikipedia contributors, "John Adams," *Wikipedia, The Free Encyclopedia*, http://en.wikipedia.org/wiki/John_Adams (accessed Dec. 31, 2011).

[19] Wikipedia contributors, "John Adams."

[20] Wikipedia contributors, "Alexander Hamilton," *Wikipedia, The Free Encyclopedia*, http://en.wikipedia.org/wiki/Alexander_Hamilton (accessed Dec. 31, 2011).

[21] Mansfield, 6-7.

[22] Dreisbach, 69.

[23] Wikipedia contributors, "Alexander Hamilton.

[24] Dreisbach, 78. Dreisbach makes the astute point: "This proclamation was issued after Jefferson had penned his famous 'Bill for Establishing Religious Freedom.'"

[25] Certainly the main reason for Jefferson's refusal to designate such days of religious observances as president was his strong conviction that religion was a matter to be dealt with by the states and the churches, a position totally consistent with his states-rights philosophy in general. Jefferson never disputed the right of the states to recognize an established church. He was so strongly opposed to the established church (Anglican) in Virginia that he, along with Madison, fought relentlessly for its disestablishment. Jefferson had become very "anti-clergy" and worried about a "Protestant Popedom."

[26] James Hutson, "A Wall of Separation: FBI Helps Restore Jefferson's Obliterated Draft," *The Library of Congress Information Bulletin* 57, no. 6 (June 1998), 137. Hutson, who has served as chief of the Manuscript Division at the Library of Congress since 1982, is the premier authority on this subject.

[27] Hutson, "A Wall of Separation," pp. 7-9.

[28] For an in-depth understanding of the drafting, editing, and purpose of this letter, see Hutson, at http://www.loc.gov/loc/lcib/9806/danbury.html.

[29] Helen E. Veit, Kenneth R. Bowling, and Charlene Bangs Bickford, eds., *Creating the Bill of Rights* (The Johns Hopkins University Press, 1991), xiii. This is a detailed 323-page documentary record of the First Federal Congress and the debates in Congress before the Bill of Rights was passed and sent to the States.

[30] Wikipedia contributors, "James Madison," *Wikipedia, The Free Encyclopedia,* http://en.wikipedia.org/wiki/James_Madison (accessed Dec. 31, 2011). Quote from Gordon S. Wood.

[31] Mansfield, 16. Quote from "The Federalist."

[32] Mansfield, 16. Quote from letter from Thomas Jefferson to James Madison, Dec. 20, 1787.

[33] Rehnquist, 8, Footnote 3. Justice Rehnquist refers to Madison's lack of enthusiasm in introducing such amendments: "In a letter he sent to Jefferson in France, Madison states that he did not see much importance in a Bill of Rights but he planned to support it because it was 'anxiously desired by others ... [and] it might be of use, and if properly executed could not be of disservice.'"

[34] Rehnquist, 4.

[35] *The New York Times* bestselling author Stephen Mansfield is a prolific writer, and his books are easily readable. *Ten Tortured Words: How the Founding Fathers Tried to Protect Religion in America...and What's Happened Since (Thomas Nelson, 2007),* which lays out the role of church and state clearly and thoroughly, is now very inexpensive. His books on the faith of George W. Bush, Barack Obama, and other present-day politicians are very interesting. His recently released book, *The Mormonizing of America* (Worthy Publishing, 2012), is a fair presentation of Mormon teachings and explains the accomplishments of modern-day Mormons.

[36] Dreisbach, 5.

[37] Mansfield, 20.

[38] Mansfield, 20.

[39] Mansfield, 20.

[40] Mansfield, see Appendix 2, 173-181.

[41] Mansfield, 68.

[42] Mansfield, 20 ff. Mansfield records highlights of congressional debate.

[43] This passage from the *1 Annals of Congress* is quoted from Mansfield, 21. The important aspects of the congressional debate are recorded in either Mansfield or Rehnquist or both. For the more dedicated scholars, find the *1 Annals of Congress* in the Library of Congress, where the entire debate is recorded.

[44] Mansfield, 23.

[45] Rehnquist, 10. *1 Annals of Cong. 914* (1789).

[46] There were no party identifications in the First Congress, but members generally were designated either as Pro-Administration or as Anti-Administration. For the most part, the "Pros" were already or became Federalists, while the "Antis" became Republicans. The philosophical Republicans sought constantly to limit the powers of the federal government.

[47] Rehnquist, 10.

[48] Rehnquist, 11.

[49] Mansfield, 14.

[50] Rehnquist, 9.

[51] Rehnquist, 12-13.

[52] Mansfield, 69. The basis of this discussion of the 14th Amendment is recorded in pp. 69 ff.

[53] Hutson, "A Wall of Separation," 9.

[54] Hutson, "A Wall of Separation," 10.

[55] Dreisbach, 152.

[56] Alan Sears and Craig Osten, *The ACLU Vs America* (B&H Publishing Group, 2005), 133.

[57] Stephen Carter makes this scholarly observation (*God's Name in Vain*, [Basic Books, 2001], 217, footnote 21): "No serious historian disputes the proposition that the antiestablishment provision in the First Amendment was included *solely* to prevent the Congress from either establishing a national church or interfering with those states that had established churches" (emphasis Carter's).

[58] Carter, 65.

[59] Carter, 35-36.

[60] Quoted on the back cover of Hutson, *Religion and the Founding of the American Republic* (Library of Congress, 1998).

[61] There is no question that the Magna Carta had a major impact on English law and subsequently on the system of law that would emerge from the American colonies in the new world. When the Magna Carta was written in 1215, it was intended to limit King John's usurpation of feudal rights and his harsh and heavy-handed administration of justice in the kingdom. Pope Innocent III immediately annulled the validity of the document on grounds that it would limit the church's authority over the king. Today, only three of the 63 clauses in the Magna Carta remain in effect as part of the law of England and Wales. "One defends the freedom and rights of the English church, another confirms the liberties and customs of London and other towns, but the third and most famous: *No free man shall be seized or imprisoned, or stripped of his rights or possessions, or outlawed or exiled, nor will we proceed with force against him, or send others to do so, except by the lawful judgment of his equals or by the law of the land. To no one will we sell, to no one deny or delay right or justice.*" This statement is provided online by the British Library (see http://www.bl.uk/treasures/magnacarta/basics/basics.html).

[62] As we discuss the few Founders who were deists or Unitarians, it will become clear that even they would be considered Christian in the broad, if not orthodox, sense of the term.

[63] In the 1790s, Muslim pirate ships from the Barbary Coast and Tripoli were viciously attacking American ships. They were stealing our cargo and taking our seamen prisoners. It was unconventional warfare and we were having great difficulty protecting our ships and men. In addition to greed, part of the Muslim motivation—then as now—was that America was perceived as a Christian nation. The young country was in no position to launch an all-out war on this area of Africa, which is now Libya. Both Presidents Washington and Adams had paid ransom (blackmail) on a few occasions to rescue some of our captured seamen. Apparently, they believed such a compromise was better than the alternative. An American diplomat by the name of Joel Barlow wrote the original draft of a peace treaty. Barlow, a former chaplain in Washington's revolutionary army, had fallen under the influence of Thomas Paine and forsaken his religious beliefs. He was now a deist at best (if not a closet atheist). He inserted language in Article 11 of the Treaty of Tripoli, which would ultimately be signed by President John Adams and touted by radical secularists in perpetuity. Article 11 reads: "*As the Government of the United States of America is not, in any sense, founded on the Christian religion; as it has in itself no character of enmity against the laws, religion, or tranquility, of Mussulmen; and as the said States never entered into any war, or act of hostility against any Mahometan nation, it is declared by the parties, that no pretext arising from religious opinions, shall ever produce an interruption of the harmony existing between the two countries.*" This language was obviously a concession based on the circumstances that certain Muslim countries would not sign a treaty with a Christian government. These Muslim pirates were a part of the lucrative Muslim slave trade involving the taking of Christians as slaves, especially in Italy. This treaty, which is rarely mentioned in American history, was totally ineffective. In 1801, President Jefferson had to take some American ships out of mothballs to blockade the ports off the African coast to stop the pirate raids on our ships.

[64] Massachusetts and Connecticut never ratified the First Amendment.

[65] Mansfield, 182-189.

[66] "... but no religious Test shall ever be required as a Qualification to any Office or public Trust under the United States."

[67] The Web site *adherents.com* compiles statistical data worldwide concerning adherent statistics and religious geography. They use primary source research, government census reports, statistical sampling surveys, organizational reports, and secondary literature. You can find out how many Lutherans live in Wisconsin or Muslims living in India. They list famous religious adherents ranging from Lutherans, Catholics, and Jehovah's

Witnesses to Zoroastrians. These references are taken from *ww.adherents.com/gov/Founding_Fathers_Religion*.

[68] Hutson must have some original evidence of religious-test act requirements in New York, since there is no evidence that Virginia ever had such a requirement. Since Hutson is widely recognized as the foremost authority on religion in the founding period, this is most likely correct.

[69] Hutson, *Religion and the Founding of the American Republic*, 68-69.

[70] Some interesting facts about religion in the original states can be found in John K. Wilson, "Religion under the State Constitutions, 1776 – 1800," *Journal of Church and State*, Volume 32, Autumn 1990, No. 4, 745-766.

[71] *Constitution of the State of Texas* (1876), Art. 1, "Bill of Rights," Sec. 4.

[72] Wikipedia Contributors, "Torcaso v. Watkins," *Wikipedia, The Free Encyclopedia*, http://en.wikipedia.org/wiki/Torcaso_v._Watkins (accessed Dec. 31, 2011).

[73] Since the *Torcaso* decision did not rule directly on the constitutionality of the Maryland law, it would not finally be declared unconstitutional until 1978.

[74] Carter, 64.

[75] Carter, 65.

[76] William Silverman, "The Exclusion of Clergy from Political Office in American States: An Oddity in Church-State Relations," *Sociology of Religion*, 2000, 61:2, 223-230. Accessed Dec. 31, 2011, at http://socrel.oxfordjournals.org/content/61/2/223.full.pdf.

[77] Silverman.

[78] Silverman.

[79] In the first two chapters of *Religion and the Founding of the American Republic* ("America as a Religious Refuge" and "Religion in Eighteenth-Century America"), Hutson concisely brings to life the religious climate in the earliest days and the founding days of our American republic. This is a most interesting and informative read.

[80] Hutson, *Religion and the Founding of the American Republic*, 124.

[81] Hutson, *Religion and the Founding of the American Republic*, 125.

[82] Hutson, *Religion and the Founding of the American Republic*, 126, Addendum 4. This entire section in Hutson's book should be read to get an accurate picture of religion at this time in American history.

[83] Alexis de Tocqueville, trans. Gerald Bevan, *Democracy in America* (Penguin Classics, 2003), 630.

[84] de Tocqueville, 630.

[85] Hutson, *Religion and the Founding of the American Republic*, Chapter 4, "Religion and the Congress of the Confederation, 1774-89."

[86] Meacham, 65-66.

[87] Meacham, back cover.

[88] Hutson, *Religion and the Founding of the American Republic*, 51.

[89] Hutson, *Religion and the Founding of the American Republic*, 51-52.

[90] Hutson, *Religion and the Founding of the American Republic*, 44.

[91] Hutson, *Religion and the Founding of the American Republic*, 39.

[92] Hutson, *Religion and the Founding of the American Republic*, 41-42.

[93] For a more detailed discussion of clerical involvement in the War of Independence see Chapter 3, "Religion and the American Revolution," in Hutson, 37 ff.

[94] Hutson, *Religion and the Founding of the American Republic*, 8.

[95] Walter D. Kennedy, *Myths of American Slavery* (Pelican Publishing, 2003), 18. Kennedy's book is an interesting read and contains considerable information and statistics even if one does not agree with all his conclusions.

[96] Reference was made in Chapter 5 to the fact that North African Muslims from the Barbary Coast took up to one million white Christian slaves, mostly from Italy, but also some from France, Spain, Holland, Great Britain, and even a few from Iceland, from the 1500s to 1800s. See Dr. Robert C. Davis, professor of Italian Social History at Ohio State University, *Christian Slaves, Muslim Masters: White Slavery in the Mediterranean, the Barbary Coast and Italy, 1500-1800* (Palgrave Macmillan, 2003).

[97] Hutson, *Religion and the Founding of the American Republic*, 51-52.

[98] Hutson, *Religion and the Founding of the American Republic*, 52.

[99] Wikipedia contributors, "Thomas Jefferson and Religion," *Wikipedia, The Free Encyclopedia*, http://en.wikipedia.org/wiki/Thomas_Jefferson_and_religion (accessed Jan. 1, 2012).

[100] Hutson, *Religion and the Founding of the American Republic*, 86.

[101] Quoted in Hutson, *Religion and the Founding of the American Republic,* 96.

[102] Wikipedia contributors, "Benjamin Franklin," *Wikipedia, The Free Encyclopedia,* http://en.wikipedia.org/wiki/Benjamin_Franklin (accessed Jan. 1, 2012).

[103] Carl Van Doren, *Benjamin Franklin* (The Viking Press, 1938), 777.

[104] Hutson, *Religion and the Founding of the American Republic,* 76. For more details on this subject, read Hutson's Chapter 6, "Religion and the Federal Government," pp. 75 ff.

[105] Hutson, *Religion and the Founding of the American Republic,* 30.

[106] Hutson, *Forgotten Features of the Founding: The Recovery of Religious Themes in the Early American 107*

[107] Hutson, *Religion and the Founding of the American Republic,* 97.

[108] Hutson, *Religion and the Founding of the American Republic,* 97.

[109] Taken from Eleanor "Nelly" Parke Custis Lewis' letter to Jared Sparks, written in 1833. George Washington adopted and raised Nelly and her brother (Martha's grandchildren) in 1781 when their father died. Nelly was just a little more than two years old at the time. The letter is available at http://www.ushistory.org/valleyforge/youasked/060.htm.

[110] Hutson, *Religion and the Founding of the American Republic,* 79. Hutson points out that the First U.S. Congress followed several of the precedents of the previous Confederation Congress in religious matters: 1) They required the appointment of two congressional chaplains, which had resulted from the Duche' defection in September 1777. The other chaplain appointed on May 1, 1788, was a Dutch Reformed minister, the Rev. William Linn. This also reflected Congress' desire to treat all Christian denominations equally. 2) The First Congress also passed legislation to implement the Northwest Ordinance, which stated that "Religion, Morality and knowledge [were] necessary to good government and the happiness of Mankind...." They also passed the previous Congress' legislation for imposing Christian morality on the army and navy.

[111] Those interested in reading undoubtedly the most comprehensive book on the question of Washington's religion should consider *Washington's God* (Basic Books, 2006). Michael Novak and his daughter, Jana Novak, give evidence of having researched every available source, concentrating on the notes and letters left behind by Washington's family and friends. This book is filled with accounts of Washington's attitude toward religion and his absolute reliance on Divine Providence.

[112] Meacham, 5.

[113] Meacham, 5.

7

The Cultural War Heats Up

The ACLU and Roger Baldwin

Many Americans probably believe that the American Civil Liberties Union—the ACLU—was a good organization, founded with noble purposes, that just went wrong over the years. A look at the stated intentions of the organization's primary and most influential founder proves otherwise.

Roger Baldwin came from a family of non-Christians and socialists from the Boston area. He was born in Wellesley, Mass., Jan. 21, 1884. His grandfather was described as an "iconoclastic and non-conformist anti-Christian crusader."[1] Baldwin was an agnostic and, like most of his family, was loosely associated with the Unitarian Church.

Among the friends whom Baldwin admired and by whom he was influenced was Margaret Sanger, who founded Planned Parenthood. Sanger was a eugenicist who believed in "selective breeding" and was admired by Adolf Hitler, who eagerly read her books. Among other friends by whom Baldwin confessed to have been influenced were many socialists, communists, and at least one radical anarchist, Emma Goldman.

"Red Emma," as Goldman was called, was the founder of the anarchist magazine *Mother Earth* and was eventually deported to Russia in 1919. From Goldman, Baldwin learned well "how to mask his true agenda and disguise it in a way to get the elites on his side."[2] After receiving his B.A. and M.A. at Harvard University, Baldwin moved to St. Louis, where he taught sociology at Washington University. It was in St. Louis that Baldwin met "Red Emma"; joined the Industrial Workers of the World; traveled to the Soviet Union in 1927; and returned to the U.S. to write *Liberty Under the Soviets*. He later denounced Soviet communism, though one might suspect this was at least partially motivated by his public relations sensitivities—these also had led him to adopt a patriotic-sounding name for his new organization, "The American Civil Liberties Union."

The ACLU was so closely tied to the communist movement in the 1920s and early 1930s that a report by a Special House Committee to Investigate Communist Activities stated:

"The American Civil Liberties Union is closely affiliated with the communist movement in the United States, and fully 90 percent of its efforts are on behalf of communists who have come into conflict with the law. It claims to stand for free speech, free press and free assembly, but it is quite apparent that the main function of the ACLU is an attempt to protect the communists."[3]

During this period, the ACLU's board was packed with prominent Communist Party members. However, Baldwin became so disenchanted with Soviet-style Communism after Stalin signed the Nazi-Soviet Non Aggression Pact of 1939 with Hitler that he was instrumental in having the ACLU board members who belonged to the American Communist Party summarily dismissed. He justified his actions by claiming that the ACLU was a private organization like a church and had a right to determine membership based on its beliefs. He said:

"The ACLU is a private organization.... And a private organization is like a church. You don't take nonbelievers into the church. We are a church; we have a creed and only true believers should lead us."[4]

It is very interesting that years later the ACLU had total amnesia about their founder's words regarding private organizations when they tried in court to force the Boy Scouts of America to accept openly gay and atheist scout leaders. For more about the founder of the ACLU and the early days of its history read *The ACLU vs. America* and the reference material it provides.[5]

Let's take a look at the ACLU agenda for America, most of which is taken from the "1992 Policy Guide of the ACLU":

1. All legal prohibitions on the distribution of obscene material—including child pornography—are unconstitutional.
2. Pornographic outlets can locate wherever they please—whether next to churches or day-care centers or near residential neighborhoods.
3. Tax-funded libraries should not restrict access of children to pornography on the Internet.
4. The military cannot stop open displays of homosexual behavior within its ranks.
5. Public schools cannot observe recognized religious, historical, or cultural holidays such as Christmas, Easter, or Hanukkah, despite hundreds of years of American tradition.
6. All legislative, military, and prison chaplaincy programs should be abolished.
7. All criminal and civil laws that prohibit polygamy and same-sex "marriages" should be done away with.[6]

These are just a few examples—taken from the ACLU's own internal documents—of what the ACLU agenda has been for more than 80 years.

The ACLU gained some prominence in the 1920s because of the "Scopes Monkey Trial," which they had initiated in Tennessee. They were not known for much else except for defending some American communists until around the middle of the 20th century, when they achieved a major success in the U.S. Supreme Court.

Hugo Black and Judicial Activism

Following the FDR landslide elections in 1932 and 1936, the country was moving to the left. As elected officials became more liberal, those appointed to judgeships, including the Supreme Court, would reflect the political change. With more liberal judges on the bench, the latent threat of judicial activism began to show signs of life. (Thomas Jefferson himself had expressed concerns about unelected judges with no direct accountability to the people distorting the will of the electorate as expressed in the founding documents and the laws passed by their elected representatives. We will discuss this further later in the chapter.)

The ACLU and its secularist allies had made only a few modest gains prior to 1947. Then came the Supreme Court decision that would open the floodgates to a comprehensive secularist assault on America's moral foundations. The 1947 decision that sought to erect a "wall of separation between church and state"— *Everson v. Board of Education of the Township of Ewing*—thrust judicial activism on the American people in much the same way as the 9/11 Islamist terrorist attacks declared Islamic *jihad* against America. Thus the "Cultural War" was formally declared!

This war on the moral and religious foundations of this nation had been in the planning for more than 25 years before the secularists won their first major victory. In *Everson*, this stark challenge to our religious freedom came in a landmark and contradictory decision.

New Jersey law allowed local governments to reimburse parents of school children who rode public buses to school. The township of Ewing, N.J., provided this bus-fee reimbursement from taxpayer dollars also for children attending Catholic schools. The Supreme Court ultimately ruled that this did not violate the Constitution, but when he wrote the majority opinion, Justice Hugo Black stated that the "First Amendment has erected a wall between church and state. That wall must be kept high and impregnable."[7]

Black's misuse of a Jefferson metaphor, taken from his letter to the Danbury Baptist Association, overturned 150 years of constitutional history and threatens the very religious liberty upon which this nation was founded.[8] Justice Black ignored the historical circumstances surrounding introduction of the constitutional amendments as well as the intent of Congress and the debate surrounding adoption of the First Amendment. How could Black not have consulted Madison's original draft of the First Amendment in trying to determine what he intended? Black didn't even consider other actions taken by this same Congress during the same time frame that would have been declared unconstitutional according to his distorted interpretation of the First Amendment that had just been adopted by this Congress.

This decision is so important in the Cultural War being waged by the ACLU and its allies in their efforts to establish a totally secular society that it begs for a closer look at the man who wrote this opinion and the history he ignored in penning this outrageous and fallacious interpretation of constitutional law.

A Troubling and Confused Life

The life and career of Justice Hugo LaFayette Black appears to be as strange and contradictory as some of his judicial opinions. He obviously was brilliant and ambitious, but at times he was either confused, unprincipled, or both.

He was born in a small wooden farm house in Harlan, Ala., which was a poor small town in the foothills of Appalachia. The youngest of eight children, he initially started out to be a medical doctor like one of his older brothers but ended up graduating from law school at the University of Alabama. After failing to make a go of a law practice in his home town, he moved to Birmingham to practice law. He served three years of a four-year term as Jefferson County prosecuting attorney before resigning to join the Army during World War I. (Black was a devout Baptist and, like his Alabama Baptist brothers, was violently opposed to the consumption of alcoholic beverages and deeply suspicious of Roman Catholicism. As prosecutor from 1914 to 1917, he made a name for himself by vigorously enforcing the Liquor Advertising Law.)

During his service in the Army, Black attained the rank of captain in two years and served all his military time stateside, after which he returned to Birmingham to become a defense attorney. This all sounds like an all-American success story, complete with patriotism. He even had represented a black man forced into some type of commercial slavery before becoming prosecuting attorney. Then, in 1921, his "big break" came when he was selected to be lead counsel for the defense in a murder trial that captivated the attention of Birmingham and the state of Alabama.

Stephen Mansfield describes the following encounter in *Ten Tortured Words.*[9] The daughter of the Rev. Edwin Stephenson (a former barber turned Methodist lay minister, who made his living helping obtain marriage licenses and marrying couples at the county court house) had been married to a Hispanic laborer by an Irish Catholic priest named Father James Coyle. Most people in Birmingham at the time were violently anti-Catholic, as was Stephenson. He suspected something was amiss when he could not find his daughter. He knew she had attended Father Coyle's church against his wishes from time to time, and so he thought he knew where to look. (In his book *Separation of Church and State,* the scholar Philip Hamburger states that Ruth Stephenson had converted to Catholicism earlier in the year.[10]) Stephenson, an intolerant Ku Klux Klan member, confronted the feisty

Irish priest, and a violent argument took place. The Methodist minister pulled a pistol and shot the Catholic priest dead.

Hugo Black became the lead of five attorneys. Hamburger points out that Jim Esdale, the grand dragon of the Alabama Klan, hired Black through the intercession of Compton Harris, one of Black's law partners.[11] The other four attorneys were members of the Klan, as was the Birmingham chief of police, the judge, and most of the jurors. The whole trial was about race and religion.

Counselor Black gained a reputation for hitting the prosecution witnesses with the question: "You're a Catholic, aren't you?" The race thing went so far as Black having Ruth's dark-skinned Puerto Rican husband, Pedro Gussman, brought in to the court room with the lights dimmed and asked the witnesses if Gussman looked like a Negro.[12] They all agreed that he did.

Stephenson was acquitted, and Black was the toast of the town. In a year or so, Black joined the Klan himself, and in 1926 he was elected to the U.S. Senate.

The Senate seat opened up because of the principled actions of Alabama Sen. Oscar W. Underwood at the 1924 Democrat Convention. Underwood, a serious contender for the Democrat nomination for president, attempted (unsuccessfully) to get the convention to adopt a motion condemning the Klan. This doomed his chances for being selected as the Democrat candidate for reelection to the U.S. Senate in 1926 in Alabama. The Alabama Klan would want one of their own. So enters Hugo Black. (For a more detailed discussion of Black's senate race see Hamburger.[13])

In 1932, Black was re-elected to the Senate as Franklin Delano Roosevelt was elected to his first term as president. Black was an avid supporter of Roosevelt's "New Deal" legislation and even strongly supported FDR's "court-packing" plan to stack the Supreme Court with an additional number of Roosevelt-friendly justices. In 1937, FDR appointed Black to fill his first vacancy on the Supreme Court.

At the time, it was customary for the Senate to approve a senator, one of its own, who was appointed to an executive- or judicial-branch position immediately and without debate. On this occasion, however, tradition was broken. A Republican senator, Warren Austin, objected on technical grounds that retirement pay for Supreme Court justices had been raised and that Black could not serve until his term of office in the Senate had been completed. The matter was referred to the Judiciary Committee, but the committee sent the nomination to the floor of the Senate a few days later on a 13-4 vote. By then, rumors of Black's Klan involvement were circulating, and two Democrat senators urged that his appointment be rejected. However, due to the lack of conclusive evidence of his Klan membership, Black was confirmed by a 63-13 vote. About a month after his confirmation, the *Pittsburgh Post-Gazette* broke the entire story of Black's Klan history. (Black had not been willing to discuss the matter up to this point.)

Such a public outcry calling for his resignation resulted that Black made his famous 11-minute radio address, one of the most widely heard broadcasts in history at the time. There is no way to put the best construction on the fact that he lied through his teeth, but it worked. He claimed that he had joined the *Robert E. Lee Klan No. 1* in Birmingham to keep it from becoming anti-Catholic and anti-Jewish, and that when he saw he was doing no good, he immediately got out.[14] Anyone who has taken even a casual look at the Klan knows that they were anti-Catholic and anti-Jewish from the beginning. They were a "white, Protestant, Christian" organization, and everyone knew it.[15] The idea that in 1923, in Birmingham, Ala., a person could join the Klan and thereby keep it from becoming anti-Catholic is the logical equivalent of denying that the Pope himself is Catholic.

Black also claimed that he joined the Klan in 1923 and attended only four meetings before he resigned in 1925. The KKK didn't exactly provide a membership list or give out a list of attendees at its meetings and rallies. It is a documented fact, however, that Black not only attended the state convention of the KKK in 1926, where Imperial Wizard Hiram Evans awarded him the very rare honor of a golden "grand passport," but he then addressed the delegates as well. In thanking the delegates for their support, he said, "I realize that I was elected by men who believe in the principles that I have sought to advocate and which are the principles of this organization."[16]

What does all this personal history have to do with a devastating decision he wrote concerning the separation of church and state in 1947? Stop and think about it for a minute! From the time Hugo Black agreed to represent the defendant in the Father Coyle murder trial, he seemed to be a man obsessed with a desire for power and fame and would take any action to achieve those goals.

Was Black so anti-Catholic that he would put the moral foundations of his country at risk to impede what he perceived to be Rome's goal to dominate America? This sounds farfetched, doesn't it? But many readers are old enough to remember the hysteria in 1960 about the pope dictating policy to America if John F. Kennedy were elected President. I reluctantly admit that as a young Lutheran pastor at the time, it bothered me, too. This is not something I'm proud of, but strong prejudices can have a major influence on one's life. Fortunately, some of us grow out of them, but some don't.

Think about the history of the settling of this country for a minute. When the Pilgrims disembarked the Mayflower in 1620, it had been only 103 years since Luther had nailed his Ninety-five Theses to the door of the Castle Church in Wittenberg. The Holy Roman Empire was still struggling over which countries would remain Catholic and which would become Lutheran, Calvinist, or some mixture of the two.

Catholics were not that numerous among the early settlers for a variety of reasons. In the early Oglethorpe settlement in Georgia, Catholics were forbidden not only for religious reasons, but for fear that they might join together with the Spanish Catholics in Florida. And, it was considered a big deal in 1701 when William Penn in the Pennsylvania Charter allowed Catholics to hold political office by limiting that privilege to those who believed in "Jesus Christ, the Saviour of the world." James Hutson explains:

> "By prohibiting the civil incapacitation of Catholics, Penn seized higher ground than other advanced thinkers of his time. In his 'Letter Concerning Toleration' (1689) his friend John Locke argued against any toleration whatsoever for Catholics. Roger Williams would have disarmed them and required them to wear distinctive clothing as a condition for worshiping freely."[17]

Roman Catholics were still a small minority in the South when I was growing up in the 1930s and 40s. There was still widespread belief among Protestants that Catholics distorted the message of Holy Scripture and that Catholics still regarded us as heretics. Many Protestants believed that the pope still ran Catholic countries, and there was a fear of Catholics gaining political prominence in America. I don't think this attitude began to change until the time of Pope Paul VI (1963-1978) or maybe not even until Pope John Paul II (1978-2005).

In any event, many religious-liberty scholars are convinced that Black's anti-Catholic bias influenced his *Everson* decision. This group would include the eminent scholar, author, and professor at American University, Daniel Dreisbach, as well as Philip Hamburger, who is John P. Wilson Professor of Law at the University of Chicago.

Hamburger, in *An American Constitutional Right,* explores in some detail the anti-Catholic sentiments in America ranging from the KKK to liberal intellectuals in the Ivy League Northeast. From the latter part of the 19th century through the first half of the 20th century, with the massive Catholic immigration, there was a wall (my word) of hostility toward Catholics and the Catholic Church erected all over America. It is well known that the Klan, the Scottish Rite Masons (especially of the Southern Jurisdiction), the Southern Baptists, and some labor unions (worried about losing their jobs to any immigrants) were vocally anti-Catholic. It is not so well known that the liberal intellectuals in academia and liberal Protestant denominations were equally as hostile, if not more so in some instances. The defense of public schools took on a religious fervor. Catholic schools were viewed with special suspicion as teaching religious "intolerance" and "anti-American" values. Demands were made for New York Governor Al Smith, as the Democrat nominee for President in 1928, to renounce his "allegiance to the pope." Hamburger writes of anti-Catholic fervor:

> "After the Depression and the Second World War, America emerged triumphant, but (as after earlier conflicts) many Protestants worried that they now face 'a head-on collision' with the Catholic Church. Substantial numbers feared that the pope planned to assert Catholic supremacy in an open struggle with secular democracies."[18]

This is the climate and culture in which Hugo Black worked in Birmingham and in the U.S Senate, as well as a justice of the Supreme Court. We do know that Black read and admired the works of the crusading anti-Catholic author Paul Blanshard. Hamburger points out that Blanshard, in *American Freedom and Catholic Power*, brought "Ivy League respectability to nativist anti-Catholicism" and notes that this book was published by the "Unitarians' Beacon Press." In addition, "The president emeritus of the Union Theological Seminary, Henry Sloane Coffin, gushed about Blanchard that 'the gratitude of all freedom-cherishing Americans goes to him' and that this volume 'should be in the hands of every thoughtful American.'"[19] I recently purchased a used copy of Blanshard's *American Freedom and Catholic Power*, originally published in 1949, just two years after Black's infamous opinion. This book was not only a best seller, but the copy I received states that this was the 19th printing, in March 1954. Hamburger quotes this pertinent passage from the previously referenced Hugo Black Jr.'s book, *My Father: A Remembrance*:

> "The Ku Klux Klan and Daddy, so far as I could tell, only had one thing in common. He suspected the Catholic Church. He used to read all of Paul Blanshard's books exposing power abuse in the Catholic Church. He thought the Pope and Bishops had too much power and property. He resented the fact that rental property owned by the Church was not taxed; he felt they got most of their revenue from the poor and did not return enough of it."[20]

The irony of all ironies is that the avid separationists violently condemned the *Everson* decision because it allowed some Catholic parochial-school students in a New Jersey town to receive government-funded bus fares. Hamburger writes:

> "The tone of the advocates of separation was set, in the days immediately after the decision, by hostile newspaper editorials, such as the Washington Post, which observed that 'the principle at issue is the most fundamental in the American concept of government—the separation of church and state.' According to the Post, Justice Black gave 'much lip-service to the principles of religious freedom' but used a 'superficial argument' to permit subsidized bus service and thereby undermined the separation of church and state. The Southern Jurisdiction of the Scottish Rite Masons, the National Education Association, and both the Southern and the Northern Baptists concurred."[21]

The Baptist Joint Conference Committee on Public Relations, composed of both Northern and Southern Baptists, had written a brief in the *Everson* case, and the day after the Black decision, they adopted a resolution denouncing it.

Those preparing to fight this decision to allow a few Catholic students in this New Jersey town to receive bus fare realized they needed a new organization for such a fight. The Baptist Joint Committee could not serve as an umbrella organization for two reasons: One, they reasoned correctly that the larger Southern Baptists would not agree with the total separation they had in mind (which shortly became a reality when prayer in public schools was banned and decisions to remove religious symbols and other free religious speech from the public square began to happen); and secondly, they needed to expand the group to include other Protestants and their purely secularist allies. Joseph Dawson, who was serving as executive secretary of Baptist Joint Committee and, like Black, was a Mason, was instrumental in founding the organization originally named "Protestants and Other Americans United for the Separation of Church and State."[22] This organization would become well known as "Americans United for the Separation of Church and State." This violently anti-religious organization would become a major ally with the ACLU[23] in their efforts to destroy the moral and religious foundation of this nation.

Stunned by the reaction of his fellow Baptists, fellow Masons, former fellow Klansmen, and other fellow Southern anti-Catholics, Black embarked on an anti-religious (initially mainly anti-Catholic) crusade: He wrote the majority opinion in *McCollum v. Board of Education* (1948), which held that the government could not provide religious education in public schools. Again he penned the majority opinion in *Engel v. Vitale* (1962), prohibiting prayer in public schools. (These and other anti-religious decisions will be discussed later in this chapter.) It is true that Klan members claimed a biblical basis for their beliefs, as distorted as their twisting of Holy Scripture turns out to be. But it is also true that not only Baptists, but many Protestant ministers in the Deep South were (or had been) members of the Klan at the time.

After we look at a few other inconsistencies in a variety of Black's decisions, we will try to look carefully at his rationale for this wall of separation between church and state. When we analyze Black's arguments for this decision, together with the historical facts he altogether neglected, it may well cause us to question whether a man of his intellect and historical knowledge could reach such a conclusion without having had a predetermined result in mind from the beginning. Stephen Mansfield in his 2007 book, *Ten Tortured Words*, raises a similar question. When making the point that it is rare for a Supreme Court ruling to be the product of one individual's thinking alone, he points out that

> "it is possible for one man to be the ruling spirit of the Court's doctrine on a specific issue, and this certainly was the case when Hugo Black wrote the majority opinion in Everson v. Board of Education. *It is one of the most troubling rulings in the Court's history, and this may well be because it was written by one of the most troubling justices in the Court's history*" (emphasis added).[24]

Justices Black's long career on the Supreme Court is filled with inconsistencies and surprises. In spite of his KKK background, he quickly established a record sympathetic to blacks and the civil rights movement. Was this a true conversion from his recent record in Alabama politics? His racism was certainly not totally dead, since in a few years he would write the court's majority opinion in *Korematsu v. United States*. This is the ruling that upheld Roosevelt's decision to intern Japanese Americans on the West Coast during World War II, resulting in 120,000 Japanese-Americans being confined in detention centers, which remains an embarrassment to our country.

In the decisions regarding communist activities in the 1950s, he usually voted with the minority in defending their rights under the freedom of speech clause. He felt that pornography and "obscene" speech were protected under the First Amendment, but flag burning was not so protected. Again Mansfield makes a telling point when he notes that Black stood "with an unswerving free speech majority in the famous Pentagon Papers case and yet burned all of his conference notes and most of the materials in his case files before he died."[25] This could be a confused man, or one rebelling against his background and dealing with his guilt. Certainly, it appears he had something to hide. (Surprisingly enough, some scholars insist that Black would have voted against *Roe v. Wade* had he been able to stay on the court a few more years. Their reasoning is that he was strongly on record that there was no "right to privacy" in the Constitution. It would have been interesting to see if he would have been able to reinvent himself one more time!)

Ignoring Congressional and Constitutional History

Whatever his reasons may have been, it is an indisputable fact that the majority opinion Black wrote in 1947 in *Everson v. Board of Education* will continue to overshadow everything else he did in his career; it will define his legacy. The decision is so bizarre and the facts are evaluated in such an inconsistent and selective manner that it appears that the specific case was immaterial and that he was just looking for a venue to attack our religious liberty, totally ban religion from the public square, and establish a godless secular state devoid of moral values and deprived of its entire history as a moral and religious nation. In this context, Stephen Mansfield astutely quotes a well-known phrase from Karl Marx, "A people without a heritage are easily persuaded."[26]

If Black's motivation was to prevent the United States from becoming a Catholic-dominated country, he was successful at great cost to his country. The liberal secularists have been the major beneficiaries of his actions. Justice Black compounds his misinterpretation of the First Amendment by defying history once again in his claim that the Fourteenth Amendment makes the First Amendment binding on the states.

* * * * *

To digress for the sake of emphasis, let me make a comparison between theology and politics. Those of us in the orthodox-Lutheran tradition believe that "all Scripture is inspired by God," without error, and is the final authority for all matters of doctrine and faith. Therefore, we adopt what we believe to be sound biblical hermeneutics and exegesis for interpreting the Bible. Starting with the axiom that "Scripture interprets Scripture," we strive to read every verse in context. In simple terms, we examine each word in each verse according to usage and grammatical considerations. We then look at the verse in the context of the chapter of the specific book of the Bible we are studying and then the context of the entire book. It is important for us to know as much as possible about who wrote the particular book, under what circumstances, etc. We search to discover what the writer actually meant. Our task as scholars is complicated by our need to be able to read Greek and Hebrew as well as by the antiquity of the documents we are studying. We do believe that our efforts are worthwhile because by following such procedures, we can truly understand God's message to us.

Sincere politicians, be they legislators, executives, judges, political scientists, or just historians, should follow similar procedures in interpreting our founding documents. Obviously, we do not claim that our primary documents—the Declaration of Independence, the Constitution, and the Bill of Rights—are inspired by God,[27] but we believe them to be unique in human history for a Republic based on freedom and justice for all. There may be some close parallels in history, but none have ever lasted as long or provided as much freedom and opportunity for as many people. The reason for the unparalleled success of this great country is that so many of the underlying principles upon which our nation was founded are based firmly on Judeo-Christian teachings of morality, compassion, and justice.

If we take the time to study the history, the debates, the parallel actions the nation's Founders took, and their writings (all of them, not just selective passages to try to prove a point), then it is simple to find out what the Founders actually intended. In studying political documents and history we have the advantage that they wrote in English, and most documents are well preserved and certainly of relatively recent date compared with the biblical documents. Most of the better-known Founders were keenly aware that they were writing for history, and they wrote often and seldom briefly. We must always be aware that virtually all of them were occasionally inconsistent, sometimes contradicted themselves, and like all mortals, changed their minds.

James Madison, for example, even went so far as to alter some of his earlier writings late in life after he retired to Montpelier, his tobacco plantation. After a number of years in retirement, he had become so obsessed with his legacy that he wanted to make sure it read the way he felt it should read. Like those of Washington and Jefferson before him, his many years of political activity had taken its toll on his personal wealth. He made the decision not to have most of his public documents and letters published, realizing they would have considerable monetary value to his beloved wife, Dolly, 17 years his junior, whom he expected to leave widowed in the not-too-distant future. He obviously felt free to make some corrections. On at least one occasion, he tried to imitate Thomas Jefferson's handwriting as he altered a few sentences in a Jefferson letter in response to a previous letter he had written to Jefferson criticizing Lafayette. Jefferson was already deceased, and Madison didn't want history to record his criticism of the Frenchman who was so important during the Revolutionary War. The fact that most of them changed their minds on certain matters, especially later in life, is one of the main reasons it is so important to take into consideration the date and circumstances of their sayings and writings.

Certainly we would expect—even demand—that men with the stature and responsibility of being members of the nation's highest court would apply such basic principles of scholarship in their deliberations that result in vital interpretations of our laws.

* * * * *

It has become commonplace in the last 40 or so years for us to talk about "activist judges" who, based on revisionist interpretations of the Constitution and the Bill of Rights, overturn the legislative intent of Congress and referendums passed by the voters. Black was not the very first activist justice on the Supreme Court, but he was one of the first and certainly the most flagrant. Most subsequent court decisions involving prayer in schools, the use of religious symbols in public places, and other expressions of religion in the public square base their conclusions, at least in part, on his majority opinion in *Everson*. This is in spite of the fact, as we have pointed out, that the ultimate ruling allowed students attending religious schools to receive tax-payer funds for bus fare in New Jersey.

Black tries to create the impression that Jefferson played a role in the drafting and adopting of the First Amendment. Lino A. Graglin, a professor of law at the University of Texas, writing a *Wall Street Journal* article in 2005, titled "Our Constitution Faces Death by 'Due Process,'" warns,

> "Judge-made constitutional law is the product of judicial review—the power of judges to disallow policy choices (i.e., the will of the people) made by other officials of government, supposedly on the ground that they are prohibited by the Constitution."

He then goes on to quote Thomas Jefferson, in a letter to Abigail Adams, Sept. 11, 1804, warning "that judges, always eager to expand their jurisdiction, would 'twist and shape' the Constitution 'as an artist shapes a ball of wax.'"[28] Then Graglin concludes, "This is exactly what has happened." How can we fail to believe that Thomas Jefferson would roll over in his grave if he knew how flagrantly Black had misapplied his "wall of separation" metaphor written to the Danbury Baptists?

The Cultural War Becomes Increasingly Hot

Building on the precedent of the *Everson* decision and Justice Black's "wall of separation" language—and frequently urged on by the ACLU—the Supreme Court proceeded on the road to abolishing all religious expression in the public schools. In *Engel v. Vitale* (1962) public school teachers were forbidden from opening class with a prayer, even if it was nonsectarian and not mandatory. In *School District of Abington Township v. Schempp* (1963) the court ruled that reciting the Lord's Prayer or any reading of Scripture in the classroom was prohibited, even if students had the right to opt out of these activities. In *Wallace v. Jaffree* (1985) a moment of silence in schools was declared unconstitutional, because the Supreme Court agreed with the ACLU that it was intended "to convey a message of state approval of prayer activities in public schools."[29] In *Lee v. Weisman* (1992) the Supreme Court once again sided with the ACLU and ruled that it violated the "Establishment Clause of the First Amendment" for ministers or rabbis to offer prayers at public high school graduation ceremonies.

We may have differing opinions about the need or appropriateness of any prayers, Scripture reading, or any other forms of religious expression in our public schools, but the ACLU and its allies have been successful in having the Supreme Court ban virtually any freedom of religious speech in our public schools. These secularists rationalize that if any religious speech, especially Christian or Jewish, is banned among the young in government-run or -supported schools, they will as adults understand that religion is not acceptable in the public square. A totally secular society will not be burdened by any moral and religious concerns to inhibit self-gratification, these secular elites reason.

Judicial Activism and *Roe v. Wade*

For nearly 170 years after adoption of the U.S. Constitution, abortion was a matter unequivocally considered to be in the domain of the states. The Founders had entrusted the federal government with powers essential to its functioning and reserved all other powers to the states. It was always their intention to keep governmental authority as close as possible to the people. The Founders had the radical and enlightened belief that the people grant powers and responsibilities to the government—not the other way around.

It was not until 1957 that organized efforts to overturn state laws regulating abortion or prohibiting doctors from performing abortions began. The first Supreme Court decision regarding abortion was issued in 1971 in *United States v. Vuitch*. The Court upheld a District of Columbia law permitting abortion to preserve a woman's life or "health." The Court decision made clear that "health" meant "psychological and physical well-being." This would in fact allow abortion for almost any reason.[30]

When the Supreme Court issued its 7-2 *Roe v. Wade* decision on Jan. 22, 1973, 31 states had laws that allowed abortion only to save the mother's life, 13 had laws regulating abortion, and four allowed abortion on demand. The *Roe* decision is so well known that it needs little discussion. It is difficult for any honest scholar or informed layman to dispute the fact that this decision was the product of seven activist judges. They obviously regarded themselves as intellectual elites who knew what was best for the people—and considered themselves superior to the intentions of the Founders! Nine men dressed in black robes, presumed experts in matters of law, sitting around discussing "trimesters" fails the laugh test.

But this was no laughing matter. The number of abortions performed more than doubled in the first 20 years after the ruling.[31] The figure had reached one million a year. By 1999, 45 percent of the abortions were being performed on women who previously had had an abortion.[32] The statistics concerning child abuse cases, a tripling of unwed mothers, major increases in suicide rates, and substance abuse by women who had received an abortion are frightening.[33]

A companion case, *Doe v. Bolton*, which is not nearly as well known, was decided the same day on similar grounds. There is a heart-rending story involved in this case that shows how unscrupulous these liberal secularists can be in their efforts to remove moral and religious restrictions on public behavior. The plaintiff, "Mary Doe," was a 22-year-old mother of three who was nine months pregnant. Sandra Cano, her real name, was a poor girl seeking a divorce from an abusive husband and the return of her children from foster care. Being poverty stricken, she sought help from Atlanta legal aid.

An ACLU lawyer, Margie Pitts Hames, was eager to help. According to Cano, her attorney lied to her because she was looking for a plaintiff to challenge the Georgia abortion law.[34] Sandra Cano further insists that she was always pro life, never intended to have an abortion—and did not have one but was tricked by this dishonest ACLU lawyer into being involved in this terrible Supreme Court case. Many of these details surfaced in an interview that Father Frank Pavone of Priests for Life had with Sandra Cano. In the conclusion to an article telling Sandra Cano's story from the interview, the writer concludes:

> "The high court's justices were not insistent in their questions. Members of that court who sided with Hames trampled the U.S. Constitution under foot. Abortion was legalized by a handful of men who were not in command of all the facts. This is precisely why the framers of the Constitution formed the legislative branch of government. Justices of the Supreme Court are supposed to rule on the constitutionality of the laws of the land, not author them."[35]

These accumulating victories by the radical secularists that were tearing down our moral foundations did not just happen. There was commitment, planning, hard work, and dedication on the part of the ACLU and its secular co-conspirators. The hard-core secular warriors had been trained and were controlling the disciplines.

This is the proper time for us to examine how this all happened. They knew who they were and what they intended to accomplish. We didn't!

Creating a Class of Secular Elites

We are all fully aware that ours is a pluralistic society with many religions and ethnic backgrounds. We have a civil government that cannot and should not be told what to do by the Christian church or by any other religious body. This government was established by the consent of the people and continues to govern by the consent of the people. The people have the right to insist that the present government continue to honor the moral values upon which this nation was founded. The Constitution and the Bill of Rights guarantee us these privileges. We dare not stand by while citizens driven by a secular agenda try to sweep the public arena completely free of religion. When an unelected activist judge, or groups of judges, threatens to invalidate the will of the people as expressed either through laws passed by our elected representatives or by referendum of the people, it is time for us to stand up and say enough is enough! There are hundreds of cases in which this is exactly what is happening.

A sociological class of "secular elites" has evolved over the last 90 or so years and firmly established itself on the secular foundations envisioned by the likes of Roger Baldwin and his anti-religious secular allies. They have established their own *religion of secularism*[36] complete with its own secular "theology." Their numbers are few but their influence is great. They have taken over most of the disciplines that influence public opinion. They do not seek to establish a large unwieldy bureaucracy. Once these secular elites dominate their field of influence, the masses can be easily controlled. Their plan of attack is simple but deceptive: the moral and religious foundations of the American people must be weakened and ultimately destroyed. They know this will not be an easy task and it will take time, since the moral and religious foundation of this country, based on Judeo-Christian principles, was laid strong and deep by the Founders.

(*It should be pointed out in bold letters that this description of secular elitist "leaders" describes only the political and ideological descendents of such hardcore secularists as Roger Baldwin and his soul mates. The well-intentioned liberals in the media, academia, politics, and other disciplines [which would include a majority of the names familiar to most of us] are simply being used unwittingly by the hardcore secularists. Like Baldwin, who urged his followers to always wrap their activities in patriotic packaging, his hardcore successors will take help from all quarters in driving their secularist agenda. If someone with credibility promotes a secularist goal, it has a much better chance of succeeding. It is hard to dispute their deceptive reasoning.*)

Meanwhile, radical secularist organizations such as the ACLU and Americans United for Separation of Church and State (or AU) have trained an "army" of cultural warriors to do the "missionary" work of chipping away at traditional American values one at a time. We have pointed out that the original secular coalitions intent on destroying our foundations were loosely composed of communists, socialists, anarchists, agnostics, atheists, and others desiring a secular, classless society free of all moral constraints. Let us take a little closer look at the hardcore types, how they have been so successful, and the extent of their influence.

I cannot imagine that any fair-minded person could dispute the fact that certain American institutions, including the press, academia, sections of the legal profession, most mainline churches and religious organizations (the National Council of Churches[37] is the best example), and some labor unions (take for example the AFL-CIO, SEIU, AFSCME, and the United Steelworkers) have had a very leftist orientation for at least six or seven decades. Some would argue that these groups form the backbone of the far left movement. Along with the trial lawyers and the feminist organizations (NARAL and Emilie's List, for example), these groups heavily influence—if not dominate—the Democrat Party.

Organizations founded by or heavily financed by George Soros, such as MoveOn (run by the extreme left-wing radical, Michael Moore); Americans Coming Together (ACT), a grass roots organization initially funded by a $10 million contribution by Soros; the Soros-founded Progressive Legislative Action Network; and Soros-funded Center for American Progress are only some examples of this billionaire's determination to control the Democrat Party and, thereby, the country. (This certainly is not unfair "name calling" since most of these individuals and organizations boldly and proudly state their intentions. It is mostly a simple matter of reading their own words. The same is true for some hard-right or libertarian organizations.)

Left-wing organizations like ACORN, which was so high profile in the voter-fraud schemes in the 2008 election, received money from all types of sources, public and private, including Soros-type radicals and even from unsuspecting moderate foundations. David Horowitz and Richard Poe, two self-confessed 1960s radicals who became alarmed at the threats such radical movements posed to the country, have co-authored a book, *The Shadow Party: How George Soros, Hillary Clinton, and Sixties Radicals Seized Control of the Democratic Party*.[38] (Certainly, it is not the case that all, or perhaps even most, of rank and file Democrats are far left or even radically liberal, however.)

As I pointed out earlier in this book, conservative Democrats ran the U.S. House of Representatives when I first came to Washington, D.C., in 1971. They were constantly at war legislatively with the much more liberal Senate. The Democratic Leadership Council (DLC) was founded in 1985 to move the Democrat Party back to the mainstream and make it look more "moderate." The DLC's founders felt the party should have learned its lessons from the failed very liberal campaigns of Hubert Humphrey, George McGovern, Jimmy Carter (after four years as a liberal president), and Walter Mondale. One of the founders and early leaders of the DLC was an Arkansas governor by the name of Bill Clinton. During the campaign of 1992, Bill Clinton enunciated such themes as the importance of free trade, welfare reform, lower taxes, and a balanced budget. It worked in spite of a multitude of charges of sexual indiscretions. (The Democrats once again moved way too far to the left in 2000 with Al Gore and in 2004 when they nominated John Kerry. They still almost won in both elections and probably would have won with a more centrist candidate.)

In October 2007, David Hill, writing in a Capitol Hill publication simply called *The Hill*, quotes some Gallup polling data that would indicate that Democrats and Independents have not overwhelmingly forsaken cultural values in spite of their anger over the economy and the war in Iraq. Fewer than half the Democrats (47 percent) and a third of the Independents (33 percent) describe the U.S. Supreme Court led by Chief Justice John G. Roberts as "too conservative."

Hill reports: "This right-leaning, Republican-influenced court is getting the approval of 41 percent of Democrats and 47 percent of Independents."[39] These Reagan "Democrats" and "Independents" are still out there. They are just disillusioned by Republican scandals (they are very few in number, but one is too many when you advertise yourselves as the "party of moral values") and the economy, which is greatly influenced by a very unpopular war. As we noted in the discussion of the 2008 election, the "financial melt-down" became such a dominant issue that the war, the Islamic-terrorist threat, and all other issues faded into the background. In any event, if the Republicans ever hope to govern again, they must recover these aptly named "value voters."[40]

The Republicans brought the value voters back into their fold in large numbers in the 2010 midterm elections. With the Obama administration supporting same-sex marriage and calling into question our religious liberties by forcing church institutions to provide birth control and mandating that Christian hospitals and personnel perform abortions against their religious convictions, Republicans are hoping for a moral revolution of voters in the 2012 elections. While the economy is likely to dominate the election, value voters could still have a major impact.

Polling data show that members of the press and college faculties are overwhelmingly registered Democrats or indicate a preference for the Democrat Party. Numerous surveys I have seen show anywhere from a 15-1 to 25-1 preference of the press for the Democrat Party over the Republican Party. I believe the numbers of professors on college campuses preferring the Democrat Party would be higher than among the press, especially in the liberal arts departments where the most influence can be exerted. Labor union leaders are virtually all Democrats. The largest teacher's union, the National Education Association, is frequently referred to as the far-left adjunct of the Democrat Party.

Why is this so important and how did it happen? Obviously, this is very important because these exercise the most influence on the information received by the American people, especially the young. They publish the most widely read newspapers. They run the TV news networks. They control the political opinions of the traditional churches. They write or influence the content of the history books and textbooks that students read.

Did all of this happen just by accident? Absolutely not! Efforts to dominate these important disciplines by committed liberals followed a very carefully developed strategy. (The strategy was not always closely coordinated, however, because it involved groups with different ultimate goals. Also, as with many movements, the leaders preyed on the masses of sincere, well-meaning, idealistic individuals who just wanted to make a contribution to society.)

One of the initial key players was the Communist Party USA. Probably by the late 1930s, and certainly by the end of World War II, the CPUSA knew they were never going to win at the ballot box in the United States. After lively debate, they adopted the policy of infiltration and influence. (It is interesting to note that the Communist Party was never able to really infiltrate the American labor unions in a meaningful way, due primarily to the strong opposition of George Meany and other equally patriotic labor leaders.)

The dedicated secularists, typified by the ACLU, adopted a similar plan as part of their overall strategy. (It is difficult to know how closely the ACLU worked together with the CPUSA. Roger Baldwin, the founder of the ACLU, had originally supported Soviet communism until Stalin signed the Nazi-Soviet Non-Aggression Pact with Hitler in 1939. Baldwin then expelled the Communist Party members from the ACLU board. In any event, they all wanted a government with God totally expelled from the public square.)

The socialists, those who believed in class warfare and redistribution of wealth, and other such anti-capitalist groups recognized the importance of controlling the communication disciplines to spread their messages. Professional "do-gooders," many living comfortably on inherited wealth, joined the infiltration tactics to change society. Once they successfully infiltrated the various professions, the media professionals, professors, and other opinion leaders could gradually alter our history by trying to find or invent clay feet for our Founders and other heroes. They search for ways to subtly ridicule our values and God-given rights. If you are going to remake a society, you must destroy the country's heritage and challenge the foundations upon which it is built. (Once again, those who have the most success winning battles in this secular war don't have to be "true believers" or "card-carrying members." They don't even have to know that a "Cultural War" is raging. Their motives may just be a desire to be "politically correct" and "multicultural" rather than a personal devotion to "the religion of secularism.")

What can we do to change these opinion leaders or at least create some balance? Well, it is not going to be easy, and it's not going to happen quickly. Once such a system is installed, it is self perpetuating. Professors encourage those who share their opinions to become professors. Departments of journalism, history, and political science, when controlled by liberal professors, can insist on hiring new professors who share their perspective (although a token conservative might be hired as window dressing). Successful liberal journalists hire like-minded young journalists. The textbooks used in our primary and secondary schools for the most part have been written by liberal scholars who harbor a desire for a totally secular society for a variety of reasons.

It is unimportant in understanding today's cultural struggle for the "soul of the country" if these "secular elitist leaders" themselves are communists (few are), socialists (not many are in the classic sense of the term), or atheists or agnostics (a few more probably fall into this category). Their motives and religious goals (in most cases) are secularist. Political correctness is one of their prime secularist "theological" doctrines. (Make no mistake about the fact that the trivialization of Christianity—other religions in the country are small and played little or no role in the Founding principles of the nation—is a basic doctrine of religious secularism. While they have made inroads, these secular elites do not yet control the people's elected officials.)

Father Richard John Neuhaus in *The Naked Public Square* makes a point that should be carefully noted by those dedicated to preserving our glorious American heritage:

> "Underlying the many crises in American life is a crisis of faith. It is not enough that more people should believe or that those who believe should believe more strongly. Rather, the faith of persons and communities must be more compellingly related to the public arena. 'The naked public square'—which results from the exclusion of popular values from the public forum—will almost certainly result in the death of democracy."[41]

This is a challenge of our times that we dare not ignore! As we examine this warning, we will be reminded of similar concerns of Benjamin Franklin, John Adams, and other prominent Founders, which were referenced in the previous chapter. Neuhaus warns that the naked public square, devoid of "transcendent" values, is a dangerous place. When religion is driven from the public square, a void is created that yearns to be filled. History teaches that this void all too often has been filled by some type of totalitarianism. Neuhaus argues that those with "the naive notion that 'it can't happen here'" fail to understand "the novelty and fragility of liberal democracy as a political system."[42]

Dr. Stephen L. Carter of Yale Law School, in *The Culture of Disbelief* and in *God's Name in Vain*, argues that churches and clergymen should avoid partisan politics lest they sacrifice their "prophetic" responsibility. He defends the proposition that churches and ministers should have such a right under our Constitution. Yet he believes such involvement tends to make them part of the system and thus to sacrifice their independence and objectivity. Carter contends they can and should exercise their right to speak out on important moral issues such as abortion. He writes that "in the case of abortion, which many different religious traditions teach to be wrong, a majority of Americans, while favoring many restrictions on abortion, reject the idea that the government should ban it. *So do I*" (emphasis added).[43]

This is consistent with the involvement of the churches and clergy in the abolition movement and civil rights struggle. On the other hand, Carter strongly opposes the contention of the secularists that an individual should leave his or her religion behind when entering the public square. (Carter contends that a religious faith that doesn't make a difference in a person's life is unworthy of the name.)

In the Introduction to *God's Name in Vain*, which Carter titles "The Politics of Disbelief," he describes why he is writing this book, the views he intends to defend, and the rift between the religious and the non-religious or secularists. If people of faith who believe that God always comes first in their lives are expected to speak only the "often meaningless language of secular liberalism" in the public square, they may well abandon "politics altogether." This is important because

> "America itself is at risk. This nation, whether ready to acknowledge it or not, faces a crisis of legitimacy. The more that the nation chooses to secularize the principal contact points between government and people—not only in public schools, but little things, like names and numbers and symbols, and big things, like taxes and marriage and ultimately, politics itself—the more it will persuade many religious people that a *cultural war* has indeed been declared, and not by the Right (emphasis added)."[44]

Richard Neuhaus argues that the secular keepers of the public square have less concern about religious individuals than about churches and religious organizations:

> "Individual religious belief can be dismissed scornfully as superstition, for it finally poses little threat to the power of the state. No, the chief attack is upon the *institutions* that bear and promulgate belief in a transcendent reality by which the state can be called to judgment. Such institutions threaten the totalitarian proposition that everything is to be within the state, nothing is to be outside the state."[45]

He then explains that when the secular elites are "screaming about why religion should not be in politics," they are simply dodging the debate the religious are demanding: "Why are your views better than ours?" Carter then makes a startling statement for a man of his intellectual stature and academic standing:

> "At a certain point, if we build too high the walls that are intended to keep religion out of politics, we will face religious people who will storm the barricades and declare the government no longer legitimate, because of its insistence on creating a single set of meanings,

a single understanding of life, that everyone must share. ... I suspect that I will be storming too."[46]

Carter hastens to add that while he is a Christian, he is standing up "for the religious freedom of all believers." He states his conviction:

> "We must never become a nation that propounds an official religion or suggests that some religions are more American than others. At the same time, one of the official religions we must never propound is the *religion of secularism*, the suggestion that there is something un-American about trying to live life in a way that puts God first. Quite the contrary: *Preserving the ability of the faithful to put God first is precisely the purpose for which freedom of religion must exist*" (emphasis added).[47]

Carter is certainly right that in today's pluralistic society we must safeguard freedom of religion for all legitimate religions. I add the word "legitimate" in perhaps a slight disagreement with Stephen Carter. I realize this could be a slippery slope and the word "legitimate" would need to be carefully defined, but I would argue that a "religion" that would advocate the *violent* overthrow of the American government or pose the threat of serious endangerment to its adherents, especially helpless children, must face some restrictions. (The Mormons "outlawed" polygamy when it became clear that their two U.S. senators from Utah were not going to be seated unless they took such action.) Again I hear and appreciate Carter's passionate arguments about public school authorities and others in positions of power challenging parents' rights to pass along their moral and religious values to their children. Parents certainly have the right to pass along their cherished beliefs to their children, but they do not have a right to abuse their children. I would also quote James Hutson, the preeminent[48] authority on religion in early America, about the use of the word "religion" in the Founding days: "In the state documents of the Founding Era religion invariably meant Christianity."[49] I add this fact simply because I think it will assist us in better understanding the culture of the country and our Founding documents as well as the men who wrote, debated, revised, and adopted them during our Founding Period.

Actually, a careful analysis of the religious demographics of America today bears some striking resemblances to the Founding Era. (This is probably true in spite of the fact that we are burdened today with a few hundred thousand of the likes of Thomas Paine and Ethan Allen.) In the first chapter of *The Culture of Disbelief*, published in 1993, Stephen Carter makes the observation:

> "Surveys indicate that Americans are far more likely to believe in God and to attend worship services regularly than any other people in the Western World.... Even though some popular histories wrongly assert the contrary, the best evidence is that this deep religiosity has

always been a facet of the American character and that it has grown consistently through the nation's history."[50]

He then offers these statistics from a 1992 Gallup poll: 96 percent of the American people say they believe in God; 82 percent identify themselves as Christian; 56 percent say they are Protestant; 25 percent claim Roman Catholic as their religion; and 2 percent are Jewish. No other religion received as much as 1 percent.[51]

On Feb. 26, 2008, *The Washington Post* published a "Pew Forum on Religion and Public Life Religious Landscape Survey" conducted May 8 thru Aug. 13, 2007. This was the largest and most in-depth ever done. Surveyed were 35,556 randomly selected adults nationwide, and the poll had a plus or minus sampling error of an amazingly low 0.6 percent. In other words, this is about as close to accurate as any poll can be. It was so detailed, that it needs some explanation.

According to the poll, 78.4 percent identified themselves as Christian in the traditional sense; 1.7 percent said they were Mormons; another 0.7 percent Jehovah's Witnesses; 0.6 percent Orthodox; and 0.3 other Christian. If you add these together (most polls make no such distinctions), you get 81.7 percent Christian. But there is more, since 16.1 percent simply said they were "unaffiliated," of which 12.1 percent identified themselves as "nothing in particular." Only 2.4 percent of the "unaffiliated" said they were "agnostic," and 1.5 percent claimed "atheist." If one makes an educated assumption that of the 12.1 percent that chose "nothing in particular" (a significant number of whom said "religion was very important to them"), a reasonable number were raised Christian, you would come up with a slightly higher figure than the 85 percent Christian usually found in other polls. Most polls list only Protestant, Catholic, Jewish, Muslim, etc. The poll was rounded out with 1.7 percent Jewish, 0.7 percent Buddhist, 0.6 percent Muslim, 0.4 percent Hindu, and the rest a scattering of Unitarian, New Age, Native American, and such.

A few of Carter's observations are of special value:

> "A nation that truly values religious freedom—a nation that truly values the constitutional separation of church and state—must welcome the religious voice into its political counsels. To do otherwise is one sure way to accomplish the task of alienating the religious from democracy, for it places official imprimatur on the cultural message that religion is an inferior human activity."[52]

In addition he astutely points out:

> "Indeed, I shall argue that, in the absence of the religious voice. American politics itself becomes unimaginable.... *Politics needs morality, which means that politics needs religion*"[53] (emphasis added).

Again, Richard Neuhaus argues that the keepers of the public square have less concern about religious individuals than about churches and religious organizations.[54]

Carter and Neuhaus certainly would seem to agree that an emerging secular state seeks to eliminate religious influence from the public square. Neuhaus' contention that the public square is hostile to religion is certainly true when you are speaking of liberal activist judges and politically correct elitists in the press. Carter's argument that the public square tends to trivialize religion is equally accurate in much of academia and some realms of political activities. All of these areas certainly overlap at times.

I would suggest that in the area of elective politics, efforts to trivialize religion are rare and hostility to religion is even rarer. My impression over the 40-plus years that I have spent in the Nation's Capital has been that the religious beliefs of our elected officials are slightly more devout than those of the population as a whole. This should not be surprising since voters tend to scrutinize a candidate's religion and frequently choose the one they perceive as most religious. I base my conclusion on having known literally thousands of U.S. congressmen and senators and a half dozen presidents and vice presidents during these years, most of them fairly well.

In this arena, religious hostility and trivialization are not the problem. Since most legislative and public-policy decisions involve compromise, we are faced with a new problem. The secularist elites, because most of them are intellectuals in their own disciplines, understand the process. Through elitist commentary in the media and "professional" suggestions to key staffers and members, they often affect the policy outcome. It would seem logical that properly informed and motivated church leaders could employ their "*prophetic*" responsibility (in Carter's words) or call the "*state to judgment*" (in Neuhaus' words) in such cases. This is what I would recognize as responsible and enlightened behavior by church leaders in a democracy established by the people—a religious people, or more accurately, a Christian people. We are a responsible Christian people who feel a responsibility to share the Gospel of Jesus Christ with all who will listen. But, at the same time, we will defend with all our might the rights of those who adhere to other religions as well.

Stephen Carter is truly a remarkable and accomplished man—a black man who earned his undergraduate degree at Stanford University and his J.D. at Yale Law School. One of his early books, *Reflections of an Affirmative Action Baby*, was written after he joined the Yale Law faculty in 1982. He confesses:

> "How strange to be a black Christian, increasingly evangelical, teaching at a traditionally white and aggressively secular academic institution. One of Yale's virtues is that it has a place for somebody like me—not me in particular, but someone like me. But not a lot of spaces."[55]

Carter is an interestingly different intellectual who ultimately comes down on the liberal side of most social issues but passionately defends the right of religious people and religious institutions to enter the public arena and defend their points of view *on religious grounds*. He fears the results of the "religion of secularism" and lays out the problems we face from the secularists in these words:

> "On America's elite campuses today, it is perfectly acceptable for professors to use their classrooms to attack religion, to mock it, to trivialize it, and to refer to those to whom faith truly matters as dupes, and dangerous fanatics on top of it. I have heard some of the wisest scholars in the country deride religious beliefs and religious believers in terms so full of stereotype and of—let us say the word—bigotry that we would be appalled were they to say similar things about just any other group.... By way of useful contrast, imagine the reaction were a professor at an Ivy League school, say, to use the classroom as a pulpit from which to evangelize urging students to march out and fight the good fight because God demands.... Do not misunderstand the point. I am not calling for professors to evangelize. But I see no reason why trying to further a religion in the classroom is worse than trying to destroy it."[56]

In a pluralistic and just society we certainly want to protect the rights of the minority. Our Founders expressed their strong intention to protect minority rights when they established the U.S. Senate. The creation of the U.S. Senate was intended to preserve states' rights by giving the smaller states an equal vote with the larger states. Two U.S. senators from each of the states, regardless of size, emphasized that this "Republic" was a union of sovereign states who willingly gave up certain designated powers to the federal government for the mutual good of the nation. The U.S. House of Representatives was to be totally democratic, based on the pure democracy theory of one man-one vote. The U.S. Senate was also intended to guard against the potential tyranny of the majority, which a pure democracy could produce.

In this representative democracy, minority rights were to be protected. How radical have elements of our society become, however, when activist judges and extreme left-wing organizations like the ACLU believe that they can trample the rights of the majority and reverse the wishes of the majority on a regular basis? Absolutely no Founder of this nation intended to establish a government that would suppress the God-given rights of the majority of its people. It is pure folly to suggest that the Constitution and the Bill of Rights were drafted to thwart the will of the people. You would have had a second revolution, before the ink was even dry on our founding documents, if such an unreasonable course of action would have ever been slightly suspected. Our Constitution certainly intended to protect minority rights, but not at the expense of majority rights.

This is a good place to discuss what our constitutional guarantee of freedom of religion means for Christian citizens—be they clergy or lay—or religious institutions as we claim our rightful place in the public square. Are we to be expected to leave our religious beliefs and moral values at home for private use only? This is certainly not what our Founding Fathers had in mind, as we have seen.

Throughout most of my adult life, beginning with my studies for a Ph.D. in philosophy (which ended without a dissertation) and during my varied political career, I have been immersed in political theory as well as politics. During this period, I have always been motivated by the question, "by what authority" do these secularists or "liberal elitists" (which is a term I have used during most of these years) think they have the unquestioned right to settle all value questions? These liberal secular elitists are in reality a small minority. They certainly have a right to be heard, but why does their word seem to carry so much weight and authority? It reminds me that Neuhaus' comment, "*of course* America is a secular society," has only recently become a tenet of conventional wisdom. He explains how fallacious that statement is: the people *are* the society, and the American people are still overwhelmingly religious. The religious affiliations gleaned from the polling data noted earlier speak volumes about the religious character of this society and how overwhelmingly Christian it still is today.

Stephen Carter compellingly raises the question of authority in two books mentioned earlier, *The Culture of Disbelief* and *God's Name in Vain*. He uses an intellectual context to discuss major cultural issues in dispute. I was pleasantly surprised to see a recognized scholar like Carter (who ends up on the liberal Democrat side of many political issues) question the usurping of the right to decide major issues by the self-appointed secular elite. A few more examples from these books, which I believe are must reads, will give the flavor of Carter's scholarly arguments that the religious certainly have equal rights with the secularists.

The question of creationism and evolution (made famous by the "Scopes Monkey Trial" in 1925) has a long history of controversy. To place this discussion in context, let us evaluate the attitudes of the people who make up America's society. Stephen Carter in *God's Name In Vain* cites a 1997 Gallup survey, which said that "44 percent of American adults believe in the literal truth of the Genesis creation story, 39 percent believe that evolution was guided by God, and 10 percent believe that God played no role."[57] A 2004 ABC News poll reported that 61 percent of adult Americans believe the account that God created the world in six days to be "literally true."[58] A recent Gallup survey revealed that 48 percent of Americans believe that God created human beings in their "present form at one time in the last 10,000 years or so." The same study found that 32 percent of the people believe that humans developed over millions of years with God guiding the process, and 15 percent believe that God played no role in the creation of humans.[59]

All of these surveys reveal that a significant plurality, if not majority, of American people believe the biblical doctrine of creation. If you choose 15 percent or 10 percent (I have seen a number of polls that find this number in single digits) who believe that God played no role in creating human life, you are talking about a small minority. The question is, should the vast majority of "we the people" who believe that God created human life have any say in what is taught in public schools, or is that decision in the sole domain of the secular authorities or secular scientists? Do they have some divine (they would not like that word) right?[60]

Carter makes it clear that he opposes teaching "scientific creation" because it is "bad science." He believes the courts were wrong, though, to disallow it on grounds that those advocating such teaching had a "religious motivation." He references the Louisiana "equal time" statute, struck down by the Supreme Court in 1987, which required that the teaching of "scientific creation" be given equal time in high schools with the teaching of evolution. Carter reminds his readers that 82 percent of American adults believe "God created human beings," and he calls into question the courts' reasoning that it was unconstitutional because the Louisiana legislature was motivated by religious beliefs.[61]

Discussing this same subject in *God's Name in Vain*, Carter discusses epistemology—the proper "method of discovering truth"—since the supporters of both creation and evolution want the public schools to teach "the truth, the whole truth, and nothing but the truth." He then makes the salient point that this debate is not so much about "what should or should not be included in the public school curriculum but *who should get to decide, and when, and how.*"[62] This is the important question, and it applies to sex education, homosexuality, pornography, and other broad moral and value questions as well.

Carter discusses many issues that should be of considerable interest to Christian readers, including prayer in public schools and denial of the right of a Colorado public-school teacher to have his Bible on his desk (which he never mentioned but occasionally read when the class was taking exams), even though the school openly displayed books on Indian religion and the occult in its library.

The final area that I have chosen to discuss is the right of churches and clergymen to defend their religious view on life. This quote from *God's Name in Vain* is a good place to begin:

> "Now to be sure, nobody threatened to lift the tax exemption of bishops back when they were trying to sway politicians away from support for school segregation or to find a way to rid the world of nuclear weapons. Indeed, before we go any further, we should take the time to note the embarrassing—or perhaps the correct word is outrageous—political bias in the enforcement of the provisions that bar political involvement by 501 (c) (3) organizations. It is a matter of simple fact that the rules are almost always invoked against churches

and other groups that fall toward the right end of our rather narrow political spectrum; the left is all but immune. One of the principal players in this little drama is the self-proclaimed watchdog known as Americans United for Separation of Church and State.... Americans United does some important work in the cause of religious liberty.... But the group has a terrible blind spot when it looks at regulation of churches involved in politics, for it is unable to see the threat to religious freedom. Americans United arguably makes things worse, for, while styling itself as protecting churches from their worst selves, the organization is probably the principal filer of complaints with the Treasury Department about religious groups overstepping the bounds of the tax code."

Then he continues:

> "As we shall see, this campaign suggests that Americans United has the wrong name, for the effort to use law to rein in the speech of clergy runs contrary to the origin and core meaning of the separation of church and state."[63]

A strong defender of the role of the churches and the clergy in such moral struggles as the abolition of slavery and the civil rights movement, Carter strongly defends the churches' rights and responsibilities in today's debate on moral issues. His insistence that the churches should not get involved in partisan politics— although he strongly defends their Constitutional right to do so—is probably sound advice up to a point. None of us wants to hear partisan politics from the pulpit. Yet our people need to be exhorted to vote for those committed to moral issues on which there can be no compromise. Presidents appoint federal judges, including Supreme Court justices; congressmen and senators vote to enact laws on moral issues. We must try to help elect those who not only profess strong moral and religious values but who also are willing to stand up and be counted on such issues.

When I meet with a candidate for Congress and ask him where he stands on abortion, and he or she says they are personally pro life[64] but don't believe they have the right to force their religious convictions on other people, my response is intended to be something like this (I usually get most of my message out): "That is surprising and a little disconcerting! Does that apply to all of your religious beliefs? How about laws regarding rape, incest, polygamy, pornography, or child abuse, just to name a few? Most of our laws regulating behavior are based solidly on religious principles. Where else do you turn? Plato, Aristotle, John Locke, and the overwhelming majority of our several hundred Founding Fathers were all religious men. Without religious authority, morals are hard to define and almost impossible to justify." (Even the belief in "natural law" is based on the presupposition that somehow God "wrote" such law in man's heart.)

Let's look now at a few of the battles that have already been lost in the Cultural War, as well as others that are raging. I will also note the good news in victories that have been won by those fighting to preserve our moral and traditional values. And, I will advocate for the need for Lutherans to get involved.

As I have said before, if we lose the Cultural War, the future looks bleak indeed for our country and our descendents.

A Few Battles Won and Lost—and the High Stakes

The ACLU and the Los Angeles County Seal[65]

In 2004, the ACLU threatened to sue Los Angeles County if the county did not change its official seal, because the seal included a small Latin cross. The county seal, adopted in 1957, included the tiny cross to represent the historical fact that this area was settled by Catholic missionaries. This seal was unconstitutional, according to the ACLU, because it represented the beliefs of one segment of the county's diverse population. (The main figure on the seal was Pomona, the Roman goddess of fruit and trees, and Pearlette, a prize cow. Apparently, the pagan goddess was not objectionable to the ACLU because it was not mentioned in the letter that threatened the lawsuit.)

The ACLU said this historic symbol, which had gone unchallenged for nearly 50 years, was objectionable and would make non-Christians feel "unwelcome." So, the ACLU threatened to take the L.A. County supervisors to court if the cross were not removed in a reasonable amount of time. Kenneth Kleinberg, the lawyer who represented the family of the artist who designed the seal—a self-avowed atheist and ACLU member—became one of the strongest critics of his own organization for tampering with art and called it pure folly on the part of the ACLU.

Dennis Prager, a well-known Jewish talk-show host, in an article titled "Taliban Come to Los Angeles," found the whole exercise absurd. He pointed out that he had talked to "Los Angeles County rabbis of every denomination" and that not one thought this historic cross should be removed or felt "unwelcome" because of it. His conclusion was that the ACLU was trying to take away all Judeo-Christian values and replace them with "leftist ones." He explains:

> "The cross represents the Christian history of Los Angeles County. It no more advocates Christianity than the Goddess Pomona advocates Roman paganism or the cow represents Hinduism. It is therefore a lie to argue Los Angeles County is pushing Christianity on its citizens."[66]

He goes on to make a very astute observation:

> "What we have here is an American version of the Taliban. The ACLU and the supervisors are leftist versions of the Taliban—

attempting to erase the Christian history of America just as the Muslim Taliban tried to erase the Buddhist history of Afghanistan when they blew up ancient Buddhist sculptures in their country."[67]

Los Angeles County Supervisor Mike Antonovich, whom I have met and believe to be a Missouri Synod Lutheran, tried to fight this attack on the seal's depiction of county history, estimating that it would cost hundreds of thousands of dollars, if not millions, to redesign and replace the official seal. Unfortunately, in spite of thousands of emails and phone calls, almost all urging them to fight to preserve the seal, the supervisors caved to the ACLU in a 3-2 vote. The supervisors had even been offered free legal support from many organizations, including the Alliance Defense Fund.

The ACLU had previously been successful in forcing the City of Redlands to remove a cross from their seal. This obviously emboldened them to take on Los Angeles County. What will these high-profile successes embolden them to do next? How long before Corpus Christi, Texas, or the Mount of the Holy Cross in the Colorado Rockies is bullied into changing their names or face some activist judge who will be glad to do it for them?

The ACLU Receives Taxpayer Dollars for Secular War

The ACLU's abuse of a little-known law passed by the Congress in 1976 has added greed to their already fanatical desire to rid America of all symbols of its religious past. This federal law, called the Civil Rights Attorney's Fee Award Act, was signed by President Ford in 1976. Its noble purpose was to help plaintiffs in civil rights cases. It taxes one's reason (not to mention pocketbooks) to figure out how it became a civil right to *not* see a cross or a monument bearing the Ten Commandments.

In the highly publicized court case in which Alabama Chief Justice Roy Moore was ordered to remove the Ten Commandments monument from the Supreme Judicial Building in Montgomery, the judge awarded $540,000 in attorneys' fees and expenses that had to be picked up by the taxpayers of Alabama. The judge who ruled against Moore and awarded the fees spoke at an ACLU conference on international law just days after issuing his opinion.[68] This system is out of control with activist judges thumbing their noses at the will of the people.

The ACLU'S Persistent Attacks on Traditional Marriage

In *Romer v. Evans* (1996), the Supreme Court ruled unconstitutional a ballot initiative approved overwhelmingly in 1993 by the voters of Colorado to deny those who practice homosexuality any special rights and privileges beyond those of ordinary citizens. For the first time, the Court used the Equal Protection Clause of the Fourteenth Amendment to bypass the will of the people and grant special status to homosexuals as a class of citizens.[69] In a 2003 ruling, *Lawrence v. Texas*, the Supreme Court struck down a Texas law banning same-sex sodomy, basing its decision partly on *Romer,* a right to privacy, and, of all things, international law to grant the right to homosexual sodomy.[70]

Although the Alliance Defense Fund (ADF)[71] and its allies had been successful in defending state laws defining traditional marriage (with some notable exceptions), it did not prevail when on May 15, 2008, the California Supreme Court in a 4-3 decision struck down a ballot initiative known as Proposition 22. Prop 22, which had been passed overwhelmingly in 2000 by California voters (61.4 percent voted for it), specifically defined a marriage to be valid only when it is between a man and a woman.

This is another example of activist judges invalidating the wishes of some 3.7 million California voters. This decision is even more threatening than the Massachusetts law that allows same-sex marriages because it has no residency requirement. In 2008, a new ballot initiative, known as Proposition 8, amending the California Constitution to define marriage as valid only between a man and a woman, passed with more than 52 percent of the vote. This California ballot initiative in defense of traditional marriage, as well as similar initiatives in Florida and Arizona, was successful due to the dedicated efforts of Christians and Christian leaders in all three states. Dr. Jerry Kieschnick, then president of The Lutheran Church—Missouri Synod, played a major role personally and motivated the church body's district presidents to get their pastors and laymen involved in this urgent effort.

Proposition 8, named "The California Traditional Marriage Initiative," has been in the courts since it was passed into law by the California voters in 2008. Homosexual activists immediately challenged this amendment to the California constitution on the grounds that it was unconstitutional. The court challenge worked its way through the very liberal U.S. Ninth Circuit Court of Appeals, the also-liberal California Supreme Court, and other courts until it was appealed to the U.S. Supreme Court early in 2012. The Supreme Court probably will not take final action on the appeal until after the 2012 election.

Homosexual activists have a proven record of promoting their agenda and will zealously continue their efforts. The Connecticut Supreme Court, in another split decision, also overturned the will of the people by ruling in 2008 that prohibiting homosexual marriage is a violation of the state constitution. (The subject of these ballot initiatives and the more recent attacks on religious liberty, in which current LCMS President Dr. Matthew Harrison has become heavily involved, will be discussed in some detail in the final chapter of this book [Chapter 8] dealing with the need for involvement of Christians in general and Lutherans in particular in theses struggles facing our nation.)

A look at how the carefully planned homosexual agenda has been advanced sheds light on how we now should confront such vicious attacks on traditional marriage. Homosexual activists understood that nothing would happen without considerable planning and effort by those who wanted society to view certain behavior simply as an acceptable alternative lifestyle.

David Kupelian's book *The Marketing of Evil* was published in 2005. His first chapter is titled "Marketing Blitz: Selling 'Gay Rights' in America."[72] Kupelian begins by pointing out that when the AIDS epidemic began to unfold in the early 1980s, homosexual behavior was being viewed with as much disdain as at any time in American history. Many readers may remember that AIDS originally was named GRID (gay-related immunodeficiency disease). Efforts by homosexual activists resulted in pressuring the medical community to change the name to AIDS (acquired immune deficiency syndrome). This was accomplished by like-minded activists who had successfully persuaded the American Psychiatric Association to remove homosexuality from the official list of mental disorders back in 1973.[73]

As the death rate from AIDS soared and big names such as Rock Hudson died from the disease, pressure mounted throughout the 1980s. When an 18-year-old Indiana boy with hemophilia, Ryan White, and tennis star Arthur Ashe contracted this horrible disease from HIV-infected blood transfusions and subsequently succumbed to AIDS, the situation reached the panic stage.[74] Homosexuals were being looked upon as modern-day lepers. Radical groups such as ACT-UP were engaged in a frenzy of activities, including demonstrations and near riots, trying to defend their sexual behavior.

Then a game-changing event took place. A group of the more rational activists decided to convene a nationwide conference to get organized to confront the threat of impending disaster facing their lifestyle. In February 1988, some 175 major activists representing the majority of "gay" organizations assembled in Warrenton, Va., to map out a plan of action. Two members of the group, Marshall Kirk and Hunter Madsen, took the ideas from the convention and turned them into a book, carefully laying out a public-relations strategy and total game plan to advance their cause. Their book was *After the Ball: How America Will Conquer Its Fear and Hatred of Gays in the '90s*. It lays out a plan of action that the gay community has followed almost to the letter with unprecedented success. A statement in the book tells the story of their success very well:

> "As cynical as it may seem, AIDS gives us a chance, however brief, to establish ourselves as a victimized minority legitimately deserving of America's special protection and care. At the same time, it generates mass hysteria of precisely the sort that has brought about public stoning and leper colonies since the Dark Ages and before.... How can we maximize the sympathy and minimize the fear? How, given the horrid hand that AIDS has dealt us, can we best play it?"[75]

They have played their hand so well that society seems to be racing to grant them special privileges and treat them with special care, as if they are an abused minority of America's finest. Certainly no American should desire to abuse anyone because of his or her beliefs or peaceful behavior. Homosexuals should have the same privileges and protections of the law as any other American. However, no special rights should be afforded them because of behavior that flies in the face of traditional American values. (No caring Americans, especially devout Christians, would oppose efforts by our compassionate nation to find a cure and ways to prevent the spread of this dread disease. Justifiably, a multitude of governmental and private programs have undertaken to fight AIDS, which has become a worldwide epidemic. In honesty many, if not most, of our serious illnesses develop as results of bad health habits.)

Homosexual activists rarely miss an opportunity to promote their cause in any forum. In June 2007, 10 homosexual organizations ran a series of ads in Capitol Hill newspapers inviting people to a reception in the Capitol to celebrate the 40th anniversary of the Supreme Court decision to strike down the anti-miscegenation laws. On June 12, 1967, in *Loving v. Virginia,* the Supreme Court declared unconstitutional the laws that existed in 16 states banning interracial marriages. The organizations ran pictures of prominent American political figures such as Republican Senate Leader Sen. Mitch McConnell, former Senator and Secretary of Defense Bill Cohen, and former Gov. Jeb Bush, all of whom are married to ladies of different racial backgrounds. They pointed out that if such discriminatory laws had still been in place, these blissful marriages could not have taken place.

This all sounded like an occasion to celebrate a significant milestone in ridding our country of a relic of its racial past. Then came the underlying sinister purpose: they were promoting gay, lesbian, and transsexual marriage. In an interview, one of the leaders of this effort called these dedicated public servants "bigots and hypocrites" for not defending their cause. Their intent is to destroy traditional marriage and family values that have been an integral part of the fabric of this country since its founding.

There is no neutral ground between right and wrong. If Christians don't stand up and say so, who will? The battle to preserve traditional values is not going to be easy with activist judges sitting on state supreme courts who are willing to overrule the will of the people. Of the 50 states, 45 have some type of law on the books that defines marriage as a union between a man and a woman. But some of these laws will likely be under attack from the courts in the not too distant future.

The ACLU Defends Online Child Pornography

The ACLU does not discriminate much about which traditional values they go after. As early as 1982, in *New York v. Feber,* they petitioned the Court to decree that child pornography is protected by the Constitution.[76] Thankfully, the Court denied their arguments and rejected their plea that child pornography is protected by the Constitution. But they never quit.

In 2004, in *Ashcroft v. ACLU,* the Supreme Court denied the implementation of the "Child Online Protection Act." This act was designed by

Congress, including several of my close friends in the U.S. House and the Senate, to protect minors from obscene material on the Internet. Implementation of this much-needed act was denied by the district court and upheld by the Third Circuit Court of Appeals. The first time the Supreme Court considered the Child Online Protection Act, it remanded (returned) it to the Third Circuit for further study. The Third Circuit affirmed its original decision to deny implementation. The act went back to the Supreme Court, which then ruled in a 5-4 decision that implementation of this law was unconstitutional. The ACLU could claim another victory in the Cultural War by making sure that children were *not protected* from pornography online.

A very recent decision that relates directly to the Internet will be discussed in the section on "good news." The Roberts Court upheld a federal law that punishes those who peddle or seek child pornography. It actually was declared constitutional with only two dissenting votes. I suspect you guessed it: one of the two dissenting votes was Justice Ruth Bader Ginsburg who previously worked for the ACLU. The ACLU is consistent!

The ACLU Takes On the Boy Scouts

In describing the ACLU's long (at least 25 years), expensive litigious fight with the Boy Scouts of America, I must make a disclaimer. As the Washington lobbyist for the BSA for almost 30 years—my firm, Hecht, Spencer and Associates, and I are the only federal lobbyists they have ever hired—I am in no way authorized to speak for them except when their board specifically authorizes me to lobby the Congress or administration on their behalf on a specific issue. I am also an active volunteer for the National Capital Area Boy Scout Council and received their "Silver Beaver" award a few years ago. With all that in mind, let me explain what has happened over the last 30 years.

The BSA is a 100-year-old, congressionally chartered, and, I might add, *private* organization with its own standards for membership and leadership. The list of requirements for membership is not long, but it has not changed over the years.[77] We believe that a scout should be "morally straight," and we try to mold scouts into young men of character and leadership who will become upright and productive citizens as adults. We seek out scoutmasters and other adult scout leaders who are "role models" for these young boys on their paths to adulthood. In our value structure, we do not believe that homosexuals and atheists are proper role models.

Over these years of court battles with the ACLU and the homosexual organizations, we have been forced to spend millions of dollars on legal fees to defend our rights as a private organization to determine our own membership requirements. This is exactly what the ACLU founder, Roger Baldwin, insisted that they had a right to do when he expelled American communists from ACLU membership in the late 1930s.

After all the money the Scouts were forced to spend, money they believed could have been much better spent on underprivileged kids in the inner cities, for example, the BSA in 2000 won a 5-4 U.S. Supreme Court decision in *Boy Scouts of America v. Dale*. The decision stated that the First Amendment right of expressive association permitted the Boy Scouts to exclude a homosexual scoutmaster. The BSA won a crucial victory for the rights guaranteed in the Constitution to private organizations to determine the standards of their membership. (The right to determine membership standards is certainly a cherished right also for all churches.)

The fight is not over by a long shot. Boy Scout troops and organizations are still confronted with denial of the use of government forums in states and communities around the country. There was an extended fight in Philadelphia, where certain city officials tried to prevent the Boy Scouts access to municipal property based on the perceived discrimination against homosexuals. These city officials tried to force the Scouts to pay the prevailing market rate of rent. Had these anti-Scout forces prevailed, the inner-city kids in Philadelphia would have paid the price for the city's political correctness. Fortunately for these kids—and the preservation of constitutional protections—a federal judge in Philadelphia ended the controversy by deciding the case in favor of the Cradle of Liberty Boy Scout Council. The City of Philadelphia was ordered to reimburse the Council for its $877,000 in legal fees. The Council was also allowed to maintain their offices in the building rent free because they had paid for construction of the building in 1929.

The BSA will probably face its biggest threat if a challenge to the "duty to God" question ever makes its way through the court system and is finally debated and decided by the Supreme Court. There are no such cases pending at the present time, and it is unlikely one will occur soon unless the Supreme Court is reconfigured with a number of new "politically correct" secularist justices.

But the Boy Scouts are always vigilant! A number of bizarre cases in state courts have been thrown out. In 2007, the U.S. Court of Appeals rejected a challenge to Department of Defense spending on national Scout jamborees at the Army's Fort A.P. Hill (*Winkler v. Gates*). The BSA was not directly involved in this case, but the ACLU argued that the Boy Scouts were a "religious organization" because of the inclusion of "duty to God" in the Scout Oath,[78] which reads: "On my honor I will do my best to do my duty to God and my country and to obey the Scout Law; to help other people at all times; to keep myself physically strong, mentally awake, and morally straight."[79]

An explanation of the 12th Scout law reads, "A Scout is reverent, he is reverent toward God. He is faithful in his religious duties and respects the convictions of others in matters of custom and religion."[80] That is the only religious statement in the Boy Scout manuals, pure and simple.

The Scout must recognize the existence of God; his religious beliefs, worship life, and religious preference are left totally to the Scout and his parents. Many, probably most, Scout troops are sponsored by churches. Based on the Boy Scouts of America's belief that a boy must be "morally straight," he cannot be an open atheist (scoutmasters don't quiz potential scouts about their religious beliefs). This has caused the ACLU and atheist organizations to challenge the BSA's right to exclude membership on these grounds.

A few examples of what Hecht, Spencer and Associates has done for the Boy Scouts in the legislative area further illustrates how the *values police* make it difficult for any organization with traditional values to function, even if they can't make them cease to exist.

For many years, there were questions about the Boy Scouts' use of public-school facilities after school hours (like many other organizations do) because of charges of discrimination. The use of such facilities is very important, particularly in rural and urban areas. The Scouts were doing pretty well in the courts. Their policy has always been to shy away from public fights over controversial issues. Sen. Jessie Helms of North Carolina, shortly before he retired in 2002, let it be known that he was going to offer an amendment to an upcoming education bill to require that the Boy Scouts be provided the same access to school facilities as any other organization. I was sent over to discourage him from offering the amendment, arguing that we were doing well in negotiations with school districts and in the lower courts, and we preferred not to have the publicity.

The elderly senator, a long-time close friend of mine, listened to my arguments and answered me something like this: "Bill, I think the Boy Scouts of America is the finest youth organization in this country and probably does more good for our young people than all the rest of them put together. I'm sick and tired of this wonderful organization having to squander their precious time and resources to use facilities that should be gladly and thankfully made available to them. I feel obligated to offer this amendment, and for maybe the first time, I'm going to have to deny your request on behalf of your client."

Once it was clear that he was going to offer the legislation, we could not let it fail. That would be a public relations nightmare.

I have rarely lobbied so hard. I talked to every senator I could reach. (I virtually camped out in a few places waiting for a senator with whom I was having difficulty getting a timely appointment.) We won by *one vote*. The "Boy Scouts of America Equal Access Act" requires public schools to provide Boy Scouts equal access to buildings and services on pain of losing federal funding. Once this amendment became law, our problem with access to school facilities went away.

Our enemies then turned to federal parks and other land preserves controlled by the Interior Department, as well as HUD-owned buildings and Defense Department facilities. Based on the success of the Helms amendment, we passed a bill in 2005, the "Support Our Scouts Act of 2005," with overwhelming bi-partisan support. This law guarantees the Scouts the same access as any other group to public lands for outdoor activities and in public buildings in urban areas owned or operated by the federal government. The ACLU couldn't seek to deny the Scouts access without also denying the same access to all of its left-wing groups.

One of the early successes I was able to help accomplish for the Boy Scouts of America also had a tremendous impact on churches. (Few of them knew about it. I probably did tell the president of the Missouri Synod about it.)

The Clinton Administration had submitted a bill to address the issue of child sexual abuse inspired by Oprah Winfrey, who herself was sexually abused as a child. The bill had very noble goals that everybody supported, but it also was a very complicated bill with a number of pitfalls.

Nobody has done more to try to protect children from pedophiles than the Boy Scouts of America. We spent untold hours trying to work with the congressional committee of jurisdiction to draft child-protection legislation that would meet constitutional muster without empowering the rights of the very people who would abuse children.

It became obvious as the 1994 session of Congress approached adjournment that the comprehensive bill was going nowhere. The Administration had some members of the House Judiciary Committee pull out a narrower provision, which was called the "Oprah Winfrey provision," to be voted on literally on the last day of the session. The provision required that all adult volunteers (professional workers were no problem) who dealt with children to have a background check. This meant that Sunday-school teachers, as well as den mothers and scoutmasters, would have to go to the local police station to be fingerprinted and pay for a background check. The estimated cost to the Boy Scouts alone would have been $30 million for the first year and $10 million to $15 million for each succeeding year. How many den mothers and Sunday-school teachers are going to be willing to go to the police station and be fingerprinted? It would have been of little benefit anyway, because the state, local, and national files weren't even integrated with any central national file at the time, and only those who had committed a sexual crime in the local area would have been identified. As in so many well-intentioned legislative cases, the cure would have been worse than the disease. It would be much worse in this case.

The bill was going to pass. I had been unable to get any of the top Democrats, who controlled the Congress at the time, to understand the seriousness of my reservations. President Clinton wanted the bill passed. It would be good publicity since it was called the "Oprah Winfrey Bill." On a Saturday morning in late October 1994, the last day of the session, I arranged to meet with a young Republican congressman by the name of John Boehner, who was serving only his second term in Congress at the time. (He is now the speaker of the House.) I met him at a bar just a few blocks from the Capitol for breakfast. I was desperate.

"If this bill becomes law in its present form and is implemented, it could destroy the Boy Scouts as we now know them," I explained. Boehner scribbled on a cocktail napkin a phrase we discussed: "shall not deter voluntarism." Boehner walked over to the floor of the House of Representatives and gave that napkin to a Republican member of the Judiciary Committee (neither one of us have been able to remember who it was as the years have gone by). This gentleman inserted it in the bill by "unanimous consent." The bill passed, including the now famous four word phrase.

I called my anxious client back at the BSA headquarters in Dallas to tell him that the "Winfrey bill" had passed but that I had been able to get a phrase inserted that might prolong the bill's implementation, even if it didn't totally solve the problem. His answer was short: "That ain't worth a darn!" (He actually used a stronger expletive.) Well, 17 years later, the Boy Scouts, and all other organizations who serve our nation's youth, including churches, have lived off of that phrase.

Let me quickly give you the rest of the story, as Paul Harvey would say. As good fortune would have it, the person in the Justice Department in charge of the agency with the responsibility for implementing laws and regulations governing youth organizations was Sheila Anthony. Sheila was the wife of former Democrat Congressman Beryl Anthony of Arkansas, a golfing buddy and fraternity brother. I had gotten to know Sheila socially through my relationship with Beryl and had developed a good enough relationship with her that she was very willing to meet and hear our point of view. She immediately recognized the flaws in this hastily passed law and the burden it would place on youth organizations. She wisely refused to implement that provision of the law and for more than a dozen years, the Boy Scouts and other youth organizations have been able to function without such a burden.

The ACLU Declares War on Christmas

The final area I would like to touch on before turning to some good news in the Cultural War is the attack on religious holidays and religious symbols connected to them.

I usually sum up this issue with the title of John Gibson's book, *The War on Christmas*. This is the number-one target of the ACLU and its secular leftist allies. They will occasionally go after Menorahs and other religious symbols, but Christmas is the biggest target by far, and if they can halt or even limit any public recognition of Christmas and its holiday traditions, they will have greatly advanced their secularist goals of pushing our religious history out of the public square.

Their attacks on Christmas have often gone beyond manger scenes, Christmas trees, saying "Merry Christmas" ("Happy Holidays" is so much more politically correct), and the singing of Christmas carols. In some bizarre instances, they have expanded this war to include the wearing of red and green clothing to "winter break" parties (in Plano, Texas, students were forbidden to wear these colors with Christmas connotations until ADF sued the school district over this lunacy) and poinsettias (banned in a courthouse in St. Paul, Minn., because someone deemed them a "Christian symbol"[81]). Some fanatics have even gone so far as to try to "baptize" "Jingle Bells" and associate this song with Christmas.

A 2000 Gallup poll found that 96 percent of all Americans—including those of non-Christian faiths—celebrate Christmas. What a target! A 2006 survey by Rasmussen Reports shows that American attitudes toward Christmas have remained fervent and special. Seventy-one percent consider Christmas the nation's most important holiday. Ninety percent celebrate Christmas, 85 percent with a special dinner. Sixty-five percent would like to see more emphasis on the birth of Christ and 60 percent planned to attend church services on Christmas Eve or Christmas Day. *Seventy-eight percent "believe that Christian holiday symbols such as baby Jesus lying in a manger should be allowed on public land, while only 9 percent disagree,"* according to the survey. Interestingly, 93 percent of Republicans and 67 percent of Democrats favored allowing Christian Christmas symbols on public spaces.[82] This subject is so vast that I can only hope to encourage you to read the books I have mentioned and others to truly understand the intensity of this war on Christmas.

In recent times, not all news is bad. There are strong indications that men and women of good will are fighting back.

In 2005, the City of Milwaukee—a Catholic and Lutheran bastion—of all places decided to call the city's Christmas tree a "holiday tree." I assume they were responding to legal threats from "the anti-Christmas police." The following year, in 2006, the Milwaukee City Council in a 9-5 vote changed the name back to "Christmas tree." I applaud the courage of these nine council members. Maybe the other five will get voted out of office.

In Tipton, Iowa, a Nativity scene had been placed on the courthouse grounds for many years without a single complaint. Other private groups had the right to put up secular displays, or even other religious displays such as a Menorah, but no one had ever asked to do so. The ACLU's Christmas police found out about the display and wrote a letter to the Cedar County Board of Supervisors threatening to sue if they did not take it down. The ACLU "generously" offered to assist them "in choosing a constitutionally appropriate method of celebrating the *solstice holidays*." The Supervisors weren't cowed; they contacted the ADF for help. An ADF attorney wrote a letter to the ACLU explaining (which I'm sure they already knew) that the law did allow the Nativity display, and the ACLU backed down.[83] I'm sure they sent their Christmas police off to find some other locations where the county supervisors were more easily bullied and didn't know about the ADF or other such organizations.

Misunderstanding and fear has poisoned the well in so many areas. We desperately need informed leaders in our local communities who will correct these false impressions. Local TV stations in the San Francisco Bay area routinely wish their listeners "Happy Kwanzaa" or "Happy Ramadan," but they would never use the dreaded C-word for fear of offending someone.

Let me just conclude this discussion by pleading with you to take a little time to look at the court rulings and decisions that can keep us from sacrificing our Christmas traditions and heritage that this country has enjoyed for hundreds of years. Such a study will make your head swim at times as you try to understand the *Lemon* test, for example, based on a 1984 Supreme Court decision (*Lynch v. Donnelly*) concerning what the present law allows with reference to placing Nativity scenes on public property. (It has to do with placing a certain number of secular symbols, such as snow men, Santa Claus, and a certain number of reindeer.) The "three reindeer rule" established by the Court may sound silly, but we cannot unilaterally surrender to the Americans United for the Separation of Church and State and the ACLU, who would destroy every vestige of our nation's long religious history.[84]

Some Good News in the Battle for this Country's Soul and Heritage

There is some good news in the fight with the left-wing anti-religious groups.

On the final day of the 2001-2002 Supreme Court term, the high court reversed an appeals court decision and ruled that a school voucher program in Cleveland, Ohio, did not infringe on the constitutional separation of church and state. In a 5-4 decision, the Court upheld a pilot program for school vouchers involving inner-city Cleveland schools, saying that it does not constitute the establishment of religion.

As you may know, vouchers use taxpayer money to underwrite tuition for private or parochial schools. President Bush had this to say: "School choice offers proven results of a better education, not only for children enrolled in the specific plan, but also for children whose public schools benefit from the competition." He continued, "This landmark ruling is a victory for parents and children throughout America."[85]

It was especially encouraging for me to read the words of Barry Lynn, who heads up the Americans United for the Separation of Church and State: "This is probably the worst church-state case in the last 50 years.... It really brings a wrecking ball to a part of the wall separating church and state."[86] Fortunately, those trying to drive every vestige of religion from the public square are experiencing some setbacks.

On May 19, 2008, the Supreme Court upheld a law known as "the PROTECT Act" (Prosecutorial Remedies and Other Tools to End the Exploitation of Children Today). Federal authorities had described this law as "vital in targeting the trafficking of online child pornography."[87] The exceptionally good news is that this was a 7-2 decision! Only Justice Ruth Bader Ginsburg, who was previously employed by the ACLU, and Justice David Souter, who consistently voted against almost everything involving traditional American values, voted no.

This law is very inclusive:

> "The law bars not only the exchange of sexually explicit images of children but also any attempt to convince another person that child pornography is available. The law covers offers that do not contain actual pornography and even offers in which no pictures exist... Its pandering provision targets the person who 'advertises, promotes, presents, distributes or solicits ... any material or purported material in a manner that reflects the belief, or that is intended to cause another to believe,' that it depicts children engaged in sexual activities."[88]

Let's hope the Supreme Court headed up by Chief Justice John Roberts will be a positive force in controlling some of the activist judges intent on destroying our moral values.

There is more good news besides these very important examples. The Alliance Defense Fund (ADF) and its growing number of allies have been able to keep the well-financed ACLU and its equally money-rich left-wing allies, such as Americans United for the Separation of Church and State, from removing public displays of religious faith all over the country, including a Ten Commandments monument in a downtown Phoenix park.

The ADF was started in 1994 by Dr. James Dobson, the late Dr. James Kennedy, the late Dr. Bill Bright, and 30 other Evangelical leaders. Alan Sears serves as the president, CEO, and general counsel of ADF. Sears held a number of positions in the Reagan administration, including serving as the executive director of the Attorney General's Commission on Pornography. Craig Osten is the vice president of Presidential Communications and Research for the ADF. He has 20 years of experience providing writing and research assistance to national religious organizations.

The ADF is now the nation's largest legal alliance dedicated to preserving religious freedom in America. I urge you to read *The ACLU v. America* in order to better understand the Cultural War that the secularists are waging at this very moment. It is time that mainline denominations who truly believe in protecting our religious freedoms and moral values get involved in this struggle. This certainly includes The Lutheran Church—Missouri Synod, its leaders, pastors, and laymen. The immediate past president of the LCMS and our current president have set good examples for us to follow.

My intention before ending this book is to discuss the critical responsibilities that Lutheran clergy and lay people, as well as other Bible-believing Christians, must accept as American citizens if this moral and religious nation is to survive as our Founding Fathers intended. In the final chapter, the case will be made that Lutherans in America have failed to understand Luther's theology of the two kingdoms. After 225 years since the founding of America, Lutherans still have the dubious distinction of having the fewest members of Congress of any major denomination other than the Greek Orthodox. Our LCMS leaders have for the most part ignored their "prophetic" role, in Stephen Carter's words, to speak out on serious moral issues facing our country since the days of Dr. Walter A. Maier until very recent times. (There have been notable exceptions, such as Dr. Jack Preus' around-the-world trip on behalf of the POWs in Vietnam and the occasions on which LCMS presidents have released statements on moral issues such as abortion and traditional marriage. In addition, Lutheran Hour speakers, such as Dr. Dale Meyer, have condemned immoral behavior by politicians and others in their messages.)

Until the last few years, LCMS leaders have been reluctant to dive into the political waters in an organized effort to remind our political leaders that "we ought to obey God" in this country founded on Judeo-Christian principles. One would hope that Dr. Jerry Kieschnick's efforts in support of three state initiatives defining marriage as between one man and one woman has awakened the staid LCMS. The LCMS has so much to offer to this traditionally moral country. Dr. Matthew Harrison, who succeeded Dr. Kieschnick as LCMS president, has picked up and intensified his efforts in getting our church seriously involved in the struggle to protect our religious freedoms under attack like never before in the history of America.

We must support and follow our leaders.

Notes

[1] Alan Sears and Craig Osten, *The ACLU vs. America* (B&H Publishing Group, 2005), 5. Most of the information about Roger Baldwin and the ACLU written in this section is based on Chapter 1 of this book. I will give page numbers for direct quotes and, of course, give credit to other sources when used.

[2] Sears and Osten, 22.

[3] Report of the Special House Committee to Investigate Communist Activities (1931), quoted on *Wikiquote*, http://en.wikiquote.org/wiki/American_Civil_Liberties_Union, accessed Jan. 2, 2012.

[4] Sears and Osten, 18.

[5] *The ACLU vs. America* is the best source on the Cultural War being directed by the ACLU I have found. The resumes of its authors, Alan Sears and Craig Osten, are very impressive. They now head up the Alliance Defense Fund (ADF), an organization founded by Christian leaders to offer legal and other assistance for those fighting to preserve our traditional values. More will be said about the ADF later in this book.

[6] Sears and Osten, 3.

[7] The full text of *Everson v. Board of Education of the Township of Ewing* is available online at http://supreme.justia.com/cases/federal/us/330/1/case.html.

[8] This is the first time the U.S. Supreme Court ever used Jefferson's metaphor as a basis for a court decision. In an 1878 decision, the Supreme Court "quoted Jefferson's letter to the Baptists to justify its rejection of a Mormon's claim that his religious obligation excused him from federal anti-polygamy law. More recently, in 1943, in a dissent, Justice Frankfurter referred in passing to 'the doctrine of separation of church and state, so cardinal in the history of this nation and for the liberty of its people'" (Philip Hamburger, *The Separation of Church and State* [Harvard University Press, 2004], 455). Two references in 150 years of Supreme Court history are not compelling, to say the least.

[9] Stephen Mansfield, *Ten Tortured Words: How the Founding Fathers Tried to Protect Religion in America ... and What's Happened Since* (Thomas Nelson, 2007), 55-58.

[10] Hamburger, 424.

[11] Hamburger, 425.

[12] Mansfield, 57.

[13] Hamburger, pp. 426 ff.

[14] Some of this discussion of Black's early history and his court decisions is taken from Wikipedia contributors, "Hugo Black," *Wikipedia, The Free Encyclopedia,* http://en.wikipedia.org/wiki/Hugo_Black (accessed Jan. 2, 2012).

[15] I became more of an expert on the Klan than I had ever intended. The House Committee on Internal Security, where I was employed when I first came to Washington, had replaced the House Un-American Activities Committee (HUAC). HUAC had virtually destroyed the KKK by infiltrating it with undercover agents. Due to a mix-up, some such agents were arrested. They chose to serve time in prison rather than to be exposed, which would have endangered their lives. I had access to this material, which was highly classified, as a high-level committee staffer. If tough informants feared for their lives in the late 1960s if they doubled crossed the KKK, you can rest assured than *no one* would have even thought about doing so in the 1920s. It would have been inviting a death sentence. HUAC never got credit for this noble undertaking. But no one died as a double-agent. Black did survive as a justice, based on his preposterous story.

[16] Hamburger, 428.

[17] James H. Hutson, *Forgotten Features of the Founding: The Recovery of Religious Themes in the Early American Republic* (Lexington Books, 2003), 135.

[18] Hamburger, 450. The chapter referred to above covers pp. 391-478 and is a very interesting read.

[19] Hamburger, 451-452.

[20] Hamburger, 463.

[21] Hamburger, 463-464.

[22] For a very interesting discussion of this entire subject, see Hamburger, 463-478, "The Aftermath of Everson."

[23] The ACLU had also filed an amicus brief in the *Everson* case. Hamburger describes their efforts: "Taking a slightly different tack, the ACLU treated separation as the First Amendment's purpose and as a pervasive American ideal. In such ways, like some nativists, the ACLU avoided the awkward reality that no American constitution mentioned separation and that the First Amendment expressly constrained the Congress rather that the states" by auguring that the "purpose of the First Amendment, seen in the perception of history, is clear enough. It was designed to bring about the complete separation of church and state. [In fact] this separation was to be achieved by guaranteeing to every person freedom from state interference in his religion or religious establishment" (p. 458).

[24] Mansfield, 58.

[25] Mansfield, 60.

[26] Mansfield, 5.

[27] Interestingly enough, with the 2012 election in mind, it should be noted that Mormons do believe that the Constitution was inspired by God. This is what Joseph Smith taught them.

[28] Sears and Osten, 135. The letter from Jefferson to Abigail Adams is included in *Writings of Thomas Jefferson* (Albert E. Bergh, ed.), published in 1905.

[29] Sears and Osten, 22-23.

[30] See National Right to Life Committee, "Abortion History Timeline." Accessed Jan. 2, 2012, at http://www.nrlc.org/abortion/facts/abortiontimeline.html.

[31] Joy Herndon, et. al., "Abortion Surveillance—United States, 1998" (Centers for Disease Control and Prevention, June 7, 2002), Fig. 1, 11. Accessed Jan. 2, 2012, at http://www.cdc.gov/mmwr/PDF/ss/ss5103.pdf.

[32] Herndon, Fig. 13, 27.

[33] See Carrie Gordon Earll, "What We Did Not Know: The Aftermath of Thirty Years of Legal Abortion." Originally published on http://www.family.org, this paper was accessed Jan. 2, 2012, at http://faith-community.org/whatwedidnotknow. Carrie Gordon Earll is the senior director of Issue Analysis for Government and Public Policy at Focus on the Family.

[34] Gayle White, "Roe v. Wade role just a page in rocky life story," *The Atlanta Journal-Constitution,* Jan. 22, 2003, A1.

[35] Bryan Lash, "The Sandra Cano Story," Priests for Life. Accessed May 3, 2011, at http://www.priestsforlife.org/testimony/ffsandracano.html.

[36] The reference to a "religion of secularism" is used by Stephen Carter, but it is also widely used by others. I used the word "secular" or some derivative several times in these first few sentences for emphasis.

[37] The National Council of Churches was founded in 1950 to replace The Federal Council of Churches, which had become heavily infiltrated by the communists.

[38] David Horowitz and Richard Poe, *The Shadow Party: How George Soros, Hillary Clinton, and Sixties Radicals Seized Control of the Democratic Party* (Thomas Nelson, 2007) is a very interesting, informative, and enjoyable read, although some of the conclusions are frightening for the future of our country. As in most, if not all, conspiracy theories, some people get included who don't really play much of a role and details or events may be slightly revised

for the sake of completeness of the theory. But the book is well documented and well written. It is ironic that in the 2008 Democrat presidential primaries, Hillary Clinton emerged as the moderate in the race. This tells a lot about how liberal Barack Obama really is and how far to the radical left he was willing to go in an effort to appease these very radical groups in the Democrat primaries.

[39] David Hill, "Poll on court encouraging for right," *The Hill*, Oct. 3, 2007. Accessed Jan. 2, 2012, at http://thehill.com/opinion/columnists/david-hill/8375-poll-on-court-encouraging-for-right.

[40] These voters basically are made up of farmers, union households (especially those of the "hard-hat" variety), Catholics, and very patriotic individuals. They didn't understand the war in Iraq and were hit hardest by the faltering economy. I argue that in some ways President Bush's record-low popularity ratings are a result of being too successful in the war against the radical Islamic terrorists. We have not had another major Islamic terrorist attack on American soil since 9/11. The radical Islamic threat no longer seemed urgent. They forgot that keeping al-Qaeda bogged down in Iraq and the counter-terrorism efforts initiated by this president have thwarted numerous terrorist plots that frequently cannot be reported for security reasons. Finally, the Republicans were unable to convince these voters that we truly are returning to our basic principles.

[41] Richard John Neuhaus, *The Naked Public Square: Religion and Democracy in America* (Wm. B. Eerdmans Publishing Company, 1996). This quote is taken from the inside cover of the jacket of the book. It is obviously placed there for the sake of emphasis.

[42] Neuhaus, 83.

[43] Stephen L. Carter, *The Culture of Disbelief: How American Law and Politics Trivialize Religious Devotion* (Basic Books, 1993), 231.

[44] Stephen L. Carter, *God's Name in Vain*, (Basic Books, 2001), 2.

[45] Neuhaus, 82.

[46] Carter, *God's Name in Vain*, 3.

[47] Carter, *God's Name in Vain*, 4.

[48] Hutson became an avid scholar on the original documents during his studies for a Ph.D. at Yale and teaching in the history departments at Yale and William and Mary. In the past 26 years as curator of manuscripts at the Library of Congress, he may have memorized many of them. He has a special interest in religion during the country's founding and is *the* preeminent scholar in this field.

[49] Hutson, p.127, note 4.

[50] Carter, *The Culture of Disbelief*, 4.

[51] Carter, *The Culture of Disbelief*, 279, footnote 2.

[52] Carter, *God's Name in Vain*, 4.

[53] Carter, *God's Name in Vain*, 5.

[54] Neuhaus, 82.

[55] Carter, *God's Name in Vain*, 188.

[56] Carter, *God's Name in Vain*, 187-188.

[57] Carter, *God's Name in Vain*, 197, footnote 2.

[58] ABC News, "Six in 10 Take Bible Stories Literally, but Don't Blame Jews for Death of Jesus," Feb. 10, 2004. Accessed Sept. 7, 2012, at http://abcnews.go.com/images/pdf/947a1ViewsoftheBible.pdf.

[59] Gallup, Inc., "Evolution, Creationism, Intelligent Design." Cited survey figures were from data collected May 3-6, 2012. Accessed Sept. 7, 2012, at http://www.gallup.com/poll/21814/evolution-creationism-intelligent-design.aspx.

[60] I am not suggesting that any Christians get involved in this fight since it has too much historic baggage. Those of us who desire to enter the fray to preserve our heritage of moral and religious values must pick and choose our fights wisely. I have read not only most of Darwin's *Origins of the Species*, but I have read *The Flood* and had the privilege to study biology under the wonderful Christian scholar "Pappy Rush" at Concordia College in Fort Wayne, Ind.

[61] Carter, *The Culture of Disbelief*, 158-168.

[62] Carter, *The Culture of Disbelief*, 152-153.

[63] Carter, *The Culture of Disbelief*, 70.

[64] If they say they are "pro choice," I express my view that they have a right to claim that description of themselves, but I believe it would be more accurate to use the phrase "pro abortion"—if the baby has no choice. Obviously, this approach doesn't often get me off on the right foot with such candidates, but at least we know where we each stand.

[65] Sears and Osten. The entire description of this attack on the Los Angeles County seal is taken from *The ACLU vs. America*, 136 – 139.

[66] Sears and Osten, 138.

[67] Sears and Osten, 139.

[68] Sears and Osten, 141.

[69] In a dissenting opinion, Justice Antonin Scalia, joined by Chief Justice William Rehnquist and Justice Clarence Thomas, makes some very astute observations on this entire subject. Scalia argues that this amendment is *"a modest attempt by seemingly tolerant Coloradans to preserve traditional sexual mores against the efforts of a politically powerful minority to revise those mores through use of the laws. That objective, and the means chosen to achieve it, are … unimpeachable under any constitutional doctrine hitherto pronounced."* He further insists that since the Constitution says nothing on the subject of homosexuality, the Court should not involve itself in the *"cultural wars,"* which should be decided by the people through the democratic process. This subject will be further discussed in Chapter 8.

[70] Sears and Osten, 26.

[71] The ADF, which I intend to discuss further when I turn to "Some Good News," is basically an organization founded by recognized Christian leaders to offer legal and other assistance in fighting the attacks by the ACLU and other secular organizations on our moral values. The ADF is headed up by Alan Sears and Craig Osten. The ADF is still relatively small compared to the likes of the ACLU, but it is having some notable successes.

[72] David Kupelian, *The Marketing of Evil: How Radicals, Elitists, and Pseudo-Experts Sell Us Corruption Disguised As Freedom* (WND Books, 2005). The following pages are based on this book. I will note page numbers when direct quotes are used.

[73] Kupelian, 20

[74] Kupelian, 22.

[75] Kupelian, 24. Kupelian quotes from Marshall Kirk and Hunter Madsen, *After the Ball: How America Will Conquer Its Fear and Hatred of Gays in the 90's* (Penguin Books, 1989), xxvii.

[76] Sears and Osten, 25.

[77] After a two-year study, a special 11-person committee appointed by the Boy Scouts of America released its report July 17, 2012, relating to the traditional position of the BSA in denying membership to scouts, volunteers, and staff who are open or avowed homosexuals. They had reached a "unanimous consensus" that the traditional position of the BSA should not be changed. As a private membership organization, the BSA has the right to establish its requirements for membership. As had always been the case, they chose to leave the discussion of this subject to a more appropriate forum.

[78] The BSA held its Centennial Jamboree in July 2010 at Fort. A.P. Hill as previously scheduled. In 2011, the BSA purchased large tracts of land in a beautiful setting in the West Virginia mountains. This land will be used for many purposes, including extreme sports on fabulous rivers and will serve as the permanent home of future jamborees.

[79] Boy Scouts of America, "Scout Oath," accessed Sept. 7, 2012, at http://www.scouting.org/sitecore/content/scoutparents/scouting%20basics/what%20scouting%20is/scout%20oath%20and%20law.aspx.

[80] Boy Scouts of America, "The Scout Law," accessed Sept. 7, 2012, at http://www.scouting.org/scoutsource/Media/Relationships/ascoutisrevernt/ss04.aspx.

[81] Sears and Osten, 157. Alan Sears and Craig Osten devote a chapter in *The ACLU vs. America* to "The ACLU vs. Christmas." This chapter of Gibson's *The War on Christmas: How the Liberal Plot to Ban the Sacred Christian Holiday Is Worse than You Thought* (Sentinel Trade, 2006) is an excellent source for understanding this area of the Cultural War.

[82] J. Harper, "Majority in U.S. believes in God," *The Washington Times*, Dec. 25, 2005.

[83] Sears and Osten, 159.

[84] Sears and Osten, 165. Please read *The ACLU vs. America* and learn about the help available from the ADF when a problem arises.

[85] Terry Frieden, "Supreme Court affirms school voucher program," CNN Justice, June 27, 2002. Accessed Sept. 7, 2012, from http://articles.cnn.com/2002-06-27/justice/scotus.school.vouchers_1_school-voucher-program-milwaukee-and-florida-parochial-school-tuition/3?_s=PM:LAW.

[86] Frieden.

[87] Robert Barnes, "Justices Uphold Child Porn Law; Case Involved Criminalization of 'Pandering," *The Washington Post*, May 20, 2008. Reprinted in *The Washington Post Supreme Court Year in Review 2009* (Kaplan Publishing, 2009), 109-110.

[88] Barnes, 109.

8

The Role Lutherans Can and Should Play in this Life and Death Struggle for the Soul of Our Country!

O f all of the noteworthy statements the world-famous evangelist Dr. Billy Graham has made in a very long career of boldly proclaiming the Gospel of Jesus Christ, none has had more impact on me than when he called The Lutheran Church—Missouri Synod a "sleeping giant."[1] Having heard this comment repeated many times, it is consistent with the view I had always held of the LCMS.

At the same time, I also know that Dr. Graham has had tremendous respect for our church body, a view based partly on a story widely circulated during my seminary days. I was told by some professors and Lutheran Hour officials about his reaction to Dr. Walter A. Maier's death in 1950. They reported that then-young evangelist Billy Graham had made inquiries about applying for the job as The Lutheran Hour speaker. He obviously was informed that this position would have to be filled by an LCMS pastor.

I felt certain Dr. Graham recognized that this "sleeping giant" had a unique potential for exerting major influence on American Christian theology as well as being a positive influence in the preservation of this moral Republic bequeathed to us by our wise Founders. Graham, as well as other conservative Christian leaders, had witnessed our Missouri Synod seminaries holding firm to our commitment to the absolute authority and integrity of God's Holy Word as higher criticism and modernism were wreaking havoc in other Christian denominations and seminaries. But we made little or no effort to enter into the debate raging in the larger Christian community in America. Early in the 20th century, men like J. Gresham Machen, who led a long fight to prevent modernists in the Northern Presbyterian Church from taking control of Princeton Theological Seminary, desperately needed the help that the biblical experts on our St. Louis seminary faculty could provide. But they seemed reluctant to publicly challenge those who wanted to destroy the authority of the Bible and bring Christianity into the modern world of social change. We had so much to offer in this fight!

A young Billy Graham no doubt was impressed by the "prophetic," urgent voice of Dr. Walter A. Maier calling America to repentance and to responsible action by her leaders as the nation experienced the Great Depression. (There can be little doubt that some aspects of Dr. Graham's ministry as an evangelist were influenced by Dr. Maier.) WAM, as he was aptly and affectionately called, had no reservations about accepting his responsibilities in Luther's left-hand kingdom and calling "Caesar" to task when Caesar was neglecting his God-given responsibilities.

But like the rest of us, Billy Graham had seen succeeding generations of LCMS leaders, laymen, and laywomen fall back into the comfortable cocoon of orthodoxy, internal debates, and thanksgiving for our blessings of being able to enjoy the fruits of pure, biblical Lutheran theology. Not that this isn't a wonderful cocoon made possible by the sacrifices of our forefathers in a country so richly blessed by our Almighty God. But we seemed to have lost the zeal to follow in our forefathers' footsteps. We diligently taught our children the doctrines necessary for their eternal salvation but we neglected, for the most part, to fulfill our civic responsibilities to help insure that our children and their children would also inherit the blessings of a country built on a moral foundation with the guarantee of religious freedom.

As they are frequently described in literature, "sleeping giants" are often hard to awaken. But once they are finally awakened, they are capable of accomplishing great things. I must admit that I grew up with an idealistic understanding of the great country our dedicated Founders left for future generations. I also grew up with a respect for The Lutheran Church—Missouri Synod that was possibly a little too idealistic for any body made up of redeemed sinners. But such ideals have served me well in my life since I was always ready to defend my country and my church.

Growing up in a small country town in South Georgia during the Great Depression and the Great War bore a striking resemblance to growing up during the founding days of our country, as I would come to understand through an in-depth study of our founding period. The flicker of hope for obtaining the American dream was never extinguished during the most difficult of times. During the Depression, people had little, but they shared, looked after one another, and they prayed without ceasing. Prayer and religious devotion were staples of our society: people in my hometown prayed on virtually every occasion in school, at football and basketball games, at virtually all celebrations such as Fourth of July events, at high school assemblies, civic clubs, PTAs, and just about everywhere imaginable. During the hard times, we prayed for God's blessings on the crops, livestock, and for the suffering and the hungry. We knew that God had not forsaken us through all our trials and tribulations.

Just as times began to improve, our fathers, grandfathers, brothers, uncles, cousins, friends, and loved ones were sent off to war. Our prayers not only did not cease but they intensified. Now most of the prayers were not for worldly goods—food or otherwise—but for the safety of those we loved and for the defeat of the evil enemy who would destroy our Christian way of life in the greatest country in the world. Patriotism was rampant! (In virtually every case our prayers were distinctively Christian. As far as I know, there were four or five Jewish families in Tifton, Ga., at the time and there was never a word of resentment spoken against Christians for honoring and asking their God for His blessings.) If you want a comparison of how similar life was at this time to life experienced by our Founding generation, just read one of Dr. James Hutson's previously referenced books on this topic!

I cannot imagine any home being more defined by Christianity than the one in which I grew up. My mother knelt by my bed with me every night as we said our prayers. (Daddy was seldom there since he was a traveling grocery salesman when I was a little boy.) We always said our table prayers before a meal. My daddy had the strongest faith and was the most devout Missouri Synod Lutheran I have ever known. He was never a person to criticize anyone but he spent untold hours telling me why the LCMS was a special church body with a special mission from God. He explained to me how we taught only what was in the Bible and that we were saved only by faith in Jesus Christ apart from any good works. When the man I loved, respected, and trusted more than any man in the world told me how special our church was, I certainly believed him.

In addition, having listened to every sermon Dr. Walter A. Maier preached on The Lutheran Hour as far back as a child could remember, his was the only face of the LCMS I knew growing up. By the time I entered high school, I had seen only two LCMS pastors in person. I am sure that I thought Dr. Maier typified all LCMS pastors. Certainly I would have expected that every LCMS pastor would have insisted that Lutheran Christians must take seriously their civic responsibilities as Americans.

When I attended Concordia College in Fort Wayne, Ind., and then the seminary in St. Louis, I was a little surprised to discover that the students were overwhelmingly Republicans, as were virtually the entire faculties at the two schools. They were all anti-communists, but few evidenced much involvement in the political process. The moral issues that would so divide our country were around in their embryonic stage but would not begin to dominate our culture until about the time I graduated from Concordia Seminary, St. Louis, in 1960. At this time in Missouri Synod history, no one had picked up Dr. Maier's mantle and raised a prophetic voice to call Americans to repentance. While I am sure many LCMS parish pastors were urging their flocks not to ignore their responsibilities as Christian citizens, there was no public church leader inspiring our people to demand that America's leaders govern based on the Judeo-Christian principles on which this nation was founded. But there are many positive signs that our most recent LCMS presidents have determined that our voice must be heard in the public square.

In fairness, we must not in any way minimize the most important fact that our dedicated LCMS pastors in America and missionaries around the world are proclaiming the Gospel of Jesus Christ in all of its truth and purity. Ministering to the flock over which the Good Shepherd has given them charge is always their primary responsibility! There is no disagreement in our church over the truth of this statement. In addition, however, our God who has so richly blessed us by allowing us to live in this great free country expects us to willingly accept our God-given responsibilities as Christian citizens. There are also many civic-minded LCMS pastors all over America urging their people to be good stewards of their God-given responsibilities as Christian citizens. There are even more LCMS pastors who are accepting their prophetic responsibility to speak out loud and clear on moral issues addressed in God's Holy Word. How can a man of God remain silent when more than 3,000 babies each day are having their God-given lives ended by government-enabled abortions? God in His wisdom established marriage as a divine institution between a man and a woman. How dare a man of God keep his counsel to himself when mere human beings shamelessly attack God's order of creation? Serious Christian laymen and laywomen listen to their pastors, and they trust them. This has been especially true among Lutherans in America.

It also should also be stressed that many LCMS church leaders, including district and Synod presidents, have not ignored the prophetic impact of speaking out on moral issues as duly elected representatives of such a highly respected church body. Most have released statements, answered press inquiries, or spoken out in a timely fashion on crucial moral issues facing this country. A few have undertaken highly publicized efforts to bring the moral authority of our church body to bear on humanitarian challenges and moral issues facing our country.

The example about which I know the most, since I was asked to do the staff work (discussed earlier in this book), was when Dr. Jack Preus led a delegation of American church leaders on an around-the-world humanitarian mission on behalf of the POWs in Vietnam. As president of the LCMS, Dr. Preus was the lead spokesman for this delegation, which represented American church bodies comprising more than 95 percent of all Christians in America. When we met with heads of state, such as Prime Minister Olof Palme in Sweden and Indira Gandhi in India, as well as church leaders including Pope Paul VI, Dr. Preus always introduced the delegation, explained our mission, and led the discussion.

The publicity surrounding the trip sent the clear message that the LCMS cared deeply about human suffering and was willing to spend whatever capital it had to alleviate as much human misery as possible. Translation: this church, known primarily for its orthodoxy and commitment to Holy Scripture, had a big caring heart!

President Nixon was so impressed with Dr. Preus that he invited him to preach a sermon and conduct a Sunday service at the White House. With the president of the United States, the vice president, most members of the Cabinet, and many prestigious U.S. senators and congressman in attendance, Dr. Preus delivered a sermon that few present would soon forget. Under the title "Blessed is the Nation Whose God is the Lord," Dr. Preus proclaimed the Law and the Gospel in clear words.

As we milled around eating pastries and drinking coffee after the service, a recognized authority told me, "That was one of the most powerful sermons I have ever heard!" That authority would be Billy Graham, who was among the dignitaries invited to the White House for this worship service. I had come to know Dr. Graham fairly well over the telephone, as I had sought his advice on the trip organized by Dr. Preus. (Just for the record, there was no "unionism" involved, since Dr. Preus read the Scriptures, gave the prayers, and conducted the entire service. We did sing a couple of agreed-upon hymns with non-Lutheran Christians.)

There was no doubt in my mind that Dr. Preus did wear Dr. Maier's mantle for at least a few months. I am also sure he had a strong interest in wearing that mantle longer in his presidency. But he felt there were so many pressing internal problems in the Missouri Synod. Those problems would dominate much of his time. I was prepared to spend more time as his special assistant had Dr. Preus decided to dedicate significant time as president bringing to bear the influence of our highly respected church on the threats of those challenging the moral foundation of our country. But the time probably was not right, since the Cultural Wars already being fought by the secularists were not well understood at this time in our history. (As will be explained later, the Southern Baptists, the largest Protestant denomination in America, did not put together an organized undertaking to become actively involved in this struggle until 1988.)

So I was off to Washington, hoping to make my contribution to this great country God had so richly blessed. I was deeply concerned about the threat of atheistic communism and the attacks by the secularists on the moral foundations of this nation. I knew if Christians were unwilling to enter the public square, it would be dominated by those who did not share our values. (Being young and idealistic, I believed God was offering me the opportunity to make my contribution to what Luther described as the "Kingdom of the Left" [the State] as a blessed member of the "Kingdom of the Right" [His Church]).

Dr. Jack Preus, whose father had been governor of Minnesota, certainly did not underestimate the importance of Lutheran Christians reaching out to those in positions of power in our government. Fortunately, having gained some notoriety as a result of his work on behalf of the POWs and MIAs, his name was known to many leaders of our government. Partly due to my pleas, he developed a pattern of visiting D.C. on his trips back East as part of his official duties. Having spent many evenings with me at social events with considerable numbers of U.S. senators, congressmen, and other government officials over the next few years, it is not an exaggeration to say that he personally knew more such leaders of our government than any Missouri Synod clergyman at the time. Jack was duly impressed with the religious convictions of many of these senators and congressmen with whom we frequently had dinner. He was always asked to offer a prayer for our government before we ate our meal.

These visits by Jack Preus and subsequent Missouri Synod officials were vitally important for a number of reasons. It is a total understatement to say that only a few dozen of the thousands of our government officials in Washington, D.C., had any idea of how the LCMS differed from the more liberal Lutheran bodies, which always had some type of government-relations organization representing them before our government. The face of Lutheranism when I arrived in the Nation's Capital was that of a church very similar to the more traditionally liberal mainline Protestant denominations. Lutherans were perceived as being moderate to liberal in theology and "progressives," if not activists, on social issues.

The one thing we always had going for us was The Lutheran Hour. I was pleasantly surprised to learn how many MCs listened to The Lutheran Hour occasionally if not regularly. It becomes understandable when you realize how many of them travel in their districts and states even on Sunday. When doing so, some would tune in to religious broadcasts on their car radios. It was good to hear that many said The Lutheran Hour was their favorite. Obviously, they heard that this program was sponsored by the LCMS. But only a few knew exactly what that meant. Some even recognized the name of Dr. Oswald Hoffmann and, by the 1990s, of Dr. Dale Meyer.

A significant event occurred after Dale Meyer became The Lutheran Hour speaker and brought The Lutheran Hour board, along with the venerable Dr. Hoffmann, to a meeting in Washington, D.C. This was the first time I met Dale in person and the only time I had a chance to have a meaningful discussion with Dr. Hoffmann. I obviously introduced the group to a number of congressmen and senators.

Dale and I would become close friends, and it was obvious from the beginning that he realized that our church has much to offer in the always-changing world of politics. Listening to his Lutheran Hour addresses, it was clear that he had no reservations about speaking out on the moral issues confronting our country. His visits to the Nation's Capital became more frequent, much more so after he became president of Concordia Seminary in St. Louis. During this time, his two dedicated and talented daughters had made their way in D.C. and were working for powerful men such as now-Speaker John Boehner and Senator Tom Coburn of Oklahoma. Dale's personality and social skills served him well as an ambassador for the LCMS. In a short period of time, Dale personally knew many more MCs than the record previously set by Dr. Preus. As a testimony to Dale's presence as a servant of Christ, he would be offered the opportunity to become the chaplain both of the U.S. Senate and the U.S. House of Representatives. On each occasion, separated by a number of years, Dale decided after prayerful consideration that the work God had called him to do at Concordia Seminary was not finished.

After giving a snapshot of how Lutherans compare to other denominations in their willingness to enter the public square, particularly in regard to holding public office, I will spend the rest of this chapter discussing the changing attitudes of our most recent LCMS leaders. Our immediate past president as well as our current LCMS president have demonstrated a desire and a willingness to pick up Dr. Walter A. Maier's mantle. This mantle is heavy, and it takes extraordinary courage to wrap it around one's shoulders. But the moral values of our great country and the religious liberty that has been held so dearly since our Founding are under greater assault than at any time in our history.

When I arrived in Washington, D.C., there were only 13 Lutherans serving in the U.S. Senate and House of Representatives. The three Lutheran senators were all Democrats—one was LCMS and attended the same Missouri Synod congregation where we became members after moving to the area. Six of the House members were Republicans and four were Democrats. I know for sure that two of the House members—possibly three—were members of LCMS churches. By contrast, there were 64 MCs in 1971 who were members of the Episcopal Church, compared with three or four who were members of the LCMS. This tells a story of civic responsibility, since the Episcopal Church had a slightly *smaller* national membership than the LCMS. To further highlight the question of the overall Lutheran emphasis on citizenship responsibilities, there were 80 Presbyterians in the U.S. Congress in 1971 and only 13 Lutherans. This in spite of the fact that there were roughly 8 million Lutherans living in America while only four and a half million Americans were Presbyterians. In statistical terms, 15 percent of the members of the U.S. Congress were Presbyterians and only 2.4 percent were Lutherans. Calvinists and Lutherans clearly had a different understanding of Christian citizenship responsibilities.

In the present 112th Congress, Lutherans have a total of 26 members—four U.S. senators and 22 members of the House of Representatives. One senator, Ron Johnson, a Republican from Wisconsin, is LCMS, and six members of the House are also LCMS. One congressman and one congresswoman are members of the Wisconsin Synod. The other three senators, all Democrats, are ELCA members. Of the 14 ELCA members of the House, seven are Republicans and seven Democrats. The six LCMS members are all Republicans, and the two WELS members are split between the two parties. (I asked the one WELS congressman if he was the only Democrat in the Wisconsin Synod. He said something like "pretty close.")

In the previous chapter, I mentioned that Lutherans have the dubious distinction of having the second fewest members of the U.S. Congress, based on national membership, of all major or mainline Christian denominations in America. Upon further study, I have learned that all Lutheran denominations are now tied with all Orthodox Church bodies but are still marginally ahead of the Greek Orthodox alone. However, the LCMS as a separate church body is now at the bottom of the list any way you count it. The LCMS is behind the Orthodox bodies grouped together or separated. The LCMS is considerably behind the congregational membership of WELS members *based on size of the church bodies*.

Numerous reasons have been offered to explain why Lutherans in general, and the more theological conservative LCMS and WELS in particular, have been so reluctant to accept more responsibilities of citizenship other than in the most basic sense. They probably have a slightly better record of obeying the laws of the country than most other groups. Anecdotal evidence indicates that Lutherans recognize a stronger responsibility to be "good Samaritans" than most. Lutherans definitely have a reputation for respecting and taking to heart the words and admonitions of their pastors. If you are going to understand the Lutheran laity's attitudes toward civic responsibilities and politics, it is essential to try to understand where their pastors come down on these issues. If we feel that more Lutherans should provide salt or leaven by serving as moral politicians and elected officials, we must get our church leaders and parish pastors involved in the process.

Jesus' words as recorded by St. Matthew after He expounded on the Beatitudes in the Sermon on the Mount afford us divine instruction on this subject. He explained to His disciples their citizenship responsibilities in unmistakable terms:

> "You are the salt of the earth, but if salt has lost its taste, how shall its saltiness be restored? It is no longer good for anything except to be thrown out and trampled under people's feet.
> "You are the light of the world. A city set on a hill cannot be hidden. Nor do people light a lamp and put it under a basket, but on a stand, and it gives light to all in the house. In the same way, let your light shine before others, so that they may see your good works and give glory to your Father who is in heaven" (Matt. 5:13-16, ESV).

I am fully aware that Jesus was primarily explaining to His disciples that their "good deeds" will motivate others to listen more carefully to the Gospel He had given them to proclaim. But I am also convinced that this message speaks volumes about Christian citizenship. When St. Paul was being held captive in Caesarea, the religious authorities in Jerusalem urged Festus, the Roman governor of Judea, to have him brought to Jerusalem so he could be put to death. St. Paul exercised his rights as a Roman citizen and appealed to Caesar. Festus respected Paul's rights to make such an appeal and he ending up spending his final years under house arrest in Rome. This enabled St. Paul to offer strength and hope to the small persecuted Christian minority in Rome.

The authors of *Lutheran Pastors and Politics* explain that "God established government, appointing Saul as the first king of Israel. Therefore, government is a divinely ordained institution with worth and merit."[2] Our wise Founding Fathers understood that God established the rule of kings at a certain time in Israel's sometime turbulent history for a specific purpose. This became necessary because of their rebellions against the covenant He had made with His chosen people. This is clearly explained in the Old Testament scriptures. These Founders further understood that in God's plan of creation He created all of His creatures free and equal. He also gave them free will, which they abused and thus sinned against their Creator. In America we are blessed to have a government in which free men, who believed they were endowed by their Creator with certain God-given rights, sought to govern themselves. The Founders realized that such a government's existence was suited only for "a moral and religious people," in John Adams' words.

So we ask, why have Lutherans been so reluctant to accept their full responsibilities as Christian citizens? Then we must ask the follow-up question: what can and should be done to change the attitudes and culture of Lutherans living in America?

I have found no better source for addressing these questions in a thoughtful a manner than *Lutheran Pastors and Politics: Issues in the Public Square* by Walz and Montreal. They look at these questions. They examine the backgrounds of the different groups of Lutherans who reached these shores. They analyze the theological differences and priorities of the various American bodies. Most answers, as expected, are found in Luther's theology of the two kingdoms. Beginning with the explanation of the Fourth Commandment in Luther's Large Catechism, the authors quote Paul Althaus' statement that "Luther believed that 'all authority is based on paternal authority.'" [3]

Having examined Richard Niebuhr's *Christ and Culture,* they turn to the Missouri Synod's Commission on Theology and Church Relations report, "Render unto Caesar ... and unto God: A Lutheran View of Church and State," and after that, to such documents as Paul Althaus' *The Ethics of Martin Luther* and Kurt Marquart's *The Church and Her Fellowship, Ministry, and Governance,* as well as portions volumes 45 to 47 of *Luther's Works.*

Walz and Montreal offer a very interesting quote from Martin Luther in the Large Catechism:

> "The same may be said of obedience to civil authority, which authority, as we have said, is all embraced in the estate of fatherhood and extends beyond other relations. Here the father is not one of a single family, but one of many tenants, citizens or subjects. Through civil rulers, as through our parents, God gives us food, home and land, protection and security. Therefore, since they bear the name and title with honor as their chief glory, it is our duty to honor them and to

esteem them as we would the greatest treasure and the most precious jewel on earth."[4]

When you read one of Dr. James Hutson's books dealing with religion in the founding period and hear the Founders' references to their civil authority as a "nursing father," it makes you wonder if some of them could possibly have read this section of the Large Catechism. But this is unlikely, since they wrote much about Calvinism and rarely mentioned Lutheranism. Maybe great minds just come to the same conclusion on certain matters. These are the words that Hutson writes in the Preface of *Forgotten Features of the Founding: The Recovery of Religious Themes in the Early American Republic*:

> "The first three chapters in this volume identify and explicate religious themes which prevailed during the Founding Period but which are of scant interest to today's scholars. These themes are: the conviction that the doctrine of a 'future state of rewards and punishments' provided religion with the means of producing social and political benefits, the assumption that the civil magistrates should play the role of 'nursing father' to religious institutions; and the belief that rights were moral powers, grounded in religion....
>
> "The forgotten themes were very old, one dating from pre-Christian times and others from the fourteenth and sixteenth centuries. That they flourished in the United States during the Founding Period demonstrates how traditional and conventional the religious mentality of the country was, *not surprising in a solidly Christian nation, as the new republic indisputably was*"[5] (emphasis added).

For a man of Hutson's stature—many scholars on early American history insist that he has read more original documents and knows more about religion in America's founding period than any man alive—to insist that such claims are indisputable is extraordinary. The examples he uses and the documentation Hutson provides in his Chapter 2, "Nursing Fathers," is a very informative read indeed.

Walz and Montreal also include a Luther quote used by Althaus that has a familiar ring: "If all men were Christians, there would be no need of secular government." Walz and Montreal note that this is sounds like the James Madison dictum: "If men were angels, no government would be necessary." Similar sentiments from Ben Franklin and John Adams were noted in earlier chapters of this book.

Using some previous studies of Lutheran attitudes toward civil government and divergent views of Luther's two-kingdom theology, the authors of *Lutheran Pastors and Politics* proceed to examine the differences in understanding of this subject among the various Lutheran church bodies in America. Very importantly, the authors had previously conducted the most extensive survey of LCMS pastors on their theological and political attitudes toward church and state. I eagerly studied the study's results. I had read many of the books they reference and had a wealth of personal anecdotal evidence based on extensive discussions with LCMS pastors. But I was now in possession of hard evidence that confirmed most of my previously held convictions.

The authors make an insightful observation about the origins of and continuing political differences of ELCA and Missouri Synod pastors. They write:

> "Part of the political divide today—ELCA pastors are largely Democrats and LCMS pastors predominantly Republican—may have its roots in immigration and value systems. Richard Jensen and Paul Kleppner suggest that in the nineteenth century, German Lutherans—the bulk of those individuals who founded the LCMS and who comprised much of the former Lutheran Church in America—subscribe to a ritualistic model, while Scandinavian Lutherans—who comprise a majority of today's ELCA—were pietistic in their value systems and politics."[6]

This was music to my ears since it validated the advice I had given over the years in my political activities. When being involved in Republican races in Iowa, Minnesota, and the two Dakotas specifically, I always insisted—sometimes until they got tired of hearing it—that we must reach out to the Scandinavian Lutherans. I always pointed out that they are basically good, God-fearing, moral people but have an inclination to be more liberal on social issues in particular because of their pietistic heritage. (They could more easily be persuaded to vote for a conservative Lutheran candidate because he or she was a Lutheran. This would include on occasion LCMS and WELS members and always was a major asset to those who belonged to one of the more liberal Lutheran bodies. The two best examples, and there are several others, are former Senator Rod Grams of Minnesota and nine-term Congressman Tom Latham of Iowa.)

Realizing that there are always numerous factors involved in any successful election, I do not believe that Rod Grams would have won his first election to the U.S. House of Representatives or his subsequent election to the U.S. Senate had he not been a Lutheran—even a conservative LCMS Lutheran. Congressman Latham, who is seeking his 10th term, is such an outstanding candidate and dedicated congressman that he would have likely won his elections as a member of any Christian denomination. But I believe that as a consistent conservative on social and moral issues as well as on fiscal and national security issues, his being a Lutheran (he was raised in an ALC congregation that is now ELCA) helped him in his close races in a district where so many Scandinavian Lutherans live. The congressional districts in which he has run had always leaned Democrat or were marginally Republican at best. I also believe that Congresswoman Michele Bachmann was helped, especially in her first election, by being a Lutheran, albeit a very conservative Wisconsin Synod Lutheran.

All of these candidates, and many others like them, would be helped if we could motivate more LCMS members to be good citizens and turn out to vote in large numbers.

Using documents produced by Frederick Luebke and Richard Jensen, the authors offer this astute observation about the history of these divergent Lutheran attitudes. They note that those with a pietistic background wanted the government to "battle sin" in the form of slavery, alcohol, or forms of discrimination against women or immigrants. On the other hand, those Lutherans described as "ritualists" wanted the government to stay out of the lives of citizens and were much less likely to oppose slavery or alcohol. They add, "In fact, some ritualists believed that 'to legislate morality was to threaten the authority of the church in spiritual matters.'"[7]

The findings reported in *Lutheran Pastors and Politics* are hardly surprising but they are very instructive. The LCMS and WELS pastors are much more conservative theologically and, therefore, are much more conservative politically than their ELCA counterparts. In partisan terms, the extensive Walz-Montreal survey of LCMS pastors revealed that "an overwhelming" 84.8 percent describe themselves as "as some kind of Republican." Almost half identified themselves as "strong Republicans." As far as party identification, there was little difference in the younger and older pastors' willingness to label themselves as "strong Republicans."

While an almost identical 84.4 percent of LCMS pastors identified themselves as conservatives to some degree, there was an age difference in identifying themselves as "very conservative" or "extremely conservative." Of LCMS pastors in the 26-40 age group, 64.5 percent identified themselves as "very conservative"; 54.4 percent of those in the 41-50 age range chose the same description; but of those pastors between 61 and 78, only 27.4 percent chose the "very conservative" description to describe themselves. Regardless of the explanation for this difference, the authors note that we can expect our LCMS pastors to be politically conservative for many years in the future. I would note that since theological conservatives tend also to become political conservatives, our seminaries must be doing a better job in giving our students a sound theological education than that for which they often get credit.

There is no similar recent survey of the theological and resulting political attitudes of WELS and ELCA pastors. But anecdotal evidence abounds. It is universally considered that the WELS clergymen are at least slightly to the right of their Missouri Synod counterparts. It is also widely speculated that the ELCA clergy is considerably more liberal theologically and polar opposites of the Missouri Synod clergy in political persuasion.

These considerations are of importance for two reasons:

One, most authorities believe that the theological and political convictions of LCMS and WELS pastors are widely shared by their parishioners. Whereas, Walz and Montreal note, "The ELCA, on the other hand, has gone the way of mainline Protestantism, in which clergy tends to be more liberal, theologically and politically, than parishioners."[8] When pastors and laity are in basic agreement on a subject, it should be easier for a pastor to motivate members of his flock to take action.

Secondly, in the bigger picture, clergymen and their church-body leaders set the agenda for their church's role in the public square. The modernist movement that took root in the early part of the 20th century created what has become known as the "social gospel." Their theme was that American churches should concentrate more on the "here" than the "hereafter." Since some of the more extreme liberals in the modernist movement no longer believed in the hereafter, their religion became one of "do-good-ism." If there happened to be a God, he would surely reward their efforts in pressuring the state to take care of its subjects. A case can be made that the liberal advocates of the social gospel wanted to influence the government to assume the role Christ had assigned to His Church—to visit the sick, feed the hungry, clothe the naked, and give alms to the poor.

But some of the mainline denominations, who had not totally forsaken Christ's command to proclaim the Gospel to sinners in need of salvation, accepted the call of the leaders of the modernist movement to demand that the American government enforce the tenets of the social gospel.

God has given the state its role and the church its role. Our Founding Fathers took decisive steps to make sure that the government never tried to tell the churches what theology they must teach or how or where Christians must worship. (Many of the colonies had tried to do just that by establishing state churches.) On the other hand, these Founders adopted a Constitution, with all types of checks and balances, establishing *how* this country was to be governed. (These same Founders were all too aware of the established churches in Europe telling their rulers how to rule. The very idea of a church body or its leaders trying to tell the government which wars to fight or how to fight them; how much to tax their citizen; what the minimum wage should be; how much foreign aid should be given to foreign governments and for what purposes it should be spent would have driven our Founders to question whether these people had forgotten in which country they lived. If such people, church leaders or laypeople, felt strongly about such issues, they were free to exercise their individual political rights as American citizens.)

Liberal Christians, as well as Bible-believing Christians, be they clerics or laypeople, have the same right to enter the political process, to choose a political party, to work as volunteers, or to run for public office. All are welcome in this great country to take their beliefs with them when they enter the public square. But they all should remember that being a Christian affords them special knowledge *only* on clear moral issues addressed in God's Holy Word. Concerning issues on which the Bible is silent they have no more—or no less—"special insight" into secular issues than those of other religions or of no religion. For a Christian church leader or layman to contend that by virtue of their religion they have a special understanding of the vigorous disputed science relating to the environment, for example, is ridiculous to say the least. However, when it comes to moral issues unequivocally addressed in the Bible, the responsibility of Christian leaders and laymen to be the "salt" and "leaven" of a free society should be beyond dispute. Our Founding Fathers not only believed that such action is permissible, but also that it is necessary for the survival of a republic governed by a free people. The words of President John Adams that "our Constitution is suitable only for a moral and religious people" cannot be quoted too frequently. We must also be reminded that the preeminent authority on the subject, Dr. James Hutson, insists that the word "religion" was virtually synonymous with "Christian" in our founding days.

The Culture Wars Enter the Political Arena Full Blast

"The Roaring '60s" left an indelible mark on American culture in many areas. Many political scientists contend that the so-called "anti-war" movement led to Lyndon B. Johnson's decision not to seek reelection as president in 1968. But arguably the most lasting effect on politics in America occurred in the chambers of the Supreme Court.

In 1962, none other than Justice Hugo Black wrote the majority opinion in *Engel v. Vitale* declaring voluntary prayer in public schools unconstitutional. A year later the Supreme Court ruled that reading Bible verses, without comment, in public schools was also unconstitutional. These were practices that had been encouraged and allowed by previous congresses and courts since the nation's Founding, as discussed earlier in this book. (Subsequent courts even struck down state laws allowing prayers and Bible readings in their public schools, even with student "opt-out" provisions. This is an eminently reasonable approach to an issue debated by some Christians as well as all secularists. Many Lutheran pastors might advise their students against participating in such prayers. Not because prayers in public schools are prohibited by the Constitution, since this is clearly not the case. But they may have a concern that these prayers would not be consistent with Lutheran doctrine.)

In any event, the battle lines were drawn indelibly on this political debate, the issue of denying prayer in public schools was so emotionally charged. The overwhelming majority of conservatives regarded such a denial as a frontal assault on America's cherished religious liberties! Anecdotally, this single issues almost cost a sitting Democrat U.S. senator his reelection in the solid Democrat state of Oklahoma at the time. In the 1966 election, the Republican candidate for the U.S. Senate, Pat Patterson, an attorney from Oklahoma City who was an avowed member of the John Birch Society, almost pulled off the upset of the century. Patterson was able to raise so little money for his campaign that those of us supporting him spent most of our time hand-painting signs that read "Pat is for Prayer in Schools!" This slogan so separated Pat from the Democrat senator that the election was not officially called until the final absentee ballot was counted at about 10:00 the morning after the election.

The denial of prayer in schools, which was regarded as a denial of the religious freedoms guaranteed to us by our Founders, was the engine that drove the Culture Wars for conservatives until around the time that I arrived in Washington. Then the second bombshell in the Culture Wars exploded in 1973 when the Supreme Court in *Roe v. Wade* declared state laws regulating abortion unconstitutional. Protecting the lives of the unborn would become a new rallying cry in the battle to preserve the moral and religious foundation of our country. Many liberal church bodies hailed *Roe* under the deceptive banner of protecting the health of women; conservative Protestant churches were slow in responding to the battle to protect human life.

The traditionally theologically and politically conservative Southern Baptists not only were late in entering this fray, they had been on the other side for a period of time. The story of the arrival on the Washington scene of Richard Land, armed with a Ph.D. from Oxford, to call his Southern Baptist denomination back to its historic biblical roots should have significant meaning for the LCMS. Dr. Land, who Religion News Service (RNS) describes as "the man who became the public face of the Southern Baptist Convention on ethical and political issues for nearly 25 years," just announced his retirement.[9] An interview with Land conducted by religion reporter Michelle Boorstein in *The Washington Post* (Aug. 10, 2012) tells a compelling story. The *Post* story notes that the Southern Baptist leadership had drifted to the political middle. Land would explain that this development occurred in part because of their desire to help Jimmy Carter become president. Carter was a Southern Baptist, even though he was a very liberal one. Land stated, "The establishment were to the left of the rank and file."[10]

In 1988, Dr. Land replaced Foy Valentine, who headed up what was then known as the Christian Life Commission. The Southern Baptist Convention established a new Ethics & Religious Liberty Commission (ERLC), of which Land has been president for the entire 25 years of its existence.

The vision of the ERLC is "an American society that affirms and practices Judeo-Christian values rooted in biblical authority." Its mission is "to awaken, inform, energize, equip, and mobilize Christians to be the catalysts for the Biblically-based transformation of their families, churches, communities, and the nation."[11]

Land describes his predecessor, Foy Valentine, as "arguing a pro-choice position" and being "a member of the ACLU." He then proclaims "we did a 180-degree turn on abortion and capital punishment." Land notes that three of every four Southern Baptists are pro-capital punishment.[12] Land became such a recognized conservative authority on abortion, no-fault divorce, and same-sex marriage that *Time* magazine would dub him "God's Lobbyist" in 2005. ERLC did engage in some selective lobbying, such as for the "Sudan Peace Act," the "Trafficking Victims Protection Act of 2000," and the "North Korean Human Rights Act of 2004," all three of which became public law.

The Religion News Service article quotes Land's letter to the acting chairman of his commission as writing that he has no intention of retiring as a culture warrior: "*I believe the 'culture war' is a titanic spiritual struggle for our nation's soul and as a minister of Christ's Gospel, I have no right to retire from that struggle*"[13] (emphasis added).

What a forceful example for LCMS leaders to carefully study as they consider their responsibility to speak out at a time when our country is facing a moral crisis and to establish a LCMS entity in Washington to give our church body a presence in the Nation's Capital. God has definitely blessed the efforts of the increasing number of pro-life organizations such as ERLC headed up by Land. Similar Roman Catholic and Evangelical organizations (Focus on the Family, for example)—added to the well-known pro-life groups, National Right to Life, Americans United for Life, and the Susan B. Anthony List—not only have driven the debate, but they have changed the attitudes of the American people.

The initial problem was that when *Roe v. Wade* was decided in 1973, those dedicated to having government-sanctioned abortions available on demand were well organized. On the other side, those who believed that innocent God-given life should be protected were not prepared for this struggle. We were always in the majority, but we were not organized. The abortion advocates astutely framed the debate in "pro-choice" terms rather than being "pro-abortion." They insisted that making abortions readily available was a women's health issue. At the time, there was no united voice of Christians to explain that pregnancy was not a disease but was God's divinely instituted order of procreation.

It should not be the least bit surprising that when polling firms, such as Gallup and Pew, started surveying the issue with the question, "Do you consider yourself 'pro-choice' or 'pro-life'?" those choosing "pro-choice" were always in a consistent majority. That people should have a choice sounds very American. It is likely that even in the early days, if the choice would have been framed as "pro-life" or "pro-abortion," the results would have been significantly different.

When Bible-believing Christians belatedly organized their efforts to protect the lives of the unborn, public attitudes began to change dramatically. (As previously noted, the government-relations wing of the Southern Baptist Convention was firmly in "pro-choice" hands until Land took control in 1988.) Pew survey results revealed for the first time in 2010 that a plurality of respondents expressed a "pro-life" choice. This response was in the majority by 2011. Recent polling by the prestigious Pew firm, which has done by far the most polling on this issue, consistently indicates that a clear majority of Americans now consider themselves "pro-life."

On Nov. 7, 2011, Fred Barnes, the respected editor of the *Weekly Standard,* published an article giving some compelling reasons why the pro-life movement is on the ascendancy. In the article, "Hidden Persuaders: The unheralded gains of the pro-life movement," Barnes points out that the mainstream media have missed "the resurgence of the pro-life crusade." Barnes contends that constantly improving science has enabled "pro-lifers" to capture "the high moral ground, chiefly thanks to advances in the quality of sonograms. Once fuzzy, sonograms now provide a high-resolution picture of the unborn child in the womb. Fetuses have become babies."[14]

Barnes instructively writes: "In 2011 alone, 24 states have enacted 52 new restrictions on abortion." He explains that most of this resulted from the fact that "Republicans gained control of 26 [state] legislatures in the 2010 election."[15]

Protecting traditional moral values under attack by the secularists should never have become a partisan political issue. It certainly was not a partisan (now wedge) issue when the secularists began the Culture Wars. There were as many conservative Christian Democrats as conservative Christian Republicans ready to take up arms when these secularists began to wage their battle on many different fronts. When the conservative Southern Democrats controlled the Congress, they had their battles with liberal Democrats as well as the liberals in the Republican ranks. For many years, the Congress tended to govern more along ideological than partisan lines.

Once again Dr. Land places abortion, same-sex marriage, and other issues in the Culture War in partisan perspective. In *The Washington Post* interview, "God's lobbyist" says "I don't endorse candidates.... If abortion has become partisan, shame on Democrats, not me. If traditional marriage has become partisan, shame on Democrats, not shame on me. I'm taking [a] stand for what I think the Bible teaches." He would then make a statement that I believe reflects his prophetic responsibility as a minister of the Gospel: "And the struggle for marriage. I do not think God blesses nations that redefine his institutions. As a Christian, I believe marriage is a divine institution. It's what Jesus said. There's a difference between equal rights and redefining marriage."[16]

By the time the two parties had their national conventions prior to the 1992 election, the issues being fought in the Culture Wars were dividing America almost completely along partisan lines. The popular Democrat Governor Bob Casey of Pennsylvania was denied the opportunity to address the Democrat National Convention at Madison Square Garden for one single reason: he was passionately committed to protecting the lives of unborn babies. Governor Casey sought to speak on behalf of the millions of Democrats he believed to be pro life. Their voices were denied the right to be heard.

A few weeks later, at the Republican National Convention, Pat Buchanan, who had been a candidate in the Republican presidential primary, delivered these remarks at the convention. Appealing to the 3 million voters that cast ballots for him in the primary, Pat said that we stand with President Bush

> "for freedom to choose religious schools, and we stand with him against the amoral idea that gay and lesbian couples should have the same standing in law as married men and women.
>
> "We stand with President Bush for right-to-life, and for voluntary prayer in public schools, and against putting American women in combat. And we stand with President Bush in favor of the right of small towns and communities to control the raw sewage of pornography that pollutes our popular culture.
>
> "My friends, this election is about much more than who gets what. It is about who we are. It is about what we believe. It is about what we stand for as Americans. There is a religious war going on in our country for the soul of America. It is a cultural war, as critical to the kind of nation we will one day be as was the Cold War itself."[17]

Twenty years later, such threats certainly have not disappeared. They have simply grown much more urgent and much more dangerous. The partisan divide has become a chasm in almost all areas. This partisan divide has been most visible as matters relating to fiscal policy have most recently dominated public debate. The frequently stark differences on moral and social policies held by the two parties are emotionally charged. Campaign rhetoric intended to fire up certain groups as elections approach often demonstrate just how strong the disagreements are on these issues. Until fairly recently, the differences on defense and foreign policy between the two parties had been less pronounced.

Virtually everyone who follows politics closely would agree that the Democrat members of the House and Senate are more liberal than at any time in their history. Likewise there would be little disagreement that their Republican counterparts are more conservative than at any time in their history. But this tells only part of the story. Most honest political analysts also would agree that *traditional* liberal Democrats are no longer the majority in their House and Senate congressional caucuses. The Democrat majority in both bodies of Congress is more accurately described as the hard left. The hard left, by its proponents' own statements analyzed earlier in this book, rejects our free enterprise economic system and believes that the federal government must have a massive role in our economy in order to more equitably distribute the nation's wealth. They categorically deny transcendent moral values and are hard-core foreign policy isolationists.

On the other hand, some liberal political pundits and politicians make the preposterous claim that the Republican congressional caucuses are controlled by the hard right. This is a politically charged outright falsehood. Based on a personal relationship with most Republican congressmen and senators, and having carefully followed the voting patterns and statements of virtually all of them, I strongly contend that the vast majority of them are traditional conservatives. (A traditional conservative has come to mean a "Reagan conservative" in my vocabulary.) Of the 47 sitting Republican senators, only four or five could be called "hard right" on some issues while five or six could be described as "moderates" or "moderate liberals." This means that at least 36 or 37 Republicans in the Senate are very consistent "Reagan conservatives."

Of the 240 Republicans currently serving in the U.S. House of Representatives, roughly 180 to 190 deserve of the title "Reagan conservative" on most occasions. Probably 10 would be better identified as "moderates" and 30 to 35 show signs of being "hard right" or "hard left," depending on the issue. (Three House Republicans are such hard-core libertarians that they have refused to endorse Mitt Romney for president.)

The Republicans do have an ideological problem but it is not nearly as serious as the one facing the Democrats. Libertarians in the Republican ranks have been discussed several times in this book because they represent a unique threat that most fail to understand. Based on a careful study, there are unquestionably more libertarians among the Republicans in the House than any previous Congress I have analyzed. This is the case because there are more total Republicans in this Congress. There may well have been as many or more on a percentage basis in the past. In any case, libertarians have never been large in numbers, but the influence they exert is always out of proportion to their numbers. As would be expected, they have infiltrated the "Tea Party" movement to the degree that they can drive the debate on many issues.

For the sake of emphasis, I note again that libertarians are "hard right" on fiscal matters since they don't really believe in government and the smaller its role the better. They have never minded being in the minority since they don't want to govern. They just want to stop as many programs as possible. (Conservatives share most of their concerns about big government, excessive government regulations, and high taxes. But conservatives realize that government also serves a necessary function in many areas. Conservatives also understand that when you are in the majority, you must govern. Otherwise you will not be in the majority after the next election.)

On the other hand, libertarians are "hard left" on most social and moral issues. They believe government has no right to control the behavior of its citizens as long they do not physically harm another person. They consider themselves to be civil libertarians, which sounds appealing and very American. But when taken to the extreme, it creates an amoral if not a totally immoral society. Such an obsession with protecting a person's privacy is dangerous when they would prevent our intelligence agencies from employing procedures to identify terrorists or potential terrorists. As foreign policy isolationists, libertarians are very hard left.

We conservative Lutherans may be late to the party. But when we get there we bring the right gifts: sound biblical theology, good judgment molded by the scrutiny of our peers, and a determination to finish a job we undertake. I want to note significant actions taken by the two most recent presidents of the LCMS. Their words and deeds indicate that they have resolved to awaken this "sleeping giant" to its God-given obligation to defend the moral foundation of this nation. Neither Dr. Jerry Kieschnick, the immediate past president of the LCMS, nor his successor, Dr. Matthew Harrison, has shown any hesitancy to climb onto the national stage when the moral foundations and religious freedoms of this nation were under siege.

Just one day after Barack Obama was inaugurated as the 44th president of the United States, Dr. Kieschnick, who had been elected three times as president of the LCMS, led a "Rally for Life" march to the U.S. Supreme Court. After the rally, this man, who was the leader of a respected but reserved church body with a membership of almost 2.5 million, preached a sermon on the sanctity of God-given life in a packed Lutheran church in Alexandria, Va. Jerry had been active in the right-to-life movement long before he was elected LCMS president. As president, Jerry had closely followed the 2008 presidential campaign and the statements made by the Democrat presidential candidate and vice presidential candidate concerning abortion. These had greatly alarmed him. Now that they had been elected, he feared that the innocent lives of unborn babies were at even greater risk than at any time in our history.

Dr. Kieschnick didn't miss much in the way of political threats to the moral foundation of this country. He called me just a week or so after the 2008 election to ask what I thought the chances were that the new Congress would pass the Freedom of Choice Act (commonly known as FOCA). Actually, I hadn't given this piece of legislation, a version of which was first introduced in 1989, much thought. Jerry proceeded to remind me that when presidential candidate Obama had addressed a Planned Parenthood gathering, he had told this audience, "The first thing I'd do as president, is sign the Freedom of Choice Act. That's the first thing that I'd do." (As I recall, he knew that this meeting had been held on July 9, 2008, and stretching an old memory, I seem to remember he also mentioned that Senator Obama cosponsored a Senate version of this bill.) In any event, he began to passionately explain to me that if this bill became law, Lutheran hospitals would have to provide an abortion to any woman seeking one or be forced to close their doors. In addition, a Lutheran doctor would either have to perform abortions against his or her religious beliefs or end their practice of medicine.

By this time in our conversation, my memory had kicked in and I remembered that this law would invalidate all state laws placing restrictions on late term and partial-birth abortions, parental notification, and all the rest. I can now reconstruct this conversation because I found a copy of a rather lengthy letter I had written to Jerry on Dec. 4, 2008, in response to his request. He had asked me to explore in depth the possibility of any such legislation being passed by Congress. He needed such information so our Lutheran hospitals and other medical facilities could begin to discuss how they would deal with such a crisis.

Knowing Dr. Kieschnick's desire for detailed information, I analyzed the voting records of pro-life Democrats in the House and the Senate to determine if it was possible for them to get enough Democrats for 218 votes in the House and 60 votes to break a filibuster in the Senate. I knew by heart the few Republicans we would lose in each body. My conclusion was that even with President Obama's persuasive powers, they could not put together enough votes to pass this legislation in either body of Congress. Everything I said in this letter proved to be totally accurate. However, I could not envision at the time how President Obama and his people would build into "Obamacare" a provision that would require all Christian doctors and nurses and Christian-run health-care facilities to participate in this procedure to kill millions of babies. I may have had suspicions, but I could not bring myself to believe that they would bypass the members of Congress elected to represent the will of the people with the U.S. Department of Health & Human Services (HHS) final rule!

As time consuming as they might be, I certainly never hesitated to undertake the assignments the president of my beloved LCMS asked me to carry out. (After all, I was not only a devout member of the church I so admired, but I was still an ordained minister of the Gospel. How could I possibly complain since I had persistently insisted that our church-body presidents bring the moral authority of the LCMS to bear on our country in the throes of a moral crisis? I didn't!) I should note, too, that Jerry had also been heavily involved in defending the divine institution of marriage, which was under attack by this administration, as will be further explained.

Just seven months after his election, Dr. Harrison agreed to become the first LCMS president to testify before a congressional committee. Sitting before the House Committee on Oversight and Government Reform Feb. 16, 2012, he delivered a statement and answered hostile as well as friendly questions in a strong defense of our cherished religious liberties. These were the very religious liberties that the Obama administration had just announced it was no longer going to respect.

These were valiant actions for leaders of a church body that had been bold in strongly defending the doctrinal teachings of Holy Scripture but reluctant to declare God's disapproval of this free government when it flagrantly violated the moral and religious principles on which this Nation was founded. I had known Jerry for almost 40 years. On my vicarage, I taught the Bible class he attended as a teenager at his home congregation. When he first visited D.C. after being elected president of the Synod, I knew he was a theological conservative and, therefore, a political conservative. I knew he was a man of courage and patriotism who would not shrink from speaking out in defense of his country when it was important. On the other hand, I had met Matt only on two occasions before we spent time together on his first trip to Washington as LCMS president. I knew from all I had heard that he, like Jerry, was also conservative theologically. I would soon learn that he, like Jerry, was also very politically conservative. It did not take long for me to conclude that he also, like Jerry, had the courage to stand up for his convictions.

As has been the case with LCMS presidents and other church leaders before them, they don't come to visit with me in D.C. to discuss Lutheran theology. Virtually everyone knows that I am a conservative, confessional Lutheran. They all had heard that one of my first questions would be "how do you intend to use the moral authority of our respected church body, known for its doctrinal orthodoxy, to defend the traditional values on which our country was founded?" Unfortunately, this question has been relevant and urgent since I first arrived on the front lines in the Nation's Capital. The cultural warfare against our country's moral and religious foundations led by the ACLU and their secular allies, both in and out of government, seem to become more intense with each passing day.

Thank God, more and more Christian leaders—lay and clergy—seem increasingly willing to enter the fray. Our foreign enemies change but never go away for long. I am thankful to God that our forefathers defeated fascism and Nazism among other "isms" long before I got involved in the political world. But communism and the Cold War dominated the foreign threats—of course infiltration of American society was always one of their weapons of choice—during most of my political life. Today, the threat of radical Islamist terrorism—employing the new tactics of massive suicide bombings along with the old tactics of infiltration and regional wars—has become arguably the most serious threat of all.

My contention is that it was the moral fiber of a free people that enabled America to succeed in our earlier conflicts. We need a renewed display of moral fiber today more than ever. When properly encouraged, the American people always respond. They need to be reminded by authorities they respect that a people who forsake their moral heritage are at great risk of losing their cherished freedoms.

The climate in the halls of government ebbs and flows with each election; some of the players change, but the pressing challenges always seem to be with us. From my beginning days with Jack Preus until now as I write these words, I have always sought to introduce every LCMS president and other church leader to as many senators and congressmen as possible. It takes desire, stamina, and a willingness to listen to many stories (it helps if the person enjoys a few glasses of wine, a sometimes drawn-out dinner, and maybe an occasional cigar) to get to know the number of government officials as I always have in mind. Virtually all such church leaders have either liked or submitted to my plan. It is with considerable pride that I can say without reservation that all of these leaders of my church have made very good impressions on these leaders of our government, many of whom are hard to impress.

Perhaps the most dramatic difference in the first visits of the two most recently elected presidents of the LCMS involved my longtime buddy (and hero) John Boehner. When I first introduced Jerry to Boehner, who was chairman of the House Committee on Education and the Workforce at the time, I told Jerry that I wanted him to meet the man whom I believed was destined to one day be the speaker of the U.S. House of Representatives. The circumstances had changed when I took Matt to meet John Boehner and proudly said, "Matt, I want you to meet the speaker of the U.S. House of Representatives, the third most powerful man in the free world."

Our Synod Presidents Are Moved to Act

In my preparation to write this chapter, I asked Jerry and Matt this question: "What motivated you to take such courageous actions as the head of a church body that has been so reluctant to enter the public square?" Their responses were so powerful that I intend to share a portion of them. It should be emphasized that by traditionally cautious LCMS standards the patriotic actions these men undertook were exceptionally bold!

It might be helpful to give a little background, based on what they told me, of how each of them became convinced that they *must* enter this struggle for the soul of our country.

I knew such a decision was a natural choice for Jerry. I clearly understood that Jerry had very conservative Lutheran training from the pastor with whom I served as a vicar. Pastor Bill Stratman minced no words in explaining orthodox Lutheran theology and citizenship responsibilities. (I had a few minor political disagreements with him as I had not yet read Barry Goldwater's *Conscience of a Conservative*. I was better prepared to understand this book having spent a year under Stratman's tutelage.) I also spent enough time in Texas to realize that most Texans believe in conservative government. (LBJ and a few other prominent Texas politicians would later prove that this trait was not shared by all Texans.)

Dr. Harrison was first required and then became a volunteer in the struggle to defend religious freedom in this country. Right from the onset of his presidency, Matt inherited a case that had begun and worked its way through the court system under the Kieschnick administration but was argued and decided by the Supreme Court after Harrison became LCMS president. This involved their roles in defending a Supreme Court case[18] brought by the Equal Employment Opportunity Commission (EEOC) on behalf of a disgruntled LCMS parochial school teacher who had been fired over a dispute with her superiors at the school. The question was whether a church entity has the right under the First Amendment to determine the qualifications of its duly called teachers and others involved in teaching religion courses, in addition to it ministers. The unanimous Supreme Court decision totally justified the LCMS' decision to fight for the religious freedom guaranteed in the First Amendment. However, the process had consumed much time and other resources that could have been better used to carry out the church's mission.

(The EEOC was established in LBJ's days with a reasonable sounding mandate to promote job opportunities for women and minorities. But as all too frequently happens, activists and crusaders soon dominated the commission. They became obsessed with quotas and other such considerations at the expense of legitimate job descriptions.)

Dr. Harrison was still upset with the wasting of the church's valuable time in this frivolous government action when he responded to my question about his willingness to invest so much effort in the fight for our religious liberties. He stated: "The Obama administration's EEOC had dragged us all the way to the Supreme Court in the Hosanna-Tabor case, only to lose a humiliating 9-0 decision in what *The New York Times* called the most significant religious freedoms case in decades. The Becket Fund took up our cause and carried the day."

It should be noted that this was not the LCMS' first confrontation over Equal Employment Opportunity regulations and religious freedom issues. Our first such battle involved Synod-owned radio station KFUO in St. Louis, a case that may have laid the groundwork for the landmark Supreme Court decision in the Hosanna-Tabor case.

In the case of KFUO, the Federal Communications Commission (FCC) contended that the radio station did not hire enough women and blacks or other minorities and that if this deficiency were not addressed, KFUO's broadcasting license could not be renewed. KFUO officials explained that the station would be happy to hire more women and minorities, but they would have to have the necessary theological backgrounds for the positions. KFUO was a part of the church's mission to proclaim the Gospel. As strange as it sounds, FCC officials contended that a Lutheran-operated radio station could not require its employees even to be Lutheran, much less have some basic understanding of Lutheran teachings. Such arrogance turned out to be a major asset in the ultimate positive decision concerning KFUO's hiring policies.

Dr. Paul Devantier, who was executive director of LCMS communications at the time, first contacted me sometime in 1994. Paul's timing was good as I was fairly confident that the Republicans were going to take control of the U.S. House and possibly the U.S. Senate. To place the case in perspective: in 1994, an FCC administrative law judge ruled that the Synod's radio station was not in compliance with the FCC's equal employment opportunity (EEO) requirements. The Missouri Synod appealed. In 1995 the FCC in a 3-2 decision upheld the judge's ruling.

Once again the battle lines were drawn. Paul and I launched what I would describe as a well organized and extensive lobbying effort. (Of course, it could not be described as lobbying since I was not paid as a lobbyist but was only a church member volunteering my time.) As I had suspected, the new Republican leadership in the House and the Senate, as well as the rank-and-file Republican members of both bodies of Congress, saw this as a blatant attack on religious liberties. In addition, most Democrats we visited were sympathetic to our concerns. As I began to spread the word, some other church bodies, especially the Roman Catholics and Mormons, who were heavily involved in radio and TV efforts, offered their help. They agreed to inform their church members in Congress. Congressman Charles Taylor, a Republican from North Carolina and a member of the powerful

Appropriations Committee that controlled the funding for all government agencies, took a special interest in our cause. He and his staff helped us draft the Religion Equality in Broadcasting Act.

Paul was also overseeing an expensive legal strategy of which the Marvin M. Schwan Charitable Foundation, under the direction of the Rev. Larry Burgdorf, provided the LCMS with some much-needed financial assistance. It is important to explain this undertaking to illustrate that The Lutheran Church—Missouri Synod has been willing to claim its citizenship responsibilities when our religious freedoms were at stake. KFUO was first charged with hiring violations when Dr. Ralph Bohlmann was president of the LCMS. The matter was not finally resolved until Dr. Alvin Barry had become president of the Synod.

There is another twist that relates to the purpose of this chapter. We had secured a comfortable majority of votes in the House and the Senate to pass our bill but the floor schedule was too packed to bring it up under regular order before Congress adjourned for the year in 1997. We had developed a plan to bring it up under unanimous consent on the final day of the session. There was going to be no objection on the House side. However, we had to get the Senate to agree, as they were adjourning a few hours before the House. Sen. Conrad Burns, a Missouri Synod Lutheran, was handling the bill in that chamber. He called me with an urgent message. A Democrat senator from South Carolina, who was an ELCA member, was refusing to allow the bill to pass by unanimous consent. Burns was prepared to refuse to allow the Senate to adjourn until a vote was held on the Religion Equality in Broadcasting Act. Some senators were already on the way to the airport, but he would call them back if I thought it was essential. I quickly called Paul and told him our dilemma. Paul told me he felt very confident that we were doing well in court and to thank Senator Burns profusely and tell him to let the senators go home.

This turned out to be a good decision (although I would have enjoyed seeing our bill signed into law after several years of hard work). On April 14, 1998, the United States Court of Appeals for the District of Columbia Circuit decided *Lutheran Church—Missouri Synod v. Federal Communications Commission and United States of America* in our church's favor. It was comforting to see my church win a major victory for religious freedom. I will always believe their decision was influenced to some degree by the knowledge that if they failed to do the right thing, the U.S. Congress would surely pass a law overturning their ruling.

Let's return to more recent history. As Matt was just settling in as the new LCMS president, the HHS issued regulations requiring all employers, religious or otherwise, that provide health insurance to provide birth control free of charge to their employees. All birth control measures, including the pill that destroys embryonic human life, must be provided to their female employees regardless of their marital status. HHS had issued an interim final rule in August 2011 that contained an exemption for non-profit religious organizations. But when they issued the final rule in January 2012, no such religious exemption was allowed. Organizations and individuals concerned about the lives of the unborn and the preservation of religious liberties, including the Roman Catholics, Evangelical groups, and pro-life members of Congress, were up in arms over such a blatant attack on religious freedom. As these groups began to mobilize for action, Dr. Harrison, who had gotten to know the speaker and many members of the House and Senate, was approached about joining these efforts. Congressman Darrell Issa, chairman of the House Oversight and Government Reform Committee, asked Dr. Harrison if he would be willing to testify before his committee on the threat to religious liberty entailed in the HHS rule. Thus, as noted, Matt Harrison would become the first LCMS president to testify before a congressional committee. That took some courage.

"On the plane to D.C. in February 2012, I carefully read HHS regulations requiring religious providers to supply contraceptives. I'd been asked to testify before the House Committee on Government Oversight and had hastily booked the flight, dropping everything in an otherwise overbooked schedule," Matt recounts. He explained to me that reading this material made it clear that "HHS and the Obama administration operate with an interpretation of the First Amendment far different from what the words themselves state. The administration, in the HHS mandates, has defined the 'free exercise' clause in terms of freedom of assembly, not the ability to operate institutions according to the dictates of one's faith and confession. It angers me that my own government is forcing the health plan of my own church body to operate under a 'grandfather clause' which severely limits our ability and flexibility into the future to serve our people."

Digesting this material obviously stirred up Matt's emotions and reminded him of the sacrifices our forefathers had made to preserve these religious liberties for future generations. His emotions became personal when he said, "Is this what my ancestors fought for? Is this why my grandfather drove his brother-in-law to the Sioux City Airport to send him off to service in the Air Force in WWII, never to return? Is this why my father-in-law fought in Europe, why he was plagued with nightmares for decades?"

Matt had a political baptism by fire when he was thrust into the hostile environment of a partisan congressional hearing (an unfamiliar setting for a minister of Christ's Gospel). He explained, "The House Oversight hearing resulted in a fiasco of spin. I was appalled as one liberal lawmaker after another stepped into the hearing room only to deliver a talking point, a potential media zinger, only to leave immediately and get another memo for the next attack. The flood of misdirection and misinformation [in efforts] to turn the event into an alleged attack on women appalled and still appalls me to the depth of my being." Then he made an unequivocal statement that I have been waiting a long time to hear a LCMS president utter: "I will never sit silent again in the face of attacks on the first amendment rights of all people, especially in this case, the rights specifically guaranteed to religious people by the Bill of Rights. We have MIAs in the [Christian] family. I and The Lutheran Church—Missouri Synod will not be MIA from the public square."

Matt Harrison is now all in as a "cultural warrior" in the struggle for the soul of this nation founded on solid Judeo-Christian principles. I firmly believe that God's powerful hand was involved. It was no accident that he experienced firsthand as a witness in the congressional hearing the devious tactics of those intent on destroying the moral and religious principles of this great nation. It was no accident that the LCMS had recently won two of the most important cases involving religious freedom in modern times. And it certainly was no accident he was able to build on the examples set by his predecessor, Jerry Kieschnick. Having experienced Matt's personality and witnessed his strongly held opinions, I am not suggesting that he would have hesitated to enter the struggle if no such background was in place. But such background certainly made his efforts easier and more likely to succeed. Dr. Walter Maier's mantle has once again been passed.

Dr. Kieschnick's efforts to defend God's institution of marriage were in evidence during the entire nine years he served as president of the LCMS. He frequently quoted the resolution passed at the 2004 LCMS convention that affirmed "on the basis of Scripture, marriage as the lifelong union of one man and one woman." In 2005, he commended the Evangelical Lutheran Church in Kenya, with whom the 2004 convention had approved altar-and-pulpit fellowship, for criticizing "same-sex blessings" recently approved by the Church of Sweden. Jerry joined 42 other U.S. church leaders in signing an open letter calling for an amendment to the U.S. Constitution defining marriage as the union of one man and one woman.

Jerry's decision to become actively involved in supporting the 2008 ballot initiatives in the states of California, Florida, and Arizona so defining traditional marriage was not surprising. The fact that he found time in his busy schedule to travel to these three states, hold press conferences, and send letters to the LCMS pastors in these states to urge support for traditional marriage was impressive. In a national press conference, which was teleconferenced into California, Florida, and Arizona, Dr Kieschnick on Oct. 22, 2008, emphasized the depth of his convictions. In an opening statement he said:

> "In less than two weeks, the American people will face a highly significant battle. United States citizens will have the opportunity to make a statement about traditional marriage that will affect the course of our nation for generations to come. In the states of Arizona, California, and Florida, marriage protection amendments are on the ballot. In these three states, The Lutheran Church—Missouri Synod, based upon our deeply held principles, will do all we can to help

protect marriage as a divinely created relationship between one man and one woman.

"As one of the largest U.S. Christian church bodies, with 2.4 million members nationwide and more than 212,000 in Arizona, California, and Florida combined, we urge our members in those states and Christians across the nation to educate themselves on the marriage issue in the short time before the election. We must protect marriage between one man and one woman for the sake of our society as we know it and as humanity has always known it. Voter participation on November 4 will be absolutely necessary and part of the responsibility to our nation that we bear as Christian citizens. It is the exercise of this duty, privilege, and honor that helps make our country great."

I asked Jerry what had motivated him to get so active and involved in the ballot initiatives regarding same sex marriage and to call our church to arms over this issue. His first response was very insightful:

"My awareness that since the beginning of history, virtually every known human society has understood marriage as a union of one man and one woman. Even religious groups differentiated and divided by disagreement on numerous foundational religious beliefs recognize the universality of marriage as it was ordained by God at the beginning of time. Incredibly, even in a country founded largely on traditional Judeo-Christian principles and values, this traditional understanding of marriage is being challenged and changed before our very eyes. I cannot simply stand by and watch the deterioration and destruction of this fundamental building block of human society."

This answer by Jerry included all of the most important reasons that all Christians *must* defend traditional marriage if they are to be true to their Creator.

In the first place, Holy Scripture, both in the Old and New Testament, clearly records God's establishment of marriage as a divine institution with the purpose of propagating the world. In the account of God's creation of the world, God specifically explains the purpose and order of His creation. After creating Adam, God determined that it was not good for man to be alone and determined to create a wife for him. Then in the last verse of the story of creation, God explains why He created woman for the man. "Therefore shall a man leave his father and his mother, and shall cleave unto his wife and they shall be one flesh" (Gen. 2:24). In an answer to the Pharisees' question about divorce, Jesus quotes this verse to explain the divine origin of marriage.[19]

Second, as a part of God's order of creation, it was clearly evident in the laws of nature.

Third, this fact is so evident in the laws of nature that every known civilization has so defined marriage. A number of civilizations have allowed a man to marry more than one wife (some many more) and a few have even allowed a woman to be married to more than one man. But until the modern-day rebellion against God and nature, no civilization ever defined marriage in homosexual terms.

The Old Testament states God's disapproval of homosexual activities so emphatically that it is totally unnecessary to recite the many references for anyone who has ever read the Old Testament. The New Testament also contains many references to the subject but it should suffice to note that in the first chapter of Romans, St. Paul describes such homosexual conduct as a rebellion against God and the laws of nature established by God. To contend that our founding documents, so carefully drafted, debated, and adopted by our Founders, carved out some type of special exemption in the name of civil rights based on sexual preference is sophistry at its worst. All a judge, or reader of this book, needs to do is pull up the Internet and search for any Founder's attitudes toward homosexual behavior. Start with Jefferson, who actually drafted a bill on the subject, and proceed to Washington who was called upon to deal with such behavior on at least one occasion as commander of the army during the Revolution. I have discovered no Founder, including Thomas Paine and Ethan Allen, who condoned homosexual behavior.

In a statement condemning the June 24, 2008, California Supreme Court decision to overturn the existing ban on same-sex marriage, Dr. Kieschnick emphasized that as Christians, we should deal with homosexuals in the spirit of Christian love in the same way we do with all sinners. Christ died for all sins and offers forgiveness for any and all sins that a repentant sinner confesses. As Americans we should also strive to insure that homosexuals, as well as any other self-defined group, enjoy the same rights and privileges afforded to all American citizens. But to create a special civil-rights exemption for homosexuals, or any other such group of people, by redefining our 225-year-old definition of traditional marriage is an affront not only to God's divine institution of marriage but to the traditions and laws established by our wise Founders.

Dr. Kieschnick's final answer to my question as to why he was willing to take such strong action in defense of traditional marriage put the issue in perspective and contains a valid warning:

> "My support for a constitutional amendment clearly defining marriage as the unique relationship between one man and one woman [is] based on the regrettable but unavoidable conclusion that the institution of marriage, the foundational cornerstone for our society, is in the process of being destroyed by extremists and radical activists in the media and by America's judicial system. We simply cannot remain silent in the face of highly motivated but wrong-headed individuals and organizations who are successfully endeavoring to redefine marriage for the entire country."

Jerry then signed off on this personal note: "My belief [is] that Edmund Burke was correct in saying that the only thing necessary for evil to triumph is for good men to do nothing!"

This leads to why I have spent a major portion of my time over the last few years to prepare this book as a resource for Lutheran pastors and lay people. (I hope it also will be of value to other Christians, as well as to other concerned citizens who profess another religion or may not be very religious at all.) It is long overdue for Missouri Synod Lutheran leaders at all levels, certainly including parish pastors, as well as members of our 6,150 congregations all over this free country, to become actively and *regularly* involved in the struggle to preserve the moral and religious soul of this great country so richly blessed by God. How can we continue to proclaim the Gospel in all its truth and purity if our Constitutional guarantees to adhere to our religious beliefs as American citizens are threatened?

The LCMS urgently needs to have a strong and well-established presence in the Nation's Capital to adequately fulfill its God-given responsibilities in this free country in which we are so privileged to live. As our Lord Jesus said, "[T]o whom much is given, from him much will be required" (Luke 12:48, NKJV).

Our country needs the moral influence of such a large church body totally committed to the teachings of Holy Scripture in this time of moral crisis. Our people must be informed and motivated to actively accept their desperately needed citizenship responsibilities. Our children and their children are depending on us to do our part to defend their future. Many of our forefathers came to this country under difficult circumstances to seek freedom and refuge in a nation that recognized the authority of God Almighty and the rights with which He had endowed His creatures. Dr. Harrison reminded us all of our LCMS heritage while testifying before the House Oversight Committee, expressing our Church's urgent concern over the HHS ruling denying our religious liberties in these words:

> "Our Church's history is rooted in religious liberty. Our Lutheran forefathers left Europe seeking religious freedom in America, and since their arrival in 1837, Missouri Synod Lutherans have rigorously guarded their beliefs and practices. We are unconditionally committed to preserving the essential teachings of our faith, to guard our religious rights, and to act as conscience dictates as informed by faith.
>
> "The recent federal mandate has prompted our church to voice public concern about federal intervention into religious beliefs and practices. Specifically, we object to the use of drugs and procedures used to take the lives of unborn children. We oppose this mandate since it requires religious organizations to pay for and otherwise facilitate the use of such drugs by their employees—a requirement that violates our stand on the biblical teaching of the sanctity of life, which is a matter of faith and conscience.

"Furthermore, we believe and teach that freedom of religion extends beyond mere houses of worship. We must be able to exercise our faith in the Public Square and, in response to Christ's call, demonstrate His mercy through our love and compassion for all people according to the clear teachings of Holy Scripture."

Such authoritative LCMS voices must be forcefully heard because Jesus Himself commanded His followers to accept their citizenship responsibilities by "rendering unto Caesar the things that are Caesar's." In addition, our voices must be clear and biblically based because of the confusion created by the majority of the "mainline" denominational leaders about what the Bible actually teaches on such questions as the defense of life and homosexuality.

The need for high-profile LCMS involvement takes on additional urgency since the larger Lutheran body, the Evangelical Lutheran Church in America (ELCA), has chosen to side with the liberal mainline denominations on such issues. This has created the impression that *all* Lutherans have abandoned the biblical teachings that God gives precious life and has established the divine institution of marriage. The former Lutheran Church in America and The American Lutheran Church had government relations during the initial years of my tenure in Washington. After they merged as the ELCA, they established the Lutheran Office of Governmental Affairs (LOGA), now known simply as the ELCA Washington Office.

(It has been a long and sometimes lonely battle as the sole voice explaining to congressmen and senators, staff members, government officials, and anybody else who would listen that the liberal Lutheran lobbying organizations spoke for only a significant minority of Lutherans in America. They certainly did not speak for LCMS and WELS members. In addition they spoke only for a decided minority of their own members, most of whom were still Bible-believing Christians. Surveys and anecdotal evidence clearly establish this latter point. Virtually all Lutheran congressmen who belonged to the LCA and ALC and who are all now members of the ELCA and have been elected as Republicans, have been and are still pro-life and pro-traditional marriage. Many of their Democrat counterparts also were pro-life and pro-family and traditional marriage. It was always a breath of fresh air when I had an LCMS dignitary at my side to forcefully help establish my claims.)

The LCMS made a serious effort to inform our clergy and laity of activities in Washington that threatened our religious liberties and beliefs when our Synod operated the Office of Government Information (OGI) in the Nation's Capital. This organization, which existed during the Bohlmann and Barry administrations, had no mandate to bring to bear the moral authority of the LCMS on government policy. OGI did enable these two presidents to meet some of the Lutheran MCs where they could explain our church's positions on moral issues. But they were careful to never give the appearance that they might be lobbying.

As the moral crisis facing our government continued to grow worse over the years, Jerry Kieschnick and then later Matt Harrison decided that our church could not stand on the sidelines and watch the moral foundations of our great nation crumble before their very eyes.

After numerous conversations with Jerry, I asked Tim Goeglein to put together a proposal for an LCMS presence in Washington. (Tim is a Missouri Synod Lutheran, former White House staffer, and currently vice president, external relations, for Focus on the Family.) In August 2008, Tim gave us a proposal he had tentatively titled "The Lutheran Institute for Cultural Affairs."

In our many conversations, we had stressed the fact that our church must avoid the morass of getting into issues that are clearly in Caesar's domain. We should deal primarily with moral issues facing our government that are clearly addressed in Holy Scripture. Obviously, the two most important such issues are our God-given obligations to respect and protect human life and to promote and protect God's divine institution of marriage and family. We also emphasized the need for our church leaders and members to speak out on and defend the transcendent moral values of human behavior following the powerful examples of our Founding Fathers. We agreed with President John Adams that our Constitution "was only suited for a moral and religious people." Our government must continue to pass and enforce laws that control immoral behavior since our country, like all others, will always be a nation of sinners until the second coming of our Lord and Savior.

We decided early on to include in our conversations the presidents of our two LCMS seminaries, Dr. Dale Meyer of St. Louis and Dr. Dean Wenthe of Fort Wayne. They both were enthusiastic about the concept. I spent much time putting together a conference call with Jerry, Tim, Dean, Dale, and me, which was not easy. Then what I consider the defining moment occurred. I found out that two of them were coming to Washington on some business, and I talked the other one into making the trip and joining us for a long dinner. I prepared an agenda and a six-page memo to myself. When you get three such powerful and smart men together, you had better be prepared to take notes and answer their questions.

After pleasantries and a few glasses of good wine, I laid the foundation for our discussion. "Gentlemen," I began, "our country is facing a spiritual crisis of greater magnitude that at any time in our history. Our country desperately needs your help! If men of your character and stature fail to answer your country's call, we are in serious danger of losing our Godly heritage." (I can roughly remember my words since I still have my notes. As they started to respond, I asked them first to let me finish my prepared statement before taking their comments and questions.)

I continued to explain that the crisis we are experiencing today is almost eerily similar to the one experienced by our nation's Founders. Then, as now, the overwhelming number of people living in America claimed to be Christians. Most of them even said that they went to church when they could—often difficult in those frontier days. But even if they still retained their faith, they were no longer practicing their Christianity as they should. Moral behavior was at a low level, and therefore the ability to establish a moral and stable government was in serious question. God sent the First and then the Second Great Awakening. As those struggling settlers were called back to their Christian faith, they were much more willing to accept their God-given citizenship responsibilities. God's intervention enabled these mostly ragtag farmers to defeat the most powerful army in the world and then to establish the freest government ever known to mankind. This happened because God in His providence sent them great preachers and wise political leaders—in many, if not most, cases they were one and the same.

Today, 85 percent of the American people identify themselves as Christians. An amazing 50 percent of those say they attend church regularly, and another 30 percent say they attend occasionally. But we are facing a moral crisis every bit as serious as the one faced in our early founding period. More than half of all marriages end in divorce, which creates problems for children being raised by a single parent; sexual immorality has become the norm, not the exception; vulgar pornography fills our TV screens and is easily accessible to our children; drug use and abuse is rampant; millions of unborn babies are facing the abortion knife; and homosexual activists have launched the most organized campaign to undermine traditional marriage and the traditional family this country has ever seen.

I further explained that polling results indicate that more Americans still consider themselves to be "pro choice" than "pro life," but their numbers are dropping and ours are rising. The margin of difference is now very narrow. Then I pointed out that this change in attitude has come as a result of the efforts of Bible-believing Christians who were now fully engaged in the debate. Once the American people would fully understand that abortions kill babies, they tended to choose life. (This prediction has now come true as a *majority* of Americans now describe themselves as "pro life.")

On the other hand, the trend concerning homosexual marriage is moving in the other direction due to the relentless barrage of misinformation being spread by the homosexual campaigns. I said that this is why Jerry has taken the bold step of making our church's voice heard in California, Florida, and Arizona. The once-overwhelming majority of Americans who opposed same-sex marriage—as well as any other special rights and privileges for homosexuals—is shrinking because people like us have not done enough to make known what the Bible emphatically teaches on this subject.

Had it not been for the efforts of Jerry and other Christian leaders like him, including many black church leaders, the constitutional amendment (Proposition 8) might not have passed in California. In liberal California in 2000, Prop 23 defining marriage as between one man and one woman passed with almost 62 percent of the vote. By 2008, Prop 8, the amendment to the California constitution establishing traditional marriage as the law of the state, passed with only 52 percent of the vote. Passing this amendment was made possible by an overwhelming "yes" vote by black voters and by a majority of Hispanic votes, in addition to the votes turned out by Christian church leaders such as Jerry Kieschnick.

I reminded the group that Americans had been so steeped in the biblical teachings and the Founders' attitude toward homosexuality that it had been only five years since the last state sodomy law (in Texas) had been ruled unconstitutional by the Supreme Court. We certainly must not get into any discussion of sodomy laws, but we must condemn homosexual sins as well as any other sexual sins. We must motivate our people to actively work to defend our God-given divine institution of marriage and the traditional family.

(There is some recent good news from what many would consider to be an unlikely source. The United Methodist Church, whose clergy is considered to be far more liberal than its membership, refused in its 2012 General Conference to change its policy on homosexuality. Daniel Burke, writing for Religion News Service, wrote May 3, 2012: "Despite emotional protests and fierce lobbying from gay rights groups, United Methodists voted on Thursday [May 2] to maintain their denomination's stance that the practice of homosexuality is "incompatible with Christian teaching."[20]   On May 7, *The Washington Post* carried a story by Burke explaining that the leadership of the United Methodists, who have 8 million U.S. members, canceled additional votes on changing their policies on same-sex marriage, including clerical blessings and gay clergy.[21] This happened after two "agree to disagree" proposals also were soundly defeated. The United Methodist Church had been a reliable partner with other liberal protestant denominations in promoting the social gospel rather than defending biblical teachings on moral issues. Some Methodist pastors and a majority of the laypeople at the conference rose up and said enough is enough.)

By the time I had finished my filibuster, as one attendant characterized my "speech," the question became, "What shall we do?" As the questions and suggestions began to flow, there was no doubt that I had the right men in the room. These three church leaders not only understood biblical theology, they also had a clear understanding of Luther's two-kingdom theology. In addition, they had a grasp of the moral threats facing our country (and might have shuffled a little in their seats while I was recounting them). Most importantly, they understood the responsibility our church has and the contribution we could make in this struggle—and the courage to say, "Let's come up with a plan."

We all agreed that our beloved Missouri Synod must bring its considerable moral authority to bear (in a prophetic role) on the moral crisis our country was facing. Those at the meeting also understood clearly that we must educate and motivate our pastors and laypeople to enter this Culture War for the soul of our country.

The next morning I called Tim Goeglein, who unfortunately had to miss the dinner due to a scheduling conflict, and informed him that all signs were go and would he please draft a plan as rapidly as his schedule permitted. Tim was able to take into consideration the suggestions offered by Jerry, Dean, Dale, and me and include them in a skillfully written and very informative document.

I should explain why such an organization as proposed in Tim's document has not been established in the intervening four years. The honest answer is simple and familiar in church circles: money! A number of things were more urgent at this time in Jerry's presidency.

In our first discussion about establishing a LCMS presence in the Nation's Capital, Tim and I agreed on certain basic guidelines. First, it had to be done carefully and precisely after due deliberation. We must adopt a clear mission and make sure we have the resources to retain the necessary professional personnel and adequate operational facilities. This could not be a shoestring undertaking. We must not try and fail. If we had to worry about paying the rent, we were doomed from the start. Second, this must be a Recognized Service Organization (an organization officially recognized by the Missouri Synod as serving its mission, but not operated by the Synod) that would not have to deal with a changing synodical bureaucracy. It must be run by a board of directors that must include the president of the Synod, the presidents of the two seminaries, and other carefully selected members. Decisions to produce documents and press releases when responding to government issues and actions must be timely. The organization must have the authority, granted by its board of directors, to produce and distribute the information necessary to inform and motivate our pastors and laypeople. In an ideal world, we needed to find a Missouri Synod layman—or two or three such laymen—with the interest and means to underwrite the operation for a reasonable period of time. Hopefully, after the organization had been successfully operating for a number of years, it might become self sufficient.

Jerry gave significant consideration to how he might be able to find the financial support we needed. But he already had so many fundraising responsibilities on his plate that he felt an obligation to set his priorities. Had he remained in office for a longer period of time, this would have remained on his "must-do" list.

On Matt Harrison's first visit to my office after assuming the Synod presidency, this proposal was at the top of my list for items to be discussed. After I explained the concept and need for such an LCMS presence in D.C., I handed him a copy of the proposal for "The Lutheran Institute for Cultural Affairs" prepared by Tim. Just as I placed the document in his hands, I received a call from a client that I had to take. Since the call lasted for 15 or 20 minutes, Matt had had time to read and think about the proposal by the time I returned to the office. He proved to be a difficult sell when I asked him what he thought of our idea—he said, "Let's do it!"

Our church leaders are not the only ones given such citizenship responsibilities. These mandates are equally pressing on our laypeople as Christian citizens. Vital information must be provided to our parish pastors to share with their flocks concerning duties as Christian citizens. If Christian citizens are unwilling to become involved in the political process, this clears the field for those who do not share our moral values to mold and run our government. This, of course, would make our Founders' worse nightmares come true.

Our vision for an LCMS office in Washington would fill a major void in fulfillment of the Missouri Synod's responsibilities to our free government. Our church body has a God-given prophetic obligation to speak out on clear moral issues and actions that in any way threaten our religious liberties. This might involve everything from an urgent letter to the American president and key members of Congress to having the LCMS president or his designee hold a press conference to address our concerns. President Harrison has already established a responsible precedent by testifying before a congressional committee when our religious liberties were being threatened by the present administration. Scholarly documents also might be produced in an effort to share our mainline church's position on moral matters clearly addressed in Holy Scripture. Such documents, press releases, or public statements, could also address our God-given liberties in matters relating to religion and morality bequeathed to us by our Founders.

Tim Goeglein offers the purpose of this organization in these elegant words:

> "Its mission will be to speak out on the most pressing social and cultural issues of our time, but the emphasis will be on issues that are distinctly rooted in Scripture. The Institute will be a decidedly activist think tank working to build a solid track record of transforming ideas into action through policy research, a regular presence on the Washington policy scene, and strategic communications. *The goal is to inject a distinctly Lutheran voice and view into Washington's bloodstream*" (emphasis added).

In addition, such a Lutheran office would have a major responsibility to provide timely and pertinent information relating to government actions, or pending actions, to our pastors and laypeople. When the secular cultural warriors are waging an all-out battle to destroy the moral and spiritual foundations of our country, information intended to emphasize our Lutheran citizenship obligations is especially crucial. Our people must be led to understand that this is a struggle to preserve a moral society founded on Judeo-Christians principles as opposed to a Godless secular society devoid of any transcendent moral values. Our people must understand that the outcome of this war will determine the fate of our moral heritage.

An LCMS institution would present a much-needed alternative moral voice to counter the loud voices of the ELCA Washington Office and the offices of other liberal Protestant denominations who almost exclusively devote their efforts in lobbying for the liberal goals of the social gospel. Such an LCMS organization will offer valuable reinforcement for the valiant efforts of the Southern Baptists, the Roman Catholics, and the multitude of Evangelical organizations fighting the good fight to defend our country's moral values and our religious freedoms.

Once again Tim finds the elegant words to explain the course this Institute or any other named LCMS presence in Washington should follow:

> "The fairly radical revolution of our values calls for a principled and confident counter-argument. The tempo, tone, and public persona of the Institute will be diplomatic and civil at all times. It is on a mission in the public square, but its mission is not to 'change' the country or the world. It will put Christ at the center and boldly defend the necessity and importance of faith, family, and freedom to the healthy way of life for Christians privileged to live free in America."

I certainly did not write this lengthy book, which involved several years of research, simply to promote the establishment of a truly needed LCMS presence in the Nation's Capital. Rather, I felt the urgency to serve as a one-man army to make available to our Lutheran pastors, laypeople, and other interested Christians vital information about the two wars we dare not lose—and we are in real danger of losing at the present time.

May God bless the United States of America and all those willing to fight in her defense.

Notes

[1] I realize that some people believe this quote attributed to Billy Graham to be nothing more than "urban legend" because it has not been documented in any of his writings. I believe he said it, however, because of a conversation I had with Dr. Graham in 1971. I had heard that he had made this comment about the Missouri Synod. I told him that I thought it accurately characterized us. I do not remember his precise response, but I do know that he in no way disputed that he had made the comment. Jeffrey Walz and Steven Montreal included Dr. Graham's comment in the Introduction of their book *Lutheran Pastors and Politics: Issues in the Public Square* (Concordia Publishing House, 2007). These two political scientists at Concordia University Wisconsin report the findings of the most scientific and largest survey of Missouri Synod pastors ever on topics relating to political, social, and moral issues. They selected 1,500 pastors based specific demographic and other polling considerations. They calculated that if they received 400 responses this would assure that the survey would be 95 percent accurate. When they received more than 650 responses, they were confident that this would be highly accurate. This information is very valuable for our purposes here.

[2] Walz and Montreal, 25.

[3] Walz and Montreal, 39.

[4] Walz and Montreal, 40. It should be remembered that Luther obviously had no experience living in a country ruled by a free people. His most vivid memories would be of living under a ruler who provided him with protection.

[5] James Hutson, *Forgotten Features of the Founding: The Recovery of Religious Themes in the Early American Republic*, (Lexington Books, 2003), ix. As documented earlier in this book, members of non-Christian religions were statistically insignificant at this time in America's history.

[6] Walz and Montreal, 60.

[7] Walz and Montreal, 60.

[8] Walz and Montreal, 61.

[9] Adelle Banks, "Southern Baptist leader Richard Land to retire after ethics probe," *Religion News Service*, Aug. 1, 2012. Accessed Sept. 13, 2012, at http://www.religionnews.com/faith/leaders-and-institutions/Southern-Baptist-leader-Richard-Land-to-retire-after-ethics-probe.

[10] Michelle Boorstein, "Richard Land: A Southern Baptist warrior bids goodbye to Washington", *The Washington Post*, Aug. 11, 2012. Accessed Sept. 13, 2012, at http://www.washingtonpost.com/local/richard-land-a-southern-baptist-warrior-bids-goodbye-to-washington/2012/08/10/d0f92880-e186-11e1-98e7-89d659f9c106_story.html.

[11] The Ethics & Religious Liberty Commission, "About Us." Accessed Sept. 13, 2012, at http://erlc.com/erlc/about/.

[12] Boorstein.

[13] Banks.

[14] Fred Barnes, "Hidden Persuaders: The unheralded gains of the pro-life movement," *The Weekly Standard*, Nov. 7, 2011. Accessed Sept. 13, 2012, at http://www.weeklystandard.com/articles/hidden-persuaders_604174.html.

[15] Barnes. It is well worth the time to pull up this well-written and instructive article.

[16] Boorstein.

[17] Patrick J. Buchanan, "1992 Republican National Convention Speech," Patrick J. Buchanan—Official Website, Aug. 17, 1992. Accessed Sept. 13, 2012, at http://buchanan.org/blog/1992-republican-national-convention-speech-148.

[18] The case is *Hosanna-Tabor Evangelical Lutheran Church and School v. EEOC*. For those who are interested, this case can easily be pulled up on the Internet. The Supreme Court's decision is available online at http://www.supremecourt.gov/opinions/11pdf/10-553.pdf.

[19] Recorded in Matt. 19:4-5 and Mark 10:6-8.

[20] Daniel Burke, "Methodists uphold policy that calls homosexuality 'incompatible with Christian teaching," *Religion News Service*, May 3, 2012. Accessed September 26, 2012, at http://www.religionnews.com/culture/gender-and-sexuality/Methodists-uphold-policy-that-homosexuality-is-incompatible-with-Christian.

[21] Daniel Burke, "Why the United Methodist Church canceled votes on same-sex marriage and gay clergy," *The Washington Post*, May 7, 2012. This article is available online at http://www.washingtonpost.com/national/on-faith/why-the-united-methodist-church-canceled-votes-on-same-sex-marriage-and-gay-clergy/2012/05/07/gIQAjoDj8T_story.html.

Selected Bibliography

ABC News. "Six in 10 Take Bible Stories Literally, but Don't Blame Jews for Death of Jesus." 10 February 2004. *ABC News* (http://abcnews.go.com/images/pdf/947a1ViewsoftheBible.pdf).

Ansari, Ali M. *Confronting Iran: The Failure of American Foreign Policy and the Next Great Crisis in the Middle East.* Basic Books, 2007.

Atwan, Abdel Bari. *The Secret History of al-Qaeda.* University of California Press, 2006.

Barnes, Fred. "Hidden Persuaders: The unheralded gains of the pro-life movement." 7 November 2011. *The Weekly Standard* (http://www.weeklystandard.com/articles/hidden-persuaders_604174.html).

Barnes, Robert. "Justices Uphold Child Porn Law; Case Involved Criminalization of 'Pandering.'" *The Washington Post Supreme Court Year in Review 2009.* Kaplan Publishing, 2009. 109-110.

Bawer, Bruce. *Surrender: Appeasing Islam, Sacrificing Freedom.* Doubleday, 2009.

—. *While Europe Slept: How Radical Islam Is Destroying the West From Within.* Anchor, 2007.

Becker, Jo and Scott Shane. "Secret 'Kill List' Proves a Test of Obama's Principles and Will." 29 May 2012. *The New York Times* (http://www.nytimes.com/2012/05/29/world/obamas-leadership- in-war-on-al-qaeda.html? pagewanted=all).

Berman, Ilan. *Winning the Long War: Retaking the Offensive against Radical Islam.* Rowman & Littlefield Publishers, 2009.

Bertone, Tarcisio. "Statement by Cardinal Tarcisio Bertone, Secretary of State." 16 September 2006. *The Holy See* (http://www.vatican.va/roman_curia/secretariat_state/card-bertone/ 2006/documents/rc_seg-st_20060916_dichiarazione_en.html).

bin Bayyah, Allamah AbdAllah bin Mahfuz, et. al. "Open Letter to His Holiness Pope Benedict XVI." 12 October 2006. *Egypt State Information Service* (http://www.sis.gov.eg/PDF/En/Arts&Culture/0726070000000000010001.pdf.)

bin Muhammad, Ghazi. "A Common Word between Us and You." 13 October 2007. *A Common Word* (http://www.acommonword.com/index.php?lang=en&page=option1).

Bishop, Bill. *The Big Sort:Why the Clustering of Like-Minded America is Tearing Us Apart*. Mariner Books, 2009.

Blazquez, Agustin. "Political Correctness: The Scourge of Our Times." 8 April 2002. *Newsmax.com* (http://archive.newsmax.com/archives/articles/2002/4/4/121115.shtml).

Bodansky, Yossef. *Bin Laden: The Man Who Declared War on America*. Prima Lifestyles, 2001.

Boehner, John. "On the Need for the Obama Administration to Quit Stonewalling & Provide All of the Facts on the Fast & Furious Operation." 21 June 2012. *John Boehner, 8th District of Ohio* (http://boehner.house.gov/news/documentsingle.aspx?DocumentID =300419).

Bowden, Mark. *Guests of the Ayatollah: The Iran Hostage Crisis: The First Battle in America's War with Militant Islam*. Grove Press, 2007.

Boykin, William G. and Harry Edward Soyster (team leaders). "Shariah: The Threat To America: An Exercise In Competitive Analysis (Report of Team B II)." 2010. *The World Security Network* (http://www.worldsecuritynetwork.com/documents/Shariah_The_ Threat_to_America_(Team_B_II_Report)_9-14-10.pdf).

Brookhiser, Richard. *Gentleman Revolutionary: Gouverneur Morris, the Rake Who Wrote the Constitution*. Free Press, 2004.

Buchanan, Patrick J. "1992 Republican National Convention Speech." 17 August 1992. *Patrick J. Buchanan – Official Website* (http://buchanan.org/ blog/1992-republican-national-convention-speech-148).

Carter, Stephen L. *God's Name in Vain*. Basic Books, 2001.

—. *The Culture of Disbelief: How American Law and Politics Trivialize Religious Devotion*. Basic Books, 1993.

Corsi, Jerome R. *Obama Nation: Leftist Politics and the Cult of Personality*. Pocket Star, 2010.

Coulter, Ann. "Obama's Cairo Speech: Funny, If It Weren't So Terrifying." *Human Events* 15 June 2009: 5.

Crile, George. *Charlie Wilson's War*. Grove Press (Reissue Edition), 2007.

Critchlow, Donald T. *The Conservative Ascendancy: How the GOP Right Made Political History*. Harvard University Press, 2007.

Davis, Gregory M. *Religion of Peace?: Islam's War Against the World*. World Ahead Publishing, 2006.

Davis, Robert C. *Christian Slaves, Muslim Masters: White Slavery in the Mediterranean, the Barbary Coast and Italy, 1500-1800*. Palgrave Macmillan, 2003.

Dinan, Stephen. "Holder balks at blaming 'radical Islam.'" *The Washington Times* 14 May 2010.

Dreisbach, Daniel. *Thomas Jefferson and the Wall of Separation of Church and State*. NYU Press, 2003.

—. "Thomas Jefferson, a Mammoth Cheese, and the 'Wall of Separation Between Church and State.'" Hutson, James H. *Religion and the New Republic: Faith in the Founding of America*. Rowman & Littlefield Publishers, 1999. 65-114.

Earll, Carrie Gordon. "What We Did Not Know: The Aftermath of Thirty Years of Legal Abortion." n.d. *Faith Community Church (House Springs, Mo.)* http://faith-community.org/whatwedidnotknow.

Emerson, Steven. *American Jihad: The Terrorists Living Among Us*. Free Press, 2003.

—. *Jihad Incorporated: A Guide to Militant Islam in the U.S.* Prometheus Books, 2006.

Flynn, Daniel J. *A Conservative History of the American Left*. Crown Forum, 2008.

Foer, Franklin. "Grover Norquist's Strange Alliance With Radical Islam." 11 November 2001. *The New Republic* (http://www.freerepublic.com/focus/fr/561786/posts).

Frieden, Terry. "Supreme Court affirms school voucher program." 27 June 2002. *CNN Justice* (http://articles.cnn.com/2002-06-27/justice/scotus. school.vouchers_1_school-voucher-program-milwaukee-and-florida-parochial-school-tuition/3?_s=PM:LAW).

Gaffney, Frank. "A Troubling Influence." 9 December 2003. *FrontPageMagazine.com* (http://archive.frontpagemag.com/readArticle.aspx?ARTID=15084).

—. "Memorandum for Members of the Board of Directors of the American Conservative Union." 14 January 2011. *Suhail Khan Exposed* (http://suhailkhanexposed.com/wp-content/uploads/2011/01/20110121_Memo_to_the_ACU_Board_115.pdf).

Gallup, Inc. "Evolution, Creationism, Intelligent Design." May 2012. *Gallup* (http://www.gallup.com/poll/21814/evolution-creationism-intelligent-design.aspx.)

Gaubatz, P. David and Paul Sperry. *Muslim Mafia: Inside the Secret Underworld that's Conspiring to Islamize America*. WND Books, 2009.

Gerges, Fawaz A. *Journey of the Jihadist: Inside Muslim Militancy*. Houghton Mifflin Harcourt, 2006.

Gerstein, Josh. "Eric Holder under seige." 12 June 2012. *Politico* (http://www.politico.com/news/stories/0612/77348.html).

Gingrich, Newt and Callista Gingrich. *Rediscovering God in America*. Thomas Nelson, 2012.

Gould, Lewis L. *The Most Exclusive Club*. Basic Books, 2006.

Guillaume, Alfred. *The Life of Muhammad: A Translation of Ibn Ishaq's Sirat Rasul Allah* . Oxford University Press, 1979.

Hamburger, Philip. *Separation of Church and State*. Harvard University Press, 2004.

Hamid, Tawfik. *The Roots of Jihad*. Top Executive Media, 2006.

Hammond, Peter. "What Islam Isn't." 21 April 2008. *FrontPageMag.com* (http://archive.frontpagemag.com/readArticle.aspx?ARTID=30675).

Holder, Eric. "Attorney General Eric Holder at the Department of Justice African American History Month Program, Wednesday, February 18, 2009, Remarks as prepared for delivery." 18 February 2009. *The United States Department of Justice* (http://www.justice.gov/ag/speeches/2009/ag-speech-090218.html?loc=interstitialskip).

Horowitz, David and Jacob Laksin. *The New Leviathan: How the Left-Wing Money-Machine Shapes American Politics and Threatens America's Future*. Crown Forum, 2012.

Horowitz, David and Richard Poe. *The Shadow Party: How George Soros, Hillary Clinton, and Sixties Radicals Seized Control of the Democratic Party.* Thomas Nelson, 2006.

Hourani, Albert. *A History of the Arab Peoples.* Belknap Press, 2010.

Hutson, James. "A Wall of Separation: FBI Helps Restore Jefferson's Obliterated Draft." *The Library of Congress Information Bulletin* June 1998: 137.

—. *Forgotten Features of the Founding: The Recovery of Religious Themes in the Early American Republic.* Lexington Books, 2003.

—. *Religion and the Founding of the American Republic.* Library of Congress, 1998.

Jordon, Hamilton. *Crisis.* Berkley, 1983.

Kennedy, Walter D. *Myths of American Slavery.* Pelican Publishing, 2003.

Kidd, Thomas S. and Matthew Harris. *The Founding Fathers and the Debate over Religion in Revolutionary America: A History in Documents.* Oxford University Press, 2011.

Kidd, Thomas S. *God of Liberty: A Religious History of the American Revolution.* Basic Books, 2010.

Kinzer, Stephen. *All the Shah's Men: An American Coup and the Roots of Middle East Terror.* Wiley, 2008.

Krauthammer, Charles. "A terrorist war Obama has denied." 1 January 2012. *The Washington Post* (http://www.washingtonpost.com/wp-dyn/content/article/ 2009/12/31/AR2009123101744.html).

—. "Obama Hovers from on High." *The Washington Post* 12 June 2009.

Kupelian, David. *The Marketing of Evil: How Radicals, Elitists, and Pseudo-Experts Sell Us Corruption Disguised As Freedom.* WND Books, 2005.

Lewis, Bernard and Buntzie Ellis Churchill. *Islam: The Religion and the People.* Pearson Prentice Hall, 2008.

Lewis, Bernard. *Crisis Of Islam: Holy War and Unholy Terror.* Random House Trade Paperbacks, 2004.

—. *The Middle East and the West.* Harpercollins College Division, 1968.

—. *The Middle East: A Brief History of the Last 2,000 Years.* Scribner, 1997.

—. *What Went Wrong?: The Clash Between Islam and Modernity in the Middle East.* Harper Perennial, 2003.

Lewis, David L. *God's Crucible: Islam and the Making of Europe, 570-1215*. W.W. Norton & Company, 2009.

Lings, Martin. *Muhammad: His Life Based on the Earliest Sources*. Inner Traditions, 2006.

Mackey, Sandra. *The Iranians: Persia, Islam and the Soul of a Nation*. Plume, 1998.

Mansfield, Stephen. "Obama's faith fits our times." *USA Today* 1 June 2009: 11A.

—. *Ten Tortured Words: How the Founding Fathers Tried to Protect Religion in America ... and What's Happened Since*. Thomas Nelson, 2007.

—. *The Mormonizing of America*. Worthy Publishing, 2012.

Mayer, Jane. "The Trial: Eric Holder and the Battle over Khalid Sheikh Mohammed." 15 February 2010. *The New Yorker* (http://www.newyorker.com/2010/02/15/ 100215fa_fact_mayer).

Meacham, Jon. *American Gospel: God, the Founding Fathers, and the Making of a Nation*. Random House, 2007.

Morris, Dick and Eileen McGann. *Fleeced*. Harper, 2008.

Nasr, Vali. *The Shia Revival: How Conflicts within Islam Will Shape the Future*. W.W. Norton & Company, 2007.

Nelson, Steven. "Holder says experiences of 'my people' not similar to contemporary voter intimidation." 3 March 2011. *The Daily Caller* (http://dailycaller.com/2011/03/03/holder-says-experiences-of-my-people-not-similar-to-contemporary-voter-intimidation/).

Neuhaus, Richard John. *The Naked Public Square: Religion and Democracy in America*. Wm. B. Eerdmans Publishing Company, 1996.

Novak, Michael and Jana Novak. *Washington's God*. Basic Books, 2006.

Obama, Barack. *Dreams from My Father: A Story of Race and Inheritance*. Broadway, 2004.

—. "Remarks by the President on a New Beginning, Cairo University, Cairo, Egypt." 4 June 2009. *The White House* (http://www.whitehouse.gov/ the-press-office/remarks-president-cairo-university-6-04-09).

—. *The Audacity of Hope: Thoughts on Reclaiming the American Dream*. Crown Publishers, 2006.

Pahlavi, Ashraf. *Faces in a Mirror: Memoirs from Exile*. Prentice Hall, 1980.

Pahlavi, Mohammad Reza. *Answer to History*. Stein & Day, 1982.

Pew Research Center for the People & the Press. "Muslim Americans: No Signs of Growth in Alienation or Support for Extremism: Mainstream and Moderate Attitudes." 30 August 2011. *Pew Research Center for the People & the Press* (http://www.people-press.org/2011/08/30/muslim-americans-no-signs-of-growth-in-alienation-or-support-for-extremism/).

Phares, Walid. *Future Jihad: Terrorist Strategies Against The West*. Palgrave Macmillan, 2006.

Polack, Kenneth M. *The Persian Puzzle: The Conflict Between Iran and America*. Random House Trade Paperbacks, 2005.

Pope Benedict XVI. "Faith, Reason and the University; Memories and Reflections" (Lecture at the University of Regensburg). 12 September 2006. *The Holy See* (http://www.vatican.va).

Rehnquist, William. "United States Supreme Court Justice Rehnquist's Dissent in Wallace v. Jaffree." 1985. *Belcher Foundation* http://www.belcherfoundation.org/wallace_v_jaffree_dissent.htm.

"Remarks by the President at Easter Prayer Breakfast." 6 April 2010. *The White House, Office of the Press Secretary* (http://www.whitehouse.gov/the-press-office/remarks-president-easter-prayer-breakfast).

Rove, Karl. "History Favors Republicans in 2010." *Wall Street Journal* 13 November 2008.

Rumsfeld, Donald (interview). *Fareed Zakaria GPS (http://transcripts.cnn.com/TRANSCRIPTS/1109/11/fzgps.01.html)* Fareed Zakaria. 11 September 2011.

Santorum, Rick. "The Elephant in the Room: A war of ideas within Islam." 22 February 2012. *Philly.com* (http://www.philly.com/philly/columnists/rick_santorum/20091105_The_Elephant_in_the_Room__A_war_of_ideas_within_Islam.html?c=r).

Schafi, Abd El. *Behind the Veil: Unmasking Islam*. Pioneer Book Company, 2002.

Scheuer, Michael. *Marching Toward Hell: America and Islam after Iraq*. Free Press, 2008.

Sears, Alan and Craig Osten. *The ACLU Vs America*. B&H Publishing Group, 2005.

Silverman, William. "The Exclusion of Clergy from Political Office in American States: An Oddity in Church-State Relations." 2000. *Sociology of Religion* (http://socrel.oxfordjournals.org/content/61/2/223.full.pdf).

Spencer, Robert. *Stealth Jihad*. Regnery Publishing, 2008.

—. *The Politically Incorrect Guide to Islam (and the Crusades)*. Regnery Publishing, 2005.

—. *The Truth about Muhammad*. Regnery Publishing, 2006.

Sperry, Paul. *Infiltration: How Muslim Spies and Subversives Have Penetrated Washington*. Thomas Nelson, 2008.

—. "Who Is Suhail Khan?" 20 January 2011. *FrontPageMag.com* (http://frontpagemag.com/2011/paul-sperry/who-is-suhail-khan/).

Stark, Rodney. *God's Battalions*. HarperOne, 2009.

Stein, Ben and Philip DeMuth. *How to Ruin the United States of America*. New Beginnings Press, 2008.

Steyn, Mark. *America Alone: The End of the World As We Know It*. Regnery Publishing, 2008.

Supreme Court of the United States. "Everson v. Board of Education of the Township of Ewing." 10 February 1947. *Justia.com* (http://supreme.justia.com/cases/federal/us/330/1/case.html).

—. "Hosanna-Tabor Evangelical Lutheran Church and School v. EEOC." 11 January 2012. *Supreme Court of the United States* (http://www.supremecourt.gov/opinions/11pdf/10-553.pdf).

Tocqueville, Alexis de and Gerald Bevan (trans.). *Democracy in America*. Penguin Classics, 2003.

Trifkovic, Serge. *Defeating Jihad*. Regina Orthodox Press, 2006.

—. *The Sword of the Prophet*. Regina Orthodox Press, 2007.

Van Doren, Carl. *Benjamin Franklin*. The Viking Press, 1938.

Veit, Helen E., Kenneth R. Bowling and Charlene Bangs Bickford. *Creating the Bill of Rights*. The Johns Hopkins University Press, 1991.

Vu, Michelle A. "Obama Sends Out Inclusive Easter Greeting." 3 April 2010. *Christian Post* (http://www.christianpost.com/news/obama-sends-inclusive-easter-greeting-44600/).

"Weekly Address: President Obama Extends Holiday Greeting." 3 April 2010. *The White House, Office of the Press Secretary* (http://www.whitehouse.gov/ the-press-office/weekly-address-president-obama-extends-holiday-greeting).

Weigel, George. *Faith, Reason, and the War against Jihadism.* Doubleday Religion, 2007.

Wenner, Jann and Eric Bates. "Roundtable: The GOP Victory—and Obama's Next Steps." 10 December 2010. *Rolling Stone* (http://www.rollingstone.com/politics/news/roundtable-the-gop-victory- the-tea-party-ascendancy-and-obamas-next-steps-20101110).

Wilson, John K. "Religion under the State Constitutions, 1776 – 1800." *Journal of Church and State* Autumn 1990: 745-766.

Woolsey, R. James, Andrew C. McCarthy and Harry E. Soyster. "Woolsey & McCarthy & Soyster: Second opinion needed on Shariah." 14 September 2010. *The Washington Times* (http://www.washingtontimes.com/news/2010/sep/14/ needed-a-second-opinion-on-shariah/?page=all).

Yale Center for Faith & Culture. "Loving God and Neighbor Together: A Christian Response to 'A Common Word Between [sic] Us and You.'" 18 November 2007. *Yale University* (http://www.yale.edu/divinity/news/071118_news_nytimes.pdf).

Yousafzai, S. and R. Moreau. "The Doctor's Grim Reward." *Newsweek* 18 June 2012: 20-22.

About Bill Hecht

B ill Hecht is thoroughly familiar—from personal experience—with church and state alike. A long-time Washington insider, Bill has worked more than 40 years in the Nation's Capital, first as a congressional aide and then as a lobbyist. He also has been a Lutheran pastor.

After his graduation from Concordia Seminary, St. Louis, Mo., Bill served as pastor of Faith Lutheran Church, Mt. Vernon, Ill., and as campus pastor at the University of Oklahoma. At OU, Bill also taught in the university's Department of Philosophy. In 1967, Bill became executive director of the Missouri State Republican Party and in 1969 served as vice president of the American Security Council. In 1971, he became executive assistant to the chairman of the House Committee on Internal Security. He then became vice president for legislative affairs at the Tobacco Institute. After working in the Reagan for President Campaign, Bill started Hecht, Spencer & Associates in 1981 and still serves as its president.

Bill's education includes B.A, B.D., and Master of Divinity degrees from Concordia Seminary, St. Louis. He also has an M.A. degree in philosophy from Washington University, St. Louis, and completed all requirements except the dissertation for a Ph.D. at the University of Oklahoma.

Among Bill's numerous awards are the *Miles Christi* (Soldier of Christ) Award from Concordia Theological Seminary, Fort Wayne, Ind.; the Distinguished Alumni Award from Concordia Seminary, St. Louis; and an honorary Doctor of Laws degree from Concordia University Wisconsin, Mequon. The National Capital Area Council of the Boy Scouts of America bestowed the Silver Beaver Award for Distinguished Service to Youth, and in 2012, Bill was chosen as one of three persons to receive an "Outstanding Georgian" commendation from the Georgia state legislature.